Concepts in
Social & Political
Philosophy

Concepts in Social & Political Philosophy

Richard E. Flathman, 1934.

University of Washington Comp.

JA
71
F54

Macmillan Publishing Co., Inc.
New York

Collier Macmillan Publishers
London

Macmillan Publishing Co., Inc.
866 Third Avenue, New York, New York 10022
Collier-Macmillan Canada, Ltd., Toronto, Ontario

Library of Congress catalog card number: 72-91268

Printing: 1   2   3   4   5   6   7   8   Year: 3   4   5   6   7   8   9

MAC 12/75   4075

Preface

The chief purpose of this book is to make it easier for, and otherwise to encourage, students of politics and society to familiarize themselves with a fruitful and increasingly prominent approach to political and social philosophy. Commonly characterized by such adjectives as "analytic," "linguistic," and "conceptual," this approach has often been identified by contrast with the approach to the study of political philosophy that has predominated in political science for a number of years. The type of research and writing most commonly done by political scientists working in the field of political philosophy has been the study of the ideas and doctrines of thinkers in the history or tradition of political philosophy. The college and university courses and training programs most commonly offered in political philosophy examine the doctrines of the most important of these thinkers. By contrast, the approach presented in this volume proceeds by analyzing concepts prominent in the politics of a number of past and present societies.

Properly understood, however, the ultimate objective of both of these approaches is the same: to gain an understanding and to prompt critical reflection concerning prominent and persistent features of the political dimensions of the life of man. Those who organize their efforts in terms of a study of leading political philosophers believe that the thinkers they examine present the most comprehensive, profound, and best-developed understandings of politics that men have achieved. The study of and reflection concerning their works, it is argued, is one of the, if not the, surest means of attaining the objectives mentioned above. On grounds that I will be examining in the introduction, proponents of the conceptual approach believe that an analysis of concepts prominent in political life can yield the same result. Nor do the similarities between the two approaches end with this point. The procedural or organizational differences between them are in themselves more superficial than might at first appear. Books, courses, and training programs of the traditional sort proceed by analyzing the works of Plato, Aristotle, Hobbes, and so on. But when one opens the works of the latter writers, one of course finds that they consist in large part of discussions of authority, obligation, freedom, justice, and equality; that is, they consist of discussions of the same topics examined in this book and throughout the literature, the courses, and the training programs produced and conducted by proponents of a conceptual approach to political and social philosophy. It should be added that books and articles written by proponents of a conceptual approach, and the college and university courses they teach, consist in no small part of examinations of the discussions of these topics by other political philosophers. In short, the contrast with which we began will not take us far in identifying or assessing the distinctive characteristics and advantages of the political philosophizing presented in this book.

I suggest, rather, that the important differences between "conceptual" or "linguistic" political and social philosophy and other kinds are not at the level of the objectives or organization and management of the enterprise, but at the philosophical level of the nature of the ground on which proponents of this approach rest their claims to know or understand something about politics. The conceptual approach is distinct in that (or insofar as) it rests upon distinctive premises about what men can know and understand about politics and how they can best arrive at the knowledge and understandings in principle available to them. It is valid or justified only if (only insofar as) these premises are defensible. And it is fully accessible only if (only insofar as) these premises are understood by those who attempt to practice it or to avail themselves of the results of the attempts of others to practice it.[1]

For present purposes the most important implication of the foregoing remarks is that to achieve the objective of encouraging and facilitating familiarity with conceptually oriented political and social philosophy, we must indicate what is involved in studying concepts and we must identify grounds on which to think that doing so can contribute to knowledge and understanding of politics and society. These questions are complex and sometimes technical, and there is great controversy concerning them.[2] My primary aim in the introduction will be to convey enough about the influential thinking concerning language and concepts to make the selections on political and social concepts accessible to students of political and social philosophy who do not have extensive training in the philosophy of language. If this objective is achieved, I may perhaps hope that some students will also be stimulated to further study of issues and positions concerning language that can be little more than outlined here.

A word is in order concerning the concepts selected for discussion and the readings presented concerning them. I hope it will be agreed that the concepts are among the standard topics not only in recent, conceptually oriented political and social philosophy but in the entire tradition of philosophizing about politics and society. It is perhaps plausible to think that they remain among the standard topics in part because they have been standard for a long time. The tradition of political and social philosophizing, as with any tradition, is self-sustaining in a number of respects. Thinker B takes up topic X because thinker A did so before him, identified interesting problems and puzzles concerning it, and left the discussion

---

[1] To return briefly to the comparison with which we began, at its best the conceptual approach is not an alternative to, or departure from, political and social philosophy as traditionally practiced but an addition to, a continuation of, that tradition. It is a continuation of the tradition in many of the same respects in which Aristotle continued and added to the work of Socrates and Plato, Aquinas continued and added to classical and early Christian political thought, and so forth. Each of these thinkers took up many of the questions and issues that had concerned their predecessors, but they approached them from different philosophical perspectives (and, of course, in different circumstances in other respects as well) and often arrived at different conclusions concerning them. If there has been a departure from the tradition in recent times, it has been effected by those who treat political philosophy in a manner that Plato, Aristotle, and Rousseau never did, namely, as first and foremost an exercise in learning what certain previous thinkers said.

[2] As will be evident to anyone who reads the selections presented here, the liveliest of these controversies are among thinkers who would properly be classified as practitioners of a conceptual or linguistic approach to philosophy. One of the unfortunate aspects of general statements such as this one is that they all too readily fall into a schematic, simplified account of developments that are many-faceted and rich in controversy.

of the topic in what B believes to be an unsatisfactory state. Changes of approach and perspective occur and sometimes yield new topics and questions for consideration. But such changes also encourage later writers to believe that they can improve on previous efforts.

There is, however, a deeper reason for the persistent concern with authority, justice, equality, and the other topics discussed in this volume. In ways that vary over time, place, and circumstance, these concepts and the questions that surround them have been prominent in the political and social life that philosophers have tried to understand and assess. This is the best reason that can be given for encouraging continuing concern with them.

But the concepts dealt with here are not the only ones that are prominent and persistent in political and social life or in political philosophy. Many others, for example "responsibility," "power," "punishment," "sovereignty," "law," "representation," "privacy," "order," and "revolution," satisfy these tests. Nor is it our intention to suggest that those which have been included here are somehow more central, more fundamental, than the many which have not. To suggest that they are would imply that political and social concepts relate to one another such that some are derivative of others, and hence that examining those which are fundamental will also give us an understanding of those that are derivative. But I am not even sure what it would *mean* to say that, for example, "responsibility" or "representation" or "law" are derivative of some or all the concepts treated. Hence I am hardly in a position to assert that in fact there is such a hierarchy or structure among our political and social concepts. There are indeed complex interconnections, and studying one concept will often enlighten us about others with which it is connected in our practice. And there are some clusters or families of concepts that relate very closely to one another, for example, "justice," "equality," and "rights." But this is not to say some are fundamental and others derivative. Hence I wish to claim no more than that the concepts dealt with here are worth study and that studying them may stimulate development of the interest and capacity to go on to the study of others.

Having recently passed through a period in which it was fashionable to suggest that—or at least to wonder whether—political and social philosophy are dead, it is encouraging that as regards most of the topics in the book the selections presented were chosen from a much larger number of attractive possibilities. Although its quality varies, as one would expect of a large literature, discussion of these matters is clearly thriving. But those who work in materials such as are reprinted here will find, I hope, few surprises. A number of the articles have been reprinted before, some of them several times. Since alternatives have been available, I take this to indicate that numerous teachers and students have found them, as I have, worth study. In any case they are referred to in most contemporary discussions of the problems to which they are addressed and, if they were omitted here, teachers would simply have to make them available from some other source. I have tried to include enough selections on each topic so that major positions are represented and so that the book itself will confront the student with controversy and hence provide a stimulus to approaching the arguments in a critical spirit. My hope is that the book will supply something close to a sufficient teaching resource for conceptually oriented courses in political and social philosophy.

Seattle, Washington   *R. E. F.*

Contents

Part V Equality

Part VI Justice

Part VII Rights

Part VIII The Public Interest

Introduction

It is evident that an enormous number of human activities take place in and by means of the use of language. Indeed this is so evident that, as long as we remain in societies in which we are fluent speakers of the particular language there employed, we ordinarily take language and our capacity to communicate by using it completely for granted. What we regard as important and sometimes problematic are the things we think, do, and desire; and the things in the world that we communicate about, not the language we use in thinking, acting, and communicating about the world.

If we pause to think about language and the ease with which we put it to such varied and important uses, however, it may well seem the most important, most extraordinary, and most problematic phenomenon of all. We switch on the radio and spin the dial, catching a sentence or two, and, learning what is on, reject one station for another. We overhear snatches of a conversation on the train and form judgments about the speakers. We write a letter to a newspaper with a circulation of thousands and never doubt that the readers will, at some level, understand what the letter says. In countless ways and circumstances we take for granted our capacity to communicate effectively with very large numbers of people, ranging from our most intimate family and friends to total strangers.

How are such things possible? How can they be explained so that we can understand not only *that* we do what Wittgenstein called a "prodigious diversity" of things with language, but *how* it is possible for us to do so? What is it, exactly, for a sentence, a phrase, or a word to *mean* something? How can sounds or marks on paper convey thoughts, understanding, and emotions most of which have never before been expressed or conveyed in the same ways and many of which are about actions, ideas, perceptions, and so on, that neither the speaker nor the auditor, the author nor the reader, have ever experienced or ever will experience except as expressed in language? These and the many questions lurking beneath their surface are not easy questions to answer.

In the twentieth century much of philosophy has taken what the philosopher Gustave Bergmann has called the "linguistic turn." Of course philosophy has always been done, could only be done, *in* language. And of course numerous philosophers from Plato forward gave thought to language itself, how it works, what can be done with it, and the implications of its prominent role in human thought and action. But it is a distinctive feature of much twentieth-century philosophizing that it not only is done in language, but is done primarily or at least often by means of the analysis of language. On the one hand, philosophers have tried to solve problems in moral and political philosophy, epistemology, and other subfields of the discipline

1

by analyzing the language that is used in nonphilosophical discourse about what is good and evil, just and unjust; about sensations, emotions, beliefs, and intentions. This type of analysis, sometimes called linguistic philosophy, is exemplified in the majority of the selections presented.

Use of the methods of linguistic philosophy, however, depends on an understanding, whether implicit or explicit, of language itself and its relationships to thought, action, and the "other realities" that philosophers try to investigate by analyzing language; it depends on answers to questions about language and communication in language, themselves. The attempt to answer such questions constitutes the chief concern of the subfield of philosophy now often designated the philosophy of language (as opposed to linguistic philosophy).[1] The philosophy of language is an attempt to clarify the notion of "meaning" itself and to understand what is involved in the ability of human beings to use language with meaning. Work of this kind has yielded comprehensive theories concerning language and meaning, and it has exercised a powerful influence on virtually all other aspects of philosophy. Our objective here will be to summarize and explore the implications of some of the propositions widely influential among the philosophers of language whose thought has had an impact upon the kind of social and political philosophizing presented in the readings. We will focus our attention on the single most important work in the philosophy of language, Ludwig Wittgenstein's *Philosophical Investigations.*[2]

1. Language and Meaning

"It is only in a language that I can mean something by something."[3] This statement expresses Wittgenstein's rejection of all theories, and particularly his own earlier theory, according to which meaning is located somewhere other than in language itself, for example, in the mind of the speaker and the auditor or in the world to which language (sometimes) refers. For this reason, when seen in the context of the work in the philosophy of language that preceded and surrounded the statement, the proposition is by no means the truism it might appear to be. It performs the essential service of directing our efforts to understand meaning to the considerations and the kinds of evidence relevant to obtaining such an understanding. If it is

[1] For this way of marking the distinction see especially John R. Searle, *Speech Acts* (New York: Cambridge University Press, 1969). See also Professor Searle's introduction to his useful anthology *The Philosophy of Language* (New York: Oxford University Press, 1971).

[2] Translated by G. E. M. Anscombe (New York: The Macmillan Company, 1953). For an account of Wittgenstein's life and work see especially Norman Malcolm, *Ludwig Wittgenstein, A Memoir,* With a Biographical Sketch by George Henrik Von Wright (New York: Oxford University Press, 1958); and K. T. Fann, ed., *Ludwig Wittgenstein, The Man and His Philosophy* (New York: Dell Publishing Co., 1967). There is a very large critical literature concerning Wittgenstein's thought. George Pitcher, ed., *Wittgenstein: The Philosophical Investigations* (Garden City, N.Y.: Anchor Books, 1966) collects a number of the papers most relevant to those aspects of Wittgenstein's thought discussed here. It also includes an extensive bibliography. More recent papers are collected in Peter Winch, ed., *Studies in the Philosophy of Wittgenstein* (London: Routledge & Kegan Paul, 1969).

[3] Ludwig Wittgenstein, *Philosophical Investigations*, Part I, Para. 38, p. 18e. Unless otherwise indicated all subsequent citations in this introduction are to the *Philosophical Investigations*. References to Part I will give the paragraph number only, references to Part II will give "II," the roman subsection of II, and the page.

only *in* language that one can mean something by something, then we will understand meaning only by looking at language and the uses to which it is put.

But how much guidance does Wittgenstein's proposition, assuming for the moment that it is true, actually give us? We are to look at language to understand meaning. But what is language? So far we are told no more than that language is where we will find meaning. But since it is meaning that we are trying to understand, this advice seems to be of limited utility. And Wittgenstein reinforces this impression when he says, for example, "Instead of producing something common to all that we call language, I am saying that these phenomena [that is uses which we make of language] have no one thing in common which makes us use the same word for all, – but that they are *related* to one another in many different ways. And it is because of this relationship, or these relationships, that we call them all 'language.' "[4] Now if we have no sure test for what counts as language, no certain way to determine that this phenomenon here before us is an example of language, it seems that we have no sure way to act upon the advice that we should examine language to understand meaning.

But of course the passage just quoted does *not* say that we have no sure way to determine that this phenomenon before us is an example of language. It says that there is no *single* characteristic common to all instances of language and hence no one criterion by which to judge *all* alleged or purported examples. Wittgenstein explains his argument about "language" by discussing the related case of "game."[5] He urges us to consider the wide variety of proceedings to which "game" is applied, for example, "board-games, card-games, ball-games, Olympic games, and so on. What is common to them all? – Don't say: 'There *must* be something common, or they would not be called games' – but *look and see* whether there is anything common to all. – For if you look at them you do not see something that is common to all, but similarities, relationships, and a whole series of them at that."[6] But then how do I, we, decide whether to call a particular proceeding a game? And how do we teach someone else what a game is? Wittgenstein responds, "I imagine that we should describe *games* to him, and we might add: 'This *and similar things* are called games.' And do we know any more about it ourselves? Is it only other people who cannot tell exactly what a game is? – But this is not ignorance. We do not know the boundaries because none have been drawn."[7]

There are several crucial ideas in these passages. First, as with games and the concept "games," there is no essence to language or the concept "language." Just as we play a great variety of games and accordingly use "game" in the course of and to talk about a great variety of activities, so we use language in a "prodigious variety" of ways and for many purposes, and we use the concept "language" for all of these. Inspection may show similarities among many of these uses but these are not quintessential to all of them.

---

[4] 65, italics in original.

[5] The quotation marks around "language" and "game" in the preceding sentence indicate that those words are being discussed, not used. Since many of the papers reprinted in this book are by British writers, it is well to explain at once that the established convention in British English is to mark such cases with inverted commas rather than quotation marks. In American English inverted commas are employed only when the words discussed rather than used occur in a sentence that is itself in quotation marks for some other reason.

[6] 66.

[7] 69.

Second, whatever difficulties philosophers or other kinds of analysts may have in explaining "games," "language," and other concepts, these difficulties do not hinder speakers from using these concepts readily and effectively in interacting with one another. If there is a fundamental fact about language, it is precisely the fact that speakers of languages do use concepts readily and effectively. This is the fact to which philosophy in all of its aspects is, as one might say, both responsible and properly responsive. If philosophers cannot account for this fact, and indeed for the extraordinary range of things that are as a matter of course done in and with language, so much the worse for philosophers.

Third, to be able to communicate with other speakers by using "game," "language," or any other concept, to understand the communications of others, to be able to explain these concepts to someone, say a child or a foreigner, who does not know the language or this or that concept in the language — to be able to do these things, as it were, day to day *is* to know what the concepts mean. To know the meaning of a concept is not to know something other than, something in addition to, or something hidden beneath what speakers of the language do with it. Rather it is to know just what they know, to have the knowledge they display and act upon in their day-to-day communication with one another. In Wittgenstein's words, "If it is asked: 'How do sentences manage to represent?' — the answer might be: 'Don't you know? You certainly see it, when you use them.' For nothing is concealed. How do sentences do it? — Don't you know? For nothing is hidden."[8]

Wittgenstein then imagines someone making the following further retort to the preceding remarks: "Yes, but it all goes by so quick, and I should like to see it as it were laid open to view."[9] That Wittgenstein is sympathetic to at least some forms of this response is evident throughout the book. He labors incessantly to lay open to view this and that use of language, to attempt to "command a clear view of the use of our words."[10] But the urge to have language "laid open" is dangerous because, once again, it might suggest that language and meaning consist of something other than what speakers of the language do with the words, something that must be uncovered by "laying open" a shell or exterior formed by ordinary use.[11] Hence Wittgenstein issues the following warning concerning the preceding retort: "Here it is easy to get into that dead-end in philosophy, where one believes that the difficulty of the task consists in this: our having to describe phenomena that are hard to get a hold of, the present experience that slips quickly by, or something of the kind. Where we find ordinary language too crude, and it looks as if we were having to do, not with the phenomena of every-day, but with ones that 'easily elude us, and, in their coming to be and passing away, produce those others as an average effect.' "[12]

Fourth, the passages we have quoted begin to suggest a crucial point concerning what for the moment we will have to call the relationship (or rather one of the important relationships) between concepts and other things — for example, between the concept "game" and games, between the concept "language" and this or that language, between the concept "meaning" and the fact that words have

---

[8] 435.

[9] 435.

[10] 122.

[11] It would perhaps be better to think of "laying out" than of "laying open."

[12] 436.

meaning. Let us recur to Wittgenstein's discussion of "games." We explain the meaning of the concept "game" by describing various activities to which that concept is applied in day-to-day speech. To describe or explain a game is *also* to describe or explain (a part of) the meaning of the concept "game." And it is obvious that there is a vital sense in which the reverse is true as well; to describe or explain the meaning of "game" is done by, and hence is, describing or explaining games. Skipping over numerous qualifications, we might say: Wherever there are games the concept "game" has application; wherever the concept "game" has application there is (are) a game(s).[13] Thus we begin to see the grounds on which it has been argued that to learn, to understand something about "game" (or "authority," or "rights," or "equality") is to learn, to understand, something about games (about authority, or rights, or equality).[14]

To sum up thus far: (1) meaning is in language; (2) language is diverse and has no essence; (3) the philosophy of language must begin with the fact that language is readily and most often successfully used to communicate; (4) a language is what its speakers do with it and to know a language and the meaning of the concepts of which it consists is to know what those speakers do with it; (5) the relationship between concepts and nonlinguistic phenomena (for example, things to which concepts refer, actions taken or talked about), although diverse in important respects, is such that knowledge or understanding of the former provides, or rather *is*, a kind of knowledge or understanding of the latter.

2. Language, Meaning, and the Purposes of Philosophy

There is evidently an antitheoretical and even antigeneralization flavor or cast to the foregoing propositions. Language is what people do with it. And when we examine what people do with their language we see great variety and diversity, little basis for generalizations or comprehensive theories. At places Wittgenstein is positively dogmatic in this respect: ". . . [W]e may not advance any kind of theory. There must not be anything hypothetical in our considerations. We must do away with *all explanation*, and description alone must take its place."[15] The purpose of philosophical investigations is not even to teach us something we did not previously know; it is merely to "assemble reminders" of what we already know, of what we know by virtue of the fact that we are speakers of a language. Assembling such reminders may occasionally help us to solve real problems, but it is more likely to dissolve pseudoproblems that plague our thinking (especially the thinking of philosophers) because we do not pay sufficient attention to the "language of every day."[16] Properly speaking, in short, philosophy is not theoretical, it is therapeutic. When successful its chief results "are the uncovering of one or another piece of

[13] A couple of obvious examples of qualifications to the preceding generalizations: (1) "Give me an example of a four-letter word in English." "Game." (2) " 'Game' is a common noun."

[14] For further discussion of this point see pp. 20–30 where we take up Wittgenstein's notion of a language game.

[15] 109. See generally 109–133 for his remarks about philosophy and its purposes and limitations.

[16] 120.

plain nonsense,"[17] and in general its aim is to teach us "to pass from a piece of disguised nonsense to something that is patent nonsense."[18]

Even if we grant, however, that the five propositions summarized earlier argue for a descriptive, therapeutic conception of philosophy,[19] it remains the case that those propositions are themselves entirely general. It is not this or that bit of meaning that is in language, but all meaning. It is not this language, this aspect of language that is what those who speak it do with it, it is all language. The situation is the same through the list of propositions we have discussed.[20] It is true that many of the discussions Wittgenstein presents have the descriptive, therapeutic flavor that the general propositions seem to recommend and that Wittgenstein explicity prescribes.[21] But the descriptive, particularistic character of these discussions can easily be exaggerated. To begin with, although specific uses of the concepts under analysis are given, Wittgenstein seldom explicitly restricts the lessons taught by those examples to the cases actually discussed or to cases with the same descriptive features. More important, the very fact that philosophy is therapeutic means that when he as a philosopher describes the use of a concept, the description "gets its light, that is to say its purpose — from the philosophical problems."[22] If this means, as I take it to mean, the problems of traditional concern to philosophers, they are not likely to be narrowly particular. The scope of the concerns of a therapist is heavily influenced if not simply given by the problems of his patients, and Wittgenstein's patients, being philosophers, are rarely afflicted by narrowly circumscribed or closely defined problems.

We must also ask how it is that these descriptions can be therapeutic in the sense of actually effecting, or at least being capable of effecting, genuine cure. Just as psychoanalytic therapy depends upon a way (or ways) of distinguishing between normal and abnormal, healthy and diseased, so philosophical therapy requires distinctions between sense and nonsense, between correct and incorrect uses of language. The philosophical therapist can uncover particular cases of nonsense and can lead his "patients" to see and escape from the nonsensical formulations only if he has criteria by which to judge. And if these criteria did not have application beyond the particular case examined, they could not tell us anything about that particular case. The propositions we have discussed thus far provide the

[17] 119.

[18] 464.

[19] We return to this question as regards political and social philosophy in Section 7 of the Introduction.

[20] The sweeping character of the five propositions can be appreciated by noting the comparable propositions in previous or concurrent (with the writing of the *Investigations*) work in the philosophy of language that they are intended to replace. Examples would be the following: (1) Meaning is not in language itself but in that to which language refers or in the minds of those who use language; (2) language *must* have an essence and the task of philosophy is to discover it; (3) communication in language may be an illusion, at best each of us "speaks" only to him or herself and no one else "really" understands; (4) what speakers of English do with that language is only a kind of epiphememenon that may or may not accurately reflect or point to the real structure or essence of language; (5) concepts are at best contingently and perhaps coincidentally related to nonlinguistic phenomena so that knowledge of how concepts are used could at best provide hypotheses about nonlinguistic phenomena, hypotheses that would in all cases have to be verified by investigation of something other than concepts.

[21] Examples might be his discussion of concepts such as "thinking," "wishing," "dreaming," and even "pain."

[22] 109.

therapeutically oriented philosopher with perfectly general instructions as to where to look, and where not to look, to find these criteria. Without them, or some substitute for them, philosophical therapy of the kind Wittgenstein recommends would be impossible.

From the perspective just discussed, indeed, the problem with the propositions about language that we have summarized thus far is not that they are narrowly descriptive or particular, but that they are so abstract, so general, that they give insufficient guidance to the would-be therapist. They tell the therapist where to look, but they give a minimum of guidance as to how to judge or assess what is found. It is of course possible that no further general guidance is available or possible, that judgments of what is sense and what nonsense, although taking place within the framework given by the five basic propositions, are and have to be context-particular in all other respects. It is possible, but according to Wittgenstein's teaching it is not in fact the case. Despite his strictures against explanations and theories, Wittgenstein offers us further generalizations about language, generalizations that are less comprehensive than those discussed earlier but that supply more substantive guidance to the philosophical therapist.

3. Meaning and Use

Meaning is in language. But language is used for a "prodigious diversity" of purposes, is part of an indefinite but very large number of activities. Where exactly in this diversity are philosophical therapists to look to find meaning, and how exactly are they to distinguish sense and nonsense and make the numerous other judgments they wish to make? Well, they should look just where, just to, those things to which we as unphilosophic speakers of language look in order to grasp, clarify, interpret, explain, question, and emphasize the meaning of the communications that we send to and receive from one another.

But where *do* speakers of a language look in order to do these things? We all know the answer in the sense that we all engage in these activities almost constantly and in large measure successfully. As with many such highly general (and highly unusual) questions, however, the fact that we know in the sense just indicated may not yet be enough to permit us to state, as opposed to acting upon or making use of, what we know. Which by no means is to say that we lack something that we need to use language and to engage in the multitude of activities of which its use is a part. Rather the fact that we can use language without being able to give a general answer to the question "Where or to what does one look to find meaning?" is itself a fundamental fact of which the philosopher of language must never lose sight. It may even suggest that there is no answer to that question; the question is inappropriate, ill-formed, or worse.

Yet Wittgenstein does offer a highly general though not unqualified answer to that question. He says, "For a *large* class of cases — though not for all — in which we employ the word 'meaning' it can be defined thus: the meaning of a word is its use in the language."[23] There is, of course, an important sense in which this answer

---

[23] 43, italics in original. Note immediately that this answer is itself put forward as an account of the way the word "meaning" is most commonly used. We learn what meaning is by examining the use of the word "meaning."

simply throws the question back to us in a little-altered form. If "use" means something like "job done by," "part played by," "role performed by," "function," "purpose," or "application" of – all terms Wittgenstein in fact employs more or less interchangeably with "use," then it might seem that the generalization is again of no more than therapeutic value; we are simply being reminded yet one more time of the extraordinary diversity in the uses to which words are in fact put and the consequent difficulty of generalizing usefully about them. Moreover, with a few exceptions that we can readily set aside, language is used by and to serve the purposes, pursue the objectives, and express the desires of individuals. Individuals and their purposes, objectives, and so forth, differ from one another; it is not surprising that their use of language differs as well. The extraordinary diversity, invention, and unpredictability in the use of language, the fact, for example, that virtually all speakers of natural languages continually and routinely construct, employ, and understand statements that have never been uttered before, is rightly treated by contemporary linguists as one of the cardinal features of language, one of the features for which any plausible philosophy of language must be able to account [24]

The meaning of a word, however, is not simply its use; it is its use *in the language.* We cannot understand language apart from the uses that speakers make of it. At the same time, *their* use of language, the use of this or that concept in a language by this or that speaker, cannot be understood apart from the place of that concept in the language of which it is part. There is no language apart from the linguistic behavior (past or present) of particular human beings, but neither, Wittgenstein insists, is there such a thing as linguistic behavior apart from the existence of a language consisting of more than the linguistic behavior of this or that human being. Language is used by individual speakers, but language, the use of language, is intrinsically more than an activity of individuals taken as such. More positively, language is intrinsically a social phenomenon, the use of language is intrinsically a social activity.

There is both a negative and a positive side to this argument, perhaps the most influential and for present purposes most important of Wittgenstein's arguments. The negative side is his argument against the (logical) possibility of a purely private language. Much of this argument is encapsulated in his remark that "an 'inner process' stands in need of outward criteria."[25] The positive side has numerous dimensions, but crucial to them all are his notions that the use of language is governed by shared rules or conventions, and shared agreements, techniques, purposes, and judgments concerning the interpretation and application of those rules and conventions. The conventions, agreements, and so on, at once regulate and constitute what Wittgenstein called "language-games." We will have to examine all these notions.

---

[24] These features of the use of language have been given particular emphasis by Noam Chomsky and his associates. For an introduction to Chomsky's views on this matter see the selections from his work in Searle, ed., op cit.

[25] 580.

4. Private Versus Public Language

The first task in understanding Wittgenstein's critique of the idea of a private language is to identify the use of "private" that concerned him. He was not arguing about private uses of language in the sense represented, for example, by A talking to himself in the privacy of his home, his study, or wherever, that is, cases in which A uses a language (as French or Russian or English) that he shares with others but, whether deliberately or not, uses it under circumstances such that other speakers of that language do not know what he is saying or even that he is speaking at all. Nor was Wittgenstein discussing private language in the sense of a special language, say a code or shorthand, that A, who also speaks a shared or public language, invents for his personal use. In such cases A could explain his code to B or C, and the latter could understand the explanations because A, B, and C share a language in which explanations can be given. As we will see, it was Wittgenstein's view that A himself could not invent or use a code that is private in this sense if he did not share a language with some others.

Wittgenstein was concerned, rather, with claims that some, or perhaps all, language is, in part or entirely, intrinsically or necessarily private, that is, in at least some respects necessarily uncommunicable to or understandable by anyone other than A himself. As Norman Malcolm puts it, "By a private language is meant one that not merely is not but cannot be understood by anyone other than the speaker."[26]

The idea of language, or parts of language, that are private in this sense arises most readily in connection with concepts that seem to refer to, seem to be used to mean, events or states of affairs that only the speaker himself can experience or otherwise know about. Leading examples are concepts that seem to refer to sensations such as pain and mental or psychological events, states, and activities such as thinking, believing, and intending. These have been thought to occur, to be experienced, somewhere internal to an individual and hence, given the way human beings are constituted, to be inaccessible to other persons. If in the nature of the case I am the only person who can experience my pains, my intentions, thoughts, and so on, and if my use of "pain," "intention," and "thought" refers to, *means*, the experience that only I can have, it would follow that I am the only one who can know the meaning of those terms as I use them. Of course, other persons hear the sounds I make, see the words I write. And for all I know or they know each of them may have experiences that are qualitatively the same as mine and they may use the same words to mark those experiences. But since I cannot experience the pains, intentions, and thoughts of others, and they cannot experience mine, there is no way we can *know* that our experiences are the same. Hence there is no way that we can *know* what another person is referring to when he uses these words.

The privacy theory is most plausible in connection with those concepts that seem to refer to what we commonly think of as sensations and mental states. But once the idea has taken hold that mental state concepts are private, the privacy theory can readily be extended to concepts we would ordinarily think of as referring to external, public, observable things and states of affairs. Trees, stone, buildings, automobiles are paradigm examples of things in the "external world." We

---

[26] Norman Malcolm, "Wittgenstein's Philosophical Investigations," in Pitcher, ed., op. cit., p. 66. Italics in original.

see them, touch them, run into them, and we do not think of doing so as involving, as it were, turning our perceptual mechanisms inward in order to examine ourselves. But the very verbs "see," "smell," and "touch" give the proponent of a private language theory an opening. These perceptual processes, it can be argued, are after all internal processes in crucial respects. When I say that I see a tree or hear a bird singing, I am reporting not only that there is a tree or a bird "out there," but that something is registering in, say, my central nervous system. The words "tree," "bird," and so forth, are simply the terms I choose, quite arbitrarily, to mark what registers in this case and to distinguish it from what is registered in other cases. Since no one else can experience my perceptual processes, no one else can know what they are like. If "tree" refers to that which the process registers in me, no one else can know the reference, the meaning, of my word "tree." In this manner the privacy thesis can be extended very widely indeed.

The private language theory, whether in a restricted or extended version, is obviously at odds with those fundamental features of Wittgenstein's philosophy of language that we sketched earlier. It is particularly important in the present context because it calls into question the idea that it is possible to study and generalize about political life, society, and so on, by studying and arriving at generalizations about the language that is part of them. First, if language is private, if each person in effect has his own language and there are and can be no more than contingent, indeed accidental, relationships among the languages of *A, B,* and *C,* then study of *A*'s language will not itself permit us any certainty about the language of *B* or *C.* Experience may teach us to expect and even to rely upon similarities for certain practical purposes, but there will be no way to determine that the similarities are genuine, that what is in *B*'s mind when he says "tree" or "headache" is actually the same as what is in *A*'s mind when he utters the same words (sounds). Second, the private language theory involves the views that the connections between *A*'s language and what *A* experiences are purely arbitrary. The event, action, or whatever is there or takes place and *A* experiences it directly, without the mediation of language. Having experienced it, having knowledge of it, he arbitrarily assigns a particular word to it. The event, action, and so on, is what it is, has the characteristics it has, quite apart from the word used to mark it. Hence study of the words used would be study of nothing more than an arbitrarily selected set of signs and would tell us nothing about the world, society, politics, or anything else.

Many of Wittgenstein's arguments against the privacy theory attempt to show that in fact, in their actual use in the languages we know, concepts such as "pain," "thinking," and "believing" do not depend for their meaning on reference to events internal to the person who uses them. There may be such events, but the use of the concepts we have is not in fact dependent upon reference to them.[27]

As I understand Wittgenstein, however, he wishes to go much beyond showing that the privacy theory does not work for this or that concept. His enterprise is the much more radical one of proving that a private language is in fact an impossibility.[28] He wants to show that one's having, knowing how to use, and understanding the meaning of a language, even a language consisting of only one

---

[27] 304–309.

[28] Another interpretation of Wittgenstein's argument is that the private language theory cannot be cogently formulated in the language we have; that all attempts at formulating the theory misuse the concepts out of which they are formulated and lapse into nonsense. See John W. Cook, "Wittgenstein on Privacy," in Pitcher, ed., op. cit., pp. 286–323.

concept, that no one else *can* understand is an impossibility. ". . . [I]f as a matter of logic you exclude other people's having something, it loses its sense to say that you have it."[29]

Much of Wittgenstein's argument here is abbreviated in the remark, "As if someone were to buy several copies of the morning paper to assure himself that what it said was true."[30] If I am in doubt of the truth of a story in the paper, appeal to a second copy is of no help because it is an appeal to the very thing that is already in question. A private language would suffer exactly the same difficulty. Wittgenstein imagines that he (and only he) has a certain sensation and wants to keep a diary of its recurrence. "To this end I associate it with the sign 'E' and write this sign in a calendar for every day on which I have this sensation." But how do I know what "E" means? Well, "I concentrate my attention on the sensation" as I speak or write the sign down, thereby impressing "on myself the connexion between the sign and the sensation." The meaning of "E" is thus established and I know what it is.

But what if, as in the case of the story in the newspaper, doubt arises in my mind as to the meaning of "E"? To say "E" has a meaning and that I know what it is requires "That I remember the connexion [between the sign and the sensation] *right* in the future. But in the present case I have no criterion of correctness." Why not? Why can't my recollection itself be such a criterion? "One would like to say: whatever is going to seem right to me is right." Wittgenstein's first response to this last remark is that it merely shows "that here we can't talk about 'right.' "[31] Now it might be responded in turn that Wittgenstein's objection is irrelevant to the issue about private language because it rests on the way "right" is used in a public language. The question whether a private language is *possible*, it might be argued, cannot be settled by showing that such a language would not satisfy criteria that are part of the use of a particular word or words in what is conceded by many to be a public language. Wittgenstein's point, however, is at least in part that concepts such as the English concepts "right" and "correct" are necessary to *any* language (including allegedly private ones) because without them there would be no sense to the claim that one knows or could know what "E" or any other concept means. To give up "right" and "correct" is also to give up "knows." Because the claim that a private language is possible is the claim that the speaker thereof (and only that speaker) can *know* what the units of the language mean, to give up "right" and "correct" is to give up that claim.

But why can't "right" and "correct" be used of "E"? Why can't I claim that my memory of the connection between "E" and the sensation not only seems but is correct? Don't we in fact rely upon our memories? Don't we in fact behave as if they give us information that is actually correct? "For example, I don't know if I have remembered the time of departure of a train right and to check it I call to mind how a page of the timetable looked. Is it the same here [that is with 'E'] ?"[32] Of course we often rely upon our memories.[33] But cases like the timetable and the case of "E" are not the same. The mental image of the timetable can be "tested for

[29] 398.
[30] 266.
[31] 258, italics in original.
[32] 265.
[33] 53.

correctness" against the printed timetable of which it is a memory. Against what can I test my memory of the connection between "E" and the sensation to which it refers? The sensation might in fact recur, but any decision I make on this point must depend entirely upon my memory, that is, on the very thing that is in doubt.[34] Hence a condition requisite to my knowing the meaning of "E" is not satisfied. Since the same difficulty obtains with any concept used privately (in the sense of "private" we are discussing), a purely private language is an impossibility. If in principle no person other than A can know the use of "E," A himself cannot know its use.

These remarks urgently raise the question of what the public character of language means, of what it consists, and of how it remedies the fatal difficulty that a private language would suffer. A schematic, general answer to these questions would be along the following lines: Languages are public in the sense that the uses of the units of which they consist are governed by conventions or rules known, accepted, and usually followed by those who speak them. Knowing a language consists of knowing the conventions that govern its units, and making sense in it consists of using it according to the conventions. There are many types of conventions or rules (for example, syntactic, semantic, orthographic) and their content varies immensely across the "prodigious diversity" of linguistic units and the uses to which they are put. But in addition to distinguishing correct from incorrect, none of these conventions refers to or depends upon phenomena (for example, perceptions or sensations) that are not in principle accessible to persons with the ordinary complement of human faculties. (For example, the rules for the use of, say, "reading" depend not on some mental event or inner state but on the capacity to perform various actions that others can observe.) A learns concepts previously unfamiliar to him by asking or observing some B (or, after his command of language has developed somewhat, by consulting a dictionary). If he is in doubt as to whether he correctly remembers the meaning of a concept he has already learned, he can consult other speakers. If he is in doubt whether a concept has been correctly used in a particular circumstance, he tests its use against the shared conventions that govern its use.

The fact that the conventions are known to and accepted by those who speak the language, and that they are keyed to public actions, events, and states of affairs, allows escape from the difficulty symbolized by the man buying a second copy of the newspaper. When A's knowledge, memory, or whatever is in doubt he can appeal to something independent of his memory, that is, to other speakers, to resolve the doubt. Since each speaker of the language can do the same, the situation in which "whatever is going to seem right *to me* is right" is avoided. Of course, most of the time individual speakers can and do rely on their own knowledge of the conventions, that is, they rarely have need explicitly to test their knowledge by consulting others. Thus someone who has learned a language, for example a Robinson Crusoe, might go on employing it without need of continuously verifying his or her knowledge by reference to other speakers. But the possibility of such verification is, at least in principle, present in the sense that what other speakers will or would say if consulted is established as the relevant criterion of correct use and meaning. And of course in practice each speaker's knowledge of the conventions is constantly refreshed and enlarged in the process of spoken and

[34] 265. "Looking up a table in the imagination is no more looking up a table than the image of the result of an imagined experiment is the result of an experiment."

written communication with others. Robinson Crusoe hardly provides the paradigm case of linguistic competence and performance, and I would conjecture that the linguistic capacities of a person in Crusoe's situation (before Friday) would undergo considerable degeneration if his isolation continued over a long period.[35]

5. Rules, Techniques, and Purposes

The foregoing schema, although not, I think, simply wrong either about Wittgenstein or our experience with language, is so general as to obscure and mislead concerning both. We cannot go into very much of the detail over which the preceding schema generalizes. But using that schema as an alternative to the equally general picture provided by the private language theory, we must elaborate somewhat on the key notion of shared rules and Wittgenstein's understanding of the several roles they do, and do not, play in language.

We will begin with two of the more explicitly labeled examples of rules of language that Wittgenstein discusses in the *Investigations*. The first is a number of rules concerning "not" and other negatives. Of these rules Wittgenstein says, "There cannot be a question whether these or other rules are the correct ones for the use of 'not.' ... For without these rules the word has as yet no meaning; and if we change the rules, it now has another meaning (or none), and in that case we may just as well change the word too."[36] The second example concerns rules governing the verb "is," namely, the "grammatical" rule that allows the use of "is" both in "the rose is red" and in "twice two is four" and the rule that allows us "to replace ... 'is' in the second sentence with the sign of equality, and forbidding this substitution in the first sentence."[37] The second of these rules, Wittgenstein says, "shows that the word 'is' has different meanings" in these two sentences.[38]

Now to begin with, merely giving an example or two provides substance for the abstract formulations we presented earlier. Every speaker of English knows that "is" is correctly used in both of the sentences Wittgenstein mentions. Equally, every such speaker knows that it would be a mistake to interpret "the rose is red" to mean "the rose = red." And that "twice two" both is and = four is pretty clearly a fact about language, not about the private mental state of this or that person.[39]

These passages seem to make a very tight connection between rules and meaning. The passage about "not" suggests that where there are no rules there is no meaning, and both passages indicate that the rules give or determine the meaning of the concepts.[40] It appears that such rules are a necessary condition of meaning and

---

[35] For further discussion of the Crusoe case, see Rush Rhees, "Can There Be a Private Language?", *Proceedings of the Aristotelian Society*, Supplementary Vol. 28 (1954), pp. 77–94.

[36] This reference is to a note that will be found at the bottom of page 147e of the *Investigations*. As with several other such notes in the volume, it is not specifically attached to any of the numbered paragraphs on the same or neighboring page. Negation is under explicit discussion from 547 to 557 and various rules governing "not" and other negatives are discussed. The note can be taken to refer to any or all of the rules discussed. The editors of the *Investigations* comment on these notes on page vie.

[37] 558.

[38] 558.

[39] Cf. 355: "And this language like any other is founded on convention."

[40] The passage concerning "is" indicates a part of the difference that is often marked by a distinction between concepts and words. One word, "is," appears in both of the sentences Wittgenstein mentions. But that one word marks or stands for two very different concepts.

that knowledge of the rules is a necessary and sufficient condition of using the concepts with meaning and of knowing their meaning when others use them. Indeed it appears, to use language Wittgenstein employs elsewhere, that the rules form a "strict calculus" and that the meaning of the statements can be "derived"[41] or "read off"[42] by anyone who knows them. Since Wittgenstein supplies no scenario to surround the statements, it might appear that knowledge of the rules is sufficient to teach their meaning no matter what the context or circumstances in which they are uttered or written (sufficient, of course, assuming certain human capacities such as to perceive, to think, to speak).

The idea that shared rules are a necessary condition of meaning is in fact a corollary of the argument against the private language theory. To say that a concept has meaning is to say that it means something, not anything. But then there must be something that determines or specifies what that meaning is, that distinguishes it from other possible meanings. "Rule" and "convention" are the terms Wittgenstein most commonly employs to mark the "something" that does this job. Since a rule can specify the meaning of concept X only if its own meaning is knowable, that is, only if the concepts of which its formulation consists have meanings, and since this condition can be satisfied only if A can test his understanding of the meaning of the rule against the understandings of other persons, it must be the case that the rule is shared among, is known by, a number of speakers. Thus "rule" and "convention" as Wittgenstein uses them have application only to things that are shared.[43] When this emendation has been added, we can rewrite the statement "Without these rules the word ['not'] has as yet no meaning" in a more general form such as "Without rules words have no meaning" and we can treat it as a general proposition in Wittgenstein's philosophy of language.

Accepting this proposition, moreover, seems to require that we also accept the propositions that knowing the rules is not only a necessary but a sufficient condition (bearing in mind the preceding proviso) of knowing the meaning of a concept; that the rules form a calculus the application of which is itself enough to allow any speaker to derive the meaning of any concept or utterance. The argument that there is no meaning without rules, after all, was exactly that rules determine or specify meaning. If rules specify meaning, then knowing the rules would seem to be a sufficient condition of knowing meaning. We might note at once that if, or insofar as, language works in this way, the possibilities of generalizing about political and social life on the basis of knowledge of language would be greatly enlarged. In order to get at what is true and false in this proposition, we will have to look more closely at the notion of a rule and of obeying, following, and being guided by a rule. These notions are before Wittgenstein throughout his work and we might as well admit at once that his account of them cannot be summarized without distortion in short compass. We will try to emphasize those features of his account that are most important to the political philosophical questions dealt with in this book.

There are many cases in which the rules governing the units of language *do in fact* specify or determine meanings with great exactness and in which persons who know the rules ordinarily can know the meanings with no hesitation and great

[41] 162.

[42] 292.

[43] Cf. 199: "Is what we call 'obeying a rule' something that it would be possible for only *one* man to do . . . ?" Italics in original.

certainty. Many rules of activities such as those for doing arithmetic, what Wittgenstein sometimes calls "calculation rules,"[44] are examples, and numerous others can be thought of.[45] The rules governing "2," "+," "=," and "4" determine that 2 + 2 = 4. Moreover, rules that work with this kind of exactness can very often be drawn for some purpose. A rule could be laid down, for example, that the concept "fair trial" can be used only of trials which are public and in which the defendant has counsel of his choice, is able to cross-examine all witnesses, and is judged by a jury of a specified composition. If so, everyone who knows the rule would know what "fair trial" means, could derive its meaning from the rule. Certain forms of conduct are characteristic of situations in which such rules have developed or have been specified. For example, use of the expression "But surely you can see . . .?", say in the context of teaching arithmetic to another person, "is just the characteristic expression of someone who is under the compulsion of a rule."[46] Again, such rules produce the feeling of "doing something or arriving at some decision or conclusion" as a matter of course. "As much," for example, "as it is a matter of course for me to call this colour 'blue.' "[47] And typically "Disputes do not break out over the question whether [such] a rule has been obeyed or not. People don't come to blows over it, for example."[48] Disputes do not often break out, for example, over whether the word "dog" has been used correctly or over whether 1970 Fords are properly called automobiles. These expressions and the activities in which they figure are a familiar part of our lives and they are witness to the degree of certainty about meaning that knowledge of rules sometimes affords us.[49]

But two very important qualifications must be entered to these remarks. First, it is by no means the case that all rules of language have the specificity and give the certainty that makes thought and action applying and following them a "matter of course." Second, not even the most clearly drawn rules of language are themselves *sufficient* to give meaning; they do not, could not, as it were stand alone as determinants of meaning. To understand these qualifications we will have to discuss at least four of Wittgenstein's most important and most closely interconnected ideas: (1) the idea of techniques of applying rules; (2) the notion of the purpose of rules and their applications; (3) the idea of language games; and (4) his notion of "general facts of nature."

"To understand a sentence," Wittgenstein says, "means to understand a language. To understand a language means to be master of a technique."[50] The concept of a "technique" appears again in a contrast between responding to an inspiration and obeying a rule: "In the cases of inspiration *I await* direction. I shall not be able to teach anyone else my 'technique' of [say] following the line. Unless, indeed, I teach him some way of hearkening, some kind of receptivity. But then, of

---

[44] See, for example, II, xi, p. 227e.
[45] See, for example, 162.
[46] 231.
[47] 238.
[48] 240.
[49] Wittgenstein's most extended treatment of such cases is in his *On Certainty*. Edited by G. E. M. Anscombe and G. H. von Wright. Translated by Denis Paul and G. E. M. Anscombe (Oxford: Basil Blackwell, 1969).
[50] 199.

course, I cannot require him to follow the line in the same way as I do."[51] Again, Wittgenstein speaks of cases, for example, learning to judge the genuineness of expressions of feeling, in connection with which what "one acquires . . . is *not* a technique; one learns correct judgments. There are also rules, but they do not form a system, and only experienced people can apply them right." One person can teach another to make such judgments, but what the teacher does is "From time to time . . . gives the right *tip*."[52]

At least a part of what Wittgenstein has in mind in talking about "techniques" is indicated by the following remarks. First, in discussing descriptions and the activity of describing something he says: "Don't always think that you read off what you say from the facts; that you portray these in words according to rules. For even so you would have to apply the rule in the particular case without guidance."[53] And later he says, "How does it come about that this arrow ⤞—➤ *points*? . . . The arrow points only in the application that a living being makes of it."[54] There are rules that govern describing something as a tree, a telephone, an obelisque, and so on, and there are rules for using an arrow to indicate a direction or to give some other instruction. A person who did not know these rules could not use words to describe and could not use an arrow or other such symbols to give directions. But to know the rules is not sufficient to perform these actions. The rules still have to be applied in particular cases and by particular persons. To be able to apply them (as opposed, for example, to being able to recite them) is to be master of a technique.

In some cases, especially those involving physical tasks, the distinction between knowing rules and being able to apply them is readily drawn. The rules for making an omelette or soufflé can be written down and I can read them or even memorize and recite them. But since I am not master of the technique of applying those rules, my omelettes and soufflés are seldom successful. I am clumsy with the implements, my timing is bad, I don't adapt effectively to minor variations in the ingredients such as the size or temperature of the eggs. But there is a technique involved. Many persons have mastered it and they can and do teach it to others. Although it may seem so to the beginner, skilled practitioners do not "await inspiration" in making a soufflé (as they might do in trying to invent a new type of soufflé or a new method of making them), and when they teach the technique to pupils they convey methods and skills relevant to all soufflé making, not only tips and judgments of highly contextual application. Nor does the teaching consist entirely of reciting rules to be followed. It includes demonstrations, examples, gestures, and approval and disapproval of the pupils efforts. This teaching and learning is not something mysterious. We observe it, we can chart its progress, we can replicate it in many instances, distinguish between effective and ineffective teaching, rapid and slow learning. But it is not sufficiently described as teaching or learning rules (although that would be an incomplete, not an inaccurate description); it is best described as teaching or learning the technique of *applying* rules.

When Wittgenstein says, "To understand a language means to be master of a technique," he is calling our attention to the respects in which learning and using language are like learning to make, and making, soufflés. There are indeed rules,

[51] 232, italics in original.

[52] 11, xl, p. 227e. Italics on "tip" in the original, other italics added. This passage should be noted as regards the question whether rules and knowledge of them are a sufficient condition of meaning.

[53] 292.

[54] 454, italics in original.

countless of them. Without rules there would be no language. Persons who do not know the rules can at best make very limited use of the language or of those parts of the language the rules of which they do not know. But our use of language involves in an essential way the techniques of applying the rules as we speak and write. Of course we are seldom aware either of the rules of our native language or of our mastery of the techniques of applying them. (It is probably part of the notion of *mastery* of a technique that the person is ordinarily no longer aware of the rules or his application of them.) The skilled maker of soufflés produces his – to the aspiring beginner – astonishing creations with little awareness of, to say nothing of deliberation about, the process of doing so. From a surprisingly early age native speakers of a language produce what, from the perspective of the adult trying to learn the language in question (who will be better able to recite some of the rules than the child), is an astonishing flow of speech. And they do so with even less awareness, deliberation, or reflection concerning the process than is characteristic of the skilled soufflé maker.

But lack of awareness at any moment in the process of applying them is not the same as lack of knowledge of the rules or lack of mastery of the technique. When people fail to communicate effectively they may be stimulated, even forced, to reflect about the language and the best way to express themselves in it in the circumstances. When disputes break out, as they sometimes do, about the meaning of a statement, the relevant rules may be stated explicitly and their application in the statement in question may be examined. Most important, as with soufflé makers, speakers of a language can teach it to other people. One of Wittgenstein's descriptions of such teaching is especially appropriate at this point:

> How do I explain the meaning of "regular," "uniform," "same" to anyone? I shall explain these words to someone who, say, only speaks French by means of the corresponding French words. But if a person has not yet got the *concepts*, I shall teach him to use the words by means of *examples* and by practice. – And when I do this I do not communicate less to him than I know myself.

> In the course of this teaching I shall show him the same colours, the same lengths, the same shapes, I shall make him find them and produce them, and so on. I shall, for instance, get him to continue an ornamental pattern uniformly when told to do so. – And also to continue progressions. . . .

> I do it, he does it after me; and I influence him by expressions of agreement, rejection, expectation, encouragement. I let him go his way, or hold him back; and so on.

> Imagine witnessing such teaching. None of the words would be explained by means of itself; there would be no logical circle.[55]

Ordinarily children learn to use concepts such as "regular," "same," and "uniform" over a period of time and in the course not of sessions devoted to teaching *them*, but of dealing with various regularities, with things that are the same as one another. (Wittgenstein seems to have in mind teaching these concepts to an adult learning a second language, but the example is hard to take literally because it is hard to imagine an adult who did not have these concepts in his native language.) The important point is that learning them involves learning more than the sort of rules called verbal definitions or explanations. It is when the student can continue a

[55] 208.

variety of patterns, do various progressions, that he can be said to "have got" the concepts. The examples, the exercises, the encouragement and criticism that Wittgenstein mentions are the means by which teachers convey the technique that they themselves know. When the student can go on applying the rules to new situations and cases without guidance, the role of the teacher is at an end because the student has mastered the technique.

Thus (1) there is no meaning without rules, and (2) following rules involves mastering and employing techniques. But just as we cannot understand rules and rule following without adding the notion of a technique, so we cannot understand those two notions together without the further notion of a purpose or point of or to, an objective served by, the rules and techniques. Rules and techniques are rules for doing something, techniques by which to do something. In the case of soufflés, for example, they are rules and techniques for making soufflés; they make no sense apart from the fact that people like to make and eat soufflés. In the examples concerning "regularity" and "same" they are rules and techniques for understanding and using these concepts correctly, that is, for doing progressions, classifying, distinguishing, and the countless other activities that involve making and understanding judgments about sameness and regularity. If human beings had no occasion to engage in these activities, the concepts "same" and "regular" would serve no purpose and the rules and techniques concerning them would have no application. A person who did not understand the purposes of the activities could learn to recite the rules governing the concepts that figure in them and even to mimic or imitate the techniques people employ in applying those rules (for example, small children imitate adults who are shaving, cooking, sewing). But it would at the very least be misleading to say that such persons had got the concepts or that they were following the rules and employing the techniques. As Wittgenstein says, "The game one would like to say, has not only rules but also a point."[56] And we are puzzled and do not know what to say about or do with rules when we do not understand their purpose: ". . . [A]s one wouldn't see the point . . . of a rule by which each piece had to be turned round three times before one moved it. If we found this rule in a board-game we should be surprised and should speculate about the purpose of the rule." (He imagines someone speculating, "Was this prescription meant to prevent one from moving without due consideration?"[57])

We can note only a few of the many qualifications and caveats that must be entered to the idea that rules, rule following, and rule application are purposive. First, to say these things is not to suggest that there is some one purpose or objective to all rules of language and all uses of language. ("The purpose of language," Wittgenstein imagines someone saying, "is to express thoughts." And he responds, "So presumably the purpose of every sentence is to express a thought. Then what thought is expressed, for example, by the sentence 'it's raining'?"[58]) The purposes served by the rules governing our concepts are as diverse as are our purposes in engaging in the myriad of activities of which use of language is an integral part. Because most of our concepts figure in numerous ways in many activities, there is no reason to think that some one purpose is served by the rules governing any single concept.

Further, we must distinguish between, on the one hand, what we might call the

[56] 564, italics in original. See generally 561–569.

[57] 567.

[58] 501.

shared, ordinary purposes of a rule, the purposes established as ordinary, and, on the other, the purposes to which that rule is put by this or that speaker in this or that context. Usually, to utter a pleonasm, the two will coincide. But this is not necessarily or always the case. For example, a usual purpose of such a use of the noun "right" as "I have a right to do X" is to advance what is thought to be a justified claim to do or have something; to assert, against others who threaten to deny it, that one is warranted in doing X. A rule governing the use of this concept is that persons advancing such a claim must be able to supply the warrant to support it (for example, the law or legal principle, the agreement or previous understanding) if others demand it of them. If no such warrant can be brought forward, others are entitled to say something like, "Well maybe you want or would like to have X, and maybe you should have a right to it, but so far you haven't shown us that you do have such a right." Another rule is that persons who have such a warrant may simply *expect* others to respect the right, may look upon respect for the right on the part of others as a matter of duty or obligation, not as a kind, generous, or otherwise superogatory action. The purpose of the latter rule might be said to be to establish and maintain the understanding that rights are to be respected as a matter of course, that persons with rights do not have to request or petition for their being respected or feel gratitude to those who do respect them. The purpose of the former rule is that the kinds of expectation encouraged by the latter one not be entertained casually or irresponsibly. These rules, the purposes they ordinarily serve, and the techniques of applying them are part of the social practice of rights; one learns them as a participant in the practice; one can convey them to others. Most of the time the purposes of particular speakers will coincide with these shared, established, ordinary purposes.

Jones may nevertheless understand these rules and ordinary purposes and yet use the concept with very different and special purposes. Perhaps he or she says, "I have a right to X," not in order to fend off threatened denials or interferences on the part of others, but in the hope of eliminating his or her own self-doubts and building the self-confidence necessary to doing X effectively. Or perhaps he or she says it (knowing that Smith won't interfere) because he or she wants to "rub in" the fact that he or she has a right that Smith does not enjoy. These latter purposes are not themselves part of the usual, shared purposes of the concepts and their rules. But A may nevertheless put the concepts to such uses, and B can understand that this is the case and indeed must do so to understand A's statements. Moreover, as Wittgenstein reminds us, a person might say "I have a right to do X" idly, with *no* purpose definite to use of these concepts in mind. Such a person might do so simply to make small talk, to enliven a lagging conversation. "And do I always talk with a very definite purpose? — And is what I say meaningless because I don't?"[59] It is part of the very notion of a rule that uses with a special purpose and uses with no definite purpose cannot be the ordinary or usual thing.[60] But given established

---

[59] II, 1x, p. 188e.

[60] "It is only in normal cases that the use of a word is clearly prescribed; we know, are in no doubt, what to say in this or that case. The more abnormal the case, the more doubtful it becomes what we are to say. And if things were quite different from what they are — ... if rule became exception and exception rule; or if both become phenomena of roughly equal frequency — this would make our normal language-games lose their point. — The procedure of putting a lump of cheese on a balance and fixing the price by the turn of the scale would lose its point if it frequently happened for such lumps to suddenly grow or shrink for no obvious reason" (142).

rules and purposes for a concept, and given that the surrounding parts of the discourse are cast in more usual form, special uses are both possible and familiar.

The phenomenon of meaning, then, cannot be understood apart from the purposes, objectives, and intentions which concepts serve and with which they are used. But just as with the equally essential notions of rules and techniques, "purpose," "objective," and related concepts must not be reified by students of language and meaning or treated as consisting of a single entity which constitutes that essence of language the existence of which Wittgenstein is at pains to deny. The purposes for which concepts are used are multiple and diverse, and they shift from context to context and from one speaker to another.

6. Language Games and General Facts of Nature

If shared rules, techniques, and purposes are necessary but not sufficient to meaningful use of language, what must be added in order to achieve a complete analysis? Once again Wittgenstein's first response is that there is no one thing and no combination of things that will complete the analysis — indeed that the notion of a complete analysis of meaning is an indication of confusion. But he does carry the discussion beyond the point to which we have followed it up to now. Much of his further thinking is presented via the elusive and difficult notions of "language-games" and "general facts of nature."

The most important point in connection with these notions, a point implicit in our entire discussion thus far, is also the most obvious and commonsensical one, namely, that language is an integral part of the things we do. Language, as we might say, is not something independent of the actions we take, something we use to talk *about* our lives and the things we do, it is *part of* our lives, our actions.[61] When we think about language, Wittgenstein counsels, the appropriate thought is not "without language we could not communicate with one another." Rather we should think "without language we cannot influence other people in such-and-such ways; cannot build roads and machines, etc."[62] Of course we do use language to communicate about things we and others do, but we do so as a part of an activity. Social scientists, to take but one example, talk about human behavior. But in doing so they themselves engage in something that is an activity in its own right, namely, the activity of doing social science. And someone else engaging in another activity, say an historian, a philosopher of social science, a government official assessing applications for research funds for social science, might talk about the activities of social scientists.

It is a characteristic of many such activities that they depend upon a more or less definite set of conditions or circumstances, the setting of particular institutions and arrangements, and the presence of delimited groups or classes of persons that share certain experiences. The actions, assumptions, procedures, and understandings characteristic of the activity are readily comprehensible within those conditions and among those persons. But if the same actions are taken, the same procedures

---

[61] "What do psychologists record? . . . Isn't it the behaviour of human beings; in particular their utterances? But these [that is the utterances] are not *about* behaviour." II, v, p. 179e, italics on "these" in original, italics on "about" added.

[62] 491.

followed, outside of the usual context they are surprising, seem odd or even bizarre, and we have difficulty comprehending and responding to them. In the context of the auction house and surrounded by items to sell and experienced auction goers to purchase them, the agitated manner, the loud, rapid-fire speech and technical terminology of the auctioneer pose no problem for us. The same conduct and terminology on the part of a salesclerk in a department store or the corner grocer behind his counter, to say nothing of the lawyer meeting clients in his office, would likely leave the auditors puzzled and perhaps dismayed. The anxious pacing, repeated inquiries, stories, and concerns exchanged that are commonplace among "expectant fathers" in the precincts of delivery rooms would be incomprehensible in a barber shop, a ticket agency, or even an employment office. Those present might know all of the words spoken, might have seen all the movements and gestures, and yet be mystified by both. Auctioneering, we might say, is a language game and various concepts, gestures, assumptions that have a clear meaning within the game are puzzling outside of its limits. And so also with awaiting the birth of one's child.

The intimate relationship between meaning, on the one hand, and the things we do and the contexts in which we typically do them, on the other, is at the heart of Wittgenstein's notion of language games.[63] "But how many kinds of sentences are there?" A common grammatical answer might be "assertion, question, and command." But this is woefully inadequate. In fact there "are *countless* kinds: countless different kinds of use of what we call 'symbols,' 'words,' 'sentences.' And this multiplicity is not something fixed, given once for all; but new types of language, new language-games, we might say, come into existence, and others become obsolete and forgotten." And "the term language-game," he goes on to say, "is meant to bring into prominence the fact that the *speaking* of language is part of an activity, or of a form of life."[64]

Some of the language games Wittgenstein mentions may involve terminology confined to the activities in question. Doing physics, playing football, living in a fraternity are distinct activities in certain respects. The technical terminology of the physicists, football players and fraternity members would be examples of words

---

[63] But he often discusses the same relationship without using the term "language game." For examples of this see 581, 583, 337, 198, 525, II, xl, p. 219e. Hoping and intending are sometimes called language games, and the other examples he gives might be as well. The important thing is not to work out defining criteria of Wittgenstein's use of the technical term "language game," but to understand the relationships between language and meaning on the one hand and types of human activities, contexts, customs, shared understandings, and so on, on the other.

[64] 23. The passage just quoted is followed by a number of examples of language games, including: "Giving orders, and obeying them," "Describing the appearance of an object, or giving its measurements," "Constructing an object from a description," "Making up a story, and reading it," "Guessing riddles," "Making a joke; telling it," "Solving a problem in practical arithmetic," "Asking, thanking, cursing, greeting, praying." 23. Leaving aside what he calls the "clear and simple" language games that he introduces early in the book as "objects of comparison" (130), among the many other examples of language games that he mentions are naming, ostensive definition, playing chess and other games, determining the truth of propositions, reading, expressing and talking about pain and other sensations, justifying various decisions, intending, believing, negating propositions, expecting, hoping, pointing, understanding, expressing grief, talking about physical objects, talking about sense impressions, reporting dreams, expressing fear, interpreting pictures, searching for the right word, using color concepts.

with such a restricted use. But distinct terminology is not the key to understanding "language game" or to distinguishing one language game from another. (It would be, for example, quite easy to compile a lengthy list of words that figure in most if not all the activities Wittgenstein mentions as examples of language games or that we have added to his list. Anyway it is its place in the activity that makes the terminology importantly distinct.) The key, rather, is the role or part that the words (and gestures, facial expression, and other means of communication) actually play in the activities we perform in playing the language games, activities which, in various ways, we distinguish one from another as a part of engaging in them. What role do the technical terms, gestures, and rapid speech play in the auction? What role do the pacing, repeated inquiries, and so forth, play in the activity of expectant fatherhood? Now, of course, these roles are determined in part by the rules, techniques, and purposes of the actions and concepts that are part of the activity. But at least a part of the point of talking about language games, of adding that concept to such terms as rule and technique, is that there is more to meaning than can be encompassed in any one of the notions discussed earlier or in a mere adding up of what is conveyed by each of them alone. We get closer to Wittgenstein's idea by saying that there is the combination of, the connections among, particular rules, techniques, and purposes. In some cases a particular rule, purposes served by it, and techniques of following it and applying it go together, and are seldom if ever used apart from one another. And the distinctive combination formed by them, the particular ways they connect up in our use of them, may be thought of as forming a language game. But there is also more: "it is our *acting*, which lies at the bottom of the language-game."[65]

What over and above rules, purposes, and techniques, and combinations thereof, does Wittgenstein have in mind when he says that acting is at the bottom of language games? Perhaps something like the following. Children who have never played card games might learn rules of poker such as the rank order of hands, might see their purpose in the game, and might be able to apply them to decide who had won a particular hand. But knowledge of such rules, purposes, and techniques would not be sufficient for them to grasp the meaning of many of the things that are said and done around poker tables. Even adults experienced with other card games and well instructed in the rules of poker will at first be awkward in their own play and will be slow to comprehend many of the remarks, gestures, facial expressions, and so on, of experienced players. Indeed seasoned poker players often have the same experience on their first encounter with a group of players. Or to use one of Wittgenstein's examples (he is talking about someone doing geometry): "What tells us that someone is seeing the drawing three-dimensionally is a certain kind of 'knowing one's way about.' Certain gestures, for instance, which indicate the three-dimensional relations: fine shades of behavior."[66] These fine shade of behavior are seldom entirely uniform among all those who participate in an activity and they are rarely if ever covered by rules governing the activity. Hence we cannot adequately explain them or the learning of them in terms of rules or rule application and following.[67] Yet regular participants in and observers of such

---

[65] *On Certainty*, op. cit., 204, p. 28e, italics in original.

[66] II, xi, p. 203e.

[67] "Where is the connexion effected," Wittgenstein asks rhetorically, "between the sense of the expression 'Lets play a game of chess' and all the rules of the game?" (197) That is, how is

activities will know their place in them. They will readily be able to distinguish between their own capacity to participate in activities in which they "know their way about" and those in which they do not, and they will be able to distinguish between others who do and who do not. Such persons, we might say, have not only mastered the rules, purposes, and techniques involved, they have mastered the language game.

There is, I think, nothing mysterious, nothing "tacit" in any specialized sense, no hidden or underlying "structure" implied in this notion of a language game. Recall again that Wittgenstein often omits the term "language-game" and simply talks of the context, the customs, the surroundings, the characteristic features, and so forth, of particular activities and uses of language. So far from being hidden or tacit, these features are known to and perpetuated by experienced participants in the activity. If they are seldom discussed or iterated explicitly by participants, it is not because they are unknown, hidden, or mysterious but because they are taken for granted in the conduct of participants, they are among the most important things new participants learn from those who are experienced in the activity, and they are among the most important things that observers must learn if they are to understand the meaning of what participants say and do. The concept "language game," to repeat, "is meant to bring into prominence the fact that the *speaking* of language is part of an activity." And since in fact, human activities differ one from another in important respects, it is meant to give prominence to the ways in which the uses of language that figure in them vary from one human activity to another. Just as games in the ordinary sense differ from one another in various ways, and it is impossible to identify a single criterion of a game or a single test by which to distinguish any one game from all others, so other human activities differ one from the others in various ways and there is no single criterion of "activity" or "language game" and no single criterion by which to distinguish any one language game from all others. What philosophers of language, social scientists, and all others who wish to understand meaning must do is look to see how the activity in question forms a "pattern which recurs, with different variations, in the weave of our life" and look

---

it that both speaker and auditor can know, from this mere statement, what is being proposed and what acting on that proposal will involve. Well they know what playing chess involves, that is, they know that there is a board, certain pieces, rules for moving those pieces, and so forth, and they know that "playing chess" refers to those things and those rules. So we can say that the connection is effected "in part in the list of the rules of the game, in the teaching of it," (197) in the persons in question having learned those rules, and so on. But the sentence just quoted does not end with "in the list of the rules of the game, in the teaching of it." Wittgenstein goes on to say "in the day-to-day practice of playing." The connection is effected "in the list of rules of the game, in the teaching of it, in the day-to-day practice of playing it (197). At 31 he says the explanation "This is the King" (in a chess set) can be helpful to someone "not because the person to whom we give the explanation already knows rules, but because in another sense he is already master of a game." And he continues as follows: "I am explaining chess to someone; and I begin by pointing to a chessman and saying 'This is the King; it can move like this, . . . and so on! . . . In this case we shall say: the words 'This is the King' . . . are a definition only if the learner already 'knows what a piece in a game is.' That is, if he has played other games, or has watched other people playing (and understood) – and *similar things*. Further, only under these conditions will he be able to ask relevantly in the course of learning the game, 'What do you call this?' – that is, this piece in a game." Italics in original.

to see how the uses of this or that concept fit into and contribute to that pattern and that weave.[68]

To sum up our results thus far, Wittgenstein argues that the meaning of a concept is its use in language, and its use is to be understood in terms of shared rules, techniques, and purposes and their role or place in a language game or activity that is part of the lives of those who speak the language. This "list" should not be thought of as giving the essence or general character of meaning. Some of the items on the list, for example, rules and a place in a language game, do seem to be necessary to meaning in Wittgenstein's view. But there are many kinds of rules, and language games vary immensely in substance and form. Hence although it is essential to have the categories "rule" and "language game" (or some equivalent terms) in one's kit of analytic tools, one must not think that this is somehow sufficient for the purpose of analyzing or even understanding meaning in this case or that.

As already indicated, however, our list still omits at least one element in Wittgenstein's analysis that is important for present purposes, namely, his notion of "general facts of nature." Meaning is in language games. When we encounter a statement or other utterance apart from the language game or games in which it plays a role, we are often puzzled by it. If the statement has no place in any language game, whether one that is already established or one that the speakers in question are setting up, it has no meaning.[69] Language games, and the rules, techniques, and purposes that figure in them, are a part of our lives, of our activities. They are something that we do. (Recall yet again his statement, "it is our *acting*, which lies at the bottom of the language-game.") In the *Investigations* he says that when someone has "exhausted the justifications" that are part of the game in which his statement was made or some other action of his was taken, he has "reached

---

[68] II, 1, p. 174. We should also note, however, that Wittgenstein sometimes uses the term "language game" in a manner that seem to refer to the entire constellation of activities in which human beings, or at least human beings who speak a single language (for example, French or English), engage. In such cases "language game" seems to be equivalent to "language." 7 and II, xi, p. 200, might be interpreted in this way. Perhaps this suggests that there is a certain "knowing one's way about" that enters into all uses of language. And it may be that something along this line is what Wittgenstein has in mind when he speaks of the "common behavior of mankind" that forms the "system of reference by means of which we interpret an unknown language" (206). This generalized knowledge allows those who have it to understand something about what is going on in activities with which they are not closely familiar but it is not enough to permit them to understand and enter into the activity as experienced participants can do. It may be enough to allow them to know that they *do not* understand in the way participants do. The main thrust of his use of "language game," however, is that activities are distinct in important ways and that meaning and understanding thereof depend upon the distinctive particulars of the activity.

[69] Wittgenstein quite often concludes that statements by philosophers are without meaning and indeed that whole philosophical theories have commonly been built upon statements that have no place in any language games and are therefore senseless. Perhaps the most prominent examples are statements such as "I know that I am in pain" that are used to support the private language theory. [It can't be said of me at all (except perhaps as a joke) that I *know* I am in pain. What is it supposed to mean — except perhaps that I *am* in pain? 245, italics in original.] But although Wittgenstein is often enough ready to say that this or that statement, *as here before us* in the work of a philosopher, plays no part in any language game and hence is nonsensical, he is very chary about saying there is not or could not be a language game in which that utterance does or could play a role. As the passage just quoted says, even "I know I am in pain" would be meaningful in the language game of telling jokes. His most general statement on

bedrock and ... [his] spade is turned. In such circumstances, Wittgenstein goes on, "I am inclined to say 'This is simply what I do.' "[70]

Owing to these statements, these views, we might call Wittgenstein's theory of language and meaning conventionalism or a conventionalist theory. Language, meaning, and the uses and limits thereof are a part of the patterns of thought and action of human beings, and they are to be understood not by examining something independent of what human beings do (for example, nature, revelation, something transcendental), but by examining the elements of those patterns of action themselves, the rules men have laid down or arrived at, the techniques, the human purposes, and so forth.[71] Certainly Wittgenstein's theory should be called a conventionalist theory. But left at the point to which we have taken it thus far, our sketch of the theory would suggest that the things human beings do, that the patterns of action found among them, are as it were altogether self-generating and self-sustaining, are in no way influenced by factors or forces the existence and operation of which do not themselves depend upon human beings and their actions. Wittgenstein's use of the notion "general facts of nature," insofar as its sketchy and oracular formulation allows us to interpret it, suggests that this would be an oversimplification.

"If the formation of concepts can be explained by facts of nature, should we not be interested, not in grammar, but rather in that in nature which is the basis of grammar?"[72] Wittgenstein agrees immediately that his interest does "include the correspondence between concepts and certain very general acts of nature." But he is doing philosophy, "not natural science ... [and not] natural history." For him this means that his interest is not in facts of nature as "possible *causes* of the formation of concepts."[73] Causal questions, for example, the causes of differences in the way persons see a picture or a puzzle, "are of interest to psychologists."[74] But as philosophers, he goes on, "We are interested [not in causes but] in the concept [in this case the concept "see"] and its place among the concepts of experience."[75] The philosopher's task is to "assemble reminders" as to the way this and related concepts are used; his aim in doing so is to clarify their use and thereby

---

this point, which should be pondered by all of those who use his authority to talk about the limits or bounds of sense or meaning, goes as follows: "To say, 'This combination of words makes no sense' excludes it from the sphere of language and thereby bounds the domain of language. But when one draws a boundary it may be for various kinds of reason. If I surround an area with a fence or a line or otherwise, the purpose may be to prevent someone from getting in or out; but it may also be part of a game and the players be supposed, say, to jump over the boundary; or it may show where the property of one man ends and that of another begins' and so on. So if I draw a boundary line that is not yet to say what I am drawing it for" (499). The most important point is that *we draw* the bounds of sense; it is something that we do.

[70] 217.

[71] I do not find in Wittgenstein a doctrine concerning the genesis of origin of language and meaning, of how it was possible for language to develop among human beings. He is analyzing what we do, not how it came about that we do what we do. For a brief attempt to sketch how a genetic analysis consistent with the Wittgensteinian theory might go, see Peter Strawson *Meaning and Truth* (London: Oxford University Press, 1970).

[72] II, xii, p. 230e.

[73] Ibid.

[74] II, xi, p. 193e.

[75] Ibid.

to help psychologists and others avoid or clear up the kinds of misunderstandings that conceptual confusion breeds.[76] And for this purpose, just as one can invent language games with which to compare those that are actually played,[77] so "we can also invent fictitious natural history" that will help to dispel misconceptions concerning language and meaning.[78]

What, then, are "general facts of nature," what other than causal relationships does Wittgenstein have in mind when he talks about the "correspondence" between such facts and concepts, and what is the philosophical interest of these "correspondences"? On the first point, in the two main comments on this subject (in the *Investigations*) Wittgenstein characterizes general facts of nature as "such facts as are hardly ever mentioned because of their great generality"[79] and "Such facts as mostly do not strike us because of their generality."[80] The first of these passages is a note that Wittgenstein added to a discussion in which he speaks of "characteristic expressions of pain, of fear, of joy." And after mentioning these items he goes on to observe that, "The procedure of putting a lump of cheese on a balance and fixing the price by the turn of the scale would lose its point if it frequently happened for such lumps to suddenly grow or shrink for no obvious reason."[81] In other places, although without using the phrase "general facts of nature," he speaks of "the primitive, the natural, expression of sensations" such as pain,[82] and of intention,[83] says it is "by nature" that we give "spontaneous expression to wishes in certain circumstances,"[84] and asserts that "commanding, questioning, recounting, chatting, are as much a part of our natural history as walking, eating, drinking, playing."[85]

Now, first, Wittgenstein does not say in these (or in any other passage), "Here is what I mean by general facts of nature, here are some examples of such facts." Thus we can only conjecture that he views the items mentioned in the passages quoted as instances of such facts. And even if we accept this conjecture, the examples are a mixed lot and it is difficult to derive a set of criteria for the use of "general facts of nature" from them. That the weight of pieces of cheese does not suddenly and mysteriously change is a different sort of fact, enters into human

[76] On the purpose of philosophy see esp. 116–133.

[77] 130.

[78] II, xii, p. 230e. Although we cannot pursue the matter here, it is worth noting that in these passages Wittgenstein seems to concede that there is some sense of "cause" in which it might be possible to show a causal relationship between facts of nature and at least some of our concepts. But it is explicit that knowledge of such a relationship would not render unnecessary or in any other way be in conflict or competition with the kinds of understandings pursued by the philosophers. Since one of the philosophers' aims is to analyze the rules governing concepts and the purposes with which concepts are used, it appears that in his view analyses of cause and analyses of rules and purposes, and the propositions that such analyses yield, are different but mutually compatible types of analysis and propositions.

[79] Note, bottom of p. 56e.

[80] II, xii, p. 230e.

[81] 142. He mentions natural numbers on the same page but he clearly is not referring to them in the note concerning general facts of nature.

[82] 244. He mentions crying as an example.

[83] The examples given are a cat stalking a bird and a beast wanting to escape from some enclosure or trap. And then he has added, "Connection with propositions about sensations."

[84] 411. But the full sentence reads "By nature and by a particular training, a particular education we are disposed to give," and so on.

[85] 25.

affairs in a way different from the fact that human beings chat and walk. To mention only the most obvious point, human beings decide whether to chat or walk in this circumstance or that, but pieces of cheese do not decide to retain their weight and shape.

One could say, however, that we human beings did not decide that we would have the capacity to chat and walk, form intentions, and express wishes, any more than we decided that we would have lungs and not gills, or eyes in the front and not on the sides of our heads. Our capacity to chat and walk is just as much a given as are our anatomical and physiological properties, as are the physical properties of matter. Perhaps, then, general facts of nature are features and properties of ourselves and the world that are not the result of choices, decisions, and actions on the part of human beings. Or rather they are a subclass of such features and properties, those which, although we know about them — or perhaps *because* we know about them so well — "are hardly ever mentioned because of their great generality" and which therefore have to be called to our attention if awareness of them would help us to be clear as to how certain concepts work.

Assuming that the foregoing is a reasonable interpretation of what Wittgenstein means by general facts of nature, how are we to interpret his remark that there is a "correspondence" between them and our concepts? It is easier to say what these correspondences do not, and on the rest of Wittgenstein's theory cannot, consist in, and we will begin with that. Perhaps we will then be in a position to piece together such elements of a more positive answer as Wittgenstein's limited remarks may permit us to identify.

First, although there may or may not be a clear sense in which "general facts of nature" *exist* independent of human conventions, decisions, and actions, they are not "facts" and they are not, as we might say, the particular facts that they are independent of conventions, decisions, and actions. "Fact," after all (that is, the concept "fact"), is not itself given by nature; as with all concepts it has meaning only in a language. And although capacities necessary to having language may be "given," the languages human beings actually speak are not. Whatever the universe may consist of, identifying and talking about any part of it as a "fact," as "general," as "natural," or in any other way is a human action that is done in a language. The action of identifying a general fact of nature as such would not be possible if none of the entities that are properly so labeled existed or were known to us (though once we had the concepts we could imagine some); but neither would that action be possible without concepts, the rules and conventions that govern their use, and the action of applying them. This point holds in a yet more obvious way concerning activities over and above merely identifying general facts of nature, for example, reflections concerning their correspondence with other things. Hence it cannot be the case that the mere existence of those things, states of affairs, or whatever that Wittgenstein calls general facts of nature is a sufficient condition of our having a concept that "corresponds" to them or a language game in which a concept figures.[86] The correspondence between concepts and general facts of nature cannot be the relationship between an X and a Y that is a sufficient condition of that X.

Can a general fact of nature be a necessary condition of a concept or a language

---

[86] Wittgenstein's discussion of "seeing" and "seeing as" is relevant here. See esp. II, xi, pp. 193e–229e.

game? Wittgenstein's answer seems to be that this question is too simple. When we have set aside the thought that general facts of nature are or could constitute sufficient conditions of concepts or language games, we see that there is no single type of relationship between them, that there are various types of correspondence between them.

To begin with, it is commonplace that one condition or state of affairs can be necessary to a number of actions and the concepts that are part of those actions. For example, the fact that I have the physical capacities necessary to writing my name is a necessary condition of giving an autograph, of writing a check, of charging merchandise at the department store, and many other actions. Thus although we can say that the correspondence between this natural capacity and, say, writing a check consists of the former being a necessary condition of the latter, we must bear in mind that this statement is hardly an exhaustive account of the correspondence between the natural capacity and concepts. Moreover, writing my name is, and can be, one of the previously mentioned actions only because certain rules and conventions, in addition to those which govern the use of "writing my name" and any other concepts involved in the statements we make, are established in society. Writing a check, for example, presupposes a complex array of institutions and procedures that are generally accepted in some society or social group. Thus the statement "the general fact of nature (that most human beings have the physical capacity to learn to write their names) is a necessary condition of the activity of writing a check" presupposes, brings along, the whole set of conventions concerning writing checks. It may be that no society would develop these conventions if certain natural capacities were not widely distributed among their members. However this may be, it is evident that the existence, even the known, identified existence, of these capacities is a necessary condition of writing a check only in a rather complex sense.

The foregoing reflection suggests a further point which may be a part of Wittgenstein's thought when he says that for his purposes fictitious natural history could do just as well as true natural history. Assume we are trying to understand the place of the concept "check" or "writing a check" among the concepts of business and commercial practice. The general fact of nature we have been discussing might enter into our discussion by way of specifying one of the conditions necessary to these practices as we now know them. (As Wittgenstein suggests, however, owing to the very generality, that is, the common, taken-for-granted character, of this fact, it is unlikely that it would enter into such a discussion.) But we can readily imagine a natural history which would allow the practices and the concept to work as they do, but in which the participants did not have the capacity to learn to write their name. Perhaps, for example, these human beings are able to register the sound of their voices on plastic disks and to play voices back simply by running a finger over the disk. Although the physical character and mode of handling "checks" would be different than they now are, the place of a check in commercial practice could be just as we know it to be. Or to take a general fact of nature that is prominent in Wittgenstein's discussions, suppose that the "natural expressions of pain" were not the cries, grimaces, and groans with which we are familiar, but rather the emission of certain odors. The indicators of pain, the marks of someone suffering pain, would be different from those we know, but in other respects the concept "pain" and the activities in which it figures could go unchanged.

In short, not only can one fact of nature be necessary to several concepts and activities, in at least some cases several different facts of nature could satisfy a condition necessary to a single activity. Perhaps this consideration lies behind Wittgenstein's choice of the logically weak word "correspondence" in his general remarks about the relationship between general facts of nature and concepts.

There are other cases, however, in which a general fact of nature is necessary to a concept in a stronger, less qualified, or less complex sense of "necessary." The fact that pieces of cheese do not suddenly and mysteriously change their weight is an example. Wittgenstein says that we have to mention such facts "in order to explain the significance, I mean the importance [as opposed to the possibility?] of a concept," and he says that if such facts changed, our normal language games would "lose their point." [87] If pieces of cheese suddenly shrank, we could still put them on a balance and record the changes in their weight. And indeed there might be a point in doing so — in scientific experiments, for example. But in such circumstances the procedure of "putting a lump of cheese on a balance and fixing the price by the turn of the scale would lose its point," that is, it would lose the point that it in fact now has in our lives.[88] The procedures and the concepts that figure in it could not be entirely understood by reference to the general facts of nature, but neither could they be understoood apart from it.

An even stronger connection is exemplified not by the particular fact of nature that human beings suffering pain cry, grimace, and groan, but by what we might call the generic fact that they show *some* "outward signs of pain."[89] On Wittgenstein's theory, our language game of pain would not merely lose its importance without this fact, it would be altogether impossible. Again, this is not to say that the generic fact of nature is a sufficient condition of our language game of pain, but it does seem that it is necessary in the strong sense that without it the game would be strictly impossible. And when we reflect on this example, it is immediately evident that there are other, indeed many other, such cases.

But Wittgenstein has at least one more qualification to make, one more warning to issue as regards the inferences we may draw from cases of the last type discussed. He is not, first of all, advancing an hypothesis to the effect that "if such-and-such facts of nature were different people would have different concepts."[90] He is not, I think, denying that such an hypothesis *could* be plausible; he is simply saying that more would have to be known in order to render it plausible. The important point he wants to make is the by now familiar one that we should not treat these general facts of nature as somehow giving us the essence, the ultimate metaphysical standing of (at least some of) our concepts. The passage we just quoted continues as follows: "But: if anyone believes that certain concepts are absolutely the correct ones, and that having different ones would mean not realizing something that we realize — then let him imagine certain very general facts of nature to be different from what we are used to, and the formation of concepts different from the usual ones will become intelligible to him."[91] Perhaps Wittgenstein is saying that the world could be other than the way we know it to be, that in this sense our

[87] Note on bottom of page 56e.
[88] 142.
[89] 257.
[90] II, xii, p. 230e.
[91] Ibid.

statements about general facts of nature are contingently not necessarily true and we should not "sublime"[92] those statements and everything tied up with them by assigning them a status they do not have. But what is more important is the suggestion, or rather the reminder, that we are *able* to imagine the general facts of nature to be other than they are; that our language permits us to form, give sensible (as opposed to nonsensical or meaningless) expression to, and make use of the thought that general facts of nature could be other than they are and specific thoughts as to how they might have been or might be. This or that general fact of nature may be said to be a necessary condition of this or that concept or language game, but our language – our thought and action – are not held in the grip of a world that is independent, and in control, of them. At the bottom of our language games are not general facts of nature but "our acting."

Meaning is in language. And language involves shared rules, techniques for interpreting and applying those rules, and purposes served by the rules and the techniques of applying them. Rules, techniques, and purposes delimit and at the same time have their use in language games, in sometimes more, sometimes less distinct patterns or clusters of activities in which, in fact, human beings engage. Among many other language games that we can play is the game, the activity, of identifying and reflecting about (what in the game is called) general facts of nature. These facts stand in a variety of relationships to and with the other elements of the language games in which they figure; just as an understanding of language and meaning requires that we understand the several roles played by rules, techniques, and so on, in our language games, so it requires an understanding of the several relationships that in practice obtain between general facts of nature and the other prominent elements of those games. For this purpose or that it will be useful to say that this or that element determines or is dependent upon some other. The most important point, however, is that all these elements are a part of what we do. Those who would understand language and meaning must look at what we do – and they must do so "from close to."[93]

7. Wittgenstein's Philosophy of Language and Political and Social Philosophy

We noted earlier that Wittgenstein presented a very restricted view of the objectives of philosophy and indeed the achievements open to philosophers. Philosophy is a purely descriptive activity, and what it describes is the obvious, what everyone knows; it should not generalize, explain, or even advance theses, and although criticism and reform are possible, they are no part of the philosopher's task. Philosophy is a therapeutic enterprise. Its aim is to help others to escape from the sort of confusions and muddles that result from inattention to language and its place in human affairs. To these ends it might clarify the use of concepts such as "authority," "obligation," and "rights" but it would do so not to teach us something we do not know about these concepts – because we already know everything there is to know about them – but to clear up difficulties that we have

[92] 38.
[93] 51.

gotten into by reminding us of things we know but to which we are not paying sufficient attention.[94]

In one respect our entire discussion of Wittgenstein has been an argument that his own philosophical practice does not conform to his preachments about what philosophy should do. The arguments we have been examining constitute a highly general account or analysis of language and meaning. Of course this account insists upon the great diversity of language games and makes no attempt to reduce that diversity or to explain it in terms of some single or very small number of quintessential factors. But the argument that language is diverse and irreducible is itself a kind of generalization, and the account contains numerous other contentions of equal generality.

For immediate purposes the two most important of these contentions are the discussions of "right," "true," and "know" in connection with the critique of the possibility of a private language and the closely connected arguments about rules, language games, and the relationships between the latter and what people do. To begin with the first discussion, recall Wittgenstein's argument that public language eliminates the difficulty with "E," the difficulty that a person using "E" would have nothing independent of his memory against which to test his use and hence could not know that he was actually using it in the correct manner. Unlike private language, in short, public language allows of such notions as a correct and incorrect, sensible and nonsensical use of concepts and in many cases allows certainty as to whether a concept has been used correctly or nonsensically.

This claim on Wittgenstein's part is essential to his view of philosophy as therapeutic. The notion of doing therapy presupposes the possibility of distinguishing between healthy and unhealthy, normal and abnormal, correct and incorrect. If there were no established, shared criteria by which to judge whether a particular use of language is sensible rather than nonsensical, there would be no grounds on which to claim that there has been confusion, misuse, and so forth, and no grounds on which to claim that therapy has been administered and a cure actually effected. Moreover, Wittgenstein's claim that "I know I am in pain" is nonsensical, that the grammars of talk about sense perception and talk about physical objects are different, or any one of the myriad of other claims he advances in his work, are claims not only that *he* knows that this is so, but that what he knows is (even if they could not say it on their own) known to be so by any speaker of the language. It is for this reason that he believes he need do, indeed can do, no more to support his claims than "assemble reminders" of how the concepts are in fact used by any speaker playing the language game or games in which they figure. Although there is a great diversity of language games and much variation in the manner in which they are played, knowing how to play them involves, at least very often, knowing rules that hold "not just once" and not just for one person, but for everyone who plays this particular game wherever and whenever they play it. In these respects, such claims as " 'I know I am in pain' is nonsensical" are put forward as truths of an entire generality, truths that hold from speaker to speaker and from one instance of playing the game or games in question to another. In short, Wittgenstein's contention that philosophy *can* be therapeutic rests upon, presupposes, the possibility of identifying recognizably true generalizations about language. And in

[94] See esp. 80–90, 108–133, 254–255, 309–464, II, xi, p. 206e, II, xii, p. 230e, II, xiv, p. 232e.

his own practice of philosophical therapy he advanced a large number of such generalizations and claimed that they are true.

If such generalizations about language are possible, the question arises as to the purpose or purposes of identifying and advancing them, the uses to which advancing them might profitably be put. Wittgenstein argues that philosophy is and should be no more than therapeutic. This is in effect an argument that the only useful purpose that could be served by advancing such generalizations would be to help us escape from muddles and confusions that we have gotten into by not attending to what we as speakers of the language know about it. (And it seems that it is primarily, though not exclusively, philosophers who get into such muddles — and this because they attempt to use concepts outside of the language games that are their natural homes.) One can readily agree that this is a valid and an important purpose, a valid and important reason for making the sort of investigations that Wittgenstein made. Numerous writers have agreed that, as it is sometimes expressed, philosophy is a "second-order" discipline or activity. It does not itself attempt to teach us about our lives and the world. Insofar as it presents statements about these subjects, they are no more than reminders of what we already know. The task of improving our knowledge of ourselves and the world falls to the various sciences and social sciences. The philosopher's task is to examine the manner in which physicists, biochemists, sociologists, and so forth, use concepts in framing, interpreting, and reporting the results of their "first-order" investigations, to help them avoid or escape from muddles, confusions, fruitless or confounded perplexities — "hangups" is the vernacular suggested by the notion of therapy — that result from misuse of the concepts they employ. Thus political and social philosophy would be a critical examination of the language of political science, sociology, anthropology. Because many of the concepts used by political and other social scientists also figure in political and social life, political and social philosophy might also contribute to clarity concerning the language of politics and social interaction. Its objectives, however, remain therapeutic; it aims to remove and avoid obstacles to an understanding of politics and society, not to supply such an understanding.[95]

To repeat, performing such therapy depends on its being possible to *know* the correct and incorrect uses of whatever concepts are in question. Wittgenstein's philosophy of language provides reasons for thinking that this condition can be satisfied. (It is not the only extant set of reasons for thinking that this condition can be satisfied. Many of the writers who have taken the view that philosophy is a second-order activity have based their position on understandings of language very different from Wittgenstein's.) But in providing reasons for thinking that a therapeutic philosophy is possible, his philosophy of language also provides reasons for thinking that philosophy, particularly political and social philosophy, can legitimately aspire to further, in some respects more ambitious, objectives and accomplishments. To make this entirely explicit we need only combine the proposition that we can *know* the proper use of concepts with Wittgenstein's argument that the "*speaking* of a language is part of an activity,"[96] that acting is at the bottom of the language game. On this view knowledge of the use of language is also knowledge of actions and activities. Understanding an activity involves

[95] For a recent and explicit endorsement of this view of political and social philosophy, see the introduction in Anthony Quinton, ed., *Political Philosophy* (New York: Oxford University Press, 1967).

[96] 23, italics in original.

understanding, being able to use, the concepts that figure in that activity; understanding concepts involves understanding the activities in which those concepts are used. Thus Wittgenstein's claim that it is possible for philosophers to perform conceptual therapy is also the claim that philosophers can know about, can understand, the human activities of which concepts are an integral part.

Now it is not to be thought that these last remarks are somehow a working out of implications in Wittgenstein's thought of which he himself was not aware or that they are in conflict with Wittgenstein's own understanding of his position. The integral relationship between and inseparability of language, meaning, and action are among the most central, the most important arguments Wittgenstein advanced. It would be altogether wrong to suggest that Wittgenstein thought the therapy performed by philosophy is insignificant or trivial, that it is concerned, in the phrase so often encountered among superficial critics, with "words" or "mere words." The confusions with which philosophical therapy is concerned, in Wittgenstein's words, "have the character of *depth*. They are deep disquietudes; their roots are as deep in us as the forms of our language and their significance is as great as the importance of our language. — Let us ask ourselves: why do we feel a grammatical joke to be *deep*? (And that is what the depth of philosophy is.)"[97]

Granting the importance of philosophical therapy, however, we must nevertheless ask why philosophy should *restrict itself* to providing therapy. If philosophers can know enough about concepts and the activities of which they are part to clear up confusions and misconceptions, what is to prevent them, what is there against, their instructing us about our concepts and activities before the confusions develop, for purposes having no definite connection with confusions. Why should they not advance the sorts of accounts of men and their activities that political and social philosophers have been putting forward from classical antiquity to the present? More specifically, if political and social philosophers can know the correct use of concepts such as "rights" and "obligation," "equality" and "justice," "liberty" and "authority," and hence can achieve a well-grounded understanding of the activities of which these concepts are an integral part, why should they not put their knowledge to more than therapeutic uses?

The discussions that form the bulk of this volume indicate that many thinkers influenced directly or indirectly by Wittgenstein have decided that they can and should do so. Many of those discussions are indeed intended (among other things) to clear up confusions and misconceptions to which previous writers have fallen victim. But most of the discussions that follow (and a much larger literature that is addressed to the same kinds of issues) proceed at least in part by analyzing the uses of concepts; most of the analysts represented argue, or at least tacitly assume, that in analyzing the uses of concepts they are also analyzing the political and social activities, practices, and arrangements of which the concepts in question are part, and few if any of them think of their enterprise as nothing more than therapeutic in character and purpose. As we argued at the outset, this literature, most of which would be impossible to understand apart from the direct or indirect influence of Wittgenstein's work in the philosophy of language, should be viewed as a continuation, on the basis of a new set of philosophical premises, of the long tradition of political and social philosophy, a tradition that aims to enlighten us concerning the political and social dimensions of our lives.

[97] 111.

On what grounds, then, did Wittgenstein criticize previous attempts to prosecute this enterprise and why did he reject it for himself? Does the work presented in this book properly stand condemned by the very philosopher to whom it owes many of the premises from which it proceeds?[98] Wittgenstein says, "If one tried to advance *theses* in philosophy, it would never be possible to question them, because everyone would agree to them."[99] And again: "In philosophy we do not draw conclusions. 'But it must be like this!' is not a philosophical proposition. Philosophy only states what everyone admits."[100] Assuming that Wittgenstein is not using "theses" and "conclusions" in some special way, there is no doubt that the philosophical writings presented here do what Wittgenstein says philosophy as he understands it does not, even cannot, do. Hence it seems that he would have to say that the writings presented here are not, properly speaking, philosophy. And the reasons he gives for his view at least appear to be consistent with the account he presents of language and meaning. Language is a part of our lives. It is what it is because we do what we do with it. The meaning of a concept is the use to which it is put by those who speak the language — by us. Since language *is* what people do with is, it must be the case that everyone (who speaks the language in question) knows what it is. Thus if philosophical theses and conclusions are about language (and if they are correct), it seems that everyone would indeed admit, would indeed agree, to them. Philosophical theses and conclusions would either be truisms or be false. Rather than advancing theses or conclusions thereof, philosophy only assembles reminders for particular purposes, that is, *reminds* people of what they already know but are neglecting.[101]

But does the argument (thesis?) that language is what people do with it require or even support the conclusion that all true theses about it must be redundant truisms?[102] This is in fact an immensely complicated question and much contemporary work in the philosophy of language is concerned with it.[103] We cannot go into the technical questions in detail but we can notice a distinction or two which cast serious doubts on Wittgenstein's view as we understand it.

[98] There is one view that we will mention only to dismiss. It is sometimes suggested that Wittgenstein would reject work such as is presented here because it concerns a type of concept, that is, ethical concepts, that cannot be analyzed. Wittgenstein does say that "our concepts in aesthetics and ethics" have blurred edges and that "if you look for definitions corresponding" to their use you will feel that "anything — and nothing — is right." But this characteristic is hardly unique to aesthetic and ethical concepts, and it is by no means Wittgenstein's view that it prevents us from analyzing them. What he says is, "In such a difficulty always ask yourself: How did we *learn* the meaning of this word ('good' for instance)? From what sort of examples? Then it will be easier for you to see that the word must have a family of meanings" (77). It is no more his view that we cannot analyze *this* family of meanings than that we cannot analyze the meanings of, say, "game."

[99] 128, italics in original.

[100] 599.

[101] 126–127.

[102] We may observe in passing that if all true theses are truisms it might be necessary to conclude that most of the "reminders" issued by Wittgenstein himself are thereby shown to be theses, not reminders, and also shown to be false. It is hard to think of any large number of Wittgenstein's reminders to which "everyone" has agreed. As influential as it has been, Wittgenstein's philosophy, like every other important philosophy, is immensely and fundamentally controversial. If his philosophy consists of reminders of what everybody knows, it is difficult to see why this should be the case.

[103] See, for example, Stanley Cavell, *Must We Mean What We Say*? esp. I (New York: Charles Scribner's Sons, 1969) and the Introductions to the books by Rorty and Katz and Fodor in the Further Readings at the end of this introduction.

First, there is the now familiar distinction between knowing how to do something and knowing what one does in doing that which one knows how to do. It is a truism that people who speak a language know how to speak it (though of course they make occasional mistakes of various kinds). But it hardly follows that everyone who knows how to speak is therefore able to give an explicit and orderly account of the rules they follow, the techniques they apply in speaking. To take a simple example, most (but not all) native speakers of English, French, and other natural languages do not regularly make mistakes with the person, number, or tense of verbs. And when they do make a mistake they will readily agree to the correction. It is by no means the case, however, that every native speaker can perform, unaided, even such simple analytic tasks as giving the conjugation of a verb or parsing a sentence (to say nothing of the more complex analyses of grammarians and linguists). They know how to use the language but they cannot give an account of what they do when they use it. If only because this is so, there are obvious utilities in having specialists who study how people speak and put together orderly and systematic accounts of what their performances consist of. There may be a sense in which the accounts they give are truistic, but they are by no means redundant or insignificant. If this is true of matters of lower school grammar, it is the more obvious and the more important as regards the sophisticated distinctions, classifications, and explanations of the linguistically oriented philosopher. Perhaps it is true that competent speakers of English would not say, "I know I am in pain," but how many of them could analyze this feature of their linguistic (non)behavior as Wittgenstein did?

The importance of this point is magnified when we attend to the fact that speaking and acting are interwoven. There is a large number of speakers who know how to use concepts such as rights, justice, obligation, and equality — who know their way about in the activities in which these concepts figure. If this were not the case there would be no concepts and activities for political philosophers to analyze. But if anyone thinks that accounts of these concepts and activities can only be truistic or obviously false, let them give such an account and see whether everyone will admit to it.

Wittgenstein's argument that speakers of a language know how to use the concepts and know their way about in activities, far from posing a problem for or a barrier to a conceptually oriented (or any other) political philosophy, is the basis on which such political philosophy is built. The problem Wittgenstein poses is not that the theses of political philosophy will be truistic and redundant, rather it is that such a political philosophy is likely to be very complicated and difficult to do. We must take seriously Wittgenstein's insistence on the prodigious diversity of uses to which language is put, the endless variety of language games in which it figures, the techniques, purposes, and fine shades of behavior that differentiate one language game and its concepts from another. Saying what people (including ourselves) do who know how to engage in these activities will often be a matter of great difficulty and complexity.[104] Political philosophers who are themselves speakers of the language and participants in the activities they are analyzing will

[104] Wittgenstein says, "The use of this word [the word happens to be "reading"] in the ordinary circumstances of our life is of course extremely familiar to us. But the part the word plays in our life, and therewith the language-game in which we employ it, would be difficult to describe even in rough outline." He then goes on to give a very lengthy description, the point of which, I take it, is to show how hard it is to capture what we do so often and so readily in everyday life (156).

know how to use the concepts and otherwise to engage in the activities. Thus in their role as political philosophers they can as it were observe their own conduct and that of fellow participants and thereby obtain what we can just as well call the evidence on which to base an account of the activity. Owing to the very detail and complexity this evidence is likely to have, putting it together into an account that is both tolerably accurate and yet contributive to the goals of political philosophy will be difficult.

Perhaps we can put the matter as follows: We can think of Wittgenstein's philosophy of language as providing epistemological premises and even a method for political and social philosophy and social science, particularly for a political and social philosophy that addresses itself to the political and social life in which the philosophers and social scientists are themselves participants. The chief premises of the epistemology are that language games are constituted by what the participants do (know how to do) and that this knowledge is necessarily shared among the participants. The "method" consists of examining what people (ergo everyone) do (does) when they do what they know how to do, that is, an examination of the rules accepted and followed, the techniques employed, the objectives and purposes pursued, and the fine shades of behavior characteristic of playing the language game. The obvious problem with the epistemology and the method is that they generate "data" that is likely to be so abundant, complex, and subtle as to be unmanageable.

There are also further problems, problems that have been more widely canvassed than the one just discussed. Not everyone participates in all language games, and not everyone who does participate does so in all aspects of the game. If it is by virtue of playing a language game that one knows how to use the concepts of that game, and if knowing how is the basis of knowing what, then it would seem to follow that only participants in a game could philosophize or do social science concerning that game. If so, the quest for generality, for a comprehensive account or understanding of political and social life, a quest that has been prominent in both philosophy and much social science, might have to be abandoned.

Readers of the selections that follow will want to inquire whether the authors who are operating (explicitly or tacitly) with the Wittgenstein premises have dealt with these difficulties. We cannot adequately specify and clarify the difficulties here, and we certainly cannot resolve them. But two general comments should be made before we conclude. First, to say that the diversity and complexity of language games is a problem for political and social philosophy is to make certain assumptions about the character and objectives of such philosophizing. The Wittgensteinian perspective teaches us to think of political philosophy as itself a distinct language game or perhaps family of such games that must be understood in its own right. We cannot conclude that the "difficulties" we mentioned are truly difficulties for political philosophy without examining this game — its concepts, questions, categories of analysis, and so on. A detailed examination of these matters is obviously impossible here. But few would argue that political philosophy has aimed at or should aim at a re-enactment of political life as experienced by participants. Thus the impossibility of such a re-enactment is not itself a difficulty for political philosophy. Yet all concerned would agree that there is some sense in which political philosophy is about political life, that it properly aims, among other things, to abstract from, generalize over, and assess politics as perpetuated and experienced by participants, not simply to ignore the latter. Whatever the particulars of one's judgment as to what this "some sense" should be (and it is a matter of great controversy), the complexity and diversity Wittgenstein stresses is going to complicate the task of political philosophy. But then why should anyone think that the enterprise of political philosophy would be anything other than complicated? If Wittgenstein teaches us something about the ways in which and why it is complicated, he does a great service. But he does another service as well. He gives us grounds for thinking that we *know* something about the complexity of political life and hence are in a position to examine the efforts of political philosophers (our own or those of someone else) and make informed and reasoned judgments about their value. Political philosophy at its best will indeed require what most of us have always believed it to require, namely, analytic and synthetic powers that are bequeathed to no more than a small number of human beings. But the efforts of such persons concern, are about, something with which, more or less, we are all familiar. For this reason Wittgenstein's teaching can be viewed as an invitation to an active, critical study of political philosophy and political philosophers. I hope that readers of this book will approach the subject in this spirit.

The second point concerns the fact that not everyone participates in all language games and that not all who participate do so to the same degree. If, or to the extent that, "knowing how" depends upon participation, it is evident that those who do not participate in a particular activity cannot make the same claims to knowledge as those who do; and this has wide and important implications for conceptually oriented political philosophy or social science. But in working out these implications we must bear in mind at least two other aspects of Wittgenstein's argument as well. The first is his insistence that language is public, not private. The rules, purposes, techniques, fine shades of behavior, circumstances, and so forth, involve, are keyed to, matters that are in principle accessible to all. They may be subtle, complicated, and hard for the unexperienced to detect, appreciate, or master. But presumably they have been mastered by the participants; and if the participants could not in principle describe, convey, *teach* them to others, that would prove that they in fact had not mastered them themselves. That is to say that political philosophers can learn about them if they take the trouble − which may indeed be considerable − to do so. Of course, the degree to which they must do so in order to carry forward their enterprise will depend upon the objectives of that enterprise as they understand it. The second point concerns Wittgenstein's remarks about the "common behavior of mankind" that we noted earlier. The common behavior of mankind, he says, "is the system of reference by means of which we interpret an unknown language."[105] This seems to mean that, in fact, whatever the explanation for it may be, there are certain ways of acting that one encounters in many diverse language games among many peoples. This suggests that there are respects in which our experience as human beings provides guidance, makes possible a sense of familiarity, even in situations most of the particulars or distinctive features of which are unfamiliar to us. Familiarity with these ways of acting is by no means a guarantee of understanding. One human being, Wittgenstein later adds, "can be a complete enigma to another. We learn this when we come into a strange country with entirely strange traditions; and, what is more, even given a mastery of the country's language. We do not *understand* the people. (And not because of not

[105] 206.

knowing what they are saying to themselves.) We cannot find our feet with them."[106] But even here, it is important to emphasize, we can at least realize that we do *not* understand them. The understandings afforded by knowledge of the common behavior of mankind, it seems fair to say, are not themselves a sufficient basis for doing political philosophy or social science concerning their activities. But it would seem to provide the possibility of realizing which steps would have to be taken in order to make political philosophy or social science possible. Some aspects of human affairs are indeed more difficult of access than others, but "*everything* lies open to view."[107] Wittgenstein's philosophy of language is very far from encouraging the thought that political philosophy is a simple, uncomplicated enterprise. But if political philosophy is about, seeks to understand, the political life of man, Wittgenstein gives us excellent grounds for optimism concerning it.

Further Reading

Wittgenstein's work hardly settled the several issues we have considered. Controversies concerning them and the new issues in the philosophy of language that have emerged in recent years remain intense. We cannot take up later developments in detail, but it may be useful to mention a few of the currently salient issues and to direct interested readers to discussions of them.

One of the early challenges to the kind of philosophizing that Wittgenstein practiced and inspired concerned the warrants needed to support claims to know the use and meaning of ordinary language and, in particular, the warrants needed to support generalizations and inferences about, and from, such claims. In its early stages this challenge took the form of arguments that the claims, generalizations, and inferences made by philosophers proceeding from the analysis of ordinary language need to be supported by the same kinds of empirical evidence gathered by empirical linguists. For this argument, see the paper by Benson Mates in the fourth item in the following list of readings and the introductions to the books by J. A. Fodor and J. J. Katz and by Richard Rorty. An influential response to these criticisms is the essay by Stanley Cavell cited in footnote 103 to the present introduction.

In its original form, the criticism just mentioned was not grounded in a well-articulated theory of language that provided an alternative to Wittgenstein's. Such a theory has developed rapidly in the ensuing years, especially in the work of Noam Chomsky. Some of Chomsky's writing is available in the books by J. R. Searle and Katz and Fodor. Searle's introduction deals with some of the major philosophical issues raised by Chomsky's work. The reader would also do well to consult the work by Peter Strawson cited in footnote 71 in this introduction.

A major development within work in the theory of language directly and positively influenced by Wittgenstein is signaled by the use of the term "speech act." As the term itself suggests, this line of development continues Wittgenstein's emphasis on the intimate relationship between the uses of language and action, but it has produced a more differentiated analysis of the types of actions we take by using language than Wittgenstein presented and a much more differentiated analysis of the key notion of rules. Some of the most important work of this type is available in Searle's *The Philosophy of Language* and is represented in the present book by his essay in Part I.

[106] II, xi, p. 233e.
[107] 126, italics added.

Finally, mention should be made of an increasingly prominent argument that is of great potential significance for social and political philosophizing influenced by Wittgenstein's views. If acting is at the bottom of language games, analyses of those games can yield knowledge and understanding concerning action and the practices and arrangements of which it is a part. Throughout the period of its development, this view was challenged not merely on the ground that we cannot achieve reliable knowledge of ordinary language by Wittgenstein's methods, but rather that ordinary language consists in large part of terms that either have no empirical referent or are so ambiguous as to render it impossible to verify the statements made by use of them. On this view, genuinely scientific work could not proceed unless ordinary language was either cleaned up or replaced entirely by language that satisfies more rigorous canons. This view continues to have its supporters. A version of it is represented in this book by Frank J. Sorauf's essay in Part VIII.

More recently, however, a new challenge has been made against the arguments of Wittgenstein and the speech act analysts. The position in question grants the intimate, indeed internal, relationship between ordinary language and action. For this reason, proponents of this view grant that analysis of ordinary language is not only possible but that it can yield knowledge and understanding of human action, that is, of the decisions, choices, intentions, and purposes of human beings. The thinkers in question, however, urge that ordinary language, and hence knowledge gained by analysis of ordinary language, may be proved to be based upon, to embody, fundamental misunderstandings and misconceptions of human beings and what they do. Ordinary language *does* embody the conceptions human beings have of themselves and the things they do; hence anyone interested in knowing about such conceptions may profitably examine it. But if someone aims to find out what human beings are really like, what human interaction really consists of, he or she will have to proceed in some other manner, and will have to analyze something other than ordinary language. Just as the physicist who wants to understand the material universe must examine that universe itself, not how other physicists — to say nothing of the uninstructed ordinary man — have conceived of it, so the political philosopher or social scientist must examine human beings and societies, not what other persons say or think about human beings and societies. A thoughtful introduction to leading versions of this argument, together with relevant bibliography, is available in Richard J. Bernstein's *Praxis and Action*, especially pp. 281–304.

Aside from the work of Wittgenstein himself, the most influential recent work in the philosophy of language has been in article form and has been conveniently anthologized. Readers who consult the following collections and their bibliographies will be apprized of the most important of all but very recent writing.

Bernstein, Richard J., *Praxis and Action*. Philadelphia: The University of Pennsylvania Press, 1971.

Black, Max, ed. *Philosophical Analysis*. Englewood Cliffs, N.J.: Prentice-Hall, Inc., 1964.

Caton, Charles, ed. *Philosophy and Ordinary Language*. Urbana: University of Illinois Press, 1963.

Chappell, V. C., ed. *Ordinary Language*. Englewood Cliffs, N.J.: Prentice-Hall, Inc., 1964.

Flew, A. N., ed. *Essays in Conceptual Analysis*. London: Macmillan & Company, Ltd., 1960.

——, ed. *Logic and Language*, First Series. Oxford: Basil Blackwell, 1951.

——. *Logic and Language*, Second Series. Oxford: Basil Blackwell, 1953.

Katz, J. J., and J. A. Fodor, eds. *The Structure of Language*. Englewood Cliffs, N.J.: Prentice-Hall, Inc., 1964.

Lewis, H. D., ed. *Clarity Is Not Enough*. New York: Humanities Press, Inc., 1963.

Linsky, Leonard, ed. *Semantics and the Philosophy of Language*. Urbana: University of Illinois Press, 1952.

Parkinson, G. H. R., ed. *The Theory of Meaning*. London: Oxford University Press, 1968.

Rorty, Richard, ed. *The Linguistic Turn*. Chicago: The University of Chicago Press, 1967.

Searle, J. R., ed. *The Philosophy of Language*. London: Oxford University Press, 1971.

Part I

Rules and Human Action

Introduction

The concept of rules is central to Wittgenstein's philosophy of language and to the later work in that subject influenced by Wittgenstein. Both Wittgenstein and later writers insisted that language and the rules followed in using it are integral to human activities — to human action. The selections in Part I explore, in greater detail than Wittgenstein or other writers working in the philosophy of language have had reason to do, the implications of this understanding for political and social life and for attempts to investigate and philosophize about various of its aspects.

The selection from Peter Winch's *The Idea of a Social Science* puts forward the sweeping thesis that "all behavior which is meaningful (therefore all specifically human behavior) is *ipso facto* rule-governed." It follows, he argues throughout the book, that to understand specifically human behavior we must understand the rules that people are following in the course of their activities. Since rule following is a reflective activity, doing so involves inquiring into the reasons people have for doing what they are doing. And since, in turn, the rules and the reasons people have for applying them as they do are part of particular contexts (language games) and have their meaning and their cogency within them, to understand the reasons we must ourselves be "at home" in those contexts. If social science and social and political philosophy are attempts to understand human behavior, these characteristics of behavior set the broad objectives and methods of, and the limitations upon, those disciplines. Many social scientists have not understood these points and have made what Winch argues is the fundamental error of modeling their efforts to understand human behavior on the natural sciences, that is, on disciplines the subject matters of which are context-independent and do not involve rules (except in the sense of regularities detected by observers) or reasoning.

Although he makes sweeping criticism of prominent understandings of social science and its objectives, Winch is very far from arguing that well-grounded and useful understandings of political and social life are impossible. Political and social life are complex and context-dependent, but the rules, reasonings, and so forth, that constitute them are known by participants and can be identified and stated by social scientists, political philosophers, and others. The second selection in this section, John R. Searle's much-discussed paper "How to Derive 'Ought' from 'Is,' " advances a further and more controversial claim. He makes a close analysis of the rules governing the practice (or institution as he calls it) of promising. His purpose in doing so is not primarily to show that such institutions *are* governed by identifiable rules, but to work out one of the important implications of the fact that human affairs include institutions governed by rules of the kind exemplified by the rules governing promising. He wants to show that these rules make possible, or rather that following these rules involves, patterns of reasoning, of inference, about moral and other normative questions that philosophers have long argued are not available to us. When we attend to the rule-governed character of our language games, he contends, we see that we can and do reach well-founded normative or evaluative conclusions by reasoning from what have traditionally been called factual or descriptive statements or premises.

If Searle is correct, his argument is of very great significance for political and social (and, of course, moral) philosophy. It suggests that philosophers working in these areas can aspire not only to well-founded knowledge concerning political and social life, but well-founded assessments and evaluations of them. Or rather, that in at least some cases well-founded knowledge concerning political and social institutions will involve evaluations and assessments, will carry such evaluations and assessments with it. Knowing how to promise involves, means, knowing that the truth of the descriptive statements "I promised" or "he promised" (together with the other conditions Searle identifies) implies the correctness of the normative statements "I have (he has) an obligation to do what I (he) promised to do." Hence the political or social philosopher who correctly identifies the rules governing promising (and who knows that someone made a promise to do X) will be able to make statements such as "He has an obligation to do X" and "It was wrong of him not to do X (because he had promised to do it.)" Political and social philosophers have certainly wanted to make statements of this type (and have in fact done so). Searle's attention to rules permits him to provide well-developed reasons for thinking that they can do so with a clear philosophic conscience, that is, with confidence that such statements can be well founded.

Winch follows Wittgenstein in recognizing that some rules are very explicit and tightly drawn and that others set only very general guidelines and require much interpretation, judgment, and reflection. Indeed, he goes so far as to call these two *kinds* of rules. Searle adds a distinction between regulative and constitutive rules. But both discussions (and especially Winch's) share a difficulty common to much of the writing concerning rules, namely that they make only very limited efforts to distinguish among the great many senses in which "rule" is used, the many ways rules enter into our activities, and the great diversity of implications and consequences that attach to our uses of them. The discussion in the third selection *begins* with the proposition that "obligation" is a rule-dependent concept. For reasons that the arguments of Wittgenstein, Winch, Searle, Hart (from whom the proposition is taken), and many others have made clear, this is an extremely important proposition; it is important if only because awareness of it eliminates difficulties encountered by analyses of "obligation" (and a host of other concepts) that do not attend to it. But as important as it is, the proposition is itself ambiguous in the extreme and requires a great deal of unpacking before it can do more than help us to avoid certain common mistakes. It is ambiguous precisely in the sense that its simple formulation does not distinguish among the many different kinds of rules that are part of the language game or (as it is called in the book from which the selection is drawn) practice of obligation. It is for this reason that much of the discussion is given to sorting out at least a few of the major kinds of rules involved in the practice, the relationships among them, the patterns of reasoning appropriate in connection with each kind, and the practical inferences that are and are not supported by the fact that a rule of a particular kind is established and followed by the participants in a practice or language game. It should be emphasized, however, that this discussion of rules remains very primitive and that much more analysis of this crucial concept remains to be done.

The analysis in the third selection owes much to the arguments of Winch and Searle (and to numerous other recent students of rules) and it does not directly contradict their major conclusions. (It is suggested that the rules of promising that Searle identifies are better classified as semantic than constitutive.) But it does suggest complications that limit what might seem to be the implications of their conclusions.

Searle's argument suggests that in many cases the one and only appropriate conclusion will be that Jones does have an obligation to do what he promised to do. And on Winch's view this implies that there is one and only one correct understanding of the practice, that a social scientist or philosopher aiming to give an account of the practice must (on pain of being mistaken) give this one account. But Searle concedes (see his footnote 8) that the constitutive rules of promising can themselves be called into question and that if this is done the conclusion required by reasoning *within* those rules would not hold. Now Searle's analysis requires that persons who have rejected the constitutive rules of promising can no longer, in their own name so to speak, use the concept "promising" of that institution. (They might call it promising and explain that, as observers, they are reporting that other actors call the institution promising. And, of course, they could use the word — the counter or marker — "promising" and explain that for them this counter marked a different concept than it does for other actors.) But they can still talk about the events and actions that occur in the institutions that others continue to call promising. They can do so, as Searle explains metaphorically, because they continue to accept and use other rules, other concepts, in the established manner.

But this shows that established language games permit of more than one way of talking about and understanding events and actions in social life. Although it is important to insist on the sense in which those events and actions are different events and actions when different concepts are used to talk about them, it is also important to insist on the sense in which they are the same events and actions. (For example, it is of the utmost importance to understanding the social conflicts involved to recognize the sense in which those who speak of "abortion" and those who speak of "murder" are talking about the same medical procedure.) To say that one description of the event is *the* correct one is not to make a conceptual point, it is to take sides in a controversy that cannot be settled on conceptual grounds alone.

Winch might agree to the foregoing argument and yet insist that philosophers and social scientists must restrict themselves to concepts that are used by *some* actor or actors in the society in question (or, as he puts it, to such concepts or to concepts that are logically tied to actor concepts; see *The Idea of a Social Science*, pp. 88—189). If alternative understandings are part of social life, philosophic or social scientific accounts thereof must of course reflect that fact. I would personally accept this view. But it must be recognized that to do so is, again, to take a position in a controversy, a controversy in which all sides are able to give expression to their position in a cogent way, in which all sides can make use of established concepts to formulate their views. To be more specific, numerous thinkers have argued that political and social philosophy and especially social science ought positively to eschew, or at least accord no special standing to, the concepts used by the actors in the social life they study. That is to say, these disciplines ought to construct their own concepts and use the latter to identify, characterize, and reason about the events and actions that occur in social life. Once they have done so, once the rules governing those concepts have been established, it is a conceptual point that those concepts and rules correctly identify the events and actions that philosophers and social scientists discuss when they apply their concepts to them in a manner that accords with the established rules for their use. The account of social life which the process yields is not true or false, correct or incorrect, by comparison with an account yielded by use of the concepts the actors employ; it is simply a different, an alternative account. Preference cannot be given to one account over the other on conceptual grounds alone; it must be given on grounds of a view concerning the purposes of social science and philosophy. Since numerous purposes can be and have been formulated in a cogent manner, there are no purely conceptual grounds on which to choose among them. But just as it is conceptual analysis, the analysis of rules, that teaches us this, so that kind of analysis can help us to see the implications of adopting and acting on one view rather than another. Viewed in this way Winch's arguments are, to this writer, extremely persuasive.

One final word. The topic of rules and action will be involved, implicitly or explicitly, throughout virtually the entire book. But it is especially integral to the discussions of authority and obligation, and the readings for those parts, particularly selections 7, 8, 10, and 11 might well have been placed in the present part.

Further Reading

Many of the important writings on rules are cited in the footnotes in the three selections presented here and no purpose would be served by repeating the information in this bibliography. The topic has been widely discussed, especially in the philosophy of language, the philosophy of logic, moral philosophy (especially discussions of utilitarianism), and what is increasingly referred to as the philosophy of action. Here again the most influential work has been in article form and much of it has been conveniently collected in the following anthologies.

Bayles, Michael D., ed. *Contemporary Utilitarianism*. Garden City, N.Y.: Doubleday & Company, Inc., 1968.

Brand, Myles, ed. *The Nature of Human Action*. Glenview, Ill: Scott Foresman and Company, 1970.

Braybrooke, David, ed. *Philosophical Problems of the Social Sciences*. New York: The Macmillan Company, 1955.

Care, Norman S., and Charles Landesman, eds. *Readings in the Theory of Action*. Bloomington, Ind.: Indiana University Press, 1968.

Dworkin, G., and J. J. Thomson, eds. *Ethics*. New York: Harper & Row, Publishers, 1968.

Foot, Philippa, ed. *Theories of Ethics*. London: Oxford University Press, 1967.

Mischel, T. R., ed. *Human Action*. New York: Academic Press, Inc., 1969.

Strawson, P. F. *Philosophical Logic*. London: Oxford University Press, 1968.

White, A. R. *The Philosophy of Action*. London: Oxford University Press, 1969.

1. Nature of Meaningful Behaviour

Peter Winch

Meaningful Behaviour

Wittgenstein's account of what it is to follow a rule is, for obvious reasons, given principally with an eye to elucidating the nature of language. I have now to show how this treatment may shed light on other forms of human interaction besides speech. The forms of activity in question are, naturally, those to which analogous categories are applicable: those, that is, of which we can sensibly say that they have a *meaning*, a *symbolic* character. In the words of Max Weber, we are concerned with human behaviour "if and in so far as the agent or agents associate a subjective *sense* (*Sinn*) with it." (33: Chapter I.) I want now to consider what is involved in this idea of meaningful behaviour.

Weber says that the "sense" of which he speaks is something which is "subjectively intended;" and he says that the notion of meaningful behaviour is closely associated with notions like *motive* and *reason*. " 'Motive' means a meaningful configuration of circumstances which, to the agent or observer, appears as a meaningful 'reason' (*Grund*) of the behaviour in question." (*Ibid*.)

Let us consider some examples of actions which are performed *for a reason*. Suppose that it is said of a certain person, *N*, that he voted Labour at the last General Election because he thought that a Labour government would be the most likely to preserve industrial peace. What kind of explanation is this? The clearest case is that in which *N*, prior to voting, has discussed the pros and cons of voting Labour and has explicitly come to the conclusion: "I will vote Labour because that is the best way to preserve industrial peace." That is a paradigm case of someone performing an action for a reason. To say this is not to deny that in some cases, even where *N* has gone through such an explicit process of reasoning, it may be possible to dispute whether the reason he has given is in fact the real reason for his behaviour. But there is very often no room for doubt; and if this were not so, the idea of *a reason for an action* would be in danger of completely losing its sense. (This point will assume greater importance subsequently, when I come to discuss the work of Pareto.)

The type of case which I have taken as a paradigm is not the only one covered by Weber's concept. But the paradigm exhibits clearly one feature which I believe to have a more general importance. Suppose that an observer, *O*, is offering the above explanation for *N*'s having voted Labour: then it should be noted that the

From Peter Winch, *The Idea of a Social Science* (London: Routledge & Kegan Paul Ltd., 1958; New York: Humanities Press, Inc., 1958), pp. 45–65, by permission of the author and publishers.

force of O's explanation rests on the fact that the concepts which appear in it must be grasped not merely by O and his hearers, but also *by N himself*. N must have some idea of what it is to "preserve industrial peace" and of a connection between this and the kind of government which he expects to be in power if Labour is elected. (For my present purposes it is unnecessary to raise the question whether N's beliefs in a particular instance are true or not.)

Not all cases of meaningful behaviour are as clearcut as this. Here are some intermediate examples. N may not, prior to casting his vote, have formulated any reason for voting as he does. But this does not necessarily preclude the possibility of saying that he has a reason for voting Labour and of specifying that reason. And in this case, just as much as in the paradigm, the acceptability of such an explanation is contingent on N's grasp of the concepts contained in it. If N does not grasp the concept of industrial peace it must be senseless to say that his reason for doing anything is a desire to see industrial peace promoted.

A type of case even farther removed from my paradigm is that discussed by Freud in *The Psychopathology of Everyday Life*. N forgets to post a letter and insists, even after reflection, that this was "just an oversight" and had no reason. A Freudian observer might insist that N "must have had a reason" even though it was not apparent to N: suggesting perhaps that N unconsciously connected the posting of the letter with something in his life which is painful and which he wants to suppress. In Weberian terms, Freud classifies as "meaningfully directed" (*sinnhaft orientiert*) actions which have no sense at all to the casual observer. Weber seems to refer to cases of this sort when, in his discussion of borderline cases, he speaks of actions the sense of which is apparent only "to the expert." This means that his characterization of *Sinn* as something "subjectively intended" must be approached warily: more warily, for instance than it is approached by Morris Ginsburg, who appears to assume that Weber is saying that the sociologist's understanding of the behaviour of other people must rest on an analogy with his own introspective experience. (See 11: pp. 153 ff.) This misunderstanding of Weber is very common both among his critics and among his vulgarizing followers; I will say more about it at a later stage. But Weber's insistence on the importance of the subjective point of view can be interpreted in a way which is not open to Ginsberg's objections: he can be taken as meaning that even explanations of the Freudian type, if they are to be acceptable, must be in terms of concepts which are familiar to the agent as well as to the observer. It would make no sense to say that N's omission to post a letter to X (in settlement, say, of a debt) was an expression of N's unconscious resentment against X for having been promoted over his head, if N did not himself understand what was meant by "obtaining promotion over somebody's head." It is worth mentioning here too that, in seeking explanations of this sort in the course of psychotherapy, Freudians try to get the patient himself to recognize the validity of the proffered explanation; that this indeed is almost a condition of its being accepted as the "right" explanation.

The category of meaningful behaviour extends also to actions for which the agent has no "reason" or "motive" at all in any of the senses so far discussed. In the first chapter of *Wirtschaft und Gesellschaft* Weber contrasts meaningful action with action which is "purely reactive" (*bloss reaktiv*) and says that purely *traditional* behaviour is on the borderline between these two categories. But, as Talcott Parsons points out, Weber is not consistent in what he says about this. Sometimes he seems to regard traditional behaviour as simply a species of habit, whereas at other times he sees it as "a type of social action, its traditionalism consisting in the fixity of certain essentials, their immunity from rational or other criticism." (24: Chapter XVI.) Economic behaviour related to a fixed standard of living is cited as an example: behaviour, that is, where a man does not exploit an increase in the productive capacities of his labour in order to raise his standard of living but does less work instead. Parsons remarks that tradition in this sense is not to be equated with mere habit, but has a *normative* character. That is, the tradition is regarded as a standard which directs choices between alternative actions. As such it clearly falls within the category of the *sinnhaft*.

Suppose that N votes Labour without deliberating and without subsequently being able to offer any reasons, however hard he is pressed. Suppose that he is simply following without question the example of his father and his friends, who have always voted Labour. (This case must be distinguished from that in which N's *reason* for voting Labour is that his father and friends have always done so.) Now although N does not act here for any reason, his act still has a definite sense. What he does is not *simply* to make a mark on a piece of paper; he is *casting a vote*. And what I want to ask is, what gives his action *this* sense, rather than, say, that of being a move in a game or part of a religious ritual. More generally, by what criteria do we distinguish acts which have a sense from those which do not?

In the paper entitled *R. Stammlers "Ueberwindung' der materialistischen Geschichtsauffassung*," Weber considers the hypothetical case of two "non-social" beings meeting and, in a purely physical sense, "exchanging" objects. (See 34.) This occurrence, he says, is conceivable as an act of *economic* exchange only if it has a sense. He expands this by saying that the present actions of the two men must carry with them, or represent, a regulation of their future behaviour. Action with a sense is symbolic: it goes together with certain other actions in the sense that it *commits* the agent to behaving in one way rather than another in the future. This notion of "being committed" is most obviously appropriate where we are dealing with actions which have an immediate social significance, like economic exchange or promise-keeping. But it applies also to meaningful behaviour of a more "private" nature. Thus, to stay with examples used by Weber, if N places a slip of paper between the leaves of a book he can be said to be "using a bookmark" only if he acts with the idea of using the slip to determine where he shall start re-reading. This does not mean that he must necessarily *actually* so use it in the future (though that is the paradigm case); the point is that if he does not, some special explanation will be called for, such as that he forgot, changed his mind, or got tired of the book.

The notion of being committed by what I do now to doing something else in the future is identical in form with the connection between a definition and the subsequent use of the word defined, which I discussed in the last chapter. It follows that I can only be committed in the future by what I do now if my present act is the *application of a rule*. Now according to the argument of the last chapter, this is possible only where the act in question has a relation to a social context: this must be true even of the most private acts, if, that is, they are meaningful.

Let us return to N's exercise of his vote: its possibility rests on two presuppositions. In the first place, N must live in a society which has certain specific political institutions — a parliament which is constituted in a certain way and a government which is related in a certain way to the parliament. If he lives in a society whose political structure is patriarchal, it will clearly make no sense to speak of him as "voting" for a particular government, however much his action may resemble in appearance that of a voter in a country with an elected government. Secondly, *N* must himself have a certain familiarity with those institutions. His act must be a participation in the political life of the country, which presupposes that he must be aware of the symbolic relation between what he is doing now and the government which comes into power after the election. The force of this condition becomes more apparent in relation to cases where "democratic institutions" have been imposed by alien administrators on societies to which such ways of conducting political life are foreign. The inhabitants of such a country may perhaps be cajoled into going through the motions of marking slips of paper and dropping them into boxes, but, if words are to retain any meaning, they cannot be said to be "voting" unless they have some conception of the significance of what they are doing. This remains true even if the government which comes into power does so in fact as a result of the "votes" cast.

Activities and Precepts

I have claimed that the analysis of meaningful behaviour must allot a central role to the notion of a rule; that all behaviour which is meaningful (therefore all specifically human behaviour) is *ipso facto* rule-governed. It may now be objected that this way of speaking blurs a necessary distinction: that *some* kinds of activity involve the participant in the observance of rules, whilst others do not. The free-thinking anarchist, for example, certainly does not live a life which is circumscribed by rules in the same sense as does the monk or the soldier; is it not wrong to subsume these very different modes of life under one fundamental category?

This objection certainly shows that we must exercise care in the use we make of the notion of a rule; but it does not show that the way of speaking which I have adopted is improper or unilluminating. It is important to notice that, in the sense in which I am speaking of rules, it is just as true to speak of the anarchist following rules in what he does as it is to say the same thing of the monk. The difference between these two kinds of men is not that the one follows rules and the other does not; it lies in the diverse *kinds* of rule which each respectively follows. The monk's life is circumscribed by rules of behaviour which are both explicit and tightly drawn: they leave as little room as possible for individual choice in situations which call for action. The anarchist, on the other hand, eschews explicit norms as far as possible and prides himself on considering all claims for action "on their merits": that is, his choice is not determined in advance for him by the rule he is following. But that does not mean that we can eliminate altogether the idea of a rule from the description of his behaviour. We cannot do this because, if I may be permitted a significant pleonasm, the anarchist's way of life is a *way of life*. It is to be distinguished, for instance, from the pointless behaviour of a berserk lunatic. The anarchist has reasons for acting as he does; he *makes a point* of not being governed by explicit, rigid norms. Although he retains his freedom of choice, yet they are still significant choices that he makes: they are guided by considerations, and he may have good reasons for choosing one course rather than another. And these notions, which are essential in describing the anarchist's mode of behaviour, presuppose the notion of a rule.

An analogy may help here. In learning to write English there are a number of fairly cut-and-dried grammatical rules which one acquires, such as that it is wrong to follow a plural subject with a singular verb. These correspond roughly to the explicit norms governing monastic life. In terms of correct grammar one does not have a choice between writing "they were" and "they was": if one can write grammatically the question of which of these expressions one should use just does not arise. But this is not the only kind of thing one learns; one also learns to follow certain stylistic canons, and these, while they guide the way in which one writes, do not *dictate* that one should write in one way rather than another. Hence people can have individual literary styles but, within certain limits, can write only correct grammar or incorrect grammar. But it would plainly be mistaken to conclude from this that literary style is not governed by any rules at all: it is something that can be learned, something that can be discussed, and the fact that it can be so learned and discussed is essential to our conception of it.

Perhaps the best way to support this point will be to consider a persuasive presentation of the case against it. Such a presentation is offered by Michael Oakeshott in a series of articles in the *Cambridge Journal*.[1] Much of Oakeshott's argument coincides with the view of human behaviour which has been presented here, and I will begin by considering this part of what he says before venturing some criticisms of the rest.

Very much in accordance with the view I have been advocating is Oakeshott's rejection of what he calls the "rationalistic" misconception of the nature of human intelligence and rationality. (See 21.) According to this misconception the rationality of human behaviour comes to it from without: from intellectual functions which operate according to laws of their own and are, in principle, quite independent of the particular forms of activity to which they may nevertheless be applied.

A good example (not discussed by Oakeshott himself) of the sort of view to which he objects is Hume's famous assertion that "Reason is, and ought only to be the slave of the passions, and can never pretend to any other office than to serve and obey them." On this view the ends of human conduct are set by the natural constitution of men's emotions; those ends being given, the office of reason is mainly to determine the appropriate means of achieving them. The characteristic activities carried on in human societies spring then, presumably, from this interplay of reason and passion. Against this picture Oakeshott is quite correct to point out that: "A cook is not a man who first has a vision of a pie and then tries to make it; he is a man skilled in cookery, and both his projects and his achievements spring from that skill." (21.) Generally, both the ends sought and the means employed in human life, so far from generating forms of social activity, depend for their very being on those forms. A religious mystic, for instance, who says that his aim is union with God, can be understood only by someone who is acquainted with the religious tradition in the context of which this end is sought; a scientist who says that his aim is to split the atom can be understood only by someone who is familiar with modern physics.

This leads Oakeshott to say, again quite correctly, that a form of human activity can never be summed up in a set of explicit precepts. The activity "goes beyond" the precepts. For instance, the precepts have to be applied in practice and, although we may formulate another, higher-order, set of precepts prescribing how the first set is to be applied, we cannot go further along this road without finding ourselves

[1] Reprinted in *Rationalism in Politics*, London, Methuen, 1962.

on the slippery slope pointed out by Lewis Carroll in his paper, justly celebrated amongst logicians, *What the Tortoise Said to Achilles* (5).

Achilles and the Tortoise are discussing three propositions, A, B, and Z, which are so related that Z follows logically from A and B. The Tortoise asks Achilles to treat him as if he accepted A and B as true but did not yet accept the truth of the hypothetical proposition (C) "If A and B be true, Z must be true," and to force him, logically, to accept Z as true. Achilles begins by asking the Tortoise to accept C, which the Tortoise does; Achilles then writes in his notebook:

'A
B
C (If A and B are true, Z must be true)
Z.'

He now says to the Tortoise: "If you accept A and B and C, you must accept Z." When the Tortoise asks why he must, Achilles replies: "Because it follows *logically* from them. If A and B and C are true, Z *must* be true (D). You don't dispute *that*, I imagine?" The Tortoise agrees to accept D if Achilles will write it down. The following dialogue then ensues. Achilles says:

> "Now that you accept A and B and C and D, *of course* you accept Z."
> "Do I?" said the Tortoise innocently. "Let's make that quite clear. I accept A and B and C and D. Suppose I *still* refuse to accept Z?"
> "Then Logic would take you by the throat, and *force* you to do it!" Achilles triumphantly replied. "Logic would tell you You can't help yourself. Now that you've accepted A and B and C and D, you *must* accept Z. So you've no choice, you see."
> "Whatever *Logic* is good enough to tell me is worth *writing down*," said the Tortoise. "So enter it in your book, please. We will call it
> (E) If A and B and C and D are true, Z must be true. Until I've granted *that*, of course, I needn't grant Z. So it's quite a *necessary* step, you see?"
> "I see," said Achilles; and there was a touch of sadness in his tone."

The story ends some months later with the narrator returning to the spot and finding the pair still sitting there. The notebook is nearly full.

The moral of this, if I may be boring enough to point it, is that the actual process of drawing an inference, which is after all the heart of logic, is something which cannot be represented as a logical formula; that, moreover, a sufficient justification for inferring a conclusion from a set of premises is to see that the conclusion does in fact follow. To insist on any further justification is not to be extra cautious; it is to display a misunderstanding of what inference is. Learning to infer is not just a matter of being taught about explicit logical relations between propositions; it is learning *to do* something. Now the point which Oakeshott is making is really a generalization of this; where Carroll spoke only of logical inference, Oakeshott is making a similar point about human activities generally.

Rules and Habits

All the above fits in very well with the position outlined in Chapter I. Principles, precepts, definitions, formulae — all derive their sense from the context of human social activity in which they are applied. But Oakeshott wishes to take a further step. He thinks it follows from this that most human behaviour can be adequately described in terms of the notion of *habit* or *custom* and that neither the notion of a rule nor that of reflectiveness is essential to it. This seems to me a mistake for reasons which I shall now try to give.

In *The Tower of Babel* Oakeshott distinguishes between two forms of morality: that which is "a habit of affection and behaviour" and that which is "the reflective application of a moral criterion" (20). He seems to think that that "habitual" morality could exist in abstraction from "reflective" morality. In habitual morality, he says, situations are met "not by consciously applying to ourselves a rule of behaviour, nor by conduct recognized as the expression of a moral ideal, but by acting in accordance with a certain habit of behaviour." These habits are not learned by precept but by "living with people who habitually behave in a certain manner." Oakeshott appears to think that the dividing line between behaviour which is habitual and that which is rule-governed depends on whether or not a rule is *consciously* applied.

In opposition to this I want to say that the test of whether a man's actions are the application of a rule is not whether he can *formulate* it but whether it makes sense to distinguish between a right and a wrong way of doing things in connection with what he does. Where that makes sense, then it must also make sense to say that he is applying a criterion in what he does even though he does not, and perhaps cannot, formulate that criterion.

Learning how to do something is not just copying what someone else does; it may start that way, but a teacher's estimate of his pupil's prowess will lie in the latter's ability to do things which he could precisely *not* simply have copied. Wittgenstein has described this situation very well. He asks us to consider someone being taught the series of natural numbers. Perhaps he has first to copy what his teacher has written with his hand being guided. He will then be asked to do the "same" thing by himself.

> And here already there is a normal and an abnormal hearer's reaction. . . . We can imagine, e.g. that he does copy the figures independently, but not in the right order: he writes sometimes one sometimes another at random. And then communication stops at *that* point. Or again he makes "*mistakes*" in the order. – The difference between this and the first case will of course be one of frequency. – Or he makes a *systematic* mistake; for example he copies every other number, or he copies the series 0, 1, 2, 3, 4, 5 . . . like this: 1, 0, 3, 2, 5, 4 . . .. Here we shall almost be tempted to say he has understood *wrong*. (37: I, 143.)

The point here is that it *matters* that the pupil should react to his teacher's example in one way rather than another. He has to acquire not merely the habit of following his teacher's example but also the realization that some ways of following that example are permissible and others are not. That is to say, he has to acquire the ability to apply a criterion; he has to learn not merely to do things in the same way as his teacher, but also *what counts* as the same way.

The importance of this distinction may be brought out by taking Wittgenstein's example a stage further. Learning the series of natural numbers is not just learning to copy down a series of figures in the order which one has shown. It involves *being able to go on* writing down figures that have not been shown one. In one sense, that is, it involves doing something *different* from what one was originally shown; but *in relation to the rule* that is being followed, this counts as "going on in the *same* way" as one was shown.

There is a sense in which to acquire a habit is to acquire a propensity to go on doing the same kind of thing; there is another sense in which this is true of learning a rule. These senses are different and a great deal hangs on the difference. Let us consider the case of an *animal* forming a habit: here there can be no question of "the reflective application of a criterion." Suppose that *N* teaches his dog to balance a lump of sugar on its nose and to refrain from eating it until *N* utters a word of command. The dog acquires a propensity to respond in a certain way to *N*'s actions; we have here a type of case which fits reasonably well into the behaviourist's cherished category of stimulus and response. *N*, however, being a simple dog-lover rather than a scientist, no doubt speaks differently: he says the dog has learned a trick. This way of speaking is worth looking at, for it opens the door to the possibility of assessing the dog's performance in terms which do not belong to the stimulus-response set of concepts at all. He can now say that the dog has done the trick "correctly" or "incorrectly." But it is important to notice that this is an anthropomorphic way of speaking; it requires a reference to *human* activities, and norms which are here applied analogically to animals. It is only the dog's relation to human beings which makes it intelligible to speak of his having mastered a trick; what this way of speaking amounts to could not be elucidated by any description, however detailed, of canine behaviour in complete isolation from human beings.

The same point is involved in pointing out that what counts as "always doing the same kind of thing when the word of command is uttered" is decided by *N* rather than by the dog. Indeed it would be nonsensical to speak of the dog's doing this. It is only in relation to *N*'s purposes, involving as they do the notion of a trick, that the statement that the dog "always does the same kind of thing" has any sense.

But whereas a dog's acquisition of a habit does not involve *it* in any understanding of what is meant by "doing the same thing on the same kind of occasion," this is precisely what a human being has to understand before he can be said to have acquired a rule; and this too is involved in the acquisition of those forms of activity which Oakeshott wants to describe in terms of the notion of habit. A legal analogy may help here. Oakeshott's distinction between the two forms of morality is in many ways like the distinction between statute law and case law; and Roscoe Pound is taking up an attitude to this distinction somewhat analogous to Oakeshott's when he refers to statute law as "the mechanical application of rules" and distinguishes it from case law which involves "intuitions" (reminiscent of Oakeshott's discussion of politics in terms of "intimations": see 22). This may sometimes be a helpful way of speaking, but it should not blind us to the fact that the interpretation of precedents, just as much as the application of statutes, involves following rules in the sense in which I have been using the expression here. As Otto Kahn-Freund puts it: "One cannot dispense with a principle which links one decision with another, which raises the judicial act beyond the realm of sheer expediency." (27: the reference to Pound is his *Introduction to the Philosophy of Law*, Chapter III. E. H. Levi gives an excellent concise account, with examples, of the way in which the interpretation of judicial precedents involves the application of rules: 14.)

It is only when a past precedent has to be applied to a new kind of rule that the importance and nature of the rule become apparent. The court has to ask *what was involved* in the precedent decision and that is a question which makes no sense except in a context where the decision could sensibly be regarded as the application, however unselfconscious, of a rule. The same is true of other forms of human activity besides law, though elsewhere the rules may perhaps never be made so explicit. It is only because human actions exemplify rules that we can speak of past experience as relevant to our current behaviour. If it were merely a question of habits, then our current behaviour might certainly be *influenced* by the way in which we had acted in the past: but that would be just a causal influence. The dog responds to *N*'s commands now in a certain way because of what has happened to him in the past; if I am told to continue the series of natural numbers beyond 100, I continue in a certain way because of my past training. The phrase "because of," however, is used differently of these two situations: the dog has been *conditioned* to respond in a certain way, whereas I *know* the right way to go on *on the basis of* what I have been taught.

Reflectiveness

Many of the statements Oakeshott makes about habitual modes of behaviour sound like the things I have been saying about rule-governed behaviour.

> Custom is always adaptable and susceptible to the *nuance* of the situation. This may appear a paradoxical assertion; custom, we have been taught, is blind. It is, however, an insidious piece of misobservation; custom is not blind, it is only "blind as a bat." And anyone who has studied a tradition of customary behaviour (or a tradition of any other sort) knows that both rigidity and instability are foreign to its character. And secondly, this form of the moral life is capable of change as well as of local variation. Indeed, no traditional way of behaviour, no traditional skill, ever remains fixed; its history is one of continuous change. (20.)

Nevertheless, the issue between us is not a merely verbal one. Whereas Oakeshott maintains that the sort of change and adaptability of which he here speaks occurs independently of any reflective principles, I want to say that *the possibility* of reflection is essential to that kind of adaptability. Without this possibility we are dealing not with meaningful behaviour but with something which is either mere response to stimuli or the manifestation of a habit which is really blind. I do not mean by this that meaningful behaviour is simply a putting into effect of pre-existing reflective principles; such principles arise in the course of conduct and are only intelligible in relation to the conduct out of which they arise. But equally, the nature of the conduct out of which they arise can only be grasped as an embodiment of those principles. The notion of a principle (or maxim) of conduct and the notion of meaningful action are *interwoven*, in much the same way as Wittgenstein spoke of the notion of a rule and the notion of "the same" being interwoven.

To see this, let us look at one of the things Oakeshott says about the contrast between his alleged two forms of morality. He says that dilemmas of the form "What ought I to do here?" are likely to arise only for someone who is self-consciously trying to follow explicitly formulated rules, not for someone who is unreflectively following an habitual mode of behaviour. Now it may well be true that, as Oakeshott alleges, the necessity for such heartsearchings is likely to be more frequent and pressing for someone who is trying to follow an explicit rule without a foundation of everyday experience in its application. But questions of interpretation and consistency, that is, matters for *reflection*, are bound to arise for anyone who has to deal with a situation foreign to his previous experience. In a rapidly changing social environment such problems will arise frequently, not just because traditional customary modes of behaviour have broken down, but because of the novelty of the situations in which those modes of behaviour have to be carried on. Of course, the resulting strain may *lead* to a breakdown in the traditions.

Oakeshott says that the predicament of Western morals is that "our moral life has come to be dominated by the pursuit of ideals, a dominance ruinous to a settled mode of behaviour." (20.) But what is ruinous to a settled mode of behaviour, of whatever kind, is an unstable environment. The only mode of life which can undergo a meaningful development in response to environmental changes is one which contains within itself the means of assessing the significance of the behaviour which it prescribes. Habits too may of course change in response to changing conditions. But human history is not just an account of changing habits: it is the story of how men have tried to carry over what they regard as important in their modes of behaviour into the new situations which they have had to face.

Oakeshott's attitude to reflectiveness is, as a matter of fact, incompatible with a very important point which he makes early on in the discussion. He says that the moral life is "conduct to which there is an alternative." Now though it is true that this "alternative" need not be consciously before the agent's mind it must be something which *could* be brought before his mind. This condition is fulfilled only if the agent could defend what he has done against the allegation that he ought to have done something different. Or at least he must be able to *understand* what it would have been like to act differently. The dog who balances sugar on its nose in response to its master's command has no conception of what it would be to respond differently (because it has no *conception* of what it is doing at all). Hence it has no alternative to what it does; it just responds to the appropriate stimulus. An honest man may refrain from stealing money, though he could do so easily and needs it badly; the thought of acting otherwise need never occur to him. Nevertheless, he has the alternative of acting differently because he understands the situation he is in and the nature of what he is doing (or refraining from doing). Understanding something involves understanding the contradictory too: I understand what it is to act honestly just so far as and no farther than I understand what it is not to act honestly. That is why conduct which is the product of understanding, and only that, is conduct to which there is an alternative.

Bibliography

1. Acton, H. B., *The Illusion of the Epoch*, Cohen & West, 1955.

2. Aron, Raymond, *German Sociology*, Heinemann, 1957.

3. Ayer, A. J., *The Problem of Knowledge*, Macmillan and Penguin Books, 1956.

4. Ayer, A. J., "Can There Be a Private Language?" *Proceedings of the Aristotelian Society*, Supplementary Volume XXVIII.

5. Carrol, Lewis, "What the Tortoise Said to Achilles," *Complete Works*, Nonesuch Press.

6. Collingwood, R. G., *The Idea of History*, OUP, 1946.

7. Collingwood, R. G., *The Principles of Art*, OUP, 1938.

8. Cranston, Maurice, *Freedom: A New Analysis*, Longmans, 1953.

9. Durkheim, Emile, *Suicide*, Routledge & Kegan Paul, 1952.

10. Geach, Peter, *Mental Acts*, Routledge & Kegan Paul, 1957.

11. Ginsberg, Morris, *On the Diversity of Morals*, Heinemann, 1956.

12. Hume, David, *Enquiry into Human Understanding*.

13. Laslett, Peter (Ed.), *Philosophy, Politics and Society*, Blackwell, 1956.

14. Levi, E. H., *An Introduction to Legal Reasoning*, University of Chicago, Phoenix Books, 1961.

15. Lynd, R. S., *Knowledge for What?* Princeton, 1945.

16. Malcolm, Norman, Article in the *Philosophical Review*, Vol. LXIII, 1954, pp. 530–559.

17. Mandelbaum, Maurice, "Societal Facts," *B. J. Sociol.*, VI, 4 (1955).

18. Mill, J. S., *A System of Logic*.

19. Newcomb, T. M., *Social Psychology*, Tavistock Publications, 1952.

20. Oakeshott, Michael, "The Tower of Babel," *Cambridge Journal*, Vol. 2.

21. Oakeshott, Michael, "Rational Conduct," *Cambridge Journal*, Vol. 4.

22. Oakeshott, Michael, *Political Education*, Bowes and Bowes, 1951.

23. Pareto, Vilfredo, *The Mind and Society*, New York, Harcourt Brace, 1935.

24. Parsons, Talcott, *The Structure of Social Action*, Allen & Unwin, 1949.

25. Popper, Karl, *The Open Society and Its Enemies*, Routledge & Kegan Paul, 1945.

26. Popper, Karl, *The Poverty of Historicism*, Routledge & Kegan Paul, 1957.

27. Renner, Karl (with Introduction by O. Kahn-Freund), *The Institutions of Private Law and Their Social Function*, Routledge & Kegan Paul, 1949.

28. Rhees, Rush, "Can There Be a Private Language?" *Proceedings of the Aristotelian Society*, Supplementary Volume XXVIII.

29. Ryle, Gilbert, *The Concept of Mind*, Hutchinson, 1949.

30. Sherif, M. & Sherif, C., *An Outline of Social Psychology*, New York, Harper, 1956.

31. Simmel, Georg, *Conflict*, Glencoe, Free Press, 1955.

32. Strawson, P. F., Critical Notice in *Mind*, Vol. LXIII, No. 249, pp. 84 ff.

33. Weber, Max, *Wirtschaft und Gesellschaft*, Tübingen, Mohr, 1956.

34. Weber, Max, *Gesammelte Aufsatze zur Wissenschaftslehre*, Tübingen, Mohr, 1922.

35. Weldon, T. D., *The Vocabulary of Politics*, Penguin Books, 1953.

36. Wittgenstein, Ludwig, *Tractatus Logico-Philosophicus*, Kegan Paul, 1923.

37. Wittgenstein, Ludwig, *Philosophical Investigations*, Blackwell, 1953.

38. Wittgenstein, Ludwig, *Remarks on the Foundations of Mathematics*, Blackwell, 1956.

2. How to Derive "Ought" from "Is" [1]

John R. Searle

I

It is often said that one cannot derive an "ought" from an "is." This thesis, which comes from a famous passage in Hume's *Treatise*, while not as clear as it might be, is at least clear in broad outline: there is a class of statements of fact which is logically distinct from a class of statements of value. No set of statements of fact by themselves entails any statement of value. Put in more contemporary terminology, no set of *descriptive* statements can entail an *evaluative* statement without the addition of at least one evaluative premise. To believe otherwise is to commit what has been called the naturalistic fallacy.

I shall attempt to demonstrate a counterexample to this thesis. [2] It is not of course to be supposed that a single counterexample can refute a philosophical thesis, but in the present instance if we can present a plausible counterexample and can in addition give some account or explanation of how and why it is a counterexample, and if we can further offer a theory to back up our counter-example – a theory which will generate an indefinite number of counter-examples – we may at the very least cast considerable light on the original thesis; and possibly, if we can do all these things, we may even incline ourselves to the view that the scope of that thesis was more restricted than we had originally supposed. A counterexample must proceed by taking a statement or statements which any proponent of the thesis would grant were purely factual or "descriptive" (they need not actually contain the word "is") and show how they are logically related to a statement which a proponent of the thesis would regard as clearly "evaluative." (In the present instance it will contain an "ought".) [3]

Consider the following series of statements:

1. Jones uttered the words "I hereby promise to pay you, Smith, five dollars."
2. Jones promised to pay Smith five dollars.
3. Jones placed himself under (undertook) an obligation to pay Smith five dollars.
4. Jones is under an obligation to pay Smith five dollars.
5. Jones ought to pay Smith five dollars.

From *Philosophical Review*, Vol. 73 (1964), pp. 43–58, by permission of the author and publisher.

[1] Earlier versions of this paper were read before the Stanford Philosophy Colloquium and the Pacific Division of the American Philosophical Association. I am indebted to many people for helpful comments and criticisms, especially Hans Herzberger, Arnold Kaufmann, Benson Mates, A. I. Melden, and Dagmar Searle.

[2] In its modern version, I shall not be concerned with Hume's treatment of the problem.

[3] If this enterprise succeeds, we shall have bridged the gap between "evaluative" and "descriptive" and consequently have demonstrated a weakness in this very terminology. At present, however, my strategy is to play along with the terminology, pretending that the notions of evaluative and descriptive are fairly clear. At the end of the paper I shall state in what respects I think they embody a muddle.

I shall argue concerning this list that the relation between any statement and its successor, while not in every case one of "entailment," is nonetheless not just a contingent relation; and the additional statements necessary to make the relationship one of entailment do not need to involve any evaluative statements, moral principles, or anything of the sort.

Let us begin. How is (1) related to (2)? In certain circumstances, uttering the words in quotation marks in (1) is the act of making a promise. And it is a part of or a consequence of the meaning of the words in (1) that in those circumstances uttering them is promising. "I hereby promise" is a paradigm device in English for performing the act described in (2), promising.

Let us state this fact about English usage in the form of an extra premise:

(1a) Under certain conditions C anyone who utters the words (sentence) "I hereby promise to pay you, Smith, five dollars" promises to pay Smith five dollars.

What sort of things are involved under the rubric "conditions C?" What is involved will be all those conditions, those states of affairs, which are necessary and sufficient conditions for the utterance of the words (sentence) to constitute the successful performance of the act of promising. The conditions will include such things as that the speaker is in the presence of the hearer Smith, they are both conscious, both speakers of English, speaking seriously. The speaker knows what he is doing, is not under the influence of drugs, not hypnotized or acting in a play, not telling a joke or reporting an event, and so forth. This list will no doubt be somewhat indefinite because the boundaries of the concept of a promise, like the boundaries of most concepts in a natural language, are a bit loose.[4] But one thing is clear; however loose the boundaries may be, and however difficult it may be to decide marginal cases, the conditions under which a man who utters "I hereby promise" can correctly be said to have made a promise are straightforwardly empirical conditions.

So let us add as an extra premise the empirical assumption that these conditions obtain.

(1b) Conditions C obtain.

From (1), (1a), and (1b) we derive (2). The argument is of the form: If C then (if U then P): C for conditions, U for utterance, P for promise. Adding the premises U and C to this hypothetical we derive (2). And as far as I can see, no moral premises are lurking in the logical woodpile. More needs to be said about the relation of (1) to (2), but I reserve that for later.

What is the relation between (2) and (3)? I take it that promising is, by definition, an act of placing oneself under an obligation. No analysis of the concept of promising will be complete which does not include the feature of the promiser placing himself under or undertaking or accepting or recognizing an obligation to the promisee, to perform some future course of action, normally for the benefit of the promisee. One may be tempted to think that promising can be analyzed in terms of creating expectations in one's hearers, or some such, but a little reflection will show that the crucial distinction between statements of intention on the one

---

[4] In addition the concept of a promise is a member of a class of concepts which suffer from looseness of a peculiar kind, viz. defeasibility. Cf. H. L. A. Hart, "The Ascription of Responsibility and Rights," *Logic and Language*, First Series, ed. by A. Flew (Oxford, 1951).

hand and promises on the other lies in the nature and degree of commitment or obligation undertaken in promising.

I am therefore inclined to say that (2) entails (3) straight off, but I can have no objection if anyone wishes to add – for the purpose of formal neatness – the tautological premise:

(2a) All promises are acts of placing oneself under (undertaking) an obligation to do the thing promised.

How is (3) related to (4)? If one has placed oneself under an obligation, then, other things being equal, one is under an obligation. That I take it also is a tautology. Of course it is possible for all sorts of things to happen which will release one from obligations one has undertaken and hence the need for the *ceteris paribus* rider. To get an entailment between (3) and (4) we therefore need a qualifying statement to the effect that:

(3a) Other things are equal.

Formalists, as in the move from (2) to (3), may wish to add the tautological premise:

(3b) All those who place themselves under an obligation are, other things being equal, under an obligation.

The move from (3) to (4) is thus of the same form as the move from (1) to (2): If E then (if *PUO* then *UO*): E for other things are equal, *PUO* for place under obligation and *UO* for under obligation. Adding the two premises E and *PUO* we derive *UO*.

Is (3a), the *ceteris baribus* clause, a concealed evaluative premise? It certainly looks as if it might be, especially in the formulation I have given it, but I think we can show that, though questions about whether other things are equal frequently involve evaluative considerations, it is not logically necessary that they should in every case. I shall postpone discussion of this until after the next step.

What is the relation between (4) and (5)? Analogous to the tautology which explicates the relation of (3) and (4) there is here the tautology that, other things being equal, one ought to do what one is under an obligation to do. And here, just as in the previous case, we need some premise of the form:

(4a) Other things are equal.

We need the *ceteris paribus* clause to eliminate the possibility that something extraneous to the relation of "obligation" to "ought" might interfere.[5] Here, as in the previous two steps, we eliminate the appearance of enthymeme by pointing out that the apparently suppressed premise is tautological and hence, though formally neat, it is redundant. If, however, we wish to state it formally, this argument is of the same form as the move from (3) to (4): If E then (if *UO* then O); E for other

---

[5] The *ceteris paribus* clause in this step excludes somewhat different sorts of cases from those excluded in the previous step. In general we say, "He undertook an obligation, but nonetheless he is not (now) under an obligation" when the obligation has been *removed*, e.g., if the promisee says, "I release you from your obligation." But we say, "He is under an obligation, but nonetheless ought not to fulfill it" in cases where the obligation is *overridden* by some other considerations, e.g., a prior obligation.

things are equal, *UO* for under obligation, *O* for ought. Adding the premises *E* and *UO* we derive *O*.

Now a word about the phrase "other things being equal" and how it functions in my attempted derivation. This topic and the closely related topic of defeasibility are extremely difficult and I shall not try to do more than justify my claim that the satisfaction of the condition does not necessarily involve anything evaluative. The force of the expression "other things being equal" in the present instance is roughly this. Unless we have some reason (that is, unless we are actually prepared to give some reason) for supposing the obligation is void (step 4) or the agent ought not to keep the promise (step 5), then the obligation holds and he ought to keep the promise. If it is not part of the force of the phrase "other things being equal" that in order to satisfy it we need to establish a universal negative proposition to the effect that no reason could ever be given by anyone for supposing the agent is not under an obligation or ought not to keep the promise. That would be impossible and would render the phrase useless. It is sufficient to satisfy the condition that no reason to the contrary can in fact be given.

If a reason is given for supposing the obligation is void or that the promiser ought not to keep a promise, then characteristically a situation calling for evaluation arises. Suppose, for example, we consider a promised act wrong, but we grant that the promiser did undertake an obligation. Ought he to keep the promise? There is no established procedure for objectively deciding such cases in advance, and an evaluation (if that is really the right word) is in order. But unless we have some reason to the contrary, the *ceteris paribus* condition is satisfied, no evaluation is necessary, and the question whether he ought to do it is settled by saying "he promised." It is always an open possibility that we may have to make an evaluation in order to derive "he ought" from "he promised," for we may have to evaluate a counterargument. But an evaluation is not logically necessary in every case, for there may as a matter of fact be no counterarguments. I am therefore inclined to think that there is nothing necessarily evaluative about the *ceteris paribus* condition, even though deciding whether it is satisfied will frequently involve evaluations.

But suppose I am wrong about this: would that salvage the believe in an unbridgeable logical gulf between "is" and "ought"? I think not, for we can always rewrite my steps (4) and (5) so that they include the *ceteris paribus* clause as part of the conclusion. Thus from our premises we would then have derived "Other things being equal Jones ought to pay Smith five dollars," and that would still be sufficient to refute the tradition, for we would still have shown a relation of entailment between descriptive and evaluative statements. It was not the fact that extenuating circumstances can void obligations that drove philosophers to the naturalistic fallacy; it was rather a theory of language, as we shall see later on.

We have thus derived (in as strict a sense of "derive" as natural languages will admit of) an "ought" from an "is." And the extra premises which were needed to make the derivation work were in no cause moral or evaluative in nature. They consisted of empirical assumptions, tautologies, and descriptions of word usage. It must be pointed out also that the "ought" is a "categorical" not a "hypothetical" ought. (5) does not say that Jones ought to pay up if he wants such and such. It says he ought to pay up, period. Note also that the steps of the derivation are carried on in the third person. We are not concluding "I ought" from "I said 'I promise,' " but "he ought" from "he said 'I promise.' "

The proof unfolds the connection between the utterance of certain words and the speech act of promising and then in turn unfolds promising into obligation and moves from obligation to "ought." The step from (1) to (2) is radically different from the others and requires special comment. In (1) we construe "I hereby promise . . ." as an English phrase having a certain meaning. It is a consequence of that meaning that the utterance of that phrase under certain conditions is the act of promising. Thus by presenting the quoted expressions in (1) and by describing their use in (1a) we have as it were already invoked the institution of promising. We might have started with an even more ground-floor premise than (1) by saying

(1b)   Jones uttered the phonetic sequence: /ai ⁺hirbai ⁺pramis ⁺təpei ⁺yu ⁺smiθ ⁺ faiv ⁺dalərz/

We would then have needed extra empirical premises stating that this phonetic sequence was associated in certain ways with certain meaningful units relative to certain dialects.

The moves from (2) to (5) are relatively easy. We rely on definitional connections between "promise," "obligate," and "ought," and the only problem which arises is that obligations can be overridden or removed in a variety of ways and we need to take account of that fact. We solve our difficulty by adding further premises to the effect that there are no contrary considerations, that other things are equal.

II

In this section I intend to discuss three possible objections to the derivation.

First Objection

Since the first premise is descriptive and the conclusion evaluative, there must be a concealed evaluative premise in the description of the conditions in (1b).

So far, this argument merely begs the question by assuming the logical gulf between descriptive and evaluative which the derivation is designed to challenge. To make the objection stick, the defender of the distinction would have to show how exactly (1b) must contain an evaluative premise and what sort of premise it might be. Uttering certain words in certain conditions just *is* promising and the description of these conditions needs no evaluative element. The essential thing is that in the transition from (1) to (2) we move from the specification of a certain utterance of words to the specification of a certain speech act. The move is achieved because the speech act is a conventional act; and the utterance of the words, according to the conventions, constitutes the performance of just that speech act.

A variant of this first objection is to say: all you have shown is that "promise" is an evaluative, not a descriptive, concept. But this objection again begs the question and in the end will prove disastrous to the original distinction between descriptive and evaluative. For that a man uttered certain words and that these words have the meaning they do are surely objective facts. And if the statement of these two objective facts plus a description of the conditions of the utterance is sufficient to entail the statement (2) which the objector alleges to be an evaluative statement

(Jones promised to pay Smith five dollars), then an evaluative conclusion is derived from descriptive premises without even going through steps (3), (4), and (5).

Second Objection

Ultimately the derivation rests on the principle that one ought to keep one's promises and that is a moral principle, hence evaluative.

I don't know whether "one ought to keep one's promises" is a "moral" principle, but whether or not it is, it is also tautological; for it is nothing more than a derivation from the two tautologies:

All promises are (create, are undertakings of, are acceptances of) obligations),

and

One ought to keep (fulfill) one's obligations.

What needs to be explained is why so many philosophers have failed to see the tautological character of this principle. Three things I think have concealed its character from them.

The first is a failure to distinguish external questions about the institution of promising from internal questions asked within the framework of the institution. The questions "Why do we have such an institution as promising?" and "Ought we to have such institutionalized forms of obligation as promising?" are external questions asked about and not within the institution of promising. And the question "Ought one to keep one's promises?" can be confused with or can be taken as (and I think has often been taken as) an external question roughly expressible as "Ought one to accept the institution of promising?" But taken literally, as an internal question, as a question about promises and not about the institution of promising, the question "Ought one to keep one's promises?" is as empty as the question "Are triangles three-sided?" To recognize something as a promise is to grant that, other things being equal, it ought to be kept.

A second fact which has clouded the issue is this. There are many situations, both real and imaginable, where one ought not to keep a promise, where the obligation to keep a promise is overridden by some further considerations, and it was for this reason that we needed those clumsy *ceteris paribus* clauses in our derivation. But the fact that obligations can be overridden does not show that there were no obligations in the first place. On the contrary. And these original obligations are all that is needed to make the proof work.

Yet a third factor is the following. Many philosophers still fail to realize the full force of saying that "I hereby promise" is a performative expression. In uttering it one performs but does not describe the act of promising. Once promising is seen as a speech act of a kind different from describing, then it is easier to see that one of the features of the act is the undertaking of an obligation. But if one thinks the utterance of "I promise" or "I hereby promise" is a peculiar kind of description — for example, of one's mental state — then the relation between promising and obligation is going to seen very mysterious.

Third Objection

The derivation uses only a factual or inverted-commas sense of the evaluative terms employed. For example, an anthropologist observing the behavior and attitudes of the Anglo-Saxons might well go through these derivations, but nothing evaluative would be included. Thus step (2) is equivalent to "He did what they call promising" and step (5) to "According to them he ought to pay Smith five dollars." But since all of the steps (2) to (5) are in *oratio obliqua* and hence disguised statements of fact, the fact-value distinction remains unaffected.

This objection fails to damage the derivation, for what it says is only that the steps *can* be reconstrued as in *oratio obliqua*, that we can construe them as a series of external statements, that we can construct a parallel (or at any rate related) proof about reported speech. But what I am arguing is that, taken quite literally, without any *oratio obliqua* additions or interpretations, the derivation is valid. That one can construct a similar argument which would fail to refute the fact-value distinction does not show that this proof fails to refute it. Indeed it is irrelevant.

III

So far I have presented a counterexample to the thesis that one cannot derive an "ought" from an "is" and considered three possible objections to it. Even supposing what I have said so far is true, still one feels a certain uneasiness. One feels there must be some trick involved somewhere. We might state our uneasiness thus: How can my granting a mere fact about a man, such as the fact that he uttered certain words or that he made a promise, commit *me* to the view that *he* ought to do something? I now want briefly to discuss what broader philosophic significance my attempted derivation may have, in such a way as to give us the outlines of an answer to this question.

I shall begin by discussing the grounds for supposing that it cannot be answered at all.

The inclination to accept a rigid distinction between "is" and "ought," between descriptive and evaluative, rests on a certain picture of the way words relate to the world. It is a very attractive picture, so attractive (to me at least) that it is not entirely clear to what extent the mere presentation of counterexamples can challenge it. What is needed is an explanation of how and why this classical empiricist picture fails to deal with such counterexamples. Briefly, the picture is constructed something like this: first we present examples of so-called descriptive statements ("my car goes eighty miles an hour," "Jones is six feet tall," "Smith has brown hair"), and we contrast them with so-called evaluative statements ("my car is a good car," "Jones ought to pay Smith five dollars," "Smith is a nasty man"). Anyone can see that they are different. We articulate the difference by pointing out that for the descriptive statements the question of truth or falsity is objectively decidable, because to know the meaning of the descriptive expressions is to know under what objectively ascertainable conditions the statements which contain them are true or false. But in the case of evaluative statements the situation is quite different. To know the meaning of the evaluative expressions is not by itself sufficient for knowing under what conditions the statements containing them are true or false, because the meaning of the expressions is such that the statements are not capable of objective or factual truth or falsity at all. Any justification a speaker can give of one of his evaluative statements essentially involves some appeal to attitudes he holds, to criteria of assessment he has adopted, or to moral principles by which he has chosen to live and judge other people. Descriptive statements are thus objective, evaluative statements subjective and the difference is a consequence of the different sorts of terms employed.

The underlying reason for these differences is that evaluative statements perform a completely different job from descriptive statements. Their job is not to describe any features of the world but to express the speaker's emotions, to express his attitudes, to praise or condemn, to laud or insult, to commend, to recommend, to advise, and so forth. Once we see the different jobs the two perform, we see that there must be a logical gulf between them. Evaluative statements must be different from descriptive statements in order to do their job, for if they were objective they could no longer function to evaluate. Put metaphysically, values cannot lie in the world, for if they did they would cease to be values and would just be another part of the world. Put in the formal mode, one cannot define an evaluative word in terms of descriptive words, for if one did, one would no longer be able to use the evaluative word to commend, but only to describe. Put yet another way, any effort to derive an "ought" from an "is" must be a waste of time, for all it could show even if it succeeded would be that the "is" was not a real "is" but only a disguised "ought" or, alternatively, that the "ought" was not a real "ought" but only a disguised "is."

This summary of the traditional empirical view has been very brief, but I hope it conveys something of the power of this picture. In the hands of certain modern authors, especially Hare and Nowell-Smith, the picture attains considerable subtlety and sophistication.

What is wrong with this picture? No doubt many things are wrong with it. In the end I am going to say that one of the things wrong with it is that it fails to give us any coherent account of such notions as commitment, responsibility, and obligation.

In order to work toward this conclusion I can begin by saying that the picture fails to account for the *different types* of "descriptive" statements. Its paradigms of descriptive statements are such utterances as "my car goes eighty miles an hour," "Jones is six feet tall," "Smith has brown hair," and the like. But it is forced by its own rigidity to construe "Jones got married," "Smith made a promise," "Jackson has five dollars," and "Brown hit a home run" as descriptive statements as well. It is so forced, because whether or not someone got married, made a promise, has five dollars, or hit a home run is as much a matter of objective fact as whether he has red hair or brown eyes. Yet the former kind of statement (statements containing "married," "promise," and so forth) seem to be quite different from the simple empirical paradigms of descriptive statements. How are they different? Though both kinds of statements state matters of objective fact, the statements containing words such as "married," "promise," "home run," and "five dollars" state facts whose existence presupposes certain institutions: a man has five dollars, given the institution of money. Take away the institution and all he has is a rectangular bit of paper with green ink on it. A man hits a home run only given the institution of baseball; without the institution he only hits a sphere with a stick. Similarly, a man gets married or makes a promise only within the institutions of marriage and promising. Without them, all he does is utter words or makes gestures. We might characterize such facts as institutional facts, and contrast them with noninstitutional, or brute, facts: that a man has a bit of paper with green ink on it is a brute fact, that he has five dollars is an institutional fact.[6] The classical picture fails to

---

[6] For a discussion of this distinction see G. E. M. Anscombe, "Brute Facts," *Analysis* (1958).

account for the differences between statements of brute fact and statements of institutional fact.

The word "institution" sounds artificial here, so let us ask: what sorts of institutions are these? In order to answer that question I need to distinguish between two different kinds of rules or conventions. Some rules regulate antecedently existing forms of behavior. For example, the rules of polite table behavior regulate eating, but eating exists independently of these rules. Some rules, on the other hand, do not merely regulate but create or define new forms of behavior: the rules of chess, for example, do not merely regulate an antecedently existing activity called playing chess; they, as it were, create the possibility of or define that activity. The activity of playing chess is constituted by action in accordance with these rules. Chess has no existence apart from these rules. The distinction I am trying to make was foreshadowed by Kant's distinction between regulative and constitutive principles, so let us adopt his terminology and describe our distinction as a distinction between regulative and constitutive rules. Regulative rules regulate activities whose existence is independent of the rules; constitutive rules constitute (and also regulate) forms of activity whose existence is logically dependent on the rules.[7]

Now the institutions that I have been talking about are systems of constitutive rules. The institutions of marriage, money, and promising are like the institutions of baseball or chess in that they are systems of such constitutive rules or conventions. What I have called institutional facts are facts which presuppose such institutions.

Once we recognize the existence of and begin to grasp the nature of such institutional facts, it is but a short step to see that many forms of obligations, commitments, rights, and responsibilities are similarly institutionalized. It is often a matter of fact that one has certain obligations, commitments, rights, and responsibilities, but it is a matter of institutional, not brute, fact. It is one such institutionalized form of obligation, promising, which I invoked above to derive an "ought" from an "is." I started with a brute fact, that a man uttered certain words, and then invoked the institution in such a way as to generate institutional facts by which we arrived at the institutional fact that the man ought to pay another man five dollars. The whole proof rests on an appeal to the constitutive rule that to make a promise is to undertake an obligation.

We are now in a position to see how we can generate an indefinite number of such proofs. Consider the following vastly different example. We are in our half of the seventh inning and I have a big lead off second base. The pitcher whirls, fires to the shortstop covering, and I am tagged out a good ten feet down the line. The umpire shouts, "Out!" I, however, being a positivist, hold my ground. The umpire tells me to return to the dugout. I point out to him that you can't derive an "ought" from an "is." No set of descriptive statements describing matters of fact, I say, will entail any evaluative statements to the effect that I should or ought to leave the field. "You just can't get orders or recommendations from facts alone." What is needed is an evaluative major premise. I therefore return to and stay on second base (until I am carried off the field). I think everyone feels my claims here to be preposterous, and preposterous in the sense of logically absurd. Of course you can derive an "ought" from an "is," and though to actually set out the derivation in this case would be vastly more complicated than in the case of promising, it is in

---

[7] For a discussion of a related distinction see J. Rawls, "Two Concepts of Rules," *Philosophical Review*, LXIV (1955).

principle no different. By undertaking to play baseball I have committed myself to the observation of certain constitutive rules.

We are now also in a position to see that the tautology that one ought to keep one's promises is only one of a class of similar tautologies concerning institutionalized forms of obligation. For example, "one ought not to steal" can be taken as saying that to recognize something as someone else's property necessarily involves recognizing his right to dispose of it. This is a constitutive rule of the institution of private property.[8] "One ought not to tell lies" can be taken as saying that to make an assertion necessarily involves undertaking an obligation to speak truthfully. Another constitutive rule. "One ought to pay one's debts" can be construed as saying that to recognize something as a debt is necessarily to recognize an obligation to pay it. It is easy to see how all these principles will generate counterexamples to the thesis that you cannot derive an "ought" from an "is."

My tentative conclusions, then, are as follows:

1. The classical picture fails to account for institutional facts.
2. Institutional facts exist within systems of constitutive rules.
3. Some systems of constitutive rules involve obligations, commitments, and responsibilities.
4. Within those systems we can derive "ought's" from "is's" on the model of the first derivation.

With these conclusions we now return to the question with which I began this section: How can my stating a fact about a man, such as the fact that he has made a promise, commit me to a view about what he ought to do? One can begin to answer this question by saying that for me to state such an institutional fact is already to invoke the constitutive rules of the institution. Is it those rules that give the word "promise" its meaning. But those rules are such that to commit myself to the view that Jones made a promise involves committing myself to what he ought to do (other things being equal).

If you like, then, we have shown that "promise" is an evaluative word, but since it is also purely descriptive, we have really shown that the whole distinction needs to be re-examined. The alleged distinction between descriptive and evaluative statements is really a conflation of at least two distinctions. On the one hand there is a distinction between different kinds of speech acts, one family of speech acts including evaluations, another family including descriptions. This is a distinction between different kinds of illocutionary force.[9] On the other hand there is a distinction between utterances which involve claims objectively decidable as true or false and those which involve claims not objectively decidable, but which are

[8] Proudhon said: "Property is theft." If one tries to take this as an internal remark it makes no sense. It was intended as an external remark attacking and rejecting the institution of private property. It gets its air of paradox and its force by using terms which are internal to the institution in order to attack the institution.

Standing on the deck of some institutions one can tinker with constitutive rules and even throw some other institutions overboard. But could one throw all institutions overboard (in order perhaps to avoid ever having to derive an "ought" from an "is")? One could not and still engage in those forms of behavior we consider characteristically human. Suppose Proudhon had added (and tried to live by): "Truth is a lie, marriage is infidelity, language is uncommunicative, law is a crime," and so on with every possible institution.

[9] See J. L. Austin, *How to Do Things with Words* (Cambridge, Mass., 1962), for an explanation of this notion.

"matters of personal decision" or "matters of opinion." It has been assumed that the former distinction is (must be) a special case of the latter, that if something has the illocutionary force of an evaluation, it cannot be entailed by factual premises. Part of the point of my argument is to show that this contention is false, that factual premises can entail evaluative conclusions. If I am right, then the alleged distinction between descriptive and evaluative utterances is useful only as a distinction between two kinds of illocutionary force, describing and evaluating, and it is not even very useful there, since if we are to use these terms strictly, they are only two among hundreds of kinds of illocutionary force; and utterances of sentences of the form (5) — "Jones ought to pay Smith five dollars" — would not characteristically fall in either class.

3. Obligation and Rules

Richard E. Flathman

... The main task of the present chapter is to analyze the concepts "rule," "rule-governed conduct," and "guiding conduct by calling attention to a rule." We will try to show that so far from excluding reason and choice from the practice of political obligation, the fact that these concepts figure in the practice renders reason and choice not only a desirable but a necessary part of it. The most difficult part of this task will be to analyze further what we will call the general rule ("Obey the law") and to show in what respects it is possible to give reasons for accepting or rejecting it.[1]

Since our discussion of these questions is lengthy, it will be well to indicate in advance the route we will follow and the major theses we will advance. We will begin by attempting (in section I) to identify some of the characteristic features of the generic phenomenon of conduct-guiding rules and to distinguish such rules and conduct guided by them from various related phenomena with which they have been confused. One purpose of this discussion is to show that rules are a feature of human action not of behavior. Rules of conduct ordinarily indicate the presence of

From *Political Obligation* by Richard E. Flathman, pp. 66–116. Copyright © 1972 by Richard E. Flathman. Reprinted by permission of Atheneum Publishers.

[1] Throughout this chapter . . . we will be assuming that Hart is correct in his thesis that in most of its conduct-guiding uses "obligation" is a rule-dependent concept; that we ordinarily use "obligation" (as distinct from "ought," "right," "good," etc.) where there is an established rule requiring or forbidding a type of conduct. [See H. L. A. Hart, *The Concept of Law* (Oxford: Clarendon Press, 1961), esp. pp. 79–88.] This thesis is obviously correct in the central class of cases before us, namely obligations defined by law. We have also suggested respects in which it is true of obligations undertaken by promising and contracting; there are rules requiring us to keep promises and fulfill contracts. In all of these cases the problem is not to decide whether there is a rule but to identify the kind or type of rule there is, to determine how the type of rule in question compares with other types, to assess the logical and practical implications and consequences of the fact that there is a rule of a certain kind. If we sort out the kinds of rules and their implications in the cases in which we would readily agree that there is a rule, we will be in a much better position to decide whether there are established uses of "obligation" which do not presuppose the presence of a rule.

a regularity or pattern in the activities of those to whom they apply. But they also presuppose that the activity to which they apply will be susceptible of guidance in the sense that the individuals to whom they apply must be able to choose or decide whether to accept them and conform to them. Similarly, rules set a standard or criterion of proper action. Hence they presuppose that the conduct in question is thought to matter sufficiently to warrant distinguishing proper from improper conduct and holding people to the former. Most important, we will argue that we can speak of rules only if those who are guided by alleged rules, or who used alleged rules in guiding the conduct of others, think that there are good reasons for accepting them and conforming to them. Developing these points will involve distinguishing rules and rule-guided conduct from the use of force, threats of force and behavior out of fear of force, from trained behavior and from habitual behavior.

Section II develops distinctions among six types of rules. The distinctions are taken with modifications from work of Max Black.... Section III is the heart of the chapter. The question at issue there is why the presence of a rule provides a ground, warrant, or justification for doing what the rule advises, directs, or requires. More particularly, why does the presence of particular legal rules and the general rule provide a ground for acting in the manner required by these rules? Does the fact that a statement that X should be done has achieved the standing of a rule add to the case for doing X? Does this fact limit the kinds of considerations that are relevent to deciding whether to do X? If it is true that political obligations are defined by rules, these questions are ways of asking whether, and if so why, political obligations should be discharged. If the latter question is to be discussed in general terms (and one of the issues before us in this section . . . is whether it is profitable to discuss it in general terms), we suggest that the above questions about rules are the best way of asking it. They are the best way of asking the question about political obligations because they direct our attention to the kinds or classes of considerations relevant to answering it.

From the standpoint of a theory of political obligation the crux of the matter is whether reasons can be given for accepting and rejecting the general rule. There is often great controversy over the merits of particular legal rules but there is little or no controversy as to whether reasons can be given for and against them. It is less obvious that the notion of giving reasons for accepting or rejecting the general rule is a cogent notion. We will grant that doing so is quite a different sort of activity from reasoning about particular legal rules. This is because of (1) the extremely abstract character of the rule and (2) the relationship between it and the semantic rules governing the concepts that figure in its formulation. The first requires that reasons for or against the rule be cast in extremely general terms, terms that can easily be so vague as to justify nothing or so inclusive as to justify too much. Owing to the relationship between the rule and semantic rules, questioning the general rule involves questioning semantic rules as well. Thus there is a sense in which merely stating the general rule, even for the purpose of questioning it, seems to reinforce and even endorse it. It is difficult, or it appears to be difficult, to find linguistic ground, as it were, on which to stand in questioning the general rule. In this chapter our attention will focus on the second of these difficulties. We will try to show that much of the difficulty can be resolved if we make the distinction just mentioned, namely between the semantic rules governing the concepts that figure in the formulation of the rule and the (conduct-guiding) general rule itself. We will also suggest that the first difficulty can be and has been overcome....

I. Characteristics of Rules

We will not get far in understanding conduct-guiding rules and rule-guided conduct without distinguishing among the major senses in which "rule" is used. But there are some characteristics common to most of the senses of "rule," and identifying them now will provide perspective on the ground that we will explore in greater detail below.

First, talk of a rule in the sense of a rule of conduct usually indicates the presence of observable regularity in the conduct to which the rule applies. This point has been a source of confusion because "regularity" is one of the things that "rule" *means* (in one of its uses). For example we say: "As a rule B does X on Saturday morning," meaning that anyone who observes B on Saturday mornings will notice that he usually does X. Of course the fact that as a rule B does X on Saturday morning is not enough to show that there is a conduct-guiding rule that B knows about and that requires or forbids that he should (must) (ought to) do X on Saturday morning. B's regularly doing X is not even a necessary condition of there being a conduct-guiding rule that he do so. But if no one to whom the conduct-guiding rule applies in fact does X on Saturday mornings, doubt will be cast on the proposition that there is a rule requiring that X be done. We usually say there is a rule (noun) requiring X only if there is evidence that the alleged rule in fact *rules* (verb) the conduct of at least some of the persons to whom it applies most of the time. At a minimum, evidence that the alleged rule does not rule the conduct of those to whom it applies will lead us to *qualify* the statement that there is a rule. We might say that there is a rule requiring X but that it has fallen into desuetude, or that a rule requiring X has been proposed but has not become effective.[2]

Second, there can be conduct-guiding rules, and talk of conduct-guiding rules, only where the conduct to which the rules apply is susceptible to guidance by second parties. This requirement means that it must be possible for the agent to whom the rules apply to choose to do what the rules require in the circumstance(s) in which the rules require it. Thus there is no sense to a rule (except in the sense of a regularity) requiring or forbidding patellar reactions or other involuntary movements and impulses.

Third, the concept "rule" involves the notion of a standard or criterion which discriminates between right and wrong, correct and incorrect, proper and improper, wise and unwise. (Which of these adjectives apply depends on the type of rule at issue. We will discuss the question further as we examine different types of rule.) The development and application of such a standard presupposes that the type of conduct in question is thought to be important enough to the society or group for there to be some point in having and enforcing the standard. The notion of right or wrong conduct has no application to conduct that everyone agrees is trivial. Thus we do not have rules governing many matters of personal taste and avocation. Of course we do have rules concerning some matters of personal taste, and other societies have rules concerning matters that we think too trivial to warrant regulation by a rule. The thesis that it must be thought to matter how people act for there to be a rule does not involve any specification of what is or could be thought to matter. It is not uncommon for it to be thought to matter that people do X *because* there is a rule requiring it. This is sometimes the case when a rule first

---

[2] On this point cf. Hart, op. cit., esp. pp. 23–24, 140–41.

develops because it is thought to matter that people do X for one reason, that reason loses its cogency, but the rule has come to be an accepted part of social arrangement. As objectionable as these views and arrangements often are, they do not upset the thesis that there are rules only where it is thought to matter how members of the society or group conduct themselves in a particular respect.

The conditions we have discussed thus far are not sufficient to distinguish making and calling attention to rules from a variety of other methods of influencing conduct, even including physical compulsion such as pulling a man from X to Y by a rope and threats of unauthorized use of force. Threatening a man with harm and deliberately pulling him by a rope presupposes a belief that it is possible to influence his behavior by doing so. They also presuppose a belief that it matters that the person act or behave in the required manner. To distinguish all ways of guiding conduct that do not involve rules would take us well beyond our present concerns. But there is one further characteristic of rules that is of the utmost importance in the present context. A can properly be said to have guided B's conduct by calling attention to a rule only if he thinks that there are good reasons for accepting the rule as a basis of conduct. B can claim to have been guided by the rule that A cited only if he (B) thinks there are good reasons for accepting the rule as a basis of conduct.

We are not suggesting that the agent's belief in the availability of good reasons for giving, accepting, and acting upon guidance is exclusive to rules. An agent may think that there are, and there may be, good reasons for making and complying with a threat. Likewise there may be good reasons for submitting to training, hypnosis, and even compulsion (though there are problems with the last) and there certainly can be good reasons for training, hypnotizing, and compelling others to do X. What we want to suggest is that absence of a belief that there are good reasons does not render talk of compulsion, threats, and trained behavior inappropriate. By contrast, belief in the availability of good reasons for an alleged rule is a necessary condition of the proper use of "rule" and "rule-guided conduct."

Clarifying and defending this thesis is the main task of the present chapter. We can make a beginning by considering some descriptions of actions of A and B which clearly do not require that A or B think they have good reasons for doing what they are doing. The clearest case is describing A as having compelled B to do X by using physical force against or upon him. A may have reasons for compelling B to do X and, logically, B can inquire into them and accept or reject them. His acceptance of them will, as a practical matter, facilitate A's task. But it is not necessary for A to have a reason (much less a good reason) for doing so in order for it to be said that he compelled B to do X. Nor is it necessary that B know and accept A's reason (assuming that he has one) for it to be appropriate to say that B's behavior was influenced or even determined by A's use of force. Presumably there is some explanation, perhaps in terms of motive or impulse, for A's compelling B to do X, and B will not understand *why* A compelled B unless he knows what the motive or impulse was. But not knowing *why* A compelled B to do X is no obstacle to knowing *that* he compelled B. We do not expect the bully or ruffian to have, much less to give, reasons for pushing other people around. Nor do we expect people pushed around by bullies and ruffians to know, much less to accept, the reasons why they are pushed around.

The same analysis applies in all but one respect to the case of influencing conduct by making unauthorized threats. B is threatened with certain consequences if he does not do X, but he is not actually compelled to do X. Therefore he must decide whether to do X. Knowing why A wants B to do X and why A is using threats may help B decide whether A will actually make good on the threats. Thus such knowledge may help him to decide whether to do X. If B has good reason to believe that A will not carry through on his threat doubt would be cast on the propriety of explaining B's action as a response to A's threat.[3]

A third and more interesting class of cases is when A trains B to do X. Assume that A trains B to do X whenever Y, such that the appearance of Y becomes a sufficient condition of B's doing X. If so, saying that A's causing Y influenced B to do X or that B did X because of the influence of A does not require evidence that A or B had good reasons. We would probably not say that A had trained B (assuming B is an adult) to do X when Y unless A gave and B accepted reasons for doing so during the training process. If A gives no reasons during the training process it would be more appropriate to say that A conditioned B to do X. (This is one of the differences between the use of training in connection with human beings and its use in connection with animals, and perhaps between training adults and training young children. It is also another area in which we need a good deal of information in order to know whether to use action concepts or behavior concepts.) But once the training had been completed having and giving reasons would become unnecessary.

An example may clarify the point here. A veteran shortstop, A, trains a rookie second baseman, B, always to angle behind him (A) when they are both pursuing a ground ball hit over second base. At the outset A explains that: (1) they must always do it the same way so as to avoid collisions; and (2) the rule he suggests is best because (i) the second baseman is necessarily moving away from the base to which he must throw the ball (first base) while the shortstop is moving more or less toward it; and (ii) the degree to which the shortstop is moving toward first base will be maximized if he cuts in front of the second baseman. The rookie then practices adjusting his angle of pursuit to that of the shortstop until he has learned to estimate the latter very quickly and to set his own course accordingly. Thus by setting his own path of pursuit A also determines B's path of pursuit (X).

Of course a conduct-guiding rule continues to be available to A and B and they might mention the rule and the reasons for it in explaining their practice to others. But we could say that A influenced B and that B's behavior was trained, even if, after several seasons, B had entirely forgotten the reasons for the arrangement. But if B had forgotten the reasons we could not say that he was following a rule when he did X. An observer could discover a rule in the sense of a regularity in B's behavior, and he might discover a rule in additional senses if he investigated the history of B's behavior. He would not now find the characteristics of conduct guided by a rule.

---

[3] Using the concept "decide" in describing B's response to A's threat slurs over a problem in the distinction between action and behavior. So long as A does not literally force B to do X there is ground for saying that B decided to do X and hence that X was an action of his. A major implication of using this description is that B can be held responsible for doing X. But if A threatens B with extremely grave consequences we sometimes say that B "had no choice" but to do X. If we say this we put X in the category of behavior rather than action. In this kind of case to say that B "had no choice" is usually to say that the choices (other than doing X) are so unpleasant or hard to accept that we could not expect B to choose them. Thus in order to make the action-behavior distinction we must know a good deal about the alternatives to doing X, the consequences of choosing them, and the circumstances in which the choice must be made.

Our reasons for his contention can be brought out more clearly if we consider the closely related case of habitual behavior. A period of training is one possible origin of a habit. When this is the case — as in the baseball example above — there is little to distinguish habitual from trained behavior. But a mode of behavior can become habitual in other ways as well, for example simply by unguided repetition of a behavior over a period of time. Most of us are not trained to smoke tobacco or drink alcoholic beverages but these are among the most commonly mentioned examples of habits. What is characteristic of habitual behavior is that the person who does X habitually has ceased to think about doing X; he has ceased to be aware of alternatives to X and to choose to do X after considering alternatives. It is not that there are no alternatives available. The availability of alternatives that *could be* chosen, objectively speaking, distinguishes habitual behavior from behavior that is compelled or determined. Nor is it that the person could not choose to do other than X in the sense in which we say that an addict could not, unaided, choose to cease using heroin or an alcoholic could not choose to give up alcoholic beverages. It is physically possible for B not to do X. But he does not consider whether to do X or not, he simply does it. Alternatives are available but he does not consider them.[4]

We have already noted that a part of the notion of a rule (save in the sense of a regularity) is the notion of a standard or criterion which distinguishes right from wrong, correct from incorrect. Stated in the most general terms, the notion of a rule involves choosing among alternatives. Thus the person who is unaware of alternatives to what he is doing cannot be following a rule. The man who unthinkingly lights up a cigarette every time he gets in the car or sits down to coffee is not following a rule. His behavior is habitual.

Following a rule, then, involves an awareness of alternatives and a choice between or among them. Combined with the point that the conduct must be thought to matter, we get the conclusion that the existence of rules that *rule* conduct presupposes a degree of reflection on the part of some substantial number of those to whom the rules apply.[5]

[4] It is true that we use the noun "habit" in cases where a person does consider alternatives but nevertheless does X. Since we have learned of its ill effects on health, smoking tobacco has become a leading example. If we say that a person has the habit of smoking we are usually saying (a) that the person thinks that smoking is undesirable and (b) that, though not addicted, he is weak-willed. Statement (a) is not a general feature of the use of "habit." There is nothing odd about the notion of good habits. Statement (b) brings out the distinctiveness of this use of the noun. It would be odd to say that a person who "had the habit" of smoking smoked "habitually." His smoking is a matter of distress to him, he worries about it, tries to avoid it or at least alleges that he is trying to avoid it, but continues to do it. A man behaving habitually does not engage in such self-examination.

[5] Later we will elaborate upon the kinds of reflection appropriate to different types of rules. But we should stress immediately that there are degrees of awareness and reflection, and that there are important distinctions to be drawn, in terms of degrees of awareness and reflection, within the category of rule-following conduct. There are many things that we do routinely, as a matter of course. Routine, matter-of-course actions are distinguished from actions we take deliberately, with close attention to each step in the process. With the most obvious marks of reflection and deliberation missing, it is sometimes difficult to distinguish such actions from habitual behavior. Contrary to Peter Winch, to whom I am indebted in the previous paragraphs, it is not enough that "it makes sense to distinguish between a right and wrong way of doing things in connection with what [the agent] ... does." (Peter Winch, *The Idea of a Social Science* (London: Routledge and Kegan Paul, 1958), p. 58). The fact that an observer can make such a distinction does not establish that the actor is aware of the distinction

If the foregoing analyses of "rule" and of compulsion, threats, trained behavior, and habitual behavior are valid, and if it is true that "obligation" is rule-dependent, it follows that compulsions, threats, trained behavior, and habitual behavior cannot be among the necessary or defining features of the practice of political obligation. They may or may not be associated with the practice in various circumstances, but their presence does not establish that the practice is operating and their absence does not establish that it is not operating. Thus we have made progress in delimiting the area in which the practice of political obligation operates and in identifying its characteristics. Since prominent theories of political obligation have analyzed the practice in terms of compulsion, threats, and trained and habitual behavior (we are thinking primarily of Plato, Austin, and Bergson) we have also made progress in disposing of influential misunderstandings of the practice. The next task is to analyze more closely the relationship between rules and rule-guided conduct on the one hand and reasons and reasoning on the other. Granting that rule-guided conduct is reflective conduct, we must try to determine what kinds of reasoning are appropriate in connection with the rules that generate and define political obligations.

II. Types of Rules

Max Black has distinguished four main senses in which "rule" is used and hence four main types of rules: (1) regularity, (2) instructions, (3) regulations, (4) precepts.[6] In addition there has been a good deal of discussion in recent years of a fifth type of rule for which there is no convenient term in ordinary language but which has been called "practice-type" (Rawls), "constitutive" (Searle) and "regulative" (Black).[7] Finally, there is a sixth type of rule which cuts across the first five categories, namely the semantic rules or conventions that we discussed in Chapter One.

For reasons already indicated, regularities are not conduct-guiding rules and will be of interest only as they figure in the formation and justification of rules of types 2–6. Instructions guide conduct but they do not generate obligations. We will be

---

or is acting upon it. The actor must give us evidence that *he* is aware of the distinction. There are a *great many* ways in which he might do this. He might recognize a mistake – whether his own or that of someone else. He might teach the activity to others. He might make adjustments in his conduct in response to changed circumstances. He might, perhaps with assistance through questioning, state the rule. And there are numerous things which he would not do which a man behaving habitually might do, for example continue with a form of behavior in inappropriate circumstances, find requests for explanations or justification puzzling or upsetting. Tests such as these often allow us to make judgments, but they do not state the defining criteria of rule-following conduct and they are often difficult to apply in actual cases. Here again we must recognize that we are working with distinctions which cannot be sharply drawn and which can often be applied only with a good deal of information about the particulars of the case to which we are applying them. On these points see L. Wittgenstein, *Philosophical Investigations*, E. Anscombe trans. (London: The Macmillan Company, 1958), esp. I, 82–83 (pp. 39–40). See also Max Black, "Rules and Routines," in Richard Peters, ed. *The Concept of Education* (London: Routledge & Kegan Paul, 1967).

[6] Max Black, *Models and Metaphors* (Ithaca: Cornell University Press, 1962), pp. 109–15.

[7] See John Rawls, "Two Concepts of Rules," *Philosophical Review* vol. 64 (1955), pp. 3 ff.; John Searle, "How to Derive 'Ought' from 'Is' " [selection 2 in this book] ; Black, "Rules and Routines," op. cit.

concerned with them only because it is enlightening to compare them with rules that do generate obligations. Regulations, of which laws, judicial decrees, and executive orders are leading examples, are of obvious importance in the present context. The question of the *kinds* of reasoning appropriate in connection with them, however, is quite straightforward and they will not occupy us for long in this chapter. The most difficult questions arise concerning precepts and their relationships to constitutive-type rules and semantic rules. We will argue that what we called the general rule is best thought of as a precept. But it takes some of its force – and acquires much of its complexity – from the semantic rules that govern the uses of the concepts that figure in its formulation. This and other precepts have some of the characteristics of constitutive rules, but we will argue that it is misleading to place them in that category. Some regulations can be thought of as constitutive rules, but they do not define obligations.

The major question before us in discussing these types of rules will be the following: in what respects, and why, does the fact that there is a rule that X be done provide a reason for deciding to do X? Does the fact that there is a rule add to the case for doing X? Does it limit the kinds of considerations that are relevant to deciding whether to do X?

We will begin by putting enough flesh on the bones of the above categories to make them useful for our purposes.

As Black has defined the term, instruction-type rules differ from regulations (as do precepts) in that they are not passed or promulgated by an authority. Rather than being "laid down" at a determinate moment of time by an authority they evolve or develop in the course of experience. It is usually impossible to say when they were formulated and when they took effect. They can and do undergo change and can and do cease to be rules, but we do not speak of their being altered or rescinded. Refusing to follow them can have adverse consequences, but it does not lead to the imposition of penalties or punishments except in a metaphorical sense. By contrast with constitutive rules, however, they do not constitute or define activities or practices and following them or not does not affect the logical status of the action. Examples of instructions are: "Do not use a screwdriver to do the work of a chisel," "In five-card stud bet heavily after the second card if you have the only ace or king showing," "Do not plant tomatoes until after the last frost."

Examples of regulations would be laws passed by a legislature and some of the rules of games that are governed by an authoritative body. About rules of this type we can usually ask such questions as: "Who *made* the rule and by what *authority*?" "How *long* has the rule been in *effect*?" "What would be required to *rescind* or *alter* the rule?"[8] We can also speak of such rules as having been enforced, obeyed,

---

[8] There are borderline cases in which it is difficult to answer the questions just mentioned and in which doubts arise as to whether the questions have point. Are these *historical* questions appropriate in the case of rules of common law that are alleged to have existed since "time out of mind?" The point of saying that they have existed since time out of mind is at once that questions of authorship cannot be answered, *and* that the rules have a lengthy history at least a part of which can be recounted. A similar difficulty arises in the case of games, for example poker, the playing of which is governed by rules but for which there is to my knowledge no recognized governing body that promulgates the rules. Shall we classify rules of common law and rules of poker as regulation-type rules? The answer is that it matters very little how we classify them so long as we are aware of their features and their significance. A system of classification should help us to identify standard cases and to manipulate them efficiently. But such a system should also increase our sensitivity to differences and special cases.

and violated, and the idea of a penalty or sanction is most at home in the case of rules of this type.

Some typical precepts are: "Do not lie," "Do not cheat," "Put charity ahead of justice," "Honor your father and mother." As with instructions, precepts are not promulgated and are not subject to alteration or rescindment. Nor do notions such as enforcement, penalties, and punishments apply to them. It is appropriate, however, for A to hold B to conformity with precepts in ways he cannot do with instructions. Blame, censure, and other nonlegal sanctions can sometimes be applied if B does not conform to them. It has been argued that precepts define or constitute practices and arrangements so that failure to conform with them, or at least to give weight to them in deciding how to act, affects the logical status of the action. Thus "Do not lie" might be thought of as a constituent part of the institution or practice of morality. To refuse to give weight to the rule *is* to show a lack of understanding of the institution and to act amorally. Again, "Obey the law" might be thought a constitutive of the practice of political obligation. If so, a person who didn't give weight to the rule in relevant circumstances would show a lack of understanding of the practice and would not be participating in it when he acted. The importance of these interpretations for present purposes is that, if valid, they limit the kinds of considerations relevant to deciding whether to tell a lie or obey a law.

Clear examples of constitutive rules would be laws that establish the procedure that must be followed in order to take a certain legal action. Thus the law of wills and testaments determines what must be done to make a will. The person who does not follow the rules simply does not make a will. The law which indicates what must be done to make a will does not create obligations to make wills. The man who fails to follow the rules laid down by the law may suffer adverse consequences but he has not failed to discharge a legal obligation and he is not subject to punishment.[9] Some rules of games also provide relatively clear cases of constitutive rules. If a man has two pairs in a poker game and his opponent has three of a kind, the man loses the hand. If he claims to have won the hand he shows that he does not know the rules of poker. The rules concerning the rank order of hands are one of the constitutive parts of the game of poker.

In this case, however, the distinction is less clear-cut, and it has less significance than in the legal example. The law of wills and testaments can be changed only if established procedures are followed by agents with proper authority. Thus what counts as a will and as making a will is quite clear-cut. But the rules of games can be changed, at least for the purpose of playing the game here and now, by those who happen to be playing it here and now. If the seven of us decide that two pairs will beat three of a kind in this evening's game, then two pairs *will* beat three of a kind. It might be argued, of course, that owing to this change in the rules the evening's game is not a game of poker. Unless this argument is just a somewhat indirect way of objecting to the change, to make it would be to claim that there exist a set of necessary conditions, perhaps necessary and sufficient conditions, of a game being called a game of poker. Hart has argued persuasively that such conditions cannot be identified for such tightly defined concepts as "valid will" and "valid contract."[10]

---

[9] For an excellent discussion of legal examples of constitutive rules, see Hart, op. cit., esp. pp. 26–48, 78–79, 238–40. Hart calls them secondary rules.

[10] See H. L. A. Hart, "The Ascription of Responsibility and Rights," *Logic and Language*, First Series, ed. A. G. N. Flew (Oxford: Basil Blackwell, 1963), esp. pp. 146–56.

It would clearly be much more difficult to identify them for "poker." Not anything will count as a game of poker, but which or how many of the usual rules can be changed or disregarded before the game ceases to be poker cannot be settled abstractly. It cannot be settled because there is no established criterion by which to settle it. Thus the logical tie between the rules of poker and "poker" is not as tightly drawn as in the case of legal rules about wills. This point, which holds for many alleged examples of constitutive rules, will be important when we discuss the kinds of reasoning that are appropriate in connection with such rules.

· · ·

III. Rules and Reasons

Apart from the case of regularities, one of the *meanings* of the noun "rule" is "guide to conduct." Can we say more than this as to why the existence of a rule provides a ground or warrant for acting in the manner directed or required by the rule?

At one level of discussion this question is most easily answered in the case of constitutive rules. Such rules provide a reason for acting because it is only by acting in the manner specified by the rules that one can engage in the practices or play the games that are constituted by the rules. If B (a batter in a baseball game) asks A (the umpire) why he should retire from the batter's box after the third strike has been called, A's proper reply is simply: "Because the rules (of baseball) require that you do so." Of course A's reply counts as a reason for B to retire only if it is indeed a game of baseball that is in progress and only if B and the other players wish to continue to play that particular game. If these conditions are satisfied, for B to question whether the rules give him a reason to retire from the batter's box would be to demonstrate a lack of understanding of baseball (or of the notions of a rule and a reason as they are used in the type of case at hand).

Put another way, in the case of constitutive rules the rule itself constitutes a reason for acting in the manner specified by the rule. It might also seem that there is no room for a distinction between a statement of the rule qua rule and reasons for the rule or for acting in conformity with it. The notion of a reason for the rule or for accepting the rule involves a misunderstanding.

We mention this argument about constitutive rules at the outset because it provides a kind of limiting case as to why the presence of a rule provides a warrant for acting in a certain manner. It is a limiting case in the sense that it says that this type of rule provides a warrant because it is a rule of this type. Put another way, it is a limiting case in that it suggests that any and all considerations other than that it is a rule of this type are irrelevant and perhaps otiose. We will be in a better position to assess this argument later, but having it in mind will facilitate the discussion of instructions, regulations, and precepts.

A. Instructions and Reasons

If B does not bet heavily after the second card when he has the only ace showing, A may rightly infer that B is not playing poker well; he is not justified in inferring that B is not playing poker. The rule does not itself constitute a reason for following the rule in the way constitutive rules have been said to do. But instructions do advise us as to how to conduct ourselves; they advise us how to maximize the likelihood of achieving our ends or purposes. Failure or refusal to conform to such rules, though it does not render our conduct irrelevant to any practice or activity, might make it self-defeating. Assume that my purpose in playing poker is to win money and my purpose in carpentry is to make useful and attractive articles out of wood. If following the rules mentioned above contributes to those ends, and if failure to conform to them causes me to lose money or to produce useless and ugly articles, I have reason to conform to the rules.

The rules themselves, however, provide a reason only in what we will call a derivative sense. "Don't use a screwdriver to do the work of a chisel" provides the carpenter with a reason for fetching the chisel from the garage only if doing so will enable him to do a job he couldn't do to his satisfaction with a screwdriver. "Bet heavily after the second card . . ." provides the poker-player with a reason to risk a large sum only if doing so maximizes his chances of coming out of the game a winner. By contrast with the relationship between "The batter shall retire from the batter's box after the third strike" and playing baseball, there is no logical relationship between the rules in question and the ends in view. The standing of the rules depends not on logic or facts about concepts but on experience in carpentry and poker playing. I accept these rules not because of any feature internal to their formulation but because experience with working with wood has shown that using a tool with the characteristics of a chisel has regularly allowed me (or others) to do certain jobs better than using a tool with the characteristics of a screwdriver. If I want to persuade another person to accept these rules, I recite the relevant experience.[11] Thus in the case of instructions the notion of giving reasons — in this respect evidence — to support the rule is not only cogent but essential to the idea of accepting and acting upon the rule. If B asks A why he should bet heavily after the second card and A replies: "Because there is a rule that says you should do so," B will do well to look for a new instructor in the fine art of poker playing.

Evidence that acting according to the rule will bring about the predicted and desired result is only a necessary, not a sufficient condition of there being good reasons for accepting and conforming to an instruction-type rule. When this condition is satisfied (and when the end-in-view is accepted) an agent has *a* reason for accepting and conforming to the rule. But for him to have good reasons for accepting it and acting upon it he must believe that there is no better way to achieve the end in view. Perhaps following rule X makes it possible to achieve Y but excludes achievement of Z, following rule X', or following no rule at all, makes it possible to achieve both Y and Z. If so, there is a reason for following X, but not a good reason. Of course if A is not aware of X' he will have a good reason for following X. Note that this distinction between a reason and a good reason has no application to constitutive rules. If I am going to play baseball, the existence of a

---

[11] By "reciting the experience," of course, we do not mean that it is necessary to recount each instance on which a carpenter messed up a job by using the wrong tool. Over time the results of experience become embodied in what we might call "abbreviations," of which instructions (and instruction books) are themselves examples but which also include the design of tools such as chisels and screwdrivers. A man learning carpentry today can be persuaded that he should use a chisel for this job and a screwdriver for that by being *shown* the differences in the design of the two tools. But he can "see" that he should use the chisel for this, the screwdriver for that only because of his experience with sharp and blunt tools; and there is something for him to "see" only because of the experience that lies behind the development and differentiation of the tools.

rule that the batter must retire after the third strike is at once a reason and a good reason for retiring. But given the availability of (well-supported) X', for a poker-player to conform to X because it is a rule would be absurd. We would suspect that following X had become habitual for him or that he was following X because A ordered him to do so, out of fear of disapproval or out of some other motive that was related to "rule" only in the sense of regularity-type rules.

Rules in the sense of instructions, in short, presuppose evidence for a rule in the sense of a regularity; a regularity which supports a prediction that following the instruction will be the most efficient means to a certain end. But reasons in the sense of this kind of evidence are not a sufficient basis for accepting an instruction (and hence not sufficient for understanding the concept "rule-governed conduct" as it is used in connection with instructions). Instructions are guides to conduct, not merely stated regularities. Accepting them involves more than accepting certain empirical generalizations as true. One cannot accept an instruction as a guide to conduct if he does not accept the end or purpose to which it directs conduct. Empirical generalizations on the one hand and ends and purposes on the other are of course distinct entities. But instructions bind the two together into a logical whole that one cannot accept without accepting both the generalization and the end or purpose. Thus in order to complete our account of instructions we must examine the notion of accepting an end or purpose.

We will do well to begin by recalling Kant's distinction between hypothetical and categorical imperatives, with instructions corresponding to the former (and, as we will see later, precepts to the latter). Both hypotheticals and categoricals advise agents how to achieve some end or goal, the difference between them, as Black puts it, is that an agent can exempt himself from a hypothetical (instruction) "by disclaiming interest in the relevant purpose."[12] Perhaps a better way to make the point is that the decision whether to accept or reject the end or purpose is not, in the pure case, subject to challenge by second parties. If I play poker simply to have an occasion to drink beer with my cronies I can rightly dismiss the rule: "Bet heavily after second card if . . ." as irrelevant. Moreover, I will be justified in regarding criticism of my decision as an unwarranted interference in my affairs.[13]

Defining "instruction" in this way has two implications. The first is that a person can accept the end served by an instruction because he deems it to be in his interest to do so, because he has an impulse to do so, because it would benefit others to do so, or for any one of a large number of reasons. In the case of instructions, proper use of the concept "rule-guided conduct" requires the availability of good reasons for accepting the rule only as regards evidence that conforming to the rule will serve an end or purpose that the agent accepts. B may

---

[12] Black, *Models and Metaphors*, op. cit., p. 112.

[13] There are few "pure" cases. My wife might object that while it is all very well that I risk family funds by playing poker, I might at least make some attempt to reduce the risk. Or another player might object that my attitude toward the (instruction-type) rules of play make the game less interesting for the other players. Insofar as my dismissal of the rule has significant consequences for others they can rightfully question it. Since there are few types of action that could never have significant consequences for others (or at least few such actions about which rules have developed) the distinction between instructions and precepts is not sharp. It is based on the fact that there are many situations in which the consequences for others of my rejecting an instruction are so insignificant – at least by comparison with their consequences for me – that challenges to my decisions or actions would be thought unwarranted.

have reasons for accepting the end but he need not have them and he need not give them if he has them.

The second implication of the definition is that instructions are not obligation-generating rules. Of course B might be *obliged* to act upon instruction X. Since it is inappropriate for others to question his decision not to do so, B cannot be said to have an obligation to act upon X. (I am not assuming that the notion of an obligation to oneself is not a cogent notion. . . .) For this reason instructions are of interest here mainly because examining them helps us to understand types of rules that do generate obligations.[14]

B. Regulations and Reasons

We turn now to the type of rule that defines most political obligations, namely regulations. . . .

. . . Legal rules can be said to define *obligations* because there is a general rule according to which there is an obligation to obey the law. If there was no such rule legislatures would have to pass a law that created an obligation to obey the other laws they passed; and doing so would only raise the question of why there was an obligation to obey the law creating an obligation to obey the other laws. But the fact that particular rules are supported by the general rule hardly excludes the possibility of supporting particular rules in other ways as well. Laws are passed by individuals or groups of individuals at a specific moment in time. Hence it is clearer than in the case of instructions and precepts that men decide to pass them. Which in turn makes it obvious that we can ask for a justification as to why they were passed. Many of the institutions and procedures characteristic of our political and governmental arrangements are designed to facilitate asking such questions, to facilitate an exchange of reasons for and against existing or prospective laws. Consider how we would respond to a legislator who thought he could give a sufficient justification for his support of bill X by pointing to the fact that after passage it would fall under the general rule. Presenting such a "justification" would constitute a conclusive demonstration that he did not understand the representative institutions under which he held his office.

Thus it is clear that reasons can be given and that we expect them to be given for or against particular legal rules. Much of the discussion of law that takes place in politics involves the exchange of such reasons. By contrast, much of the discussion of law and obedience that takes place in treatises on political obligation concerns the argument that the absence of good reasons for a particular law is not enough to

[14] Note the relationships between the foregoing discussion of instructions and the case of constitutive rules such as the legal rules as to how to make a will and rules of baseball such as retiring after the third strike. In the latter two cases we said that one must follow the rules only if one wanted to make a will or play baseball. Just as the instruction "Don't use a screwdriver to do the work of a chisel" applies only to the person who wants to achieve certain objectives in working with wood, so the law of wills and testaments and the rule of baseball apply only to the person who wants to make a will or to play baseball. The cases differ, of course, in that in the one the relationship between following the rule and achieving the objective is empirical, in the other it is logical. But in neither case does the rule itself provide a sufficient reason for following the rule or for thinking there is an obligation to follow the rule. Thus if, say, "There is an obligation to keep promises" or "There is an obligation to obey the law" are practice-type rules, something more than the characteristics which make them rules of this type must be brought forward if it is to be said that there is an obligation to follow them.

show that that law should not be obeyed. Once passed the law falls under what we are calling the general rule. This rule creates an obligation to obey the particular law even if there are no good reasons for, or if there are good reasons against, the particular rule as such. Thus the question arises whether it is possible to give reasons for accepting and obeying the general rule and how such reasons relate to reasons for doing the action which the particular rule in question requires us to take.

C. Precepts and Reasons: The Case of "Obey the Law"

The general rule is not made or passed by an authority and it would make no sense to say that it had been rescinded or even amended. For these reasons it should not be classified as a regulation-type rule as we are using that category. In this respect it is similar to "Promises should be kept" and to rules of games which are not governed by an authoritative ruling body. Yet, with the qualifications noted above, a man who does not understand and accept the rule "Promises should be kept" cannot participate in the practice or activity of promising and a man who does not understand and accept the rules establishing the rank order of poker hands cannot play poker. The institution or practice of ruling conduct by law, and of having one's own conduct governed or ruled by law, is more complex than promising or than the the most complicated of games. Accordingly, the relationship of the rule "Obey the law" to law is more complex than the relationship of "Promises should be kept" to promising. As with promising and playing games, however, one does not understand the practice of governing conduct by law unless he understands that to say of a rule that it is a law is to say of it that there is an obligation to obey it. To say of a rule that it is a law is to say that it has been promulgated by an authoritative agent or agency who or which has the authority to promulgate the particular rule in question. And to say that a rule has been promulgated by an agent or agency with the authority to pass the rule is to say that there is ordinarily an obligation to obey the rule. As Pitkin, to whom I am indebted on these points, puts it: "It is part of the concept, the meaning of 'authority' that those subject to it are required to obey, that it has a right to command. It is part of the concept, the meaning of 'law,' that those to whom it is applicable are obligated to obey it."[15] The best way to see this is to notice that denying it would create the difficulty noted above, namely that legislatures would not only have to pass laws, they would have to pass laws that required obedience to the laws that they had passed. Thus although the general rule "Obey the law" or "There is an obligation to obey the law" is not itself a law or any other species of authoritative command, use of the concept "law" (and hence implicitly the concept "authority") in the rule make it impossible to reject the rule without challenging the rules governing the (relevant) use of "law" and "authority." "There is ordinarily an obligation to obey the law" is an explication of one feature of "law" and "authority." A person who doesn't understand this doesn't understand the semantic rules governing the concepts in question.

Given these features of "law" and "authority" it might seem to follow that we are faced with a case in which there is and can be no logical distance between the rule and the reason for accepting the rule. The formulation of the rule (or any

[15] Hanna Pitkin, "Obligation and Consent – II" [selection 11 in this book].

formulation of equivalent meaning) itself seems to constitute the reason for accepting the rule.

1. Applying the Rule. Pitkin, Searle, Rawls, and the other writers who, to my knowledge, have discussed these matters, do not conclude that these characteristics of "Obey the law" and "Keep promises" justify the conclusion that conduct governed by them is or even could be entirely mechanical. Difficult questions arise in applying the rule to particular cases. These writers insist, however, that such difficulties are properly resolved by examination of the rule itself, not by appeal to considerations external to the rules. There are occasions on which promises need not or even should not be kept and laws not obeyed. But whether a law is to be obeyed is a question to be decided by looking to see what exceptions or excusing conditions are allowed by or established as part of the rules, not by looking to considerations external to the rules. If this argument is correct it shows that there is at least one important sense in which the rule and the reason for accepting the rule are one and the same.

This position assumes rather more clarity concerning the boundaries of the practice constituted by the rules than is often justified. Any rule-constituted activity is itself a part of and is meaningful only because it is a part of a larger context of human practices, arrangements, institutions, and relationships. Baseball, chess, and poker, for example, are distinct activities constituted by rules unique to each of the games in question. But none of these games could be understood by a person with no grasp of the general concept of a game that is at once cooperative and competetive.[16]

In the case of political obligation these problems have most often been brought to our attention in connection with the work of courts in interpreting and applying constitutional provisions and statutes. A man would be a poor judge indeed if he did not understand that the fact that the provision before him was a constitutional or statutory provision constituted a reason for accepting and conforming to it. But a judge who knew nothing but the letter of the constitution or the statute books, who refused to consider anything "external" to those sources in interpreting and applying the latter, would be little better. (Again, if we take the first clause literally, he would be no better at all since in both cases the judge would be unable to do the work of a judge.) It is worth mentioning that the problems of the judge typically reach him only after they have first been faced by the legislator, the citizen, and the policeman. In law we have an authoritative agent to whom we look to "decide" issues in the interpretation of rules. But this does not free the citizen of the need to make judgments on the same issues, judgments that he makes in a more final way in the case of promising and other moral and social practices that have not been made a part of a system of law. Thus the citizen who accepts and attempts to conform to "Obey the law" must also understand and take account of features of the larger setting in which that rule exists, that is of considerations that are, in various degrees, external to that rule. His reasoning concerning his political obligations, like the judge's reasoning, must include consideration of matters external to the rules that define them. To argue that it is inappropriate, logically or otherwise, for him to consider such matters is to reduce conduct guided by the general rule and the particular rules that fall under it to a logical impossibility or to

[16] Cf. Wittgenstein, op. cit., I, 29–33 (pp. 14–16).

an absurdity. The conceptual connections between "authority," "law," and "obligation" do not support the inference that decisions to accept and act upon the general rule in this case or that must or even can be based exclusively upon features or characteristics internal to the rule.

2. Accepting the Rule. The foregoing discussion deals with problems of applying rules to particular cases. Since the question of applying a rule does not arise in a practical way unless the rule has been accepted, the discussion tacitly assumed that the rule had been accepted. We now come to the question whether sense can be made of the notion of giving reasons for or against accepting the general rule categorically. Pitkin and others have argued that this notion is based on confusions, is evidence of "philosophical disorder." If this is true, the fact that the general rule is an integral part of the practice of political obligation means that there are definite limits on the use of reason in making judgments about one's political obligations. As we noted at the end of Chapter One, this argument is also an instance of a thesis about ways in which language sets limits to thought and action.

a. "Obey the law" as a semantic rule. Pitkin begins her argument by distinguishing the two questions just identified: "Why should I obey this law in these circumstances?" and "Why should I ever obey laws?" She accepts the view that the first question will be familiar to any person with a modicum of awareness of his role as a moral and political agent. Although there are hard cases in which there is dispute about the answer, we know how to go about finding an answer and we reach agreement in a large number of cases. The second question, on the other hand, has been raised mainly in philosophical works and there is great disagreement among those who have tried to answer it. She then suggests that "if none of the theories of political obligation is able to deal adequately with that question, it must be quite peculiar, not nearly as straightforward as it looks. Perhaps it is a question that cannot be fully answered in the ordinary way. But what sort of question is that; . . . I would suggest . . . that it is a symptom of philosophical disorder, the product of a philosophical paradox."[17] If this is the case the most immediate task is not to resolve the problem or answer the question, but to dissolve the paradox.[18] This can be done by placing the appropriate emphasis upon facts that those caught up in the paradox are fully familiar with, indeed which are available to them from their knowledge of the very concepts in which they state the question, but which they haven't brought to bear on the question that is bothering them. The "answer" to the question "Why am I (ever) obligated to . . . obey laws?" is "that this is what

---

[17] Pitkin, loc. cit., p. 46. For a very similar argument see Margaret Macdonald, "The Language of Political Theory," in *Logic and Language*, First Series. We might note in passing that most of the philosophers who have put forward answers to this question give every indication of being quite satisfied with their answers to it. They typically criticize previous answers (thereby indicating that they thought previous theories meaningful but mistaken) and give what they take to be cogent reasons for accepting their own answer. Moreover they seem to think it out of considerable practical importance that other men accept their answer. It is perhaps also worthwhile to remind ourselves of what we all know, namely that the failure of all previous attempts to answer a question does not itself entail the conclusion that the question is meaningless and for that or some other reason unanswerable.

[18] In Pitkin's words, the task is to "show how and why it [the paradox] arises, why anyone should so much as suppose that political obligation in general needs (or can have) a general justification." This would "require a discussion of the nature of philosophical puzzlement" (Pitkin, loc. cit.).

'legitimate government,' 'genuine authority' *mean*. It is part of the concept, the meaning of 'authority' that those subject to it are required to obey, that it has a right to command. It is part of the concept, the meaning of 'law,' that those to whom it is applicable are obligated to obey it. As with promises, so with authority, government and law: there is a prima facie obligation involved in each, and normally you must perform it."[19] The theorist who is not satisfied with this answer, who quests "for some 'higher,' absolute, deductive, justification is misguided. Insofar, then, as the grammatical point does not seem to still the question, does not get at what someone philosophically puzzled wants to ask, what is needed is not a better justification, but an account of why the philosopher is driven to ask the question in the first place."[20]

We have no quarrel with Pitkin's account of "authority," "law," and "obligation." The correctness of that account explains why legislatures do not have to state that there is an obligation to obey their laws. It bears repeating that we cannot come to grips with the practice of political obligation if we do not understand "law," "authority," and "obligation" as they are used in the ordinary language(s) in which that practice is conducted. Any attempt to discuss the question "Why am I obligated to obey the law?" — whether in this case or ever — that is not grounded in an understanding of the uses of these concepts will not be discussion of that practice. Insofar as it is intended to be discussion of that practice it will be meaningless. As H. A. Prichard put it, to ask why I have an obligation is to assume that there is some sense in which I have one, which is possible only if I understand the concept "obligation."[21] Thus far Pitkin's argument is correct and important.

It is a long and unwarranted step from these premises to the radical conclusion that any and all attempts to answer or even to discuss seriously the question "Why do I (ever) have an obligation to obey the law?" no matter how firmly grounded in understanding of the linguistic facts to which Pitkin points, must be misguided and must be meaningless except as a symptom of a philosophical disorder. The first problem in assessing the argument is to determine just how to interpret the crucial but ambiguous notion "philosophical disorder." What precisely is the nature of the disorder involved in categorical questioning of the obligation to obey the law? The strongest interpretation, which is suggested by the fact that the conclusion is built upon an analysis of concepts, would be that it is impossible to raise this question without systematically misusing concepts so as to render the discussion literally without meaning or sense. Interpreted in this way, Pitkin's argument constitutes no less than a delineation of the "bounds of sense" in one (not so little) corner of human activity; an attempt to identify, as Plato would have put it, the limits of intelligibility.

This strong interpretation is not the only one that finds a warrant in Professor Pitkin's text. Siding with Cavell against Rawls's view that there could be intelligible

---

[19] Ibid., p. 48.

[20] Ibid., p. 49. Cf. Wittgenstein's remarks that when we have stated and taken to heart the meaning of the concepts involved we have identified a "form of life." And forms of life are "What has to be accepted, the given. . . ." Wittgenstein, op. cit., II, xi (p. 226). Again, "If I have exhausted the justifications I have reached bedrock, and my spade is turned. Then I am inclined to say: 'This is simply what I do.' " Ibid., I, 217 (p. 85).

[21] See H. A. Prichard, *Moral Obligation* (London: Oxford University Press, 1949), esp. essays 4 and 5.

discourse about the utility of the practice of promising qua social practice, she says that Rawls's view "implies a degree of freedom of choice on our parts which we do not in fact have. To evaluate the practice of promising pro and con, we would have to envision alternatives. And how shall we envision a society which knows no obligation to keep one's word? . . . We seem to have no choice about the pros and cons of such an institution. It is not socially useful; it is indispensable to the very concept of society and human life."[22]

Now this passage is itself ambiguous and could be used to support the first interpretation we suggested. To say that the institution is indispensable to the *concept* of society might be construed as a remark not about human needs or the way men interact in a society but about the conventions governing the use of "society"; a remark in the formal mode to the effect that "society" is misused if it is applied to arrangements or relationships that do not include the practice of ascribing and assuming obligations and holding people to their word. The point at issue would not be whether men have lived or could live together without this institution, but whether it would be proper to describe such an arrangement as a society. And that issue would be settled by looking not at how men live together but how the concept "society" is used.

The passage could also be interpreted to be about some kind of contingent, perhaps physical necessity; to be an assertion that it would be impossible for men to live together without the institutions in question, or perhaps impossible to attain the benefits that result from life in a society with those institutions. This interpretation is most clearly suggested by Pitkin's extension of her remarks about the necessity of the institution of keeping one's word to the case of law, government, and authority. She concedes that "here, I suppose, there may be somewhat more room for discussion [of the merits of these institutions qua-institutions] than with promises. For it is not at all obvious that government and law are indispensable to human social life."[23] The passage continues in a manner that could be taken to withdraw the concession as regards authority. But the important point is that the phrase "*concept* of society and human life" has been dropped in favor of "human social life." This phrase creates problems of its own, but there is nothing in Pitkin's use of it that tempts us to interpret her remarks as an abbreviated analysis of the use of "society" (as remarks in the formal mode). Thus any necessities or impossibilities that are discovered will have to be the consequence of facts about man or society and thus contingent not necessary. The "philosophical disorder" involved in categorical questioning of the obligation to obey authoritative commands will be a result of mistakes concerning facts about human beings and societies, not mistakes in the use of language.

The third and weakest interpretation of "philosophical disorder" is bound up with Pitkin's discussion of the quest for and impossibility of an "absolute, deductive justification" of such institutions as promising, law, government, and authority and hence of the obligations generated by those institutions and practices. Having noted that "classical consent theories" did attempt to provide a utilitarian justification for authority and obligation by first describing a society which lacked them, Pitkin passes directly to the assertion that "even a recognition of the necessity or utilitarian advantages of such things as authority, law, and

[22] Pitkin, loc. cit., p. 48.
[23] Ibid., p. 48.

government is no absolute answer to the man who is questioning his particular obligation to obey. . . . There is no such absolute answer, and can be none. Nothing we say is absolutely beyond question."[24] Here Pitkin does not deny the possibility of meaningful categorical questioning of authority and obligation. Her criticisms are directed against a particular type of categorical questioning and more especially to a particular type of attempt to reply to such questioning. A man who was dissatisfied with Pitkin's grammatical answer to the question "Why should I (ever) obey the law?" but who was not in quest of an "absolute, deductive answer," could attempt to assess the institution of law, authority, and obligation without evidencing the philosophical disorder that Pitkin has in mind. If it could be shown that Plato, Hobbes, Locke, Green, etc., did not hope to provide an "absolute, deductive" answer to the questions they raised about obligation, their philosophizing could be, so far as Pitkin's criteria go, meaningful and free of "disorder." On this interpretation Pitkin's argument, at least insofar as it is concerned with categorical questioning of obligations, is primarily directed not to obligation but to a particular sort of perplexity or puzzlement, the kind that persists in the face of every sort of answer or response save the one that logically is unavailable.[25] As she says — and we agree with her although it would require an immense digression even to begin to state clearly and defend our position — "nothing we say is absolutely beyond question." (But then we must ask whether this ringing declaration applies to Pitkin's own assertions concerning the impossibility of meaningful categorical questioning of political obligations. Unfortunately we must also ask whether it applies to the ringing declaration "Nothing we say is absolutely beyond question.") If this is the case, the sort of perplexity with which she is concerned is not unique to obligation or to normative matters. The same sort of perplexity and questioning could arise concerning "$2 + 2 = 4$" or "The atomic weight of lead is X." Thus the arguments about impossibility should be understood as indicating what it is, in the case of obligation, that this particular form of perplexity and questioning overlooks or fails to take to heart, not as establishing a bar to any and all categorical questioning of obligation. This is a "weak" version or interpretation of the argument in that it does not establish a bar to all categorical questioning of the institutions in question and in that it does not distinguish the problem of justifying these institutions from the problem of justifying or supporting any other practice, rule, proposition, or conclusion. Interpreted in this way the argument is of no interest here and we will say no more about it.

Let us now imagine the merits of the argument interpreted in the first and strongest sense we identified, namely as asserting that all attempts to question categorically the obligation to obey the law involve conceptual errors that render the discussion meaningless.[26] Insofar as this argument depends on the assertion that it is logically or conceptually impossible to conceptualize an alternative to the present arrangement, the argument has no serious claim to our allegiance. We are talking about the concepts "authority," "obligation," "law," and "society." For

[24] Ibid., p. 49.

[25] She is interested, in other words, in the sort of puzzlement that was of great concern to Wittgenstein and which has been discussed so brilliantly by John Wisdom.

[26] Pitkin never asserts this of attempts to question the obligation to obey the law and our judgment is that it is not her intention to assert it concerning the obligation to keep promises. The challenge thrown up by her discussion suggests the question — which is of obvious importance — and provides a convenient opportunity to examine it.

there to be concepts that we can use there must be rules or conventions establishing the proper use or uses of those concepts. As we argued above, the notion of a rule of conduct presupposes an alternative to the required conduct; the notion of following a rule presupposes awareness of an alternative. Rules establishing the proper use of a concept necessarily exclude some uses as improper. Thus to know how to use "authority" is, among other things, to know how not to use it, to know how to distinguish the use of authority from the use of other concepts. Which is to be able to conceive of alternatives to arrangements involving authority at least in the sense of being able, so far as logic is concerned, to conceive of arrangements that do not involve authority, including entire societies in which no authority is to be found. More pointedly, people who know the English language are not tempted to apply "authority" to anything and everything to which it does not apply. They are tempted to apply it to phenomena that bear certain similarities to authority, for example power or influence or prestige. In learning how to use it we learn how to distinguish its use from the use of related concepts. A man who lives in a society in which there is both authority and power and who knows how to use both "authority" and "power" is in an excellent position to conceive of a society in which there would not only be no application for "authority" but in which he would properly use "power" in all the situations that resemble those in which, in his society, he properly uses "authority."

Assuming, then, that it is possible to conceptualize an alternative to the arrangement that involves the relationships between "authority," "law," and "obligation" as we now use them, let us inquire whether there is any other sense in which categorical questioning of that arrangement necessarily leads us into "philosophical disorder." Interpreted in the "strong" sense, the argument before us is an example of a type of argument that has been called — not altogether out of a benevolent attitude toward it — "descriptivism."[27] It involves the contention that it is possible to derive a normative conclusion (T), that B has a prima facie obligation to do X (obey a law), from two factual premises, namely: (1) There is a law that is authoritative for A that requires X; and (2) The statement (which is a statement of the semantic rules governing the concepts in question) "R is an authoritative law" entails the statement "All those for whom the law is authoritative have a prima facie obligation to obey the law." Indeed the argument implies that in such cases premises other than 1 and 2 are irrelevant to supporting T and otiose in any argument intended to support T. Once again this is an impeccable account of the inferences allowed by the concepts as they are now used. Moreover, these inferences must be understood in order to participate in the practice in question. A man who did not understand that these are valid inferences could not fully understand the actions, verbal and otherwise, of participants in the practice; a man who simply chose to ignore the inferences would not be understood by other participants.

But a man need not simply ignore the inferences. He might deny that he (ever) should have had or should ever have an obligation to obey the law, explain that he issues his denial in full knowledge that it flies in the face of established conventions, and try to *justify* his denial by presenting arguments intended to show that the conventions that allow the inference T, including the linguistic conventions, are unfortunate or pernicious and should be altered or repudiated. If he simply said,

---

[27] See R. M. Hare, "Descriptivism," *Proceedings of the British Academy* XLIX (1963).

flat out, so to speak, that he had no obligation, other members of the society might find it difficult to understand him.[28] If he explained what he meant and tried to justify his position we might find his views unpersuasive, wrongheaded, or even shocking and pernicious. Is there any ground whatever for thinking that we would find them unintelligible? We would, rather, realize that the man was engaged in the radical enterprise of questioning and trying to alter some of the most fundamental conventions — both linguistic and otherwise — in our society. It is a logical point that we cannot question and/or try to change all of the conventions, linguistic or otherwise, of our society at one time. If we tried to do so we would have no usable concepts in which to form our questions. But holding most of the concepts constant, that is using them in the conventional manner to think about the uses of selected concepts, we can question and try to change the use of any given concept.[29] Given the elaborate web of conceptual relationships that extend out from a concept such as "authority" this is a sensitive task.[30] But there is no reason to think it a logically impossible undertaking. Wherein lies the logical or conceptual error in the following statement; "The more I reflect about political authority and the obligations generated by its exercise the more convinced I become that society as a whole would do better to imitate the example of my poker club and do without it. According men a claim to obedience independent of the reasons they can give for the particular rules they suggest hampers and erodes the process of discussion and diminishes our humanity. Leadership, influence, even power, these we need. But there is nothing I would like better than a society in which the concept of authority as we now know it would have no application."[31]

We will conclude the discussion of the first and strongest interpretation of Pitkin's thesis by quoting . . . a passage that supplies a general perspective from which to view the thesis and the points we have tried to make against it.

> In discussing the logic of ordinary language I have frequently used the word "rule." . . . The word is not inappropriate: for to speak of . . . "rules" is to speak of ways in which language may be *correctly* or *incorrectly* used. But though not inappropriate the word may be misleading. We do not judge our linguistic practice in the light of antecedently studied rules. We frame rules in the light of our study of our practice. Moreover, our practice is a very fluid affair. If we are to speak of rules at all, we ought to think of them as rules which everyone has a license to violate if he can show a point in doing so. In the effort to describe our experience we are continually putting words to new uses, connected with, but not identical with, their familiar uses; applying them to states of affairs which are both like and unlike those to which the

---

[28] But of course if this happened, and if the conversation were a serious one, couldn't they, and wouldn't they be likely to, ask him what he meant? When a man says something that we find puzzling don't we ordinarily assume that he is trying to say something meaningful — if not necessarily something sensible — and try to discover what it is? And aren't we usually successful?

[29] See Searle, loc. cit., p. 52, n. 8.

[30] Recall Wittgenstein, op. cit., I, 106 (p. 46). "We feel as if we had to repair a torn spider's web with our fingers."

[31] Even Hare, to whom I am indebted here, gives too little weight to the possibility of questioning and trying to change the uses of concepts which in present use represent cases of a logical tie between what he calls the descriptive and commendatory meaning. That I cannot (now) describe a rule as an authoritative law without implying that there is an obligation to obey it does not prevent me from questioning and trying to change the conventions that constitute the basis of that tie. Cf. Hare, loc. cit., esp. p. 127.

words are most familiarly applied. Hence we may give a meaning to sentences which, at first sight, seem self-contradictory. And hence . . . it is in fact hard to frame a grammatical sentence to which it is impossible to imagine some sense being given; and given, not by arbitrary *fiat*, but by an intelligible, though probably figurative, extension of the familiar senses of the words and phrases concerned.[32]

Strawson's point is that the rules governing ordinary language do not constitute a rigid or strict calculus such as is constituted by the rules of a system of formal logic. We must be able to account not only for the stability and continuity of ordinary language, for the respects in which its development to the present influences the ways in which we talk, but also for its fluidity and the possibilities of variation and change that are contained in it.[33]

We turn now to the argument that categorical questioning of the obligation to obey the law is impossible because, for some reason other than logical impossibility, we are unable to "conceive of alternatives" to the existing practice, unable to conceive of men living together without law or authority and an obligation to obey them. This argument looks suspiciously like the argument of the naturalist who watched the bumblebee fly away and said: "It's impossible." For what else is the state of nature described by Glaucon, Hobbes, Locke, and Hume but such a conception? And what else have anarchists been putting forward as an ideal? These thinkers have not only conceived of an alternative, they have worked an alternative out in considerable detail and have *put it to use* in thinking about society and politics. Indeed they have used it for the very purpose that the argument we are considering dismisses as a symptom of philosophical disorder, namely as a means of evaluating, in general or categorically, the practice involving authority, law, and obligation. Given the fact that to all appearances men *have* conceived of an alternative, and given the absence of logical or conceptual barriers to doing so, the least we are entitled to say is that the person who argues that it is impossible to do so takes on the burden of showing in detail what is wrong in each of the numerous cases that seem to refute his position.

But this is not all we are entitled to say. We are also entitled to inquire into the status of the proposition "It is (nonlogically) impossible for men to conceive of men living together without authority, law, and obligation." The most obvious point here is that since the impossibility we are now considering is contingent, not logical, it is contingent upon something or some set of things that might change. Thus the proposition can only be a (somewhat hyperbolic) way of saying "It is impossible for men *as they are* living in the world *as it is* to conceive of an alternative." But further, what does it mean to say that it is (nonlogically) impossible for men to *conceive* of something? Grammatically the statement looks like "It is impossible for men as they are (and the gravitational forces being what they are) to jump twenty-five feet straight up." As is often the case, however, grammatical similarity is not a good guide to logical similarity. In the case of jumping twenty-five feet straight up we know what would count as evidence that the act in question is or is not impossible. Is the same true in the case of the contention that it is impossible to conceive of an alternative to the practice we are discussing? Can we measure and

---

[32] Peter Strawson, *Introduction to Logical Theory* (London: Methuen and Co., 1952), p. 230.

[33] Cf. Wittgenstein, *The Blue and Brown Books*, pp. 24–25, 82; *Philosophical Investigations*, I, 64–75 (pp. 31–35), and esp. I, 107–9 (pp. 46–47).

determine the present limits of our "powers of imagination" in the way that we can measure and determine the present limits of the strength of our muscles? If we cannot do so, what sense (other than that no one has yet done so – if contrary to fact that was the case) are we to give to the idea that it is impossible for men as they are to conceive or to imagine something. The conditions necessary to the use of "impossible" and "cannot" are not satisfied in this case.

At the very best, then, the assertion that it is (nonlogically) impossible to conceive of men living together without authority, law, and obligation (to conceive of an alternative to present arrangements) is an assertion about the past that cannot bind the future. At worst the assertion depends on a misuse of "cannot" and "impossible." Thus the arguments we have been considering do not show that we cannot conceive of alternatives to present arrangements. If the capacity to question those arrangements categorically carries with it the possibility of distinguishing between the rules that constitute those arrangements and reasons for or against accepting those rules, these arguments do not show that there is no logical room for such a distinction.[34]

This conclusion is of great importance. It means that there are alternatives to simply thinking and doing what the semantic rules governing our language, even very fundamental features of our language, influence us to think and do. It means that our thought and action in the area of law and authority are not bounded by impassable conceptual or logical restraints. In order to know *what* we are faced with when faced with a law and *what* we are doing when we obey it or disobey it we must understand the concepts involved. But to understand them is to understand the possibilities open to us concerning them.

  b. "Obey the law" as a precept.   The general rule is potentially of great significance in our lives. There are a very large number of laws requiring and forbidding a very large number of actions. If the general rule gave us good reasons for obeying all laws it would be the basis of a substantial part of our conduct. If it is logically and conceptually possible to ask for reasons for accepting the general rule we certainly have good reason to do so.

The first question that arises is whether those features of the rule that Pitkin has rightly emphasized provide good reasons, or reasons at all, for obeying the law. If we treat these linguistic facts as materials for answering the question rather than stilling it, should they have weight with us? Does the existence of these linguistic rules add anything to the case for obeying the law?

The answer is pretty obviously "No." Pitkin reminds us of what the words "law" and "authority" mean. But the fact that the words have a certain established use is in itself hardly a reason for acting in a manner that affects other people. If instead of saying "That was what I was ordered to do" Eichmann had said "That is what the words 'authoritative command' mean" he would hardly have added to the strength of his case. "That is what the words mean; therefore that is what I have an obligation to do" is so abject a form of conformism as to be altogether outside of

---

[34] The matter is nicely disposed of by Jane Austen . . .: "My dear Jane, Mr. Collins is a conceited, pompous, narrowminded, silly man; you know he is, as well as I do; and you must feel, as well as I do, that the woman who marries him cannot have a proper way of thinking. You shall not, for the sake of one individual, change the meaning of principle and integrity, nor endeavor to persuade yourself or me, that selfishness is prudence, and insensibility of danger security for happiness." Jane Austen, *Pride and Prejudice* (New York: The Pocket Library, 1940), p. 149.

the realm of moral reasoning. Of course Eichmann could not reason about whether he had an obligation to obey if he did not know what the words meant. He could not do so because he could not know *what* he was reasoning about. But to know what one is reasoning about is a precondition of reasoning about it; it is not the same thing as reasoning about it. (This is not to deny that in fact we are often *influenced* by the semantic rules governing the concepts that we use in reasoning.)

If the fact that "This is a law" means "There is an obligation to obey it" is to count as a reason for obeying the law it must be shown that it is desirable that the words be used in this way. Or better, it must be shown that it is desirable that society have arrangements that include laws and the rule that people have an obligation to obey them. In terms of the breakdown of types of rules that we are using, the semantic rule must coincide with a precept-type rule for which there are good reasons.[35]

Putting the matter this way helps us to see that the question "Why should I ever obey the law?" is indeed a very special kind of question. As Pitkin says, we are familiar with it primarily from the work of political philosophers who have been concerned to understand and evaluate political practices seen in a very general perspective. The infrequency with which the question is asked is perhaps now explained in part by the conceptual facts we have been discussing. Language is often misused in ordinary speech (that is this or that part of language is misused) but few men step outside of and self-consciously assess (part of) language in the manner now involved in categorical questioning of the obligation to obey the law. But it may also be that a very large number of people would agree with the view that authority, law, and obligation are "indispensable" to social life. Since they would have in effect answered the question we are considering, they would have no reason to discuss it explicitly.

A more important sense in which the question is special can be seen by recurring to the distinction between the general rule and particular legal rules. The very grammar of the general rule conveys the impression that there is some one thing, law, that people are to obey, and hence that there is some one reason for obeying it or not. This is profoundly misleading. There is one concept that has numerous applications, all of which may share certain features (for example, having authoritative standing), but which may differ from one another in important respects. We have already noted the distinction between laws that require or forbid

---

[35] This would be true of constitutive rules (if they are a distinct category). It should be clear from the discussion in the text that we regard "There is an obligation to obey the law" as a semantic rule which coincides with a precept. To digress briefly concerning the general question of constitutive rules, we suggest that a number of the examples that have been put forward as instances of such rules are better thought of as semantic rules. "There is an obligation to keep promises" is a case in point. It is not clear how this rule is distinguished from "Do not lie," "Do not cheat," "Do not act in a rude manner," and many other rules which can be viewed as explications of the concepts of which their formulation consists. The person who does not know that lying and cheating are things that one should not do does not know how to use the concepts "lie" and "cheat." We could not engage in the practice of lying or cheating, or criticize it, if we did not have the concepts. (Cf. Philippa Foot, "Moral Arguments," *Mind* [1958], pp. 502–13, and "Moral Beliefs." *Proceedings of the Aristotelian Society* 59 [1958–59], pp. 83–104.) We would reserve the category "constitutive rules" for rules which not only identify what must be done to engage in a certain activity but which can be laid down, and changed, only by an authoritative procedure. Compare in this respect John Rawl's remark that "the practice conception [of rules] is more relevant to understanding legal and legal-like arguments than it is to the more complex moral arguments" (Rawls, loc. cit., final footnote).

and laws that enable or empower. The corollary of this distinction is that the notions of obedience and obligation have no application to laws of the latter type. In addition, some obligation-generating laws are vastly more important than others. It is not only implausible but pernicious to think that the reasons for obeying laws against homicide are in all respects the same as the reasons for obeying parking ordinances; that the reasons for obeying the laws of contract are in all respects the same as those for obeying the laws forbidding mistreatment of children. We have to ascend to an extremely high and general level, to a level to which our ordinary experience with law rarely takes us, to find a single purpose or set of purposes common to all laws or a single set of reasons for obeying all laws. Categorical questioning of the obligation to obey the law draws us away from the considerations involved in day-to-day thinking about law. Insofar as such questioning obscures the differences among laws, it is not impossible or meaningless, it is dangerous.

It does not follow that we should dismiss such questioning. To dismiss it would be to exclude an important part of the practice of political obligation from our consideration. If we rarely encounter men *asking* the question "Why should I ever obey the law?" and if we rarely find men actually rejecting the obligation to obey the law categorically (as opposed to reflecting, say in writing political philosophy, about whether there are good reasons for rejecting it), it is not at all uncommon for men to *answer* the question affirmatively. This is in fact what is happening when acceptance of the general rule "Obey the law" is inculcated in the young, extolled in discussions of the achievements of a society, or offered as a reason for obeying laws that are thought to be objectionable. Offering this kind of advice presupposes not reasons for thinking that a particular law is a good or defensible law, but reasons for thinking that the practice which includes authority, law, and obligation is a good practice. There is no reason to think that the very large number of people who hold this view and give such advice can only be or in fact are merely explaining the meaning of the concepts they use in giving the advice.[36] Such people might accept the view that authority and law are indispensable to society, but this could just as well mean (as Pitkin recognizes) that there are a great many reasons that support it, not that it cannot be supported (except by giving facts about language). These reasons do not add up to an absolute, deductive justification; but they might provide a cogent argument for accepting the rule, an argument that would have to be met by anyone who claimed that he was justified in rejecting the rule. Political philosophers have tried very hard to state such reasons. That we find some of these reasons unpersuasive does not show that they are not reasons or that the exercise of working them out is futile or misguided. Reasons of the sort philosophers have presented have persuaded a great many men that authority and law qua authority and law are valuable and should be maintained even at the cost of considerable sacrifice of other values in particular cases. Competing reasons have persuaded a much smaller number of men that authority and law are of little value and that nothing should be sacrificed to maintain them (this seems to be Thoreau's view) or

---

[36] Pitkin's view in this regard is very much like the position of David Hume. Hume said that moral guidance is often no more than reports about the meaning of words. "The merit of delivering true general precepts in ethics is very small. Whoever recommends any moral virtues really does no more than is implied in the terms themselves." David Hume, "Of the Standard of Taste," *Essays: Moral, Political, and Literary* (London: Oxford University Press, 1963), pp. 233–34.

even that they are of no value or are a positive evil that should be done away with (this seems to Bakunin's view). Thus categorical questions and answers about authority and law taken alone, that is independent of their relation to the more particular questions that arise in connection with authority and law, not only have meaning and sense but have practical application and significance.

It is not the case, however, that reasoning about law and authority qua law and authority is only possible about or relevant to categorical acceptance or rejection of them. The categorical question "Why should I ever obey the law?" does not have to be answered with reasons why I should *always* obey the law or why I should *never* obey the law. Reflection about the categorical question can lead to the conclusion, did lead Socrates to the conclusion, that there are important benefits and advantages to be derived from the practice and that it is worth maintaining. As the case of Socrates also shows, it can equally lead to the conclusion that there are difficulties and dangers that arise in connection with the practice, difficulties that sometimes justify disobedience. If the fact that a rule is a law is relevant to deciding whether to obey it, it is difficult to see why the reasons that make law important, and hence contribute to making the fact that the rule is a law a relevant fact, would be irrelevant. For most of us most of the time the value of categorical questioning is not that it will help us to decide whether to become anarchists, but that it gives us general considerations to bring to the less than categorical choices and judgments which we all must make throughout out lives.

3. Summary Concerning the Precept "Obey the Law." From one perspective "Obey the law" is a semantic rule. Stating it serves to explicate one feature of the use of the concepts "authority," "law," and "obligation." A person who does not understand the rule does not understand the relevant uses of these concepts or the social and political practices of which they are an integral part. It is impossible to understand the concepts that are used to formulate the rule, the rule itself, or the practice constituted by the concepts and the rule without also understanding a larger network of concepts, rules, and social and political practices of which the practice involving political authority, law, and political obligations are but one. Applying the rule to particular cases often requires explicit attention to that larger network as well as to the characteristics of the situation at hand.

Owing to the uses of the concepts "law," "authority," and "obligation," merely to apply those concepts to a particular rule without questioning their ordinary use is to imply that there is an obligation to obey them. The precept-type rule that coexists with the semantic rules is also well established in numerous societies and disputes about obedience often center on the case for the regulation-type rule in question not the semantic- or the precept-type rule. For these reasons the normative implications of the use of the concepts is often not explicitly defended. Because the regulation-type rules to which the general rule applies are diverse in content and purpose, it is difficult to identify a single reason or set of reasons for accepting the general rule. Indeed there is a danger of oversimplification in reasoning about the general rule and much to be said for a political process which emphasizes reasoning about the particular regulation-type rules. But it is neither impossible nor meaningless to defend or question the general rule; it is defended or questioned whenever it is recommended or attacked independently of its application to a particular legal rule, and it has been defended and attacked in a systematic manner by a number of political philosophers.

IV. Concluding Remarks

We can now draw conclusions concerning the questions with which we began the chapter, namely what the existence of rules of various types adds to the case for doing an action that falls under them, and what sorts of reasoning are appropriate to supporting acceptance of and conformity with the various types we have examined.

1. An instruction-type rule supports B's acting in a manner that accords with the rule if B wants to achieve the goal or objective which is served by following the rule. Whether B will try to achieve that objective is up to him. Such rules are appropriately supported by giving evidence (from experience) that following the rule is the most efficient way to achieve the objective or objectives that B has. However B may in fact act, if he does not believe that there is such evidence it is inappropriate to say that he is following the rule.

2. Constitutive rules support B's acting in a manner that accords with the rule in that they establish what must, logically speaking, be done in order to achieve an objective or engage in an activity. The only sense in which they can be supported in a particular case is by showing that they have been correctly identified and applied. Reasons could be given for or against changing the rules and hence the practice they constitute but until such changes have been ratified by established procedures it will remain the case that B can engage in the activity only by following the rule as it is. In their character as constitutive rules such rules support B's following the rule only if B wants to achieve the objective or engage in the activity constituted by the rules. Some of the rules that have been characterized as constitutive rules have social standing such that it is thought that individuals have an obligation to follow the rules if they have once entered into the activity. Thus if I have made a promise or contract I have an obligation to keep it or perform it. But this feature is not a general characteristic of rules with the logical properties that distinguish the category. Having entered a game of baseball does not put me under an obligation to keep on playing. Or rather, if I do have such an obligation it is generated by rules other than the rules of baseball. Hence where the feature is present it is best to say that one and the same formulation states both a constitutive rule and a rule of some other kind — for example a precept or regulation. Thus if promising is treated as a practice constituted by constitutive rules, "There is an obligation to keep promises" is *both* a constitutive rule which constitutes a part of the practice *and* a precept. Using the first to guide conduct is "supported" by showing that the rule is in fact established and has been correctly cited; use of the second is supported by showing that it is good or desirable that there is a practice of promising which includes the constitutive-type rule. B might want to engage in the practice despite the fact that he disapproved of it or disapproved of that characteristic of it which is given by the existence of the precept-type rule. If so he could be guided by the constitutive rule but not by the precept. In such a case his conduct would be reasoned in the sense that he chose to follow the rule as against alternative actions and believed that following the rule was the most efficient means to his objective. If he did not have reasons for following the rule in this sense he could not be said to have followed it.

3. The semantic rules we have examined in this chapter have a number of the features of constitutive rules. We must understand such rules if we are to know *what* we are doing in taking a particular action. Use of them in guiding speech is "supported" by evidence that they have been correctly identified. Since to speak is

sometimes to act in ways over and above speaking, semantic rules sometime guide conduct in the sense of indicating what we must do if we are to act in a manner consistent with the implications of the ways we have previously spoken. Or more precisely, they indicate what we must do if, when our actions have been properly characterized, those characterizations are to be consistent with the ways we originally spoke. Thus if B says that X is an authoritative law that applies to him, he must also say that he has an obligation to obey that law. And if he says he has an obligation to obey that law he must discharge that obligation unless he can show that the obligation is defeated or that he is excused from it in the circumstances. The force of the "must" in the three previous sentences, however, is "must do it if he is to speak and otherwise act in a manner consistent with the established semantic rules." And to show that an action is consistent with semantic rules is not to show that the action is justified.

In the cases we have considered it is useful to think of the semantic rule as coinciding with regulations or precepts. To show that the *action* of obeying the law is justified one must show that the regulations and/or the precept that coincides with the semantic rule are justified. It is logically possible to conform to the semantic rule despite rejecting the precept or regulation; someone might do so simply to facilitate communication. This fact is sufficient to show that following the one is logically independent of following the other. B can be said to be following the semantic rule if he shows that he knows the rule and shows that he knows that following it is the most efficient means to his end of facilitating communication.

In fact, of course, following the one ordinarily coincides with following the other. Moreover, semantic rules can be changed without recourse to established, authoritative, procedures. Hence the person who dislikes a precept that coincides with a semantic rule begins the process of challenging and changing the latter at the same time that he challenges the precept. (The case of regulations is more like the case of constitutive rules in this respect.) By the same token the person who follows the precept, that is shows that he acts in accord with it because he thinks there are good reasons for doing so, also follows the semantic rule. The fact that the semantic rule is so intimately related to the precept makes it appear that the semantic rule is itself a reason for accepting and following the precept. Indeed it makes it appear that there is no room for a distinction between a semantic rule and a precept and hence that the only general reason for obeying the law is "that is what the words mean." A main purpose of our argument has been to show that this is nothing more than appearance.

A rule is a regulation in the sense in which we are using the term only if it is authoritative in the sense of "promulgated by an agent or agency with the authority to do so." The question whether a particular rule is authoritative will often be decided by looking to some higher rule such as a charter or constitution. But the fact that a rule is authoritative affects its significance for conduct only because there is a precept-type rule according to which there is an obligation to obey authoritative rules. Regulations presuppose such a precept in the sense that if there were no such precept the implications of saying that regulations are authoritative would be different than they now are. Thus part of the conduct-guiding force of regulations stems from the fact that the precept "Obey the law" lies behind them. In this respect the advice that B should obey a particular law is supported by giving reasons for accepting the precept. B can be said to be guided by the rule only if he thinks there are good reasons for the precept.

But there is no such thing as obeying the law in the abstract. Any action properly described as obeying the law will also be describable as some other action as well — for example submitting an income tax return or attaching a pollution control device to one's automobile. The concept "law" and the rule "Obey the law" identify and govern only one feature of the particular legal rule and actions taken under it; they identify and govern the action under only one of the characterizations appropriate to it. Hence there is a possibility of reasoning about the rule and the conduct taken under characterizations other than "law" and "Obey the law." Putting a pollution control device on one's car can be defended or attacked independent of the fact that there is a law requiring it. Moreover, since any form of conduct that we can describe could be required or prohibited by law, the reasoning that supported or attacked "Obey the law" could be known a priori to be conclusive as to whether to obey any particular law only if it could be established that obeying the law, as such, is the greatest possible good (or evil) in all circumstances. It is something of an understatement to say that this is implausible. Thus if B is to defend what he is doing in obeying or disobeying a law he must be able to defend what he is doing under characterizations other than "obeying (disobeying) a law." Since he is obeying a rule (in addition to the rule "Obey the law") he must be able to defend that rule. Since he *is* obeying or disobeying the rule "Obey the law," being able to defend doing so gives him reasons for doing what he is doing and allows him to claim that his conduct is guided by a rule. But being able to defend "Obey the law" is not a sufficient condition of being able to defend his conduct and it is not sufficient to show that his conduct is guided by any rule other than "Obey the law."

Precepts such as "Keep your promises" and "Do not lie" are widely accepted in numerous societies and are thought to be extremely important. Indeed they are so widely accepted that to describe an action as lying, or as breaking a promise, is in itself to condemn that action. It is perfectly appropriate to regard "Do not lie" and "Do not break promises" as semantic rules governing some of the uses of "lie" and "promise." A person who does not understand these rules does not understand the use of "lie" and "promise" in the language. "Obey the law" is more controversial than "Do not lie" and "Do not break promises" but to so characterize the action is also to assess it normatively; but here too to call a rule a law which applies to B is to say that B has an obligation to obey it. The person who does not understand this fact does not understand the present use of "law" in the language.

But the case against lying, breaking promises, and obeying the law does not consist of these linguistic facts. The person who does not know these facts cannot make a case for or against these rules or for or against acting in accord with them. This is because he does not know *what* he is making a case for or against. Moreover, making a case for or against them can be viewed as, among other things, making a case for continuing to use the concepts as they are now used. But to describe the arguments of Socrates, Plato, Hobbes, Thoreau, etc., in this way would be to trivialize them. These thinkers recognized that the rules in question concerned forms of conduct that have substantial consequences in human affairs. They were strongly for or against the rules because they thought the consequences were very good or very bad. They accepted or rejected, obeyed or disobeyed the rules because they thought that there are good reasons for doing so; because they thought that obeying and disobeying them are effective ways to achieve certain ends and because they thought that there are good reasons for valuing and trying to achieve those ends. Once we have examined the relationship between these precepts and other types of rules it is clear that they understood the matter correctly. The existence of a precept-type rule adds to the case for acting in accord with the rule to the degree that there are good reasons for thinking that doing so is an effective way to achieve certain ends and that the ends are desirable. It can be said that a person's conduct has been guided by such rules to the extent that there is evidence that the person knows what conforming to the rule consists of and thinks that there are good reasons for doing so.

Part II

Authority

Introduction

The selections on authority speak to and about one another in a number of ways, sometimes explicitly, sometimes implicitly. But it is symptomatic of the difficulties that attend the analysis of authority that it would be difficult to summarize briefly or in any very orderly way the substantive relationships among the selections and among the themes, agreements, and disagreements that recur in them. The attempt to do so would produce less of a pattern than a list — and a rather disparate list at that.

The reason for this may be the same one that Richard B. Friedman gives for his view that the "meaning of authority seems to be the subject of ceaseless and acrimonious controversy in both political philosophy and social science," namely, that "authority is a notion bound up with most, if not all, of the central questions of political philosophy." There may be a suggestion in Professor Friedman's remarks that the importance of authority has been exaggerated, that philosophers and others have thought that questions about it arise in context, in which they do not in fact do so. However this may be, it is obvious that the concept figures prominently in a great many contexts, a great many aspects of life. Notice that we speak not only of political and legal, but of military, religious, parental, educational, and even moral authority and that, although authoritative *commands* appear mainly in legal, political, and military circumstances, there can be authorities and authoritative views, judgments, and even persons on an immense range of subjects and aspects of life. "Authority" is a concept that plays a prominent role in a large number of language games. For this reason alone, it is hardly surprising that it has been difficult to win wide agreement for any single analysis of the concept and that the analyses we have do not fit together like pieces in a puzzle. (There may be other reasons as well, for example, that authority is a controversial subject. Many people are strongly "for it" or "against it," think it is an extremely valuable feature of human affairs that should be strengthened and extended or an indefensible or doubtful feature that should be eliminated or kept within the narrowest possible limitations.)

Given the complexity and controversy that attend the topic, it is doubtful that any substantive issues concerning it can be clarified in these introductory remarks. But it may be possible to distinguish a few of the main questions that have been raised about it and hence to facilitate access to the following discussions.

Perhaps the most commonly discussed question, at least in political and moral philosophy, is whether, and if so why, authority·can be justified and whether the directives, judgments, and so forth, that issue from it should be obeyed, accepted, or whatever. There is no doubting the importance of this question. But it is worth reminding ourselves that answers presuppose knowledge of what authority *is*, of *what* we are justifying or rejecting when we take a position on this matter. The following selections make it abundantly clear that, at least if "know" means "can say," this condition is not very clearly satisfied.

But saying that we must know what authority is suggests that it is some one thing or entity and that understanding it involves searching that entity out and examining it. (And if one doesn't find the entity, or the one expected, one might reach the conclusion that there is no such thing as authority, that the word does not refer to anything, is a piece of mythology. Or perhaps that it once existed but has now disappeared from the earth.) We might, on the other hand, follow Wittgenstein's suggestion and treat "What is authority?" as a question best answered by examining the uses of the concept "authority," the roles it plays in the several language games of which it is a part. Since it figures in many language games this is likely to be a difficult business (and hence to provide a good example of the difficulties of a political and social philosophy proceeding from Wittgensteinian premises). But since the concept *is used* in our language, and since as speakers of the language we know how to use it, this approach gives us a way to proceed and some reason to think that it is a sensible way to proceed (and hence provides an example of the advantages of a political and social philosophy that proceeds from Wittgensteinian premises).

The most general question we want to suggest, then, is, "When, by whom, and for what purposes is 'authority' properly used?" We want to urge readers of the following selections on the topic to, as it were, "translate" those discussions into answers to these questions. To that end we will present a few examples of ways in which such "translations" might be made.

Alasdair MacIntyre discusses the secularization of British society and the resultant disappearance of the basis or bases of social and moral agreement which common religious beliefs had earlier provided. The resultant disagreement, according to him, goes so deep as to reach the uses of major concepts of social, political, and moral life. Because of it the "notion of moral authority is no longer a viable one" in the society. Most people, I presume this means, are not likely to use the concept "authority" as regards moral questions, and those who do so only show thereby that they "are living in a past that has survived in our society in the life of a particular class." MacIntyre is offering an answer to one form of the question, "When is 'authority' properly used?"; he is specifying some of the *conditions* that in his view must obtain in order for the concept to have a meaningful place or role in human affairs. (This question is also discussed in other selections, especially in Friedman's paper.)

The question of the conditions necessary to the use of "authority" can be distinguished from questions about the purposes for which it is used when those conditions are satisfied and the implications or consequences of its use. Versions of the question about purpose are at issue in the several discussions (Richard B. Friedman, Richard G. Peters, and Carl J. Friedrich) of the similarities and differences between authority, on the one hand, and coercion, force, advice or counsel, and reasoned argument, on the other. All these are used, at least very often, for the broad purpose of influencing belief or action. But it is unsatisfactory to leave the matter with this remark because it seems obvious that the particular kind of influence that one hopes to have by exercising authority, or that society hopes to sanction by establishing authority, is different from what one hopes to have by using force, giving advice, and so on. So the analyst goes on to attempt finer distinctions among the purposes that bring the several concepts into play. (The issue about *de jure* versus *de facto* authority discussed by Peters can be viewed as one aspect or version of this question. The suggestion seems to be that both "types" of authority are species of influence but that they share purposes with one another that they do not share with other species of influence.) Such distinctions are presumably based upon the things people say when exercising or responding to authority as opposed to power, the varying expectations they entertain in connection with the several types of influence, and so forth.

Since Max Weber's work on the subject (selection 4) there has been a great deal of discussion of "types" of authority. By contrast with the distinction between *de jure* and *de facto*, Weber's distinctions among types are drawn in terms of who has the authority and the basis on which authority is accorded to those who have it by the persons over whom it is exercised. In other words, Weber identifies the generic phenomenon of authority by examining the *conditions* under which and the *purposes* for which it is exercised, claimed, and accorded, and then he attempts to distinguish among types or species of the genera in terms of the reasons it is accorded to particular types or classes of people. If the distinctions are important it is presumably because authority works somewhat differently, enters into social and political life in somewhat different ways, depends upon somewhat different conditions, in each of the major types that Weber distinguishes. And Weber's discussion is indeed an attempt to show that this is the case. (Attention should be given to the similarities and differences between Weber's distinctions among traditional, rational-legal, and charismatic authority and Friedman's distinction between "in authority" relations and "an authority" relations.)

At a minimum, then, we should distinguish among questions concerning the conditions under which authority has a place in social life, the purposes or objectives for which it is used, and the bases or basis on which it is accorded to and claimed by various persons or classes of persons. If the meaning of "authority" is its use in the language, answers to these questions as regards the various language games in which "authority" plays a role will tell us a good deal about its meaning; and if we can learn about political and social life by learning about concepts, learning the meaning (in the sense of use) of "authority" should teach us a good deal about the place of authority in social and political life.

The foregoing remarks bring us back to the first question we mentioned, the question about justifying authority. We said that we cannot justify or reject authority unless we know what it is. Now to know what it means is to know its use, its place in a society. Or to use the shorthand that Searle employs in his discussion of promising, it is to know the rules concerning "authority." Searle and more particularly Hanna Pitkin argue that knowledge of these rules permits normative or evaluative as well as descriptive statements about the activity in question. (Pitkin's argument is presented in her article in the following part. Her formulations are discussed at length in selection 11.) On Pitkin's interpretation of "authority," for example, to know what authority is is to know that A has a (prima facie) obligation to obey commands that are authoritative for him or her. Just as "I promised" means "I have an obligation to do what I promised to do," so "X is an authoritative command (for me)" means "I have a (prima facie) obligation to obey that command." On this view, to know and to act within the rules of the practice *is* to accept the authority established by those rules. To reject authority it is necessary to step back from the rules and call them into question. One can do this as regards the rules establishing this particular authority and that. The deep dilemma that seems to exist for thoroughgoing critics of authority is that in stepping back from and criticizing authority and authoritative arrangement X or Y, one must accept as authoritative, if only for the moment, at least those rules, those language games, in which one acts when criticizing and rejecting X and Y.

Further Reading

The footnotes to Richard B. Friedman's articles constitute an excellent bibliography of recent discussions of authority, and the reader is referred to them.

4. The Types of Authority and Imperative Co-ordination

Max Weber

I. The Basis of Legitimacy[1]

I: The Definition, Conditions, and Types of Imperative Control

"Imperative co-ordination" was defined above[2] as the probability that certain specific commands (or all commands) from a given source will be obeyed by a given group of persons. It thus does not include every mode of exercising "power" or "influence" over other persons. The motives of obedience to commands in this sense can rest on considerations varying over a wide range from case to case; all the way from simple habituation to the most purely rational calculation of advantage. A criterion of every true relation of imperative control, however, is a certain minimum of voluntary submission; thus an interest (based on ulterior motives or genuine acceptance) in obedience.

Not every case of imperative co-ordination makes use of economic means; *still less* does it always have economic objectives. But normally (not always) the imperative co-ordination of the action of a considerable number of men requires control of a staff of persons.[3] It is necessary, that is, that there should be a relatively high probability that the action of a definite, supposedly reliable group of persons will be primarily oriented to the execution of the supreme authority's general policy and specific commands.

The members of the administrative staff may be bound to obedience to their superior (or superiors) by custom, by affectual ties, by a purely material complex of interests, or by ideal (*wertrational*) motives. *Purely* material interests and calculations of advantage as the basis of solidarity between the chief and his administrative staff result, in this as in other connexions, in a relatively unstable situation. Normally other elements, affectual and ideal, supplement such interests. In certain exceptional, temporary cases the former may be alone decisive. In everyday routine life these relationships, like others, are governed by custom and in addition, material calculation of advantage. But these factors, custom and personal

---

Reprinted with permission of The Macmillan Company from *The Theory of Social and Economic Organization* by Max Weber, translated by A. M. Henderson and Talcott Parsons, edited by Talcott Parsons, pp. 324–333, 341–345, 358–366, 382–386. Copyright 1947 by Talcott Parsons.

[1] In this chapter Weber departs from his previous practice and, in addition to the usual division into numbered sections, has a system of somewhat more comprehensive subdivisions. These will be designated by capital letters.—Ed.

[2] Chap. i, p. 152, [of *The Theory of Social and Economic Organization*]. The translation problem raised by the term *Herrschaft* was commented upon at that point.—Ed.

[3] An "administrative staff." See chap. i, 12.

advantage, purely affectual or ideal motives of solidarity, do not, even taken together, form a sufficiently reliable basis for a system of imperative co-ordination. In addition there is normally a further element, the belief in legitimacy.

It is an induction from experience that no system of authority voluntarily limits itself to the appeal to material or affectual or ideal motives as a basis for guaranteeing its continuance. In addition every such system attempts to establish and to cultivate the belief in its "legitimacy." But according to the kind of legitimacy which is claimed, the type of obedience, the kind of administrative staff developed to guarantee it, and the mode of exercising authority, will all differ fundamentally. Equally fundamental is the variation in effect. Hence, it is useful to classify the types of authority according to the kind of claim to legitimacy typically made by each. In doing this it is best to start from modern and therefore more familiar examples.

1. The choice of this rather than some other basis of classification can only be justified by its results. The fact that certain other typical criteria of variation are thereby neglected for the time being and can only be introduced at a later stage is not a decisive difficulty. The "legitimacy" of a system of authority has far more than a merely "ideal" significance, if only because it has very definite relations to the legitimacy of property.

2. Not every "claim" which is protected by custom or by law should be spoken of as involving a relation of authority. Otherwise the worker, in his claim for fulfilment of the wage contract, would be exercising "authority" over his employer because his claim can, on occasion, be enforced by order of a court. Actually his formal status is that of party to a contractual relationship with his employer, in which he has certain "rights" to receive payments. At the same time the concept of a relation of authority naturally does not exclude the possibility that it has originated in a formally free contract. This is true of the authority of the employer over the worker as manifested in the former's rules and instructions regarding the work process; and also of the authority of a feudal lord over a vassal who has freely entered into the relation of fealty. That subjection to military discipline is formally "involuntary" while that to the discipline of the factory is voluntary does not alter the fact that the latter is also a case of subjection to authority. The position of a bureaucratic official is also entered into by contract and can be freely resigned, and even the status of "subject" can often be freely entered into and (in certain circumstances) freely repudiated. Only in the limiting case of the slave is formal subjection to authority absolutely involuntary.

Another case, in some respects related, is that of economic "power" based on monopolistic position; that is, in this case, the possibility of "dictating" the terms of exchange to contractual partners. This will not, taken by itself, be considered to constitute "authority" any more than any other kind of "influence" which is derived from some kind of superiority, as by virtue of erotic attractiveness, skill in sport or in discussion. Even if a big bank is in a position to force other banks into a cartel arrangement, this will not alone be sufficient to justify calling it a relation of imperative co-ordination. But if there is an immediate relation of command and obedience such that the management of the first bank can give orders to the others with the claim that they shall, and the probability that they will, be obeyed purely as such regardless of particular content, and if their carrying out is supervised, it is another matter. Naturally, here as everywhere the transitions are gradual; there are all sorts of intermediate steps between mere indebtedness and debt slavery. Even the position of a "salon" can come very close to the borderline of authoritarian domination and yet not necessarily constitute a system of authority. Sharp differentiation in concrete fact is often impossible, but this makes clarity in the analytical distinctions all the more important.

3. Naturally, the legitimacy of a system of authority may be treated sociologically only as the probability that to a relevant degree the appropriate attitudes will exist, and the corresponding practical conduct ensue. It is by no means true that every case of submissiveness to persons in positions of power is primarily (or even at all) oriented to this belief. Loyalty may be hypocritically simulated by individuals or by whole groups on purely opportunistic grounds, or carried out in practice for reasons of material self-interest. Or people may submit from individual weakness and helplessness because there is no acceptable alternative. But these considerations are not decisive for the classification of types of imperative co-ordination. What is important is the fact that in a given case the particular claim to legitimacy is to a significant degree and according to its type treated as "valid"; that this fact confirms the position of the persons claiming authority and that it helps to determine the choice of means of its exercise.

Furthermore a system of imperative co-ordination may — as often occurs in practice — be so completely assured of dominance, on the one hand by the obvious community of interests between the chief and his administrative staff as opposed to the subjects (bodyguards, Pretorians, "red" or "white" guards), on the other hand by the helplessness of the latter, that it can afford to drop even the pretence of a claim to legitimacy. But even then the mode of legitimation of the relation between chief and his staff may vary widely according to the type of basis of the relation of authority between them, and, as will be shown, this variation is highly significant for the structure of imperative co-ordination.

4. "Obedience" will be taken to mean that the action of the person obeying follows in essentials such a course that the content of the command may be taken to have become the basis of action for its own sake. Furthermore, the fact that it is so taken is referable only to the formal obligation, without regard to the actor's own attitude to the value or lack of value of the content of the command as such.

5. Subjectively, the causal sequence may vary, especially as between "submission" and "sympathetic agreement." This distinction is not, however, significant for the present classification of types of authority.

6. The scope of determination of social relationships and cultural phenomena by authority and imperative co-ordination is considerably broader than appears at first sight. For instance, the authority exercised in the school has much to do with the determination of the forms of speech and of written language which are regarded as orthodox. The official languages of autonomous political units, hence of their ruling groups, have often become in this sense orthodox forms of speech and writing and have even led to the formation of separate "nations" (for instance, the separation of Holland from Germany). The authority of parents and of the school, however, extends far beyond the determination of such cultural patterns which are perhaps only apparently formal, to the formation of the character of the young, and hence of human beings generally.

7. The fact that the chief and his administrative staff often appear formally as servants or agents of those they rule, naturally does nothing whatever to disprove the authoritarian character of the relationship. There will be occasion later to speak of the substantive features of so-called "democracy." But a certain minimum of

assured power to issue commands, thus of "authority," must be provided for in nearly every conceivable case.

2: The Three Pure Types of Legitimate Authority

There are three pure types of legitimate authority. The validity of their claims to legitimacy may be based on:

1. Rational grounds — resting on a belief in the "legality" of patterns of normative rules and the right of those elevated to authority under such rules to issue commands (legal authority).
2. Traditional grounds — resting on an established belief in the sanctity of immemorial traditions and the legitimacy of the status of those exercising authority under them (traditional authority); or finally,
3. Charismatic grounds — resting on devotion to the specific and exceptional sanctity, heroism or exemplary character of an individual person, and of the normative patterns or order revealed or ordained by him (charismatic authority).

In the case of legal authority, obedience is owed to the legally established impersonal order. It extends to the persons exercising the authority of office under it only by virtue of the formal legality of their commands and only within the scope of authority of the office. In the case of traditional authority, obedience is owed to the *person* of the chief who occupies the traditionally sanctioned position of authority and who is (within its sphere) bound by tradition. But here the obligation of obedience is not based on the impersonal order, but is a matter of personal loyalty within the area of accustomed obligations. In the case of charismatic authority, it is the charismatically qualified leader as such who is obeyed by virtue of personal trust in him and his revelation, his heroism or his exemplary qualities so far as they fall within the scope of the individual's belief in his charisma.

1. The usefulness of the above classification can only be judged by its results in promoting systematic analysis. The concept of "charisma" ("the gift of grace") is taken from the vocabulary of early Christianity. For the Christian religious organization Rudolf Sohm, in his *Kirchenrecht*, was the first to clarify the substance of the concept, even though he did not use the same terminology. Others (for instance, Hollin, *Enthusiasmus und Bussgewalt*) have clarified certain important consequences of it. It is thus nothing new.

2. The fact that none of these three ideal types, the elucidation of which will occupy the following pages, is usually to be found in historical cases in "pure" form, is naturally not a valid objection to attempting their conceptual formulation in the sharpest possible form. In this respect the present case is not different from many others. Later on (§11ff.) the transformation of pure charisma by the process of routinization will be discussed and thereby the relevance of the concept to the understanding of empirical systems of authority considerably increased. But even so it may be said of every empirically historical phenomenon of authority that it is not likely to be "as an open book." Analysis in terms of sociological types has, after all, as compared with purely empirical historical investigation, certain advantages which should not be minimized. That is, it can in the particular case of a concrete form of authority determine what conforms to or approximates such types as "charisma," "hereditary charisma" (§10, 11), "the charisma of office," "patriarchy" (§7),

"bureaucracy" (§4), the authority of status groups,[4] and in doing so it can work with relatively unambiguous concepts. But the idea that the whole of concrete historical reality can be exhausted in the conceptual scheme about to be developed is as far from the author's thoughts as anything could be.

II. Legal Authority with a Bureaucratic Administrative Staff[5]

3: Legal Authority: The Pure Type with Employment of a Bureaucratic Administrative Staff

The effectiveness of legal authority rests on the acceptance of the validity of the following mutually inter-dependent ideas.

1. That any given legal norm may be established by agreement or by imposition, on grounds of expediency or rational values or both, with a claim to obedience at least on the part of the members of the corporate group. This is, however, usually extended to include all persons within the sphere of authority or of power in question — which in the case of territorial bodies is the territorial area — who stand in certain social relationships or carry out forms of social action which in the order governing the corporate group have been declared to be relevant.

2. That every body of law consists essentially in a consistent system of abstract rules which have normally been intentionally established. Furthermore, administration of law is held to consist in the application of these rules to particular cases; the administrative process in the rational pursuit of the interests which are specified in the order governing the corporate group within the limits laid down by legal precepts and following principles which are capable of generalized formulation and are approved in the order governing the group, or at least not disapproved in it.

3. That thus the typical person in authority occupies an "office." In the action associated with his status, including the commands he issues to others, he is subject to an impersonal order to which his actions are oriented. This is true not only for persons exercising legal authority who are in the usual sense "officials," but, for instance, for the elected president of a state.

4. That the person who obeys authority does so, as it is usually stated, only in his capacity as a "member" of the corporate group and what he obeys is only "the law." He may in this connexion be the member of an association, of a territorial commune, of a church, or a citizen of a state.

5. In conformity with point 3, it is held that the members of the corporate group, in so far as they obey a person in authority, do not owe this obedience to him as an individual, but to the impersonal order. Hence, it follows that there is an obligation to obedience only within the sphere of the rationally delimited authority which, in terms of the order, has been conferred upon him.

The following may thus be said to be the fundamental categories of rational legal authority:—

(1) A continuous organization of official functions bound by rules.

(2) A specified sphere of competence. This involves (a) a sphere of obligations to perform functions which has been marked off as part of a systematic division of

---

[4] *Standische.* There is no really acceptable English rendering of this term.—Ed.

[5] The specifically modern type of administration has intentionally been taken as a point of departure in order to make it possible later to contrast the others with it.

labour. (b) The provision of the incumbent with the necessary authority to carry out these functions. (c) That the necessary means of compulsion are clearly defined and their use is subject to definite conditions. A unit exercising authority which is organized in this way will be called an "administrative organ."[6]

There are administrative organs in this sense in large-scale private organizations, in parties and armies, as well as in the state and the church. An elected president, a cabinet of ministers, or a body of elected representatives also in this sense constitute administrative organs. This is not, however, the place to discuss these concepts. Not every administrative organ is provided with compulsory powers. But this distinction is not important for present purposes.

(3) The organization of offices follows the principle of hierarchy; that is, each lower office is under the control and supervision of a higher one. There is a right of appeal and of statement of grievances from the lower to the higher. Hierarchies differ in respect to whether and in what cases complaints can lead to a ruling from an authority at various points higher in the scale, and as to whether changes are imposed from higher up or the responsibility for such changes is left to the lower office, the conduct of which was the subject of complaint.

(4) The rules which regulate the conduct of an office may be technical rules or norms.[7] In both cases, if their application is to be fully rational, specialized training is necessary. It is thus normally true that only a person who has demonstrated an adequate technical training is qualified to be a member of the administrative staff of such an organized group and hence only such persons are eligible for appointment to official positions. The administrative staff of a rational corporate group thus typically consists of "officials," whether the organization be devoted to political, religious, economic — in particular, capitalistic — or other ends.

(5) In the rational type it is a matter of principle that the members of the administrative staff should be completely separated from ownership of the means of production or administration. Officials, employees, and workers attached to the administrative staff do not themselves own the non-human means of production and administration. These are rather provided for their use in kind or in money, and the official is obligated to render an accounting of their use. There exists, furthermore, in principle complete separation of the property belonging to the organization, which is controlled within the sphere of office, and the personal property of the official, which is available for his own private uses. There is a corresponding separation of the place in which official functions are carried out, the "office" in the sense of premises, from living quarters.

(6) In the rational type case, there is also a complete absence of appropriation of his official position by the incumbent. Where "rights" to an office exist, as in the case of judges, and recently of an increasing proportion of officials and even of workers, they do not normally serve the purpose of appropriation by the official, but of securing the purely objective and independent character of the conduct of the office so that it is oriented only to the relevant norms.

(7) Administrative acts, decisions, and rules are formulated and recorded in

---

[6] *Behörde.*

[7] Weber does not explain this distinction. By a "technical rule" he probably means a prescribed course of action which is dictated primarily on grounds touching efficiency of the performance of the immediate functions, while by "norms" he probably means rules which limit conduct on grounds other than those of efficiency. Of course, in one sense all rules are norms in that they are prescriptions for conduct, conformity with which is problematical.—Ed.

writing, even in cases where oral discussion is the rule or is even mandatory. This applies at least to preliminary discussions and proposals, to final decisions, and to all sorts of orders and rules. The combination of written documents and a continuous organization of official functions constitutes the "office"[8] which is the central focus of all types of modern corporate action.

(8) Legal authority can be exercised in a wide variety of different forms which will be distinguished and discussed later. The following analysis will be deliberately confined for the most part to the aspect of imperative co-ordination in the structure of the administrative staff. It will consist in an analysis in terms of ideal types of officialdom or "bureaucracy."

In the above outline no mention has been made of the kind of supreme head appropriate to a system of legal authority. This is a consequence of certain considerations which can only be made entirely understandable at a later stage in the analysis. There are very important types of rational imperative co-ordination which, with respect to the ultimate source of authority, belong to other categories. This is true of the hereditary charismatic type, as illustrated by hereditary monarchy and of the pure charismatic type of a president chosen by plebiscite. Other cases involve rational elements at important points, but are made up of a combination of bureaucratic and charismatic components, as is true of the cabinet form of government. Still others are subject to the authority of the chief of other corporate groups, whether their character be charismatic or bureaucratic; thus the formal head of a government department under a parliamentary regime may be a minister who occupies his position because of his authority in a party. The type of rational, legal administrative staff is capable of application in all kinds of situations and contexts. It is the most important mechanism for the administration of everyday profane affairs. For in that sphere, the exercise of authority and, more broadly, imperative co-ordination, consists precisely in administration.

III. Traditional Authority

6: Traditional Authority

A system of imperative co-ordination will be called "traditional" if legitimacy is claimed for it and believed in on the basis of the sanctity of the order and the attendant powers of control as they have been handed down from the past, "have always existed." The person or persons exercising authority are designated according to traditionally transmitted rules. The object of obedience is the personal authority of the individual which he enjoys by virtue of his traditional status. The organized group exercising authority is, in the simplest case, primarily based on

---

[8] *Bureau.* It has seemed necessary to use the English word "office" in three different meanings, which are distinguished in Weber's discussion by at least two terms. The first is *Amt*, which means "office" in the sense of the institutionally defined status of a person. The second is the "work premises" as in the expression "he spent the afternoon in his office." For this Weber uses *Bureau* as also for the third meaning which he has just defined, the "organized work process of a group." In this last sense an office is a particular type of "organization," or *Betrieb* in Weber's sense. This use is established in English in such expressions as "the District Attorney's Office has such and such functions." Which of the three meanings is involved in a given case will generally be clear from the context.—Ed.

relations of personal loyalty, cultivated through a common process of education. The person exercising authority is not a "superior," but a personal "chief."[9]

His administrative staff does not consist primarily of officials, but of personal retainers.[10] Those subject to authority are not "members" of an association, but are either his traditional "comrades" or his "subjects." What determines the relations of the administrative staff to the chief is not the impersonal obligation of office, but personal loyalty to the chief.

Obedience is not owed to enacted rules, but to the person who occupies a position of authority by tradition or who has been chosen for such a position on a traditional basis. His commands are legitimized in one of two ways: (a) partly in terms of traditions which themselves directly determine the content of the command and the objects and extent of authority. In so far as this is true, to overstep the traditional limitations would endanger his traditional status by undermining acceptance of his legitimacy. (b) In part, it is a matter of the chief's free personal decision, in that tradition leaves a certain sphere open for this. This sphere of traditional prerogative rests primarily on the fact that the obligations of obedience on the basis of personal loyalty are essentially unlimited.[11] There is thus a double sphere: on the one hand, of action which is bound to specific tradition; on the other hand, of that which is free of any specific rules.

In the latter sphere, the chief is free to confer "grace" on the basis of his personal pleasure or displeasure, his personal likes and dislikes, quite arbitrarily, particularly in return for gifts which often become a source of regular income. So far as his action follows principles at all, these are principles of substantive ethical common sense, of justice, or of utilitarian expediency. They are not, however, as in the case of legal authority, formal principles. The exercise of authority is normally oriented to the question of what the chief and his administrative staff will normally permit, in view of the traditional obedience of the subjects and what will or will not arouse their resistance. When resistance occurs, it is directed against the person of the chief or of a member of his staff. The accusation is that he has failed to observe the traditional limits of his authority. Opposition is not directed against the system as such.

It is impossible in the pure type of traditional authority for law or administrative rules to be deliberately created by legislation. What is actually new is thus claimed to have always been in force but only recently to have become known through the wisdom of the promulgator. The only documents which can play a part in the orientation of legal administration are the documents of tradition; namely, precedents.

7: Traditional Authority — (Continued)

A traditional chief exercises authority with or without an administrative staff. The typical administrative staff is recruited from one or more of the following sources:

  a. From persons who are already related to the chief by traditional ties of

---

[9] *Herr.*

[10] *Diener.*

[11] This does not seem to be a very happy formulation of the essential point. It is not necessary that the authority of a person in such a position, such as the head of a household, should be unlimited. It is rather that its extent is unspecified. It is generally limited by higher obligations, but the burden of proof rests upon the person on whom an obligation is laid that there is such a conflicting higher obligation.—Ed.

personal loyalty. This will be called "patrimonial" recruitment. Such persons may be kinsmen, slaves, dependents who are officers of the household, clients, coloni, or freedmen.

b. It may be recruited from other sources on an "extra-patrimonial" basis. This category includes people in a relation of purely personal loyalty, such as all sorts of "favourites," people standing in a relation of fealty to their chief — "vassals" — and, finally, those who have of their own free will entered into a relation of personal loyalty as officials.

In traditionalistic organizations, it is very common for the most important posts to be filled with members of a ruling family or clan.

In patrimonial administrations, it is common for slaves or freedmen to rise even to the highest positions. It has not been uncommon even for Grand Viziers to have been at one time slaves.

The typical household officials have been the following: the senechal, the marshal (once in charge of horses), the chamberlain, the carver, the steward, who was the head of the service personnel and possibly even of the vassals. These are to be found everywhere in Europe. In the Orient, in addition, the head eunuch, who was in charge of the harem, has been particularly important. In the African kingdoms, the executioner is often included. Universally, the body physician, the astrologer, and various others have been common.

In China and in Egypt, the principal source of recruitment for patrimonial officials lay in the clientele of the king. Armies of coloni have been known throughout the Orient and were typical of the Roman nobility. Even in modern times, in the Mohammedan world, armies of slaves have existed.

The regime of "favourites" is characteristic of every patrimonial system and has often been the occasion for "traditionalistic" revolutions.

The status of "vassal" will be dealt with separately.

Bureaucracy has first developed in patrimonial states with a body of officials recruited from extra-patrimonial sources; but, as will be shown presently, these "officials" have originally been personal followers of their chief.

In the pure type of traditional authority, the following features of a bureaucratic administrative staff are absent: (a) a clearly defined sphere of competence subject to impersonal rules, (b) a rational ordering of relations of superiority and inferiority, (c) a regular system of appointment and promotion on the basis of free contract, (d) technical training as a regular requirement, (e) fixed salaries, in the type case paid in money.

In place of a well-defined impersonal sphere of competence, there is a shifting series of tasks and powers commissioned and granted by a chief through his arbitrary decision of the moment. They then tend to become permanent and are often traditionally stereotyped. An important influence is exerted by competition for sources of income and advantage which are at the disposal of the persons acting on behalf of the chief or of the chief himself. It is often in the first instance through these interests that definite functional spheres are first marked off and, with them, genuine administrative organs.

In the first instance, those with permanent functions are household officials of the chief. Their functions outside the administration of the household itself are often in fields of activity which bear a relatively superficial analogy to their household function, or even which have originated in a completely arbitrary act of the chief, and have later become traditionally stereotyped. In addition to household officers, there have existed primarily only persons with *ad hoc* specific commissions.

The absence of clear spheres of competence is clearly evident from a perusal of the list of the titles of officials in any of the Ancient Oriental states. With rare exceptions, it is impossible to associate with these titles a set of functions rationally delimited in the modern Western sense which has remained stable over a considerable period.

The process of defining permanent functions in terms of competition among and compromise between interests seeking favours, income, and other forms of advantage is especially clearly evident in the Middle Ages. This phenomenon has had very important consequences. The interests in fees of the powerful Royal courts and of the powerful legal profession in England was largely responsible, partly for breaking the influence of Roman and Canon law, partly for limiting it. Existing irrational divisions of official functions have frequently in all periods been stereotyped by the existence of an established set of rights to fees and perquisites.

In contrast to the rational hierarchy of authority in the bureaucratic system, the question who shall decide a matter — which of his officials or the chief himself — or who shall deal with complaints, is, in a traditional regime, treated in one of two ways. (1) Traditionally, on the basis of the authority of particular received legal norms or precedents. (2) Entirely on the basis of the arbitrary decision of the chief. Whenever he intervenes personally, all others give way to him.

In Germanic law, apart from the traditionalistic system of adherence to precedent, there is a principle which is derived from the arbitrary power of the political chief; namely, that in the presence of the chief himself the jurisdiction of any court is suspended. This principle has the same source as the *jus avocandi*, in the arbitrary grace of a monarch and its modern derivative, chamber justice. A court rendering judgment in terms of precedents was in the Middle Ages very often the agency which declared and interpreted the law and was thus the principal source from which the law of a locality was taken.

As opposed to the bureaucratic system of free appointment, household officials and favourites are very often recruited on a purely patrimonial basis from among the slaves or serfs of the chief. If, on the other hand, the recruitment has been extra-patrimonial, they have tended to be holders of benefices which he has granted as an act of grace without being bound by any formal rules. A fundamental change in this situation is first brought about by the rise of free vassals and the filling of offices by a contract of fealty. Since, however, such relations of fealty have been by no means primarily determined by considerations of objective function, this has not altered the situation with respect to definite spheres of competence or clearly determined hierarchical relationships. Except under certain circumstances when the administrative staff is organized on a basis of praebends, there is such a thing as "promotion" only according to the arbitrary grace of the chief.

Rational technical training as a basic qualification for office is scarcely to be found at all among household officials or the favourites of a chief. Where there is even a beginning of technical training for appointees, regardless of what it consists in, this fact everywhere makes for a fundamental change in the development of administrative practice.

For many offices a certain amount of empirical training has been necessary from very early times. This is particularly true of the "art" of reading and writing which was originally truly an art with a high scarcity value. This has often, most strikingly in China, had a decisive influence on the whole development of culture through the mode of life of persons with a literary education. Among other things, it has eliminated the recruiting of officials from intra-patrimonial sources and has thus limited the power of the chief by making him dependent on a definite social group.

In place of regular salaries, household officials and favourites are usually supported and equipped in the household of the chief and from his personal stores. Generally, their exclusion from the lord's own table means the creation of benefices, at first usually benefices in kind. It is easy for these to become traditionally stereotyped in amount and kind. Along with the elements supported by benefices or in place of them, there are various agencies commissioned by the lord outside his own household, as well as various fees which are due him. The latter are often collected without any regular rate or scale, being agreed upon from case to case with those seeking favours.[12]

IV. Charismatic Authority

10: The Principal Characteristics of Charismatic Authority and Its Relation to Forms of Communal Organization

The term "charisma" will be applied to a certain quality of an individual personality by virtue of which he is set apart from ordinary men and treated as endowed with supernatural, superhuman, or at least specifically exceptional powers or qualities. These are such as are not accessible to the ordinary person, but are regarded as of divine origin or as exemplary, and on the basis of them the individual concerned is treated as a leader. In primitive circumstances this peculiar kind of deference is paid to prophets, to people with a reputation for therapeutic or legal wisdom, to leaders in the hunt, and heroes in war. It is very often thought of as resting on magical powers. How the quality in question would be ultimately judged from any ethical, aesthetic, or other such point of view is naturally entirely indifferent for purposes of definition. What is alone important is how the individual is actually regarded by those subject to charismatic authority, by his "followers" or "disciples."

For present purposes it will be necessary to treat a variety of different types as being endowed with charisma in this sense. It includes the state of a "berserker" whose spells of maniac passion have, apparently wrongly, sometimes been attributed to the use of drugs. In Medieval Byzantium a group of people endowed with this type of charismatic war-like passion were maintained as a kind of weapon. It includes the "shaman," the kind of magician who in the pure type is subject to epileptoid seizures as a means of falling into trances. Another type is that of Joseph Smith, the founder of Mormonism, who, however, cannot be classified in this way with absolute certainty since there is a possibility that he was a very sophisticated type of deliberate swindler. Finally it includes the type of intellectual, such as Kurt Eisner,[13] who is carried away with his own demagogic success. Sociological analysis, which must abstain from value judgments, will treat all these on the same

---

[12] The concept of "benefices" will be taken up presently.
[13] The leader of the communistic experiment in Bavaria in 1919.—Ed.

level as the men who, according to conventional judgments, are the "greatest" heroes, prophets, and saviours.

1. It is recognition on the part of those subject to authority which is decisive for the validity of charisma. This is freely given and guaranteed by what is held to be a "sign" or proof,[14] originally always a miracle, and consists in devotion to the corresponding revelation, hero worship, or absolute trust in the leader. But where charisma is genuine, it is not this which is the basis of the claim to legitimacy. This basis lies rather in the conception that it is the *duty* of those who have been called to a charismatic mission to recognize its quality and to act accordingly. Psychologically this "recognition" is a matter of complete personal devotion to the possessor of the quality, arising out of enthusiasm, or of despair and hope.

No prophet has ever regarded his quality as dependent on the attitudes of the masses toward him. No elective king or military leader has ever treated those who have resisted him or tried to ignore him otherwise than as delinquent in duty. Failure to take part in a military expedition under such leader, even though recruitment is formally voluntary, has universally been met with disdain.

2. If proof of his charismatic qualification fails him for long, the leader endowed with charisma tends to think his god or his magical or heroic powers have deserted him. If he is for long unsuccessful, above all if his leadership fails to benefit his followers, it is likely that his charismatic authority will disappear. This is the genuine charismatic meaning of the "gift of grace."[15]

Even the old Germanic kings were sometimes rejected with scorn. Similar phenomena are very common among so-called "primitive" peoples. In China the charismatic quality of the monarch, which was transmitted unchanged by heredity, was upheld so rigidly that any misfortune whatever, not only defeats in war, but drought, floods, or astronomical phenomena which were considered unlucky, forced him to do public penance and might even force his abdication. If such things occurred, it was a sign that he did not possess the requisite charismatic virtue, he was thus not a legitimate "Son of Heaven."

3. The corporate group which is subject to charismatic authority is based on an emotional form of communal relationship.[16] The administrative staff of a charismatic leader does not consist of "officials"; at least its members are not technically trained. It is not chosen on the basis of social privilege nor from the point of view of domestic or personal dependency. It is rather chosen in terms of the charismatic qualities of its members. The prophet has his disciples; the war lord his selected henchmen; the leader, generally, his followers. There is no such thing as "appointment" or "dismissal," no career, no promotion. There is only a "call" at the instance of the leader on the basis of the charismatic qualification of those he summons. There is no hierarchy; the leader merely intervenes in general or in individual cases when he considers the members of his staff inadequate to a task with which they have been entrusted. There is no such thing as a definite sphere of authority and of competence, and no appropriation of official powers on the basis of social privileges. There may, however, be territorial or functional limits to charismatic powers and to the individual's "mission." There is no such thing as a salary or a benefice. Disciples or followers tend to live primarily in a communistic relationship with their leader on means which have been provided by voluntary gift.

[14] *Bewährung.*
[15] *Gottesgnadentum.*
[16] Weber uses the term *Gemeinde,* which is not directly translatable.—Ed.

There are no established administrative organs. In their place are agents who have been provided with charismatic authority by their chief or who possess charisma of their own. There is no system of formal rules, of abstract legal principles, and hence no process of judicial decision oriented to them. But equally there is no legal wisdom oriented to judicial precedent. Formally concrete judgments are newly created from case to case and are originally regarded as divine judgments and revelations. From a substantive point of view, every charismatic authority would have to subscribe to the proposition, "It is written . . . , but I say unto you. . . ."[17] The genuine prophet, like the genuine military leader and every true leader in this sense, preaches, creates, or demands *new* obligations. In the pure type of charisma, these are imposed on the authority of revolution by oracles, or of the leader's own will, and are recognized by the members of the religious, military, or party group, because they come from such a source. Recognition is a duty. When such an authority comes into conflict with the competing authority of another who also claims charismatic sanction, the only recourse is to some kind of contest, by magical means or even an actual physical battle of the leaders. In principle, only one side can be in the right in such a conflict; the other must be guilty of a wrong which has to be expiated.

Charismatic authority is thus specifically outside the realm of everyday routine and the profane sphere.[18] In this respect, it is sharply opposed both to rational, and particularly bureaucratic, authority, and to traditional authority, whether in its patriarchal, partimonial, or any other form. Both rational and traditional authority are specifically forms of everyday routine control of action; while the charismatic type is the direct antithesis of this. Bureaucratic authority is specifically rational in the sense of being bound to intellectually analysable rules; while charismatic authority is specifically irrational in the sense of being foreign to all rules. Traditional authority is bound to the precedents handed down from the past and to this extent is also oriented to rules. Within the sphere of its claims, charismatic authority repudiates the past, and is in this sense a specifically revolutionary force. It recognizes no appropriation of positions of power by virtue of the possession of property, either on the part of a chief or of socially privileged groups. The only basis of legitimacy for it is personal charisma, so long as it is proved; that is, as long as it receives recognition and is able to satisfy the followers or disciples. But this lasts only so long as the belief in its charismatic inspiration remains.

The above is scarcely in need of further discussion. What has been said applies to the position of authority of such elected monarchs as Napoleon, with his use of the plebiscite. It applies to the "rule of genius," which has elevated people of humble origin to thrones and high military commands, just as much as it applies to religious prophets or war heroes.

4. Pure charisma is specifically foreign to economic considerations. Whenever it appears, it constitutes a "call" in the most emphatic sense of the word, a "mission" or a "spiritual duty." In the pure type, it disdains and repudiates economic exploitation of the gifts of grace as a source of income, though, to be sure, this often remains more an ideal than a fact. It is not that charisma always means the

---

[17] Something contrary to what was written, as Jesus said in opposition to the Scribes and Pharisees.—Ed.

[18] Weber used the antithesis of *Charisma* and *Alltag* in two senses. On the one hand, of the extraordinary and temporary as opposed to the everyday and routine; on the other hand, the sacred as opposed to the profane. See the editor's *Structure of Social Action*, ch. xvii.—Ed.

renunciation of property or even of acquisition, as under certain circumstances prophets and their disciples do. The heroic warrior and his followers actively seek "booty"; the elective ruler or the charismatic party leader requires the material means of power. The former in addition requires a brilliant display of his authority to bolster his prestige. What is despised, so long as the genuinely charismatic type is adhered to, is traditional or rational everyday economizing, the attainment of a regular income by continuous economic activity devoted to this end. Support by gifts, sometimes on a grand scale involving foundations, even by bribery and grand-scale honoraria, or by begging, constitute the strictly voluntary type of support. On the other hand, "booty," or coercion, whether by force or by other means, is the other typical form of charismatic provision for needs. From the point of view of rational economic activity, charisma is a typical anti-economic force. It repudiates any sort of involvement in the everyday routine world. It can only tolerate, with an attitude of complete emotional indifference, irregular, unsystematic, acquisitive acts. In that it relieves the recipient of economic concerns, dependence on property income can be the economic basis of a charismatic mode of life for some groups; but that is not usually acceptable for the normal charismatic "revolutionary."

The fact that incumbency of church office has been forbidden to the Jesuits is a rationalized application of this principle of discipleship. The fact that all the "virtuosi" of asceticism, the mendicant orders, and fighters for a faith belong in this category, is quite clear. Almost all prophets have been supported by voluntary gifts. The well-known saying of St. Paul, "If a man does not work, neither shall he eat," was directed against the swarm of charismatic missionaries. It obviously has nothing to do with a positive valuation of economic activity for its own sake, but only lays it down as a duty of each individual somehow to provide for his own support. This because he realized that the purely charismatic parable of the lilies of the field was not capable of literal application, but at best "taking no thought for the morrow" could be hoped for. On the other hand, in such a case as primarily an artistic type of charismatic discipleship, it is conceivable that insulation from economic struggle should mean limitation of those who were really eligible to the "economically independent"; that is, to persons living on income from property. This has been true of the circle of Stefan George, at least in its primary intentions.

5. In traditionally stereotyped periods, charisma is the greatest revolutionary force. The equally revolutionary force of "reason" works from without by altering the situations of action, and hence its problems finally in this way changing men's attitudes toward them; or it intellectualizes the individual. Charisma, on the other hand, may involve a subjective or internal reorientation born out of suffering, conflicts, or enthusiasm. It may then result in a radical alteration of the central system of attitudes and directions of action with a completely new orientation of all attitudes toward the different problems and structures of the "world."[19] In prerationalistic periods, tradition and charisma between them have almost exhausted the whole of the orientation of action.

[19] Weber here uses *Welt* in quotation marks, indicating that it refers to its meaning in what is primarily a religious context. It is the sphere of "worldly" things and interests as distinguished from transcendental religious interests.—Ed.

V. The Routinization of Charisma

II: The Routinization of Charisma and Its Consequences

In its pure form charismatic authority has a character specifically foreign to everyday routine structures. The social relationships directly involved are strictly personal, based on the validity and practice of charismatic personal qualities. If this is not to remain a purely transitory phenomenon, but to take on the character of a permanent relationship forming a stable community of disciples or a band of followers or a party organization or any sort of political or hierocratic organization, it is necessary for the character of charismatic authority to become radically changed. Indeed, in its pure form charismatic authority may be said to exist only in the process of originating. It cannot remain stable, but becomes either traditionalized or rationalized, or a combination of both.

The following are the principal motives underlying this transformation: (a) The ideal and also the material interests of the followers in the continuation and the continual reactivation of the community, (b) the still stronger ideal and also stronger material interests of the members of the administrative staff, the disciples or other followers of the charismatic leader in continuing their relationship. Not only this, but they have an interest in continuing it in such a way that both from an ideal and a material point of view, their own status is put on a stable everyday basis. This means, above all, making it possible to participate in normal family relationships or at least to enjoy a secure social position in place of the kind of discipleship which is cut off from ordinary worldly connexions, notably in the family and in economic relationships.

These interests generally become conspicuously evident with the disappearance of the personal charismatic leader and with the problem of succession, which inevitably arises. The way in which this problem is met — if it is met at all and the charismatic group continues to exist — is of crucial importance for the character of the subsequent social relationships. The following are the principal possible types of solution:—

a. The search for a new charismatic leader on the basis of criteria of the qualities which will fit him for the position of authority. This is to be found in a relatively pure type in the process of choice of a new Dalai Lama. It consists in the search for a child with characteristics which are interpreted to mean that he is a reincarnation of the Buddha. This is very similar to the choice of the new Bull of Apis.

In this case the legitimacy of the new charismatic leader is bound to certain distinguishing characteristics; thus, to rules with respect to which a tradition arises. The result is a process of traditionalization in favour of which the purely personal character of leadership is eliminated.

b. By revelation manifested in oracles, lots, divine judgments, or other techniques of selection. In this case the legitimacy of the new leader is dependent on the legitimacy of the technique of his selection. This involves a form of legalization. It is said that at times the *Schofetim* of Israel had this character. Saul is said to have been chosen by the old war oracle.

c. By the designation on the part of the original charismatic leader of his own successor and his recognition on the part of the followers. This is a very common form. Originally, the Roman magistracies were filled entirely in this way. The system survived most clearly into later times in the appointment of "dictators" and in the institution of the "interrex." In this case legitimacy is acquired through the act of designation.

d. Designation of a successor by the charismatically qualified administrative staff and his recognition by the community. In its typical form this process should quite definitely not be interpreted as "election" or "nomination" or anything of the sort. It is not a matter of free selection, but of one which is strictly bound to objective duty. It is not to be determined merely by majority vote, but is a question of arriving at the correct designation, the designation of the right person who is truly endowed with charisma. It is quite possible that the minority and not the majority should be right in such a case. Unanimity is often required. It is obligatory to acknowledge a mistake and persistence in error is a serious offence. Making a wrong choice is a genuine wrong requiring expiation. Originally it was a magical offence.

Nevertheless, in such a case it is easy for legitimacy to take on the character of an acquired right which is justified by standards of the correctness of the process by which the position was acquired, for the most part, by its having been acquired in accordance with certain formalities, such as coronation. This was the original meaning of the coronation of bishops and kings in the Western World by the clergy or the nobility with the "consent" of the community. There are numerous analogous phenomena all over the world. The fact that this is the origin of the modern conception of "election" raises problems which will have to be gone into later.

e. By the conception that charisma is a quality transmitted by heredity; thus that it is participated in by the kinsmen of its bearer, particularly by his closet relatives. This is the case of hereditary charisma. The order of hereditary succession in such a case need not be the same as that which is in force for appropriated rights, but may differ from it. It is also sometimes necessary to select the proper heir within the kinship group by some of the methods just spoken of; thus in certain Negro states brothers have had to fight for the succession. In China, succession had to take place in such a way that the relation of the living group to the ancestral spirits was not disturbed. The rule either of seniority or of designation by the followers has been very common in the Orient. Hence, in the house of Osman, it has been obligatory to eliminate all other possible candidates.

Only in Medieval Europe and in Japan universally, elsewhere only sporadically, has the principle of primogeniture, as governing the inheritance of authority, become clearly established. This has greatly facilitated the consolidation of political groups in that it has eliminated struggle between a plurality of candidates from the same charismatic family.

In the case of hereditary charisma, recognition is no longer paid to the charismatic qualities of the individual, but to the legitimacy of the position he has acquired by hereditary succession. This may lead in the direction either of traditionalization or of legalization. The concept of "divine right" is fundamentally altered and now comes to mean authority by virtue of a personal right which is not dependent on the recognition of those subject to authority. Personal charisma may be totally absent. Hereditary monarchy is a conspicuous illustration. In Asia there have been very numerous hereditary priesthoods; also, frequently, the hereditary charisma of kinship groups has been treated as a criterion of social rank and of eligibility for fiefs and benefices.

f. The concept that charisma may be transmitted by ritual means from one bearer to another or may be created in a new person. The concept was originally magical. It involves a dissociation of charisma from a particular individual, making it an objective, transferrable entity. In particular, it may become the charisma of office. In this case the belief in legitimacy is no longer directed to the individual, but to the acquired qualities and to the effectiveness of the ritual acts. The most important example is the transmission of priestly charisma by anointing, conse-cration, or the laying on of hands; and of royal authority, by anointing and by coronation. The *caracter indelibilis* thus acquired means that the charismatic qualities and powers of the office are emancipated from the personal qualities of the priest. For precisely this reason, this has, from the Donatist and the Montanist heresies down to the Puritan revolution, been the subject of continual conflicts. The "hireling" of the Quakers is the preacher endowed with the charisma of office.

.   .   .

13: Combinations of the Different Types of Authority

The above discussion makes it quite evident that imperatively co-ordinated groups, which belong only to one or another of these pure types, are very exceptional. Furthermore, in relation to legal and traditional authority especially, certain important types, such as the collegial form and some aspects of the feudal, have either not been discussed at all or have been barely suggested. In general, it should be kept clearly in mind that the basis of every system of authority, and correspondingly of every kind of willingness to obey, is a *belief*, a belief by virtue of which persons exercising authority are lent prestige. The composition of this belief is seldom altogether simple. In the case of "legal authority," it is never purely legal. The belief in legality comes to be established and habitual, and this means it is partly traditional. Violation of the tradition may even be fatal to it. Furthermore, it has a charismatic element, at least in the negative sense that persistent and striking lack of success may be sufficient to ruin any government, to undermine its prestige, and to prepare the way for charismatic revolution. For monarchies, hence, it is dangerous to lose wars since that makes it appear that their charisma is no longer genuine. For republics, on the other hand, striking victories may be dangerous in that they put the victorious general in a favourable position for making charismatic claims.

Communal groups[20] approximating the purely traditional type have certainly existed. But they have never been stable indefinitely and, as is also true of bureaucratic authority, have seldom been without a head who had a personally charismatic status by heredity or office. Under certain circumstances, the charismatic chief can be different from the traditional one. Sometimes everyday economic needs have been met under the leadership of traditional authorities; whereas certain exceptional ones, like hunting and the quest of "booty" in war, have had charismatic leadership. The idea of the possibility of "legislation" is also relatively ancient, though for the most part it has been legitimized by oracles. Above all, however, whenever the recruitment of an administrative staff is drawn from extra-patrimonial sources, the result is a type of official which can be differentiated from those of legal bureaucracies only in terms of the ultimate basis of their authority and not in terms of formal status.

[20] *Gemeinschaften.*

Similarly, entirely pure charismatic authority, including the hereditary charismatic type, etc., is rare. It is not impossible, as in the case of Napoleon, for the strictest type of bureaucracy to issue directly from a charismatic movement; or, if not that, all sorts of praebendal and feudal types of organization. Hence, the kind of terminology and classification set forth above has in no sense the aim — indeed, it could not have it — to be exhaustive or to confine the whole of historical reality in a rigid scheme. Its usefulness is derived from the fact that in a given case it is possible to distinguish what aspects of a given organized group can legitimately be identified as falling under or approximating to one or another of these categories. For certain purposes this is unquestionably an important advantage.

For all types of authority the fact of the existence and continual functioning of an administrative staff is vital. For the habit of obedience cannot be maintained without organized activity directed to the application and enforcement of the order. It is, indeed, the existence of such activity which is usually meant by the term "organization." For this to exist in turn, it is essential that there should be an adequate degree of the solidarity of interests, both on the ideal and material levels, of the members of the administrative staff with their chief. It is fundamental in understanding the relation of the chief to these members that, so far as this solidarity exists, the chief is stronger than any individual member but is weaker than the members taken together. It is, however, by no means necessary for the members of an administrative staff to enter into any deliberate agreement in order to obstruct or even consciously oppose their chief so successfully that the leadership of the chief becomes impotent. Similarly, any individual who sets out to break up a system of imperative control must, if he is going to take over the position of power, build up an administrative staff of his own, unless he is in a position to count on the connivance and co-operation of the existing staff against their previous leader.

Solidarity of interest with a chief is maximized at the point where both the legitimacy of the status of the members and the provision for their economic needs is dependent on the chief retaining his position. For any given individual, the possibility of escaping this solidarity varies greatly according to the structure. It is most difficult where there is complete separation from the means of administration, thus in purely traditional patriarchal structures, under pure patrimonialism and in bureaucratic organizations resting on formal rules. It is easiest where fiefs or benefices have been appropriated by socially privileged groups.

It is most important, finally, to realize that historical reality involves a continuous, though for the most part latent, conflict between chiefs and their administrative staffs for appropriation and expropriation in relation to one another. For the development of culture as a whole, it has been crucial in what way this struggle has worked out and what has been the character of the class of officials dependent upon him which has helped the chief win out in his struggle against the feudal classes or other groups enjoying appropriated powers. In different cases it has been a ritually trained type of educated class, the clergy, purely secular clients, household officials, legally trained persons, technically specialized financial officials, or private individuals without official status.[21]

---

[21] *Honoratioren.* There is no good English equivalent term. It refers to persons performing functions and exercising authority who do not depend on the position as a major source of income and generally enjoy an independent status in the social structure.—Ed.

One of the reasons why the character of these struggles and of their outcome has been so important, not only to the history of administration as such, but to that of culture generally, is that the type of education has been determined by them and with it the modes in which different social strata have been subject to different types of educational influence.

1. Both the extent and the way in which the members of an administrative staff are bound to their chief will vary greatly according to whether they receive salaries, opportunities for profit, allowances, or fiefs. It is, however, a factor common to all of these that anything which endangers the legitimacy of the chief who has granted and who guarantees them, tends at the same time to endanger the legitimacy of these forms of income and the positions of power and prestige in the social system which go with membership in the administrative staff. This is one of the reasons why legitimacy, which is often so much neglected in analysing such phenomena, plays a crucially important role.

2. The history of the dissolution of the older system of legitimate authority in Germany during and immediately after the World War is instructive in this connexion. The War, on the one hand, went far to break down the authority of tradition; and the German defeat involved a tremendous loss of prestige for the government. These factors combined with systematic habituation to illegal behaviour, undermined the amenability to discipline both in the army and in industry and thus prepared the way for the overthrow of the older authority. At the same time, the way in which the old administrative staff continued to function and the way in which its system of order was simply taken over by the new supreme authorities, is a striking example of the extent to which, under rationalized bureaucratic conditions, the individual member of such a staff is inescapably bound to his technical function. As it has been noted above, this fact is by no means adequately explained by the private economic interests of the members – their concern for their jobs, salaries, and pensions – although it goes without saying that these considerations were not unimportant to the great majority of officials. In addition to this, however, the disinterested ideological factor has been crucial. For the breakdown of administrative organization would, under such conditions, have meant a breakdown of the provision of the whole population, including, of course, the officials themselves, with even the most elementary necessities of life. Hence an appeal was made to the sense of duty of officials, and this was successful. Indeed the objective necessity of this attitude has been recognized even by the previous holders of power and their sympathizers.

3. In the course of the present revolution in Germany, a new administrative staff came into being in the Soviets of workers and soldiers. In the first place it was necessary to develop a technique of organizing these new staffs. Furthermore, their development was closely dependent on the War, notably the possession of weapons by the revolutionary element. Without this factor the revolution would not have been possible at all.[22] It was only by the rise of charismatic leaders against the legal authorities and by the development around them of groups of charismatic followers, that it was possible to take power away from the old authorities. It was furthermore only through the maintenance of the old bureaucratic organization that power once achieved could be retained. Previous to this situation every

[22] This and its historical analogies will be discussed further below [in *The Theory of Social and Economic Considerations*].

revolution which has been attempted under modern conditions has failed completely because of the indispensability of trained officials and of the lack of its own organized staff. The conditions under which previous revolutions have succeeded have been altogether different.[23]

4. The overthrow of authority on the initiative of the administrative staff has occurred in the past under a wide variety of conditions. Some form of organization of the members of the staff has always been a necessary prerequisite. According to the circumstances, it might have more the character of a conspiracy or more that of a general solidarity with corresponding organization. The latter is, under the conditions to which the modern official is subject, peculiarly difficult; but as the Russian case has shown, it is not altogether impossible. As a general rule, however, such types of organization do not go further than the kind which is open to workers through the ordinary procedure of the strike.

5. The patrimonial character of a body of officials is above all manifested in the fact that admission involves a relation of personal dependency. In the Carolingian system, one became a *puer regis*, under the Angevins, a *familiaris*. Survivals of this have persisted for a very long time.

[23] See below, the chapter on the theory of revolutions. (This projected chapter was apparently never written and no systematic account of revolutions is available either in *Wirtschaft und Gesellschaft* or elsewhere in Weber's published works.—Ed.)

5. On the Concept of Authority in Political Philosophy

Richard B. Friedman

The concept of authority is one of the rare ideas that has remained stubbornly central both to political philosophy and to empirical social science in spite of their divergence in the twentieth century. The highly self-conscious interest that political philosophy has in authority is obvious. For authority is a notion intimately bound up with most, if not all, of the central questions of political philosophy, especially the so-called problem of political obligation. And as for social science, the heavy intellectual burden placed on the notion of authority may be seen in the pre-eminent role played by the concepts of legitimacy and legitimate power in the study and definition of such "subjects" as the stability of political systems, the transition from traditional to modern society, organizational behavior, political socialization, etc.

This is a revised and enlarged version of a paper delivered at the 1971 Annual Meeting of the American Political Science Association. However, it still remains a provisional sketch of ideas that form part of a work in progress. Reprinted by permission of the author.

At the same time, the "meaning" of authority has been the subject of ceaseless and acrimonious controversy in both political philosophy and social science. This controversy is invariably cast in the form of a dispute over the relation between the notions of authority, power, and legitimacy; and a large variety of approaches to authority have been forged out of these elements.[1] Moreover, since Weber, this controversy has come to effect the very question of what politics is and what the field and the scope of political study consists in. In addition to all this, there is also the peculiar but interesting and important claim that the very concept of authority has been corrupted or even lost in the modern world, and that it is this loss of understanding that lies behind the confusion over authority prevailing in contemporary thought. This is an opinion frequently expressed in some of the most well-known discussions of authority in recent years,[2] though in fact it first became something like a common view during the great debate over the dissolution of traditional authority in early nineteenth-century European thought. Kierkegaard expressed a view that may be found among most critics of "modern" society, when he spoke of the "confusion involved in the fact that the concept of authority has been entirely forgotten in our confused age."[3]

Authority, then, has proved to be an elusive concept, as well as an indispensable one, and perhaps there is no single view of authority that can serve as the model for understanding all the different uses to which it is put. But rather than attempt to survey the various different views of authority that may be found in contemporary thought, I propose to set out in a series of brief remarks what I take to be the main elements of the concept of authority. This procedure will perhaps obscure some of the subtleties and may seem to neglect some of the larger problems traditionally coupled with the examination of authority. But, one hopes it will make clear the main lines of interpretation.

1. The Scope of the Concept of Authority: Belief and Action

Discussions of authority, especially by political scientists and legal philosophers, often deal exclusively with authority over conduct. But the scope of the concept as it is actually used is in fact a good deal broader. For although a man who exercises authority does indeed influence other men, this influence may be over beliefs as well as conduct. Thus, the *Oxford English Dictionary* gives for "authority" not only the "right to command" and "power to influence action," but also "power over the opinions of others," "intellectual influence," "power to inspire belief," and "title to be believed." Concomitantly, a person may be said to "have authority" in two distinct senses. For one, he may be said to be "in authority," meaning that he occupies some office, position, or status which entitles him to make

---

[1] For surveys of various definitions, see John Schaar, "Reflections on Authority," *New American Review*, No. 8 (New American Library, New York, 1970); Young C. Kim, "Authority; Some Conceptual and Empirical Notes," *Western Political Quarterly*, Vol. 19 (June, 1966), 223–234; Robert Peabody, "Authority," *International Encyclopedia of the Social Sciences* (New York, 1968), Vol. I, 473–477.

[2] E.g., Hannah Arendt, "What Is Authority?" in *Between Past and Future* (Cleveland and New York, 1963); Bertrand de Jouvenel, *Sovereignty* (Chicago, 1957), p. 30; John Schaar, *op. cit.*; Alasdair MacIntyre, *Secularization and Moral Change*, The Riddell Memorial Lectures, 1964 (London, 1967), pp. 50–55.

[3] *On Authority and Revelation: The Book on Adler*, trans. Walter Lowrie (Princeton, 1955), p. XVI.

decisions about how other people should behave. But, secondly, a person may be said to be "an authority" on something, meaning that his views or utterances are entitled to be believed (including, to complicate matters, beliefs about the right and wrong way of doing things). And so we speak of teachers, priests, parents, and experts (of various kinds) as having authority over beliefs as well as of legislators, judges, and generals having authority over conduct.

Now the broad scope of the concept of authority is closely connected to the central and controversial role it plays in political philosophy. For the concept of authority has been characteristically invoked in political philosophy to help define the nature of the cohesion or unity characteristic of human societies. Neither coercion nor rational argument, nor both together, seem capable of accounting for the coordination of wills required for a society to exist. Additional concepts appear to be required for this task, and authority has been preeminent among these other concepts. But, in this connection, it is possible to distinguish two very different approaches to the way in which the concept of authority has entered into the attempt to conceive the unity of a human society. One approach concentrates on the nature and role of authoritative beliefs, maintaining that society cannot exist in the absence of a consensus of authoritative beliefs about the meaning of human life and the ends of human conduct. ". . . [W]ithout common belief," Tocqueville claims, "no society can exist," and he makes quite clear in an extended discussion of this matter that he means beliefs held on the "principle of authority," that is, "on trust and without discussion."[4] On this view, the notions of "authority" and "legitimacy" have a derivative application in politics. Political institutions are said to have "authority" or "legitimacy" to the extent to which the members of society regard those institutions as reflecting, embodying, or promoting their shared beliefs; and the dominant theme of this approach is that, although a common set of authoritative beliefs is constitutive of the social order, the weakening or dissolution of those beliefs is bound to generate destructive acts directed against the values and practices of the established social order and even ultimately against the self, e.g., suicide, madness. It is usually some version of this approach to authority — in terms of shared beliefs — that those writers have had in mind who claim that the notion of authority has been lost or distorted in modern times.

The second approach, by contrast, concentrates on the authoritative regulation of conduct by the state. Its central theme is that social life is impossible in the absence of the authority of the state. It is political authority that is needed just because men are "individuals" who do not share the same values or, what is the same thing, who conceive themselves to have different and often conflicting purposes in life, so that no social order whatever could be maintained among such individuals if each were to insist that government reflect his "values," as a condition of acknowledging the duty of obedience to government. All men, then, must submit to common rules, regardless of their own "private" opinions as to the worth

---

[4] Bradley (ed.), *Democracy in America* (New York, 1955), two volumes, Vol. II, pp. 9–10. See also, for example, Auguste Comte, "Considerations on the Spiritual Power" in *System of Positive Polity* (London, 1877), four volumes, Vol. 4, especially pp. 619–621 and 636–638, and Emile Durkheim, *The Elementary Forms of the Religious Life* (New York, 1965), pp. 236–245. Cf. Parsons: "Without attachment to the constitutive common values the collectivity tends to dissolve. . . . That the stability of any social system . . . is dependent on a degree of such integration may be said to be the fundamental dynamic theorem of sociology." *The Social System* (Glencoe, Ill., 1951), pp. 41–42.

of those rules: the authority necessary to the existence of society is not conceived in terms of common beliefs, but in terms of a common framework of rules of conduct, within which the individuals can then pursue their own ends. On this view, then, the authority required for social cohesion is defined against the background of the absence or loss of shared beliefs, and so appears as a kind of compensation for that absence or loss.[5]

Now these two approaches to authority have been mentioned at the outset of this paper for two reasons. First of all, to point out what I take to be, in rough outline, the general character of the debate which has provided the intellectual context of the discussion of authority at least in modern political philosophy since, say, Hobbes, and especially in the last two centuries. It is hard to think of a significant discussion of authority in modern times that has not been inspired by the confrontation of these two approaches. But, in the second place, I have called attention to them in order to indicate, perhaps in an overly dramatic manner, the scope of philosophical inquiry into the idea of authority. I am suggesting, in other words, that it would be a gratuitous limitation on the proper scope of inquiry to restrict analysis in advance to authority over conduct, or, on the other hand, to assume that a modern system of legal authority constitutes the paradigm for understanding all forms of authority. Even if legal authority is made the principal focus of inquiry, that particular form of authority can, I suggest, be fully understood only by way of contrast with a system of authoritative belief. Indeed, the elimination of any element of authoritative belief from our present conception of political and legal authority needs to be seen as an historical achievement profoundly tied up with the work of certain modern political philosophers – if indeed it can now be taken for granted. To call attention to these two approaches should at least serve as a precaution against an unduly narrow restriction on the scope of inquiry.[6]

2. Authority and "Legitimate Power"

However, the broad scope of the concept of authority is not the only thing that has made that notion so intricate and controversial. For political philosophy and social science have both been preoccuppied with the problem of the difference between authority and other forms of influence. Indeed, it is now commonplace in political philosophy as well as in social science to assume that the notion of authority belongs to a network of concepts having to do with the various ways in which some men get other men to do what they wish, such as power, domination, coercion, force, manipulation, persuasion, etc. Authority thus appears as a species of the genus "social control" or "influence" and hence as a concept coordinate with yet distinct from, say, coercion or persuasion through rational argument. From this perspective, then, an account of the nature of authority must be cast in the form of

---

[5] As examples of this view, consider Hobbes, *Leviathan,* Spinoza, *Theologico-Political Treatise,* ch. 16ff., and Mill, *On Liberty* in connection with Utilitarianism, ch. 5.

[6] There has been almost no discussion of authority over beliefs in contemporary philosophy. One illuminating exception is E. Anscombe, "Authority in Morals," in John M. Todd (ed.), *Problems of Authority* (Baltimore, 1962), 179–188. I will return to the iscussion of the distinction between being "in authority" and being "an authority" in the last three sections of this paper.

an exploration of the relationship between authority and the other notions forming this network of influence-terms, and the main task of analysis thus becomes that of exhibiting the distinctive type of influence involved in the idea of authority.[7]

In keeping with this general program of analysis, the dominant approach to authority in contemporary social science has been to construe authority in terms of the notion of "legitimacy" and, accordingly, to define authority as "power that is legitimized."[8] Here again, what has been at issue is the use of "authority" to help come to terms with political and social cohesion. For modern social science has been especially concerned with the maintenance of cohesion not simply by force, but by the sense of "legitimacy" attached to power, and this has led to the development of the view of authority as "legitimate power" or, as Weber put it in initiating this development, the "legitimate use of physical force" or even "legitimate violence."[9] Given this approach, it is not surprising to be told that, "The principal analytical problem is to clarify the relationship between political authority and coercion."[10]

To forestall confusion over the relation between the concepts of authority and coercive power that might be introduced into my discussion of authority by the dominance of the Weberian approach in modern social science, it is necessary to observe a familiar distinction between two uses of the word "authority" in everyday political discourse. For there is still another distinction embedded in the notion of a person's having authority, besides that between being "in authority" and being "an authority." In the first place, when we state that a particular person has authority, we often mean that he has the right, or is entitled, to issue commands, make decisions, enforce obedience, etc. This is to use the word "authority" in the *de jure* sense, and it presupposes some sort of legal conventions, system of rules, or method of entitlement, whereby it may be determined who shall have this particular right. It is in this sense that Justice Frankfurter, for example, used the term "authority" when he denied that the presidency had the right to seize the steel industry: "Absence of authority in the president to deal with a crisis does not imply want of power in government." Hobbes was defining authority in

---

[7] This is the approach to authority taken by a wide variety of contemporary political philosophers and social scientists. In this connection, compare, for example, R. S. Peters, "Authority," in Anthony Quinton (ed.), *Political Philosophy* (Oxford, 1967) and Hannah Arendt, *On Violence* (New York, 1969), pp. 43–47 with Robert Dahl, "Power," *International Encyclopedia of the Social Sciences,* Vol. 12, pp. 405–415 and Dorwin Cartwright, "Influence, Leadership, Control," in James March (ed.), *Handbook of Organizations* (New York, 1965). As different as all these writers may be in other respects, they all share the assumption that authority can only be understood by differentiation from other influence terms. Most of the differences between these writers have to do with the relationship between authority and coercive power. I should add that there is no single agreed-on name for the entire class of concepts in question: "power." (Dahl, *op. cit.*) and "social control" (H. L. A. Hart, *The Concept of Law* [Oxford, 1961]) are often used, but it seems to me that "influence" is perhaps less likely to mislead because it does not as readily suggest coercion and hence the deprivation of liberty.

[8] G. A. Theodorson and A. G. Theodorson, *A Modern Dictionary of Sociology* (New York, 1969), p. 21. Cf. Dorwin Cartwright, *op. cit.,* p. 150.

[9] Max Weber, *The Theory of Social and Economic Organization,* trans. Talcott Parsons (New York, 1947), p. 154, and "Politics as a Vocation" in Gerth and Mills (eds.), *From Max Weber* (New York, 1958), p. 78.

[10] C. W. Cassinelli, "Political Authority: Its Exercise and Possession," *Western Political Quarterly,* XIV (Sept. 1961), pp. 635–646, 637.

this *de jure* sense when he said in a famous passage of *Leviathan*: ". . . and as the right of possession, is called dominion; so the right of doing any action is called AUTHORITY. So that by authority, is always understood a right of doing any act; and *done by authority*, done by commission, or license, from him whose right it is."[11] "Authority" used in this fashion characteristically forms part of a judgment, and it is a judgment passed on the *source* of a man's claim to act (or to speak), not on the *content* of his action. Thus, to concede or to deny that some particular person has the authority to perform some action is not precisely to approve or to disapprove of that action itself, but rather to affirm or reject his warrant (his "authorization") to be the one entitled to do such a thing.

However, in the second place, the statement that a person has authority is also used in a *de facto* sense, to indicate that that person is quite capable of eliciting a distinctive kind of obedience, allegiance, or belief, involving (let us say roughly and provisionally) deference or respect or trust. Here the term "authority" is being used to call attention to the peculiar type of influence or control or sway that one person does in fact exert over others, and the term "authority" thus serves the purpose of distinguishing that mode of influence from such other modes of procuring compliance as the threat of punishment or the offer of reward. However, this particular type of influence is not identical with authority in the *de jure* sense, nor is it even necessarily the consequence of the recognition of that authority. Thus, a man may receive deference from others because they recognize and respect his legal right to govern or instead because of his "personal" qualities. So James Mill wrote to Brougham, "You already hold such a station in the minds of men, that office can add nothing to your dignity." And de Gaulle, it was said, had *de facto* authority in the Fifth Republic partly because his *de jure* authority was acknowledged and respected and partly because he was a man *of* authority able to stimulate deference on his own account. (This is, of course, part of the point Weber is making when he contrasts charismatic authority with legal-rational authority.)

Now it should be noticed that to say that a person has authority in the *de jure* sense of the right to rule does not imply that his will is necessarily effective, nor even if it is, why it is. To be more specific, the fact that a person has the right to rule does not mean that those under his jurisdiction acknowledge his title to ascendancy over them, so that his commands may be either ignored (in which case he lacks influence of any sort) or else obeyed, but out of fear, prudence, hope of reward, etc. (in which case he lacks authority in the *de facto* sense).[12] Likewise, a person who holds a position which entitles him to use force to secure compliance with his decisions may be obeyed because he is recognized to be entitled to command or for the very different reason that he exercises the force he rightfully possesses. That a person possesses the authority to use force does not alter the fact that if he does use force to exact obedience, his subjects are not then obeying him out of respect for his authority. That force is rightfully or lawfully exercised does not alter the cause of obedience, though it may *justify* the use of coercion.

Essentially the same point may be made about the notion of legitimate power.

[11] *Leviathan*, ch. XVI (Oakeshott ed., pp. 105–106). Cf. *Luke*, 20, 2 (King James): "Tell us, by what authority doest thou these things? or who is he that gave thee this authority?"

[12] On this matter, see the useful discussions of Anthony de Crespigny, "Power and Its Forms," *Political Studies* (1968), pp. 192–205; D. D. Raphael, *Problems of Political Philosophy* (London, 1970), pp. 66–75; John Day, "Authority," *Political Studies* (1963), pp. 257–271.

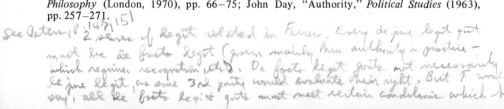

For the use of that notion exhibits an ambiguity parallel to the one already pointed out in the use of the term "authority." Thus, to introduce the idea of legitimate power as a way of explaining the fact the X obeys Y sometimes means that X obeys because he regards Y as legitimately in command; but at other times it means that X gets Y to obey by exercising coercive power although the use of coercion is regarded as legitimate (by X himself or by some third party).[13] In the first case, obedience is voluntary, and the term "legitimacy" serves the function of pointing to the reason why the subject obeys; in the second case, obedience is compelled, and the term "legitimacy" serves the very different function of pointing to the fact that the use of compulsion is regarded with approval. Thus, the term "legitimate power" sometimes serves to point to the operation of a type of influence distinct from coercion, sometimes to the fact that it is precisely coercive influence that is operating, though with the approval of at least some of the people involved.

The basic difficulty here is that the word "authority" is, or has come to be (confusingly), used in ordinary political discourse to mark a pair of quite different distinctions. First, it is used to distinguish between the legitimate and illegitimate use of coercion. Second, it is used to distinguish between coerced obedience (whether legitimately imposed or not) and noncoerced deferential obedience. Take, for example, the statement that, "the authority of the government has broken down." This may mean that respect, trust, deference for the government has collapsed, although people may still be obeying as a result of fear of punishment, self-interest, bargaining, apathy, cynical resignation, etc. Or it may mean that those "in authority," who are legally entitled to maintain order, cannot do so, even by the exercise of force and the threat of punishment. Thus, the word "authority" is used both to refer to the rightful use of force in order to procure obedience and to characterize a particular mode of submission or subordination that excludes compulsion. The criterion for the correct application of the term "authority" in the first case is the legal status of the person who uses force, and the legal standing of his actions (e.g., whether or not they are *ultra vires*); whereas, in the second case, the criterion is the type of allegiance accorded rulers by their subjects. Depending, then, on which sense of the word "authority" is employed, it can be correct usage either to affirm or to deny that authority is exhibited in one and the same activity of compelling obedience. The point, then, is not that it is somehow improper to use the word "authority" to mean "legitimate power" or "legitimate use of force," but rather that it is essential to distinguish between the two very different explanations of why people obey that are embedded confusingly in our current terminology.

3. Authority, Reason, and the "Surrender of Private Judgment"

The preceding section was not intended to suggest that the general program of analyzing authority as a distinctive mode of influence was itself necessarily misguided. In fact, the word "authority" is frequently used to point to a special kind of influence that some persons exert over others in contrast to other kinds of influence; and, on this score, I believe a useful point of departure for further analysis may be found in a position adopted by several recent writers on authority.

[13] Cf. Terry Nardin, *Violence and the State: A Critique of Empirical Political Theory*, Sage Professional Papers in Comparative Politics (Beverly Hills, Calif., 1971), pp. 38–40.

believe essential for de jure legit as well.

R. S. Peters writes,

> Maybe the term "authority" is necessary for describing those situations where conformity is brought about *without* recourse to force, bribes, incentives or propaganda and *without* a lot of argument and discussion. . . . we describe such situations by saying that an order is obeyed or a decision is accepted *simply because X* gave it or made it. . . . The use of authority, in other words, is a manner of regulating human behaviour which is an intermediary between moral argument and the use of force. . . . The main function of the term "authority" in the analysis of a social situation is to stress . . . ways of regulating behaviour by certain types of utterance in contrast to the other ways of regulating behaviour.[14]

Hannah Arendt states that,

> If authority is to be defined at all, then, it must be in contradistinction to both coercion by force and persuasion through argument.

And elsewhere she goes on to supply the following vivid example:

> Its hallmark is unquestioning recognition by those who are asked to obey; neither coercion nor persuasion is needed. (A father can lose his authority either by beating his child or by starting to argue with him, that is, either by behaving to him like a tyrant or by treating him as an equal.)[15]

On this view, authority is distinguished from coercion as a mode of influence because it involves some sort of "recognition" on the part of the subject that the person to whom he submits is "entitled" to obedience and it is distinguished from persuasion in that obedience is not procured by "argument." Now this view seems to me correct as far as it goes, but susceptible of further development and explication; and to bring out most sharply what is involved in this approach to authority, it is necessary, first of all, to reintroduce an idea that had traditionally been regarded as absolutely central to the understanding of authority by political philosophers. This is what used to be called "deference" or (better) the "surrender of private judgment" or "individual judgment" in discussions of authority up until quite recently. To take a single example, the following passage from Mill's essay on Tocqueville provides an exemplary statement of this understanding of authority.

> The Americans, according to M. de Tocqueville . . . carry into practice the habit of mind which has been so often inculcated as the one sufficient security against mental slavery — the rejection of authority, and the assertion of the right of private judgement. . . . They are not accustomed to look for guidance either to the wisdom of ancestors, or to eminent contemporary wisdom, but require that the grounds on which they act shall be made level to their own comprehension."[16]

[14] "Authority," *op cit.*, p. 92. See also Peters, *Authority, Responsibility and Education* (New York, 1960), p. 15.

[15] "What Is Authority?" *op. cit.*, p. 93, and *On Violence, op. cit.*, p. 45. For this same approach, see also Anthony de Crespigny, "Power and Its Forms," *op. cit.*; R. F. Khan, "A Note on the Concept of Authority," in G. Wijeyawardene (ed.), *Leadership and Authority* (Singapore, 1968).

[16] "Tocqueville on Democracy in America, Vol. II (1840) in Gertrude Himmelfarb (ed.) *Essays on Politics and Culture* (Garden City, N.Y., 1963), p. 241. Mill is here talking about authority over belief, but the general point applies also to authority over action, as argued below. Compare Tocqueville's own discussion of authority in the opening chapters of Vol. II: this discussion is conducted in terms of the "philosophical method of the Americans" which is "to submit to the private judgement of each man all the objects of his belief."

The idea being conveyed by such notions as the surrender of private judgment or individual judgment is that in obeying, say, a command simply because it comes from someone accorded the right to rule, the subject does not make his obedience *conditional* on his own personal examination and evaluation of the thing he is being asked to do. Rather, he accepts as a sufficient reason for following a prescription the fact that it is prescribed by someone acknowledged by him as entitled to rule. The man who accepts authority is thus said to surrender his private or individual judgment because he does not insist that reasons be given that he can grasp and that satisfy him, as a condition of his obedience. Conversely, to have authority is not to have to offer reasons in behalf of what one has prescribed as a condition of being paid obedience. In this sense, obedience to a command "simply because X gave it" (Peters) entails abdication of one's own judgment as to the particular act in question and the adoption in its place of the judgment of someone else as guiding one's conduct.[17]

This view of authority may be briefly illustrated by considering one especially significant kind of authoritative utterance — a command. What is the difference between a prescription coming from someone acknowledged to have authority and a prescription coming from, say, a friend? If your friend tells you to stop smoking you may well listen to his reasons, think his advice good, and so take it; but there is nothing in this that makes it obligatory. His prescription is a piece of advice; acquiescence is conditional on your own judgment of the contents of the prescription. By contrast, the point of claiming that an imperative comes from authority is to put a person under an obligation to obey it, and what this involves is that the subject is supposed to obey it apart from his own opinion of its merits. The point of claiming that a prescription comes from authority is to waive the requirement of justifying it, as a condition of is being something that ought to be followed, and instead to offer as sufficient "reason" for following the prescription the fact that it comes from a certain person. Hobbes draws the distinction between command and advice as follows:

> ... counsel is a precept, in which the reason of my obeying it is taken from the thing itself which is advised; but command is a precept, in which the cause of my obedience depends on the will of the commander. For it is not properly said.... I command, except the will stands for reason. Now when obedience is yielded to the laws, not for the thing itself, but by reason of the advisor's will, the law is not a counsel but a command. ...[18]

This quote from Hobbes brings out the basic difference between command and counsel upon which the element of authority involved in a command depends for its distinctive meaning. In the case of advice or counsel, the "reason" for going along with the prescription depends on the content of the prescription. To explain why one did an act advised by another person is to show one's reasons for doing *this* particular act rather than some other act. One's explanation remains at the level

---

[17] I believe this analysis is what underpins the view, to be found among many political thinkers, that to be under the sway of authority is to be (literally) unself-determined, because guided by another self in the manner indicated. (On the sense in which authority involves lack of self-guidance, see also sections 5 and 6 below.) This is one sense in which freedom and authority have been thought to be opposed: note Mill's use of the imagery of "mental slavery" to bring home not his own view, but that of the Americans. Note also the parallel between authority and coercion in that both involve "reasons" for doing an act extraneous to a direct personal assessment of the merits of the act itself.

[18] *De Cive*, 14, 1. Cf. *The Elements of Law*, I, 13, 6 and II, 10, 4.

of the action itself. But a command carries weight not because of what is said, but because of the fact that what is said is an order given by a particular person. To explain why one did the act is to show that one falls under the jurisdiction of the person who prescribed it at least as regards the act in question, and if that explanation is challenged, then the next step in explanation is to show the importance of submitting to his authority. But in either case, and however far one's explanation goes, the explanation does not take place on the level of the particular act itself: the point of this conception of authority is precisely to bypass the action itself in giving "reasons" for doing it. The "reason" for doing the act is thus transferred from the "thing itself" to the "will" of the person who prescribes the act so that, as Hobbes put it, the "will stands for the reason"; and this in turn makes it possible for the person who submits to authority to abdicate his own judgment of the merits of the prescription as a condition of obedience. What is therefore essential to the concept of an authoritative command is the opening up of a distinction between the person who prescribes and what he prescribes, so that the content of the prescription becomes irrelevant, and the person becomes the factor that endows the prescription with its distinctive appeal.

At this point, the question arises whether the command is to be taken as the model for all types of authoritative utterance. In particular, what about the case of believing someone who is an "authority"? Is the command-obedience relationship to be taken as the model for understanding the relationship between the believer and the authority he believes? Now far from denying that there are crucial differences between authority over belief and authority over conduct, I shall in fact lay a great deal of stress on the differences. Indeed, the distinction between these two forms of authority seems to me absolutely critical for understanding political authority, and I shall take up this matter further on. Nevertheless, it seems to me that both forms of authority share in common the feature so far emphasized in this discussion, namely, the surrender of private judgment. In the case of a command obeyed on authority, the subject complies without making his conduct dependent on his own judgment of the act commanded. When a person accepts a belief on authority, he is to be understood to be abdicating his own judgment as to the basis of the belief, i.e., the grounds on which it is supposed to rest, out of deference to the judgment of someone else. In his *Essay on the Influence of Authority in Matters of Opinion* (1849), G. C. Lewis supplies the following useful definition:

> When any one forms an opinion on a question either of speculation of practice, without any appropriate process of reasoning really or apparently leading to that conclusion, and without compulsion or inducement of interest, but simply because some other persons, whom he believes to be competent judges on the matter, entertain that opinion, he is said to have formed his opinion on authority.... The principle of authority ... (is) the principle of adopting the belief of others, on a matter of opinion without reference to the particular grounds on which that belief may rest.[19]

In authoritative belief, then, the same two features reappear once again as paramount: on the one hand, it is some particular person rather than his utterance itself that determines assent; on the other hand, the subject does not make his

---

[19] George Cornewall Lewis, *An Essay on the Influence of Authority in Matters of Opinion* (London, 1849), pp. 6–7. Note again the division of influence into basically three types – authority, rational argument, and coercion.

immutable

assent conditional on his own private judgment of the proposal. This analysis is scarcely new. Aquinas says, in discussing authoritative belief, that the "decisive factor is who it is whose statement is assented to; by comparison the subject matter which is assented to is in a certain sense secondary."[20]

To defer to authority, then, is to refrain from insisting on a personal examination and acceptance of the thing one is being asked to do (or to believe) as a necessary condition of doing it (or believing it). And what I am claiming, therefore, is that we have to see the notion of authority in connection with the idea of a very special sort of reason for action (or belief). To cite authority as a reason for doing an act (or believing an opinion) is to put a stop to the demand for reasons at the level of the act itself, and to transfer one's reason to another person's "will" or judgment. From this standpoint, then, it is the contrast between authority and persuasion through rational argument (rather than the contrast between authority and coercive power) that is essential to the delineation of the distinctive kind of dependence on the will or the judgment of another person involved in an authority relationship. That is, the crucial contrast is between the case in which one man influences another to adopt some course of action by helping him to see the merits of that particular action and the case in which no reasons have to be given to a person to gain his compliance with a prescription because he "accepts" the person who prescribes it. In what we might conceive as the pure or ideal case of persuasion through rational argument, only the substance of the argument matters. Who the speaker is – his social status, position, office, or "personality" – is in principle strictly irrelevant to the agent's reasons for adopting the action. In an authority relation, by contrast, it is precisely the status of the speaker which is decisive. We might think of it in this way. To the extent to which the social identity or "personality" of the individual who prescribes an act becomes incidental to the reason for complying with it, the relationship between the parties moves away from the case of authoritative influence; to the extent to which the content of the prescription becomes incidental, the relationship moves away from the case of persuasion through rational argument. Kierkegaard brings out the central point succinctly: "To ask whether the king is a genius, with the implication that in such a case he is to be obeyed, is really *lèse majesté*, for the question contains a doubt concerning subjection to authority."[21]

4. The "Mark" of Authority

The authority relation, however, has another dimension besides that special and distinctive kind of dependence on the will or judgment of another so well conveyed by the notion of a "surrender of private judgment." It also involves a certain kind of "recognition" that the person to whom one defers is entitled to this sort of submission. In the vocabulary of discourse about authority, a number of different terms are used on this score, such as "recognition," "acceptance," and "acknowledgment"; and in contemporary social science it has become a stock practice to speak

[20] *Summa Theologica,* Second Part of the Second Part, II, i. Cf. Newman: "it is not a direct assent to the proposition, still it *is* an assent to the authority which enunciates it." *The Grammar of Assent* (Garden City, N.Y., 1955), p. 53.

[21] Soren Kierkegaard, *On Authority and Revelation The Book on Adler* (Princeton, 1955), p. 113. Cf. "Of the Difference Between a Genius and an Apostle" in Walter Kaufmann (ed.), *The Present Age* (New York, 1962), p. 100.

of the "belief" in the "legitimacy" of the person accorded authority, a phrase intended to express the so-called subjective element of opinion that goes along with the "objective" element of "behavior" to make up the authority relation. This "subjective" element of "belief" or "recognition" has been the subject of a good deal of analysis and classification; and it has proved easy to become confused about it. In a recent discussion of authority, it has been contended that:

> Authority . . . always implies a belief as to right; and we need to add that this belief may be either one in the correctness of someone's view on a matter of fact or theory or, alternatively, one in the correctness of someone's practical judgement or advice. Any account of authority must cover both kinds of case and it seems to me that this can only be done by bringing out the general dependence of the concept on beliefs as to right in general.[22]

The difficulty with this view is that it obscures the distinction between two quite distinct types of belief involved in the authority relation — the belief that a person is entitled to rule and the belief in the correctness of his commands or utterances. To confound these two beliefs is to fail to recognize that belief can enter into the authority relation at two distinct points and can be directed on two distinct objects, the source of the authoritative utterance and the content.[23] But, furthermore, the failure to distinguish these two beliefs tends to obscure the more serious problem as to whether every form of authority must involve belief in the correctness of the utterances of authority: in section 7 of this paper, the argument will be made that it is a definitive feature of the commands of someone "in authority" to be dissociated from any claim to belief in their correctness, as contrasted with the claim merely to external conformity.

To bring out the precise character and role played by the element of "recognition" or "belief" that a person is entitled to rule (or to speak) within the authority relation, it is necessary to observe that that relationship must possess another feature in addition to the element of deference or "surrender of private judgment" so far stressed. And this is that there must be some public way of identifying the person whose utterances are to be taken as authoritative. In legal systems, this is often explicitly provided for by formal conventions or what H. L. A. Hart calls "rules of recognition." But the point I wish to make is that some public way of identifying authority is a *logical* requirement of deferential obedience wherever it is to be found in society. I can explain what I mean as follows. Since in an authority relationship a command is obeyed, a pronouncement accepted, etc., on account of who it comes from, rather than as a result of an evaluation of its merits, there must be some way of identifying the person who has authority apart from an evaluation of his utterances. For if there is no way of telling whether an utterance is authoritative, except by evaluating its contents to see whether it deserves to be accepted in its own right, then the distinction between an authoritative utterance and advice or rational persuasion will have collapsed. The appeal of the utterance will lie in such rationality as it may be seen to possess in its own right, rather than in its derivation from some particular person. In that event,

---

[22] David R. Bell, "Authority" in G. N. A. Vesey (ed.), *The Proper Study*, Royal Institute of Philosophy Lectures, Vol. 3 (London, 1971), p. 197.

[23] On the two sorts of belief in relation to authority, see the long discussion by Hobbes of the idea "that in belief are two opinions; one of the saying of the man; the other of his virtue." *Leviathan,* ch. 7 (Oakeshott [ed.], pp. 41–42).

the subject's reason for accepting the utterance may well be more secure, but his confidence will now be placed in his own independent judgment of the merits of the utterance. What is therefore essential to an authority relationship is a distinction between statement and speaker such that the latter can endow the former with its appeal. And for this, the speaker must be capable of somehow being known as "having authority" apart from a personal assessment of the merits of his utterances. So there must be some way of identifying authority that is independent of the act of inspecting his proposals in their own right.

In an interesting paper on authority, the social psychologist Milton Rokeach states that:

> . . . every communication received from an external authority source contains two kinds of information. It contains information of a substantive nature and it contains information about the authority source itself. Substantive information is typically obtained from the sheer content of the message. The prestige aspects of the source are obtained from the expressive and evaluative aspects of the message.[24]

What I am arguing is that these two elements of an authoritative communication are not a contingent, empirical feature of the authority relationship, but rather part of the very meaning of the concept of authority. It is essential that an authoritative communication transmit both the substantive proposal the subject is supposed to follow and information about the communicator himself by virtue of which he can somehow be identified as entitled to speak. In the absence of some means of identifying authority apart from an assessment of the content of his commands, the notion of authority would be dissipated, being reduced to a kind of advice which could only be accepted or rejected on the basis of a judgment of its merits.

Now, historically, this means of identification was usually called the "mark" of authority. (Alternatively it was referred to as the "sign," "symbol," "certificate," or "credentials" of authority.) As Hobbes put it, there must be "marks, whereby a man may discern in what man, or assembly of men, the sovereign power is placed and resideth."[25] Or, in Bentham's words, there must be a "common signal . . . notorious and visible to all."[26] Of course, many different things have been viewed by human beings as "marks" of authority: office, social station, property, "great" power, pedigree, religious claims, "miracles" (Augustine[27]), etc. In formal legal systems, there are often explicit rules or conventions defining the conditions that must be satisfied in order for the declarations of a man or body of men to count as authoritative. But throughout social life there are less explicitly formulated but nonetheless established marks of authority, such as Bagehot's "wealth and rank,"

---

[24] "Authority, Authoritarianism, and Conformity," in Irwin A. Berg and Bernard M. Bass (eds.), *Conformity and Deviation* (New York, 1961), p. 235.

[25] *Leviathan,* ch. 18 (Oakeshott [ed.], p. 118). Cf. "Nor is it enough the law be written, and published; but also that there be manifest signs, that it proceedeth from the will of the sovereign. For private men, when they have, or think they have force enough to secure their unjust designs, and convey them safely to their ambitious ends, may publish for laws what they please, without, or against the legislative authority. There is therefore requisite, not only a declaration of the law, but also sufficient signs of the author and authority. The author, or legislator is supposed in every commonwealth to be evident. . ." (ch. 26, p. 178).

[26] Wilfrid Harrison (ed.), *A Fragment on Government* (Oxford, 1960), p. 99.

[27] *City of God,* XXII, 8.

"tradition and custom" which, according to the author of *The English Constitution*, did in fact identify authority and "excite reverence" in nineteenth-century England.[28] The "mark" of authority may then be understood as the criteria that men do in fact accept as designating who is to have authority, that is, whose judgment is to be deferred to.

The concept of authority can thus have an application only within the context of certain socially accepted criteria which serve to identify the person(s) whose utterances are to count as authoritative. For it is logically possible for a man to take as his "reason" for doing an act the fact that it was prescribed by another person, bypassing the question of the merits of the act itself, only if the person who prescribes is somehow "recognized" as entitled to this sort of ascendancy. The act of deferring to authority contains as an essential part of its meaning for the actor, a recognition of what went before as an order issued by some particular person. From this perspective, then, the authority relation may be depicted as a complex structure consisting to two tiers: at the first level, there is the special kind of influence one person is exerting over another person, at the second level, there is the recognition and acceptance of certain criteria for designating who is to possess this kind of influence.[29] But now it may be noticed that this analysis has a direct bearing on the widespread view of authority as an "influence" concept. For it follows that to use the concept of authority to explain the influence one man has over another always implies that there exists between those persons something more than that the one is "influencing" the other. It implies that there exists some mutually recognized normative relationship giving the one the right to command or speak and the other the duty to obey. Authority thus involves a form of influence that can only be exercised from within a certain kind of normative arrangement accepted by both parties. Therefore to explain how one man can exercise authoritative influence over another always calls for an explanation of the existence (acceptance) of the arrangement within which the parties conceive themselves to be embraced. However, this does not necessarily imply that this arrangement itself exists because of the exercise of influence by the authority over his subject. We should not jump to the conclusion that because the exercise of authority is the exercise of influence, it follows that the structure within which this kind of influence can alone be exercised itself exists (i.e., is accepted) because of the exercise of influence. It is this consideration that calls into question the attempt in so much contemporary political science to construe authority relations on the model of individualist-power relations which are wholly reducible without remainder to a matter of influence, that is, reducible to the capacity of some individuals to work their wills over other individuals.[30]

[28] *The English Constitution* (London, 1928), pp. 238–239, 6–7.

[29] The authority relation is a two-tiered structure, and this is what makes it possible to conceive the activity of "civil disobedience" (or "conscientious objection") as an activity in which disobedience to a particular law is joined together with some sort of sign on the part of the disobedient person that he does not mean his disobedience to imply a repudiation of the authority whose law it is. This particular notion of civil disobedience at any rate is logically dependent on the structure of the concept of authority, and it is because of this dependence that it has come to seem plausible to maintain that it is not even a necessary condition of the existence (acceptance) of an authority relation for there to be compliance in every instance.

[30] It will be readily recognized that there are a number of interlocking issues here, through which political philosophy tends to get entangled with problems now taken up in "philosophy of social science." First, it is at this point that the analysis of authority becomes bound up with the controversy over "methodological individualism," viz., whether (in this case) the kinds of

5. "Traditional Authority"

In this discussion I have laid a great deal of stress on the notion of a surrender of private judgment. But this key idea covers several possibilities which now call for discrimination.

In the first place, many writers on authority speak indiscriminately of "unthinking submission" (Bergson),, "unquestioning recognition" (Arendt), "uncritical acceptance," and the like.[31] And indeed the notion of authority is often popularly associated with the idea of "blind obedience." It should therefore be made clear that the notion of a surrender of private judgment covers two separate possibilities. For there is a difference between the case in which a person submits to authoritative utterances without evaluating them at all because he automatically concedes them an unchallengeable normative validity and the case in which a person does judge, but submits anyway, irrespective of his own judgment. In the former case, what is surrendered is judgment itself: the subject does not judge but simply obeys. In the latter case, what is suspended is not judgment but choice: the subject desists from acting on his own judgment, even though he may "privately" dissent from the authoritative utterance. Here the authority relationship is characterized by what Oakeshott, in discussing Hobbes, calls the "will not to will."

Now it should be observed that this same distinction does *not* apply to authority over beliefs. For it seems contradictory to speak of a person believing some opinion on authority irrespective of his own judgment of its validity or regardless of the fact that he dissents from that opinion. Belief on authority calls for internal assent, whereas the notion of acting in conformity to the commands of authority allows for the dissociation of thought and action. It is necessary, then, to recognize that the authority relationship can involve different sorts of submission which should not all be lumped together under the category of "blind obedience," although the key issue for political philosophy in this respect has been whether it is necessary for specifically political authority to claim unquestioning obedience and internal assent, or only external conformity. Both Hobbes and Spinoza, for example, were deeply concerned with this issue, and they were able to arrive at the conclusion that political authority need not require internal assent only as a result of a comprehensive critique and reconstruction of received views of political authority in which the element of authoritative belief had remained central.[32]

---

explanation we are able to give to account for the existence (or dissolution) of authority structures are or can be couched wholly in terms of individualist influence concepts, such as force. Secondly, there is the controversy over the character of explanation in social science, in this case, whether explanation in terms of "causes" or "meaning" is possible or appropriate as to the existence/acceptance of authority structures. Cf. Peter Winch: "Authority is not a sort of influence. It is not a kind of *causal* relation between individual wills but an *internal* relation." "Authority" in Quinton (ed.), *Political Philosophy, op. cit.,* p. 98.

[31] Henri Bergson, *The Two Sources of Morality and Religion* (Garden City, N.Y., 1956), pp. 9–26; Hannah Arendt, *On Violence, op. cit.,* p. 45; Compare David Easton's definition of authority: "if A sends a message to B and B adopts this message as the basis of his own behavior without evaluating it in terms of his own standards of what is desirable under the circumstances, we can say that A has exercised *authority* over B." "The Perception of Authority and Political Change," in Carl J. Friedrich (ed.), *Authority,* Nomos I (Cambridge, Mass., 1958), p. 179.

[32] Some facets of this achievement are suggested below in Sections 7 and 8. Hobbes says "by the captivity of our understanding is not meant a submission of the intellectual faculty to the opinion of any other man; but of the will to obedience, where obedience is due." *Leviathan,* ch. 32 (Oakeshott [ed.], p. 243). See also Hobbes, *Elements of Law,* II, 6, 3 and Spinoza, *Theologico-Political Treatise,* ch. 20.

These remarks point to a form of authority that has been the subject of prolonged inquiry in political philosophy. So far, the authority relationship has been specified as a relation in which the subject *refrains* from demanding a satisfactory justification of the proposal he is being asked to accept, as a condition of his acceptance. Authority thus involves the absence of justification (at the level of the particular action or belief in question). But the point is that justification may be absent not because the subject desists from demanding one, but because it does not occur to him that he is capable of evaluating the demands authority makes on him. That is, he may not conceive the possibility that he could stand back from the established ways of society and make up his own mind whether or not those ways are deserving of his allegiance. The grip that the established authority structure has over a person's mind may be so complete that it does not occur to him that that structure could be judged in the light of any standards external to it, e.g., natural rights. The authority relationship will then be characterized not by the deliberate abstention from acting on one's own judgment, but by the absence of the recognition that one has the capacity to judge. From this perspective, then, the point is not that "private judgment" or "individual judgment" is surrendered or suppressed, but that it has not appeared because the experience in which it can gain a foothold has not appeared, viz., the recognition of alternatives and the experience of tension and conflict between established practices and independent moral standards. It is in this sense that Hegel speaks of a certain "objective" or preautonomous stage of human consciousness in which men are unaware of their own capacity for moral judgment and choice, and unquestioningly concede to established social arrangements an unconditional validity to which they are not conscious of making any contributions of their own.[33] Again, it is in this sense that Mill, in the opening pages of *On Liberty*, speaks of a "customary" or "traditional" morality in which "The rules which obtain among themselves appear to them self-evident and self-justifying ... because the subject is one on which it is not generally considered necessary that reasons should be given either by one person to others or by each to himself."[34] Here, then, roughly, is a type of authority in which justification is absent for a very different reason than that men somehow recognize the point in certain circumstances of deliberately abstaining from requiring a justification acceptable to them.

I think it is undeniable that something like this conception of "traditional" authority has always been of central concern to political philosophy. It has been especially important to those political philosophers who have set their treatments of authority within the context of the decay of traditional beliefs and the rise of a self-conscious mode of morality to fill the vacuum. Nevertheless, I shall not discuss this type of authority any further in this paper.[35] It raises difficult and intricate questions that require extended treatment in their own right. I have mentioned it

[33] For a most illuminating discussion of this side of Hegel's thought, see Frederick A. Olafson, *Principles and Persons an Ethical Interpretation of Existentialism* (Baltimore, 1967), ch. III, from which the above formulation of Hegel's view is taken.

[34] *On Liberty* (London, 1910), p. 69. On certain aspects of this notion in Mill's thought, see my article "A New Exploration of Mill's Essay *On Liberty*," *Political Studies*, XIV (October, 1966), pp. 281–304.

[35] Especially instructive materials for thinking about this aspect of authority are provided by studies of the dissolution of systems of authoritative belief; see, for example, the discussions of the erosion of "traditional" authority in eighteenth-century Europe by Klaus Epstein, *The Genesis of German Conservatism* (Princeton, 1966) and Bernard Groethuysen, *The Bourgeois*

only in order to clarify the preceding account of authority and to point to a topic that would have to be developed in any comprehensive examination of authority.

6. Authority and "Auctoritas"

one of meanings of legit

Recently a number of political philosophers working on the topic of authority have devoted a considerable amount of attention to the Latin origins of the term "authority." Indeed, Peters speaks of "auctoritas as the key to authority," a view expressed in several other recent discussions of authority.[36] It is worth pausing briefly at this juncture to consider this matter as it bears on the view of authority being developed in this paper.

The word "authority" and its cognates, such as "authorize," "author," "authentic," stem from the Latin "auctoritas" and "auctor."[37] "Auctoritas" was the legal term for a surety in a transaction, the testimony of a witness or the means for the verification of some fact, e.g., a document. It apparently then came to mean the respect or dignity or weight attached to the person or document involved; and later yet, the Roman Senate was said to have the "authority" to be heard, though not the "power" to govern which was held by the "people." The word "auctor" apparently derives from the lost verb "augere": to augment, increase, enrich, tell about. An "auctor" was "he that brings about the existence of any object, or promotes the increase or prosperity of it, whether he first originates it, or by his efforts gives greater permanence or continuance to it," and thus according to the different objects brought about or augmented, an auctor could be, on the one hand, a creator, inventor, producer, founder, etc., or on the other hand, the "author of a writing, a writer . . . in general one that gives an account of something, a narrator, reporter, informant."[38] The Latin "auctor" thus points to both senses of the English "author": (1) a writer and (2) an actor in the sense of the person responsible for an action or for starting a line of action. Now, in this connection, what has been selected for emphasis in contemporary philosophical discussions of authority, that look back to the Roman notion of an "auctor" for insight into our idea of authority, is the notion of an "auctor" in the second sense of an actor who originates, begins, founds, etc. From this perspective, a person with authority has been understood to be someone to whom a decision or opinion can be traced back as the source of that decision or opinion or else as someone who carries forward into the present, continues or "augments" some foundling act or line of action started in the past. However, it is equally important not to ignore the notion of an

---

Catholicism vs. Capitalism in Eighteenth-Century France (New York, 1968) and the discussion of the "way of authority" in the "intellectual crisis of the reformation" by Richard H. Popkin, *The History of Scepticism from Erasmus to Descartes* (New York, revised edition, 1968).

[36] Peters, "Authority," *op. cit.*, p. 85. See also C. J. Friedrich, "Authority, Reason, and Discretion," in Friedrich (ed.), *Authority*, Nomos I (Cambridge, Mass., 1958), pp. 29–31; Arendt, "What Is Authority?" *op. cit.*, pp. 120–128; Schaar, "Reflections on Authority," *op. cit.*, p. 55.

[37] In the following discussion I have relied on C. T. Lewis and C. Short, *A Latin Dictionary* (Oxford, 1966); Henry Nettleship, *Contributions to Latin Lexicography* (Oxford, 1889); J. P. V. D. Balsdon, "Auctoritas, Dignitas, Otium," *The Classical Quarterly*, X (May, 1960), pp. 43–50; R. Heinze, "Auctoritas," *Hermes*, LX (1925), 348–366.

[38] Lewis and Short, *op. cit.*

"auctor" in the first sense of a writer, witness, or someone who gives an account of something. The significance of this aspect of an "auctor" for our concept of authority is brought out in the following passage from what is the best discussion of the relation between authority and "auctor" that I have come across. This discussion is by none other than William Gladstone and was part of a prolonged debate over authority in Victorian England started by John Auston's original lectures on jurisprudence (1829). As Gladstone's own contribution to this debate, as well as the debate itself, are almost completely forgotten today, it is especially worth quoting at length from the key passage:

> The proper idea (of "auctor") is that of one who *adds*. In strictness, this must be adding to what existed before, as a witness adds to the thing his testimony about the thing. . . . From this original form the meaning passes on to a gradual creation, the creation of something that receives successive increment . . . the use of the word author for writer is strictly correct, and belongs to the original sense. An "author" comes between us and the facts or ideas, and adds to them a . . . ground of belief, in his own assurance to us respecting them. . . . And hence perhaps we obtain the largest and clearest idea of "authority," as that which comes between us and an object, and in relation to us adds something to the object which is extrinsic to it, which is apart from any examination of it by ourselves, but which forms a motive, of greater or lesser weight as the case may be, for belief or action respectively in their several spheres.[39]

In speaking of the "idea of authority" in this fashion, the examples Gladstone offered were those of an authority in religion in the sense of a witness to some unique historical event or revelation, such that others are in the position of being dependent on his testimony about that occurrence; or a scientific authority whose views must be taken on trust by laymen in so far as they cannot comprehend the reasoning which supports those views. In both cases of authority, there is dependence on the "account" of another person, and it is this special kind of dependence that, on Gladstone's analysis, links our idea of authority to the notion of an "auctor" in the sense of a writer whose "words" or report about some thing others must rely on for their own (vicarious) knowledge of that thing.[40] On Gladstone's scheme, then, an authority is an intermediary between the thing he is an authority on and the persons who accept him as an authority on that thing. He has access to it and they have access of his augmentation of or testimony about that thing. Authority in this sense always involves differentiated access: direct, personal access, on the one hand, and vicarious, mediated access, on the other hand. Authority and author thus share in common the notion of a special type of reliance of one person on another, whereby one person is dependent for his experience or knowledge of some thing upon the account of the person who has direct access to

[39] "On the Influence of Authority in Matters of Opinion," *The Nineteenth Century*, I (March, 1877), pp. 3–4. Among the other participants in the debate were G. C. Lewis, J. F. Stephen, J. S. Mill, and Nasau Senior. On Austin's and Mill's views on authority, see my article, "An Introduction to Mill's Theory of Authority," in J. B. Schneewind (ed.), *Mill: A Collection of Critical Essays,* "Modern Studies in Philosophy" (New York, 1968), pp. 379–425.
[40] Cf. Hooker's definition: "By a man's authority we here understand the force which his word hath for the assurance of another's mind that buildeth upon it. . . . For so it is said in St. John's Gospel, 'Many of the Samaritans of that city believed in him for the saying of the woman, which testified, He hath told me all things that ever I did.' " *Laws of Ecclesiastical Polity*, II, ch. VII, 2.

or knowledge of it. Gladstone's discussion thus brings out the connection between the Roman notion of an "auctor" and the modern concept of authority as involving the surrender of one's own judgment and the adoption in its place of the judgment of someone else.

Now, while the preceding remarks need not be regarded as anything more than a heuristic suggestion for thinking further about authority, they do require qualification in one crucial respect. For the above analysis does not fit all forms of authority, at least in the modern world, but only some. The idea that to have authority is to be *interposed* between something on which one speaks and the persons who accept that speech as credible is retained in our concept of being "an authority." It is above all in the idea of believing an authority that the central element of an intermediary is retained. In the notions of a religious authority or a scientific authority (Gladstone's two examples), there are still preserved the essential element of differentiated access, which makes one person dependent on another for his knowledge or experience of the thing in question. However, not everyone who has authority is said to be "an authority" on something. A person may rather be "in authority," and this notion does not necessarily imply an authoritative interpretation of some antecedent experience, but only an authoritative *decision*. Someone who is "in authority" need not derive his claim to deference from having access to something from which his subject is debarred. Nevertheless, he does claim deference; he does claim obedience that is not conditional on an examination of the merits of his commands – and so a certain residue of the Roman notion of an "auctor" as involving dependence on the "word" of another is still preserved even in the notion of being "in authority."[41]

These brief remarks on the terms "auctoritas" and the contrast they point up between the notions of "in authority" and "an authority" may, then, constitute a preface to what follows.

7. The Concept of Being "in Authority"

I have so far presented the authority relation as a complex structure in which a person desists from demanding a justification of the thing he is being asked to do (or to believe) as a condition of his doing it (or believing it). However, this does not mean that the entire authority relation is incapable of justification. It only means that the form assumed by an argument for authority must possess a special character, and to make a beginning on this matter, I now want to show the importance of distinguishing between the kind of entitlement or justification implied in being "in authority" from that implied in being "an authority" *on* something. These two types of authority, and their respective justifications, should not be confused with one another. Each rests on a different pattern of argument,

[41] Note the difference between an "auctor" as someone who writes or testifies about his experience of something he did not himself create and a modern understanding of an "author" as "creative," *ex nihilo*. Then compare the notion of "auctoritas" as involving "augmentation" of a prior foundation through the continuous handing down of the original accounts of that foundation with, say, Hobbes's notion of a sovereign authority as someone who makes law by "will," against the background of natural chaos. The crux of the change in both cases is the disappearance or elimination of the pre-existing thing which the author or authority does not himself create, but only augments or interprets.

and so far from either one being a necessary condition of the other, they involve conflicting presuppositions.

To begin with, it should be observed that the justification or point of having someone "in authority" is to be discovered by considering the predicament it is designed to remedy. This predicament occurs whenever men cannot agree on what is to be done, so that, to avoid chaos, there must be agreement about who is to decide what is to be done. That is, the predicament occurs whenever there is a situation in which a collection of individuals wish to engage in some common activity requiring a certain degree of coordinated action but they are unable to agree on what the substance of their common behavior should be. And because they cannot agree, it follows that if each insists on following his own views, the common activity will be made impossible. Since the cost of insisting on following one's own judgment is chaos, it may then appear reasonable for each man to sacrifice his own judgment as the basis of (some part of) his behavior and also to forego pressing his own views on all the others, even though he regards his own views as fully justified and their's as mistaken; and instead accept someone to make binding decisions for all, or to establish some procedure, such as election lottery or hereditary lineage, designed to define who is to have the right to make binding decisions upon all. In other words, to a rational man, despairing of agreement at the substantive level, it may appear reasonable to step up to the procedural level in order to reach agreement on who is to be obeyed, on whose utterances are to count as authoritative. However, this move will be reasonable for a man to adopt only on two conditions. First, the coordination of activity achieved by the abandonment of one's own judgment must be more important than the values thereby sacrificed, including the value of being free to pursue one's views and to try to win other men over to them. (For Hobbes and Spinoza, it is the existence of society itself which depends on the acceptance of authority, and since the security provided by a social order is a necessary condition of the freedom to pursue one's values, whatever they may be, it is always a rational sacrifice to accept such an authority.) Second, it must be sufficiently unlikely or even impossible for consensus to be brought about at the substantive level, whereby no one will have to sacrifice his own judgment because each will have come to concur with all the others. If it is held that people really do agree at some deep, unapparent level, and that disagreement is merely a superficial surface phenomenon that can be supplanted by consensus brought about through persuasion, education, or an historical transformation, then the establishment of a system of authority of this sort will have lost its point because the desired coordination of activity can be achieved without the sacrifice of individual judgment. (This is why the criticism of this type of authority in the history of political theory has always taken the form of an argument that there really is underlying consensus among men – whether that consensus is conceived to be "natural," though concealed from men's eyes by corrupt institutions and superstitious beliefs, as in certain strains of eighteenth-century thought, or "social," though obliterated by "individualism," as in certain strains of nineteenth-century thought.)[42]

[42] For the eighteenth-century strain, see, for example, Condorcet, in S. Hampshire (ed.), *Sketch for an Historical Picture of the Progress of the Human Mind* (New York, 1955), pp. 17–18, 50–53, 109, and Paine, *Age of Reason*, ch. 17; for the nineteenth century, *The Doctrine of Saint-Simon*, 1st sess., and Comte, "Plan of the Scientific Operations Necessary For Reorganizing Society" in *System of Positive Polity* (London, 1875–77), Vol. 4, Appendix.

So the point of having someone "in authority" is to be discovered by considering what would happen if each person insisted on making up his own mind as a condition of coordinating his actions with his fellows. From this perspective, the authority relationship will then appear as an elaborate contrivance designed to achieve agreement at the procedural level in the face of disagreement at the substantive level — by defining whose judgment is to count as "public" and whose judgment is to be deemed "private." In this connection, it is worth noting the meaning acquired by the term "private" within the framework of this type of system of authority. "Private judgment" is *not* a judgment exercised on private matters such as family life or business affairs; it is not a privatized or apolitical judgment. It is rather a nonauthoritative judgment, which may be highly political in content but which is nevertheless not entitled to prescribe behavior. Indeed, it is precisely because of the highly contentious public character of human opinions that from the standpoint of this view of authority it becomes necessary to have a public definition of whose judgment is to be designated as merely private. It is therefore a serious though common misunderstanding of this type of system of authority to assume that it presupposes a type of person who restricts himself to a nonpolitical existence: the privatized, apolitical character that has so often been given a central role in nineteenth- and twentieth-century criticisms of "liberalism" constitutes an inversion of the original premises of the individualistic theory of authority.

From this standpoint, then, the basis of the claim to obedience made by a person "in authority" is of a very special kind. This claim does not derive from any special personal characteristics of the person invested with authority, such as superior powers of judgment or special knowledge (as in the case of being "an authority"). His claim to be obeyed is simply that he has been put "in authority" according to established procedure, rather than that his decisions are, on independent grounds, sound, meritorious, or superior decisions. What makes an act obligatory is that it has been declared obligatory by the person invested with authority over that class of actions. (We might well wish to consider the view, therefore, that there is a "performative" element involved in this conception of authority, which is no part of the concept of "an authority."[43]) The merits and demerits of the actual decisions are strictly irrelevant to the "obligation" to obey, and therefore the claim to obedience is not compromised by showing that it is inferior to some other decision that might have been taken. Indeed, the whole point of setting up this sort of authority is to dissociate the claim to obedience from the question of the merits of the particular decisions one is being asked to accept. For as long as the claim to obedience is left contingent on a judgment of merits, the disagreement among men at the substantive level is bound to reintroduce the chaos the system of authority was set up to avoid in the first place. At the same time, it is not contradictory to defer to the decisions of this sort of authority and yet also to disapprove of those decisions. For if a person's private judgment has become irrelevant to his duty to obey, it is also the case that his internal assent is also irrelevant. This type of authority produces a decision to be followed, not a

---

[43] Cf. J. R. Lucas's definition of authority: "A man, or body of men, *has authority* if it follows from his saying 'Let X happen,' that X ought to happen." *The Principles of Politics* (Oxford, 1966), p. 16. See also Max Black, "Notes on the meaning of 'rule,' " *Theoria*, XXIV (1958), pp. 142–144.

statement to be believed.[44] Belief is both unjustified (since no decision can make something true, but only obligatory) and unnecessary (since it is common action not common opinion that constitutes the purpose behind the establishment of this type of authority).[45]

8. The Concept of Being "an Authority"

I now turn to the very different kind of title to authority implied in being "an authority." Here the justification for deferring to some person is that he is thought to have special knowledge, wisdom, or insight or to be the recipient of a revelation or unique experience not available to other men. What is essential to this sort of authority is that something be accessible to one person that is inaccessible or less accessible to others, whether this special access involves expertise, learning, singular experience or skill, revelation, etc. It is this special knowledge that constitutes the vindication of the layman's deferential acceptance of the authority's utterances even though he does not or even cannot comprehend the grounds on which those utterances rest. Examples of this sort of authority are plentiful, ranging from rather mundane cases drawn from everyday life to extraordinary religious and political examples. So we speak of an authority on ancient history, modern physics, and economic problems of employment as well as such extraordinary cases as Weber's charismatic leader whose authority rests on the "normative patterns or order revealed by him."[46] Perhaps, however, the exemplary case of this type of authority for Western political philosophy has been that of religious authority whether of priests or prophets. Ullmann states that the concept of *auctoritas* was rather swiftly taken over from Roman thought in order to define the special ascendancy claimed for the papacy:

> What is evil and what is not evil in a Christian world . . . can clearly enough be pronounced only by those who are in a special sense qualified to pronounce upon this crucial issue. It was here that the concept of the papal *auctoritas sacrata* played its decisive role. . . . The king so it was held, had not sufficient *scientia* to enable him to state authoritatively what was, and what was not, evil, what was, and what was not, sinful. . . .[47]

This example brings out the basic elements of the concept of "an authority": on the one hand, the special knowledge or "scientia" claimed by one man; on the other hand, the contention that other men are debarred from this special knowledge, so that they are dependent on those who do possess the knowledge in question, if they are not to be left in ignorance. Thus the basic purpose of this sort of authority is to substitute the knowledge of one person for the ignorance or lesser knowledge of another person, although what the person who defers thereby comes

[44] Cf. John Rawls, "Legal Obligation and the Duty of Fair Play" in Sidney Hook (ed.), *Law and Philosophy: A Symposium* (New York, 1964), pp. 8–9.

[45] On this, see especially E. Anscombe, "Authority in Morals," *op. cit.*

[46] *Theory of Social and Economic Organization*, trans. Parsons, p. 301.

[47] Walter Ullmann, *Principles of Government and Politics in the Middle Ages* (London, 1961), p. 64; also pp. 67, 272, 257–2n, 305. See also J. M. Cameron, *Images of Authority: A Consideration of the Concepts of "Regnum" and "Sacerdotium"* (New Haven, 1966), pp. 4, 14–15, 36.

to possess as a surrogate for his ignorance is not knowledge, but "true belief" in the sense of belief that is indeed justified, though the believer knows not why.

The justification of this sort of authority must, then, always be cast in the form that X knows something that Y does not know: for if X does not know, Y has no reason to defer; whereas if Y knows also, there is no need to defer. Moreover, it is precisely the particular ground on which the claim to authority rests in this case, namely, superior knowledge or insight, that makes belief, and not merely external conformity, the appropriate response to authority. Here what is produced is not merely a decision to be followed, but a statement to be believed. The claim that a person makes to authority in this case is not, then, based on the bare fact that he has been put "in authority" in accordance with an established procedure, but on his being qualified to speak because of certain special personal characteristics that set him apart from other men. Accordingly, his claim to be deferred to is logically independent of his "having authority," and this amounts to a fundamental difference from the case of being "in authority." In the latter case, a person claims that his decisions should be deferred to because he has authority: if he does not have authority, there is no reason to defer to him. By contrast, in the case of being "an authority," the person claims he should have authority because of his special capacities: if people do not acknowledge his authority, it remains the case that they ought to, since his special knowledge does not cease just because he lacks acknowledgment.[48]

In the former case, the system of authority is logically prior to the person; in the latter case, the person is prior to the system.[49] (Presumably, this is the logical basis of the distinction Weber draws between charismatic authority, which is personal, and legal-rational authority, which is based on rules. The typical expression of the charismatic authority is, according to Weber, "It is written that. . . . But I say unto you. . . ."[50])

The concept of "an authority" can thus be recognized to rest on two connected presuppositions. The first presupposition is inequality. One person defers to another on some matter because he lacks the knowledge or insight that he assumes the other possesses. Believing an authority thus presupposes a recognized inequality between the parties, and it is this that provides the justification for the abdication of judgment. The assumption always is, in Mill's words, that "some are wise, and some are otherwise." However, the key consideration is that this recognized inequality is *logically* prior to the authority relationship itself. It is *because* of the

---

[48] Cf. Kierkegaard: "the man who is called by a revelation and to whom a doctrine is entrusted, argues from the fact that it is a revelation . . . it remains St. Paul's responsibility to see that he produces that impression, whether anybody bows before his authority or not." "Of the Difference Between a Genius and an Apostle," in W. Kaufmann (ed.), *The Present Age* (New York, 1962, p. 93.

[49] However, this is oversimplified. For the question remains how someone with special knowledge is to be recognized by those who lack it. Here the notion of publicly accepted "marks" of authority must re-enter the discussion, and with it the difficult concept of "faith in authority." But this is an intricate problem, requiring extended treatment that cannot be undertaken within the confines of this paper. Further, the notion of papal authority must also complicate this analysis because here the claim to "auctoritas" is made to depend on the occupancy of a special office. Yet plainly this conception of authority is not based on the Hobbesian predicament which forms the basis of the notion of "in authority"; it rather satisfies the two presuppostions (mentioned below) that are always involved in the idea of being entitled to speak authoritatively.

[50] *Theory of Social and Economic Organization, op. cit.*, p. 301.

superior insight of some person that he should be acknowledged as "an authority" by others: the deference relation is thus supposed to reflect the antecedent concrete "personal" differences between the parties. In this respect, there is a fundamental difference between the concept of "an authority" and the concept of "in authority." In the latter case, there is certainly inequality too, for every authority relation involves (by definition) the direct inequality of command and obedience, someone influencing and someone being influenced. However, it is only in this limited sense that it is correct to say that every authority relation is "hierarchical."[51] For the fact that one person is "in authority," whereas the other obeys, does not imply an inequality antecedent to the authority relation itself. On the contrary, what it does imply is a particular sort of equality, recognized by all parties. For as we saw in discussing the notion of being "in authority," it is precisely in the context in which men cannot agree on what is to be done that it can be rational for them to accept someone to decide what is to be done. But this will appear as a rational solution to their predicament only if each is prepared to acknowledge the impossibility of producing consensus at the substantive level by somehow winning others over to his own views. If, for instance, one of them can somehow get himself recognized as "an authority" on the basis of, say, religious charisma, then consensus becomes possible on a very different basis. The equality assumption involved in the concept of being "in authority" is, therefore, of a subtle order. The assumption is not that nobody actually knows any more than anyone else, that no one is wiser, better or superior; but rather that no one can "persuade" the others that his judgment is superior, such as to justify deference. The equality involved here, therefore, is the equal abandonment by each person of the presumption that a consensus can be produced in conformity to his own individual views. Each must thus recognize his own opinions as merely "private," and the claim that they are more as a conceit.[52]

The key point is, then, that it is only one particular type of authority that necessarily presupposes a recognized antecedent inequality or hierarchy: there is a second type of authority that presupposes that men acknowledge one another as equals in precisely the respect in which the first type of authority demands acknowledgment of inequality.

The second presupposition is what I shall call the "epistemological" presupposition. For the claim that a person should defer to the superior knowledge or insight of another person presupposes that such knowledge or insight is in principle available — at least to some humans. And, in turn, the person who defers must share with his authority this same "epistemological" framework which defines what sorts of things are accessible to the human mind or to human experience, even though he is himself debarred from that knowledge or experience through lack of the requisite learning, wisdom, grace, revelation, opportunity, etc. The first-order claim to be an authority on some matter implies the second-order claim that the matter in

---

[51] E.g., Arendt, "What Is Authority?" *op. cit.,* p. 93.

[52] Cf. Hobbes: "If nature therefore have made men equal, that equality is to be acknowledged: or if nature have made men unequal; yet because men that think themselves equal, will not enter into conditions of peace, but upon equal terms, such equality must be admitted. ... The breach of this precept is pride," *Leviathan,* ch. 15 (Oakeshott [ed.], pp. 100–101). Cf. *Elements of Law,* I, 17, 1. Hence the suppression of a certain kind of intellectual pride becomes a condition for the liberation of the individual's intellect from the requirement of internal assent involved in a system of authoritative belief.

question belongs to the class of things capable of being known, and the acceptance of the first-order claim implies acceptance of the second-order claim. Thus, between the person who is an authority on some matter and the person who accepts his statements as credible, there is a double system of belief: belief in the utterances of authority and belief that the mind of man can have contact with the reality on which that authority speaks. Thus, to revert to the example from Ullmann on papal authority, it is the assumption of a "Christian world" in which knowledge or understanding of "evil" and "sin" is possible, that makes it intelligible to think of some person as being an authority on such matters. Again, in his illuminating discussion of authority in *Secularization and Moral Change,* Alasdair MacIntyre writes:

> In our society the notion of moral authority is no longer a viable one. For the notion of authority can only find application in a community and in areas of life in which there is an agreed way of doing things according to accepted rules. There being an agreed right way of doing things is logically prior to the acceptance of authority as to how to do things. It is possible for there to be people who can function as authorities upon chess either in saying what the rules are which define the game, or what the most effective ways to play chess are, only because the game of chess exists as a set of established and agreed practices, both in respect of following the rules and in respect of legislating about them. Were it not for this prior social agreement the notion of an authority in chess would be a vacuous one. What is true of chess is also true of morality; unless there is an established and right way of doing things, so that we have social agreement on how to follow the rules and how to legislate about them, the notion of authority in morals is empty.[53]

MacIntyre is here concerned ·with the way in which the concept of "moral authority" becomes vacuous, and his contention is that this occurs when the "prior social agreement" on which that authority rests breaks down, so that fundamental moral principles no longer appear to belong to the class of things capable of being known, but are instead viewed as relative to human choices and desires (as, say, Hobbes regarded them[54]). However, what I especially wish to point out about MacIntyre's argument as to the dissolution of moral authority is that it applies strictly to the case of being "an authority" because it is here only that authority need be a spokesman or interpreter of a prior system of beliefs. But someone who is "in authority" is not necessarily an authority *on* anything: his decisions do not have to be presented as authoritative expressions, deliverances, or interpretations of logically prior beliefs or principles. On the contrary, it is precisely the key point about the concept of "in authority" to be *dissociated* from any background of shared beliefs. It is, then, in those circumstances in which a society has lost the sense of a common framework of substantive moral beliefs and has grown sceptical of the idea of a homogenous moral community, that the notion of being "in authority" may present itself as the appropriate form of authority for defining the general rules all men must conform to. But this does not imply that there is no "social agreement" lying behind the practice of being "in authority." For as we saw, the establishment or existence of someone "in authority" presupposes a complex *recognition* of dissensus and equality at the substantive level over against

---

[53] *Secularization and Moral Change, op. cit.,* p. 53.
[54] For example, *Leviathan,* ch. 4.

which men are prepared to step up to the procedural level and abide by the decisions of the person designated as being "in authority," whether or not those decisions happen to coincide with their "private" opinions. And it is therefore essential to differentiate between the two kinds of "prior social agreement" which lie behind the two kinds of authority.[55]

To sum up, then, the relationship between a person who is "in authority" and the person who defers presupposes a very different sort of context than that presupposed by the relationship between a person who is "an authority" and the person who defers to him. In the latter case, it is a world of common beliefs and the recognition of inequality in the capacity of men to understand those beliefs. In the former case, it is a world of conflicting opinions and the recognition that all opinions are equally "private," no one of them having a claim in its own right to organize society.

[55] The passage from MacIntyre is thus misleading to the extent to which it suggests application to authority in general, and not just "an authority." The same error, it seems to me, is committed by Peter Winch when he runs together "in authority" and "an authority," and indiscriminately claims that both involve a "system of ideas" ("Authority" in Quinton [ed.], *Political Philosophy, op. cit.,* pp. 101, 105–106).

6. Authority

Richard S. Peters

1. Authority and Artifice

There are good reasons as well as personal excuses for ushering in Hobbes at the outset of a discussion on "authority"; for Hobbes himself introduced the concept to deal with difficult problems connected with the analysis of human institutions. And there is little point in making a list of the different ways in which the term "authority" can be used unless the distinctions are made with an eye on the problem or cluster of problems that can be clarified by means of them.

Hobbes was impressed by the fact that a civil society is not a natural whole like a rook or a beehive; yet it is not a mere multitude of men. A multitude of men becomes an artificial person when each man *authorizes* the actions of a representative. "Of persons artificial, some have their words and actions owned by those whom they represent. And then the person is the *actor*; and he that owneth his words and actions is the AUTHOR: in which case the actor acteth by authority ... and as the right of possession, is called dominior; so the right of doing any action, is called AUTHORITY. So that by authority, is always understood a right of doing any act; and *done by authority*, done by commission, or licence, from him whose right it is." (*Leviathan,* Ed. Oakeshott pp. 105–6). De Jouvenel, also, uses

From *Proceedings of The Aristotelian Society,* Vol. 32 (1958), pp. 207–224. Reprinted by courtesy of the Editor of The Aristotelian Society. © 1958 The Aristotelian Society.

the concept of "authority" in the context of the same type of problem. Having rejected the view that civil societies come into being through voluntary association or through domination from without, he claims that authority is "the efficient cause of voluntary associations" ... "Everywhere and at all levels social life offers us the daily spectacle of authority fulfilling its primary function – of man leading man on, of the ascendancy of a settled will which summons and orients uncertain wills. ... Society in fact exists only because man is capable of proposing and affecting by his proposals another's dispositions; it is by the acceptance of proposals that contracts are clinched, disputes settled and alliances formed between individuals. . . . What I mean by 'authority' is the ability of a man to get his proposals accepted." (*Sovereignty* pp. 29–31.)

2. The De Jure and De Facto Senses of "Authority"

I have chosen to start off with these quotations from Hobbes and de Jouvenel partly because they both introduce the concept of "authority" in the context of the attempt to elucidate what is meant by a society as distinct from a multitude of men, and partly because the two quotations illustrate an important difference in the ways in which the term "authority" is used in the context of the same sort of problem. For Hobbes "authority" is what might be called a *de jure* concept; for de Jouvenel it seems to be a *de facto* one. In other words, for Hobbes the term indicates or proclaims that someone has a *right* to do something. "Done by authority" means "done by commission or licence from him whose right it is." Now I am not concerned to defend Hobbes' odd conception of the handing over of rights or his account of "authorization." But, whatever the correct analysis of the connexion between "authority" and "right," it is quite clear that there is a very important use of the term "authority," which is favoured by Hobbes, which connects the two concepts. A man who is "in authority" for instance, clearly has a right to do certain sorts of things. This use of "authority" is to be contrasted with the *de facto* favoured by de Jouvenel. For he says "What I mean by 'authority' is the *ability* of a man to get his proposals accepted." The Oxford English Dictionary seems to permit both usages; for it gives "power or right to enforce obedience." It also speaks of "power to influence the conduct and actions of others; ... personal or practical influence; power over the opinion of others; intellectual influence"; as well as "moral or legal supremacy; the right to command or give an ultimate decision ... title to be believed." And in ordinary conversation the two senses can be used without danger of misunderstanding in one sentence when we say things like "The headmaster and others in authority had, unfortunately, no authority with the boys." The question quite naturally arises how these two senses of "authority" are related and whether both senses are important, as Hobbes and de Jouvenel maintain, for saying certain sorts of things about specifically human relationships and organizations.

3. Hobbes' Rendering of the De Jure Sense

The *de jure* concept of authority presupposes a system of rules which determine who may legitimately take certain types of decision, make certain sorts of pronouncements, issue commands of a certain sort, and perform certain types of symbolic acts. Hobbes brings this out by saying that the actions of a representative are authorized. He relies on the sense of "authorize" which assimilates it to commissioning or giving a warrant to a man to do certain types of things. The subjects are conceived of as having words and actions which they own, of which they are the "authors," and to which they have a right. They then appoint a representative to whom they transfer their right. He is now commissioned or "authorized" to act on their behalf. "So that by authority is always understood a right of doing any act; and done by authority, done by commission or licence from him whose right it is." Now Hobbes, as is well known, and as Mr. Warrender has recently shown in such stimulating detail, had a very strange view of natural rights which permeates this picture of authority. He was led by it to conceive of authority *in general* in terms of the particular case where a man is the author of a word or act, to which he also has a right, and where he commissions someone else to act in this matter on his behalf. This is indeed a case of an authorized act; but there is a more general meaning of "authorize" which is to set up or acknowledge as authoritative; to give legal force or formal approval to. Similarly "authorized" in its most general meaning is equivalent to "possessed of authority." "Authorization" is better understood in terms of the general concept of "authority" rather than vice-versa. Hobbes pictured "authority" in terms of "authorization" which is one of its derivatives. But he did bring out the obvious connexion between "authority" and the existence of an "author" in the realm of acts and words, which is the key to seeing how the concept works.

4. "Auctoritas" as the Key to "Authority"

The concept of "authority" is obviously derived from the old concepts of "auctor" and "auctoritas." An "auctor" was, to quote Lewis and Short, "he that brings about the existence of any object, or promotes the increase or prosperity of it, whether he first originates it, or by his efforts gives greater permanence or continuance to it." "Auctoritas" which is a producing, invention, or cause, can be exercised in the spheres of opinion, counsel or command. The point of this little excursion into philology is to stress not only the sphere of opinion, command and so on, in which "auctoritas" is regarded as being exercised, but also the connexion of the concept with "producing," "originating," "inventing" − in short, with there being an author.

Now in some spheres of social life it is imperative to have such "auctores" who are producers or originators of orders, pronouncements, decisions and so on. It is also the case that in social life, whether we like it or not, there are such "auctores" to whom commands, decisions and pronouncements are to be traced back in any factual survey of how social regulation is brought about. This is the sense of "authority" stressed by de Jouvenel. The notion of "authority" involves therefore either a set of rules which determine who shall be the *auctor* and about what, or, in its *de facto* sense, a reference to a man whose word in fact goes in these spheres. The *de jure* sense of "authority" proclaims that a man has a right to be an "auctor"; the *de facto* sense states that he is a matter of fact one. Hobbes' account of "authorization" relates to the particular case where a man has a right to be an "auctor," as laid down by a set of rules, and where he commissions someone else to do what he himself has a right to do. Indeed, often, as in a bureaucratic system, there are subordinate sets of rules which lay down procedures for the granting of such warrants and commissions. But all authority cannot adequately be conceived in this fashion.

5. Weber's Legal-Rational and Traditional Rules for Determining Who Is IN Authority

Indeed, one of the great services done by the sociologist, Max Weber, has been to stress the *different* types of normative systems which are connected with different types of authority. For legitimacy may be bestowed in different ways on the commands or decisions or pronouncements issuing from an "auctor." In what he calls a legal-rational system the claim to legitimacy rests on "a belief in the 'legality' of patterns of normative rules and the right of those elevated to authority under such rules to issue commands." (*Theory of Economic and Social Organizations*, Ed. Talcott Parsons, pp. 300/1.) There is also, however, traditional authority "resting on an established belief in the sanctity of immemorial traditions and the legitimacy of the status of those exercising authority under them."

There are most important and interesting differences between these types of authority but this is not the place to investigate the difference between traditional and legal rules, or to comment on the adequacy of Weber's analysis – but in both cases to speak of "the authorities" or "those in authority" or those who "hold authority" is to proclaim that on certain matters certain people are entitled, licensed, commissioned or have a right to be *auctores*. And the right is bestowed by a set pattern of rules.

6. Weber's Charismatic Authority

This type of authority is to be distinguished clearly from other types of authority where the right derives from personal history, personal credentials, and personal achievements, which, as will be argued later, are intimately bound up with the exercise of authority in its *de facto* sense. There is a gradation from the pure *de jure* sense of "authority" as when we say that "Wittgenstein held a position of authority in Cambridge," through the notion of *an* authority" as when we say "Wittgenstein was an authority on William James" to the *de facto* sense as when we say "Wittgenstein exerted considerable authority over the Moral Science Club." Both the last two senses of "authority," unlike the first, imply something about the attributes or qualifications of the individual in question. But the details of this transition are very difficult to make explicit.

Weber, as a matter of fact, made much of authority deriving from personal characteristics when he spoke of "charismatic authority" – "resting on devotion to the specific and exceptional sanctity, heroism or exemplary character of an individual person, and of the normative patterns or order revealed or ordained by him" (op. cit., p. 301). He was thinking primarily of the outstanding religious and military leaders like Jesus and Napoleon. He therefore pitched his account rather high and personal "authority" is decked with the trappings of vocation, miracles and revelation. Nevertheless, there is something distinctive about the charismatic leader which he shares in an exaggerated form with other "natural" leaders who exercise authority in virtue of personal claims and personal characteristics. For he is unlike the moral reformer who gives reasons of a general kind for his innovations, reasons which he expects everyone to appreciate. He appeals to revelation or claims that he has a call. These are not really justifications of his innovations; they are ways of stressing that he need give no justification because he is *a special sort of man.*

7. Gradations in the Concept of "AN Authority"

This notion of presenting credentials of a *personal* sort is an intermediary between the purely *de jure* and the *de facto* senses of "authority." For the reference to personal characteristics is a way of establishing that a man has a right to make pronouncements and issue commands because he is a special sort of person. And, although in some societies a man who sees visions and goes into trance states is in danger of electric shock treatment, in other societies pointing to such peculiarities of personal biography are ways of establishing a man as *an* authority in certain spheres. In societies where the claim to vocation or revelation is acceptable there are also, usually, collateral tests for eliminating charlatans and the mentally deranged. But his claims rest, as it were, on some kind of personal initiation into mysteries that are a closed book to most men. In a similar way years of study of inaccessible manuscripts would establish a man as "an authority" on a special period of history, or years spent in Peru might establish a man as "an authority" on the Incas. Collateral tests would, of course, be necessary to vouch for his trustworthiness. But in many fields people become "authorities" by some process of personal absorption in matters that are generally held to be either inaccessible or inscrutable. Dodds suggested that the Forms were objects of this sort for Plato — objects which the initiated had to scrutinize by a kind of bi-location of personality as practised by shamans. And the scrutiny of such objects gave the philosopher kings a right to make decisions and issue commands — in short, made them authorities. (*The Greeks and the Irrational*, pp. 210/11.)

Weber stresses the importance of success as a necessary condition for the maintenance of charismatic authority. If success deserts the leader he tends to think of his god as having deserted him or his exceptional powers as failing him. And his authority will be correspondingly reduced. The disciples, it is said, were in despair when Jesus had been crucified. It was only when he accomplished the supreme feat of rising from the dead that they recovered their faith in him and in his claims. To a certain extent the charismatic leader is in the position of a man who keeps spotting Derby winners without a system. His authority depends on always being right by virtue of a "flair" or a "hunch" — words which point to his inability to give grounds for his pronouncements. It is because his authority derives from such *personal* peculiarities that failure tends to be fatal. This is a very important empirical generalization about a necessary condition for the exercise of authority which applies at much more mundane levels.[1]

The point, however, is that in the case of these extreme types of charismatic

---

[1] Ernest Gellner has pointed out to me that in many societies there are institutional devices for covering up failure so that the authority *can't* be wrong.

authority revelation and success are not simply necessary conditions for the exercise of authority *de facto*. They are also *grounds* for establishing the right to be an *auctor*. This can be shown, too, in more mundane spheres where we speak of a person being *an* authority. He has not been put *in* authority; he does not hold authority according to any system of rules. But because of his training, competence and past success in this sphere he comes to be regarded as *an* authority. He has a right to speak. It may be the case that people do not exercise authority in various spheres unless they are competent and successful *as a matter of fact*; but it is also the case that they come to be regarded as authorities because these necessary conditions come to be regarded as grounds for a right. The notion of *an* authority, therefore, implies as it were, a self-generating system of entitlement which is confined to specific spheres of pronouncement and decision. We speak of an authority on art, music or nuclear physics. The grounds which entitle a man are directly connected with his *personal* history and achievements in a specific sphere. These grounds vary from the extremes of revelation, initiation and vocation, through less esoteric grounds like study of inaccessible material in history, to the more public and accessible training of a scientist. But in all these spheres success seems to be a usual ground of entitlement.

8. De Facto Authority: Its Necessary Conditions and Meaning

It was suggested by reference to the Wittgenstein example, that there was a gradation from the purely *de jure* sense of "authority," through the concept of "an authority" to the *de facto* sense of "authority." The analysis of *de facto* authority must now be tackled and the question faced whether the term "authority" can ever be used properly if there is no suggestion of a *right* to make decisions and issue commands or pronouncements. Does the exercise of authority *de facto* presuppose that the person who exercises it must be in authority or an authority? In the Admirable Crichton situation the butler, in fact, exercised authority, though the lord was in authority. Are we to assume that, in some sense the butler had a right to make decisions? Or does saying that the butler had authority over the lord mean simply that the lord accepted the butler's decisions just because they issued from a particular man in whose presence his "genius was rebuked"?

Of course most people who exert authority *de facto* do so because of the deference paid to their office or status rather than because of any outstanding personal characteristics. But there is often a mixture of both as in the case of Julius Caesar or Queen Elizabeth the First. Indeed there is subtle interweaving of these institutional and personal conditions for the exercise of authority *de facto*. For, as we say, the office makes the man; and often the man gives dignity to the office. The same tendency is to be observed in cases where it is more appropriate to speak of there being *an* authority. The entitlement accorded has a snowball effect. Often the outcome is disastrous — portentous pronouncements which are unquestionably accepted but which turn out to be erroneous. The generalization to other spheres is also a well-known phenomenon — one which Socrates spent so much time attacking.

There is, therefore, a widespread connexion between being in authority or an authority and the *de facto* exercise of authority. But this is a contingent connexion, not a necessary one. And as Admirable Crichton situations are not unusual, it looks as if being in authority or an authority are only frequently conditions for exercising authority; it does not look as if they are even necessary conditions.

What then of the cases where a man exercises authority *de facto* purely because of certain personal characteristics — when either there is no deference paid to his office if he is an official, or when he is not in a position of authority at all? There are two questions here which need to be distinguished. The first is about the conditions other than being in authority or an authority which are necessary to the exercise of authority *de facto*. The second is the logical question of what it *means* to exercise authority *de facto* in this tenuous sense. Is it the case that always the exercise of authority implies that in *some* sense, a man must be regarded as entitled to command, make decisions and so on? Are there necessary conditions which, as in the case of "an authority" come to be regarded as grounds for a right? To answer this it will be as well to deal briefly with the sorts of things which might be suggested as necessary conditions.

A variety of generalizations can be made about necessary conditions for bringing about unquestioning conformity — for instance, that a man's decisions tend to be accepted in proportion to the extent to which he has been proved right before. Success, too, strengthens another necessary condition for the exercise of authority — the expectation of being believed, followed or obeyed. People will tend to accept decisions and obey orders in proportion as the man who makes them or gives them expects that they will. The more successful he is, the less questioning there will be and the greater will be the confidence with which he utters them. We have phrases like "an air of authority," "an authoritative voice," and Jesus, it is said, produced consternation because as a boy he spoke "with authority" in the temple. Such descriptions draw attention to the outward signs of the inner certitude which is usually necessary for the exercise of authority. For it is not sufficient for a man to be in fact wise or shrewd or a felicitous prophet, if he is to exercise authority. He must also be known to be so. It is said that Attlee's authority in the country suffered in his early days as Prime Minister because he did not have a good public relations officer. A man cannot exercise authority if he hides his light under a bushel.

Such empirical generalizations are the province of the social psychologist. The question of philosophical interest is whether any such empirical conditions must come to be regarded as *grounds* for a right if a man is to be said properly to exercise authority without being in authority or an authority. A concrete case will help here. Suppose there is an explosion in a street or a fire in a cinema. Someone comes forward who is not a policeman or a fireman or manager of the cinema and who is quite unknown to all present — i.e. he is not regarded as "an authority" in virtue of his personal history or known competence in an emergency. Suppose he starts issuing orders and making announcements. And suppose that he is unquestioningly obeyed and believed. Would we say that such a man exerted authority in a crisis? I think we would only say so if we thought that his orders were obeyed *simply because they were his*. There would have to be something about him in virtue of which his orders or pronouncements were regarded as being in some way legitimately issued. Maybe it would be his features; maybe it would be the tone of his voice.[2] Maybe he would have a habit of command. But those who heard him

---

[2] Cf. *King Lear*, Act. 1 Sc. IV. *Lear*: Who wouldst thou serve? *Kent*: You. *Lear*: Dost thou know me fellow? *Kent*: No sir: but you have that in your countenance which I would fain call master. *Lear*: What's that? *Kent*: Authority.

would have to think in an embryonic way that he was the sort of man who could be trusted. It would put the matter altogether too strongly to say that they thought he had a right to take control. For obviously, in any useful sense of "right," he has not got a right. He has not been appointed; he is not a status-holder; he possesses no credentials of a more personal sort. All that can be said is that there is something about him which people recognize in virtue of which they do what he says simply because he says it. Perhaps the word "faith" is required here; for, as Hobbes put it, the word "faith" is required when our reasons for assent derive "not from the proposition itself but from the person propounding."

It may be, however, that the search for some vague ground for the acceptance of orders in this unquestioning way is to approach the analysis of "authority" in its *de facto* sense in too positive a manner. Perhaps the use of the term "authority" is to *deny* certain characteristic suggestions rather than to assert a positive ground for unquestioning obedience. People often do what they are told because they are threatened or bribed or physically forced. After all, obedience in a crisis can be produced by a fire-hose or machine gun, irrespective of who is manning it. Maybe the term "authority" is necessary for describing those situations where conformity is brought about *without* recourse to force, bribes, incentives or propaganda and *without* a lot of argument and discussion, as in moral situations. We describe such situations by saying that an order is obeyed or a decision is accepted *simply because* X gave it or made it. This is a way of excluding *both* that action was taken on moral grounds *and* that the person acted under constraint or pressure or influence. The use of authority, in other words, is a manner of regulating human behaviour which is an intermediary between moral argument and the use of force, incentives and propaganda.

9. Common Features of All Uses of "Authority"

There are, therefore, features which all uses of the term "authority" have in common. In so far as the *de facto* sense implies that, in an indeterminate and embryonic sense, the person who exercises authority is regarded as "having a right" to be obeyed, and so on, the *de facto* sense is parasitic on the *de jure* sense. But the common features of both senses are, perhaps, best brought out by summarizing and making explicit the peculiar nature and role of authority in the regulation of human behaviour – the point at which I embarked on this analysis in the company of Hobbes and de Jouvenel.

(a) In Contrast to "Power." The first feature to stress is the connexion between "authority" and the use of certain types of regulatory utterances, gestures and symbolic acts. A person *in* authority has a right to make decisions, issue pronouncements, give commands and perhaps perform certain sorts of symbolic significant acts. To *have* authority with another man is to get him to do things by giving orders to him, by making pronouncements and decisions.

The main function of the term "authority" in the analysis of a social situation is to stress these ways of regulating behaviour by certain types of utterance *in contrast* to other ways of regulating behaviour. This is to reject the more usual attempts to analyse "authority" in terms of "power" as exemplified by Weldon, for instance, who claims that "authority" means power exercised with the general approval of those concerned. (*Vocabulary of Politics*, p. 56.) This, of course, is not to deny that it may be important, as Warrender stresses, to distinguish physical power from political power, the latter being confined to cases where an element of "consent" is involved, as when a man does something because he is threatened, cajoled or duped, in contrast to when he is physically coerced — e.g. bound and put into prison. (See *The Political Philosophy of Hobbes* pp. 312/3.) It might, therefore, be tempting to regard the exercise of authority as a species of the exercise of political power distinguished by approval as opposed to mere acceptance on the part of the victim. But this, surely, is an over-simplification. For often what we want to bring out when we say that men are in authority or exert authority over other men is that they get their way or ought to get their way by means *other than those* of force, threats, incentives and propaganda, which are the usual ways of exercising *power*. It is only when a system of authority breaks down or a given individual loses his authority that there must be recourse to power if conformity is to be ensured. The concept of "authority" is necessary to bring out the ways in which behaviour is regulated *without* recourse to power — to force, incentives and propaganda. These ways are intimately bound up with issuing pronouncements, making decisions and giving commands. I suppose the concept of "power" can be extended to cover these ways of influencing people. But my claim is that "power" usually has meaning by contrast with "authority" rather than as a generic term of which "authority" is just one species.

In so far as there is a *positive* connexion between "power" and "authority" it is better conceived along other lines. For instance, it might well be true that a common condition for the exercise of authority *de facto* is the ability to dispose of overwhelming power, if necessary. Or, alternatively, power might be regarded as a ground of entitlement. The old saying that there can be no legitimacy without power might be interpreted in this second way — as claiming that one of the grounds which give a man a right to command must always be, directly or indirectly, the ability to dispose of power, if necessary. Or it could be interpreted in the first way as an assertion that the possession of power is a necessary condition for the *de facto* exercise of authority, the legitimacy of which might be established in other ways. And, of course, this necessary condition, like others which I have mentioned before, can come to be regarded as a ground of entitlement. There is, however, no need to explore this positive connexion in detail. For my claim is that these are answers to other questions — questions about the grounds of entitlement or about the necessary conditions for the exercise of authority, not questions about the meaning of "authority."

There is little mystery about why authority should be so intimately connected with the problem of the analysis of human institutions. For men, *pace* Aristotle, are rule-following animals; they talk and regulate their own behaviour and that of others by means of speech. Men perform predictably in relation to each other and form what is called a social system to a large extent because they accept systems of rules which are infinitely variable and alterable by human decision. Such systems can only be maintained if there is general acceptance of procedural rules which lay down who is to originate rules, who is to decide about their concrete application to concrete cases, and who is entitled to introduce changes. In other words, if this peculiarly human type of order is to be maintained there are spheres where it is essential that decisions should be accepted simply because *somebody*, specified by rules of procedure, has made them. It is very difficult to play cricket without an umpire, just as it is difficult to conceive of an army working without a hierarchical system of command. The term "authority" is essential in those contexts where a pronouncement, decision or command must be accepted simply because some person, conforming to specifications laid down by the normative system, has made or given it — where there must be a recognized "auctor." More liberal societies, of course, guard against injustice and stupidity by instituting further procedures for appealing against decisions of those in authority. But this is merely a device whereby a higher authority is instituted to correct the mistakes of a lower one. It is still a regulatory device which relies on the institution of authority and in no way abrogates the duty of obedience to the lower authority, provided that the lower authority is acting *intra vires*.

(b) In Contrast to Moral and Scientific Regulation of Conduct and Opinions. This analysis of "authority" accounts also for a long tradition which stresses the incompatibility between authority and certain specific human enterprises like science and morality. For it would be held that in science the importance of the "auctor" or originator is at a minimum, it never being justifiable in scientific institutions to set up individuals or bodies who will either be the originators of pronouncements or who will decide finally on the truth of pronouncements made. The procedural rules of science lay it down, roughly speaking, that hypotheses must be decided by looking at the evidence, not by appealing to a man. There are also, and can be, no rules to decide who will be the originators of scientific theories. In a similar way, it would be held that a rule cannot be a moral one if it is to be accepted just because someone has laid it down or made a decision between competing alternatives. Reasons must be given for it, not originators or umpires produced. Of course, in both enterprises provisional authorities can be consulted. But there are usually good reasons for their choice and their pronouncements are never to be regarded as final just because they have made them. In science and morality there are no appointed law-givers or judges or policemen. This is one of the ways in which life in the laboratory differs from life in the army and law-courts.

This analysis of "authority" readily explains, too, the connexions so often made between "authority" and "command." For commands, roughly speaking, are the sorts of regulatory utterances for which no reasons need to be given. A man can only give a command if he is in a position of authority or if he exerts authority in a *de facto* sense. For as an occupant of an office or as a status holder he has a right to make decisions which are binding and to issue orders. Similarly, if the *de facto* sense of authority is being used, to say that a man has authority over other men is to say, amongst other things, that they will do what they are told without questioning the prudence, wisdom and good sense of the decision. They may, of course, question its legality; for questions can be raised about a man's right to issue commands in general or in a particular sphere. These are questions about his right to an office or status, or about the sphere of its competence or his prerogative. But once it is granted that he occupies an office or holds a status legitimately, and once it is made clear that he is not straying from its sphere of competence or exceeding his prerogative, there can be no further question of justifying his commands. For commands just are the type of regulatory utterance where questions of justification are ruled out.

Authority, however, is not exercised *only* in the giving of commands. There are also the spheres of making pronouncements and decisions and the performance of symbolic acts. Behaviour or opinion in these spheres is regulated by the utterance of a man which carries with it the obligation for others to accept, follow or obey. The claim put forward by Hobbes and Austin, that law is command, is right in stressing the connexion between law and authority but wrong in conceiving of commands as the only form of authoritative utterance. Similarly those who speak of "the authority of the individual conscience" cannot be supposed merely to be saying that in moral matters a man must give himself orders, which sounds, in any case, a little quaint; rather they are saying that in moral matters a man must decide himself between conflicting claims and principles and not accept the pronouncements and decisions of others simply because they issue from determinate sources. In morals a man must be his own "auctor."

10. Conclusion

To conclude: my thesis is that the concept of "authority" can be used in a *de jure* and a *de facto* sense. Amongst the former uses it is very important to distinguish the kind of entitlement implied in being *in* authority from that implied in being *an* authority. Authority in a *de facto* sense is parasitic on the *de jure* sense in that it implies that decisions are in fact accepted or commands obeyed simply because they issue from a certain person whose attributes are in some way regarded as bestowing legitimacy on them. The grounds for this legitimacy are often much more indeterminate than those more impersonal grounds characteristic of *de jure* authority. There are, however, more general negative features which all senses of "authority" share. The term is always used to speak of ways in which conduct is regulated as distinct from the mere use of power – e.g. the giving of commands, the making of decisions and pronouncements, as distinct from the use of force, incentives and propaganda. Secondly, within the sphere of decisions, pronouncements and other such regulatory utterances, authority is confined to those which are or must be obeyed simply because someone has made them. This second feature of "authority" brings out the contrast between laws, commands and religious utterances, on the one hand, and those of science and morality on the other. Both these features or "authority" are rooted in the Latin word "auctoritas" which implies an originator in the sphere of opinion, counsel and command.

7. Authority in Morals

Elizabeth Anscombe

To many, at least of those who study philosophy, there are difficulties about any notion of authority in morals. There are, of course, various forms of authority. There is the right to declare to someone else what is true — in this case what is right and what wrong, and to demand that he accept what one says and act accordingly. There is the authority of superior knowledge — in this case, it would be the authority, i.e. the outstanding credibility, of an expert on right and wrong, virtue and vice. There is again the authority of someone exercising his prophetical office, who teaches *qua* one set up by God to teach; in this case, declaring what is right or wrong, virtuous or vicious.

Now the first of these, however distasteful it may be, is a sort of authority that can hardly be denied to exist by the most recalcitrant modern philosopher. For it is exercised by people in bringing up children; and if there is such a thing as authority of a commanding kind at all, or if there is such a thing as a right, this authority and this right can hardly be denied, since it is quite necessary, if children are to be brought up, that their bringers-up act as if they were exercising such an authority; and since what is a necessity can hardly fail to be a right, so anyone who has to bring children up must have this right.

This authority, however, is not accompanied by any guarantee that someone exercising it will be right in what he teaches. When he is wrong, then, what is the position as regards his authority? To say he still has the right to demand that he be believed is absurd; for there can be no right to be believed when what one says is not right, and no right to demand what one does not have a right to obtain. It would commonly be said that such a person — a parent, say, with erroneous convictions about right and wrong — has a right to be obeyed as far as external actions were concerned, so long as what he demanded was not wrong, or very burdensome and unreasonable. However, I am not interested in that, but only in the character of his authority in declaring what is right or wrong and requiring that his children accept what he says. Authority seems a relatively clear notion when it means the right to be obeyed, even if you are wrong in giving the order, as it does when authority over actions is what we are considering. But it is much more difficult to explain authority to teach, such as a parent exercises in bringing up his children. If this is an authority that he only has when he is right, then, it may be asked, how is it authority at all? The child only has to think him wrong, in order to have to reject his authority: this is to say, for the child to think him wrong must lead to the child's rejecting his authority, if the child is logical. But then how can it be a reproach to the child that it did not believe what he said, and so dishonoured its father's authority? And in that case, in what sense is there authority here?

Or does authority to teach, such as a parent has — and which he must have inasmuch as he positively has a duty to teach — *not* after all carry with it a right to

From John M. Todd, ed., *Problems of Authority* (London, England, and Baltimore, Md.: Darton Longman & Todd Ltd., 1962), pp. 179–188, by permission of the author and publisher.

be believed? But does it not carry a right to demand belief? A right, for example, to order a child to stop being silly?

Nevertheless there is a difference between saying: You did not do as I told you, and that is bad, because it was I, whom you ought to obey, who told you, and: You did not believe what I said, and that is bad, because it was I, whom you ought to believe, who told you.

The difference lies in this: that the one with authority over what you do, can decide, within limits, what you shall do; his decision is what makes it right for you to do what he says — if the reproach against you, when you disobey him, is only that of disobedience. But someone with authority over what you think is not at liberty, within limits, to decide what you shall think among the range of possible thoughts on a given matter; what makes it right for you to think what you think, given that it is your business to form a judgment at all, is simply that it is true, and no decision can make something a true thing for you to think, as the decision of someone in authority can make something a good thing for you to do.

This comes out in the fact that one tells the person under one's authority to do thus and so, but, more often, not to believe this and that, so much as: that this and that is true. The demand that a child accept what one says is based on the claim to know what he does not and to have the job of telling him. "Why ought I to do that?" — "Because I say so"; if "Why ought I to believe that?" is answered by "Because I say so," that can only be because my saying so is good evidence that the thing is true, and in general it would not be so answered.

Thus, while it is possible to beg or counsel someone to believe something while admitting that one does not believe it oneself, it is not possible authoritatively to order someone to believe something while admitting that one does not believe it oneself. (There are plenty of situations in which one may intelligibly order someone to believe or not to believe something; I will not elaborate them.)

This is connected with the fact that to teach authoritatively is primarily to declare the things one is teaching, demanding attention and mastery of what one says from one's pupil. Now "such-and-such is the case, but I do not believe it is" is notoriously a contradiction, even though of a rather curious sort.

So far, our problems have been concerned with the authority of a fallible teacher, whatever he is teaching, not especially with the teaching of morals. But morals I suppose are what is most universally taught by fallible teachers informally at least, by praising and blaming other people, by reining the child in or giving him free rein in various ways (encouragement, reward, etc. and their opposites).

It looks both necessary and impossible that there should be teaching authority on the part of fallible people. A professional teacher, however, presumably has authority to teach; and this does not seem so difficult. Naturally he cannot justifiably claim his teaching commission in support of his teaching when what he teaches is untrue. So he too has a commission only to teach what is true. But the child who will not learn what the teacher teaches — is he not guilty of rejection of authority? And to learn is necessarily to accept, i.e. to believe, a good deal of what one is taught. If a child were liable not to believe his teacher, how could it happen that he selected only those things to disbelieve that were in fact untrue? So he needs to be liable to believe his teacher. If he is, he will learn at any rate some truth; by its aid he will eventually be able to reject what he is taught that is false so far as it is important that he should: or so it is to be hoped.

The right that a fallible teacher has, in that he has authority, then, is the right that those he has to teach should be generally prepared to believe their teachers. At all frequent disbelief when what he says is true will be, then, an injury done to the authority of a teacher – as well as having about it whatever badness attaches to being wrong without excuse.

The great assumption lying behind this is that no one who is taught at all can fail to be taught a great deal that is true and that to a great extent *verum index sui et falsi.*

We sometimes imagine someone with a terribly bad upbringing, who is taught all sorts of misbehaviour as right, and taught to despise much that is good, and we think: what about such a person? – But people of the most horrible principles know quite well how to cry out against injustice and lying and treachery, say, when their enemies are guilty of them. So they in fact know quite a lot.

There need not be some common kernel of morals that everyone learns who learns anything. The moral law is a range; some people have one part of the range, some another.

But is there something essentially less teachable about morals than, say, chemistry or history or mathematics – or, again, religious dogma? This view might be maintained in connexion with that *autonomy of the will* about which Kant wrote. To take one's morality from someone else – that, it might be held, would make it not morality at all; if one takes it from someone else, that turns it into a bastard sort of morality, marked by heteronomy.

Now it was wrong, in the list of teachable things with which to contrast morality, to put mathematics alongside the others. "Be ye doers of the word and not hearers only" I once saw as the motto of a chapter in a big text book of higher mathematics, and it was right; one does not learn mathematics by learning that mathematical propositions are truths, but by working out their proofs. Similarly it might be held that one's morality *must* be something one has formulated for oneself, seeing the rightness and wrongness of each of the things one judges to be right or wrong; so that if ever anyone else taught one, he was the occasion of one's formulating for oneself what he taught, rather than the source of information.

There is tied up with this view the idea that one's own personal conscience is necessarily the supreme arbiter in matters of right and wrong. And here we are often not clear whether the necessity is a logical necessity, or a necessity under pain of doing ill: whether, in entertaining the idea of not going by one's own conscience, one is supposed to be guilty of a linguistic absurdity or a reprehensible departure from the right way.

There is a confusion here. Let conscience be one's judgment of right and wrong, i.e. of good and evil in conduct, of what is virtuous and what vicious to do. Then to say that one's own conscience is necessarily supreme arbiter in such matters is to say that necessarily what one judges right and wrong, one judges right and wrong.

One could similarly say that one cannot think anything to be true without thinking it. But that does not tend to shew that one cannot think a thing on the strength of what someone else says, judging that that is much more likely than what one could have been inclined to think if left to oneself.

The confusion can perhaps be best cleared up if we consider the parallel case of memory. I can make no judgment about the past without some reliance on my own memory. But only a fool thinks that his own memory is the last word, so far as he is concerned, about what happened. A man may have reason to judge that other men's memory is more reliable than his, and will in any case be well advised to check his own memory against theirs; he may also have reason to believe that some public record is more reliable than his own memory. Of course he would not have any basis for such judgments if he did not already rely on his own memory to some extent; but it would not be reasonable to argue from this that his own memory must after all be for him the last word about what has happened in the past.

Similarly, in practical matters, a man must put some reliance on his own conscience: that is to say, on those judgments of right and wrong which he makes for himself. I call it a judgment that he makes for himself when he judges on a ground that he can see for himself; he does not merely judge "that is wrong," he judges "that is wrong because . . ." and then follows some further account of the action which he can judge and which he also judges to make the action wrong. To rely exclusively on one's own conscience (one's "unaided" conscience) is to refuse to judge anything in practical matters unless in this sense one is able to judge for oneself. Now in this sense of "one's own conscience" only a foolish person thinks that his own conscience is the last word, so far as he is concerned, about what to do. For just as any reasonable man knows that his memory may sometimes deceive him, any reasonable man knows that what one has conscientiously decided on one may later conscientiously regret. A man may have reason to judge that another man's moral counsel is more reliable than his own unaided conscience; he will in any case be well advised to take counsel with others; he may, moreover, have reason to believe that some public source of moral teaching is more reliable than his own unaided judgment. Of course he would not have any basis for such judgments if he did not already rely on his own moral judgments to some extent; but it would be sophistical to argue from this that his own conscience must after all be for him the last word about what he ought to do. This sophism, though, aided by confusion with the sense in which it is indeed impossible to take anything but one's conscience as arbiter of right and wrong, has led people to embrace Kant's thesis on the autonomy of the will and to attack, either as illogical or as reprehensible, those who, say, consult the Divine Law and accept its judgments, though themselves unable to see why, say, something forbidden by that law is wrong.

A strong sense of duty may attach to the deliveries of one's conscience — whether they are the deliveries of the "unaided" conscience or are one's ultimate decision. Some people think that this sense of duty is to be unquestioningly obeyed and that such obedience is a moral vindication. But it is not reasonable to hold that one can so easily get away with having thought good what was bad and bad what was good, and acted accordingly — by having had a sense of duty in connexion with what one did. It would have an adverse effect on the seriousness of one's concern to avoid sinning, if one was guaranteed against it by following one's sense of duty — no matter what road it led one on. I do not mean that it would necessarily make one worry less; in some circumstances it might make one worry more; for only an endlessly conscientious style in one's behaviour, only endless bellyaching could reassure one that one was exercising the sense of duty. Nevertheless that isn't seriousness.

To return to the comparison with mathematics. That suggested that as one cannot just take mathematical information but must think for oneself, so one cannot just take moral information but must think it for oneself; this would be reason to think that one could not be taught morality except in the sense that one can be taught mathematics.

Now there is something right about the comparison. But it is rightly made, not as I made it, by speaking of formulating one's morality for oneself, but as the mathematical text book made it, by quoting the text from St. James: "Be doers of the word and not hearers only."

You have to do the mathematics; and the teacher can get you to do it: that is what teaching mathematics is. Similarly teaching morals will be, not getting the pupil to think something, not giving him a statement to believe, but getting him to act; this can be done by someone who brings up children. One does not learn mathematics, I said, by learning that certain propositions – mathematical ones – are true, but by working out their proofs. Similarly one does not learn morality by learning that certain propositions – ethical ones – are true, but by learning what to do or abstain from in particular situations and getting by practice to do certain things, and abstain from others.

However, the reckoning what to do or abstain from in particular circumstances will constantly include a reference, implicit or explicit, to generalities. So much so, that this seems to be an important part of what makes morality. Because of it human conduct is not left to be distinguished from the behaviour of other animals by the fact that in it calculation is used by which to ascertain the means to perfectly particular ends. The human wants things like health and happiness and science and fair repute and virtue and prosperity, he does not simply want e.g. that such and such a thing should be in such and such a place at such and such a time. Such generalities or principles are: to do good and avoid doing harm; not to do what will get you disrepute; not to do what will make you poorer; not to take other people's property. And the questions arise, which of such principles are true and which false, which quite general and which to be modified in suitable circum-stances; whether indeed they can be called true and false, right and wrong, and why; what should be the application of this or that one in describable particular situations. Even if the purpose of such a theory is, as Aristotle says, not knowledge but practice, the considerations are theoretical in the sense that they are capable of being argued in the study. A human being can be brought up without any such study-theory, but the study-theory of some of the people who have gone in for that kind of thing is liable in the long run to exert an influence on the practical principles of the general run of people. If parents teach their children to be reflective, they may themselves teach them a certain amount of moral theory, and if there is such a thing as a public teaching, it is likely to be in great part theoretical, i.e. general, leaving individuals and their advisers to make applications.

Now there is indeed a sense in which only the individual can make his own decisions as to what to do, even if his decision is to abide by someone else's orders or advice. For it is he who acts and therefore makes the final application of whatever is said to him.

It may be said, concerning his judgments in the field of theoretical morals, that in the same way it is he who thinks what he thinks, and so too only he can make his own decisions as to what to think. No doubt; but here there is such a thing as believing what he is told without reflection, consideration or interpretation; doing what one is told is an interpretation and so with doing, however obedient one is, one can hardly escape being one's own pilot. I have said that a man would be foolish who would not take advice; but there comes a point where he must act and that is the end of listening to advice. But with believing it is otherwise; a man may decline to be his own pilot for certain of his beliefs and altogether rely on authority, without doing anything on his own account to digest and assimilate the beliefs. This would be possible in moral matters only to the extent that his beliefs were idle, without consequences, i.e. if they concerned matters that he never had to deal with.

Now some dogmatic beliefs are revealed and could not be known otherwise. The question arises whether this could be essential to some moral beliefs. That is to say, whether there are any that are *per se* revealed.

There are two different ways in which a moral belief may be *per accidens* revealed. One way is when someone relies on an authority for something that a man could have thought out for himself. He does not know, let us suppose, whether it is all right at all to beat a child for its misbehaviour. So he asks a modern educationist, supposing him to know, and gets the answer: no; or, if he has different predilections, he consults the Bible and gets the answer: yes. He forms his opinion accordingly. Note that if he is to *act* on it, and the opinion he has adopted is the positive one, he has got to be his own pilot in deciding when and where. But at present we are speaking only of belief, which may perhaps never come to practice. Here, then, is one way in which a moral belief may rely *per accidens* on authority, whether on the authority of an expert (someone supposed to be wise in the field, though of course not supposed to be infallible) or on that of someone with a prophetical office.

Another way is this: some of the facts, of what is the case, will help to determine moral truth – i.e. some of the truth about what is the case will help to determine the truth about what kinds of thing ought and ought not to be done. Now some such truths about what is the case are revealed; original sin for example. There are also revealed some conditional promises, to disregard which is to despise the goodness of God. Both of these things lead us to infer the rightness of an asceticsm which would otherwise have been morbid or founded on a false view of life. Here then is something one could not have worked out for oneself: the furthest one could have got would be to see the advisability of weighting the scales a certain amount against the pleasures and enjoyments of life, as they can be seen to have a practical tendency to corrupt people, i.e. to soften them, make them greedy and pervert and coarsen their judgment. But this would not justify anything severely ascetical.

Here there is room for accepting authority also on the moral conclusions to be drawn from the facts; but *this* acceptance – the acceptance of *consequences* as following – is similar to the acceptance in the first type of *per accidens* revelation of moral truth, just as the grounds on which the authority itself tells you moral truth may be either *per se* revealed truth as to facts, or facts discoverable by reason's unaided investigation.

What there does not seem to be room for is moral truths which are *per se* revealed. Given the facts about original sin and the promise of the possibility of a man's joining his sufferings to those of Christ, the goodness of severely ascetical practices, so long as they do not damage the body or its faculties, is obvious; there is no such thing as a revelation that such and such is good or bad not for any reason, not because of any facts, not because of any hopes or prospects, but simply: such and such is good to do, this is to be believed, and could not be known or inferred from anything else. How can one instruct an archer to aim at an unseen target? There would be no room for that knowledge by connaturality which is characteristic of the understanding of a virtuous person, in such a case; no room, therefore, for understanding application of what one believed to be right or wrong.

Mr. Michael Dummett, reasoning on the topic of cause and effect, came to the conclusion that but for the goodness of God in revealing it to us, it could not have been known that it would be wrong to engage in certain practices whose object it was to procure that such and such should *have* been the case; we might have discovered that something always turned out to have been the case if we subsequently recited some formula, and so recite the formula in order to secure that the past was as we wanted it to have been. Now this is a case in point. If it is not unreasonable, if it is not foolish and superstitious to do this, then there could be nothing wrong with it and there is no room for the exercise of the goodness of God simply in forbidding it. To do it would only be *malum quia prohibitum.*

It was objected that the "new law" of Christ was indeed a revelation in the domain of morality. The speaker admitted this in the sense that the motives, spirit, meaning and purpose of the moral life of Christians depended on revelation, while insisting both that the law of love had already been taught in the Old Testament and that the content *of the moral law, i.e. the actions which are good and just, is not essentially a matter of revelation.*

8. Secularization and Moral Change
Alasdair MacIntyre

... There is an argument about the analysis of moral concepts in which the division is between those who want to stress that words like "good" and "ought" are essentially expressions of standards chosen by the agent who utters these words, and those who take the view that moral concepts are such that they can only be used intelligibly by those who are prepared to endorse standards that are already written into our moral language. So on the one side there is the claim that our key moral expressions are and cannot ever be anything more than the expression of the agent's own choice of standards, that they have no more authority over the agent than the agent himself chooses to confer upon them; and on the other view is that if we take, for example, the virtue words, words such as "courage," "generosity," and the like, or the vice words, words such as "rudeness," or "cowardice," we shall find that the rules for the use of these expressions are such that we cannot choose what is to count as courageous, or what is to count as cowardly, but we have to accept a framework of concepts which is given in our moral vocabulary. This argument is very often presented as though each side was claiming to characterize the whole range of moral concepts, as these must be in all

From *Secularization and Moral Change* by Alasdair MacIntyre, published by Oxford University Press for the University of Newcastle-upon-Tyne, pp. 49–57. Reprinted by permission of the author and publisher.

times and all places, in such a way that one side must be altogether right and the other must be altogether wrong; but if one looks sociologically at the facts about this particular society now, the suspicion is born that what we find in this dispute are perhaps not two rival descriptions of the same moral phenomena, but instead, descriptions of two quite different sets of phenomena, which do as a matter of fact coexist within our society.

There are on the one hand the language and the concepts of those people who have continued to live within a tolerably well-established moral framework with a tolerably well-established moral vocabulary; this may be any one of the moralities which I have tried to outline, or it may be some synthesis between them, or it may indeed be some other moral alternative. Members of this type of social group possess a list of what they take to be the virtues and vices; moreover they possess a concept of the virtues such that the authority which requires their practice is not conferred by the agent's choice. To understand that generosity or courage or thrift is a virtue is to understand that one ought to be generous or brave or thrifty, and this "ought" has a force prior to any choice of moral standards that we make. Indeed choices of moral standards are judged correct or incorrect in the light of their understanding of the virtues and vices.

There are, however, other individuals who have a different kind of moral vocabulary. They do not belong to a single homogeneous moral community with a shared language and shared concepts. Instead they find themselves solicited from different standpoints. They cannot avoid choice, and what moral standards they adopt depends upon their own choices. So choice is the fundamental moral concept and there are no objective impersonal standards in the light of which ultimate choices can be criticized. The fact that there are these two sorts of people in our society underlies a paradoxical element in many moral discussions. To understand this element we need to grasp two essential points about the use of moral concepts. There is something inherently odd as well as something compelling about any doctrine which claims that the meaning of moral expressions can be expressed in terms of the notions of the agent's acts of approval or expressions of feeling or choices. Any analysis which, no matter with what sophistication, suggests that the meaning of "This is good" or of "I ought to do this" is roughly equivalent to "This is what I choose to approve of" or "This is what I do approve of" raises the question of why we have distinctively moral expressions in the language anyway. If what I want to say is "This is what I choose to approve of" why should I not say just that, instead of saying "This is good" or "This is right"? The answer is that it is quite clear that when I use moral concepts I do at least try to make a claim which goes beyond the expression of my own choices or feelings. If I tell you that "You ought to do this" or use some other expression of this kind, I present to you a claim which by the very use of these words implies a greater authority behind it than the expression of my feelings or choices could ever give to it. I claim, that is, that I could point to a criterion in virtue of which you too ought to recognize the authority of the standard presented. It is obvious that this activity of appealing to impersonal and independent criteria only makes sense within a community of discourse in which such criteria are established, are shared. Outside such a community the use of moral expressions is only a kind of private gesture. In any situation where that use has not been socially established there is no recognized criterion to appeal to. The distressing fact about our own society is that we are in just this situation: the effective and honest use of moral predicates does presuppose a shared moral vocabulary in an established moral community, but we do not as a whole community share such a single moral vocabulary. The extent to which different moral criteria are established in common amongst us is extremely uncertain, and therefore the kind of appeal that we are able to make when we use moral predicates is also uncertain.

What is the relevance of this to the theme of secularization? In a society which is able to give expression to its common life in religious forms — as contrasted with a society where a number of individuals or sub-groups happen to have religious beliefs — what gives the society a common life must include the acceptance of certain shared moral standards as authoritative. A society could have a common morality and accept a common moral authority without that authority taking a religious form or having any religious backing. But if religious forms are to have a hold upon life and upon practice, then there must be room for some appeal to a religious authority in moral matters. In our society the notion of moral authority is no longer a viable one. For the notion of authority can only find application in a community and in areas of life in which there is an agreed way of doing things, according to accepted rules. There being an agreed right way of doing things is logically prior to the acceptance of authority as to how to do things. It is possible for there to be people who can function as authorities upon chess either in saying what the rules are which define the game, or what the most effective ways to play chess are, only because the game of chess exists as a set of established and agreed practices, both in respect of following the rules and in respect of legislating about them. Were it not for this prior social agreement the notion of an authority in chess would be a vacuous one. What is true of chess is also true of morality; unless there is an established and shared right way of doing things, so that we have social agreement on how to follow the rules and how to legislate about them, the notion of authority in morals is empty.[1] It therefore follows that any programme according to which we could re-establish moral community by first getting some sort of authority accepted is absurd. For there is far more to the concept of moral authority than simply that of someone issuing fiats in an impressive way. Suppose that tomorrow some religious spokesman, claiming to speak with *ex cathedra* authority, was to stand up and say what the solution to Britain's moral problems is on the subject of the hydrogen bomb, or on sexuality, nothing that he said would have any more hold over us than what contending parties say to each other now, until he had produced some criterion which enabled us to understand that he was appealing to a standard which we had *already* accepted — and could therefore recognize, which was somehow established in our ways of behaving and in the goals we pursued. For only then could we possibly see point in following his advice.

If it is true that without established moral agreement the notion of moral authority is vacuous, then light is thrown both upon the history of the Church's loss of moral authority and also upon certain contemporary religious claims. For it is not the case that men first stopped believing in God and in the authority of the Church, and then subsequently started behaving differently. It seems clear that men first of all lost any over-all social agreement as to the right ways to live together, and so ceased to be able to make sense of any claims to moral authority. Consequently they could not find intelligible the claims to such authority which were advanced on the part of the Church. The historical evidence about the

[1] P. G. Winch, *Authority*, Arist. Soc. Supp. Vol., 1960, is an excellent discussion.

development of secularization bears this out. Social change and with it moral change is chronologically prior to the loss of belief effected by intellectual argument, except where a very small minority are concerned. Intellectual argument only takes on a key role at a point at which social change and moral change have made it very difficult to know what the substance of the Christian claim involves in the choice of a way of life, and what the distinctive content of being a Christian in one's behaviour is. It is, of course, possible for men to say that the distinctive thing about a Christian is that he joins with others in distinctively religious activities — especially rituals and ceremonies — and nothing more. But the Christian churches go on making wider moral claims. On the problems of sexual behaviour, of the morality of war, and of delinquency, for example, the bishops of the Church of England have spoken as though it only needed the application of what they allege to be clear Christian moral standards for these problems to be solved. I hope I have given some reasons for showing that what the bishops said must be false. But one wants to go on to ask, "Why do they speak as they do?" I think the answer is by asking, "Who are these people who talk like this?" Bishops and church spokesmen in general tend to be drawn from sections of society, and from a generation within those sections, in which the highly articulated forms of morality that I discussed earlier still survive. They still live within a moral framework and use a moral vocabulary that has been eroded and lost elsewhere in society; like other survivors of shipwreck they live on deserted islands. One finds some confirmation of this suggestion by looking at the only other comparable group who similarly treat morality as though it was still what it once had been: the judges. If we look at the social origins of judges and also at the ages at which they take office we find similarities to bishops and other church leaders. Both tend to have been at public schools. Both tend to secure the kind of office from which they issue utterances which claim moral authority at a relatively high age. The result is a continuous supply of utterances by judges in which moral authority is claimed in just the way in which the bishops claim it. "The Courts," said Lord Simmons, "have a residual power to conserve not only safety and order, but also the moral welfare of the state." "I would say most emphatically," said Lord Denning ungrammatically, "that standards and morals are the concern of the law and that whether done in private or in public," and Lord Chief Justice Parker talking to the journalists in the Vassall case said: "How can you say there is any dishonour on you, if you do what is your duty in the ordinary way as a citizen, in putting the interests of the State above everything?" (What is interesting is not merely that the Lord Chief Justice should hold this monstrous doctrine, but that clearly he felt it to be obviously true.)

As do bishops, judges tend to assert not only that the Courts have a responsibility for maintaining moral standards, but that it is possible for them to say unambiguously what the solution to most of the vexed moral problems of our time is. This could only be maintained by people who are living in a past that has survived in our society in the life of a particular class. The inability of this social class to communicate with the rest of society is not a phenomenon private and restricted to that class but is something experienced by all those who speak from within a particular surviving moral community to those outside it. English society today is at best morally pluralistic in a way that makes the notion of authoritative moral utterance inapplicable; at worst it is a society in which the lack of a shared moral vocabulary makes the use of explicit moral assertion positively pernicious.

What is pernicious is the illusion that is created of a society united not as in fact it is by harsh utilitarian necessities, but by common standards and ideas.

It is not of course the case that moral achievement is ruled out. The greatest contemporary moral achievement is the creation of the type of community where shared ends and needs make possible the growth of a common life and a common commitment, which *can* be expressed in a common language. But religious forms provide us with no guidance here. From the standpoint of morals the secularization of our society can be seen as one side of a process, the other side of which has been a certain moral disintegration. But it does not follow that it would be right to view the first as cause, the second as effect.

9. Authority, Reason, and Discretion[1]

Carl J. Friedrich

Ever since the eighteenth-century revolt against the established authorities in church and state, there has been a marked tendency among freedom-loving intellectuals to view "authority" with a jaundiced eye, if not to denounce it. When Charles S. Peirce wrote a generation ago that "when the method of authority prevailed, the truth meant little more than the Catholic faith,"[2] he was echoing this intellectual sentiment. Conservatives have maintained that the implication here is that what Peirce called "the method of authority" was some kind of unreasoning superstition, some foolishness which must be superseded by the clear voice of "reason." When the Jacobins erected altars to the Goddess of Reason, they had proudly assumed that they were abandoning authority for reason. Little did they realize how authoritative was their outlook, and how much depended upon their authority for their particular reasoning to prevail.

In reaction, conservatives since Bonald and de Maistre have made a fetish of authority beyond all reason. The ringing phrases in which de Maistre denounced the rationalism of the enlightenment center upon the issue of authority against reason. He would claim infallibility for the pope in the same phrase in which he would

Reprinted with permission from Carl J. Friedrich, ed., *Authority: Nomos I.* (Indianapolis: The Bobbs-Merrill Co., Inc., 1958), pp. 28–48.

[1] An earlier attempt at a formulation of the position of this study may be found in an article, "Loyalty and Authority," in *Confluence* (1954), vol. III, pp. 307ff. Cf. Miss Hannah Arendt's challenging article, "Was ist Autorität? " reprinted from an unspecified journal (1955), and Francis G. Wilson's "The Prelude to Authority," in *The American Political Science Review*, 31:12ff. (1937); see also George S. Langrod, "Liberty and Authority," ch. XIV of *Freedom and Authority in Our Time*, ed. Lyman Bryson, Louis Finkelstein, R. M. MacIver, and Richard McKeon (1953); and Sebastian de Grazia, "Authority and Rationality," *Philosophy*, 27 (1952). See also footnote 20, below.

[2] Charles S. Peirce, "How to Make Our Ideas Clear" as reprinted in *Love, Chance and Logic* (1923), p. 55.

vindicate an unqualified monarchical sovereignty.[3] Because reasoning, *raisonne-ment*, can lead to the dissolution of all social order, to anarchy and terror, men ought to and are in fact ready to subject themselves to authority without asking the "reasons why." Similar sentiments are frequently expressed in contemporary American conservatism.

But are reasoning and authority so antithetical? Does authority have no basis in reason? The following analysis seeks to elucidate the proposition that authority and reason are closely linked, indeed that authority rests upon the ability to issue communications which are capable of reasoned elaboration.

In common usage, authority is often confused with power or taken to be a synonym of power. In more learned discourse, authority has been defined as a particular kind of power, such as "formal power" or "rightful power." It has been spoken of in relation to persons, as well as to other entities, such as law or the dictionary. The problem of what makes people "accept" authority, by obeying commands or believing a message, has given rise to a variety of interpretations of authority. Authority has been juxtaposed to freedom, or to force, or to reason. It has been praised and condemned in all these contexts, and as a result, the word has been incorporated in a pejorative adjective, "authoritarian," and linked as a general characteristic to "personality" as an objectionable and eradicable trait. In most of these discussions, both on the popular and the learned level, it has been assumed that authority is a peculiar something that can be possessed, and gained or lost, as the case may be. Against such views it has been argued through the ages that there is only power based on some sort of constraint, and that authority is merely a make-belief, based upon religious faith at best.

It is illuminating to cast a glance at the Roman antecedents from which the word "authority" is derived. *Auctoritas* is, according to Mommsen,[4] not readily definable in its original meaning. It has predominantly the sense related to the verb from which it is derived: *augere*, to augment. *Auctoritas* thus supplements a mere act of the will by adding reasons to it. Such augmentation and confirmation are the results of deliberation by the "old ones." The *patrum auctoritas* is, for that reason, more than advice, yet less than a command. It is, as Mommsen comments, advice which cannot be properly disregarded, such as the expert gives to the layman, the leader in Parliament to his followers. This augmentation or implementation and confirmation had in ancient Rome, as did indeed authority elsewhere, religious overtones. While it was not intended to set limits to the free decision of the community, it was intended to prevent violations of what was sacred in the established order of things. It was believed that because such violations were a crime (*nefas*) against the divine order, they might jeopardize the divine blessing. Thus, the preservation of good auspices probably was the basic idea underlying the *patrum auctoritas*, the authority of the fathers, that is to say, of the Senate. It was a matter of adding

---

[3] "L'infaillibilité dans l'ordre spirituel, et al souveraineté dans l'ordre temporel, sont deux mots parfaitement synonymes." *Du Pape*, Book I, ch. I.

[4] Theodor Mommsen, *Römisches Staatsrecht* (2nd ed., 1888), III, 1033ff. I should like to call attention in this connection to the fact that Apollo was the "augmenter." When one considers the symbolism of Apollo as the God of the Sun, of reason and moderation, this serves as a most revealing symbolic *datum*. Cf. W. K. C. Guthrie, *The Greeks and Their Gods* (1950), pp. 183ff. Guthrie writes of "Apollo's primary aspect, his championship of law and order . . . limit, moderation, obedience to authority, and condemning excess in all its forms" (p. 203). There are also the precepts which this augmenter represented.

wisdom to will, a knowledge of values shared and traditions hallowed, to whatever the people wanted to do. (Later on, the *auctoritas* became a more general notion, and something of what our modern word "author," meaning a maker or originator, suggests.)

Why bother with these ancient verbal connotations? Because they suggest the role of reasoning, they thereby help to get clearly into focus what is probably the central fact to which a great many of the situations refer in which the word "authority" is employed. When there are good reasons for doing or believing something, such action or thought acquires a quality which is otherwise lacking. This has been overlooked by that rather numerous group of writers and philosophers who thought they could build law upon power alone. The power of him who willed something was, they thought, what gave someone's decision authority. Hobbes, as well as Rousseau and many others, thought that the sovereign will was the source of all law.[5] Much Anglo-American legal tradition has, by contrast, retained the older notion – a notion that can be traced back through the Middle Ages to the Stoics – that reason, and more especially Coke's "artificial reason of the law" are of decisive importance in providing law with the necessary authority.[6] It is this view which assigns to the judge such a central position in a legal system: he, as a man "learned in the law," is conceived as lending the statutory "decisions" of an elected legislature an additional quality, by relating them to the basic principles of the law and thus making them authoritative. Only by fitting the willed statutory law into such a broader framework of "reason" does it become fully right, that is to say, authoritative.

In his forthright little study on political verbiage, T. D. Weldon makes an effort at clearing away some of the thick underbrush that has grown up around the word "authority." He remarks that until recent times, no clear distinction has been drawn between power and authority, and that it is "too simple to identify 'authority' with 'force rightly or justly applied.'" He differentiates four kinds of authority, ranging from pure force to unquestioning confidence, and hence asserts that "force exercised or capable of being exercised with the general approval of those concerned is what is normally meant by 'authority.'" Thus, if the followers *want* wickedness, they will obey a wicked authority.[7] And yet, at the start of his analysis, Weldon had pointed out that authority somehow is related to the face that he who possesses it could produce reasons, if challenged. Such was the case of the Roman Senate, such is the case of the modern judge. To say, as Weldon does, that "the proper use of force is always authoritative" is quite inadmissible, unless this statement is made into a tautology by giving to the adjective "proper" the meaning of "reasonable," in the sense of possessing adequate reasons for him to whom the force is applied. What is more, Weldon himself seems to know this, for he tells us that when people begin to ask the question, "Why should I obey X?" X is on the way to losing his authority.

This last observation deserves further exploration. For when such a question is

---

[5] Hobbes, *Leviathan*, ch. X, vi–viii; Rousseau, *Contrat Social*, book II. For Hobbes the key of "authority" is "the right of doing any act."

[6] Sir Edward Coke, *Reports*, VIII, Bonham's case; see C. J. Friedrich, *Philosophy of Law in Political and Historical Perspective* (University of Chicago Press, 1958), ch. X. Cf. also C. D. Brown, *The Lion and the Throne – The Life and Times of Sir Edward Coke 1552–1634* (1957), pp. 302ff.

[7] T. D. Weldon, *The Vocabulary of Politics* (Pelican Books, 1953), pp. 50–56.

raised, a number of answers may be given. One answer would be in terms of hierarchy and status — because he is your king or your father. Another might be in terms of religion and faith — because God has commanded you to do so. A third would be in terms of interest and advantage — because he may make you his heir and successor. A fourth would be in terms of personal emotions and loyalties — because he loves you and you are devoted to him. A fifth would be in terms of law — because article so-and-so of the civil code requires you to do it. Such a recital, though incomplete, suggests some of the values and beliefs involved in reasoning upon authority, and at the same time, it gives a first hint of the fluid, indeed the fugitive quality of power based on authority. However, these five answers do not enable us really to get at the distinctive phenomenon which the augmentation and confirmation of will by some sort of reasoning accomplishes. The escape into the psychological con-comitants of this datum of political experience suggests that a crucial aspect belonging to its ontological core has not yet been laid bare.[8]

We have, in the previous paragraph, spoken of authority in terms of obedience. This is very commonly done; indeed, in action-related situations, obedience is the predominant aspect. But there is another phase of authority which is paramount in such situations as those involving the teacher, the scholar, and the dictionary. As to the last, some very interesting special problems are presented by the authority of nonpersonal entities, such as dictionaries, laws, and the like. It might be argued that one could bracket these entities and their "authority," because their authority may be traced back to the human "authors" who created them. There is, furthermore, often a question as to who were the makers: the fathers at Philadelphia, or the long line of judges who adorned the Supreme and other courts, or yet the presidents and congressmen. From a certain standpoint, it may even be said that the Constitution as it exists today is the work of the entire American people. The problem of the "authority" of impersonal entities will, I believe, become more comprehensible, once the analysis of the rational component of authority has been further advanced.

Leaving aside, then, the authority of such impersonal entities, we return to the situation of the teacher, the scholar, the doctor, or the lawyer. Here authority seems to be related to the fact that the person wielding authority possesses superior knowledge or insight. Frequently — for instance, among scholars accepting each other's authority — the authority of X rests upon the fact that he could give extended reasons for the opinions he expounds.[9] It is not essential for such authority, however, that these opinions are conclusively demonstrable; indeed only where they are not thus demonstrable, the phenomenon of authority in the strict sense is involved. In any case, the authority of the teacher, the scholar, the doctor, and the lawyer is infused with a rational element, and the belief in it includes the belief in superior "reasoning." It is challenged on the part of those who accept it, by asking, not, why should I obey? but, why should I agree?

[8] The close relation between the psychological and the nominalist misinterpretation of phenomena like authority is strikingly illustrated in the approach of Max Weber, who, confusing authority with legitimacy, misses one of the key aspects of authority, by minimizing its rational aspect.

[9] This aspect of the matter is strikingly illuminated by the role that agreement upon methods of work and modes of demonstration plays among scientists. For an elaboration of this factor, as far as science is concerned, see my paper, "Political Philosophy and Political Science," in the collective volume to be published (1958) by Northwestern University Press under the title *Approaches to the Study of Politics.*

Before I proceed with this analysis, it might be well to turn to a kind of primordial authority which has been particularly controversial in our time, namely parental authority. In the course of each child's development, the growth of authority may be studied and experienced. It might be remarked in passing that it is in this sphere that misunderstandings about the nature of authority have been most frequent. Along with the teacher-pupil relationship, the parental relationship has been jeopardized by ideas that in the last generation have played havoc with genuine community in the name of "progress."[10] And yet there was much good in these youth movements and "progressivisms" of our younger days; it was really the manner of stating the issue, rather than the criticism of outmoded patterns of living, that was at fault. In a nutshell, it might be said that these movements challenged "authority" as such, when they should have asked for the replacement of outworn and unreal authority by genuine authority. What this means, I should like to illustrate by the parental problem. In the beginning, the child is helplessly dependent and in the power of the parents. Indeed, their power is absolute force to such a degree that the legislator has seen fit to step in and regulate by law, to control and limit, the unlimited power of the parents, at least to some extent. But this absolute power does not continue, as the child grows. A wise parent will increasingly prefer to explain what needs to be done and to be believed, to give reasons, thus replacing subjection by understanding. He will respond to the questions, "why?" and "wherefore?" and seek to develop in the child an understanding of, a participation in, the *reasons* which animate the parent in asking for obedience as well as for agreement. It is in this process that a new relationship, different from that of power and force, comes into being, and it is this relationship which I should like to designate as authority. Such authority rests upon the fact that the child increasingly gains insight into parental orders and regulations, into parental opinions and beliefs. The child learns to relate both to basic values, and thereby comes to share these values with his parents. Such insight anticipates the insight into the regulations and opinions of the larger community, the church, the school, and eventually the polity. What is important is to realize that all such discourse provides for participation of the child. By coming to understand these regulations and beliefs, the child is helped, so to speak, to shape them into proper possessions, to make them his own. Thus discipline is transformed into self-discipline. It may well happen, and often does in fact happen, that this process takes place only partially and incompletely. Power and force continue to play their role, often to the point where they create dangerous tensions and frustrations about which modern psychology and psychoanalysis have taught many revealing lessons. For, if the power of parents is wielded without such growing participation and insight on the part of the child, then either the community of the family is destroyed by the rebellion of the child, or the child's personality is destroyed by the imposition of the meaningless opinions, rules, and regulations. It is this latter situation which has been the focal point of attack by many thoughtful critics who have written about the "authoritarian personality" and "authoritarian family relations," when actually what they mean is better termed "totalitarian

---

[10] This particular pitfall was the crux of the more radical extravaganzas committed in the name of progressive education some years ago. See, for a statement of the opposing position, my paper, "This Progressive Education" in *The Atlantic Monthly*, 154: 421ff. (October 1934), which became a stormy petrel of controversy for a while, but was never really refuted.

personality," and "totalitarian family."[11] But I do not care, to speak with Locke, about the words, as long as the matter be clearly understood. What seems to me significant about this well-known development within the family is that the phenomenon of authority is associated with "reasoning." And by reasoning I do not mean the absolute rationality alleged to be possessed by mathematics and logic, that is to say, the reasoning which calls no value judgments into play, but rather the reasoning which relates actions to opinions and beliefs, and opinions and beliefs to values, however defined.[12] It has, I hope, become apparent that I not only reject the use of the word "authority" for the purpose of designating any kind of power, but that when I speak of authority, I wish to say that the communications of a person possessing it exhibit a very particular kind of relationship to reason and reasoning. Such communications, whether opinions or commands, are not demonstrated through rational discourse, but they possess the *potentiality of reasoned elaboration* – they are "worthy of acceptance."[13] Seen in this perspective, authority is a *quality* of communication, rather than of persons, and when we speak of the authority of a person, we are using a shorthand expression to indicate that he possesses the capacity to issue authoritative communications. And furthermore, when we say X possesses authority, we thereby propose to suggest that the communications which X addresses to A, B, and C are based upon reasoning that has meaning not only to X, but also to A, B, and C, in the sense of being related to knowledge which they all possess, or to opinions, beliefs, and values which they all share. But we are not concerned with the problem of persuasion; it is not a matter of X's ability to "influence" the thinking or acting of the others, though this usually is involved in the situation. What matters is that this capacity to issue communications which may be elaborated by reasoning is a decisive phenomenon in a great many social and more particularly political relationships. We should like to call it authority, but, whatever it is called, this potentiality of reasoned elaboration would appear to play a vital role in situations which involved authority. Perhaps one should be content to call it the "rational factor" in authority.

As far as the opinions, beliefs, and values involved in such reasoned elaboration are concerned, they may be one or many, readily identifiable or highly speculative and abstract. One value, such as truth or justice or health, may predominate, or there may be an infinitely complex array of values[14] such as is represented by a

---

[11] See Theodor W. Adorno, *et al., The Authoritarian Personality* (1951), especially the section written by Adorno himself. See also the discussion on the issue with Else Brunswick, a contributor to *Totalitarianism*, ed. Carl J. Friedrich (1953), pp. 171ff. and 274f.

[12] Cf., for example, Raymond Polin, *La Création des Valeurs* (1945; 2nd ed., 1952), *passim.*

[13] This suggestive term was proposed by Morton White in a discussion of the group mentioned in footnote 20. It makes it clear that authority in its reasoning dimension is primarily a quality of the bearer of authority and of his communications, rather than those subject to it. But while it helps to express the thought I am concerned with, it does not sufficiently stress the rational component to suffice for this purpose.

[14] I do not use the term "system" here, nor in related contexts, although this is now frequently done, because the term should be avoided, unless the actual presence of a system can be demonstrated – which is rarely the case. On system analysis, cf. Ludwig von Bertalanffy, "Problems of General System Theory" in *General System Theory – A New Approach to the Unity of Science*, from *Human Biology* (1951).

culture or a way of life.[15] What matters is that some propositions, whether judgments or commands, can be elaborated by suitable reasoning in terms of these values, opinions, or beliefs, while others cannot, or only imperfectly. The capacity of men to speak in meaningful terms, to say the things which may be thus elaborated, varies enormously. This capacity, I think, is implied when we speak of some of them as authorities.

Now it is important that this "reasoning" is not necessarily, nor even usually, employed in fact, though it may be hinted at or suggested by symbols. But it is important that the "potentiality of reasoned elaboration" of the communication exists. In other words, not the psychological concomitant of a *belief* in the capacity of the authority for such reasoned elaboration is decisive, but the actual existence of such a capacity. This does not mean that there could not arise situations wherein the capacity was erroneously believed to exist. Such errors are a common occurrence in relations among men. But such situations are properly and meaningfully described as involving "false" or "faked" authority. Genuine authority, on the other hand, requires that the capacity actually is present. The respect, esteem, or other psychological concomitants, while undoubtedly present as well, are not a distinctive feature of authority. Power, wealth, and a host of other qualities likewise occasion these psychological reactions.

It is evident that the capacity to communicate authoritatively, that is, to be able to enlarge upon what is being communicated in terms meaningful to those who are being addressed, has a vital relation to the phenomena of power. Indeed, there can be no question but that this capacity always gives some power to him who possesses authority, and therefore authority is one of the sources of power. But just as the dagger by which I can kill a man and thus force him to surrender his purse is in any strict sense not power but the source of it, so likewise authority is *not* power, but it may cause it. This explains the undoubted fact that has been the occasion of much political comment, namely the continuance of power without authority, as well as the continuance of authority without power. Nero exercised power without authority, while the Senate of his time possessed authority yet little or no power. In precise terminology, which would speak of authority only when thinking of communications, this is readily comprehensible.[16]

The phenomenon which we have thus identified as a crucial aspect of authority explains why authority is a necessary part of all human relationships and communities. Such relationships are unmanageable without authority, because communication would become impossibly cumbersome. Wife and husband, no less than government and citizen, could not carry on for long if all the reasoning involved in saying what they have to say to each other would have to be stated or reproduced each time a communication were to be made. It is enough that the potentiality of such reasoning, the relating of actions to opinions, and of opinions to values, exists and is readily recognized. Indeed, in complementary relationships,

[15] I have no objection to anyone wishing to employ the term "authority" for designating some other social phenomenon, such as "rightful power" or "legitimate power" or yet "power based on esteem or respect." But I do insist that in that case some other term will have to be suggested or invented for designating the social reality which I am describing and have labeled "authority," believing this to be its specific meaning.

[16] Harold Lasswell and Abraham Kaplan, by contrast, having defined authority as "formal power" (see *Power and Society*, 1950, pp. 133ff.), leave this kind of situation in the dark. For how does it help to describe the situation in which the Senate found itself as "formal power"?

such as that of husband and wife in contemporary American society, or that of fellow scholars or colleagues in related professional pursuits, there occurs what might be called the phenomenon of mutual authority. What I mean by "mutual" authority is that each of the persons in such a relationship is an authority to the other, but in divergent fields of work. This phenomenon is nearly incomprehensible when the relationship is merely seen in terms of power in its various forms.[17]

The foregoing analysis also helps in understanding better the peculiarly fluid quality of power based on authority. Since opinions, values, and beliefs are continually changing, in response to changes in the environment and to creative innovations, whether of a political, aesthetic, or religious nature, it is quite possible, indeed a recurrent experience, that a person may lose his power based on authority, not because the commands he gives or the opinions he utters are less "authoritative" in the sense that they may be elaborated by reasoning, but because such reasoning is related to opinions, beliefs and values that have lost their validity. When one, in such situations, says that a man has "lost his authority," this is really a shorthand expression; he has lost power because his authority, or rather the authority of his communications, is disintegrating, because this rational component which is crucial is deteriorating.

Another perplexing situation that becomes clearer, it is hoped, as a result of the analysis attempted here is the role of authority in totalitarian societies. If authority is interpreted as some kind of power, whether "formal," or "legal" or "rightful," the role of authority in totalitarian systems remains controversial and indeed obscure. Some say, with reference to a totalitarian regime, if they identify themselves with it and its rulers, that the authority of the ruler is very great. Others, identifying themselves with the subject elements of the population who are coerced into obedience, insist that there is no authority or very little in such a totalitarian society. The rational aspect of authority which we identified as the potentiality for reasoned elaboration of communications, whether they be commands or opinions or beliefs, makes it possible to understand these societies better. In contrast to constitutional societies where authority is diffuse and pluralistic, since authoritative communications issue from many centers of authority, such as churches, schools, trade unions, parties, all kinds of associations, as well as the government, authority in totalitarian societies is strikingly polarized and intensified at the center of the totalitarian movement. Thus the authority of a Lenin, a Stalin, or a Hitler when confronting his followers is very much greater than that of a democratic leader, while at the same time his authority in confronting the rest of the society is very much weaker. To put it another way, governmental authority is both enlarged and reduced: enlarged, when one considers the followers, reduced, when one considers the rest of the people. Authority is not being centralized, or as the National Socialists called it, *gleichgeschaltet*, but it is being concentrated at the center of

---

[17] This proposition provides the clue to the nature of political authority under democratic conditions. Only the mutual respect of the citizens can give meaning to the acceptance of majority decisions, and the difficulty of mass democracy of the great urban concentrations of the present day must be seen as springing from this dissolution of the neighborhood and the disappearance of the respect associated with it. See my *The New Image of the Common Man* (1941 and later) for an exploration of the problems involved here. The contrast to present-day conditions can be seen in such processes as the New England town meeting; for this see John Gould, *New England Town Meeting* (1940), which, while a bit romantic, conveys well the point of mutuality of which I am speaking.

such a society. The explanation, in terms of our analysis, is not far to seek. The opinions and the commands of a Stalin or a Hitler, oriented to the regime's ideology, to the values and beliefs embodied in *Das Kapital* or *Mein Kampf*, could as a rule be elaborated by extensive reasoning.[18] It is important to bear in mind that such reasoning may well appear wholly "irrational" to anyone outside the particular belief and value system.[19]

Still another phenomenon, and one of paramount importance to democratic constitutional government which our theory of authority is able to elucidate, is that of discretion. Authority interpreted as involving the potential reasoning in interpersonal communications, that is to say as the capacity for reasoned elaboration, provides the clue to the problem of why discretion is both indispensable and manageable in all political and legal systems. In what follows, I shall concentrate on the phenomenon of discretion in constitutional democracies, that is, governments according to law made with popular participation.

It is worth remembering that John Locke discusses the problem of discretion when he comes to consider the prerogative. "This power to act according to discretion for the public good, without the prescription of the law and sometimes even against it, is that which is called prerogative," he writes in the *Second Essay* (160). And further that "the good of society requires that several things should be left to the discretion of him that has the executive power" (*Second Essay*, 159). There is an interesting similarity between Locke's approach and the Chinese tradition of "tsung-tung" or legitimate authority: no authority can be legitimate that fails to fulfill the function for which it was created — the public good.

Discretion may be defined in various ways, but what is always involved is (1) the notion that a choice between several alternatives can, indeed must, be made; and (2) the notion that such a choice is not to be made arbitrarily, wantonly, or carelessly, but in accordance with the requirements of the situation.[20] There is the further notion (usually) that discretion ought to come into play within the framework of rules, implementing them, carrying them through, elaborating them. Thus a court, when using discretion in imposing a penalty, is acting within the framework of the rules of the penal law according to which the criminal has been adjudged guilty, and an administrative body, in fixing a rate, is acting within the framework of the rules of, say, the law of public utilities which fixes the way such utilities should be operated, after defining them and so forth. When a court or a commission or an administrative official acts in accordance with such general

---

[18] The recent tergiversations of Khrushchev in trying to explain his adherence to the objectives and purposes of Stalin, while rejecting some of his methods, seemed to me a striking illustration of the point here made: by attaching himself to the "reasoning" of Stalin in terms of the communist ideology, he evidently sought to preserve, and if possible, to strengthen his authority, at the same time reducing that of Stalin, whom he shows to have done things which *he could not have justified by reasoned elaboration.* Hence the juxtaposing of Lenin to Stalin.

[19] This instance is particularly worthy of attention, because Hitler's position appears to any outsider to have been that of utter madness. His conduct was not only irrational, but contrary to all common sense and reason. But reason in the general sense and "reasoning" in the sense here suggested, namely, relating to values, opinions, and beliefs, are not the same thing.

[20] The author wishes here to acknowledge his general indebtedness to an informal discussion group of Harvard faculty members, mostly from the Law School, who met during 1956–1957 and explored the general problems of "rule versus discretion" as a problem of legal philosophy. The group owed its existence to the initiative of Lon Fuller.

standards as "reasonableness" or "good morals," it is supposed to be doing this within the range of rules established by the law.[21]

To put it another way, discretion comes into play whenever no rules (or principles) can be, or have been, formulated, while at the same time, mere whim cannot be allowed. For a concrete example, one might turn to the choice of personnel. A legislative body or other principal may give fairly elaborate rules and establish precise regulations for the selection of personnel, as is done in civil service legislation. There always will remain, in many instances, an element of discretionary choice. The candidates may all be of a certain age, may all have a certain education and experience, come from certain localities, and possess a variety of other specified traits. There will often be candidates who are identical in all these respects, yet a choice has to be made between them. The selection board may have to decide whether to prefer a man from Yale or from Harvard, they may have to assess the precise meaning of words used in letters of recommendation, and so forth. The law will, therefore, give specified persons "discretion" to select the candidate. In doing so, the expectation will be that the person or persons given discretion will use it "to the best of their ability." What this means is that they will give careful thought to all the factors involved. They may, to stay with our illustration, evaluate the writers of the letters of recommendation, considering their reliability, their past record of assessing men's ability, and other factors. They may consider that there are already several Harvard men in the organization and that there should be some diversity; or they may, reversely, consider that experience with Yale men has been so good that preference should be given to another Yale man.

At the same time, it will be generally assumed that a person vested with power to exercise discretion will be able to give reasons for what he has done. This aspect is particularly evident where a superior gives a subordinate discretion. He will ordinarily assume that the subordinate will use good sense, experience, stick to established precedent, and so on. But he will also expect the subordinate to be able to "explain," if for any reason he finds that the decision made ought to be subjected to review. The superior will rarely be satisfied with an explanation such as "I just felt that way" or "my instinct told me this was the right man," let alone an explanation which would say "I liked his face" or "she had such a lovely voice."

If one inspects such "reasoned elaboration" or inquires into what is expected under such a heading, he finds that the reasoning involved is both "instrumental" and "valuational," or to put it another way, it proceeds to argue both in terms of means and ends. The personnel man may suggest that the person chosen believes in democracy, or he may insist that the man rejected is possibly a believer in socialism or a fellow traveler. He may say that the candidate is steady and a good family man, or reversely that he is a drunkard and a bachelor. But besides such value judgments, there may be instrumental judgments, dwelling upon the man's ability, his

---

[21] Here we are face to face with the problem of the general clauses which are carried to such disastrous lengths in totalitarian (as indeed in many autocratic) regimes. A German jurist, J. W. Hedemann, stressed the dangers of such a "flight" in the German judicial decisions preceding Hitler's advent to power in his book *Die Flucht in die Generalklauseln* (1933); but the issue is much more pointedly developed by Fritz von Hippel, in *Die Perversion von Rechtsordnungen* (1955), giving many concrete illustrations of how such general clauses (and some not so general) may be carried beyond the limits allowed by the system. These are instances of the abuse of discretion.

knowledge of foreign languages, or what have you. The discretion as used is, in other words, tied to the opinions, values, and beliefs shared by members of the organization, as well as to the tasks to be performed.

It is by now becoming apparent why discretion is so valuable and indeed also why it is so inescapable an aspect of not only all government and administration, but all human relationships. Philosophers have since time immemorial dwelt upon the fact that rules can never cope with the infinite variety and detail of the concrete situations. To cope with the resulting inadequacy of all law, they have at times sought to find persons of exceptional wisdom, to identify as it were a natural elite of persons who would be so wise as to be able to exercise limitless discretion. Plato went perhaps further than any other thinker in this respect, at least the younger Plato of the *Republic*. Nor is it easy to argue against him, once the crucial concession is made that such men can be found by some reliable method. Plato himself took refuge in the hope of some kind of providential coincidence by which the philosopher and the holder of absolute power are brought together. Most of the rest of us have rejected his notion of the philosopher-king, precisely because the problem which he minimized, namely how to find the persons worthy of being entrusted with so much discretion, seems to be the most difficult.[22] For in the choice of personnel, as our humble illustration suggested, some of the most persistent discretionary problems present themselves. But though one rejects Plato's notion of a natural elite, and most of what goes with it, the fact remains that precisely where the novel, the unprecedented situation arises, calling for creative innovation and invention, all rules and regulations break down and discretion comes to the fore. And when such discretion is used in such a way as to benefit society, when, as the ancient verbiage has it, the "general good" is served, then government and administration are most universally acclaimed. Eisenhower deciding to cross the channel, Congress deciding to grant Puerto Rico commonwealth status, Truman deciding to act in Korea — these are recent instances of the exercise of discretion in dramatic situations calling for creative initiative, and utterly removed from the possibility of being handled by precedent or established rule.

Whenever discretion is thus used, whenever the factors relevant to a decision are obviously numerous and at least in part unforeseeable, it will seem to most men that an attempt to limit such discretion by pre-established rule or regulation would be unwise and in its consequences probably unjust.[23] But it appears similarly unwise and unjust to entrust such discretionary power to persons not qualified to

---

[22] Cf. Plato, *Republic*, especially at 473d. Aristotle, dubious of this doctrine, has an approach to the problem of discretion which is more nearly in keeping with our views, especially in connection with his doctrine of *epieikeia*. Cf. my *Philosophie des Rechts* (1954), ch. II. Note the sage comment of Kant on this doctrine of the limitless discretion of the philosopher-king: "It is not to be expected that kings philosophize or that philosophers become kings, nor is it to be desired because the possession of power corrupts the free judgment of reason inevitably." See my *The Philosophy of Kant* (1949), p. 456, and *Inevitable Peace* (1948), *passim*. The passage on the royal lie, or "noble falsehood" as A. D. Lindsay translates it, is found in *Republic*, 414.

[23] This point was especially emphasized by Henry Hart, in the discussions referred to in footnote 20. The argument has been elaborated from time to time by various authors. The political thought of writers like Machiavelli and Hegel is dominated by this problem, and its range overemphasized by them. Much of the literature of the New Deal in one way or another carries this implication. It is equally true of British labor thought. For the latter, see the scholarly work of W. A. Robson, especially his *Justice and Administrative Law* (3rd ed., 1951).

exercise good judgment, that is to say, not acting in such a way that their reasoning could afterwards be examined and found defensible. At this point, we are confronting the vital relationship of discretion to responsibility. Irresponsible discretion is not what is ordinarily wanted. But what constitutes "responsible discretion"? Essentially it is discretion which is exercised with due regard to all the considerations that enter into the situation. This will usually mean that the person exercising such discretion is duly qualified. He will seem to act responsibly when he acts in accordance with the full knowledge of the particular science, art, craft, or operation involved in the situation calling for discretion. That is why the selection of personnel appears as the core of the problem of how to arrange for the exercise of discretion. (It is, incidentally, the sound residue in Plato's notion of the philosopher-king.) And that is why administrative responsibility turns to such a large extent upon evaluation of the performance in terms of objective standards prevalent in a particular field of work and the sense of workmanship connected with it.[24]

At this point, the relation of discretion to the rational aspect of authority we have stressed becomes almost self-evident. When a person possesses the capacity to act in such a way that his communications concerning his actions possess by implication the potentiality of being supported by effective reasoning, he would appear to be eminently suited to occupy a position of discretionary power. To put this proposition in terms of our previous analysis, it follows that the exercise of discretionary power presupposes the possession of authority. Whenever a person possesses authority, in the sense in which we have here been employing the term, he is capable of using discretion. The fact that his decisions, commands, or other communications could be reinforced by reasoned elaboration relating them to established values and beliefs will lend his acts that "authority" without which discretion becomes arbitrary abuse of power.

If what has just been said is correct, it explains why authority is so often seen in the perspective of its psychological penumbra. For it is important, if authority is to be the source of power, that is, if the potentiality for reasoned elaboration is to manifest itself by people willing to "go along" without such reasoned elaboration, that those subject to the command, or expected to conform in opinion or belief, recognize this potentiality. It is this undoubted fact which has led many to mistake the respect, esteem, or administration involved for the very nature of authority. Actually, as already mentioned, these psychological concomitants are unsatisfactory if made the sole or primary criterion for identifying the nature of authority, because they occur in other comparable situations. For example, power generates esteem, and wealth respect, and holiness admiration, so that if these psychological concomitants are made the heart of the matter, authority tends to be confused with any or all of these.

At this point, it might be well to explore further the difficulties resulting from making authority antithetical to reason and truth. There is some ground for this kind of antithesis on an elementary level; for as we saw earlier, authority as defined by us does not come into play when the communication rests upon self-evidence, or the rigid rationality of demonstrable truth. But truth has a wider connotation and

[24] Cf. *Constitutional Government and Democracy* (1951), ch. XIX, and *The New Belief in the Common Man* (1941), ch. VI, "Responsibility and the Sense of Workmanship."

embraces many kinds of existential situations.[25] Incidentally, truth is one of the key values to which authority in many contexts is vitally linked. It is the sharing of this value which allows scholars to accept each other's authority, where they would not accept that of a journalist or a preacher. We might add that theology is a striking instance of reasoned elaboration of a patently transcendental system of belief. Ecclesiastical authority is vitally related to it. Thus the Catholic faith is just one of numerous possible grounds for reasoned elaboration. Every body of thought – pragmatism and skepticism as well as "the faith" – must build upon some unexplained major premises. Actually, the great *Summa* of Thomas Aquinas is one of the most ambitious efforts at reasoned elaboration ever attempted by the mind of man, and it stands to reason that those who share with Thomas Aquinas his basic opinions, beliefs, and value judgments should look upon anyone who is fairly conversant with his thought as possessed of a certain authority. The case is really not very different when the authority is rooted in a full knowledge of Karl Marx or John Dewey.

But, we are told by thoughtful men, most of the people who accept authority, whether of the church or of the government, have no idea of these elaborate reasonings, would not understand them if they heard them, and do not care to learn about them. This may well be true, up to a point, as it is when we consult a doctor or engineer, but I submit that it is the potentiality of such reasoned elaboration that matters. The communications are intrinsically "worthy of acceptance." Much institutionalized authority is maintained without the persons involved being able to elaborate. Here are the points where the "interlarding" of authority and power is most frequent. Hence these institutionalized situations are the most fertile source of the confusion between authority and power. For there is always a considerable number of people around who are obeying, believing, or conforming, because they submit to power in its various forms, including physical violence, but talk about it as obeying authority. Far be it from me to insist that all obedience and other kinds of conformity are the result of authority, since I incline toward the view that this is the error involved in the views on authority I am questioning – views which confound authority with power. All I really insist upon is that the potentiality for reasoned elaboration of communications, that is, the potentiality of supporting communications by valuational and instrumental reasoning, since it usually elicits belief, provides a potent ground for maintaining conformity in matters of action, opinion, and belief where a community exists. It is a fundamental aspect of social and more particularly of political relations. Without it no community or society can function, because no discretionary power can for long be exercised, and hence all creative, innovating, inventive activity would cease. It seems to me that this fundamental potentiality of reasoned elaboration is the differentiating characteristic of what men have talked about since the days of the *auctoritas* of the fathers of the Roman Senate, when they have spoken of authority as contrasted with

[25] Cf. Karl Jaspers, *Von der Wahrheit* (1947), where incidentally a position concerning authority is developed which has some points of contact with that here stated, at least in general. Cf. especially pp. 862ff., where an authority which reason "grasps" (*ergreift*) is contrasted with an authority that is "catholic," and hence transcendent and absolute. Jaspers' notion that such authority may be "grasped" and thus mastered by "reason" underestimates the amount of reason involved in catholic authority, on one hand and the "power of reason" in mastering authority, on the other.

power. It is related to truth as much as to any other value about which men can and do reason. It is related to freedom, because without it there can be no discretion, and without discretion there can be no freedom, in private or public life. It is the result of the fact that man, endowed with reason, is yet a finite being, whose reason is likewise finite and enclosed within definite limits. An extravagant belief in human reason is apt to lead (as it has led in the past) to extravagant claims on behalf of authority. But the reach of authority is forever confined to the reach of reasoning. There can be no absolute, no total authority, because there does not exist any absolute truth or total reason. The belief in such absolute truth is associated with a claim to absolute authority, transcending the analysis here given, as faith transcends science.

What then is "false" authority? It is that phantom which recurs in human society when men issue communications as authoritative which are believed to allow for reasoned elaboration when actually they do not. That is why the psychological interpretation of authority leads astray; for people may well *believe* that communications could be effectively elaborated and are therefore worthy of acceptance when no such potentiality exists. The falseness of such authority is revealed the moment the pretended potentiality has to be actualized. There is nothing subtle or surprising in these observations: "genuine" and "false" are terms which customarily refer to the possibility that the appearance may be deceptive. In a remarkable study on the influence of authority in matters of opinion, a nineteenth-century liberal concluded that "in the present state of the civilized world, the progress of society will depend in part upon legislative improvements, and upon those measures which a government can command or influence; but it will depend still more upon the substitution of competent for incompetent guides of public opinion; upon the continued extension of their influence; and upon the consequent organization of a sound authority in all the departments of theory and practice."[26] Cast into the less hopeful mood of our skeptical age, one might say instead that the maintenance of a measure of civilized existence depends upon the continued operation of authority as outlined in this essay. As long as we can maintain a measure of authority, that is to say, as long as those who wield power recognize their responsibility for discretionary acts in the sense of an obligation to retain the regard for the potentiality of reasoned elaboration, a constitutional order can be maintained. Once this regard is lost — and it may be lost by man at large no longer accepting reason as a guide — the night of meaningless violence is upon us. In conclusion, I should like to quote a little-known passage from an *Address to the King* by Edmund Burke which was written at the time certain members of Parliament who had opposed the measures of the government in the contest between Britain and the American colonies thought of seceding from that venerable body. "We have been too early instructed, and too long habituated to believe, that the only firm seat of all authority is in the minds, affections, and interests of the people, to change our opinions ... for the convenience of a mere temporary

[26] See George Cornwall Lewis, *An Essay on the Influence of Authority in Matters of Opinion* (London, 1849). Lewis, in a striking sentence, lends support to the position here developed: "He who believes upon authority, entertains the opinion simply because it is entertained by a *person* who appears to him *likely to think correctly on the subject*." He defines the "principle of authority" as that of "adopting the belief of others, on a matter of opinion, without reference to the particular grounds on which that belief may rest" (pp. 6–7), where the stress is on the *particular*.

arrangement of state."[27] Only when what is commanded and maintained can be thus reasoned upon and defended is authority secure. Only then can the five answers given above to the question, "why should I agree or obey?" be stated in a manner worthy of acceptance in the eyes of those who give as well as those who receive them.

[27] Edmund Burke, *Works* (Boston, 1839), vol. V, p. 135.

Part III

Political Obligation

Introduction

H. L. A. Hart and Hanna Pitkin, in the first two selections of this part, make further contributions to the discussion of language and rules, and the implications and consequences of their place in social life. Hart examines such considerations in order to locate those aspects or areas of social and political practice in which questions about duty and obligation arise and to distinguish such questions from issues involving other moral concepts.[1] Pitkin's reflections on the rules governing "obligation" and "authority" lead to the conclusion that questions prominently discussed in the theory of political obligation are not genuine issues; they are issues that are in fact settled by the grammar of the concepts used in formulating them. When this is realized, the search for other sorts of answers to the questions will cease. In this respect Pitkin's article is an example of philosophical therapy of the kind Wittgenstein recommended.[2]

The bulk of the following discussion of obligation, however, is concerned with intensely practical questions about obedience and disobedience to law and government. Hart's remarks on this subject offer little more than a hint of a theory, but that theory has had considerable influence. Hart himself elaborates the theory slightly in selection 28, and the theory which John Rawls develops in his article in this part bears substantial resemblance to it. Pitkin takes up the question of obedience in much greater detail. She begins with an examination of the consent or contract theory according to which one has an obligation to obey because in some sense he has consented, contracted, or agreed to do so. Pitkin attempts a reformulation of this argument (some might think she abandons it completely) according to which (to oversimplify seriously) one has an obligation to obey if the government in question is such that he *ought to* consent, that is, if the government is and does what a government should be and should do. Pitkin admits that this theory looks a good deal like utilitarian theories of political obligation, but she rejects utilitarianism on the ground (very roughly) that it is unable to account for the conceptual facts about "authority" and "obligation" and the role they play in actual practice.

In his paper reprinted in this part, Rawls' particular purpose is to develop a defense for civil disobedience in a constitutional democracy. But he insists that this defense must be congruent with a general theory of political obligation in such democracies. As with Pitkin, he begins his sketch of such a theory from a contractarian position and attempts to reformulate the basic contentions of

[1] For a more fully developed version of Hart's argument in this respect, see his *The Concept of Law* (Oxford: Clarendon Press, 1961).

[2] Her argument is discussed at length in selection 3 of this book.

traditional forms of that theory so as to avoid objections to it. Although he does not discuss the matter explicitly in this paper, he views the social contract theory and utilitarianism as the main competitors for our allegiance in moral and political philosophy. His decision in favor of the former is based on his conviction that it is the only theory that can deal satisfactorily with justice. His theory of political obligation is derived from the fundamental propositions of his theory of justice, and the reader should consult his article on that subject (selection 25) in connection with his paper in this part. A number of his criticisms of utilitarianism are presented there.[3]

Richard Wasserstrom attacks what he calls the absolutist theory of political obligation, the doctrine according to which one is *never* justified in disobeying the law. This might be regarded as such an extreme and implausible view as to be unworthy of detailed consideration. But something very close to this position seems to be accepted by numerous people, and in any case in attacking the position Wasserstrom considers and criticizes a number of arguments commonly employed by those who do not themselves accept the absolutist position. Wasserstrom's argument is broadly utilitarian and he presents counterarguments to attacks on utilitarianism such as Pitkin and Rawls have put forward.

The last selection in this part, *The Crito*, is the first systematic discussion of political obligation, but it remains one of the very best we have. In very short compass Socrates takes up a surprising number of the major arguments for obedience and disobedience that have been advanced in a discussion that has continued for more than 2,000 years. Elsewhere the present writer has argued that if interpreted via the categories in which the discussions of our own day have taken place, his position is basically utilitarian.[4] However this may be, what is most important about Socrates' discussion is his attempt to order and assess the wide range of considerations relevant to decisions to obey or disobey the great diversity of laws and commands with which the citizen is presented.

Further Reading

Bedau, Hugo, ed. *Civil Disobedience*. New York: Pegasus, 1969.

Brandt, Richard. "The Concepts of Obligation and Duty," *Mind*, Vol. 73 (1964), pp. 374–393.

Flathman, Richard E. *Political Obligation*. New York: Atheneum Publishers, 1972.

Goldwin, Robert A., ed. *On Civil Disobedience*. Chicago: Rand McNally & Co. 1969.

Hare, R. M. "The Lawful Government," in Peter Laslett and W. G. Runciman, eds., *Philosophy, Politics and Society*, 3rd Series. Oxford: Basil Blackwell, 1967.

Pennock, J. R., and J. C. Chapman, eds. *Political and Legal Obligation*. New York: Atherton Press, Inc., 1970.

Plamenatz, J. P. *Consent, Freedom and Political Obligation*. London: Oxford University Press, 1968.

Prichard, H. A. *Moral Obligation*. London: Oxford University Press, 1949.

[3] Professor Rawls' recently published book *A Theory of Justice* (Cambridge, Mass.: Harvard University Press, 1971) presents the most fully developed and integrated statements of his views on the subjects of his articles reprinted in this volume.

[4] See my *Political Obligation*, op. cit., Chapter Eight. And see Chapter Seven of the same work for a defense of the utilitarian view against various recent attacks.

Rawls, John. "Legal Obligation and the Duty of Fair Play," in Sidney Hook, ed., *Law and Philosophy*. New York: New York University Press, 1964.

Tussman, Joseph. *Obligation and the Body Politic*. New York: Oxford University Press, 1960.

Walzer, Michael. *Obligations*. Cambridge, Mass: Harvard University Press, 1970.

10. Legal and Moral Obligation

H. L. A. Hart

Moral philosophers in both England and America have long spoken and written as if the phenomenon under investigation was primarily, if not exclusively, moral *obligation* or moral *duty*; very few have questioned the suitability of the expressions "obligations" and "duty" to describe the principal subject of their study. Yet, as their examples show, these philosophers have been very much concerned with such actions as the gratuitous infliction of pain on children or animals, the killing of human beings, the heartless abandonment of friends, lying and other forms of deception. Something more, I hope, than a blind wish to adhere to our common speech prompts the protest that it is absurd to speak of having a moral *duty* not to kill another human being, or an *obligation* not to torture a child. Surely when we are moved by moral repugnance and shrink from some squalid action the situation is ill-conveyed by saying that here we are acknowledging a *duty*; and surely it is at least misleading to say that we have acknowledged (or recognized) an *obligation* when in difficult circumstances, not provided for by anything that could reasonably be called a rule, we think out the consequences of alternative lines of conduct and decide what on the whole is best to do.

The point of such a protest is not, or at any rate not merely, that "duty" or "obligation" are too weak, too feeble in condemnatory force, for the blacker moral offenses. "Obligation" and "duty" are not inappropriate here because they are reserved for the relatively minor matters on a single moral scale to which belong also more serious elements (moral crimes). The point, rather, is that they do not belong to the same scale and the extension of these terms to the whole field of morality blinds us to its variety and complexity.

Two considerations might perhaps alert us to this fact. The first is that among the examples used by moral philosophers there are certainly some where the expressions "obligation" and "duty" sit quite happily. Moral obligations do arise from promises, from the position of parent, and there may be a moral obligation to obey the law. So, too, moral duties do spring from positions of trust like that of a confidential servant, or from recognized positions or roles in a social group such as that of being a host or a neighbor, a husband or a father. Such cases where the terminology of obligation and duty is so obviously appropriate have, I think, discernible common or related features, and these contrast with the kind of thing at stake when we insist that we ought not to inflict gratuitous pain. What tends to obscure the difference is that "ought" (and in some contexts both "must" and "should") may be used in urging others to abstain both from breaking their promises and from torturing children, and in moral criticism of these offenses when committed. Yet this is no better ground for the identification of what are disparate, though of course related, segments of morality than is the fact that, given

From A. I. Melden, ed., *Essays in Moral Philosophy* (Seattle: University of Washington Press, 1958), pp. 82–107, by permission of the author and publisher.

appropriate contexts, "ought," "must," and "should" may be used when it is patent that nothing moral is at stake. You ought to, you should, you must change your wet clothes.

Second, and more important, there is a whole world where duties and obligations are really at home. This is the legal world; for here both expressions are almost always appropriate for whatever the rules of an actually existing legal system forbid. If a statute forbids cruelty to children or animals, then we have a legal duty to forbear from such cruelty. In speaking of the legal obligation to do what we have bound ourselves by contract to do, we make no more felicitous use of the word "obligation" than when we speak of the legal obligation to keep off other people's land, or to refrain from assaulting or libeling them; but in ordinary nonlegal discourse and in morals it is different. So in the succeeding sections of this paper I propose first to inquire into the character of legal obligation and then to determine why in referring to certain moral situations we naturally make use of the legally colored concepts of obligation and duty.

I

It may perhaps help with the understanding of legal obligation and duty if we begin, not with an onslaught on definition, but by noting some of the remarkable things that can, in any developed legal system, be done about them, and hence be said about them. First and foremost, it is the case (and perhaps more obviously true of obligations than of many other features of a legal system) that legal obligations are very often (though not always) human artifacts in the sense that they may be deliberately created by the appropriate action of human beings and subjected to various modes of change and manipulation. Their status as obligations may be independent of their content for we not only may *have* legal duties and obligations, but we may *create*, or *impose* them (e.g., by legislation), or *incur* or *assume* them (e.g., by making contracts). They may be *varied* and *modified* and *extinguished*; and persons may (notably where obligations are created by contract) be *released* from them.

Of course, in any developed legal system, not only obligations or duties but other legal entities (rights, powers, immunities, and disabilities) may be similarly created, modified, or extinguished; and rights may be transferred, e.g., when property is alienated upon a sale. The most prominent and important example of the deliberate *creation* of legal duties and obligations is the creation of a legal obligation by legislative enactment. In any modern society legislation is a very complex operation. The legislative process involves not only the cooperation of numerous persons qualified under existing legal rules to take part, but also their compliance with a complex procedure determined by legal rules, which exist and are accepted as governing the process. Normally, the crucial step is a vote for or against a legislative proposal usually presented in written form. Given such circumstances, the upshot of the vote and of certain subsequent formalities (assent by the Queen, or signature by the President, or lapse of a certain time without notice of disapproval) is that a law is *made* or *enacted*, introducing, say, two years of military service for all males between the ages of twenty-one and thirty-five, or prohibiting the sale of intoxicating liquors. In this manner legislators create obligations and impose them on others (and on themselves in their personal capacity) who are thenceforth legally bound to do or forbear doing certain things. Subordinate authorities may also by enactment be given a derivative legal *power* to create further obligations and duties within a certain area.

It is perhaps useful to compare and contrast these legislative operations with those operations whereby a person also creates obligations but imposes them, not on others, but only upon himself. The most notable example of this is, of course, the bilateral or consensual contract which is the legal analogue of the promise where, e.g., one man binds himself to deliver a ton of bricks to another by a certain date in consideration of the other's binding himself to pay £100 for them. But there are other forms of self-imposition of obligation: both in the English and in the American systems a person may declare himself a trustee of property perhaps for persons yet unborn, and immediately thereupon is under obligation or duty not to deal with it in certain ways which were open to him up to that point.

How are the creation, imposition, modification, and extinction of obligations and other operations on other legal entities such as rights possible? How can such things be done? This Kantian-sounding question can only be answered by describing in detail how in fact they are done. The lawyer, so used to this kind of thing, would reply in his own terminology, "These things can be done because the law confers *powers* upon persons to do these things: they do them in the exercise of legal powers." But the philosopher may well inquire: What are these powers? What is it for a law to confer a power and for someone to exercise such a power? "Power" here does not mean capacity to bring about observable physical change, and certainly to some these operations have appeared a sort of legal (and moral) alchemy, not susceptible of any explanation. Hagerström,[1] faced with the difficulties of analyzing the simplest one of such operations, namely, the transfer of ownership, concluded that the character of all such operations could only be elucidated by reference to a widespread belief in the magical powers of words to bring about changes in a suprasensible world of legal rights and duties. He developed his theories mainly in relation to Roman law, starting from the acute observation that the crucial words used by the purchaser in the *mancipatio*, the Roman formal transfer of property ("I say this slave is mine according to the law"), could not be intended as a statement of ordinary fact since the words, if treated as a statement, would be false at the time they were spoken, for the ownership did not "pass" to the purchaser till later.

This certainly was a flash of insight, but Hagerström's approach suffered badly from the failure to notice that the theory that the creation, transfer, or modification of obligations and rights was "magical" had just as much (so just as little) force in relation to the central operative words used in the enactment of a modern statute imposing obligations, or the operative words (words of grant) in a private document such as conveyance or will. The modern legislative formulas ("Now it is hereby enacted") and the operative words ("X hereby conveys unto Y," "I hereby bequeath to B") taken as statements of facts are also false, for the "acts," "deeds," or "instruments" in which they appear do not "take effect" until further formalities (signing, sealing, witnessing, delivery, and so forth) are completed or often until some later event happens, such as the testator's death in the case of a will.

[1] See Axel Hagerström, *Inquiry into the Nature of Law and Morals,* ed. Karl Olivecrona, trans. C. D. Broad (Stockholm: Almqvist & Wiksell, 1953), and the present writer's review in *Philosophy,* XXX (1955), 369–73.

So Hagerström leaves us with the residual problem: How can words have legal effects, and what are the effects that they have? Our concern is only with a special part of his question: How can words create legal obligations, and what are the legal obligations they create? But even this necessarily involves consideration of the foundation of any legal system, and of part of what is involved in the assertion that a legal system exists; for any answer that stops short of this will leave the original problem on our hands. Thus we might, indeed, we must, begin by saying that, if words are to be used to create legal obligations, rules of the system must exist providing that if they are used (by the appropriate persons in the appropriate circumstances) these persons designated by these words shall be legally bound or have a legal obligation to do or to abstain from certain actions. It is easy to see that both behind the words used by a municipal corporation enacting a bylaw imposing an obligation on occupiers of land to drain or to fence it in from the highway, and behind the words used in a lease under which the tenant has an obligation to pay rent, there must be rules of the system providing that if certain words are used in this way then the occupiers of land in the one case and the tenant in the other case shall have these obligations. But what does it mean to say of those rules that they exist and that they provide that persons shall have such obligations? In the case of subordinate rules of the system, such as the statutes conferring legislative powers on a municipal corporation, the assertion that the rules exist means that they belong to a class of rules marked off as valid rules of the particular system by criteria specified in the fundamental rules of the system, such as the English rule that what the Queen in Parliament enacts is law, or in the United States the rule of the Constitution that (subject to certain restrictions) what Congress enacts is law in certain fields. But to say of these fundamental rules (which provide and specify the legislative competence of the legislative authority) that they *exist* is to say something different. "Exist" here cannot mean "valid, given the system's criteria of validity" as, roughly, it does in the case of subordinate rule of the system. In this case "exists" must refer to the *actual practice* of the particular social group whose legal system is under consideration. Even in the case of the simplest imaginable legal system where a monarch has unrestricted legislative authority to enact law imposing legal obligations by pronouncing or writing down what he requires to be done, the actual practice of the group presupposed by the assertion that he has this authority is complex and not shortly describable. It was too shortly described by Austin[2] as a general habit of obedience to a person or persons not in a like habit of obedience to others. Kelsen,[3] seeing the inadequacies of this formulation, divorced the "basic norm" of a legal system from any actual practice by misleadingly characterizing it as a fundamental "hypothesis" or "postulate" made by the jurist examining the system. The inadequacies of both these extremes have led others to insist that what is at the root of every legal system is a general recognition of a *moral* obligation to obey the law so that there is a necessary[4] or analytic connection and not merely an

---

[2] See John Austin, *The Province of Jurisprudence Determined,* ed. H. L. A. Hart (London: Weidenfeld & Nicolson, 1954), Lecture VI, pp. 198–205.

[3] See Hans Kelsen, *General Theory of Law and State* (Cambridge, Mass.: Harvard University Press, 1949): ". . . a juristic hypothesis – that is, a basic norm, to be established by a logical analysis of actual juristic thinking" (p. xv); "The basic norm of a legal order is the postulated ultimate rule according to which the norms of this order are established and annulled, receive and lose their validity" (p. 116).

[4] See, for example, A. L. Goodhart, *English Law and the Moral Law* (London: Stevens & Sons, 1953): "By blandly suggesting that this basic norm must be 'presupposed to be binding'

empirical one between the statement that a legal system exists and the statement that most of the population recognizes a moral obligation to obey the law.

To steer between these aberrations of juristic theory it is necessary first to see why "habit" and "obedience" are not enough to characterize the situation in which we say legal obligations are created by legislation. If members of a group merely have a *habit* of obeying an individual, X, who threatens them and is able to harm them in the event of disobedience, this situation might be described by saying they are *obliged* or *compelled* to obey him or to do what he says, but not by saying that they have or recognize an *obligation* to do what X says. If we are to speak of their having or recognizing an obligation to do what X says, their attitude to X's words must be more than habitual obedience. The minimum requirement in *addition* to general obedience, if we are to speak of the group's recognizing or having a legal obligation to do something specified by X, is (1) that X's words should generally be accepted as constituting a standard of behavior so that deviations from it (unlike the mere failure to follow a mere habit current in the society, such as that of drinking tea or coffee) are treated as occasions for criticism of various sorts; (2) that references to X's words are generally made as *reasons* for doing or having done what X says, as supporting *demands* that others should do what he says, and as rendering at least permissible the application of coercive repressive measures to persons who deviate from the standard constituted by X's words.

How many of the social group (subjects or officials) must do these things, how continuously, and how long to constitute "general" obedience and "general" use of X's words in this way admits of no determinate answer, just as we are not called on to say exactly how old a man must be to be middle-aged. But in any social group where obligations are created by legislation, and the expressions "I have a legal obligation to do this" and "He has a legal obligation to do that" have their present force, there must be a social practice at least as complex as I have described and not merely habitual obedience on the part of the members of the group. Anyone who uses such forms of expression as "I (you) have an obligation to" implies that his own attitude to the legislator's words is that described, for these statements of obligation are used to draw conclusions from legal rules on the footing that the rules are authoritative for the speaker. One who repudiated the authority altogether might of course recognize that he would be made to suffer if he disobeyed the rules, but the natural expression for this point of view would be not "I (you) have an obligation to" but "I am (you are) obliged to" or "under this system I (you) will suffer if I (you) do not."

The foregoing perhaps sufficiently shows the inadequacies of the characterization of the root of a legal system in terms of a *habit* of obedience. Kelsen was right in insisting that there must be more than habits or regularities of behavior in the narrow sense of regularly doing what the authority says. Yet his conception of the basic norm as a rule, "hypothesis," or "axiom," the "validity" of which is

---

Kelsen avoids the most important problem in legal philosophy" (p. 18); "If . . . we regard the law as a rule which is recognised as obligatory then the element of force becomes of minor importance. We then realise that the obligatory nature of these rules is based on other grounds, and that one of the most important of these is that of moral law. It is for this reason that the moral sense is one of the dominant forces not only in establishing the efficacy of law, but also in its very existence. The jurist cannot ignore the moral law as irrelevant to his subject because if he does so then he will be ignoring one of the grounds on which the basic idea of obligation is based" (p. 28).

"assumed" or "postulated"[5] brings in a set of quite inappropriate quasi-mathematical expressions that we might indeed adopt if those were the only alternatives to describing the relevant facts in terms of "habits of obedience." But there is a third alternative, and this is to describe the relevants facts in terms not of habits but of the rules actually accepted by a social group. The question whether a group does accept a given rule is different in the ways already indicated from the question whether it habitually obeys a person, though the two questions are alike in that both are questions of fact and Austin is to be preferred to Kelsen for seeing that a statement of fact and not an "assumption of validity" is presupposed in any statement that someone has a legal obligation. If a group of persons behaves in the way we have distinguished as accepting what a legislator says as constituting a standard of behavior, then they accept the rule that he is to be obeyed, and then the rule that his word is law exists. The rule that what the Queen in Parliament enacts is law exists in this way. Once such a rule is thus found to exist in the actual practice of a group, it is absurd to speak of it as a *valid* rule, equally absurd to speak of it as *invalid* or of *assuming* or *postulating* its *validity*. We might as well speak of postulating or assuming the validity of an actually existing social rule that we take hats off on entering a house. Of course we can raise a number of different questions about such rules, e.g., whether it is a good or desirable thing that members of a group should accept them or have a moral obligation to go on with them, but it is most confusing to discuss this question in terms of "validity."

The third misconception, namely, that if a legal system exists there must (logically) be a general recognition of a *moral* obligation to obey the law, is an excessive reaction to Kelsen's geometrical characterization of the basic norm. Of course it is probably true that unless a majority voluntarily cooperated in obeying the rules of a coercive legal system it could not endure; it may even be true that unless a great number conceived themselves and others morally bound to obey, the system might be quite unstable. But this is insufficient to demonstrate the alleged *logical* connection between "There is a legal system in England" and "In England there is a general recognition of a moral obligation to obey the law," though the first of these is certainly true and the second is probably true. Equally irrelevant to the precise point are the undoubted facts that the development of the law by courts and legislature has been powerfully influenced by the moral convictions of the population and always will be. This does not show that no legal system exists unless obedience is motivated by a conviction that there is a moral obligation to obey. The assertion that there is a legal system in England (or anywhere else) does entail that there is in fact general acceptance of a fundamental rule such as the rule that what the Queen in Parliament enacts is law, though its form may be far more complex than this: general acceptance of such a rule does consist in more than habitual obedience for it includes the further use of, and attitude to, the enacted law which I have described. But both this general obedience and the further use of and attitudes to the law may be motivated by fear, inertia, admiration of tradition, or long-sighted calculation of selfish interests as well as by recognition of moral obligation. As long as the general complex practice is there, this is enough to answer

[5] See Kelsen, *General Theory of Law and State,* as cited above and as follows: "The validity of this first constitution is the last presupposition, the final postulate, upon which the validity of all the norms of our legal order depends" (p. 115); "The basic norm is an indispensable assumption because, without it, the normative character of the basic historical event could not be established" (p. 396).

affirmatively the inquiry whether a legal system exists. The question of what motivates the practice, though important, is an independent inquiry.

Once the complex social practice is established whereby a person's words are accepted as constituting a standard of behavior to the group, the legislative authority thereby constituted need not (though it may) be limited to the simple case of direct creation of obligation by legislation enjoining or forbidding specific actions or classes of action. The legislator may have authority to enact further rules conferring authority on others similar to his own for the regulation of limited areas of conduct (subordinate legislation) or rules empowering private individuals to create obligations for themselves, e.g., by contract. But the obligations created in those derivative ways under enacted rules owe their status as obligations ultimately to the underlying practice of the social group in accepting the legislative enactments as constituting standards of behavior and can be understood only if we understand the simple fundamental case of the creation of obligation by direct enactment and its dependence on the complex social practice that constitutes this basic authority.

We now can consider shortly those cases where legal obligations are not *created* at all but arise directly not under rules that have been deliberately introduced by legislation but under customary rules, and also those obligations that are created by the exercise of power conferred by such customary rules. Hitherto we have concentrated attention on those legal obligations that are brought into existence by deliberate legislation in order to demonstrate certain important features: it is, however, true that in most legal systems many rules under which obligations arise are not deliberately created but are customary in origin. "Custom" is usually a subordinate criterion of validity in modern legal systems in the sense that such customary rules may be deprived of their validity by legislative enactment while the converse in most cases is not true; but there is no *logical* reason (though every practical reason) why a legal system should not have as its sole criterion of validity the rule that only those rules are valid which represent the customary long-established practice of the group in certain matters or the practice of some subgroup. In such cases authority is not attributed to the holder of any office and obligations are not conceived as created by deliberate acts but as owing their status to the fact of traditional practice: *this practice* is taken as the standard. Sometimes even the degree of generalization involved in the recognition of "custom" as a general criterion of validity may not be achieved. There may be no recognition of any general principle as rendering actions legally obligatory but only a discrete set of rules may exist, which means that the social group simply accepts certain distinct types of conduct as standards of behavior and for the criterion of behavior in the way described. This plainly would be near the vanishing point of legal *system.*

It remains only to draw attention to the fact that, even where legal rules are customary, powers to create obligations may arise under such rules. The power to create obligations by simple contract in many Anglo-American jurisdictions arises under common law rules that were not introduced by deliberate legislation, but are conceived of as representing the long-established customary practice of the courts. Of course where a legal system exists containing among its criteria of validity a rule of precedent, i.e., that those rules are valid which are extracted from past cases by loosely defined rules of interpretation, the line between those rules that owe their validity to an authority's deliberate act and those that do not becomes blurred though not (as some Realists have argued) nonexistent.

II

We have yet to discuss in detail what most people would regard as *the* salient feature of an obligation and to some extent of duties: this is the important connection between obligation and coercion or compulsion. If we have an obligation to do something there is some sense in which we are bound to do it, and where we are bound there is some sense in which we are or may be compelled to do it. To probe these notions it is important to distinguish three things: (1) being physically compelled to do something, (2) being obliged to do something, (3) having an obligation to do something. The difficulty of the topic is that of stating without exaggeration the relation between the third member of this trio and the others, and Austin, who made in the introductory sections of *The Province of Jurisprudence Determined* the most painstaking effort to understand the notion of obligation, did fatally exaggerate this relation. He perceived correctly that when a man is dragged to prison, and so in some sense compelled to enter it, this is not a case of having an obligation or dury to go there. But, though he avoided this mistake, Austin defined obligation and duty in terms of the sanction or evil which one who commands (signifies his desire to another that he should do something) threatens to inflict in the event of disobedience.[6] To have a duty or an obligation, according to Austin, is to be liable or obnoxious to an evil so threatened where "liable" or "obnoxious" means "likely to incur." The most obvious defect of this definition is that it would be satisfied by the case of a gunman's ordering me to hand over my purse at the point of a gun, where we would *not* say, "I had an obligation to hand over my purse"; what encourages the mistake is that we *would* say in such a case, "I was *obliged* to hand over my purse." So at first sight Austin's account looks like a fairly accurate definition of "being obliged" to do something and a very poor definition of "having an obligation" to do something. But we must take into account Austin's additions to and refinements upon his starting point. His account of specifically *legal* obligation differs from the primitive example of the gunman in a number of respects. Instead of the gunman, we have the sovereign defined as the person or persons whom the bulk of society generally obey, and who is himself not in a like habit of obedience to anyone else; further, commands of the sovereign are to follow "general"[7] courses of conduct and are addressed usually to numbers of persons. Apart from these qualifications for the special case of legal obligation, Austin also insists that his definition would be satisfied even if the chance of incurring the threatened evil was very small, and the evil itself was very small: "the slightest chance of the slightest evil" is enough to constitute obligation

---

[6] See Austin, *The Province of Jurisprudence Determined:* "Being liable to evil from you if I comply not with a wish which you signify, I am *bound* or *obliged* by your command, or I lie under a *duty* to obey it" (p. 14); ". . . wherever a duty lies, a command has been signified; and whenever a command is signified, a duty is imposed" (p. 14); "The evil which will probably be incurred in case a command be disobeyed or (to use an equivalent expression) in case a duty be broken, is frequently called a *sanction,* or an *enforcement of obedience.* Or (varying the phrase) the command or duty is said to be *sanctioned* or *enforced* by the chance of incurring the evil" (p. 15); "When I am talking *directly* of the chance of incurring the evil, or (changing the expression) of the liability or obnoxiousness to the evil, I employ the term *duty,* or the term *obligation* . . ." (p. 18).

[7] *Ibid.:* "Now where it obliges *generally* to acts or forbearances of a *class,* a command is a law or rule" (p. 19).

or duty.[8] Lastly, Austin, albeit with hesitation, suggests that if a person has an obligation or duty he must have the threatened evil "in prospect," i.e., fear it,[9] though certainly this psychological element is little stressed.

Unfortunately these additions and refinements cause Austin's analysis to fall between two stools. It ceases to be a plausible analysis of "being obliged" to do something and remains an inadequate analysis of "having an obligation." To see precisely where it fails we must concede something which may be disputed: Austin would not allow any system of rules to count as a legal system unless its rules provided for the infliction of evil in the case of disobedience. We may for the purpose of the argument concede this as a part of the definition of "legal," though it was deduced by Austin from propositions that we might wish to reject: he thought laws were commands, and he thought commands were significations of desire by one who had the intention and some ability to inflict some evil in the event of disobedience. But, even if we concede the analytical connection between the notion of a legal system and that of a sanction in the form of evil or harm, the definition of having an obligation in terms of the *chance* of incurring the threatened evil, and of the individual's having this evil in prospect, leads to absurdities.

We may deal first with the psychological element (prospect of evil), which Austin only very uncertainly uses. The statement that a thief has a legal obligation not to take the purse is not a psychological statement about him. He may have no fear at all of the threatened evil, and yet his obligation remains. If he is deterred by fear we may say, rather oddly, that he was obliged to leave it alone. Second, the statement that a person has an obligation on a particular occasion is quite independent of any assessment of the chances of his incurring the evil though these may be very important in considering where he could be said to be obliged to do something that he did on a particular occasion. There is no contradiction or even oddity in saying, "It's your duty to report for military service, but, since you're living in Monte Carlo and there's no extradition treaty, there's not the slightest chance of their getting you."

Third, there is something quite ludicrous in Austin's first stressing the importance of the threatened evil and then reducing it to "the slightest chance of the slightest evil." This ruins his analysis as an analysis even of being obliged to do something. Only where a choice is made less eligible by some substantial disadvantage do we speak of being obliged.

The most general cricitism of Austin's analysis of obligation is that his inadequate notions of chance of incurring evil, prospect of threatened evil, are misleading because they obscure a central element, and this is simply the existence of rules of the appropriate kind. The most charitable view of Austin's talk of the chances of incurring evil is to regard it as expressing in inappropriate predictive terminology the following two facts: (1) if a legal system is to exist under which obligations are created there must at its root be the complex social practice we have

---

[8] *Ibid.:* "But where there is the smallest chance of incurring the smallest evil, the expression of a wish amounts to a command, and, therefore, imposes a duty. The sanction, if you will, is feeble or insufficient; but still there *is* a sanction, and, therefore, a duty and a command" (p. 16).

[9] *Ibid.:* "If, in spite of that evil in prospect, I comply not with the wish which you signify, I am said to disobey your command, or to violate the duty which it imposes" (p. 14); ". . . *superiority* signifies *might:* the power of affecting others with evil or pain, and of forcing them, through fear of that evil, to fashion their conduct to one's wishes" (p. 24).

already described; (2) the system must contain rules providing for the application of sanctions in the event of disobedience though not all rules need have sanctions "annexed" to them. Without the notion of a system of rules resting on that complex social practice, the difference between "obliging" and "imposing or creating an obligation" cannot be made clear.

Hence the important connection between the concept of coercion and obligation cannot be clearly stated in Austinian terms with its impoverished vocabulary of habit and its inadequate analysis of command in terms of the expression of a wish that people should act in certain ways made by one who intends and has some power to visit disobedience with some evil. The coercion in question may indeed take the form of the infliction of evil as it does in the case of a municipal legal system, but if it does the application of the evil must be something for which the rules of the system itself provide. However clear the actual power of a legislator was to visit certain conduct with pains, his threat and even use of force to coerce people to obey him would not constitute an obligation unless these were provided for by means of the appropriate legislative forms. At the most people would be obliged to do what he said. So the essential element of coercion is not the fact (the chance or the prospect) that evil will follow disobedience, but there should be an existing system of rules conferring authority on persons to prohibit behavior and to visit breaches of the prohibition with the appropriate coercive, repressive, or punitory techniques of the system.

Some qualification though not abandonment must be made of this last point. In all municipal legal systems there are some cases where there is no provision for sanctions in the event of a breach of a rule. Though perhaps no logical vice or infinite regress would attach to a self-referring rule that all officials should exact sanctions for all offenses including any breach of this rule itself, it is quite common for legal rules to require officials to do certain things and for the system to provide no sanction in the case of their breach. This is for example the case with the obligation imposed by the United States Constitution on the President to take care for the due execution of the laws. Yet we do not hesitate to refer to such cases as cases of official duty or obligation. They show that even within a legal system the complex features that characterize the standard case of obligation may come apart. This is reflected in juristic terminology, such as that of "duties of imperfect obligation," which the Romans invented for just such cases; and it helps to generate part of the skeptical doubts whether international law is "really" law or better classified as a branch of morality.

III

Within the vaguely bounded field of morality, there is certainly a sector (no doubt also vaguely bounded) in which we make use of a concept characterized by three salient features distinctive of the concept of a legal obligation. These features I shall refer to by terms that I hope will be found self-explanatory: (1) dependence on the actual practice of a social group, (2) possible independence of content, and (3) coercion. Outside philosophy, the expressions "obligation" and "duty" are used mainly for the appraisal or criticism of conduct by standards that have these three features and are not used indifferently for all forms of moral judgment. But certainly even nonphilosophical usage sometimes extends beyond this, and my concern is not to legislate in favor of a more restricted use of these expressions but only to determine the differences between different sorts of moral phenomena obscured by this extension. This is worth doing for perhaps two reasons: first, there is undoubtedly a standing temptation in philosophy to assimilate all types of moral judgment to a single type; second, we can best understand other areas of morality if we *first* focus clearly on the three salient features of obligation as they appear in the actual morality of a social group. To characterize morality (as, e.g., R. M. Hare does in his illuminating book, *The Language of Morals*[10]) as *primarily* a matter of the application to conduct of those ultimate principles which the individual accepts or to which he commits himself for the conduct of his life seems to me an excessively Protestant approach. Important as this aspect or kind of moral judgment is, we need to understand it as a development from the primary phenomenon of the morality of a social group.

In suggesting that we distinguish one type of moral judgment from another, I do not in the least wish to deny that the conduct that they require may often be identical. It is often the case that one and the same particular action is required by different moral principles. If I promise to look after and protect a neighbor's child I have an obligation to do this which arises from my promise; but I may also think it inconsistent with my moral principles to permit unnecessary suffering of this as of any other child though I should not naturally phrase my recognition of this latter principle in terms of recognizing an obligation. Here is one way in which different principles of moral conduct overlap. But they may also coincide in a different and more important way. It may be that the social group in which we live and accept the institution of a promise as breeding obligations also endorses the different and wider principle that it is wrong to inflict gratuitous suffering. Even here, so long as we think that the force of this wider principle does not depend on its actual acceptance by the social group (but is something by which we may judge the actual morality of social groups), we have again to distinguish two different kinds of principle requiring the same action on a particular occasion. The area of morality I am attempting to delineate is that of principles which would lose their moral force unless they were widely accepted in a particular social group.

Promises constitute the obvious case of moral obligation, and here certainly we have all the three salient features that we have noticed. If we are to incur such obligations there must be some established procedure generally accepted by some specific social group whereby the utterance or writing of a certain range of expressions is sufficient to render actions specified by them obligatory for the speaker or writer. If no such procedures exist, promising is logically impossible, just as saluting would be logically impossible if there were no accepted conventions specifying the gestures of formal recognition within a military group. When we promise we make use of specified procedures in order to change the moral situation; in lawyer's language we exercise a "power" conferred by rules to change moral relations.

Promises have pre-eminently the feature I have called independence of content: the obligation springs not from the nature of the promised action but from the use of the procedure by the appropriate person in the appropriate circumstances. This independence is further manifested by the fact that the obligation thus deliberately created may also be deliberately extinguished by the promisee. This independence

---

[10] R. M. Hare, *The Language of Morals* (Oxford: Clarendon Press, 1952).

of content does not, however, entail that there is no restriction whatsoever upon the classes of action that a person may make obligatory for himself by promising to do them. Morals like law may have principles of "public policy" and render "void" a promise that from the start involved doing something patently immoral; but we should distinguish from such cases those where we subsequently discover moral reasons (perhaps in changed circumstances) against doing what we have promised to do. In these latter cases we have a moral obligation arising from the promise, but one that we consider in the light of other principles we ought not to carry out.

The third element of *coercion* needs careful scrutiny in this and other cases of moral obligation. In the case of legal obligation, rules typically provide that, in the event of failure or threatened failure to do what other primary rules require, there must be some official determination of the fact of this failure (judgment of a court) and then a variety of official steps taken to punish the failure or, in civil cases, to secure performance or its nearest equivalent. These steps include imprisonment used as punishment or used differently as a means of inducing obedience in a particular case or the forcible seizure of money or goods (execution) for compensation – and there are many other variants. By contrast (and this is one major distinction between moral and legal obligation), the coercion characteristic of moral obligation takes the form not of the infliction of harm or the use of force but primarily of the exposure of the individual to reminders that he has failed to comply with rules regarded by the social group as a matter of serious importance and to demand that he should comply. The typical moral pressure takes the form of an appeal not to fear of harmful consequences or to the futility of refusing to do what in the end one will be forced to do but to the delinquent's presumed respect for the rules he has broken. "You have broken your promise." "That would involve breaking your promise." The assumption inherent in such criticism is that what is most needed is a reminder of what the rules require and that the guilt or shame engendered by the contemplation of their breach will suffice or at least tend to inhibit future or continued failure to comply. Of course there are ancillary techniques: blame, praise, exhortation, severance of social relations, temporary exclusion from the group may be used, and these may shade off into something very like threats of harm and punishment. Yet, as soon as an appeal is made primarily to fear even of unorganized "sanctions," we are on the way from moral to legal obligation. The fact that moral pressure is characteristically exerted through an appeal to the delinquent's assumed respect for the institution violated, together with the fact that the plea, "I could not help it," is, if substantiated, always an excuse, jointly constitute the "internality" of morals as compared with the "externality" of law. This has sometimes been grossly misrepresented by the contention that whereas laws require us to do certain actions morals only require us to be in certain states of mind (or soul).

If we now consider not promises but the moral duties attached to an office or role in social life, these differ most notably in that the particular duties attached to these roles (a husband's duty to support his wife, the father's to look after his children) are not conceived of as truly created by the deliberate choice of the individual. The independence of content that these duties have is therefore rather different in that they are conceived of as *assumed* by entry upon the particular role so that one who takes up the role is thereby specially committed to discharging these duties. They are not principles of universal application to all societies alike but are conceived of as something that may vary from society to society together with a whole mass of associated institutions. Hence the obligation to maintain wife or children may not attach to husband or father in societies that think of it as normal for the wife to work and for children to be provided with support at the public expense. As noted above, though wider principles of morality may require a man to look after any child in need of care, the *duty* on a parent to do this springs from the fact that this particular society attaches moral importance to persons occupying such a position doing this.

If we consider the notion of a moral obligation to obey the law, we find that there are a number of issues requiring separation. One of them we have already discussed: viz., the claim that if a legal system exists then it follows that there must logically be a general recognition of moral obligation to obey the law so that if there is no such general recognition of a moral obligation to obey the law it would be a mistake to say that a legal system existed. Apart from this, however, there is some ambiguity in the notion of an obligation to obey *the law*. Presumably, if we consider that we should obey only those laws whose effects are likely to be (morally) good or the lesser of two (moral) evils, this would not be the recognition of a moral obligation to obey the law but only the application of some general principle that we should maximize good and minimize evil. The recognition of an obligation to obey *the law* must as a minimum imply that there is at least some area of conduct regulated by law in which we are not free to judge the moral merits of particular laws and to make our obedience conditional on this judgment. In a modern state it seems most plausible to suggest that this area is that which includes matters of defense and economic welfare but excludes, say, matters of religion or esthetic taste. Do we in fact recognize that we are bound within some such area to obey the law as such? There is at least a plausible argument that we do not in fact recognize any such obligation to obey the law as such but that our moral scruples against disobeying those laws whose effects we may think bad is due to the consideration that our disobedience might encourage general disorder and would therefore be the greater of two evils. Yet, though plausible, this is not convincing: it ignores, first, the fact that if we are ready to go to prison rather than obey our attitudes might very well strengthen the system as a whole and not weaken it; second, it ignores the very important fact that obedience often appears to most not as something required by a general principle that we should not harm human beings unnecessarily but as something required by the consideration that the particular members of our own society have obeyed the law and expect it to be obeyed. Where obedience to the law is motivated by such considerations, there is recognition of a moral obligation to obey with the three salient features that characterize it.

IV

In conclusion, I shall shortly consider certain motives for extending the use of "obligation" or "duty" to a much wider field so as to include those principles by reference to which we criticize adherence to or departures from the accepted morality of a social group. In the little-read second and third chapters of *The Province of Jurisprudence Determined*, Austin described the area of morality with which I have been concerned as that of "positive morality";[11] with it he contrasted

---

[11] Austin, *The Province of Jurisprudence Determined*, pp. 12 and 125–29.

the Law of God, which constituted in his view the proper standard for the criticism of both positive law and positive morality and to which the principles of general utility are our "index." On such a view the ultimate principles of morality are the commands of God, and on this view we shall have no difficulty in conceiving of all the actions that they require as obligations. This is so because of the strength of the analogy between fundamental principles so conceived and the three salient features of obligation. For, first, fundamental moral principles on this view will be independent of content since they will owe their status not to what they require but to their being the commands of God. Second, God has every power and, on some accounts, every intention to punish disobedience or render it futile. But God's authority is not on such a view constituted by the actual practice of a social group, and it is this which renders the analogy imperfect so that the claim that "I have a moral obligation to do X" means the same as "God has commanded me to do X" may be a source of confusion even among those who share this view.

A very different motive for the extension of the concept of obligation is to be found in J. S. Mill's *Utilitarianism*[12] and probably still inspires most of those who wish to use the term widely. Mill says that

> ... the idea of penal sanction, which is the essence of law, enters not only into the conception of injustice, but into that of any kind of wrong. We do not call anything wrong, unless we mean to imply that a person ought to be punished in some way or other for doing it; if not by law, by the opinion of his fellow-creatures; if not by opinion, by the reproaches of his own conscience. This seems the real turning point of the distinction between morality and simple expediency. It is a part of the notion of Duty in every one of its forms, that a person may rightfully be compelled to fulful it.

Here, it seems to me, Mill very accurately fastens on the notion of coercion as essential to both legal and moral obligation, but this is accurate where coercion refers to the attitudes or actions of other human beings and where compulsion has a similar meaning. There is, however, a step of some magnitude from the notion of being punished or compelled by "the law and the opinion of fellow creatures" to the notion of "punishment or compulsion by the reproaches of conscience." Some analogy there is; yet it may well be felt that its utility is limited, and that the line between all "morality" and "simple expediency" is far too complex to be drawn in this way.

---

[12] See J. S. Mill, *Utilitarianism* (Everyman's Library ed.; New York: E. P. Dutton & Co., 1910), chap. v, p. 45.

11. Obligation and Consent—II

Hanna Pitkin

A reexamination of even the most venerable traditional problems of political theory can sometimes yield surprisingly new and relevant results.[1] The problem of political obligation, for example, and its most popular "solution," based on consent, turn out on reexamination to be rather different from what we have come to assume about them. The problem of political obligation resolves itself into at least four mutually related but partially independent questions:

1. The limits of obligation (" *When* are you obligated to obey, and when not?")
2. The locus of sovereignty ("*Whom* are you obligated to obey?")
3. The difference between legitimate authority and mere coercion ("Is there *really* any difference; are you ever *really* obligated?")
4. The justification of obligation ("*Why* are you ever obligated to obey even a legitimate authority?")

And the consent theory of obligation, as exemplified in Locke's *Second Treatise* and Joseph Tussman's *Obligation and the Body Politic*, turns out to yield a new formulation – perhaps a new interpretation of consent theory, perhaps an alternative to it – that might be labelled either the doctrine of the "nature of the government" or the doctrine of "hypothetical consent."[2]

It teaches that your obligation depends not on any actual act of consenting, past or present, by yourself or your fellow-citizens, but on the character of the government. If it is a good, just government doing what a government should, then you must obey it; if it is a tyrannical, unjust government trying to do what no government may, then you have no such obligation. Or to put it another way, your obligation depends not on whether you have consented but on whether the government is such that you *ought* to consent to it, whether its actions are in accord with the authority a hypothetical group of rational men in a hypothetical state of nature would have (had) to give to any government they were founding. Having shown how this formulation emerges from Locke's and Tussman's ideas, I want now to defend it as a valid response to what troubles us about political obligation, and as a response more consonant than most with the moral realities of human decisions about obedience and resistance. At the same time the discussion should also demonstrate how many different or even conflicting things that one might want to call "consent" continue to be relevant – a fact which may help to explain the tenacity of traditional consent theory in the face of its manifest difficulties. Such a defense and demonstration, with a detailed attention to such decisions, are difficult; the discussion from here on will be more speculative, and will raise more questions than it answers.

From *American Political Science Review,* Vol. 60 (1966), pp. 39–52, by permission of the author and publisher.

[1] This and part of the following paragraph are intended to summarize the argument of "Obligation and Consent – I," This *Review,* 59 (December, 1965), pp. 990–999.

[2] John Locke, *Second Treatise of Civil Government*; Joseph Tussman, *Obligation and the Body Politic* (New York: Oxford, 1960).

I. The Theory Applied

Our new doctrine seems most obviously satisfactory as a response to question three, concerning the difference between legitimate authority and mere coercion. For it teaches that legitimate authority is precisely that which *ought* to be obeyed, to which one ought to consent, which deserves obedience and consent, to which rational men considering all relevant facts and issues would consent, to which consent can be justified. Anything or anyone else who tries to command us is then merely coercing, and is not entitled to our obedience. This answer to the question is essentially what Wittgenstein calls a "point of grammar;" it reminds us of the way concepts like "authority," "legitimacy," "law" are related in our language (and therefore in our world) to concepts like "consent" and "obedience."[3] To call something a legitimate authority is normally to imply that it ought to be obeyed, You cannot, without further rather elaborate explanation, maintain simultaneously *both* that this government has legitimate authority over you *and* that you have no obligation to obey it. Thus if you say that you consent to it (recognize it as an authority), that statement itself is normally a recognition of the obligation to obey, at least at the moment it is uttered. Part of what "authority" means is that those subject to it are obligated to obey. As an answer to question three, then, this doctrine tells us (something about) what legitimate authority *is* by reminding us of something about what "legitimate authority" *means*. But of course that is not yet to provide criteria for telling apart the two species — legitimate authority and mere coercion — when you encounter them in reality.

Thus, insofar as our *real* need is for a practical way of deciding whether to obey or resist this government right now, or which of two rival authorities to follow, our new theory seems less adequate. Its response to our question three does not seem immediately helpful with questions one and two; and surely those are of the most concern to real people confronted with decisions about action. It just does not seem very helpful to tell a man considering resistance to authority: you must obey if the government is such that you ought to obey. But neither is traditional consent theory very helpful to this man; indeed, one of its weaknesses has always been this matter of detailed application. Perhaps it is even a mistake to assume that a theory of political obligation is supposed to tell a man directly what to do in particular cases.[4]

One might argue, however, that such a theory should at least tell him what sorts of considerations are relevant to his decision, direct his attention and tell him where to look.[5] And in that regard, I suggest that traditional consent theory is defective, for it directs such a man's attention to the wrong place. It teaches him to look at himself (for his own consent) or at the people around him (for theirs), rather than at the merits of the government. Where it demands obedience, consent theory does so on the grounds that he or the majority have consented; where it justifies

---

[3] Ludwig Wittgenstein, *Philosophical Investigations* (New York: Macmillan, 1953). See also Stanley Louis Cavell, "The Claim to Rationality" (Unpublished Ph.D. dissertation, Harvard University, 1961), esp. Chapter I.

[4] See, for example, Margaret Macdonald, "The Language of Political Theory," in A. Flew, ed., *Logic and Language: First Series* (Oxford: Basil Blackwell, 1960), pp. 167–186.

[5] This suggestion is advanced, against Miss Macdonald's argument, in S. I. Benn and R. S. Peters, *Social Principles and the Democratic State* (London: George Allen & Unwin, 1959), pp. 299–301.

resistance, it does so on the grounds that consent was never given or has been exceeded. Thus the man who must choose is directed to the question: have I (we) consented to this? The new doctrine formulated in this essay seems at least to have the virtue of pointing such a man in the right direction. For it tells him: look to the nature of the government — its characteristics, structure, activities, functioning. This is not much of a guide, but it is a beginning much more usefully related to what men need to think about when they make such choices.

Let us consider seriously what sorts of things people really think about when they confront a genuine decision about obedience and resistance, and what sorts of things they ought to think about. But anyone who undertakes to do that is immediately overwhelmed by the complexity and multiplicity of what seems relevant, and by the many different imaginable cases. We need to consider a list of specific cases at least as diverse as these:

Socrates, as presented in the *Crito* and the *Apology*.
An ordinary criminal.
An American student engaging in civil disobedience.
A Mississippi Negro who decides to join a revolutionary group.
A South African Negro who decides to join a revolutionary group.
A minor official in Nazi Germany, who continues to carry out his functions.

Even a brief review of such cases teaches at least this much: the occasions for contemplating and possibly engaging in disobedience are extremely varied; and a great many kinds of non-obedience are available, from flight through crime to attempted revolution.[6] Some forms of non-obedience are violent, others not; some are personal and others organized; some are isolated actions and others a systematic program of action; some are directed against a particular law or decree and others against an entire system of government. To a person confronted with a real decision about resistance or obedience, it makes an enormous difference what kind of action is contemplated. Circumstances that may justify escape or isolated refusal to obey a particular law may not suffice to justify revolution; indeed, some forms of resistance (like civil disobedience) may even be provided for within a political system.

Next, we may notice that all of our examples are, or could reasonably be, people in conflict. Socrates may never have been in doubt as to what he would do, but his friends certainly disagreed with him at first; and he cast his own argument in the form of a confrontation between the desire "to play truant" and the admonitions of the laws. All of our examples (with the exception of the criminal?) might have good, serious reasons for resistance. None of them ought to feel entirely free to pursue those reasons without first weighing them against something else — his *prima facie* obligation to obey. One might say: all these men ought to feel a certain tie to their governments, their societies, in the sense in which Socrates feels such a tie, but some of them might nevertheless be justified in disobeying or resisting. That he does not sufficiently feel such a tie, that he has no (good) reason, no justification for disobedience, is precisely what makes the case of an "ordinary" criminal different from the rest. This is at least in accord with the formula offered by our new theory: normally law, authority, government are to be obeyed and resistance requires justification. You are not morally free to resist as a matter of whim.

---

[6] Something like this point is suggested by Tussman, *op. cit.,* p. 43.

The real person confronted by a problematic situation about obedience needs to know that, but he obviously needs to know much more. He needs to know much more specifically when resistance is justified and what might count as a justification. Does he learn this by thinking about his own past consent or that of his fellow-citizens, as traditional consent theory would suggest? Or does he learn it by assessing the nature and quality of the government?

Our cases of potential disobedience show an interesting division in this respect. Three of them — the student and the two Negroes — seem quite unlikely to think much about their own past consent — when and whether they consented, how often and how seriously, expressly or tacitly, and so on. What they are likely to think about is the "outrageous" conduct and "oppressive, unjust" structure of the government, and of the possible consequences of resistance. The criminal (since we have defined him as "ordinary") is not likely to think about either obligations to obey or justifications for his action. The Nazi might well cite his consent to the Fuehrer, his oath of office, pledges of absolute obedience, and so on, as a justification for continued obedience despite "certain unpleasant government measures that perhaps ought not to have been taken." And Socrates is passionately aware of his ties to the Athenian laws, the gratitude he owes them for past favors, the power of his past consent to them.

Thus both Socrates and the Nazi do seem to look to past consent rather than to the nature of the government. But the significance of this fact has yet to be assessed; for on closer examination, each of their cases reveals an important weakness in traditional consent theory. From the case of the Nazi we can learn that even express consent may not be enough; and from that of Socrates, the difficulties of applying past consent as a guide to action.

It might be tempting to say that of our six cases, only Socrates is truly moral, for only he thinks about his obligations and commitments to the laws. But the example of the Nazi saves us from this simplistic response, by showing that sometimes past promises and oaths are not enough to determine present obligations. Sometimes a man who cites even an express oath to obedience, is being not admirable but hypocritical, refusing to recognize where his real duty lies. We would not want to say that past oaths and promises count for nothing, that they can be ignored at will. We all feel the power of the argument that you ought to be consistent, that it isn't fair to pick up your marbles and go home just because it's your turn to lose under the rules you have accepted so far. But that is partly because such a partisan assessment of the rules is likely to be biased. If you can in fact show that the rules are really unfair, then any time is a good time to change them. Again, normally rules and authorities are to be obeyed; when occasions for questioning this obligation arise, what is ultimately needed is an assessment of the rules or authorities. Mere reference to your "going along with them" in the past is not enough.

No doubt if a man had no political obligation he could acquire one by a promise or contract. But that by no means proves that political obligation can be acquired *only* by promise or contract; it may be that a quite independent political obligation is sometimes reinforced by an oath to obey, at other times (partly) countered by a promise to resist. A personal past commitment to obey need not settle the matter.

Indeed, the case of the Nazi calls attention to something traditional consent theory seems to have overlooked: the duty to resist. There are times in human history when men are not merely free(d) from an obligation to obey, but positively obligated to oppose the powers that be. The authors of the Declaration of Independence recognized this, despite their heavy reliance on Locke; for they saw resistance to tyranny not merely as man's right but as his duty. Locke, and traditional consent theory in general, make no provisition for such a duty, nor can it be easily accommodated within their framework. There is provision in Locke's system for majority resistance to a tyrannical government, and a duty to follow such a majority. But *individual* resistance has a highly ambiguous status at best, and is certainly *not* a duty.[7] For if political obligation arises from contract, the violation or overstepping of this contract leaves each individual free to do as he likes with regard to the tyranny. True, the individual is still then bound by natural law; but natural law does not command the punishment of offenders, it only permits it. And amending the Lockeian system on this score would obviously require fundamental changes in its individualistic presuppositions.

Similarly, traditional consent theory teaches that at times of civil war or successful revolution, when an old authority structure collapses, each individual is free to place his consent anew wherever he wishes and thinks best for himself. If he thinks fit to follow a highway robber then, he is free to do so. But when we contemplate real cases, would we not rather want to maintain that even in chaos there is responsibility, that even then the individual has some obligation to think of others as well as himself, the welfare of society or mankind as well as his own?

It seems that insufficient attention has been given to the failure of traditional consent theory to provide for any obligation to resist, or any obligation to choose responsibly when new authorities must be chosen. Indeed, divine right, prescription and utilitarianism can accommodate such obligations far more easily than a contract theory can. As for the "nature of the government" or "hypothetical consent" doctrine developed in this essay, it too would presumably require amendment on this score. An enlarged version might hold: your obligation is to obey what deserves obedience and consent, and to resist what deserves resistance and rejection (leaving the important possibility that many persons or agencies deserve neither obedience nor resistance). But it is not obvious to me whether the obligation to resist tyranny should be construed as a part of political obligation at all, or as an occasional alternative to it. The question seems related to that of whether revolution is a special part of political life or a breakdown of the political.

II. The Case of Socrates

Though the Nazi may continue to obey on the grounds that he has sworn to do so, we may find that he thereby fails to perform his true obligations. Why, then, does Socrates' position — equally founded on past personal consent — strike us as so exemplary and moral? I would suggest that the distinguishing thing about Socrates' situation is this: he can find no fault with the Athenian laws, nor even with the Athenian way of administering them. Only his own particular conviction and sentence are (almost fortuitously) unjust. And his dialogue with the laws is essentially a way of expressing or establishing this fact. Socrates' past consent is not so much compelling in its own right, as it is a way of expressing and reinforcing his present judgment that there is nothing basically wrong with the system, no

[7] Locke, *op. cit.,* pars. 121, 149, 168, 203–4, 208–9, 211–12, 220, 232, 240–3.

justification for resistance. What amazes us about him is not this judgment, nor the refusal to accept a single case of injustice as a justification for disobedience. These are relatively ordinary positions to take. What amazes us about him is that he construes disobedience so widely, to include even flight; and that he is willing to perform his obligation down to the minutest detail, even at the cost of his life.[8]

The suggestion is, then, that Socrates' focus on his past acceptance of the laws and his gratitude to them is in fact an evaluation of the Athenian government (or the expression of such an evaluation). We need to recall that this same moral Socrates refused to carry out an "authoritative" order given him in the time of the Thirty Tyrants, because it was unjust, and would apparently have refused to carry out injustice voted by a democratic majority as well.[9] In those earlier situations, one may suppose, what Socrates thought about was the injustice of what he had been ordered to do, and of those who issued the order, not his own (tacit?) consent to them.

To this line of argument a traditional consent theorist might respond: Socrates looks to his own past consent in order to find and determine its limits, in order to see whether this new governmental action does not exceed what he had consented to. But if we take that seriously as a model of what the moral man must do when he contemplates resistance, we set him an extremely difficult task. How is Socrates to know *to what* he has consented, particularly if his consent has been tacit? Surely it is not enough to say that he has consented only to those precise things the government did in the past, so that any new or unprecedented action is automatically *ultra vires*. But if not that, then to what does one give tacit consent? Is it to the particular people then in authority, or to the authority of the office they hold, or to the laws that define and limit that office, or to the body that makes those laws, or to the Constitution that lays down rules and procedures for the making of laws, or to the principles behind that Constitution, or to the fellow-members of the society, or even to all of mankind? In particular cases, these various foci of loyalty may come into conflict; then knowing that one has consented to them all at a time when they were in agreement is no help for deciding what to do.

In short, though two of our examples do look to their own past consent in deciding what to do, one of them thereby fails to perform his true obligation, and the other seems to be using the language of consent to express a favorable assessment of the government. Furthermore, we have noted at least two disadvantages of personal consent as a criterion: the difficulty of knowing *to what* you have consented (especially if consent was tacit), and the fact that even an express oath to obey may sometimes be outweighed by an obligation to resist.

Besides an individual's personal consent, traditional consent theory offers as an alternative criterion the "consent of the governed," the consent of all, or a majority of one's fellow-citizens. Of such consent, too, we would have to say that it cannot simply be dismissed as irrelevant. Even our Negro in Mississippi or South Africa might think about how widely shared his grievances are. But again, the consent or dissent of the majority cannot by itself be decisive for defining your obligation. Majorities are sometimes wrong, and have been known to do evil. Resistance might

---

[8] Plato, *Crito* [50]: "are you not going by an act of yours to overturn us — the laws, and the whole state, as far as in you lies?" B. Jowett translation (New York: Random House, 1937).

[9] Plato, *Apology,* 32.

be justified in Athens under the Thirty Tyrants or in Nazi Germany despite the majority.

But majority consent does enter the argument at another level, in a way quite different from the relevance of personal consent. Majority consent may be relevant as a *way* of assessing, as *evidence about* the nature of the government, given that the nature of the government bears on political obligation. In fact, a variety of considerations each of which we might want to call "consent of the governed" can be used in the process of evaluating a government. They may come into conflict with each other, and their relative weight and importance will be a matter of one's political values, of what kind of government he thinks desirable or even tolerable.

It is useful to distinguish here between the "procedural" criteria yielded by the consent of the governed for assessing a government, and the "substantive" ones. Procedural criteria are those which concern the institutional structure and political functioning of the government, the way in which it makes decisions and takes actions. To assess its nature, we want to know about the way a government functions in relation to the governed — whether it is responsive to them or forces its policies on them. Thus we look for machinery for the expression of popular desires; we look for the degree of popular participation in or control over decisions, for channels for the redress of grievances, for access to power. At the same time we look also for signs of repression, of propaganda, of coercion. We look, of course, not merely at the institutions defined on paper, but at their actual functioning in the largest social sense. Denial of suffrage to Negroes in South Africa is very different from denial of suffrage to women in Switzerland (and theorists would do well to think about why this is so). But roughly speaking, a government is likely to seem to us deserving if it is open to the governed, reprehensible if it rules them against their will. This general criterion may well be expressed by some formula like "the consent of the governed;" but that formula must not be taken too simply, and that criterion must not be regarded as our only one.

Besides this vague cluster of procedural criteria, we have in addition substantive ones. We may look also at the substance of what the government does — whether it pursues good, benevolent, justifiable policies. A government that systematically harms its subjects, whether out of misguided good intentions or simply for the selfish gain of the rulers, is to that extent illegitimate — even if the subjects do not know it, even if they "consent" to being abused. But even here "the consent of the governed" is *relevant* as important evidence, for one of the main ways we estimate whether people are being well treated is by whether they seem to like what they get. Only we may sometimes need to consider other evidence as well; the consent or dissent of the governed need not be decisive as to the goodness or justness of a government's policies.

It is the relationship between at least these two kinds of criteria that is likely to determine our assessment of a government, whether it deserves support or opposition. Thus we may all agree that a government pursuing very bad policies and forcing them on its subjects, so that it is obviously doing great harm to them and other countries, and doing so despite their attempts at protest and without their consent — such a government clearly is the occasion for resistance. Conversely, if we find a government that truly has the consent of its subjects although they have wide sources of information and true opportunities to dissent and criticize, and if that government pursues only the most praiseworthy policies, then few of us would urge revolution or resistance to it. The problematic cases are, of course, the ones in between, where procedure and substance are partly good, partly bad, and you need to make evaluations and decisions. Here it begins to be a matter of your metapolitics – how you think of men and societies, what positions you are willing to take and defend, and take responsibility for.

Suppose, for example, that a government is procedurally open, with genuine channels for controlling policy from below, but it engages in vicious policies. Then, one might want to say, the citizen is not free to engage in revolution; he has channels available and it is his duty to use them, to change the policy. But what if he tries to do so, and fails because the majority continues to approve of the wickedness? What if he is a member of a permanent minority group, being systematically abused and exploited by an eager, consenting majority? Then the seemingly open channels of consent are not truly open to him. Might there not come a point when violent minority resistance of some sort is justified?

Or suppose that a government is benevolent, so no one can criticize its actions, but in procedure it is simply autocratic and dictatorial. Is revolution justified against a benevolent dictatorship? This might be the case, for example, if men need political participation in order to be really well, in order to reach their full human potential. Then bad procedure would itself become a substantive grievance.

The theoretical complications possible here are legion, but at least this much seems clear: evaluating a government in order to decide whether it deserves obedience or resistance, requires attention both to the way it works and to what it does. In both cases something like consent is relevant; it may be a formula for expressing some rather complex requirements concerning opportunities for dissent and participation, or it may be evidence of good policies. Thus even if we adhere to the doctrine of hypothetical consent or the nature of government, majority consent may still be relevant in a subordinate capacity for assessing a government, for working out more detailed answers to our questions one and two about consent, the specific practical "when" and "whom" of obedience. But here "the consent of the governed" is not one simple thing, decisive for obligation; rather, it is relevant in a number of different, potentially conflicting ways.

And all of these ways put together differ, in turn, not merely from personal consent, but also from the doctrine of hypothetical consent developed in this essay.[10] That legitimate authority is such that one ought to consent to it, is a precept built into English grammar, into the meanings of these terms. That a legitimate government is one which has the consent of (a majority of) the governed – is procedurally responsive to them or looks after their interests, or both – is one particular position about what kind of government is desirable for men. More accurately, it is a cluster of positions, depending on the relative weight given to procedural and substantive criteria. Though these positions are very widely shared today, and though they were shared by almost all traditional consent theorists, they are not the only conceivable positions on this subject. Someone might undertake to argue, for example, that a government is legitimate only to the extent that it fosters high culture, or to the extent that it promotes the evolution of a master race. That would be to reject majority consent as any sort of criterion for assessing a government. But the doctrine of hypothetical consent holds even for someone taking such an unorthodox position; even for him, a legitimate government would be the one that deserves consent, to which everyone ought to

[10] For the latter distinction, compare Benn and Peters, *op. cit.*, pp. 329–31.

consent. Both the philosophical weakness and the historical persistence and strength of traditional consent theory rest in its failure to distinguish these very different arguments.

Finally, even if we succeed in evaluating a government, that does not seem fully to settle how we must behave toward it. One final, important consideration seems relevant: the action taken must be appropriate. To the diversity of ways in which one can obey or support, resist or overthrow a government, there correspond a diversity of conditions when the various actions may be appropriate or justified. The fact that some action is justified, that some abuse has taken place, does not mean that just any action will do. A man mistreated by his superior may kick his dog. We can understand, and perhaps even sympathize, but surely the action is not justified. Not just any violation of law will qualify as civil disobedience or attempted revolution. This observation is presumably related to the traditional assertion of consent theorists, that it is necessary to "exhaust the remedies" available, to suffer "a long train of abuses" before violent resistance is justified. Where other actions are appropriate, revolution may not be called for.

Thus it begins to seem that a decision about obedience and resistance ought to be measured not merely against the character of the government, but against all the relevant social circumstances — what alternatives one can envision, and what consequences resistance is likely to have. Revolution would not seem justified, for example, if one had no hope of its being followed by an improvement in conditions. If it would simply substitute one tyranny for another, or if it would annihilate the human race through the resulting violence, then it does not seem justified.[11]

But a doctrine that casts its net so wide, making all social circumstances at least potentially relevant, that sees both an obligation to obey and an obligation to resist, and that stresses so much the individual burden of decision, seems very close to the social utilitarianism examined in the first half of this essay. It seems to say, with the social utilitarian, you are obligated to obey when that is best on the whole for society (all of mankind?), and obligated to resist when *that* is best on the whole. But that formula, and social utilitarianism, seem to neglect again the obligatory nature of law and authority in normal circumstances, the *prima facie* obligation to

[11] One difficulty of this discussion is that it seems to make human decisions look excessively rational. Are any abstract principles of this kind really relevant to what real people think about when they must decide? Is a man on the point of rebellion or revolution not much more likely to be moved by strong emotion — by an overwhelming anger or sense of outrage?

But I would like to suggest that the human capacity for outrage is, as it were, the emotional correlate to rational moral principles. It is our inner, helpless response to a violation of principles of right and wrong, as we sense them, perhaps quite inarticulately. Outrage (unlike mere anger), is an emotion of principle. I take it that this is what Albert Camus means when he insists that "the act of rebellion is not, essentially, an egoistic act," even though it can, "of course" have "egoistic motives." *The Rebel* (New York: Vintage, 1956), p. 16. The rebel, the man who acts from a sense of outrage, says not merely "I don't want to put up with this," but "No man ought to have to put up with this." And by feeling "no man ought . . ." he acts, in a sense, on principle. Compare Tussman, *op. cit.,* pp. 78–79.

Of course a man's feeling that his situation is outrageous is one thing; whether the situation is in fact outrageous is another. A three-year-old may feel outraged at not being allowed to drink the detergent. We may sympathize with his feelings, but cannot condone the resulting violence. Not every feeling of outrage is a valid assessment of the world; but then, not every rational judgment that the limits of contractual obligation have been exceeded is valid either. No doubt rational judgments are more likely to be right; that is one advantage of rationality.

obey. Being subject to law, government, authority means precisely an obligation (normally) to do what *they* say is best, rather than judge the welfare of society for yourself and act on your private judgment. Yet there are times when you must resist in the name of something very like the welfare of society. Whether these two positions are compatible remains somehow problematic; but before we can make a final stab at the matter, we must finish applying our new doctrine to our four questions about political obligation.

III. Justifying Political Obligation

We come now to question four, the matter of justification: "why are you ever obligated to obey even legitimate authority?" Here again our "nature of the government" doctrine does not at first seem a very useful answer. For it can only say: because of the nature of the government, because the government is such that you ought to obey it and consent to it, because a rational man would do so. But that answer is not likely to still the question. For someone genuinely puzzled about obligation in this (philosophical) way is likely to persist: "how does that 'ought' bind me, *why* must I do what a rational man would do, what if I don't *want* to be rational?"

But the reader may have noticed by now that all of the theories and versions of theories we have considered are subject to this same difficulty to some extent. Some seem better designed to cope with it than others; yet we can always push the question further back: why must I do what God commands, why must I do what history teaches, why must I do what is best for me personally, why must I do what I have promised? Even traditional consent theory is liable to this difficulty; and it is remarkable that despite Hume's early criticism, we continue to believe in consent theory while ignoring this problem. For Hume had already told the consent theorist:

> You find yourself embarrassed when it is asked, *Why we are bound to keep our word?* Nor can you give any answer but what would, immediately, without any circuit, have accounted for our obligation to allegiance.[12]

The obligation to keep one's word is no more "natural" and self-evident and indubitable than political obligation itself; though either may sometimes reinforce the other, neither can give the other absolute justification. The two obligations are essentially separate and equal in status.[13] Why, then, does the traditional consent theorist, so doubtful about the validity of political obligation, take the obligation of keeping contracts as obvious? Why, if he imagines a state of nature, is it always

[12] David Hume, "Of the Original Contract," in Sir Ernest Barker, ed., *The Social Contract* (New York: Oxford, 1960), p. 161.

[13] This assertion is not about the relative claims that the two obligations – political obedience and promise-keeping – have on us, where they come into conflict. It seems obvious to me that no single, binding principle could be found to govern such a question. There are occasions when a vitally important promise is clearly a more important obligation than obedience to some minor law; on the other hand, the keeping of a minor promise is no excuse whatsoever for treason. But the assertion that the two obligations are separate and equal is not meant to bear on this question. It is meant only to say: there is no reason to suppose that promising is more "natural" or basic than obeying authority, and hence no reason to derive the latter from the former.

stripped of political authority but inevitably equipped with a natural law that dictates the keeping of one's word? Hume uses these questions as a rhetorical device to attack consent theory, but they can also be taken seriously as a way of learning something more about the consent theorist.

For a theorist does not choose his beliefs and his doubts. The traditional consent theorist simply finds himself in doubt about (the justification of, or limits of, or validity of) political obligation; it just seems obvious to him that there is a problem about it. And he simply is not in doubt about promises or contracts; it just seems obvious to him that they oblige.

At one level one can argue that both the consent theorist's doubt and his assumption spring from the peculiar picture of man and society he seems to hold. If your picture of man in the abstract is of a man fully grown, complete with his own private needs, interests, feelings, desires, beliefs and values, and if you therefore never think about how he grew up and became the particular person he became, then he may well seem to you an ineluctably *separate* unit, his ties to other individuals may seem mysterious or illusory and will require explanation. Given man as such a separate, self-contained unit, it does indeed seem strange that he might have obligations not of his own choosing, perhaps even without being aware of them, or even against his will. Furthermore, self-assumed obligations may then strike you as a way of overcoming this separateness. For it is easy to confuse the fact that promises and contracts are self-assumed, with the idea that the *obligation to keep* them is self-assumed as well. That is, the person who makes a promise seems to recognize and commit himself to the institution of promises; the person who makes a contract seems to acknowledge thereby the binding character of contracts, so that a later refusal to accept them as binding strikes one as a kind of self-contradiction. But of course this is a confusion. The making of particular promises or contracts presupposes the social institution of promising or contracts, and the obligation to keep promises cannot itself be founded on a promise.

In truth, there is something profoundly wrong with the consent theorist's picture of man. Every free, separate, adult, consenting individual was first shaped and molded by his parents and (as we say) society. It is only as a result of their influence that he becomes the particular person he does become, with his particular interests, values, desires, language and obligations. The only thing truly separate about us is our bodies; our selves are manifestly social. But surely even the consent theorist knows this, so the problem becomes why he nevertheless holds, or is held captive by, a different and peculiar picture. Could that picture be not so much the cause as the by-product of his philosophical doubt?

After all, consent theorists are not the only ones troubled about political obligation. Political theorists of other persuasions have also been led, or have led themselves sometimes to ask "why are you ever obligated to obey even legitimate authority?" But if none of the theories of political obligation is able to deal adequately with that question, it must be quite peculiar, not nearly as straight-forward as it looks. Perhaps it is a question that cannot be fully answered in the ordinary way. But what sort of question is that; and if it cannot be answered, how should it be treated? Tussman rejects it as a symptom of "moral disorder"; I would suggest instead that it is a symptom of philosophical disorder, the product of a philosophical paradox. If so, it will not disappear — the theorist will not stop being bothered by it — unless we can show how and why it arises, why anyone should so much as suppose that political obligation in general needs (or can have) a general justification. But that would require a discussion of the nature of philosophical puzzlement far beyond the scope of this essay.

What can be done here is something much more limited and less effective. Having suggested that the status of political obligation and of the obligation to keep promises is essentially the same — that neither is more "natural" than or can serve as an absolute justification for the other — we can approach our question four about political obligation by first pursuing a parallel question about promises. For in the area of promises some extremely useful work has been done in philosophy in recent years — work which can be applied to the problem of political obligation.[14]

Philosophers have sometimes asked a question like our question four about promises: "why are you (ever) obligated to keep (any of) your promises (whatsoever); why do promises oblige?" This question, too, can be answered in terms of divine commandment or utilitarian consequences, social or individual; and here, too, the answers are less than satisfactory. "God commands you to keep your word" is no answer to the nonbeliever, nor to someone heretical enough to demand proof of God's will. The utilitarian response tends to dissolve the obligation altogether, so that your duty is always to do what produces the best results, quite apart from whether you have made any promises on the subject. And, of course, a consent argument is out of the question here ("you have promised to keep your promises?").

What has been suggested by philosophers is this: "promise" is not just a word. Promising is a social practice, something we *do*, something children have to learn *how* to do. It has rules, penalties, roles and moves almost in the way that games have them. Children do not learn what a promise is by having one pointed out to them; they learn gradually about what it means to "make a promise," "keep (or break) a promise," "be unable to promise but certainly intend to try," "have said something which, in the circumstances, amounted to a promise," and so on. Promising is not just producing certain sounds ("I promise"), for a phonograph might make those sounds, or a man rehearsing a play, or a philosopher explaining the practice, yet none of these would actually be promising. Promising, rather, is taking on an obligation. That is, "to promise" does not mean "to make certain sounds," but rather "to take on an obligation."

Now, of course, we do not always do what we have promised. Sometimes we act contrary to our obligations, and sometimes we are wholly or partly excused from performing what we had promised. If for example, keeping a promise would frustrate the purpose for which it was made, or would lead to great evil, or has become impossible, we may be excused from performing. So about any particular promise we have made it may sometimes be relevant to ask: am I still obligated to perform or not? That is, normally, in principle promises oblige; a promise is a certain kind of obligation. But sometimes, under certain circumstances, there is reason to question or withdraw or cancel that obligation in a particular case. In such circumstances we weigh the alternatives, the possible consequences of performance and failure to perform. But our obligations, including that of the promise, continue to be among the factors that must be weighed in the decision.

---

[14] See particularly J. L. Austin, *Philosophical Papers* (Oxford: Clarendon, 1961), chs. 3, 6 and 10; John Rawls, "Two Concepts of Rules," *Philosophical Review*, LXIV (January, 1955), 3–32; and S. L. Cavell, "Must We Mean What We Say?" in V. C. Chappell, *Ordinary Language* (Englewood Cliffs, N. J.: Prentice-Hall, 1964), esp. pp. 94–101.

The obligation of a promise does not simply disappear when there is occasion to question it; it only is sometimes outweighed.

But philosophers are sometimes led to wonder *categorically*, about *all* promises: do they oblige; what are the reasons pro and con; why am I ever obligated to keep any promise? And here, of course, there are no *particular* circumstances to weigh in the balance; the question is abstract and hypothetical. What sort of answer is possible to this question? First, that this is what a promise *is*, what "promise" means. A promise is a self-assumed obligation. If you *assume* an obligation and have not yet performed it, nor been excused from it, then you *have* an obligation; in much the same way as someone who puts on a coat, has a coat on.[15] To ask why promises oblige is to ask why (self-assumed) obligations oblige. And to the question why obligations oblige the only possible answer would seem to be that this is what the words mean.

Beyond this one can only paraphrase Wittgenstein: there are a hundred reasons; there is no reason. There is no absolute, deductive answer to the question "why does any promise ever oblige?" beyond calling attention to the meaning of the words. There is no absolute, indubitable principle from which the obligation can be deduced. It is, to be sure, related to any number of other principles, obligations and values; but the relationship is more like a network (or patchwork) than like a hierarchical pyramid. It is simply a mistake to suppose that there might be such an absolute principle, such a deductive proof. We have no right to expect one. (Why, then, does the philosopher expect one; why can we ourselves be led to share his expectation when we are in a "philosophical mood"?)

John Rawls has pointed out that utilitarianism will not do as a criterion for the keeping of particular promises – as a standard for *when* promises oblige.[16] To say "keep your promises only when that maximizes pleasure and minimizes pain" is to miss precisely the *obligatory* nature of a promise; having once promised you are not free to decide what to do merely on utilitarian grounds. But, Rawls says, utilitarian considerations *are* relevant at a different level of argument, for assessing the social practice of promising. For we can ask "must we (should we) have an institution like promising and promise-keeping at all?" And here utilitarian reasons seem relevant; we may try to justify the social practice by its useful consequences.

Stanley Cavell has argued that this implies a degree of freedom of choice on our parts which we do not in fact have.[17] To evaluate the practice of promising pro and con, we would have to envision alternatives. And how shall we envision a society which knows no obligation to keep one's word? (For it is not, of course, the particular English locution "I promise" that is being assessed, but the practice of assuming obligations and holding people to their word.) We seem to have no choice about the pros and cons of such an institution. It is not socially useful; it is indispensable to the very concept of society and human life.

But even if we could and did evaluate as Rawls suggests, and "decide" that the institution of promising is on balance socially useful, even this would not provide an absolute justification for the keeping of particular promises. For what are we to answer the man who says: "granted that we must have the practice of promising, and granted promising means taking on an obligation; still, why am *I* obliged to

[15] Compare Cavell, "Must We Mean What We Say?" *op. cit.,* pp. 96, 99.
[16] *Op. cit.,* Part II.
[17] "The Claim to Rationality," Chapter VIII.

keep my promise? Why can't *I* be an exception?" To him we can only say, that is how obligation and promises work. Of course you *can* refuse to keep your promise, but then you are failing to perform an obligation.

Now the same line of reasoning can be applied to the question "why does even a legitimate government, a valid law, a genuine authority ever obligate me to obey?" As with promises, and as our new doctrine about political obligation suggests, we may say that this is what "legitimate government," "valid law," "genuine authority" *mean*. It is part of the concept, the meaning of "authority" that those subject to it are required to obey, that it has a right to command. It is part of the concept, the meaning of "law," that those to whom it is applicable are obligated to obey it. As with promises, so with authority, government and law: there is a *prima facie* obligation involved in each, and normally you must perform it. Normally a man is not free to decide on utilitarian grounds whether or not he will do a certain thing, if that thing happens to be against the law or required by law; he is not free to make a decision on his own the way he would be free where the law is silent. The existence of the law on this subject normally constitutes an obligation, just as having promised normally constitutes an obligation, so that one is not free to decide what to do just as if no promise had been made. (This is not, of course, to say that everything claiming to be law is law, that everyone claiming to have authority has it, that every statement alleged to be a promise is in fact one. It says only: *if* something is a promise, law, obligation, *then* normally it obliges.) This kind of response to question four is obviously almost the same as the one our doctrine of hypothetical consent yielded to question three: government and authority are concepts grammatically related to obligation and obedience. A legitimate government is one that you ought to obey and ought to consent to because that is what the words mean. But as before, this answer is likely to seem purely formal, and empty. It will not satisfy someone genuinely puzzled about the justification of political obligation.

But as with promises, all that one can say beyond calling attention to the meanings of the words, is that no absolute, deductive justification exists or is necessary. There are no absolute first principles from which this obligation could be derived. It is related to all kinds of other obligations in all kinds of ways, to be sure, but the relationship is not hierarchical and deductive. In particular, as we have seen, the obligatory nature of promises is no more or no less absolute and indubitable than the obligation to obey laws. Again, following Rawls' suggestion, one might attempt a utilitarian assessment of such institutions or practices as law, government and authority. And here, I suppose, there may be somewhat more room for discussion than with promises. For it is not at all obvious that government and law are indispensable to human social life. But can we conceive society without any such thing as authority? One function of the idea of the state in nature in classical consent theories does seem to be a kind of indirect demonstration of the utilitarian advantages of having governments and laws. If such things did not exist, Locke seems to argue, we would have to invent them.[18]

But as with promises, even a recognition of the necessity or utilitarian

---

[18] It is significant, in this respect, that consent theorists so often speak of contracts or covenants, rather than simple promises or oaths. For of course the idea of a contract or convenant implies that you get something in return for the obligation you take on, and in a way at least suggests the informal additional ties of gratitude. But there are other differences as well, a contract being more formal and usually more explicit than a promise.

advantages of such things as authority, law and government is no absolute answer to the man who is questioning his particular obligation to obey, who wants to be an exception. There is no such absolute answer, and can be none. Nothing we say is absolutely beyond question. Again, you *can* disobey but in the absence of excuses or justifications you violate an obligation when you do so.

The parallel between promises and authority as obligations is not perfect. For one thing, promises are explicitly taken on oneself; political obligation (I have argued) need not be. Furthermore, promises are normally made to particular persons, whereas political obligation is sometimes confounded by our question two, by the problem of rival authorities. We have noted the difficulty of determining to whom or what consent is given: particular officials, their positions, the laws, the Constitution, the people of the society. This means, among other things, that political obligation is open to a kind of challenge not normally relevant to promises. We saw that, following Rawls, both promises and political obligation can be challenged at two very different levels: sometimes we may claim to be excused from performing in a particular case (for instance because of conflicting obligations or overwhelming difficulties). And sometimes we may want to challenge and assess the whole institution with the obligations it defines. But in addition, political obligation can be challenged also on a third level. Sometimes we may refuse to obey neither because our particular case is exceptional, nor because we question such obligation categorically, but because the one who is claiming authority over us does not in fact have it. We may resist a government that has become tyrannical not as a special, personal exception, and not because we are against government, but because *this* government no longer deserves obedience. Such a challenge is made on principle, *in accord* (as it were) with the "rules" of political obligation.

But the differences between promises and political obligation do not affect the point to be made here. That point concerns our question four, the search for a justification for having to obey (or having to keep a promise); and it is essentially twofold. First, we have said, "authority," "law," and "government" are grammatically, conceptually related to obligation, as is "promise." And beyond this, the quest for some "higher," absolute, deductive justification is misguided. Insofar, then, as the grammatical point does not seem to still the question, does not get at what someone philosophically puzzled wants to ask, what is needed is not a better justification, but an account of why the philosopher is driven to ask the question in the first place.

IV. The Duality of Obligation

As Locke suggests in his preface, the consent theorist's purpose is a dual one. He wants both to show that men are sometimes justified in making revolutions, and to show that men are normally bound to obey governments and laws. And this is, indeed, what must be shown, since both these things are in fact true. The fact is that on one hand men are in some sense above or outside the institutions of their society, its laws, its government. They can measure and judge these institutions. Though they have not themselves made them they can change them; and sometimes even violent change may be justified. On the other hand, men are also part of and subject to their society, bound by its norms and authorities. Not every attempt at revolution is justified.

To say that men are both superior to their government and subject to it is to express a paradox. Because it seems so paradoxical, the traditional social contract theorists saw it instead as a temporal sequence: *first* men were free and could make a commonwealth, *then* they became bound by it (within the limits of a contract). We have seen some of the difficulties that result. Finding an accurate and unparadoxical way to express this paradoxical truth seems to me the most interesting problem connected with political obligation, but it is important to notice that this problem is not confined to political obligation. We are both superior to and subject to *all* our obligations, and *that* is what requires an accounting. Discussing it will reveal one final, rather subtle way in which obligation both is and is not a matter of consent — but all obligation, not just the obligation to obey.

We are familiar enough from ethics with the view of a number of philosophers (notably Kant) that an action is not fully moral unless the actor knows what he is doing and does it for the right reasons. An action done for selfish motives but accidentally producing some charitable result is not (really, fully) a charitable action. A moral action is one taken *because* it is right, on principle. On analogy we might want to say that a man cannot (really, fully) obey an order unless he recognizes that it is an order that the man issuing it has authority over him. He cannot (really, fully) obey a law or a government unless he recognizes it as valid law or legitimate government; only then will what he does (really, fully) *be* obeying. If I "order" a leaf to fall from a tree, and the leaf immediately does so, it is not obeying my order; if I silently and secretly "order" my neighbor to mow his lawn and he does so, he is not (really, fully) obeying my order. Even if he hears and understands what I am saying, he is not (really, fully) obeying me unless he recognizes what I say as an order, considers me as having authority to order him about, and mows the lawn *because* of my order.

Consequently, the capacity for this kind of awareness and intention is a precondition for being fully obligated. This is why leaves cannot be obligated (except in storybooks, where they are anthropomorphized), and children cannot fully do so. It may be right to punish or reward a child, but the child is not yet fully a moral agent capable of recognizing and therefore of having obligations.

It is not difficult to regard this kind of awareness and intention as a form of consenting to one's obligation. If (really, fully) obeying an order presupposes the recognition of it as an order and of the man who issues it as having authority, then surely that recognition resembles a kind of (perhaps tacit) consent to his authority. And then it becomes easy to take a final further step, and say you are not (really, fully) obligated unless you recognize, acknowledge, accept, acquiesce in, consent to that obligation. Such a line of reasoning undoubtedly has heightened the appeal of consent theory for a number of writers, and it clearly is the main basis for Tussman's stress on consent. He chooses agreement rather than force or habit as the nature of political association precisely because,

> "I have a duty to . . ." seems to follow from "I have agreed to" in a way that it does not follow from "I am forced to" or "I am in the habit of." This is sometimes expressed as the view that obligations are, or even must be voluntarily assumed.[19]

But even if one accepts these transitions and concludes that obligation in the full moral sense always requires consent, it by no means follows that obligation consists

[19] *Op. cit.,* p. 8.

only of this inner awareness and intent. For that would imply that anyone failing or refusing to consent for any reason whatsoever is thereby excused from the obligation in question, does not have that obligation, cannot meaningfully be blamed or criticized for failing to perform it.[20] But no major ethical theorist, least of all Kant, would be willing to accept that consequence, any more than Tussman is willing to let the morally unaware clods in society disobey laws whenever they please.

It is necessary to recognize that obligation has not one, but two fundamental aspects — the inner, "awareness" aspect stressed by Tussman, and an outer aspect having to do with the way others see what we do, how it looks objectively. These two aspects of obligation may be seen as corresponding to two familiar strains in ethical theory: the teleological, concerned with the consequences of action, and the deontological, concerned with its motives.[21] The former deals primarily in the outer, shared world of facts and events, and takes as fundamental the concept of the *good*: the latter deals primarily in the inner, personal world of thoughts and feelings, and takes as fundamental the concept of *right*. I would suggest, following Cavell, that both are a necessary part of any valid account of morality and obligation, that neither can be ignored outright in assessing action.

Those moral philosophers who have stressed the deontological side of moral appraisal have been concerned particularly with the matter of giving praise: a person does not deserve full credit for an act of charity, of courage, of obedience, unless his intentions were charitable, courageous, obedient. He should not get full credit for an action that merely looks charitable "from the outside," if his own perception of what he was doing was quite otherwise. To a lesser extent this is also true of blame: you are responsible for the damage you do, no matter how good your intentions were, but good intentions may be a *partial* excuse. Those philosophers who have stressed the teleological orientation of moral appraisal have been more concerned with blame or responsibility, but most particularly with duty. Your duty is not merely to intend good behavior, but to behave well; the performance and its results are what define your duty.

But in a way this dichotomization — deontology for praise, teleology for duty — misses the point. For the real difficulty is in determining *what* action has been performed, what actually was done. It is naming the action (correctly) that is the problem: was it, should we call it, an act of charity, an act of obedience, considering what took place, considering his intentions? Having put it that way, one wants to say that the two modes of assessment are always both relevant, but not equally relevant to all actions. To the assessment of certain actions, inner intention is much more relevant; to the assessment of others, outer events will seem decisive. Lying is more a matter of inner intent, deceiving more a matter of outward results. Moreover it may be that, in a broader sense, whole categories of action vary in this respect. It may be, for example, that inner awareness is categorically more relevant in face-to-face, personal relationships than in public, political conduct. We do care more about motive and intention in assessing personal relationships and actions — love, anger and forgiveness — than in assessing political actions in the public realm.

If this is so, it deserves more attention than it has received from political theorists. No doubt it has something to do with the fact that in personal morality

---

[20] Benn and Peters, *op. cit.*, p. 322.

[21] This and the next three paragraphs lean heavily on Cavell, "The Claim to Rationality," p. 323 and all of Part II.

there is no umpire, no arbiter or judge; it is of the essence of morality that we confront each other directly. In the political, public realm, on the other hand, the normal situation is one where official "interpreters" are supplied by the society to tell the individual what the law or Constitution says, whether he has or has not committed grand larceny. But what happens at times of resistance or revolution is precisely that these normal official interpreters are themselves called into question. We are both bound by, and yet sometimes free to challenge or change all our obligations; but political obligation has an additional complexity, in that its *content* seems to be a subordination to the judgment of others.[22]

But if normally law and authority oblige and resistance requires justification, and if normally judgment is to some extent subordinated to that of the authorities, and if revolutionary situations are precisely the ones that are not normal in these respects, then the crucial question seems to be: *who is to say*?[23] Who is to say what times are normal and what times are not, when resistance is justified or even obligatory? If we say "each individual must decide for himself," we seem to deny the normally binding character of law and authority. If we say "society" or "the majority" or "the duly constituted authorities decide," then we seem to deny the right to resist, since it may be the majority or the authorities themselves that need to be challenged. Yet these seem to be the only two alternatives.

The matter is very difficult, though the question seems so simple. This essay will only briefly indicate a direction in which a solution might be sought. What needs to be said seems to be this: the decision both is and is not up to each individual. Each individual does and must ultimately decide for himself and is responsible for his decision; but he may make a wrong decision and thereby fail to perform his obligations. But then who is to say someone has made a wrong decision? Anyone can say, but not everyone who cares to say will judge correctly; he may be right or wrong. And who decides that?

Each person decides for himself what to say and do; yet people sometimes speak and act in ways that are cowardly or cruel, thoughtless or irresponsible. And it is not merely up to the actor to assess his own action in this respect. Other people

---

[22] Compare Tussman, *op. cit.*, pp. 86–95. It is tempting to construe the problem in relation to Hannah Arendt's discussion of action: *The Human Condition* (1958), Part V. The human situation is precarious, and human action fallible in unpredictable ways. Both privately as individuals, and collectively as a society, we try to some extent to overcome this uncertainty, this fallibility. We make commitments, tie ourselves down for the future. As individuals, for example, we make promises. As a society, for example, we try to act and plan beyond the lifetimes of individuals, through the education of our children, or through the establishment of laws and institutions. As we reduce the uncertainty of private future action by telling others what we will do so that they can count on it, so we reduce the uncertainty of public future action by telling others and ourselves what we will do and how, so that we all can count on it. Yet in both private and collective action, uncertainty remains and things go wrong. We do not always live up to our commitments, and promised actions do not always accomplish their intended purpose. Institutions do not always function as intended either; they produce quite different goals, pursue other principles than those they were supposed to embody. Thus sometimes we need to review, replace or reject commitments we have made; sometimes it must be right for us to do so.

And where do human beings get the standards by which on such occasions they assess their government and find it wanting? Well, surely from the very society which they criticize with these standards. That this is possible – that we learn both the existing rules and criteria for assessing rules *together*, and yet can use the latter on occasion to criticize the former – may well be the most important single fact about social life.

[23] Compare Tussman, *op. cit.*, pp. 44–6.

who want or need to assess the action may also do so; each of them will make a decision for which he bears responsibility, yet none of these decisions is absolutely definitive. The judge trying a would-be rebel makes a decision; the foreign onlooker asked to give money for a revolutionary cause makes a decision; the historian examining the record in a later generation makes a decision.[24] Each of us who talks or thinks or acts with regard to the situation assesses it, and no theory or God or Party can get us off that hook.

But that does not mean that all judgments are arbitrary or merely a matter of personal preference or whim. Some decisions are made arbitrarily or whimsically or selfishly or foolishly; others are made on principle, rationally, responsibly. These are ways or modes of deciding; none of them characterizes decision as such. And an individual's decision does not become rational, responsible or right merely because he thinks it is, merely because he urgently wants it to be. What is ultimately needed here is a better understanding of the role played in our language and our lives by assessments like "he was right," "he made a bad decision," "he betrayed the cause," and the like.

Who is to say? I want to answer, each person who cares to, will say — not merely the one who acts, not merely his associates, not merely those in authority over him, not merely the detached historian or observer. No one has the last word because there is no last word. But in order to make that clear, one would have to say a great deal more about how language functions, and why we are so persistently inclined to suppose that there must be a last word.

---

[24] Thus not only citizens, but also bystanders and commentators may need to decide about a government. Their problems are not the same, to be sure. The citizen must decide whether to obey or resist; the bystander never had an obligation to obey, so he at most must decide whether or whom to assist; the commentator only makes a judgment. Therefore the evaluation of governments as to their legitimacy, their entitlement-to-be-obeyed-by-their-subjects, is a topic that ranges beyond problems of political obligation.

12. The Justification of Civil Disobedience

John Rawls

I. Introduction

I should like to discuss briefly, and in an informal way, the grounds of civil disobedience in a constitutional democracy. Thus, I shall limit my remarks to the conditions under which we may, by civil disobedience, properly oppose legally

Originally presented at the meetings of the American Political Science Association, September 1966. Some revisions have been made and two paragraphs have been added to the last section. Copyright © 1968 by John Rawls.

established democratic authority; I am not concerned with the situation under other kinds of government nor, except incidentally, with other forms of resistance. My thought is that in a reasonably just (though of course not perfectly just) democratic regime, civil disobedience, when it is justified, is normally to be understood as a political action which addresses the sense of justice of the majority in order to urge reconsideration of the measures protested and to warn that in the firm opinion of the dissenters the conditions of social cooperation are not being honored. This characterization of civil disobedience is intended to apply to dissent on fundamental questions of internal policy, a limitation which I shall follow to simplify our question.

II. The Social Contract Doctrine

It is obvious that the justification of civil disobedience depends upon the theory of political obligation in general, and so we may appropriately begin with a few comments on this question. The two chief virtues of social institutions are justice and efficiency, where by the efficiency of institutions I understand their effectiveness for certain social conditions and ends the fulfillment of which is to everyone's advantage. We should comply with and do our part in just and efficient social arrangements for at least two reasons: first of all, we have a natural duty not to oppose the establishment of just and efficient institutions (when they do not yet exist) and to uphold and comply with them (when they do exist); and second, assuming that we have knowingly accepted the benefits of these institutions and plan to continue to do so, and that we have encouraged and expect others to do their part, we also have an obligation to do our share when, as the arrangement requires, it comes our turn. Thus, we often have both a natural duty as well as an obligation to support just and efficient institutions, the obligation arising from our voluntary acts while the duty does not.

Now all this is perhaps obvious enough, but it does not take us very far. Any more particular conclusions depend upon the conception of justice which is the basis of a theory of political obligation. I believe that the appropriate conception, at least for an account of political obligation in a constitutional democracy, is that of the social contract theory from which so much of our political thought derives. If we are careful to interpret it in a suitably general way, I hold that this doctrine provides a satisfactory basis for political theory, indeed even for ethical theory itself, but this is beyond our present concern.[1] The interpretation I suggest is the following: that the principles to which social arrangements must conform, and in particular the principles of justice, are those which free and rational men would agree to in an original position of equal liberty; and similarly, the principles which govern men's relations to institutions and define their natural duties and obligations are the principles to which they would consent when so situated. It should be noted straightway that in this interpretation of the contract theory the principles of

---

[1] By the social contract theory I have in mind the doctrine found in Locke, Rousseau, and Kant. I have attempted to give an interpretation of this view in: "Justice as Fairness," *Philosophical Review* (April, 1958); "Justice and Constitutional Liberty," *Nomos*, VI (1963); "The Sense of Justice," *Philosophical Review* (July 1963). [Ed. note. See also "Distributive Justice," in Peter Laslett and W. G. Runciman, eds., *Philosophy, Politics and Society* (1967).]

justice are understood as the outcome of a hypothetical agreement. They are principles which would be agreed to if the situation of the original position were to arise. There is no mention of an actual agreement nor need such an agreement ever be made. Social arrangements are just or unjust according to whether they accord with the principles for assigning and securing fundamental rights and liberties which would be chosen in the original position. This position is, to be sure, the analytic analogue of the traditional notion of the state of nature, but it must not be mistaken for a historical occasion. Rather it is a hypothetical situation which embodies the basic ideas of the contract doctrine; the description of this situation enables us to work out which principles would be adopted. I must now say something about these matters.

The original doctrine has always supposed that the persons in the original position have equal powers and rights, that is, that they are symmetrically situated with respect to any arrangements for reaching agreement, and that coalitions and the like are excluded. But it is an essential element (which has not been sufficiently observed although it is implicit in Kant's version of the theory) that there are very strong restrictions on what the contracting parties are presumed to know. In particular, I interpret the theory to hold that the parties do not know their position in society, past, present, or future; nor do they know which institutions exist. Again, they do not know their own place in the distribution of natural talents and abilities, whether they are intelligent or strong, man or woman, and so on. Finally, they do not know their own particular interests and preferences or the system of ends which they wish to advance: they do not know their conception of the good. In all these respects the parties are confronted with a veil of ignorance which prevents any one from being able to take advantage of his good fortune or particular interests or from being disadvantaged by them. What the parties do know (or assume) is that Hume's circumstances of justice obtain: namely, that the bounty of nature is not so generous as to render cooperative schemes superfluous nor so harsh as to make them impossible. Moreover, they assume that the extent of their altruism is limited and that, in general, they do not take an interest in one another's interests. Thus, given the special features of the original position, each man tries to do the best he can for himself by insisting on principles calculated to protect and advance his system of ends whatever it turns out to be.

I believe that as a consequence of the peculiar nature of the original position there would be an agreement on the following two principles for assigning rights and duties and for regulating distributive shares as these are determined by the fundamental institutions of society: first, each person is to have an equal right to the most extensive liberty compatible with a like liberty for all; second, social and economic inequalities (as defined by the institutional structure or fostered by it) are to be arranged so that they are both to everyone's advantage and attached to positions and offices open to all. In view of the content of these two principles and their application of the main institutions of society, and therefore to the social system as a whole, we may regard them as the two principles of justice. Basic social arrangements are just insofar as they conform to these principles, and we can, if we like, discuss questions of justice directly by reference to them. But a deeper understanding of the justification of civil disobedience requires, I think, an account of the derivation of these principles provided by the doctrine of the social contract. Part of our task is to show why this is so.

III. The Grounds of Compliance with an Unjust Law

If we assume that in the original position men would agree both to the principle of doing their part when they have accepted and plan to continue to accept the benefits of just institutions (the principle of fairness), and also to the principle of not preventing the establishment of just institutions and of upholding and complying with them when they do exist, then the contract doctrine easily accounts for our having to conform to just institutions. But how does it account for the fact that we are normally required to comply with unjust laws as well? The injustice of a law is not a sufficient ground for not complying with it any more than the legal validity of legislation is always sufficient to require obedience to it. Sometimes one hears these extremes asserted, but I think that we need not take them seriously.

An answer to our question can be given by elaborating the social contract theory in the following way. I interpret it to hold that one is to envisage a series of agreements as follows: first, men are to agree upon the principles of justice in the original position. Then they are to move to a constitutional convention in which they choose a constitution that satisfies the principles of justice already chosen. Finally they assume the role of a legislative body and guided by the principles of justice enact laws subject to the constraints and procedures of the just constitution. The decisions reached in any stage are binding in all subsequent stages. Now whereas in the original position the contracting parties have no knowledge of their society or of their own position in it, in both a constitutional convention and a legislature, they do know certain general facts about their institutions, for example, the statistics regarding employment and output required for fiscal and economic policy. But no one knows particular facts about his own social class or his place in the distribution of natural assets. On each occasion the contracting parties have the knowledge required to make their agreement rational from the appropriate point of view, but not so much as to make them prejudiced. They are unable to tailor principles and legislation to take advantage of their social or natural position; a veil of ignorance prevents their knowing what this position is. With this series of agreements in mind, we can characterize just laws and policies as those which would be enacted were this whole process correctly carried out.

In choosing a constitution the aim is to find among the just constitutions the one which is most likely, given the general facts about the society in question, to lead to just and effective legislation. The principles of justice provide a criterion for the laws desired; the problem is to find a set of political procedures that will give this outcome. I shall assume that, at least under the normal conditions of a modern state, the best constitution is some form of democratic regime affirming equal political liberty and using some sort of majority (or other plurality) rule. Thus it follows that on the contract theory a constitutional democracy of some sort is required by the principles of justice. At the same time it is essential to observe that the constitutional process is always a case of what we may call imperfect procedural justice: that is, there is no feasible political procedure which guarantees that the enacted legislation is just even though we have (let us suppose) a standard for just legislation. In simple cases, such as games of fair division, there are procedures which always lead to the right outcome (assume that equal shares is fair and let the man who cuts the cake take the last piece). These situations are those of perfect procedural justice. In other cases it does not matter what the outcome is as long as the fair procedure is followed: fairness of the process is transferred to the result (fair gambling is an instance of this). These situations are those of pure procedural justice. The constitutional process, like a criminal trial, resembles neither of these; the result matters and we have a standard for it. The difficulty is that we cannot frame a procedure which guarantees that only just and effective legislation is enacted. Thus even under a just constitution unjust laws may be passed and unjust policies enforced. Some form of the majority principle is necessary but the majority may be mistaken, more or less willfully, in what it legislates. In agreeing to a democratic constitution (as an instance of imperfect procedural justice) one accepts at the same time the principle of majority rule. Assuming that the constitution is just and that we have accepted and plan to continue to accept its benefits, we then have both an obligation and a natural duty (and in any case the duty) to comply with what the majority enacts even though it may be unjust. In this way we become bound to follow unjust laws, not always, of course, but provided the injustice does not exceed certain limits. We recognize that we must run the risk of suffering from the defects of one another's sense of justice; this burden we are prepared to carry as long as it is more or less evenly distributed or does not weigh too heavily. Justice binds us to a just constitution and to the unjust laws which may be enacted under it in precisely the same way that it binds us to any other social arrangement. Once we take the sequence of stages into account, there is nothing unusual in our being required to comply with unjust laws.

It should be observed that the majority principle has a secondary place as a rule of procedure which is perhaps the most efficient one under usual circumstances for working a democratic constitution. The basis for it rests essentially upon the principles of justice and therefore we may, when conditions allow, appeal to these principles against unjust legislation. The justice of the constitution does not insure the justice of laws enacted under it; and while we often have both an obligation and a duty to comply with what the majority legislates (as long as it does not exceed certain limits), there is, of course, no corresponding obligation or duty to regard what the majority enacts as itself just. The right to make law does not guarantee that the decision is rightly made; and while the citizen submits in his conduct to the judgment of democratic authority, he does not submit his judgment to it.[2] And if in his judgment the enactments of the majority exceed certain bounds of injustice, the citizen may consider civil disobedience. For we are not required to accept the majority's acts unconditionally and to acquiesce in the denial of our and others' liberties; rather we submit our conduct to democratic authority to the extent necessary to share the burden of working a constitutiontl regime, distorted as it must inevitably be by men's lack of wisdom and the defects of their sense of justice.

IV. The Place of Civil Disobedience in a Constitutional Democracy

We are now in a position to say a few things about civil disobedience. I shall understand it to be a public, nonviolent, and conscientious act contrary to law usually done with the intent to bring about a change in the policies or laws of the

---

[2] On this point see A. E. Murphy's review of Yves Simon's *The Philosophy of Democratic Government* (1951) in the *Philosophical Review* (April, 1952).

government.[3] Civil disobedience is a political act in the sense that it is an act justified by moral principles which define a conception of civil society and the public good. It rests, then, on political conviction as opposed to a search for self or group interest; and in the case of a constitutional democracy, we may assume that this conviction involves the conception of justice (say that expressed by the contract doctrine) which underlies the constitution itself. That is, in a viable democratic regime there is a common conception of justice by reference to which its citizens regulate their political affairs and interpret the constitution. Civil disobedience is a public art which the dissenter believes to be justified by this conception of justice and for this reason it may be understood as addressing the sense of justice of the majority in order to urge reconsideration of the measures protested and to warn that, in the sincere opinion of the dissenters, the conditions of social cooperation are not being honored. For the principles of justice express precisely such conditions, and their persistent and deliberate violation in regard to basic liberties over any extended period of time cuts the ties of community and invites either submission or forceful resistance. By engaging in civil disobedience a minority leads the majority to consider whether it wants to have its acts taken in this way, or whether, in view of the common sense of justice, it wishes to acknowledge the claims of the minority.

Civil disobedience is also civil in another sense. Not only is it the outcome of a sincere conviction based on principles which regulate civic life, but it is public and nonviolent, that is, it is done in a situation where arrest and punishment are expected and accepted without resistance. In this way it manifests a respect for legal procedures. Civil disobedience expresses disobedience to law within the limits of fidelity to law, and this feature of it helps to establish in the eyes of the majority that it is indeed conscientious and sincere, that it really is meant to address their sense of justice.[4] Being completely open about one's acts and being willing to accept the legal consequences of one's conduct is a bond given to make good one's sincerity, for that one's deeds are conscientious is not easy to demonstrate to another or even before oneself. No doubt it is possible to imagine a legal system in which conscientious belief that the law is unjust is accepted as a defense for noncompliance, and men of great honesty who are confident in one another might make such a system work. But as things are such a scheme would be unstable; we must pay a price in order to establish that we believe our actions have a moral basis in the convictions of the community.

The nonviolent nature of civil disobedience refers to the fact that it is intended to address the sense of justice of the majority and as such it is a form of speech, an expression of conviction. To engage in violent acts likely to injure and to hurt is incompatible with civil disobedience as a mode of address. Indeed, an interference with the basic rights of others tends to obscure the civilly disobedient quality of one's act. Civil disobedience is nonviolent in the further sense that the legal penalty for one's action is accepted and that resistance is not (at least for the moment) contemplated. Nonviolence in this sense is to be distinguished from nonviolence as a religious or pacifist principle. While those engaging in civil disobedience have often held some such principle, there is no necessary connection between it and

[3] Here I follow H. A. Bedau's definition of civil disobedience. See his "On Civil Disobedience," *Journal of Philosophy* (October, 1961).

[4] For a fuller discussion of this point to which I am indebted, see Charles Fried, "Moral Causation," *Harvard Law Review* (1964).

civil disobedience. For on the interpretation suggested, civil disobedience in a democratic society is best understood as an appeal to the principles of justice, the fundamental conditions of willing social cooperation among free men, which in the view of the community as a whole are expressed in the constitution and guide its interpretation. Being an appeal to the moral basis of public life, civil disobedience is a political and not primarily a religious act. It addresses itself to the common principles of justice which men can require one another to follow and not to the aspirations of love which they cannot. Moreover by taking part in civilly disobedient acts one does not foreswear indefinitely the idea of forceful resistance; for if the appeal against injustice is repeatedly denied, then the majority has declared its intention to invite submission or resistance and the latter may conceivably be justified even in a democratic regime. We are not required to acquiesce in the crushing of fundamental liberties by democratic majorities which have shown themselves blind to the principles of justice upon which justification of the constitution depends.

V. The Justification of Civil Disobedience

So far we have said nothing about the justification of civil disobedience, that is, the conditions under which civil disobedience may be engaged in consistent with the principles of justice that support a democratic regime. Our task is to see how the characterization of civil disobedience as addressed to the sense of justice of the majority (or to the citizens as a body) determines when such action is justified.

First of all, we may suppose that the normal political appeals to the majority have already been made in good faith and have been rejected, and that the standard means of redress have been tried. Thus, for example, existing political parties are indifferent to the claims of the minority and attempts to repeal the laws protested have been met with further repression since legal institutions are in the control of the majority. While civil disobedience should be recognized, I think, as a form of political action within the limits of fidelity to the rule of law, at the same time it is a rather desperate act just within these limits, and therefore it should, in general, be undertaken as a last resort when standard democratic processes have failed. In this sense it is not a normal political action. When it is justified there has been a serious breakdown; not only is there grave injustice in the law but a refusal more or less deliberate to correct it.

Second, since civil disobedience is a political act addressed to the sense of justice of the majority, it should usually be limited to substantial and clear violations of justice and preferably to those which, if rectified, will establish a basis for doing away with remaining injustices. For this reason there is a presumption in favor of restricting civil disobedience to violations of the first principle of justice, the principle of equal liberty, and to barriers which contravene the second principle, the principle of open offices which protects equality of opportunity. It is not, of course, always easy to tell whether these principles are satisfied. But if we think of them as guaranteeing the fundamental equal political and civil liberties (including freedom of conscience and liberty of thought) and equality of opportunity, then it is often relatively clear whether their principles are being honored. After all, the equal liberties are defined by the visible structure of social institutions; they are to be incorporated into the recognized practice, if not the letter, of social arrangements. When minorities are denied the right to vote or to hold certain political offices, when certain religious groups are repressed and others denied equality of opportunity, in the economy, this is often obvious and there is no doubt that justice is not being given. However, the first part of the second principle which requires that inequalities be to everyone's advantage is a much more imprecise and controversial matter. Not only is there a problem of assigning it a determinate and precise sense, but even if we do so and agree on what it should be, there is often a wide variety of reasonable opinion as to whether the principle is satisfied. The reason for this is that the principle applies primarily to fundamental economic and social policies. The choice of these depends upon theoretical and speculative beliefs as well as upon a wealth of concrete information, and all of this mixed with judgment and plain hunch, not to mention in actual cases prejudice and self-interest. Thus unless the laws of taxation are clearly designed to attack a basic equal liberty, they should not be protested by civil disobedience; the appeal to justice is not sufficiently clear and its resolution is best left to the political process. But violations of the equal liberties that define the common status of citizenship are another matter. The deliberate denial of these more or less over any extended period of time in the face of normal political protest is, in general, an appropriate object of civil disobedience. We may think of the social system as divided roughly into two parts, one which incorporates the fundamental equal liberties (including equality of opportunity) and another which embodies social and economic policies properly aimed at promoting the advantage of everyone. As a rule civil disobedience is best limited to the former where the appeal to justice is not only more definite and precise, but where, if it is effective, it tends to correct the injustices in the latter.

Third, civil disobedience should be restricted to those cases where the dissenter is willing to affirm that everyone else similarly subjected to the same degree of injustice has the right to protest in a similar way. That is, we must be prepared to authorize others to dissent in similar situations and in the same way, and to accept the consequences of their doing so. Thus, we may hold, for example, that the widespread disposition to disobey civilly clear violations of fundamental liberties more or less deliberate over an extended period of time would raise the degree of justice throughout society and would insure men's self-esteem as well as their respect for one another. Indeed, I believe this to be true, though certainly it is partly a matter of conjecture. As the contract doctrine emphasizes, since the principles of justice are principles which we would agree to in an original position of equality when we do not know our social position and the like, the refusal to grant justice is either the denial of the other as an equal (as one in regard to whom we are prepared to constrain our actions by principles which we would consent to) or the manifestation of a willingness to take advantage of natural contingencies and social fortune at his expense. In either case, injustice invites submission or resistance; but submission arouses the contempt of the oppressor and confirms him in his intention. If straightway, after a decent period of time to make reasonable political appeals in the normal way, men were in general to dissent by civil disobedience from infractions of the fundamental equal liberties, these liberties would, I believe, be more rather than less secure. Legitimate civil disobedience properly exercised is a stabilizing device in a constitutional regime, tending to make it more firmly just.

Sometimes, however, there may be a complication in connection with this third condition. It is possible, although perhaps unlikely, that there are so many persons or groups with a sound case for resorting to civil disobedience (as judged by the foregoing criteria) that disorder would follow if they all did so. There might be serious injury to the just constitution. Or again, a group might be so large that some extra precaution is necessary in the extent to which its members organize and engage in civil disobedience. Theoretically the case is one in which a number of persons or groups are equally entitled to and all want to resort to civil disobedience, yet if they all do this, grave consequences for everyone may result. The question, then, is who among them may exercise their right, and it falls under the general problem of fairness. I cannot discuss the complexities of the matter here. Often a lottery or a rationing system can be set up to handle the case; but unfortunately the circumstances of civil disobedience rule out this solution. It suffices to note that a problem of fairness may arise and that those who contemplate civil disobedience should take it into account. They may have to reach an understanding as to who can exercise their right in the immediate situation and to recognize the need for special constraint.

The final condition, of a different nature, is the following. We have been considering when one has a right to engage in civil disobedience, and our conclusion is that one has this right should three conditions hold: when one is subject to injustice more or less deliberate over an extended period of time in the face of normal political protests; where the injustice is a clear violation of the liberties of equal citizenship; and provided that the general disposition to protest similarly in similar cases would have acceptable consequences. These conditions are not, I think, exhaustive but they seem to cover the more obvious points; yet even when they are satisfied and one has the right to engage in civil disobedience, there is still the different question of whether one should exercise this right, that is, whether by doing so one is likely to further one's ends. Having established one's right to protest one is then free to consider these tactical questions. We may be acting within our rights but still foolishly if our action only serves to provoke the harsh retaliation of the majority; and it is likely to do so if the majority lacks a sense of justice, or if the action is poorly timed or not well designed to make the appeal to the sense of justice effective. It is easy to think of instances of this sort, and in each case these practical questions have to be faced. From the standpoint of the theory of political obligation we can only say that the exercise of the right should be rational and reasonably designed to advance the protester's aims, and that weighing tactical questions presupposes that one has already established one's right, since tactical advantages in themselves do not support it.

VI. Conclusion: Several Objections Considered

In a reasonably affluent democratic society justice becomes the first virtue of institutions. Social arrangements irrespective of their efficiency must be reformed if they are significantly unjust. No increase in efficiency in the form of greater advantages for many justifies the loss of liberty of a few. That we believe this is shown by the fact that in a democracy the fundamental liberties of citizenship are not understood as the outcome of political bargaining nor are they subject to the calculus of social interests. Rather these liberties are fixed points which serve to limit political transactions and which determine the scope of calculations of social advantage. It is this fundamental place of the equal liberties which makes their systematic violation over any extended period of time a proper object of civil disobedience. For to deny men these rights is to infringe the conditions of social cooperation among free and rational persons, a fact which is evident to the citizens of a constitutional regime since it follows from the principles of justice which underlie their institutions. The justification of civil disobedience rests on the priority of justice and the equal liberties which it guarantees.

It is natural to object to this view of civil disobedience that it relies too heavily upon the existence of a sense of justice. Some may hold that the feeling for justice is not a vital political force, and that what moves men are various other interests, the desire for wealth, power, prestige, and so on. Now this is a large question the answer to which is highly conjectural and each tends to have his own opinion. But there are two remarks which may clarify what I have said: first, I have assumed that there is in a constitutional regime a common sense of justice the principles of which are recognized to support the constitution and to guide its interpretation. In any given situation particular men may be tempted to violate these principles, but the collective force in their behalf is usually effective since they are seen as the necessary terms of cooperation among free men; and presumably the citizens of a democracy (or sufficiently many of them) want to see justice done. Where these assumptions fail, the justifying conditions for civil disobedience (the first three) are not affected, but the rationality of engaging in it certainly is. In this case, unless the costs of repressing civil dissent injures the economic self-interest (or whatever) of the majority, protest may simply make the position of the minority worse. No doubt as a tactical matter civil disobedience is more effective when its appeal coincides with other interests, but a constitutional regime is not viable in the long run without an attachment to the principles of justice of the sort which we have assumed.

Then, further, there may be a misapprehension about the manner in which a sense of justice manifests itself. There is a tendency to think that it is shown by professions of the relevant principles together with actions of an altruistic nature requiring a considerable degree of self-sacrifice. But these conditions are obviously too strong, for the majority's sense of justice may show itself simply in its being unable to undertake the measures required to suppress the minority and to punish as the law requires the various acts of civil disobedience. The sense of justice undermines the will to uphold unjust institutions, and so a majority despite its superior power may give way. It is unprepared to force the minority to be subject to injustice. Thus, although the majority's action is reluctant and grudging, the role of the sense of justice is nevertheless essential, for without it the majority would have been willing to enforce the law and to defend its position. Once we see the sense of justice as working in this negative way to make established injustices indefensible, then it is recognized as a central element of democratic politics.

Finally, it may be objected against this account that it does not settle the question of who is to say when the situation is such as to justify civil disobedience. And because it does not answer this question, it invites anarchy by encouraging every man to decide the matter for himself. Now the reply to this is that each man must indeed settle this question for himself, although he may, of course, decide wrongly. This is true on any theory of political duty and obligation, at least on any theory compatible with the principles of a democratic constitution. The citizen is responsible for what he does. If we usually think that we should comply with the law, this is because our political principles normally lead to this conclusion. There is a presumption in favor of compliance in the absence of good reasons to the contrary. But because each man is responsible and must decide for himself as best he can whether the circumstances justify civil disobedience, it does not follow that he may decide as he pleases. It is not by looking to our personal interests or to political allegiances narrowly construed, that we should make up our mind. The citizen must decide on the basis of the principles of justice that underlie and guide the interpretation of the constitution and in the light of his sincere conviction as to how these principles should be applied in the circumstances. If he concludes that conditions obtain which justify civil disobedience and conducts himself accordingly, he has acted conscientiously and perhaps mistakenly, but not in any case at his convenience.

In a democratic society each man must act as he thinks the principles of political right require him to. We are to follow our understanding of these principles, and we cannot do otherwise. There can be no morally binding legal interpretation of these principles, not even by a supreme court or legislature. Nor is there any infallible procedure for determining what or who is right. In our system the Supreme Court, Congress, and the President often put forward rival interpretations of the Constitution. Although the Court has the final say in settling any particular case, it is not immune from powerful political influence that may change its reading of the law of the land. The Court presents its point of view by reason and argument; its conception of the Constitution must, if it is to endure, persuade men of its soundness. The final court of appeal is not the Court, or Congress, or the President, but the electorate as a whole.[5] The civilly disobedient appeal in effect to this body. There is no danger of anarchy as long as there is a sufficient working agreement in men's conceptions of political justice and what it requires. That men can achieve such an understanding when the essential political liberties are maintained is the assumption implicit in democratic institutions. There is no way to avoid entirely the risk of divisive strife. But if legitimate civil disobedience seems to threaten civil peace, the responsibility falls not so much on those who protest as upon those whose abuse of authority and power justifies such opposition.

[5] For a presentation of this view to which I am indebted, see A. M. Bickel, *The Least Dangerous Branch* (Indianapolis, 1962), especially Chapters 5 and 6.

13. The Obligation to Obey the Law*

Richard A. Wasserstrom

I

The question of what is the nature and extent of one's obligation to obey the law is one of those relatively rare philosophic questions which can never produce doubts about the importance of theory for practice. To ask under what circumstances, if any, one is justified in disobeying the law, is to direct attention to problems which all would acknowledge to be substantial. Concrete, truly problematic situations are as old as civil society.

The general question was posed — though surely not for the first time — well over two thousand years ago in Athens when Crito revealed to Socrates that Socrates' escape from prison could be easily and successfully accomplished. The issue was made a compelling one — though once again surely not for the first time — by Crito's insistence that escape was not only possible but also *desirable*, and that disobedience to law was in *this* case at least, surely justified. And the problem received at the hand of Socrates — here perhaps for the first time — a sustained theoretical analysis and resolution.

Just as the question of what is the nature and extent of one's obligation to obey the law demanded attention then — as it has throughout man's life in the body politic — it is no less with us today in equally vexing and perplexing forms. Freedom rides and sit-ins have raised the question of whether the immorality of segregation may justify disobeying the law. The all too awesome horrors of a nuclear war have seemed to some to require responsive action, including, if need be, deliberate but peaceful trespasses upon government-owned atomic testing grounds. And the rightness of disobedience to law in the face of court-ordered school integration has been insisted upon by the citizens of several states and acted upon by the governor of at least one.[1]

The problem is one of present concern and the questions it necessarily raises are real. But even if the exigencies of contemporary life were not such as to make this topic a compelling one, it is one which would still be peculiarly ripe for critical inquiry. In part this is so because despite their significance many of the central issues have been relatively neglected by legal or political philosophers and critics.

From *UCLA Law Review*, Vol. 10 (1963), pp. 780–807, by permission of the author and publisher. © 1963 by The Regents of the University of California.

* This is an expanded and substantially revised version of a paper, "Disobeying the Law," which was presented at the December, 1961, meeting of the Eastern Division of the American Philosophical Society and which was published in 58 *J. Philosophy* 641 (1961).

This revision has been benefitted by the helpful comments and suggestions of my colleagues, Professors Herbert Packer and Gerald Gunther; and especially of Professor Arnold Kaufman of the Department of Philosophy of the University of Michigan, presently a Fellow at the Center for Advanced Study in the Behavioral Sciences.

[1] This is to say nothing of the stronger claim, involved in many of the war crimes prosecutions, that one does have a duty to disobey the law and, therefore, that one can be properly punished for having obeyed the law.

Many of the important questions which bear upon the nature and extent of one's obligation to obey the law have been dealt with summarily and uncritically; distinguishable issues have been indiscriminately blurred and debatable conclusions gratuitously assumed.

More important is the fact that historically the topic has generally been examined from only one very special aspect of the problem. Those philosophers who have seriously considered questions relating to one's obligation to obey the law have considered them only in the context of revolution. They have identified the conditions under which one would, if ever, be justified in disobeying the law with the conditions under which revolution would, if ever, be justified; and they have, perhaps not surprisingly, tended thereby to conclude that one would be justified in disobeying the law if, and only if, revolution itself would in that case be justified.[2]

To view the problem in a setting of obedience or revolution is surely to misconstrue it. It is to neglect, among other things, something that is obviously true — that most people who disobey the law are not revolutionaries and that most acts of disobedience of the law are not acts of revolution. Many who disobey the law are, of course, ordinary criminals: burglars, kidnappers, embezzlers, and the like. But even of those who disobey the law under a claim of justification, most are neither advocates nor practitioners or revolution.[3]

If the traditional, philosophical treatment of this subject is unduly simplistic and restrictive, contemporary legal thought is seldom more instructive. It is distressing, for one thing, that those whose daily intellectual concern is the legal system have said so little on this subject. And it is disturbing that many of those who have said anything at all appear so readily to embrace the view that justified disobedience of the law is a rare, if not impossible, occurrence. What is so disturbing is not the fact that this view is held — although I think it a mistaken one — but rather that such a conclusion is so summarily reached or assumed.[4]

[2] See, e.g., Austin, *The Province of Jurisprudence Determined* 53–55 (1954); Hume, *A Treatise of Human Nature*, bk. III, § § 9, 10; Locke, *The Second Treatise of Government*, chs. 18, 19.

[3] A subject which has surely not received the philosophical attention it deserves is that of the nature of revolution. What, for instance, are the characteristics of a revolution? Must the procedures by which laws are made or the criteria of validity be altered? Or is it sufficient that the people who occupy certain crucial offices be removed in a manner inconsistent with existing rules? Must force or resistance accompany whatever changes or alterations are made? Whatever the answers may be to questions such as these, it is, I think, plain that particular laws may be disobeyed under a claim of justification without any of these features being present. One can *argue* that for one reason or another, any act of disobedience must necessarily lead to revolution or the overthrow of the government. But then this is an argument which must be demonstrated.

[4] Professor Henry Hart, for example, in his extremely stimulating analysis of the aims of the criminal law seems to hold such a view. Professor Hart believes, that the criminal law ought only be concerned with that conduct which is morally blameworthy. From this he infers that no real problem can ever be presented by laws which make knowledge of the illegality of an action one of the elements of the offense. And this is so because the "knowing or reckless disregard of legal obligation affords an independent basis of blameworthiness *justifying the actor's condemnation as a criminal*, even when his conduct was not intrinsically antisocial." Hart, "The Aims of the Criminal Law," 23 *Law & Contemp. Prob.* 401, 418 (1958). (Emphasis added.) Some such view can also be plausibly attributed to, among others, Professor Lon Fuller, see text at section II, and Professor Herbert Wechsler, see text at section IV. Of course, all of these scholars, or any other person holding such a view, might well insist that the position is tenable only if an important qualification is made, namely, that the legal system in question be that of an essentially democratic society. For a discussion of this more restricted claim, see text at section IV.

I must make it clear at the outset that it is not my purpose to devote the remainder of this article to a documentation of the claims just made concerning either historical or contemporary thought. I do not wish to demonstrate that people in fact do believe what they appear to believe about the possibility of justified disobedience to law. Nor do I wish to show why it is that people have come to believe what they appear to believe. Rather, in very general terms I am concerned here with *arguments* — with those arguments which have been or which might be given in support of the claim that because one does have an obligation to obey the law, one ought not ever disobey the law.

To describe the focus of the article in this manner is, however, to leave several crucial matters highly ambiguous. And thus, before the arguments can be considered properly, the following matters must be clarified.

A. There are several different views which could be held concerning the nature of the stringency of one's obligation to obey the law. One such view, and the one which I shall be most concerned to show to be false, can be characterized as holding that one has an *absolute* obligation to obey the law. I take this to mean that a person is never justified in disobeying the law; to know that a proposed action is illegal is to know all one needs to know in order to conclude that the action ought not to be done;[5] to cite the illegality of an action is to give a sufficient reason for not having done it. A view such as this is far from uncommon. President Kennedy expressed the thoughts of many quite reflective people when he said not too long ago:

> ... [O]ur nation is founded on the principle that observance of the law is the eternal safeguard of liberty and defiance of the law is the surest road to tyranny.
>
> The law which we obey includes the final rulings of the courts as well as the enactments of our legislative bodies. Even among law-abiding men few laws are universally loved.
>
> But they are universally respected and not resisted.
>
> Americans are free, in short, to disagree with the law, but not to disobey it. For in a government of laws and not of men, no man, however prominent or powerful, and no mob, however unruly or boisterous, is entitled to defy a court of law.
>
> If this country should ever reach the point where any man or group of men, by force or threat of force, could long deny the commands of our court and our Constitution, then no law would stand free from doubt, no judge would be sure of his writ and no citizen would be safe from his neighbors.[6]

A more moderate or weaker view would be that which holds that, while one does have an obligation to obey the law, the obligation is a prima facie rather than absolute one. If one knows that a proposed course of conduct is illegal then one has a good — but not necessarily a sufficient — reason for refraining from engaging in that course of conduct. Under this view, a person may be justified in disobeying the

---

[5] Because I am concerned with the question of whether one is ever *morally justified* in acting illegally, I purposely make the actor's knowledge of the illegality of the action part of the description of the act. I am not concerned with the question of whether ignorance of the illegality of the action ought to excuse one from moral blame.

[6] *N.Y. Times*, Oct. 1, 1962, p. 22, col. 6. The same qualification must be made here as was made in note 4 *supra* — President Kennedy may well have meant his remarks to be applicable only to the legal system which is a part of the set of political institutions of the United States.

law, but an act which is in disobedience of the law does have to be justified, whereas an act in obedience of the law does not have to be justified.

It is important to observe that there is an ambiguity in this notion of a prima facie obligation. For the claim that one has a prima facie obligation to obey the law can come to one of two different things. On the one hand, the claim can be this: the fact that an action is an act of disobedience is something which always does count against the performance of the action. If one has a prima facie obligation to obey the law, one always has that obligation — although, of course, it may be overridden by other obligations in any particular case. Thus the fact that an action is illegal is a relevant consideration in every case and it is a consideration which must be outweighed by other considerations before the performance of an illegal action can be justified.

On the other hand, the claim can be weaker still. The assertion of a prima facie obligation to obey the law can be nothing more than the claim that as a matter of fact it is *generally* right or obligatory to obey the law. As a rule the fact that an action is illegal is a relevant circumstance. But in any particular case, after deliberation, it might very well turn out that the illegality of the action was not truly relevant. For in any particular case the circumstances might be such that there simply was nothing in the fact of illegality which required overriding — *e.g..*, there were no bad consequences at all which would flow from disobeying the law in this case.

The distinction can be made more vivid in the following fashion. One person, A, might hold the view that any action in disobedience of the law is intrinsically bad. Some other person, B, might hold the view that no action is intrinsically bad unless it has the property, P, and that not all actions in disobedience of the law have that property. Now for A, the fact of disobedience is *always* a relevant consideration,[7] for B, the fact of disobedience may always be initially relevant because of the existence of some well-established hypothesis which asserts that the occurrence of any action of disobedience is correlated highly with the occurrence of P. But if in any particular case disobedience does not turn out to have the property, P, then, upon reflection, it can be concluded by B that the fact that disobedience is involved is not a reason which weighs against the performance of the act in question. To understand B's position it is necessary to distinguish the relevance of *considering* the fact of disobedience from the relevance of the fact of disobedience. The former must always be relevant, the latter is not.

Thus there are at least three different positions which might be taken concerning the character of the obligation to obey the law or the rightness of disobedience to the law. They are: (1) One has an absolute obligation to obey the law; disobedience is never justified. (2) One has an obligation to obey the law but this obligation can be overridden by conflicting obligations; disobedience can be justified, but only by the presence of outweighing circumstances. (3) One does not have a special obligation to obey the law, but it is in fact usually obligatory, on other grounds, to do so; disobedience to law often does turn out to be unjustified.

B. It must also be made clear that when I talk about the obligation to obey the law or the possibility of actions which are both illegal and justified, I am concerned

---

[7] To repeat, though, it surely is not necessarily conclusive, or sufficient, since an action in obedience to the law may under some other description be worse, or less justifiable, than disobedience.

solely with *moral obligations* and *morally justified* actions. I shall be concerned solely with arguments which seek to demonstrate that there is some sort of a connection between the legality or illegality of an action and its morality or immorality. Concentration on this general topic necessarily renders a number of interesting problems irrelevant. Thus, I am not at all concerned with the question of why, in fact, so many people do obey the law. Nor, concomitantly, am I concerned with the nonmoral reasons which might and do justify obedience to law — of these, the most pertinent, is the fact that highly unpleasant consequences of one form or another are typically inflicted upon those who disobey the law. Finally there are many actions which are immoral irrespective of whether they also happen to be illegal. And I am not, except in one very special sense, concerned with this fact either. I am not concerned with the fact that the immorality of the action itself may be a sufficient reason for condemning it regardless of its possible illegality.

C. My last preliminary clarification relates to the fact that there is a variety of kinds of legal rules or laws and that there is a variety of ways in which actions can be related to these rules. This is an important point because many moral philosophers, in particular, have tended to assimilate all legal rules to the model of a typical law or legal order which is enforced through the direct threat of the infliction by the government of severe sanctions, and have thereby tended to assume that all laws and all legal obligations can be broken or disobeyed only in the manner in which penal laws can be broken or disobeyed. That this assimilation is a mistake can be demonstrated quite readily. There are many laws that, unlike the typical penal law, do not require or prohibit the performance of any acts at all. They cannot, therefore, be disobeyed. There are laws, for example, that make testamentary dispositions of property ineffective, unenforceable, or invalid, if the written instrument was not witnessed by the requisite number of disinterested witnesses. Yet a law of this kind obviously does not impose an obligation upon anyone to make a will. Nor, more significantly, could a person who executed a will without the requisite number of witnesses be said to have disobeyed the law. Such a person has simply failed to execute a valid will.[8]

The foregoing observations are relevant largely because it is important to realize that to talk about disobeying the law or about one's obligation to obey the law is usually to refer to a rather special kind of activity, namely, that which is

---

[8] See Hart, *The Concept of Law* 27–48 (1961), particularly for the clearest and fullest extant philosophical analysis of the important distinguishing characteristics of different kinds of legal rules.

In this connection a stronger point than the one made above can be made. It is that there are many laws which, if they can be disobeyed at all, cannot be disobeyed in the way in which the typical criminal law can be disobeyed. For there are many laws that either impose or permit one to impose upon oneself any number of different legal obligations. And with many of these legal obligations, regardless of how created, it seems correct to say that one can breach or fail to perform them without thereby acting illegally or in disobedience of the law. One's obligation to obey the law may not, therefore, be coextensive with one's legal obligations. In the typical case of a breach of contract, for example, the failure to perform one's contractual obligations is clearly a breach of a legal obligation. Yet one can breach a contract and, hence, a legal obligation without necessarily acting illegally. This last assertion is open to question. And arguments for its correctness would not here be germane. It is sufficient to recognize only that failing to honor or perform some types of legal obligations may be a quite different kind of activity from violating or disobeying a law or order which is backed up, in some very direct fashion, by a governmentally threatened severe sanction.

exemplified by, among other things, actions in violation or disobedience of a penal law. It is this special type of activity which alone is the concern of this article.

II

One kind of argument in support of the proposition that one cannot be justified in disobeying the law is that which asserts the existence of some sort of *logical* or conceptual relationship between disobeying the law and acting immorally.[9] If the notion of illegality entails that of immorality then one is never justified in acting illegally just because part of the meaning of *illegal* is *immoral*; just because describing an action as illegal is — among other things — to describe it as unjustified.[10]

A claim such as this is extremely difficult to evaluate. For one has great difficulty in knowing what is to count as truly relevant — let alone decisive — evidence of its correctness. There is, nevertheless, a supporting argument of sorts which can be made. It might go something like this:

It is a fact which is surely worth noticing that people generally justify action that *seems to be* illegal by claiming that the action *is not really* illegal. Typically an actor who is accused of having done something illegal will not defend himself by pointing out that, while illegal, his conduct was nevertheless morally justified. Instead, he will endeavor to show in one way or another that it is really inaccurate to call his conduct illegal at all. Now it looks as though this phenomenon can be readily accounted for. People try to resist the accusation of illegality, it might be argued, for the simple reason that they wish to avoid being punished. But what is interesting and persuasive is the fact that people try just as hard to evade a charge of illegality even in those situations where the threat of punishment is simply not an important or even relevant consideration.

The cases of the recent sit-ins or freedom rides are apt. To be sure, the claim was that the preservation of segregated lunch-counters, waiting rooms, and the like was

---

[9] It is worth emphasizing that I am not at all interested in the claim — which in many ways is an odd one to belabor — that there is a logical relationship between disobeying the law and acting illegally. See, e.g., Carnes, "Why Should I Obey the Law? 71 *Ethics* 14 (1960).

[10] Professor Fuller may hold to some version of this view in his article, "Positivism and Fidelity to Law — A Reply to Professor Hart, 71 *Harv. L. Rev.* 630, 656 (1958), where, after characterizing the position of legal positivism as one which says that "On the one hand, we have an amoral datum called law, which has the peculiar quality of creating a moral duty to obey it. On the other hand, we have a moral duty to do what we think is right and decent." Professor Fuller goes on to criticize this bifurcation of law and morality on the grounds that "The 'dilemma' it states has the verbal formulation of a problem, but the problem it states makes no sense. It is like saying I have to choose between giving food to a starving man and being mimsey with the borogroves. I do not think it unfair to the positivistic philosophy to say that it never gives any coherent meaning to the moral obligation of fidelity to law."

Others who at least suggest adherence to such a position are: Baier, *The Moral Point of View* 134 (1958); Nowell-Smith, *Ethics* 236−37 (1959); and Weldon, *The Vocabulary of Politics* 57 , 62, 66−67 (1953). And there are surely passages in Hobbes that could also be read in this way. See, e.g., Hobbes, *Leviathan*, chs. XIII, XVIII. The claim that *illegal* entails *immoral* is closely related to, but surely distinguishable from, the position that Professor Fuller, among many others, may also hold, namely, that there are certain minimum "moral" requirements that must be met before any rule can be a law.

morally indefensible. But an important justification for the rightness of the actions employed in integrating these facilities in the fashion selected rested upon the insistence that the perpetuation of segregation in these circumstances was itself illegal. One primary claim for the rightness of freedom rides was that these were not instances of disobeying the law. They were instead attempts to invoke judicial and executive protection of legal, indeed constitutional, rights. While there were some, no doubt, who might have insisted upon the rightness of sit-ins even if they were clearly illegal, most people were confident of the blamelessness of the participants just because it was plain that their actions were not, in the last analysis, illegal. Were it evident that sit-ins were truly illegal many might hold a different view about the rightness of sitting-in as a means to bring about integrated facilities.

Language commonly invoked in the course of disputes between nations furnishes another equally graphic illustration of the same point. In the continuing controversy over the status of Berlin, for instance, both the United States and Russia have relied upon claims of legality and have been sensitive to charges of illegality, to an appreciably greater extent than one would otherwise have supposed. And much the same can be said of the more recent dispute between India and China. Now if nations which have little to fear in the way of the imposition of sanctions for acting illegally are nevertheless extraordinarily sensitive to charges of illegal conduct, this also may be taken as evidence of the fact that *illegality* implies *immorality*.

Wholly apt, too, was the controversy over the Eichmann trial. To some, the fact that the seizure and trial of Eichmann by Israel was illegal was sufficient to cast grave doubts upon the justifiability of the proceedings. To others, the charge of illegality made it necessary to demonstrate that nothing really illegal had occurred. What is significant about all this is the fact that all of the disputants implicitly acknowledged that illegality was something which did have to be worried about.

Such in brief is the argument which might be advanced and the "evidence" which might be adduced to support it. I think that such an argument is not persuasive, and I can best show this to be so in the following fashion.

Consider the case of a law that makes it a felony to perform an abortion upon a woman unless the abortion is necessary to preserve *her* life. Suppose a teenager, the daughter of a local minister, has been raped on her way home from school by an escapee from a state institution for mental defectives. Suppose further that the girl has become pregnant and has been brought to a reputable doctor who is asked to perform an abortion. And suppose, finally, that the doctor concludes after examining the girl that her life will not be engangered by giving birth to the child.[11] An abortion under these circumstances is, it seems fair to say, illegal.[12] Yet, we would surely find both intelligible and appealing the doctor's claim that he was nonetheless justified in disobeying the law by performing an abortion on the girl. I at least can see nothing logically odd or inconsistent about recognizing both that there is a law prohibiting this conduct and that further questions concerning the rightness of obedience would be relevant and, perhaps, decisive. Thus I can see

---

[11] These facts are taken from Packer & Gampell, "Therapeutic Abortion: A Problem in Law and Medicine," 11 Stan. L. Rev. 417 (1959), where they are introduced in a different context.

[12] Such would seem to be the case in California, for example, where Cal. Pen. Code § 274 makes the performance of an abortion a felony unless the abortion is necessary to preserve the life of the pregnant woman.

nothing logically odd about describing this as a case in which the performance of the abortion could be both illegal and morally justified.[13]

There is, no doubt, a heroic defense which can be made to the above. It would consist of the insistence that the activity just described simply cannot be both illegal and justified. Two alternatives are possible. First, one might argue that the commission of the abortion would indeed have been justified if it were not proscribed by the law. But since it is so prohibited, the abortion is wrong. Now if this is a point about the appropriateness of kinds of reasons, I can only note that referring the action to a valid law does not seem to preclude asking meaningful questions about the obligatoriness of the action. If this is a point about language or concepts it does seem to be perfectly intelligible to say that the conduct is both illegal and morally justified. And if this is, instead, an *argument* for the immorality of ever disobeying a valid law, then it surely requires appreciable substantiation and not mere assertion.

Second, one might take a different line and agree that other questions can be asked about the conduct, but that is because the commission of the abortion under these circumstances simply cannot be illegal. The difficulty here, however, is that it is hard to understand what is now meant by *illegal.* Of course, I am not claiming that in the case as I have described it, it is clear that the performance of the abortion must be illegal. It might not be. But it might be. Were we to satisfy all the usual tests that we do invoke when we determine that a given course of conduct is illegal, and were someone still to maintain that because the performance of the abortion is here morally justified it cannot be illegal, then the burden is on the proponent of this view to make clear how we are to decide when conduct is illegal. And it would further be incumbent upon him to demonstrate what seems to be highly dubious, namely, that greater clarity and insight could somehow be attained through a radical change in our present terminology. It appears to be a virtually conclusive refutation to observe that there has never been a legal system whose criteria of validity — no matter how sophisticated, how rational and how well defined — themselves guaranteed that morally justified action would never be illegal.

Thus an argument as strong as any of the above must fail. There is, of course, a weaker version which may be more appealing. If it is true that there is something disturbing about justifying actions that are conceded to be illegal, then one way to account for this is to insist that there is a logical connection between the concepts involved, but it is something less than the kind of implication already discussed. Perhaps it is correct that *illegal* does not entail *immoral; illegal* might nevertheless entail *prima facie immoral.* The evidence adduced tends to show that among one's moral obligations is the prima facie duty to obey the law.[14]

---

[13] I am supposing, of course, that one would regard the performance of the abortion — in the absence of the relevant penal law — is clearly morally justified. If one disagrees with this assessment of the morality of the case, then some other example ought to be substituted. One likely candidate, drawn from our own history, is that of the inherent rightness in refusing to return an escaped Negro slave to his "owner." If one believes that refusing to do so would be clearly justifiable, then consider whether the existence of the fugitive slave laws necessarily rendered a continued refusal unjustified.

[14] Sir W. David Ross, for example, suggests that the obligation to obey the law is a prima facie obligation which is a compound of three more simple prima facie duties. Ross, *The Right and the Good* 27–28 (1930).

Once again, it is somewhat difficult to know precisely what to make of such a claim. It is hard to see how one would decide what was to count as evidence or whether the evidence was persuasive. At a minimum, it is not difficult to imagine several equally plausible alternative explanations of the disturbing character of accusations of illegal activity. In addition, to know only that one has a prima facie duty to obey the law is not to know a great deal. In particular, one does not know how or when that obligation can be overridden. And, of course, even if it is correct that acting illegally logically implies acting prima facie immorally, this in no way shows that people may not often be morally justified in acting illegally. At most, it demands that they have some good reason for acting illegally; at best, it requires what has already been hypothesized, namely, that the action in question, while illegal, be morally justified.

Thus, it is clear that if the case against ever acting illegally is to be made out, conceptual analysis alone cannot do it. Indeed, arguments of quite another sort must be forthcoming. And it is to these that I now turn.

III

One such argument, and the most common argument advanced, goes something like this: The reason why one ought never to disobey the law is simply that the consequences would be disastrous if everybody disobeyed the law. The reason why disobedience is never right becomes apparent once we ask the question "But what if everyone did that?"

Consider again the case of the doctor who has to decide whether he is justified in performing an illegal abortion. If he only has a prima facie duty to obey the law it looks as though he might justifiably decide that in this case his prima facie obligation is overridden by more stringent conflicting obligations. Or, if he is simply a utilitarian, it appears that he might rightly conclude that the consequences of disobeying the abortion law would be on the whole and in the long run less deleterious than those of obeying. But this is simply a mistake. The doctor would inevitably be neglecting the most crucial factor of all, namely, that in performing the abortion he was disobeying the law. And imagine what would happen if everyone went around disobeying the law. The alternatives are obeying the law and general disobedience. The choice is between any social order and chaos. As President Kennedy correctly observed, if any law is disobeyed, then no law can be free from doubt, no citizen safe from his neighbor.

Such an argument, while perhaps overdrawn, is by no means uncommon.[15] Yet, as it stands, it is an essentially confused one. Its respective claims, if they are to be fairly evaluated, must be delineated with some care.

At a minimum, the foregoing attack upon the possibility of justified disobedience might be either one or both of two radically different kinds of objection.

[15] Socrates, for instance, supposes that were he to escape he might properly be asked: "[W]hat are you about? Are you going by an act of yours to overturn us — the laws and the whole state, as far as in you lies? Do you imagine that a state can subsist and not be overthrown, in which the decisions of law have no power, but are set aside and overthrown by individuals?" Plato, Crito. Analogous arguments can be found in, for example: Austin, *The Province of Jurisprudence Determined* 52–53 (1954); Hobbes, *Leviathan*, ch. XV; Hume, *A Treatise of Human Nature*, bk. III, pt. II, 3, 6, 8, 9; Toulmin, *An Examination of the Place of Reason in Ethics* 151 (1950).

The first, which relates to the consequences of an act of disobedience, is essentially a *causal* argument. The second questions the *principle* that any proponent of justified disobedience invokes. As to the causal argument, it is always relevant to point out that any act of disobedience may have certain consequences simply because it is an act of disobedience. Once the occurrence of the act is known, for example, expenditure of the state's resources may become necessary. The time and energy of the police will probably be turned to the task of discovering who it was who did the illegal act and of gathering evidence relevant to the offense. And other resources might be expended in the prosecution and adjudication of the case against the perpetrator of the illegal act. Illustrations of this sort could be multiplied, no doubt, but I do not think either that considerations of this sort are very persuasive or that they have been uppermost in the minds of those who make the argument now under examination. Indeed, if the argument is a causal one at all, it consists largely of the claim that any act of disobedience will itself cause, to some degree or other, general disobedience of all laws; it will cause or help to cause the overthrow or dissolution of the state. And while it is possible to assert that any act of disobedience will tend to further social disintegration or revolution, it is much more difficult to see why this must be so.

The most plausible argument would locate this causal efficacy in the kind of example set by any act of disobedience. But how plausible is this argument? It is undeniable, of course, that the kind of example that will be set is surely a relevant factor. Yet, there is nothing that precludes any proponent of justified disobedience from taking this into account. If, for example, others will somehow infer from the doctor's disobedience of the abortion law that they are justified in disobeying *any* law under *any* circumstances, then the doctor ought to consider this fact. This is a consequence — albeit a lamentable one — of his act of disobedience. Similarly, if others will extract the proper criterion from the act of disobedience, but will be apt to misapply it in practice, then this too ought to give the doctor pause. It, too, is a consequence of acting.[16] But if the argument is that disobedience would be wrong even if no bad example were set and no other deleterious consequences likely, then the argument must be directed against the principle the doctor appeals to in disobeying the law, and not against the consequences of his disobedience at all.

As to the attack upon a principle of justified disobedience, as a principle, the response "But what if everyone disobeyed the law?" does appear to be a good way to point up both the inherent inconsistency of almost any principle of justified disobedience and the manifest undesirability of adopting such a principle. Even if one need not worry about what others will be led to do by one's disobedience, there is surely something amiss if one cannot consistently defend his right to do what one is claiming he is right in doing.

In large measure, such an objection is unreal. The appeal to "But what if everyone did that?" loses much, if not all, of its persuasiveness once we become clearer about what precisely the "did that" refers to. If the question "But what if everyone did that?" is simply another way of asking "But what if everybody disobeyed the law?" or "But what if people generally disobeyed the laws?" then the question is surely quasi-rhetorical. To urge general or indiscriminate disobedience to laws is to invoke a principle that, if coherent, is manifestly indefensible. It is equally plain, however, that with few exceptions such a principle has never

---

[16] For a very special and related version of this argument, see text at section V.

been seriously espoused. Anyone who claims that there are actions that are both illegal and justified surely need not be thereby asserting that it is right generally to disobey all laws or even any particular law. It is surely not inconsistent to assert both that indiscriminate disobedience is indefensible and that discriminate disobedience is morally right and proper conduct. Nor, analogously, is it at all evident that a person who claims to be justified in performing an illegal action is thereby committed to or giving endorsement to the principle that the entire legal system ought to be overthrown or renounced. At a minimum, therefore, the appeal to "But what if everyone did that?" cannot by itself support the claim that one has an absolute obligation to obey the law — that disobeying the law can never be truly justified.

There is, however, a distinguishable but related claim which merits very careful attention — if for no other reason than the fact that it is so widely invoked today by moral philosophers. The claim is simply this: While it may very well be true that there are situations in which a person will be justified in disobeying the law, it is surely not true that disobedience can ever be justified solely on the grounds that the consequences of disobeying the particular law were in that case on the whole less deleterious than those of obedience.[17]

This claim is particularly relevant at this juncture because one of the arguments most often given to substantiate it consists of the purported demonstration of the fact that any principle which contained a proviso permitting a general appeal to consequences must itself be incoherent. One of the most complete statements of the argument is found in Marcus Singer's provocative book, *Generalization in Ethics:*

> Suppose, . . . that I am contemplating evading the payment of income taxes. I might reason that I need the money more than the government does, that the amount I have to pay is so small in comparison with the total amount to be collected that the government will never miss it. Now I surely know perfectly well that if I evade the payment of taxes this will not cause others to do so as well. For one thing, I am certainly not so foolish as to publicize my action. But even if I were, and the fact became known, this would still not cause others to do the same, unless it also became known that I was being allowed to get away with it. In the latter case the practice might tend to become widespread, but this would be a consequence, not of my action, but of the failure of the government to take action against me. Thus there is no question of my act being wrong because it would set a bad example. It would set no such example, and to suppose that it must, because it would be wrong, is simply a confusion. . . . Given all this, then if the reasons mentioned would justify me in evading the payment of taxes, they would justify everyone whatsoever in doing the same thing. For everyone can

---

[17] This is a particular illustration of the more general claim that for one reason or another utilitarianism cannot be a defensible or intelligible moral theory when construed as permitting one's moral obligation to do any particular action to be overridden by a direct appeal to the consequences of performing that particular action. For recent statements of the claim see, e.g., Nowell-Smith, *op. cit. supra* note 10; Rawls, "Two Concepts of Rules," 64 *Philosophical Rev.* 3 (1955), in Olafson, *Society, Law and Morality* 420 (1961); Singer, *Generalization in Ethics* 61–138, 178–216 (1961); Toulmin, *op. cit. supra* note 15, at 144–65; Harrison, Utilitarianism, Universalisation, and Our Duty to Be Just, 53 *Aristotelian Soc'y Proceedings* 105 (1952–53).

For some criticisms of this restriction on utilitarianism see, *e.g.,* Wasserstrom, *The Judicial Decision* 118–37 (1961). But see Hart, "Book Review," 14 *Stan. L. Rev.* 919, 924–26 (1962).

argue in the same way — everyone can argue that if he breaks the law this will not cause others to do the same. The supposition that this is a justification, therefore, leads to a contradiction.

I conclude from this that, just as the reply "Not everyone will do it" is irrelevant to the generalization argument, so is the fact that one knows or believes that not everyone will do the same; and that, in particular, the characteristic of knowing or believing that one's act will remain exceptional cannot be used to define a class of exceptions to the rule. One's knowledge or belief that not everyone will act in the same way in similar circumstances cannot therefore be regarded as part of the circumstances of one's action. One's belief that not everyone will do the same does not make one's circumstances relevantly different from the circumstances of others, or relevantly different from those in which the act is wrong. Indeed, on the supposition that it does, one's circumstances could never be specified, for the specification would involve an infinite regress.[18]

Singer's argument is open to at least two different interpretations. One quite weak interpretation is this: A person cannot be morally justified in acting as he does unless he is prepared to acknowledge that everyone else in the identical circumstances would also be right in acting the same way. If the person insists that he is justified in performing a certain action because the consequences of acting in that way are more desirable than those of acting in any alternative fashion, then he must be prepared to acknowledge that anyone else would also be justified in doing that action whenever the consequences of doing that action were more desirable than those of acting in any alternative fashion. To take Singer's own example: A person, A, could not be morally justified in evading the payment of his taxes on the grounds that the consequences of nonpayment were *in his case* more beneficial, all things considered, than those of payment, unless A were prepared to acknowledge that any other person, X, would also be justified in evading his, *i.e.*, X's taxes, if it is the case that the consequences of X's nonpayment would in X's case be more beneficial, all things considered, than those of payment. If this is Singer's point, it is, for reasons already elaborated, unobjectionable.[19]

But Singer seems to want to make a stronger point as well. He seems to believe that even a willingness to generalize in this fashion could not justify acting in this way. In part his argument appears to be that this somehow will permit everyone to justify nonpayment of taxes; and in part his argument appears to be that there is a logical absurdity involved in attempting to make the likelihood of other people's behavior part of the specification of the relevant consequences of a particular act. Both of these points are wrong. To begin with, on a common sense level it is surely true that the effect which one's action will have on other people's behavior is a relevant consideration. For as was pointed out earlier, if A determines that other people will be, or may be, led to evade *their* taxes even when the consequences of nonpayment will in their cases be less beneficial than those of payment, then this is

---

[18] Singer, *op. cit. supra* note 17, at 149–50.

[19] Neither Singer nor I have adequately refuted the confirmed ethical egoist who insists that he is prepared to generalize but only in the sense that X's nonpayment is justified if, and only if, the consequences of X's nonpayment would in X's case be more beneficial *to A* than those of payment. This is a problem which surely requires more careful attention than it typically receives. It will not do simply to insist that the egoist does not understand ordinary moral discourse. Instead, what must be demonstrated are the respects in which the egoist's position is an inherently unjust one. But to make this showing is beyond the scope of this article.

a consequence of A's action which he must take into account and attempt to balance against the benefits which would accrue to society from his nonpayment. Conversely, if for one reason or another A can determine that his act of nonpayment will not have this consequence, this, too, must be relevant. In this sense, at least, other people's prospective behavior is a relevant consideration.

More importantly, perhaps, it is surely a mistake — although a very prevalent one in recent moral philosophy — to suppose that permitting a general appeal to consequences would enable everyone to argue convincingly that he is justified in evading his taxes. Even if I adopt the principle that everyone is justified in evading his taxes whenever the consequences of evasion are on the whole less deleterious than those of payment, this in no way entails that I or anyone else will always, or ever, be justified in evading my taxes. It surely need not turn out to be the case — even if no one else will evade his taxes — that the consequences will on the whole be beneficial if I succeed in evading mine. It might surely be the case that I will spend the money saved improvidently or foolishly; it might very well be true that the government will make much better use of the money. Indeed, the crucial condition which must not be ignored and which Singer does ignore is the condition which stipulates that the avoidance of one's taxes in fact be optimific, that is, more desirable than any other course of conduct.

The general point is simply that it is an empirical question — at least in theory — what the consequences of any action will be. And it would surely be a mistake for me or anyone else to suppose that that action whose consequences are most pleasing to me — in either the short or long run — will in fact be identical with that action whose consequences are on the whole most beneficial to society. Where the demands of self-interest are strong, as in the case of the performance of an unpleasant task like paying taxes, there are particular reasons for being skeptical of one's conclusion that the consequences of nonpayment would in one's own case truly be beneficial. But once again there is no reason why there might not be cases in which evasion of taxes would be truly justified, nor is there any reason why someone could not consistently and defensibly endorse nonpayment whenever these circumstances were in fact present.

There is one final point which Singer's discussion suggests and which does appear to create something of a puzzle. Suppose that I believe that I am justified in deliberately trespassing on an atomic test site, and thereby disobeying the law, because I conclude that this is the best way to call attention to the possible consequences of continued atmospheric testing or nuclear war. I conclude that the consequences of trespassing will on the whole be more beneficial than any alternative action I can take. But suppose I also concede — what very well may be the case — that if everyone were to trespass, even for this same reason and in the same way, the consequences would be extremely deleterious. Does it follow that there is something logically incoherent about my principle of action? It looks as though there is, for it appears that I am here denying others the right to do precisely what I claim I am right in doing. I seem to be claiming, in effect, that it is right for me to trespass on government property in order to protest atomic testing only if it is the case that others, even under identical circumstances, will not trespass. Thus, it might be argued, I appear to be unwilling or unable to generalize my principle of conduct.

This argument is unsound, for there is a perfectly good sense in which I am acting on a principle which is coherent and which is open to anyone to adopt. It is simply the principle that one is justified in trespassing on government property whenever – among other things – it happens to be the case that one can say accurately that others will not in fact act on that same principle. Whether anyone else will at any given time act on any particular principle is an empirical question. It is, to repeat what has already been said, one of the possible circumstances which can be part of the description of a class of situations. There is, in short, nothing logically self-contradictory or absurd about making the likelihood of even identical action one of the relevant justifying considerations. And there is, therefore, no reason why the justifiability of any particular act of disobedience cannot depend, among other things, upon the probable conduct of others.

IV

It would not be at all surprising if at this stage one were to feel considerable dissatisfaction with the entire cast of the discussion so far. In particular, one might well believe that the proverbial dead horse has received still another flaying for the simple reason that no one has ever seriously argued that people are never justified in disobeying the law. One might insist, for instance, that neither Socrates nor President Kennedy were talking about all law in all legal systems everywhere. And one might urge, instead, that their claims concerning the unjustifiability of any act of disobedience rest covertly, if not overtly, on the assumption that the disobedience in question was to take place in a society in which the lawmaking procedures and other political institutions were those which are characteristic of an essentially democratic, or free, society. This is, of course, an important and plausible restriction upon the original claim, and the arguments which might support it must now be considered.

While there are several things about a liberal, democratic or free society which might be thought to preclude the possibility of justified disobedience, it is evident that the presence of all the important constitutive institutions *cannot* guarantee that unjust or immoral laws will not be enacted. For the strictest adherence to principles of representative government, majority rule, frequent and open elections and, indeed, the realization of all of the other characteristics of such a society, in no way can insure that laws of manifest immorality will not be passed and enforced. And if even the ideal democratic society might enact unjust laws, no existing society can plausibly claim as much. Thus, if the case against the possibility of justified disobedience is to depend upon the democratic nature of the society in question, the case cannot rest simply on the claim that the only actions which will be made illegal are those which are already immoral.

What then are the arguments which might plausibly be advanced? One very common argument goes like this: It is, of course, true that even democratically selected and democratically constituted legislatures can and do make mistakes. Nevertheless, a person is never justified in disobeying the law as long as there exist alternative, "peaceful" procedures by which to bring about the amendment or repeal of undesirable or oppressive laws. The genuine possibility that rational persuasion and argument can bring a majority to favor any one of a variety of competing views, both requires that disapproval always be permitted and forbids that disobedience ever be allowed. This is so for several reasons.

First, it is clearly unfair and obviously inequitable to accept the results of any social decision-procedure only in those cases in which the decision reached was one of which one approves, and to refuse to accept those decisions which are not personally satisfying. If there is one thing which participation, and especially voluntary participation, in a decision-procedure entails, it is that all of the participants must abide by the decision regardless of what it happens to be. If the decision-procedure is that of majority rule, then this means that any person must abide by those decisions in which he was in a minority just as much as it means that he can insist that members of the minority abide when he is a member of the majority.

As familiar as the argument is, its plausibility is far from assured. On one reading, at least, it appears to be one version of the universalization argument. As such, it goes like this. Imagine any person, A, who has voted with the majority to pass a law making a particular kind of conduct illegal. A surely would not and could not acknowledge the right of any person voting with the minority justifiably to disobey that law. But, if A will not and cannot recognize a right of justified disobedience here, then A certainly cannot consistently or fairly claim any right of justified disobedience on his part in those cases in which he, A, happened to end up being in a minority. Thus, justified disobedience can never be defensible.

This argument is fallacious. For a person who would insist that justified disobedience was possible even after majoritarian decision-making could very plausibly and consistently acknowledge the right of any person to disobey the law under appropriate circumstances regardless of how that person had voted on any particular law. Consider, once again, the case already put of the doctor and the pregnant girl. The doctor can surely be consistent in claiming both that circumstances make the performance of the illegal abortion justified and that any comparable action would also be right irrespective of how the actor, or the doctor, or anyone else, happened to have voted on the abortion law, or any other law. The point is simply that there is no reason why any person cannot consistently: (1) hold the view that majority decision-making is the best of all forms of decision-making; (2) participate voluntarily in the decision-making process; and (3) believe that it is right for *anyone* to disobey majority decisions whenever the relevant moral circumstances obtain, *e.g.,* whenever the consequence of obedience to that law at that time would on the whole be more deleterious than those of obedience.

But this may be deemed too facile an answer; it also may be thought to miss the point. For it might be argued that there is a serious logical inconsistency of a different sort which must arise whenever a voluntary participant in a social decision-procedure claims that not all the decisions reached in accordance with that procedure need be obeyed. Take the case of majority rule. It is inconsistent for anyone voluntarily to participate in the decision-process and yet at the same time to reserve the right to refuse to abide by the decision reached in any particular case. The problem is not an inability to universalize a principle of action. The problem is rather that of making any sense at all out of the notion of having a majority decide anything — of having a procedure by which to make group decisions. The problem is, in addition, that of making any sense at all out of the fact of voluntary participation in the decision-procedure — in knowing what this participation can come to if it does not mean that every participant is bound by all of the decisions which are reached. What can their participation mean if it is not an implicit promise to abide by all decisions reached? And even if the point is not a logical one, it is surely a practical one. What good could there possibly be to a scheme, an institutional means for making social decisions, which did not bind even the participants to anything?

The answer to this argument — or set of arguments — is wholly analogous to that which has been given earlier. But because of the importance and prevalence of the argument some repetition is in order.

One can simply assert that the notion of any social decision-making procedure is intelligible only if it entails that all participants always abide by all of the decisions which are made, no matter what those decisions are. Concomitantly, one can simply insist that any voluntary participant in the decision-process must be consenting or promising to abide by all decisions which are reached. But one cannot give as a plausible reason for this assertion the fact that the notion of group decision-making becomes incoherent if anything less in the way of adherence is required of all participants. And one cannot cite as a plausible reason for this assertion the fact that the notion of voluntary participation loses all meaning if anything less than a promise of absolute obedience is inferred.

It is true that the notion of a group decision-making procedure would be a meaningless notion if there were no respects in which a group decision was in any way binding upon each of the participants. Decisions which in no way bind anyone to do anything are simply not decisions. And it is also true that voluntary participation is an idle, if not a vicious, act if it does not commit each participant to something. If any voluntary participant properly can wholly ignore the decisions which are reached, then something is surely amiss.

But to say all this is not to say very much. Group decision-making can have a point just because it does preclude any participant from taking some actions which in the absence of the decision, he might have been justified in performing. And voluntary participation can still constitute a promise of sorts that one will not perform actions which, in the absence of voluntary participation, might have been justifiable. If the fact of participation in a set of liberal political institutions does constitute a promise of sorts, it can surely be a promise that the participant will not disobey a law just because obedience would be inconvenient or deleterious to him. And if this is the scope of the promise, then the fact of voluntary participation does make a difference. For in the absence of the participation in the decision to make this conduct illegal, inconvenience to the actor might well have been a good reason for acting in a certain way. Thus, participation can create new obligations to behave in certain ways without constituting a promise not to disobey the law under any circumstances. And if this is the case, adherence to a principle of justified disobedience is not inconsistent with voluntary participation in the decision-making process.

Indeed, a strong point can be made. The notion of making laws through voluntary participation in democratic institutions is not even inconsistent with the insistence that disobedience is justified whenever the consequences of disobedience are on the whole more beneficial than those of obedience. This is so because a promise can be a meaningful promise even if an appeal to the consequences of performing the promise can count as a sufficient reason for not performing the promise.[20] And if this is the case for promises generally, it can be no less the case for the supposed promise to obey the law.

Finally, even if it were correct that voluntary participation implied a promise to obey, and even if it were the case that the promise must be a promise not to disobey on consequential grounds, all of this would still not justify the conclusion that one ought never to disobey the law. It would, instead, only demonstrate that disobeying the law must be prima facie wrong, that everyone has a prima facie obligation to obey the law. This is so just because it is sometimes right even to break one's own promises. And if this, too, is a characteristic of promises generally, it is, again, no less a characteristic of the promise to obey the law.

The notions of promise, consent, or voluntary participation do not, however, exhaust the possible sources of the obligation to obey the laws of a democracy. In

---

[20] The point here is analogous to that made in the discussion of Singer's argument. Moral philosophers have often argued that one cannot appeal simply to the consequences of performing or not performing a particular promise as a reason for not performing that promise. And the reason why this is so is that the notion of having promised to do something would be unintelligible if the promisor could always, when the time came for performance, be excused if it were the case that the consequences of nonperformance were more beneficial than those of performance. This would make promising unintelligible, so the argument goes, because promising entails or means obligating oneself to do something. But if the appeal to consequences is what is to be determinative of one's obligations, then the promise becomes a wholly superfluous, meaningless act. Rawls, for instance, puts the point this way: "Various defenses for not keeping one's promise are allowed, but among them there isn't the one that, on general utilitarian grounds, the promisor (truly) thought his action best on the whole, even though there may be the defense that the consequences of keeping one's promise would have been *extremely* severe. While there are too many complexities here to consider all the necessary details, one can see that the general defense isn't allowed if one asks the following question: what would one say of someone who, when asked why he broke his promise, replied simply that breaking it was best on the whole? Assuming that his reply is sincere, and that his belief was reasonable (i.e., one need not consider the possibility that he was mistaken), I think that one would question whether or not he knows what it means to say 'I promise' (in the appropriate circumstances). It would be said of someone who used this excuse without further explanation that he didn't understand what defenses the practice, which defines a promise, allows to him. If a child were to use this excuse one would correct him; for it is part of the way one is taught the concept of a promise to be corrected if one uses this excuse. The point of having the practice would be lost if the practice did allow this excuse." Rawls, *supra* note 17, at 17, in Olafson, *op. cit. supra* note 17, at 429–30.

Now I am not concerned to dispute Rawls' remark if taken as descriptive of our institution of promising. For what I am here concerned with is the claim, implicit throughout, that promising would be a meaningless or pointless activity if the excuse were permitted. I should say though that the passage quoted from Rawls is not, I think, central to his main argument. I think I can show this to be a mistake through the following two examples.

(1) *A* has promised *B* that he will mow *B*'s lawn for *B* on Sunday. On Sunday, *A* is feeling lazy and so he refuses to mow the lawn.

(2) *A* is sitting home on Sunday, feeling lazy, when *B* calls him up and asks him to come over and mow *B*'s lawn. *A* refuses to mow the lawn.

Ceteris paribus, it would be the case that *A* is wrong in refusing to mow *B*'s lawn in example (1) but not blamable for refusing to mow *B*'s lawn in example (2). Why is this so? Because *A*'s promise to mow *B*'s lawn creates an obligation which in the absence of such a promise is nonexistent. If this is so, then permitting the general utilitarian defense does not make a promise a meaningless gesture. This is so because there are many situations in which, in the absence of having promised to do so, we are not, for example, obligated to inconvenience ourselves simply for another's convenience. Personal inconvenience then might be one excuse which must be inconsistent with the practice of promising, even if the general appeal to consequences is not. Thus, promising would and could have a real point even if the general appeal to consequences were a good defense.

particular, there is another set of arguments which remains to be considered. It is that which locates the rightness of obedience in the way in which any act of disobedience improperly distributes certain burdens and benefits among the citizenry. Professor Wechsler, for example, sees any act of disobedience to the laws of the United States as "the ultimate negation of all neutral principles, to take the benefits accorded by the constitutional system, including the national market and common defense, while denying it allegiance when a special burden is imposed. That certainly is the antithesis of law."[2 1]

On the surface, at least, Professor Wechsler's claim seems overly simple; it appears to be the blanket assertion that the receipt by any citizen, through continued, voluntary presence of benefits of this character necessarily implies that no act of disobedience could be justified. To disobey any law after having voluntarily received these benefits would be, he seems to suggest, so unjust that there could never be overriding considerations. This surely is both to claim too much for the benefits of personal and commercial security and to say too little for the character of all types of disobedience. For even if the receipt of benefits such as these did simply impose an obligation to obey the law, it is implausible to suppose that the obligation thereby imposed would be one that stringent.

But there is a more involved aspect of Professor Wechsler's thesis — particularly in his insistence that disobedience of the law, where benefits of this kind have been received, is the negation of all neutral principles. I am not at all certain that I understand precisely what this means, but there are at least two possible interpretations: (1) Unless everyone always obeyed the law no one would receive these obviously valuable benefits. (2) Since the benefits one receives depend upon the prevalence of conditions of uniform obedience, it follows that no one who willingly receives these benefits can justly claim them without himself obeying. The first has already been sufficiently considered.[2 2] The second, while not unfamiliar, merits some further attention.

In somewhat expanded form, the argument is simply this. What makes it possible for any particular person to receive and enjoy the benefits of general, personal and economic security is the fact that everyone else obeys the law. Now, if injustice is to be avoided, it is surely the case that any other person is equally entitled to these same benefits. But he will have this security only if everyone else obeys the law. Hence the receipt of benefits at others' expense requires repayment in kind. And this means universal obedience to the law.[2 3]

[2 1] Wechsler, "Toward Neutral Principles of Constitutional Law," 73 *Harv. L. Rev.* 1, 35 (1959).

[2 2] See text at section III.

[2 3] For a somewhat related characterization of the source of the obligation to obey the law, see Hart, "Are There Any Natural Rights?" 64 *Philosophical Rev.* 175, 185 (1955), in Olafson, *Law, Society, and Morality* 173, 180–81 (1961): "A third very important source of special rights and obligations which we recognize in many spheres of life is what may be termed mutuality of restrictions. . . . In its bare schematic outline it is this: when a number of persons conduct any joint enterprise according to rules and thus restrict their liberty, those who have submitted to these restrictions when required have a right to a similar submission from those who have benefited by their submission. The rules may provide that officials should have authority to enforce obedience and make further rules, and this will create a structure of legal rights and duties, but the moral obligation to obey the rules in such circumstances is *due to* the co-operating members of the society, and they have the correlative moral right to obedience. In social situations of this sort (of which political society is the most complex example) the obligation to obey the rules is something distinct from whatever other moral obligations there

There are two features of this argument which are puzzling. First, it is far from clear that the benefits of security received by anyone necessarily depend upon absolute obedience on the part of everyone else. It just might be the case that an even greater quantum of security would have accrued from something less than total obedience. But even if I am wrong here, there is a more important point at issue. For reasons already discussed, it is undeniable that even in a democracy a price would be paid for universal obedience — the price that might have to be paid, for instance, were the doctor to refuse to perform the abortion because it was illegal. If this is so, then the fact that a person received benefits from everyone else's obedience does not necessarily entail that it is unjust for him to fail to reciprocate in kind. The benefit of general security might not have been worth the cost. A greater degree of flexibility on the part of others, a general course of obedience except where disobedience was justified, might have yielded a greater benefit. People may, in short, have done more or less than they should have. And if they did, the fact that anyone or everyone benefitted to some degree in no way requires that injustice can only be avoided through like and reciprocal conduct. If it is better, in at least some circumstances, to disobey a law than to obey it, there is surely nothing unjust about increasing the beneficial consequences to all through acts of *discriminate* disobedience.

If the argument based upon the effect of receipt of certain benefits is therefore not very persuasive, neither in most cases is the argument which is derived from the way in which any act of disobedience is thought to distribute burdens unfairly among the citizenry. The argument can be put very briefly: If there is one thing which any act of disobedience inevitably does, it is to increase the burdens which fall on all the law-abiding citizens. If someone disobeys the law even for what seems to be the best of reasons, he inevitably makes it harder — in some quite concrete sense — on everyone else. Hence, at a minimum this is a good reason not to disobey the law, and perhaps a sufficient reason as well.

This argument is appealing because there is at least one kind of case it fits very well. It is the case of taxation. For suppose the following, only somewhat unreal, conditions: that the government is determined to raise a specified sum of money through taxation, and that, in the long, if not the short, run it will do so by adjusting the tax rate to whatever percentage is necessary to produce the desired governmental income. Under such circumstances it could plausibly be argued that one of the truly inevitable results of a successfully executed decision to evade the payment of one's taxes — a decision made, moreover, on ostensibly justifiable grounds — is that every other member of society will thereby be required to pay a greater tax than would otherwise have been the case. Thus in some reasonably

---

may be for obedience in terms of good consequences (*e.g.,* the prevention of suffering); the obligation is due to the co-operating members of the society as such and not because they are human beings on whom it would be wrong to inflict suffering."

I would point out only two things. First, as Professor Hart himself asserts — in a passage not quoted — the existence of this right in no way implies that one is never justified in disobeying the law. The right which any participating member has in others' obedience can justifiably be infringed in appropriate circumstances. Second, and here perhaps Professor Hart disagrees for reasons already elaborated, there is no reason that I can see why an appeal to the consequences of disobeying a particular law cannot be a sufficient justification for infringing upon that right. It is surely conceivable, at least, that this is all the submission to rules which anyone ought to have given, and hence all the submission which anyone is entitled to expect from others.

direct and obvious fashion any act of disobedience — particularly if undetected — does add to the burdens of everyone else. And surely this is to make out at least a strong case of prima facie injustice.

Now, for reasons already elaborated, it would be improper to conclude that evasion of one's taxes could never be justified. But the argument is persuasive in its insistence that it does provide a very good reason why evasion always must be justified and why it will seldom be justifiable. But even this feature of disobedience is not present in many cases. Tax evasion, as opposed to other kinds of potentially justified disobedience, is a special, far from typical case. And what is peculiar to it is precisely the fact that any act of disobedience to the tax laws arguably shifts or increases the burden upon others. Such is simply not true of most types of acts of disobedience because most laws do not prohibit or require actions which affect the distribution of resources in any very direct fashion.

Thus, if we take once again the case of the doctor who has decided that he is justified in performing an illegal abortion on the pregnant girl, it is extremely difficult, if not impossible, to locate the analogue of the shifting of burdens involved in tax evasion. How does the performance of the abortion thereby increase the "costs" to anyone else? The only suggestion which seems at all plausible is that which was noted earlier in a somewhat different context. Someone might argue that it is the occurrence of illegal actions which increase the cost of maintaining a police force, a judiciary and suitable correctional institutions. This cost is a burden which is borne by the citizenry as a whole. And hence, the doctor's illegal acts increase their burdens — albeit very slightly. The difficulty here is threefold. First, if the doctor's act is performed in secret and if it remains undetected, then it is hard to see how there is any shift of economic burden at all. Second, given the fact that police forces, courts and prisons will always be necessary as long as unjustified acts of disobedience are a feature of social existence, it is by no means apparent that the additional cost is anything but truly de minimus.[24] And third, the added costs, if any, are in the doctor's case assumed by the doctor *qua* member of the citizenry. He is not avoiding a burden; at most he adds something to everyone's — including his own — existing financial obligations. Thus, in cases such as these, it is not at all evident that disobedience need even be prima facie unjust and hence unjustified.

V

There is one final argument which requires brief elucidation and analysis. It is in certain respects a peculiarly instructive one both in its own right and in respect to the thesis of this article.

It may be true that on some particular occasions the consequences of disobeying a law will in fact be less deleterious on the whole than those of obeying it — even in a democracy. It may even be true that on some particular occasions disobeying a law will be just whereas obeying it would be unjust. Nevertheless, the reason why a person is never justified in disobeying a law — in a democracy — is simply this: The chances are so slight that he will disobey only those laws in only those cases in

---

[24] Curiously, perhaps, given a legal system in which laws are in general good and hence in which the possibility of justified disobedience is rare, the special or added cost of an occasional act of justified disobedience is diminished still further.

which he is in fact justified in doing so, that the consequences will on the whole be less deleterious if he never disobeys any law. Furthermore, since anyone must concede the right to everyone to disobey the law when the circumstances so demand it, the situation is made still worse. For once we entrust this right to everyone we can be sure that many laws will be disobeyed in a multitude of cases in which there was no real justification for disobedience. Thus, given what we know of the possibilities of human error and the actualities of human frailty, and given the tendency of democratic societies to make illegal only those actions which would, even in the absence of a law, be unjustified, we can confidently conclude that the consequences will on the whole and in the long run be best if no one ever takes it upon himself to "second-guess" the laws and to conclude that in his case his disobedience is justified.[25]

The argument is, in part, not very different from those previously considered. And thus, what is to be said about it is not very different either. Nonetheless, upon pain of being overly repetitive, I would insist that there is a weak sense in which the argument is quite persuasive and a strong sense in which the argument is quite persuasive and a strong sense in which it is not. For the argument makes, on one reading, too strong an empirical claim — the claim that the consequences will in the long run always in fact be better if no one in a democracy ever tries to decide when he is justified in disobeying the law. As it stands, there is no reason to believe that the claim is or must be true, that the consequences will always be better. Indeed, it is very hard to see why, despite the hypothesis, someone might still not be justified in some particular case in disobeying a law. Yet, viewed as a weaker claim, as a summary rule, it does embody a good deal that is worth remembering. It can, on this level, be understood to be a persuasive reminder of much that is relevant to disobedience: that in a democracy the chances of having to live under bad laws are reduced; that in a democracy there are typically less costly means available by which to bring about changes in the law; that in a democracy — as in life in general — a justified action may always be both inaptly and ineptly emulated; and that in a democracy — as in life in general — people often do make mistakes as to which of their own actions are truly justified. These are some of the lessons of human experience which are easy to forget and painful to relearn.

But there are other lessons, and they are worth remembering too. What is especially troubling about the claim that disobedience of the law is never justified, what is even disturbing about the claim that disobedience of the law is never justified in a democratic or liberal society, is the facility with which its acceptance can lead to the neglect of important moral issues. If no one is justified in disobeying the Supreme Court's decision in *Brown v. Board of Educ.*[26] this is so because, among other things, there is much that is wrong with segregation. If there was much that was peculiarly wrong in Mississippi this fall, this was due to the fact, among other facts, that a mob howled and a governor raged when a court held that a person whose skin was black could go to a white university. Disobeying the law is often — even usually — wrong; but this is so largely because the illegal is usually restricted to the immoral and because morally right conduct is still less often illegal. But we must always be sensitive to the fact that this has not always been the case, is

---

[25] For fuller analyses and assessments of this argument in different contexts see, *e.g.*, Rawls, *supra* note 17; Wasserstrom, *op. cit. supra* note 17, at 118–71.

[26] 347 U.S. 483 (1954).

not now always the case and need not always be the case in the future. And undue concentration upon what is wrong with disobeying the law rather than upon the wrong which the law seeks to prevent can seriously weaken and misdirect that awareness.

14. The Crito

Plato

Socrates: Here already, Crito? Surely it is still early?

Crito: Indeed it is.

Socrates: About what time?

Crito: Just before dawn.

Socrates: I wonder that the warder paid any attention to you.

Crito: He is used to me now, Socrates, because I come here so often. Besides, he is under some small obligation to me.

Socrates: Have you only just come, or have you been here for long?

Crito: Fairly long.

Socrates Then why didn't you wake me at once, instead of sitting by my bed so quietly?

Crito: I wouldn't dream of such a thing, Socrates. I only wish I were not so sleepless and depressed myself. I have been wondering at you, because I saw how comfortably you were sleeping, and I deliberately didn't wake you because I wanted you to go on being as comfortable as you could. I have often felt before in the course of my life how fortunate you are in your disposition, but I feel it more than ever now in your present misfortune when I see how easily and placidly you put up with it.

Socrates: Well, really, Crito, it would be hardly suitable for a man of my age to resent having to die.

Crito: Other people just as old as you get involved in these misfortunes, Socrates, but their age doesn't keep them from resenting it when they find themselves in your position.

Socrates: Quite true. But tell me, why have you come so early?

Crito: Because I bring bad news, Socrates — not so bad from your point of view, I suppose, but it will be very hard to bear for me and your other friends, and I think that I shall find it hardest of all.

Socrates: Why, what is this news? Has the boat come in from Delos — the boat which ends my reprieve when it arrives?

Crito: It hasn't actually come in yet, but I expect that it will be here today, judging from the report of some people who have just arrived from Sunium and left it there. It's quite clear from their account that it will be here today, and so by tomorrow, Socrates, you will have to . . . to end your life.

Pages 28 to 39 from Plato: *The Last Days of Socrates* translated by Hugh Tredennick (Penguin Classics). Copyright © Hugh Tredennick, 1954, 1959, 1969.

Socrates: Well, Crito, I hope that it may be for the best. If the gods will it so, so be it. All the same, I don't think it will arrive today.

Crito: What makes you think that?

Socrates: I will try to explain. I think I am right in saying that I have to die on the day after the boat arrives?

Crito: That's what the authorities say, at any rate.

Socrates: Then I don't think it will arrive on this day that is just beginning, but on the day after. I am going by a dream that I had in the night, only a little while ago. It looks as though you were right not to wake me up.

Crito: Why, what was the dream about?

Socrates: I thought I saw a gloriously beautiful woman dressed in white robes, who came up to me and addressed me in these words: Socrates, "To the pleasant land of Phthia on the third day thou shalt come."[1]

Crito: Your dream makes no sense, Socrates.

Socrates: To my mind, Crito, it is perfectly clear.

Crito: Too clear, apparently. But look here, Socrates, it is still not too late to take my advice and escape. Your death means a double calamity for me. I shall not only lose a friend whom I can never possibly replace, but besides a great many people who don't know you and me very well will be sure to think that I let you down, because I could have saved you if I had been willing to spend the money. And what could be more contemptible than to get a name for thinking more of money than of your friends? Most people will never believe that it was you who refused to leave this place although we tried our hardest to persuade you.

Socrates: But my dear Crito, why should we pay so much attention to what "most people" think? The really reasonable people, who have more claim to be considered, will believe that the facts are exactly as they are.

Crito: You can see for yourself, Socrates, that one has to think of popular opinion as well. Your present position is quite enough to show that the capacity of ordinary people for causing trouble is not confined to petty annoyances, but has hardly any limits if you once get a bad name with them.

Socrates: I only wish that ordinary people *had* an unlimited capacity for doing harm; then they might have an unlimited power for doing good, which would be a splendid thing, if it were so. Actually they have neither. They cannot make a man wise or stupid; they simply act at random.

Crito: Have it that way if you like, but tell me this, Socrates. I hope that you aren't worrying about the possible effects on me and the rest of your friends, and thinking that if you escape we shall have trouble with informers for having helped you to get away, and have to forfeit all our property or pay an enormous fine, or even incur some further punishment? If any idea like that is troubling you, you can dismiss it altogether. We are quite entitled to run that risk in saving you, and even worse, if necessary. Take my advice, and be reasonable.

Socrates: All that you say is very much in my mind, Crito, and a great deal more besides.

Crito: Very well, then, don't let it distress you. I know some people who are willing to rescue you from here and get you out of the country for quite moderate sum. And then surely you realize how cheap these informers are to buy off; we shan't need much money to settle them, and I think you've got enough of my

[1] *Iliad* 9.363.

money for yourself already. And then even supposing that in your anxiety for my safety you feel that you oughtn't to spend my money, there are these foreign gentlemen staying in Athens who are quite willing to spend theirs. One of them, Simmias of Thebes, has actually brought the money with him for this very purpose, and Cebes and a number of others are quite ready to do the same. So, as I say, you mustn't let any fears on these grounds make you slacken your efforts to escape, and you mustn't feel any misgivings about what you said at your trial – that you wouldn't know what to do with yourself if you left this country. Wherever you go, there are plenty of places where you will find a welcome, and if you choose to go to Thessaly, I have friends there who will make much of you and give you complete protection, so that no one in Thessaly can interfere with you.

Besides, Socrates, I don't even feel that it is right for you to try to do what you are doing, throwing away your life when you might save it. You are doing your best to treat yourself in exactly the same way as your enemies would, or rather did, when they wanted to ruin you. What is more, it seems to me that you are letting your sons down too. You have it in your power to finish their bringing-up and education, and instead of that you are proposing to go off and desert them, and so far as you are concerned they will have to take their chance. And what sort of chance are they likely to get? The sort of thing that usually happens to orphans when they lose their parents. Either one ought not to have children at all, or one ought to see their upbringing and education through to the end. It strikes me that you are taking the line of least resistance, whereas you ought to make the choice of a good man and a brave one, considering that you profess to have made goodness your object all through life. Really, I am ashamed, both on your account and on ours, your friends'. It will look as though we had played something like a coward's part all through this affair of yours. First there was the way you came into court when it was quite unnecessary – that was the first act. Then there was the conduct of the defense – that was the second. And finally, to complete the farce, we get this situation, which makes it appear that we have let you slip out of our hands through some lack of courage and enterprise on our part, because we didn't save you, and you didn't save yourself, when it would have been quite possible and practicable, if we had been any use at all.

There, Socrates, if you aren't careful, besides the suffering there will be all this disgrace for you and us to bear. Come, make up your mind. Really it's too late for that now; you ought to have it made up already. There is no alternative; the whole thing must be carried through during this coming night. If we lose any more time, it can't be done; it will be too late. I appeal to you, Socrates, on every ground; take my advice and please don't be unreasonable!

Socrates: My dear Crito, I appreciate your warm feelings very much – that is, assuming that they have some justification. If not, the stronger they are, the harder they will be to deal with. Very well, then, we must consider whether we ought to follow your advice or not. You know that this is not a new idea of mine; it has always been my nature never to accept advice from any of my friends unless reflection shows that it is the best course that reason offers. I cannot abandon the principles which I used to hold in the past simply because this accident has happened to me; they seem to me to be much as they were, and I respect and regard the same principles now as before. So unless we can find better principles on this occasion, you can be quite sure that I shall not agree with you — not even if the power of the people conjures up fresh hordes of bogies to terrify our childish minds, by subjecting us to chains and executions and confiscations of our property.

Well, then, how can we consider the question most reasonably? Suppose that we begin by reverting to this view which you hold about people's opinions. Was it always right to argue that some opinions should be taken seriously but not others? Or was it always wrong? Perhaps it was right before the question of my death arose, but now we can see clearly that it was a mistaken persistence in a point of view which was really irresponsible nonsense. I should like very much to inquire into this problem, Crito, with your help, and to see whether the argument will appear in any different light to me now that I am in this position, or whether it will remain the same, and whether we shall dismiss it or accept it.

Serious thinkers, I believe, have always held some such view as the one which I mentioned just now, that some of the opinions which people entertain should be respected, and others should not. Now I ask you, Crito, don't you think that this is a sound principle? You are safe from the prospect of dying tomorrow, in all human probability, and you are not likely to have your judgment upset by this impending calamity. Consider, then, don't you think that this is a sound enough principle, that one should not regard all the opinions that people hold, but only some and not others? What do you say? Isn't that a fair statement?

Crito: Yes, it is.

Socrates: In other words, one should regard the good ones and not the bad?

Crito: Yes.

Socrates: The opinions of the wise being good, and the opinions of the foolish bad?

Crito: Naturally.

Socrates: To pass on, then, what do you think of the sort of illustration that I used to employ? When a man is in training, and taking it seriously, does he pay attention to all praise and criticism and opinion indiscriminately, or only when it comes from the one qualified person, the actual doctor or trainer?

Crito: Only when it comes from the one qualified person.

Socrates: Then he should be afraid of the criticism and welcome the praise of the one qualified person, but not those of the general public.

Crito: Obviously.

Socrates: So he ought to regulate his actions and exercises and eating and drinking by the judgment of his instructor, who has expert knowledge, rather than by the opinions of the rest of the public.

Crito: Yes, that is so.

Socrates: Very well. Now if he disobeys the one man and disregards his opinion and commendations, and pays attention to the advice of the many who have no expert knowledge, surely he will suffer some bad effect?

Crito: Certainly.

Socrates: And what is this bad effect? Where is it produced? I mean, in what part of the disobedient person?

Crito: His body, obviously; that is what suffers.

Socrates: Very good. Well now, tell me, Crito — we don't want to go through all the examples one by one — does this apply as a general rule, and above all to the sort of actions which we are trying to decide about, just and unjust, honorable and dishonorable, good and bad? Ought we to be guided and intimidated by the opinion of the many or by that of the one — assuming that there is someone with expert knowledge? Is it true that we ought to respect and fear this person more than all the rest put together, and that if we do not follow his guidance we shall spoil and mutilate that part of us which, as we used to say, is improved by right conduct and destroyed by wrong? Or is this all nonsense?

Crito: No, I think it is true, Socrates.

Socrates: Then consider the next step. There is a part of us which is improved by healthy actions and ruined by unhealthy ones. If we spoil it by taking the advice of nonexperts, will life be worth living when this part is once ruined? The part I mean is the body. Do you accept this?

Crito: Yes.

Socrates: Well, is life worth living with a body which is worn out and ruined in health?

Crito: Certainly not.

Socrates: What about the part of us which is mutilated by wrong actions and benefited by right ones? Is life worth living with this part ruined? Or do we believe that this part of us, whatever it may be, in which right and wrong operate, is of less importance than the body?

Crito: Certainly not.

Socrates: It is really more precious?

Crito: Much more.

Socrates: In that case, my dear fellow, what we ought to consider is not so much what people in general will say about us but how we stand with the expert in right and wrong, the one authority, who represents the actual truth. So in the first place your proposition is not correct when you say that we should consider popular opinion in questions of what is right and honorable and good, or the opposite. Of course one might object, All the same, the people have the power to put us to death.

Crito: No doubt about that! Quite true, Socrates. It is a possible objection.

Socrates: But so far as I can see, my dear fellow, the argument which we have just been through is quite unaffected by it. At the same time I should like you to consider whether we are still satisfied on this point, that the really important thing is not to live, but to live well.

Crito: Why, yes.

Socrates: And that to live well means the same thing as to live honorably or rightly?

Crito: Yes.

Socrates: Then in the light of this agreement we must consider whether or not it is right for me to try to get away without an official discharge. If it turns out to be right, we must make the attempt; if not, we must let it drop. As for the considerations you raise about expense and reputation and bringing up children, I am afraid, Crito, that they represent the reflections of the ordinary public, who put people to death, and would bring them back to life if they could, with equal indifference to reason. Our real duty, I fancy, since the argument leads that way, is to consider one question only, the one which we raised just now. Shall we be acting rightly in paying money and showing gratitude to these people who are going to rescue me, and in escaping or arranging the escape ourselves, or shall we really be acting wrongly in doing all this? If it becomes clear that such conduct is wrong, I cannot help thinking that the question whether we are sure to die, or to suffer any other ill effect for that matter, if we stand our ground and take no action, ought not to weigh with us at all in comparison with the risk of doing what is wrong.

Crito: I agree with what you say, Socrates, but I wish you would consider what we ought to *do*.

Socrates: Let us look at it together, my dear fellow; and if you can challenge any of my arguments, do so and I will listen to you; but if you can't, be a good fellow and stop telling me over and over again that I ought to leave this place without official permission. I am very anxious to obtain your approval before I adopt the course which I have in mind. I don't want to act against your convictions. Now give your attention to the starting point of this inquiry — I hope that you will be satisfied with my way of stating it — and try to answer my questions to the best of your judgment.

Crito: Well, I will try.

Socrates: Do we say that one must never willingly do wrong, or does it depend upon circumstances? Is it true, as we have often agreed before, that there is no sense in which wrongdoing is good or honorable? Or have we jettisoned all our former convictions in these last few days? Can you and I at our age, Crito, have spent all these years in serious discussions without realizing that we were no better than a pair of children? Surely the truth is just what we have always said. Whatever the popular view is, and whether the alternative is pleasanter than the present one or even harder to bear, the fact remains that to do wrong is in every sense bad and dishonorable for the person who does it. Is that our view, or not?

Crito: Yes, it is.

Socrates: Then in no circumstances must one do wrong.

Crito: No.

Socrates: In that case one must not even do wrong when one is wronged, which most people regard as the natural course.

Crito: Apparently not.

Socrates: Tell me another thing, Crito. Ought one to do injuries or not?

Crito: Surely not, Socrates.

Socrates: And tell me, is it right to do an injury in retaliation, as most people believe, or not?

Crito: No, never.

Socrates: Because, I suppose, there is no difference between injuring people and wronging them.

Crito: Exactly.

Socrates: So one ought not to return a wrong or an injury to any person, whatever the provocation is. Now be careful, Crito, that in making these single admissions you do not end by admitting something contrary to your real beliefs. I know that there are and always will be few people who think like this, and consequently between those who do think so and those who do not there can be no agreement on principle; they must always feel contempt when they observe one another's decisions. I want even you to consider very carefully whether you share my views and agree with me, and whether we can proceed with our discussion from the established hypothesis that it is never right to do a wrong or return a wrong or defend oneself against injury by retaliation, or whether you dissociate yourself from any share in this view as a basis for discussion. I have held it for a long time, and still hold it, but if you have formed any other opinion, say so and tell me what it is. If, on the other hand, you stand by what we have said, listen to my next point.

Crito: Yes, I stand by it and agree with you. Go on.

Socrates: Well, here is my next point, or rather question. Ought one to fulfill all one's agreements, provided that they are right, or break them?

Crito: One ought to fulfill them.

Socrates: Then consider the logical consequence. If we leave this place without first persuading the state to let us go, are we or are we not doing an injury, and doing it in a quarter where it is least justifiable? Are we or are we not abiding by our just agreements?

Crito: I can't answer your question, Socrates. I am not clear in my mind.

Socrates: Look at it in this way. Suppose that while we were preparing to run away from here — or however one should describe it — the laws and constitution of Athens were to come and confront us and ask this question, Now, Socrates, what are you proposing to do? Can you deny that by this act which you are contemplating you intend, so far as you have the power, to destroy us, the laws, and the whole state as well? Do you imagine that a city can continue to exist and not be turned upside down, if the legal judgments which are pronounced in it have no force but are nullified and destroyed by private persons?

How shall we answer this question, Crito, and others of the same kind? There is much that could be said, especially by a professional advocate, to protest against the invalidation of this law which enacts that judgments once pronounced shall be binding. Shall we say, Yes, I do intend to destroy the laws, because the state wronged me by passing a faulty judgment at my trial? Is this to be our answer, or what?

Crito:What you have just said, by all means, Socrates.

Socrates: Then what supposing the laws say, Was there provision for this in the agreement between you and us. Socrates? Or did you undertake to abide by whatever judgments the state pronounced?

If we expressed surprise at such language, they would probably say, Never mind our language, Socrates, but answer our questions; after all, you are accustomed to the method of question and answer. Come now, what charge do you bring against us and the state, that you are trying to destroy us? Did we not give you life in the first place? Was it not through us that your father married your mother and begot you? Tell us, have you any complaint against those of us laws that deal with marriage?

No, none, I should say.

Well, have you any against the laws which deal with children's upbringing and education, such as you had yourself? Are you not grateful to those of us laws which were instituted for this end, for requiring your father to give you a cultural and physical education?

Yes, I should say.

Very good. Then since you have been born and brought up and educated, can you deny, in the first place, that you were our child and servant, both you and your ancestors? And if this is so, do you imagine that what is right for us is equally right for you, and that whatever we try to do to you, you are justified in retaliating? You did not have equality of rights with your father, or your employer — supposing that you had had one — to enable you to retaliate. You were not allowed to answer back when you were scolded or to hit back when you were beaten, or to do a great many other things of the same kind. Do you expect to have such license against your country and its laws that if we try to put you to death in the belief that it is right to do so, you on your part will try your hardest to destroy your country and us its laws in return? And will you, the true devotee of goodness, claim that you are justified in doing so? Are you so wise as to have forgotten that compared with your mother and father and all the rest of your ancestors your country is something far more precious, more venerable, more sacred, and held in greater honor both among gods and among all reasonable men? Do you not realize that you are even more bound to respect and placate the anger of your country than your father's anger? That if you cannot persuade your country you must do whatever it orders, and patiently submit to any punishment that it imposes, whether it be flogging or imprisonment? And if it leads you out to war, to be wounded or killed, you must comply, and it is right that you should do so. You must not give way or retreat or abandon your position. Both in war and in the law courts and everywhere else you must do whatever your city and your country command, or else persuade them in accordance with universal justice, but violence is a sin even against your parents, and it is a far greater sin against your country.

What shall we say to this, Crito — that what the laws say is true, or not?

Crito: Yes, I think so.

Socrates: Consider, then, Socrates, the laws would probably continue, whether it is also true for us to say that what you are now trying to do to us is not right. Although we have brought you into the world and reared you and educated you, and given you and all your fellow citizens a share in all the good things at our disposal, nevertheless by the very fact of granting our permission we openly proclaim this principle, that any Athenian, on attaining to manhood and seeing for himself the political organization of the state and us its laws, is permitted, if he is not satisfied with us, to take his property and go away wherever he likes. If any of you chooses to go to one of our colonies, supposing that he should not be satisfied with us and the state, or to emigrate to any other country, not one of us laws hinders or prevents him from going away wherever he likes, without any loss of property. On the other hand, if any one of you stands his ground when he can see how we administer justice and the rest of our public organization, we hold that by so doing he has in fact undertaken to do anything that we tell him. And we maintain that anyone who disobeys is guilty of doing wrong on three separate counts: first because we are his parents, and secondly because we are his guardians, and thirdly because, after promising obedience, he is neither obeying us nor persuading us to change our decision if we are at fault in any way. And although all our orders are in the form of proposals, not of savage commands, and we give him the choice of either persuading us or doing what we say, he is actually doing neither. These are the charges, Socrates, to which we say that you will be liable if you do what you are contemplating, and you will not be the least culpable of your fellow countrymen, but one of the most guilty.

If I asked why, they would no doubt pounce upon me with perfect justice and point out that there are very few people in Athens who have entered into this agreement with them as explicitly as I have. They would say, Socrates, we have substantial evidence that you are satisfied with us and with the state. You would not have been so exceptionally reluctant to cross the borders of your country if you had not been exceptionally attached to it. You have never left the city to attend a festival or for any other purpose, except on some military expedition. You have never traveled abroad as other people do, and you have never felt the impulse to acquaint yourself with another country or constitution. You have been content with us and with our city. You have definitely chosen us, and undertaken to observe us in all your activities as a citizen, and as the crowning proof that you are satisfied with our city, you have begotten children in it. Furthermore, even at the time of your trial you could have proposed the penalty of banishment, if you had chosen to do so – that is, you could have done then with the sanction of the state what you are now trying to do without it. But whereas at that time you made a noble show of indifference if you had to die, and in fact preferred death, as you said, to banishment, now you show no respect for your earlier professions, and no regard for us, the laws, whom you are trying to destroy. You are behaving like the lowest type of menial, trying to run away in spite of the contracts and undertakings by which you agreed to live as a member of our state. Now first answer this question. Are we or are we not speaking the truth when we say that you have undertaken, in deed if not in word, to live your life as a citizen in obedience to us?

What are we to say to that, Crito? Are we not bound to admit it?

Crito: We cannot help it, Socrates.

Socrates: It is a fact, then, they would say, that you are breaking covenants and undertakings made with us, although you made them under no compulsion or misunderstanding, and were not compelled to decide in a limited time. You had seventy years in which you could have left the country, if you were not satisfied with us or felt that the agreements were unfair. You did not choose Sparta or Crete – your favorite models of good government – or any other Greek or foreign state. You could not have absented yourself from the city less if you had been lame or blind or decrepit in some other way. It is quite obvious that you stand by yourself above all other Athenians in your affection for this city and for us its laws. Who would care for a city without laws? And now, after all this, are you not going to stand by your agreement? Yes, you are, Socrates, if you will take our advice, and then you will at least escape being laughed at for leaving the city.

We invite you to consider what good you will do to yourself or your friends if you commit this breach of faith and stain your conscience. It is fairly obvious that the risk of being banished and either losing their citizenship or having their property confiscated will extend to your friends as well. As for yourself, if you go to one of the neighboring states, such as Thebes or Megara, which are both well governed, you will enter them as an enemy to their constitution, and all good patriots will eye you with suspicion as a destroyer of law and order. Incidentally you will confirm the opinion of the jurors who tried you that they gave a correct verdict; a destroyer of laws might very well be supposed to have a destructive influence upon young and foolish human beings. Do you intend, then, to avoid well-governed states and the higher forms of human society? And if you do, will life be worth living? Or will you approach these people and have the impudence to converse with them? What arguments will you use, Socrates? The same which you used here, that goodness and integrity, institutions and laws, are the most precious possessions of mankind? Do you not think that Socrates and everything about him will appear in a disreputable light? You certainly ought to think so.

But perhaps you will retire from this part of the world and go to Crito's friends in Thessaly? That is the home of indiscipline and laxity, and no doubt they would enjoy hearing the amusing story of how you managed to run away from prison by arraying yourself in some costume or putting on a shepherd's smock or some other conventional runaway's disguise, and altering your personal appearance. And will no one comment on the fact that an old man of your age, probably with only a short time left to live, should dare to cling so greedily to life, at the price of violating the most stringent laws? Perhaps not, if you avoid irritating anyone. Otherwise, Socrates, you will hear a good many humiliating comments. So you will live as the toady and slave of all the populace, literally "roistering in Thessaly," as though you had left this country for Thessaly to attend a banquet there. And where will your discussions about goodness and uprightness be then, we should like to know? But of course you want to live for your children's sake, so that you may be able to bring them up and educate them. Indeed! By first taking them off to Thessaly and making foreigners of them, so that they may have that additional enjoyment? Or if that is not your intention, supposing that they are brought up here with you still alive, will they be better cared for and educated without you, because of course your friends will look after them? Will they look after your children if you go away to Thessaly, and not if you go away to the next world? Surely if those who profess to be your friends are worth anything, you must believe that they would care for them.

No, Socrates, be advised by us your guardians, and do not think more of your children or of your life or of anything else than you think of what is right, so that when you enter the next world you may have all this to plead in your defense before the authorities there. It seems clear that if you do this thing, neither you nor any of your friends will be the better for it or be more upright or have a cleaner conscience here in this world, nor will it be better for you when you reach the next. As it is, you will leave this place, when you do, as the victim of a wrong done not by us, the laws, but by your fellow men. But if you leave in that dishonorable way, returning wrong for wrong and evil for evil, breaking your agreements and covenants with us, and injuring those whom you least ought to injure — yourself, your friends, your country, and us — then you will have to face our anger in your lifetime, and in that place beyond when the laws of the other world know that you have tried, so far as you could, to destroy even us their brothers, they will not receive you with a kindly welcome. Do not take Crito's advice, but follow ours.

That, my dear friend Crito, I do assure you, is what I seem to hear them saying, just as a mystic seems to hear the strains of music, and the sound of their arguments rings so loudly in my head that I cannot hear the other side. I warn you that, as my opinion stands at present, it will be useless to urge a different view. However, if you think that you will do any good by it, say what you like.

Crito: No, Socrates, I have nothing to say.

Socrates: Then give it up, Crito, and let us follow this course, since God points out the way.

Part IV

Freedom and Liberty

Introduction

As with "authority," "liberty" and "freedom" (which we will treat as inter-changeable) are concepts that are used very widely, in many language games. It is a commonly held view, represented here by Franz Neumann's essay, that there is no single analysis of "freedom," that we must chart the diversity of uses, senses, indeed the concepts of freedom, distinguish among the rules governing each, and attempt to assess the value of freedom in each of the main senses in which it is used. Thus Neumann, restricting himself to uses that are politically relevant, distinguishes three conceptions that have been especially prominent in political thought, the juridical, the cognitive, and the volitional. Similarly, Sir Isaiah Berlin, whose influential essay "Two Concepts of Liberty" is discussed in the other two papers in this part, finds two senses, "negative" freedom or freedom from interference and restraint, and "positive" freedom or freedom to do or to be something, to be central and irreducible one to the other.[1]

Neumann thought that all three of the concepts he discussed are important and defensible, but he urged that it is only when the volitional concept has been given its due weight that a normatively acceptable understanding of political freedom has been reached. On this view there is a very close connection between political freedom and democracy. Because democracy as Neumann understood it involves freedom to participate in political life, this third concept is an example of positive freedom in the terms of Berlin's distinction. A main thesis of Berlin's essay is that, historically, conceptions of positive freedom have in fact been used not to defend or advance democratic politics such as Neumann favored, but rather for despotic and even totalitarian purposes. Briefly, when freedom is treated as being or doing something that *A* presently is not or does not do, may not want to be or do, it becomes possible to say that actions or policies, even if coercive, that lead, influence, or cause *A* to be or to do *X*, increase *A*'s freedom. The history of the positive concept of freedom, Berlin argues, is so dominated by such uses that we should eschew it altogether; restrict ourselves to the negative concept; and argue for political participation, democracy, and numerous other values on the many better grounds that support them. If we follow this advice, it will be possible for us to say, for example, that societies can be democratic (or just, or virtuous, or egalitarian) and yet allow little freedom in the "negative" sense of freedom from interferences

---

[1] See Sir Isaiah Berlin, "Two Concepts of Liberty" in his *Four Essays on Liberty* (New York: Oxford University Press, 1969). This essay was originally published separately by Oxford University Press (London, 1958). It is also available in an abridged version in Anthony Quinton, ed., *Political Philosophy* (New York: Oxford University Press, 1967).

and impositions. Since democratic societies do interfere with and make impositions upon their members, this is a definite advantage.

S. I. Benn and W. L. Weinstein, and Gerald C. MacCallum, Jr., respond differently to the prevalence of "freedom" in ordinary discourse. Both selections argue that in fact there is one *concept* of "freedom" with a quite definite set of rules governing its use (or rather that there is only one concept of freedom when freedom is used of agents and their actions). MacCallum argues that freedom always involves a "triadic" relationship involving an agent (X), something that X is free *from* or free *of* (Y), and something that X is thereby free *to* do, be, or become (Z). This analysis, which Benn and Weinstein accept as their starting point, is specifically directed against Berlin's distinction between "negative" and "positive" freedom. MacCallum argues that talk about freedom is "intelligible" only when all three elements, and hence *both* Berlin's freedom from and freedom to are either explicitly or implicitly identified. Disputes about freedom are not between or among different concepts of freedom but about the range over which the $X, Y,$ and Z can and should move, that is, about what counts as being an agent, an interference, something that one can do or be. (And, of course, about the value or disvalue of this interference versus that objective, of this X being free to do that Z as against some other agent continuing to act in a manner that interferes with X, and so on.)

Berlin was not very insistent concerning the logical status of his distinction, admitting that the two concepts "may . . . seem . . . at no great logical distance from each other — no more than negative and positive ways of saying much the same thing." But in a later response to critics of his essay he did contend that MacCallum's analysis is faulty. "A man struggling against his chains," he argued, "or a people against enslavement need not consciously aim at any definite future state. A man need not know how he will use his [negative] freedom; he just wants to remove the yoke. So do classes and nations."[2] Thus it is "intelligible" to speak of negative freedom, of freedom from interferences and restrictions, without entering into the question of what one will be free to do or be after the restrictions have been removed.

MacCullum might reply that some objective or good, even if very general, is always implicit in the discussions of throwing off a yoke. Benn and Weinstein furnish a more specific reply. In general their argument goes beyond MacCallum in that, in the latter's terms, they specify the range within which MacCallum's "term variables" (that is the $X, Y,$ and Z) must remain. We cannot, they argue, "assign just *any* value to these variables, for there are certain characteristics of the concept ["freedom"] that limit what in general one can appropriately say one is free from, and free to do." As regards free *to* do, they contend that "it is apposite to discuss whether . . . [an agent] is free to do . . . [a particular action] only if it is a possible object of reasonable choice. . . . It is not a question of logical absurdity; rather, to see the point of saying that one is (or is not) free to do X, we must be able to see that there might be some point in doing it. Our conception of freedom is bounded by our notions of what might be worthwhile doing; it is out of its element when we find its objects bizarre." If we apply this analysis to Berlin's response to MacCallum, we see that, though Berlin supplies no context and no particular objective, we can so readily imagine so many "objects of reasonable choice," so many objectives to throwing off one's chains, that we have no problem

---

[2] Ibid, p. 43.

understanding the statement. If Berlin's example had been equally without context and had been, say, "he just wants to remove three hairs from the back of his leg," we would indeed have difficulty understanding the statement as a demand for freedom.[3]

The analysis of Benn and Weinstein also bears on the (implicit) controversy between Neumann and Berlin concerning what Neumann calls the cognitive and volitional conceptions of freedom. Berlin treats these as part of positive freedom, enters harsh strictures against the uses to which they have been put in political thought and practice, and argues that they lend themselves to such uses. Benn and Weinstein agree that unfreedom is created by (certain kinds of) restrictions placed upon choice. But to say that choice has been restricted is to say that, apart from the restrictions, a choice could have been made. And "choice presupposes a chooser; only a man who can be seen as a chooser is qualified as the subject of a free act." Hence we need an analysis of the conditions necessary to seeing a person (or other agent) as a chooser. Features of Benn's and Weinstein's analysis of these conditions, for example that choosers must have a realistic understanding of the alternatives among which they choose and must be capable of criticizing and rejecting proposals made to them, may suggest that the kinds of considerations Neumann identifies as part of the cognitive and volitional dimensions of freedom are necessary to choice. If so, they are part of talk about "freedom" because of what MacCallum calls the first of the term variables, namely, the agent. Thus if there is a viable distinction between negative and positive freedom, Neumann's considerations are part of both sides of it. But this point could not be settled without a closer specification of the considerations that Neumann mentions and a much fuller analysis of agency and choice than is available in these selections.

One final point. However well or badly the distinction between negative and positive freedom may stand up to logical scrutiny, this writer at least is in full sympathy with what I take to be a primary concern of those who have argued for it. Whatever else may be involved in an adequate analysis of the concept, it is clearly the case that deliberate interferences with human choice and action, however motivated, restrict or eliminate freedom. That such restrictions are often necessary and justified must not be allowed to blind us to this fact. Much thinking about "positive" freedom has had exactly this effect. It encourages us to say not only that an interference or restriction is in the public interest, contributes to equality, welfare, morality, security, or whatever, but that it enhances freedom. If we submit to the temptation to talk this way, the felt necessity of justifying the interference will have lost all basis. If our concepts really do encourage us to talk this way, we ought to change our concepts.

---

[3] Actually I am not sure that Benn's and Weinstein's point here is specific to the concept of "freedom." It goes back, rather, to Wittgenstein's much more general argument about the purposive character of the use of language and the arguments of Winch and others concerning the human actions of which language is a part. We should also note that we understand the fact that a person is under a yoke in terms of the purposes of those who have put him or her in that condition. Presumably, there is something that we want to make the person unfree to do.

Further Reading

Austin, J. L. "A Plea for Excuses," in J. L. Austin, *Philosophical Papers*, edited by J. O. Urmson and G. J. Warnock. Oxford: Clarendon Press, 1961.

Friedrich, Carl J., ed. *Liberty*. New York: Atherton Press, Inc., 1962.

Hampshire, Stuart, *Freedom of the Individual*. New York: Harper & Row, Publishers, 1965.

Hart, H. L. A. *Law, Liberty and Morality*. Stanford: Stanford University Press, 1963.

Hayek, F. A. *The Constitution of Liberty*. Chicago: The University of Chicago Press, 1960.

Hook, Sidney, ed. *Determinism and Freedom*. New York: Collier Books, 1961.

Kaufman, A. S. "Professor Berlin on Negative Liberty," *Mind*, Vol. LXI (1962), pp. 241–244.

MacFarlane, L. J. "On Two Concepts of Liberty," *Political Studies*, Vol. 14 (1963), pp. 77–81.

Nichols, D. "Positive Liberty, 1880-1914," *American Political Science Review*, Vol. LVI (1962), pp. 114–128.

Oppenheim, Felix A. *Dimensions of Freedom*. New York: St. Martin's Press, Inc., 1961.

White, D. M. "Power and Liberty," *Political Studies*, Vol. 22 (1971), pp. 37–48.

15. The Concept of Political Freedom[1]

Franz Neumann

It is a fairly widespread academic doctrine that political theory is concerned with determining the limits of the citizen's obedience to the state's coercive powers. In this formula coercion appears legitimate, and the sole function of political theory is to erect a fence around such political power. The analysis of political power — its origin, manifestations and techniques — belongs to another discipline, sociology. In both disciplines political power seems to be accepted as an ontological datum, a natural fact, and the role of political theory is to see to it that political power behaves with relative decency.

Insofar as political theory is concerned with the legitimacy of political power, it has, according to prevailing opinion, a mere ideological function. Political theory is conceived as a rationalization of existing power relationships. A theory's validity is thus determined by a pragmatic-utilitarian appraisal in terms of the assistance it gives in defending or conquering an existing power position, with its propagandistic-manipulative success the criterion of its truth.

This position expresses, often unwittingly, the political alienation of contemporary man: the fact that man considers political power a force alien to him, a force which he cannot control and with which he cannot identify himself, and which at best can be made barely compatible with his existence. The extraordinary decline in prestige of the political philosophies of Plato and Rousseau — theorists who attempted to solve the problem of man's political alienation — seems to confirm this view.

There is, of course, no doubt for any realistically minded person that politics is a struggle for power — a struggle between persons, groups, and states. The assertion that in politics Right fights Might, Idea combats Power — with the frequent addition that, after all, Right and Idea will ultimately be victorious — may be edifying and comforting to many but seems impossible of proof. In fact, whenever Right has had to contend with Power, Right has been defeated. Were we to stop at this formula, we ought to abandon political theory altogether (save as a technique of manipulation) and accept what one commonly understands by Machiavellianism:

Reprinted with permission of The Macmillan Company from *The Democratic and the Authoritarian State* by Franz Neumann. © by The Free Press, A Corporation, 1957.

[1] This article is a continuation of my paper "Approaches to the Study of Political Power." A German version, in an abbreviated form, was published under the title "Zum Begriff der Politischen Freiheit," *Zeitschrift für die Gesamte Staatswissenschaft* 25 (1953). Parts of it were read as papers in Arthur W. Macmahon's Columbia University Seminar on The State, and before the Twelfth Symposium on Science, Philosophy and Religion, New York (1953). The discussions provoked by the papers helped greatly in the clarification of my ideas.

that nothing really changes in politics, that the "outs" always fight the "ins" for profit, prestige and security. The wise observer will add that you cannot expect anything else, human nature being what it is — basically selfish and evil.

In a period of conflicts, of uncertainty, hatred, and resentment, this view — like pessimistic theories in general — seems especially attractive. St. Augustine's theory of man (as commonly interpreted), Machiavelli's view of politics, Metternich's conception of foreign relations, are all unquestionably fashionable today, and if contrasted with a shallow misinterpretation of enlightenment philosophy they are certainly more realistic. Modern sociology and political science do not weary of stressing the view that politics consists in nothing but the manipulation of large masses by small elites, particularly through clever use of symbols: in order to beat an enemy, one must merely be cleverer. A theory then becomes an ideological statement which, if repeated often enough, will by its own weight change the political situation and produce victory.

But the ordinary man is repelled by these conceptions. Distinguishing the promotion of an idea from the sale of soap he refuses to accept the view that the legitimation of political power is a matter of individual preference. As a political man he deeply feels that his preference must be part of a more universally valid value system, a system of natural law or justice or national interest or even humanity.

Politics is indeed a struggle for power — but in this struggle persons, groups, and states may represent more than their egoistic interests. Some may really defend national interests or those of humanity, while their opponents may merely rationalize their egoistic-particular demands. The thought structure of the former would be termed an idea; the latter, an ideology — an *arcanum dominationis* designed to hide and rationalize concerns which are actually egoistic.

This formula, of course, answers no questions. How does one determine whether an interest is more than a particular one? The answer is difficult, more difficult today than perhaps at any other period of history, precisely because our thinking is so heavily permeated by propaganda that it sometimes seems hopeless to attempt to pierce the layers of symbols, statements, ideologies and thus to come to the core of truth.[2]

Yet this is precisely the task of political theory. It is in this enterprise that political theory parts company with the sociology of knowledge. Sociology is concerned with description of the factual; political theory is concerned with the truth. The truth of political theory is political freedom.[3] From this follows one basic postulate: Since no political system can realize political freedom fully, political theory must by necessity be critical. It cannot justify and legitimize a concrete political system; it must be critical of it. A conformist political theory is no theory.

Thus the concept of political freedom needs clarification. The present discussion has primarily a didactic function: to dissect the concept of political freedom into its three constituent elements — the juridical, the cognitive, and the volitional — with the hope that they may be re-integrated into an overall theory of political freedom.

---

[2] The preceding paragraphs form the transition from my article "Approaches to the Study of Political Power," *supra* note 1.

[3] See Humboldt, *Ideen zu einem Versuch die Grenzen der Wirksamkeit des Staates zu Bestimmen* c. 16 (1851).

The Concept of Juridical Liberty

Freedom is first and foremost the absence of restraints. There is little doubt that this view underlies the liberal theory of freedom, that it is the key concept of what one understands by constitutionalism, that it is basic to the understanding of what, particularly in the Anglo-American tradition, one understands by juridical liberty.[4] This is the formula of Hobbes (although he formulated it as a natural science theory), and of Locke, Montesquieu[5] and Kant. Thus understood, freedom may be defined as negative or "juristic" freedom. In referring to this concept as negative we do not mean bad or objectionable, but rather that it is in the Hegelian sense[6] one-sided and therefore inadequate. The negative element may not be thrown out — to do so leads to the acceptance of totalitarianism — but it cannot, of itself, adequately explain the notion of political freedom. Translated into politics, the negative aspect of freedom necessarily has led to the formula of citizen versus state. The real meaning of this formula needs clarification.

Its basic presupposition is philosophic individualism — the view that man is a reality quite independent of the political system within which he lives.[7] The positing of man against political power implies, in varying degrees, an acceptance of man's political alienation. Political power, embodied in the state, will always be alien to man; he cannot and should not fully identify himself with it. The state must not completely swallow up the individual; the individual cannot be understood merely as a political animal.[8] A political theory based upon an individualistic philosophy must necessarily operate with the negative-juridical concept of freedom, freedom as absence of restraint.

[4] On this, see particularly Corwin, *Liberty Against Government — The Rise, Flowering and Decline of a Famous Juridicial Concept* (1948).

[5] Montesquieu's formula, however, has a certain ambiguity. See my Introduction to *The Spirit of the Laws.*

[6] See Hegel, *Philosophy of Right* ∫ 5 Addition (Knox transl. 1942).

[7] This, most certainly, was not the view of Plato, at least not in the *Republic*. But in the Aristotelian political philosophy, as revealed in his discussions of the rule of law in his *Politics, Ethics and Rhetoric*, the individualistic element begins to enter. Plato's architectonic or organic conception of justice meant that the individual can have no claim against the social whole. Aristotle, in contrast, defines justice as distributive, as the restoration of proportionate equality, and he is thus compelled to consider the claim of man against man as an individual. Aristotle anticipates an individualistic conception, but for him the criterion of justice is still the order of the *Polis*. The history of the growth of the competing anti-Platonic individualistic conception initiated by the Sophists, taken up by Epicurus and the Sceptics, and transformed by the Stoics, is too well known to deserve another treatment here, see Sabine, *A History of Political Thought*, c. 8 (rev. ed. 1950), but one may say that with Aristotle's death man's history as an individual begins. See Tarn, *Hellenistic Civilization* 69 (1927). Cicero's legal philosophy is probably the first full-fledged individualistic-Stoic presentation of a natural law doctrine which, in Christianity, was extended and deepened as well as narrowed and diverted into the spiritual realm — the equality of souls before God.

[8] This is obvious in the case of the individualistic-liberal theories, since they have been conceived with this aim in mind. But it applies equally to the individualistic-absolutist theories of Hobbes and Spinoza. Both assert that the individual, threatened in the state of nature, is driven by the law of self-preservation to organize a state to which he surrenders his natural freedom. Both writers, however, qualify their radicalism: Hobbes by constructing the social contract as a kind of business agreement obligating the sovereign to maintain peace, order, and security, the contract lapsing when the sovereign fails to carry out his duty; Spinoza by identifying right and might, a formula which permits every social group to transform itself from an *alienus iuris* into a *sui iuris* and thus to become sovereign.

The idea that there are individual rights which political power may restrain and restrict but never annihilate is concretized in the civil rights catalogues of the various constitutions. Indeed, for practical purposes, juridical freedom largely coincides with these charters. An analysis of civil rights provisions thus seems equivalent to an analysis of the concept of juridical freedom. Legally, civil liberties establish a presumption in favor of the rights of the individual and against the coercive power of the state. They are no more than presumptions because there is not, and obviously cannot be, a political system which recognizes the individual's sphere of freedom absolutely and unconditionally. Thus the state may intervene with the individual's liberty — but first it must prove that it may do so. This proof can be adduced solely by reference to "law" and it must, as a rule, be submitted to specific organs of the state: courts or administrative tribunals. There are thus three statements inherent in this analysis of civil rights:

The burden of proof for intervention rests always with the state.
The only means or proof is reference to a law.
The method by which a decision is to be reached is regulated by law.

Clearly the political significance of this formula depends upon the meaning of the term "law." Abstractly, there are three possible definitions:

1. Law may mean a set of rules of behavior asserted to be objectively valid within any political system (as is the case in the Thomastic view).
2. Law may mean the sum total of individual rights allegedly existing prior to the political system and not being, in their essence, affected by it (the Lockean position).
3. Law may mean the positive law of the state, valid if enacted in accordance with a written or unwritten constitution.

The first two meanings of the term "law" can be dispensed with in our analysis. In the reality of political life, natural rights (in either meaning) have validity only if they are institutionalized, only if there is an authorized agency capable of enforcing them against opposing provisions of positive law. Thus medieval natural-law norms were valid if the Church or the vassals were successful in asserting what they considered natural rights against imperial or royal legislation. The right of resistance was then indeed the institutionalization of "natural law."[9] With the emergence of the state, with its institutional monopolization of the means of coercion, "natural law" or "inalienable natural rights" have a political meaning only if they are recognized by organs of the state — and to this extent they become positive law. This is precisely the case with civil rights when they are incorporated into a written constitution or are recognized, as in the English system, in constitutional and legal practice.[10] The philosophic theories concerning civil rights may have shaped their enactment and may still be necessary for interpreting them in ambiguous situations, but they do not determine their legal validity.

---

[9] See Kern, *Gottesgnadentum und Widerstandsrecht im früheren Mittelalter* 161–284, 310–12, 367–71, 394–96, 412–15, 432–34 (1914). See also Magna Carta, c. 61.

[10] See on this my two papers: "Types of Natural Law" and "On the Limits of Justifiable Disobedience." For the sake of accuracy it may be wise to stress that civil liberties in Great Britain owe probably less to either the Thomistic or the Lockean system than to the common law conception of historic rights of the Englishman and the techniques and the skill of the common lawyers.

Thus the "law" by which the state proves its right to interfere with individual rights can only be positive law.

Yet the meaning of the term "positive law" is in itself a problem. Genetically, the validity of positive law is determined solely by the fact that it is enacted in accordance with certain written or unwritten procedural rules. Thus the Hobbes-Austin-Kelsen definition is correct, translating the concept of sovereignty into legal terms. Law is simply *voluntas*, or will.

But historically there has been a second definition, concerned with the formal structure of positive law, one which emphasizes its generality. Were law merely *voluntas*, the concept of a "rule of law" would have no ascertainable meaning for the protection of individual rights, for sovereignty and law would then be synonymous. Actually there exists a steady tradition, stemming from Plato[11] and Aristotle,[12] holding that no matter what the law's substance its form must be general (or universal, as it is sometimes termed). Even when natural law has been rejected, insistence upon the law's formal structure survives as a minimal requirement of reason for restraint of power. The generality of the law may thus be called secularized natural law.[13]

The generality of law means logically a hypothetical judgment by the state on the future behavior of legal subjects, its basic manifestations being the legislative statute or the *ratio decidendi* of the common law.

Two determinants are contained in this definition: first, law must be a rule which does not mention particular cases or individual persons but which is issued in advance to apply to all cases and all persons in the abstract; and second, it must be specific, as specific as possible in view of its general formulation.[14] This view of the nature of law determined legal and political thought from the 17th century on. It was common to Hooker and Locke and was most accurately formulated by Rousseau, in whose political philosophy this notion of law is virtually the sole institutionalized limit upon the community's sovereignty. This is how he defines the law:

> When I say that the object of the law is always general, I mean that the law considers the subjects in their totality and their actions in the abstract, but never a man as a single person and never an individual act. Therefore, the law may well provide that there shall be privileges but it must never grant them to a named person . . . in a word: each statement referring to an individual object does not belong to the legislative power.[15]

France and England adopted this position. Even Austin, protagonist of the volitional theory of law, says: "Now where the law obliges generally to acts and forbearances of a class, a command is a law or rule."[16] Almost every theorist

---

[11] Plato, *Laws* *713–15 (Jowett transl. 1871).

[12] Aristotle, *Ethica Nicomachea*, Bk. 5, c. 9, *1137^b (Ross transl. 1925).

[13] A detailed analysis of this problem appears in my dissertation *The Governance of the Rule of Law* (unpublished thesis in London University Library, 1936).

[14] See 1 Malberg, *Contribution à la Théorie Générale de l'Etat* 289 (1920).

[15] Rousseau, *Contrat Social*, Bk. 2, c. 6.

[16] 1 Austin, *Lectures on Jurisprudence* 94 (5th ed. 1929).

asserts that this ought to be the theory of law[1][7] even where one has to admit that positive constitutional law permits the enactment of individual measures.[1][8]

From the simple proposition that there exists a presumption in favor of the individual's freedom there follows every element of the liberal legal system: the permissibility of every act not expressly forbidden by law; the closed and self-consistent nature of the legal system; the inadmissibility of retroactive legislation; the separation of the judicial from the legislative function. These concepts were – and seem still to be – accepted by the civilized world without question, with their logical connection with the doctrine of the law's generality well perceived.

If there is a presumption for the individual's right, it logically follows that only behavior that is expressly forbidden by law is punishable. This statement is universally recognized as being the foundation of legal liberty. Hence follows the inadmissibility of bills of attainder, which deny that a presumption exists for right against power and which permit power to enact individual measures directed against specifically named persons. By this token the bill of attainder is a legislative and judicial act in one.[1][9] The doctrines *nullum crimen sine lege* and *nulla poena sine lege* are latinistic formulations of the basic principle[2][0] against retroactivity.[2][1] Its inadmissibility follows logically from the structure of the general law as a hypothetical judgment about future behavior – a rule, therefore, for an indefinite number of concrete cases. A retroactive law covers, hidden behind the language of a general law, countable concrete cases, and is thus in reality a mechanical addition of individual measures.[2][2] The famous Nazi *Lex van der Lubbe* of March 29, 1933, retroactively introducing the death penalty for arson, was enacted for the sole purpose of dealing with the alleged arsonist of the Reichstag.

Moreover, the generality of the law implies the doctrine of a separate judiciary. If the law is to be abstract, if it is to regulate an unknown number of future cases, then its application to concrete cases cannot be in the hands of those who make the general rule. Thus judicial or administrative functions are legally subordinated (no matter what may be the sociological theory of the judicial function) in such a way that the judge or administrator performs the routine function of subsuming a concrete case under a general law.

The liberal legal tradition rests, therefore, upon a very simple statement: individual rights may be interfered with by the state only if the state can prove its

[1][7] I am not concerned with the intellectual history of this theory from Plato and Aristotle to the Stoics, and to the Thomistic system, and from there to the Descartian-Newtonian philosophy, but rather with its actual functions.

[1][8] As in England and France.

[1][9] This is clearly demonstrated in the rider to the appropriation bill denying salaries to Lovett *et al*. See United States v. Lovett, 328 U.S. 303 (1946).

[2][0] Despite their latinity, the rules were born only in the 18th century. See Hall, "Nulla Poena Sine Lege," 47 *Yale L.J.* 165 (1937).

[2][1] "Retroactivity is the greatest crime the law can commit; it is the tearing up of the social pact, the annullment of the conditions by virtue of which society may demand obedience from the individual. . . . Retroactivity takes away from the law its character; the retroactive law is no law." With these words did one of the apostles of liberalism, Benjamin Constant, attack retroactivity. *Le Moniteur Universel*, June 1, 1828, p. 754, col. 3.

[2][2] Today, the rule against retroactivity has virtually a meaning only in criminal law. On the American doctrine see Corwin, *op. cit. supra* note 4, at 60–61.

claim by reference to a general law which regulates an indeterminate number of future cases; this excludes retroactive legislation and demands a separation of legislative from judicial functions. The underlying assumption of the liberal legal system is the logical consistency of the law. The legal system is deemed to be closed so that new law can be created only by legislation; the judge or administrator must answer each case by reference to existing law.[23]

I have little doubt that this formula expresses, so far as any formula can, the creed of liberal legal thought. Yet there remains the question of what this theoretical system actually guarantees. I have distinguished three functions of the generality of law: a moral, an economic, and a political function.[24]

The moral (or ethical) function consists in the inherent elements of equality and security which it presupposes. A minimum of equality is guaranteed, for if the law-maker must deal with persons and situations in the abstract he thereby treats persons and situations as equals and is precluded from discriminating against any one specific person. By the same token a minimum of security exists in the relation between the individual and the state. The individual knows in advance that an act, once performed, cannot be made punishable by a later law and that he alone cannot be made to suffer, unless others, for similar reasons, are also made to suffer. This is the ethical content of the prohibition against bills of attainder — a prohibition by which the Anglo-American countries have, on the whole, scrupulously abided. Even Great Britain, where the sovereignty of Parliament theoretically permits the enactment of attainder bills, has never since the 17th century resorted to them save in colonies against natives.[25]

Thus it seems correct to say that an ethical minimum is inherent in this formal structure. This basic idea is well expressed in Cicero's statement, "The magistrates who administer the law, the jurors who interpret it — all of us in short — obey the

[23] These principles are equally applicable to common law. I have attempted to show this in my London dissertation, *supra* note 13. The ratio *decidendi* of the judicial decision fills the role of the code or statute; English judges deny that they create new law and assert that they merely apply the general principle contained in the *ratio decidendi*. For important statements on this problem see Vinogradoff, *Common Sense in Law* (2d ed. 1946); Goodhart, "Precedent in English and Continental Law," 50 *L.Q. Rev.* 4 (1934).

[24] The following is based on my article "Der Funktionswandel des Gesetzes im Recht der burgerlichen Gesellschaft," in *Seitschrift fur Sozialforschung* 542 (1937).

[25] The one case which I could discover illustrates well the ethical significance of the general principle. In Rex v. Earl of Crewe, [1910] 2 K.B. 576, approved in Sobhuzae II v. Miller, [1926] A.C. 518, 524 (P.C.), the Court had to deal with the proclamation of a Colonial High Commissioner for detention of a native under an Order in Council based upon the Foreign Jurisdiction Act, 53 & 54 *Vict.*, c. 37 (1890), by which the Habeas Corpus Act was suspended. Farwell, L. J., in giving the judgment, said: "The truth is that in countries inhabited by native tribes who largely outnumber the white population such acts, although bulwarks of liberty in the United Kingdom, might, if applied there, well prove the death warrant of the whites," *id*. at 615, thus admitting the legality of suspending the Habeas Corpus Act not only generally, but also "in respect of a particular individual," *id*. at 616; and Kennedy, L. J., adds that the Proclamation is " 'a privilegium' — legislation directed against a particular person, and generally, as I hope and believe, such legislation commends itself as little to the British legislators as it did to the legislators of ancient Rome . . .," *id*. at 628, while Rowlatt, for the defense, pointed to the relationship between the Proclamation and a bill of attainder, *id*. at 583–88.

The Supreme Court decision United States v. Lovett, 328 U.S. 303 (1946) applies the very same principle not only to legislative deprivation of the freedom of named individuals but to deprivation of every right.

law to the end that we may be free,"[26] and still more precisely in Voltaire's dictum, "*La liberté consiste à ne dépendre que des lois.*"[27] Both have in mind the general law. If the sovereign may enact measures interfering with an individual's rights, the role of judge becomes transformed into that of a policeman or bailiff. The generality of the law is thus the precondition of judicial independence, which, in turn, makes possible the realization of that minimum of liberty and equality that inheres in the formal structure of the law.

The formal structure of the law is, moreover, equally decisive in the operation of the social system of a competitive-contractual society. The need for calculability and reliability of the legal and administrative system was one of the reasons for the limitation of the power of the patrimonial monarchy and of feudalism. This limitation culminated in the establishment of the legislative power of parliaments by means of which the middle classes controlled the administrative and fiscal apparatus and exercised a condominium with the crown in changes of the legal system. A competitive society requires general laws as the highest form of purposive rationality, for such a society is composed of a large number of entrepreneurs of about equal economic power.[28] Freedom of the commodity market, freedom of the labor market, free entrance into the entrepreneurial class, freedom of contract, and rationality of the judicial responses in disputed issues – these are the essential characteristics of an economic system which requires and desires the production for profit, and ever renewed profit, in a continuous, rational, capitalistic enterprise.[29] The primary task of the state is the creation of a legal order which will secure the fulfillment of contractual obligations; the expectation that contractual obligations will be performed must be made calculable. This calculability can be attained only if the laws are general in structure – provided that an approximate equality in power of the competitors[30] exists so that each has identical interests. The relation between state and entrepreneur, particularly in regard to fiscal obligations and interferences with property rights, must also be as calculable as possible. The sovereign may neither levy taxes nor restrain the exercise of entrepreneurial activity without a general law, since an individual measure necessarily prefers one to another and thus violates the principle of entrepreneurial equality. For these reasons the legislator must remain the sole source of law. Thus seen, the alleged contradiction in the attitude of liberalism toward legislation vanishes. Roscoe Pound[31] maintained that the Puritans' view of legislation contained an inherent contradiction: on the one hand, hostility to legislation; on the other, firm belief in it and rejection of customary law and equity. But this is precisely the attitude of the whole liberal period, which, for obvious reasons, desires as little governmental intervention as possible – since intervention, by definition, interferes with private rights – but if intervention at all, then in the form of the legislative statute with clear, precise, unambiguous general terms.

[26] Cicero, "Pro Cluentio" in *The Speeches of Cicero* ∫ 53, *146 (Hodge transl. 1927).

[27] Voltaire, "Pensées sur le gouvernement" in *23 Oeuvres Complètes* 526 (Garnier ed. 1879).

[28] See Weber, *Wirtschaft und Gesellschaft* 174 (1922).

[29] See Weber, *The Protestant Ethic and the Spirit of Capitalism* 17 (Parsons transl., 2d ed. 1950).

[30] See particularly 1 Adam Smith, *A Theory of Moral Sentiments*, Part 3, c. 3 (5th ed. 1781).

[31] See Pound, *The Spirit of the Common Law* 46 (1925).

The political function of the general law is manifested in the Anglo-American slogan: a government of laws and not of men,[32] and in the Prussian-German notion of the *Rechtsstaat* (state based upon law). Both formulations contain, obviously, an ideological element. The law cannot rule. Only men can exercise power over other men. To say that laws rule and not men may consequently signify that the fact is to be hidden that men rule over other men. While this is correct, the ideological content of the phrase "the rule of law" differs sharply according to the political structure of the nation which coins it. The English rule of law and the German *Rechtsstaat*[33] doctrines have really nothing in common. To the Germans, the *Rechtsstaat* merely denotes the legal form through which every state, no matter what its political structure, is to express its will.

> The state is to be a Rechtsstaat; that is the watchword, and expresses what is in reality the trend of modern developments. It shall exactly define and inviolably secure the direction and the limits of its operation, as well as the sphere of freedom of its citizens by means of law. Thus it shall realize directly nothing but that which belongs to the sphere of law. This is the conception of the Rechtsstaat, and not that the state shall only apply the legal order without administrative aims, or even only secure the right of the individuals. It signifies above all not the aims of the state, but merely the method of their realization.

This is the formula of Friedrich Julius Stahl,[34] founder of the theory of the Prussian monarchy. The last sentence is the decisive one; it has been fully accepted by the German liberal theorists. It means, of course, that neither the origin nor the goals of the law are relevant; but that the form of a general law gives to every state its legal (*Rechtsstaat*) character. That a conservative monarchist coined this theory is, of course, understandable; that the liberals adopted it merely expresses the collapse of German political liberalism in 1812, in 1848, and during the constitutional conflict with Bismarck in 1862. German liberalism remained content to defend its rights against the monarchy, particularly its property rights, but was no longer concerned with the conquest of political power. Indeed, as this formula indicates, it had traded political freedom for economic advance and security.[35]

In contrast, the English doctrine of the rule of law comprises two different propositions: that Parliament is sovereign, thus possessing the monopoly of law-making (the democratic legitimation of political power); and that the legislation enacted will comply with the requirements of a liberal legal system as defined above. Dicey recognizes the logical incompatibility of the two statements but believes that "this appearance is delusive; the sovereignty of Parliament as contrasted with other forms of sovereign power, favors the supremacy of the law, whilst the predominance of rigid legality throughout our institutions evokes the

---

[32] The formula (according to Corwin, *op. cit. supra* note 4, at 13) was coined by Harrington, *Harrington, Oceana* 37 (Toland ed. 1747), who ascribes it to Aristotle and Livy. Cicero uses much the same term.

[33] According to Rudolf Gneist the word *Rechtsstaat* has been coined by Robert von Mohl, 1 *Geschichte und Literatur der Staatswissenschaften* 296 (1855). On the differences between Germany and England see Burin, *The Rule of Law in German Constitutional Thought: A Study in Comparative Jurisprudence* (unpublished thesis in Columbia University Library, 1953).

[34] 2 Stahl, *Rechts- und Staatslehre* 137 (3d ed. 1878).

[35] Robert von Mohl himself, see note 33 *supra*, however, did not accept the Stahl formula. To him, the character of a state as a *Rechtsstaat* is equally determined by the political and social goals expressed in the legal system. His view did not find acceptance.

exercise, and thus increases the authority of parliamentary sovereignty."[36] The fact is that Dicey was, and probably still is, correct. The reason for this does not lie in a kind of pre-established harmony between power and right in the United Kingdom but probably in the self-restraint of Parliament, which in turn is the result of a functioning party system and a balanced and stable social structure.

The United States system lies between the two marginal cases of the *Rechtsstaat* and the English rule of law, the two elements often being, as now, in a rather precarious balance.

To sum up: The general character of the law and the presumptions in favor of the right of the individual and against the state play three roles in modern society: a moral, in that they guarantee a minimum of freedom, equality and security; an economic, in that they make possible a competitive-contractual society; a political, in that in varying degrees they hide the locus of power. I should stress here that the moral function transcends both the economic and political contexts within which it operates. This is the legal value, the sole legal value, inherent in a legal system so structured. All other values realized in a legal system are introduced from outside, namely by power.

It is clear, I think, that our political, social, and economic life does not consist solely of rational — that is, calculable — relationships. Power cannot be dissolved in legal relationships. The dream of the liberal period was precisely that it could. From the end of the 18th century to the first half of the 19th this view of a rational society assumed, one may say, utopian characteristics. All relevant relationships were deemed to be legal; the law was to be general in character; the judge was merely "the mouthpiece of the law," applying it through a logical process of subsumption.[37] Legal positivism is not only, as is commonly taught, the acceptance of political power as it is, but also the attempt to transform political and social power relationships into legal ones.

But this, of course, does not work. It never did and never could. If our social, economic and political life were merely a system of rational, calculable relationships, the rule of law would of course cover everything. While power can at times be restrained, it cannot be dissolved. The nonrational element, power, and the rational element, law, are often in conflict.

The conflict may be resolved in two ways: the general law may, in its very formulation, contain an escape clause permitting purely discretionary decisions

---

[36] Dicey, *Introduction to the Study of the Law of the Constitution* 402 (8th ed. 1915).

[37] Thus Jeremy Bentham demanded a code because it "would not require schools for its explanation, would not require casuists to unravel its subtleties. It would speak a language familiar to everybody; each one might consult it at his need. ... Commentaries, if written, should not be cited. ... If a judge or advocate thinks he sees an error or omission, let him certify his opinion to the Legislature," "General View of Complete Code of Laws" in 3 Bentham, *Works* 210 (Bowring ed. 1843). What Bentham advocated, the French carried out. See Gény, *Méthode d'Interprétation et Sources du Droit Privé Positif* 77, 84 (2d ed. 1932), and 1 Malberg, *op. cit. supra* note 14, at 719. The French forbade the judges to interpret laws and created, in 1790, the *référé législatif*, a mandatory of the legislative power, to interpret ambiguous provisions of law (abolished only 1828–1837). The "enlightened despots" Frederick II of Prussia and Joseph II of Austria flatly forbade legal interpretations of laws; a Bavarian instruction of 1813, probably drafted under the influence of Paul Johann Anselm Feuerbach, forbade officials and private scholars the writing of commentaries to the Bavarian penal code. See Radbruch, *Feuerbach* 85 (1934). Savigny took the same line.

which are not the product of the subsumption of a concrete case under an abstract rule; or, if power so desires, the general law may be suspended altogether.

I shall consider only the first case. Every legal system employs legal standards of conduct — statements permitting the agencies of the state to act in a purely discretionary fashion while outwardly complying with the liberal tradition of a general law. These legal standards of conduct may be explicit (that is, written into codes or statutes) or implicit (that is, may be interpreted by courts into statutes). One may perhaps say that power enters rational private law through equity; and rational constitutional law through prerogative (or some similar term).

I shall first take examples from private law, in order to show that the principle prevails even in the most rational section of the legal system.

Liberal legal theory was once violently opposed to equity (in the Aristotelian meaning: as a corrective to rigid general laws). Whether one reads Selden's Table Talk[38] or Blackstone's Commentaries,[39] or Kant's Legal Philosophy[40] — to mention but a few — equity is denounced as incompatible with the calculability which is the primary requirement of liberal law. England, the home of modern European equity, was at once her gravedigger. According to Maitland, equity had become since 1875 merely "that body of rules which is administered only by those Courts which are known as Courts of Equity."[41] And in Lord Eldon's judgment, "The doctrines of this court ought to be as well settled and made as uniform almost as those of the common law, laying down fixed principles, but taking care that they are applied according to the circumstances of each case."[42] Similar statements by other English judges show basic agreement on the necessity of transforming equity into a rigid system of law in order to secure the calculability which economic transactions require.

But the rejection of equity is germane only to a competitive economic system. Equity considerations increase with the increase in concentrations of economic power and in interventionist activities of the state.

We may generally say that equitable rules are and must be applied where one has to deal with power positions.[43] When an interest approaches monopolistic control, its private power becomes quasi-legislative and therefore public. Since each such interest affects public welfare in a unique way, the state can regulate it only through some form of individual measure. This is introduced into the liberal legal system through the equity approach. The English conspiracy doctrine as applied to restraints of trade, the American concept of "reasonableness" as applied to economic combinations, the German doctrine of "good morals" as applied to industrial disputes, are all clear evidence of this. The whole of the German law regarding the legality of strikes and lockouts is contained in the Civil Code provision that an act which inflicts damage upon another and violates good morals is a tort. Our whole anti-trust law is really nothing but the statement that an unreasonable combination is illegal. Yet how can one rationally define such

[38] See *Table Talk of John Selden* 43 (Pollock ed. 1927).

[39] See 1 *Bl. Comm.* *62.

[40] See Kant, *Philosophy of Law* 51 (Hastie transl. 1887), where equity is defined as a "dumb goddess who cannot claim a hearing of right. Hence it follows that a Court of Equity, for the decision of disputed questions of right, would involve a contradiction."

[41] Maitland, *Equity* 1 (Chaylor and Whitaker ed. 1928).

[42] Gee v. Pritchard, 2 Swan. Ch. 402, 414, 36 Eng. Rep. 670, 674 (1818).

[43] But not only there. There is a second set of circumstances which I do not discuss here: the problem of colliding interests of equal value to society (e.g., divorce law).

standards? They can be illustrated and described but never defined. Nor, without risking extreme rigidity, could we seek to do otherwise. The general law therefore operates best when it regulates the behavior of a vast number of competitors of about equal strength. If it has to deal with power concentrations it will be replaced by clandestine individual measures.

Similar methods are employed in the field of public law, appearing in three sets of problems:

1. No political system will fully uphold the legal value of calculability and legal security if it deems its own security endangered by it. Power will thus strive to set aside the juristic notion of freedom.
2. The fundamental presupposition of liberal legal theory is that the right of one will coincide with the right of others, and that in case of conflicting rights the state will fulfill its arbiter function through the application of precisely defined general laws. But quite often the colliding interests seem to be of equal weight and the conflict can then be solved only by a discretionary decision.
3. No political system is satisfied with simply maintaining acquired rights. The juristic concept of freedom — as we have developed it — is naturally conservative.[44] But no system, even the most conservative one (in the literal meaning of the term) can merely preserve; even to preserve it must change. The values that determine the character of the changes are obviously not derived from the legal system. They come from outside, but for propagandistic reasons they are presented as legal demands, often allegedly derived from natural law.

To answer the first two of these problems it becomes necessary to define more accurately the amount of freedom which civil rights actually guarantee. To this end the traditional civil liberties must be classified, for it would be dangerous to speak of only one right: individual freedom. While all civil rights ultimately go back to this basic philosophical conception, historical development has led to a distinction among various types of rights with different functions and different sanctions.

Civil rights, as restraints upon power, are necessary as a means of preserving freedom. This formulation implies two statements: civil rights are indispensable for the realization of freedom; but civil rights do not exhaust freedom — they are but one of its elements. Freedom is more than the defense of rights against power; it involves as well the possibility of developing man's potentialities to the fullest. Only because we do not trust any power, however well-meaning, to decide what is good or bad for us, do we insist on a realm of freedom from coercion. This is the fundamental and inalienable (the so-called negative or juristic) aspect of our freedom.

But what, concretely, is it that is inalienable? We may distinguish three types of traditional rights: personal, societal, and political.

Rights may be called personal if their validity is bound solely to man as an isolated individual.[45] The security of the person, of houses, papers and effects,[46] the right to a fair trial,[47] the prohibition of unreasonable searches and seizures[48]

---

[44] Thus, correctly, Corwin, *op. cit. supra* note 4, at 6.

[45] Not quite happily, Professor Freund calls them "passive liberties." See Freund, *On Understanding the Supreme Court* 23 (1949).

[46] *U.S. Const. Amend. IV.*

[47] *U.S. Const. Amend. II, VI.*

[48] *U.S. Const. Amend. IV.*

do not depend upon man's association with other men. Their protection is not dependent (or should not be) upon changes in the socio-economic system, such as the change from competitive to organized capitalism, nor upon political expediency. What precisely constitutes a fair trial may be open to interpretation;[49] but reasons of state can never justify inroads into these principles. The criminal law provisions of our constitution are absolute personal rights; and probably no country has as many detailed constitutional provisions concerning these personal rights.[50]

Societal civil rights can be exercised only in relation to other members of society, They are, in a proper sense, rights of communication. Freedom of religion (as distinguished from religious conscience), freedom of speech, of assembly, and of property are such rights. One limitation is inherent in them: the exercise of these rights must not deprive others of theirs; in the language of Kant the rights of one must coexist with the rights of others. It is through such general laws as those of libel, slander and trespass that this coordination is perfected.

There is a demonstrable relationship between personal and societal rights. While the personal rights are, so to speak, an end in themselves, they are also ancillary to the societal rights. Without security of the person there can be no free communication, since a person subject to arbitrary arrest and without the prospect of a fair trial will be reluctant to engage in free communication. But the additional ancillary character of the personal rights must not lead to the view that they are subject to the inherent limitations of the societal rights.

This seems simple, but the two problems raised above − the conflict of political power with juristic freedom, and the conflict of two interests − create difficulties that, if conceived solely as legal problems, seem really insurmountable. The second problem is best illustrated by the Supreme Court decision in *Kovacs* v. *Cooper*,[51] in which the Court upheld a local ordinance forbidding the use of sound trucks emitting "loud and raucous" noises.

But it is the first problem which is the really important one. *Feiner v. New York*[52] is a typical case, appearing in precisely the same form in every nation: the citizen exercises his right to free speech, the audience protests, disorder ensues, the police are called in, they arrest the speaker for breach of the peace or for disorderly conduct and thus restore order. A study of the decisions of administrative or criminal courts in Germany and France will, as a rule, show that these courts, like our Supreme Court, uphold the discretionary power of the police to take such measures as they think fit to prevent disorder. In Germany, resistance by the speaker to such police action would be punishable as "resistance to the state power," while here the Supreme Court upheld the conviction for breach of the peace. Thus free speech is everywhere qualified by the proviso[53] that the agent of political power may determine at his discretion whether he will protect free speech or side with the power of the mob against it.

[49] See the statement on principles by Justice Cardozo, Palko v. Connecticut, 302 U.S. 319 (1937).

[50] In light of this the *Rabinowitz* decision, covering unreasonable searches and seizures, is very hard to take. United States v. Rabinowitz, 339 U.S. 56 (1950).

[51] 336 U.S. 77 (1949).

[52] 340 U.S. 315 (1951).

[53] But for the United States, consider the more favorable decisions, Terminiello v. Chicago, 337 U.S. 1 (1949), and Thomas v. Collins, 323 U.S. 516 (1945), and the discussion in Chafee, *Free Speech in the United States* 409−35 (1941).

Some constitutional lawyers and political scientists detect a decisive difference between the United States and continental Europe in the different constitutional formulae: the First Amendment with its statement: "Congress shall make no law . . . abridging the freedom. . . ." as against the typical continental formula: the right of free opinion is guaranteed within the framework of the laws.

There is indeed a difference, and there seems little doubt that the American pattern is preferable. Under our constitutional provision freedom of the press has developed remarkably better than under the numerous continental European press laws. But the decisive difference must be attributed less to different formulae than to more sensitive attitudes toward civil liberties, particularly on the part of the courts.

Beyond any shadow of a doubt the *calculable* relation between the rights of the individual and the power of the state is everywhere governed by an escape clause. In continental Europe it is the so-called reservation of the law; in the United States it is the "clear and present danger" formula.[54]

The clear and present danger test demonstrates the impossibility of clarifying the precise meaning of legal standards of conduct. David Riesman[55] goes so far as to assert that the *Schenck* decision does not permit the court to weigh the value of free speech against that of any governmental policy. This is probably an extreme interpretation but it does seem, in considering the range of decisions from *Near* v. *Minnesota*,[56] *Board of Education* v. *Barnette*,[57] *Thomas* v. *Collins*[58] to the *Dennis* case,[59] that the test has been watered down from "clear and present" to "clear and probable" danger, allowing the non-calculable element of political power to assert itself against the calculable limitation upon that power. Thus power, or "necessity," or "reason of state" cannot be effectively eliminated or restrained by constitutional law.[60]

Furthermore, not only do the objectively necessary or alleged requirements of political power interfere with the rule of general law; they may even occasion the total suspension of civil liberties. The state of siege, martial law, emergency powers—these merely indicate that reasons of state may actually annihilate civil liberties altogether. Common to these institutions in most countries is the fact that the discretionary power of those who declare an emergency cannot be challenged. It is they who determine whether an emergency exists and what measures are deemed necessary to cope with it.

Civil rights (personal and societal) are to be distinguished from political rights, though they are closely related. Continental theory frequently distinguishes "human" and "civil" rights—the former, it is asserted, are inherent in the nature of man as a free and equal being, enjoyed by citizens, denizens, and visitors; the latter are derived solely from the political structure of the state.

[54] Schenck v. United States, 249 U.S. 47 (1919).
[55] See Riesman, "Civil Liberties in a Period of Transition" in 3 *Public Policy* 33, 39 (1942).
[56] 283 U.S. 697 (1931).
[57] 319 U.S. 624 (1943).
[58] 323 U.S. 516 (1945).
[59] Dennis v. United States, 341 U.S. 494 (1951).
[60] In Germany the famous Arts. 10, 17 of the Prussian General Code (*Allgemeines Landrecht*) gave almost complete discretionary power to the police, and the institution of "protective custody" rested on this provision. Legally the situation is similar in all countries. The differences between the various countries are thus caused by different attitudes of the courts and of the law-makers, and not by the formulations.

This is correct if the term "political structure" is properly defined. If it simply says that a citizen has as many political rights as those wielding political power are willing to grant, it is meaningless. What is really meant is that the nature and extent of political rights are determined by the nature of the political system — that is, by what the political system claims to be.

Thus if a political system claims to be a democracy, specific rights must be implemented. On the whole, there is agreement on the minimal basic rights: equal franchise and equal access to all public offices, and equality of treatment in regard to occupations, professions and callings.

The rights of the *status activus* (as these political rights are sometimes called) presuppose, as I have mentioned, the personal and societal rights. There can be no formation of the national will on the basis of equal suffrage without freedom of the person and without free communication. By definition, therefore, any abrogation of personal or societal rights necessarily involves an intervention with political rights — though not vice versa.

So far, quite traditional problems have been discussed — although it is hoped that they have been discussed in a more systematic setting than usual. The problems are traditional because they revolve around the old formula of citizen versus state, which is primarily thought of in a context of criminal-law. In this setting civil rights can be, or at least could be, more or less effectively protected. But in modern society three new problems arise which are difficult or perhaps impossible to fit into this theoretical model: the effect upon civil rights of far-reaching changes in the socio-economic structure; the application of social sanctions against dissenters; and the attempt to legitimize positive demands upon the state by means of "civil rights."

These questions indicate that the juristic notion of freedom covers only one element of freedom, and cannot include all of political freedom. The confrontation citizen versus state is inadequate for several reasons.

If political freedom were mere legal freedom, it would be difficult to justify democracy as that political system which maximizes freedom. A constitutional monarchy would do as well, and indeed there are continental historians and political scientists who take precisely this position and even assert its superiority over democracy. This view we believe to be untenable — but this compels us to define political freedom more concretely.

Furthermore, juristic freedom is static and conservative, while society changes. The problem was well stated by Justice Jackson:

> [T]he task of translating the majestic generalities of the Bill of Rights, conceived as part of the pattern of liberal government in the eighteenth century, into concrete restraints on officials dealing with the problems of the twentieth century, is one to disturb self-confidence. These principles grew in soil which also produced a philosophy that the individual was the center of society, that his liberty was attainable through mere absence of governmental restraints, and that government should be contented with few controls and only the mildest supervision over man's affairs. We must transplant these rights to a soil in which the *laissez faire* concept or principle of non-interference has withered at least as to economic affairs, and social advancements are increasingly sought through closer integration of society and strengthened governmental controls.[61]

[61] Board of Education v. Barnette, 319 U.S. 624, 639–40 (1943).

Justice Jackson's view, moreover, leads to these doubts: the formula liberty versus government seems to comprehend two statements: that individual liberty increases with the decrease of governmental power (and vice versa); and that liberty has but one enemy: government. Neither of these implications can be accepted. It is historically impossible to maintain that governmental interventionism of itself decreases the scope and effectiveness of the citizen's freedom. A mere superficial acquaintance with history is quite enough to show that there is no logical connection between the two factors. A less interventionist Imperial Germany protected freedom far less effectively than a far more more interventionist Weimar Republic. England during the less total World War I was not as sensitive to civil rights as during the more total World War II. In the United States, the Supreme Court decisions extending the scope of civil rights protection began in 1931. The historical links between interventionism and civil rights are but little investigated by the historians and political scientists. The theoretical falsity of the statement that liberty decreases with the increase of governmental intervention is obvious since the term "intervention" neither indicates its purpose nor the interests against which intervention is directed. The connection between the two situations is a political-historical one, requiring analysis of each concrete situation, for it is undeniable that a minimum of intervention — the maintenance of "law and order" — is always indispensable to the preservation of individual rights, so that the very existence of the state is a precondition for their exercise.

This, in turn, is closely tied up with the second implication of the formula liberty versus government, namely, that the state is the sole enemy of liberty. That this is fallacious reasoning should be obvious from the fact that private social power can be even more dangerous to liberty than public power. The intervention of the state with respect to private power positions may be vital to secure liberty.

Thus the juristic notion of liberty is inadequate in the following respects:

1. The protection of liberty through general laws does not take into account the content of the laws. The general law may be repressive in content. A state may brutalize its penal system and, for instance, threaten the death penalty for all petty crimes. Nothing in the theory of juristic liberty could possibly prevent this. Even Rousseau, the fanatic believer in the generality of the law, was compelled to admit[62] that the law may create privileges although it must not grant them to individual persons. Thus we cannot but repeat that the juristic notion of liberty can guarantee only a minimum of liberty. That minimum may mean much or very little, depending on factors nonlegal in character.

2. Even within the scope of the juristic concept of liberty, escape clauses like the clear and present danger formula permit political power to prevail over individual rights. Thus Justice Frankfurter's statement in the *Dennis* case that "[C]ivil liberties draw at best only limited strength from legal guarantees . . ."[63] adequately formulates our position.

In short, the juristic notion of liberty, based upon the philosophic formula that freedom is the absence of restraint, opposes freedom to necessity, the two allegedly belonging to two different realms. There is no need here to resume the age-old debate on the correlation between freedom and necessity, but it seems necessary to restate the stages in the development of what we call the cognitive concept of liberty in order to show its political relevance.

[62] See Rousseau, *Contrat Social*, Bk. 2, c. 6 (1672).
[63] Dennis v. United States, 341 U.S. 494, 555 (1951).

The Cognitive Element in Freedom

The first step is to be found in Greek natural philosophy culminating in the philosophy of Epicurus. To him, as to Lucretius, the "terror then and darkness of mind must be dispelled not by the rays of the sun and glittering shafts of day, but by the aspect and the law of nature."[64] Their problem was to free men from the terror inspired by the superstitious belief that natural phenomena are due to the arbitrary intervention of the Gods — precisely the religious superstition that Plato[65] desired to maintain and even strengthen in order to keep the masses in hand. In opposition to this view Epicurus taught that external nature was governed by necessity, that is, by immutable natural laws. Understanding of this necessity makes man free, liberates him from the fear which the phenomena of external nature instil into the ignorant. "A man cannot dispel his fear about the most important matters if he does not know what is the nature of the universe but suspects the truth of some mythical story. So that without natural science it is not possible to attain our pleasures unalloyed";[66] and still more precisely, "necessity is an evil, but there is no necessity to live under the control of necessity."[67] Ever since Epicurus the development of natural science has occupied a decisive place in the growth of man's freedom; not only does the understanding of external nature free man from fear, but, as again indicated by Epicurus, it permits the utilization of natural processes for the betterment of man's material life. This powerful Epicurean tradition has continued to our day in the philosophy of Hobbes, Spinoza, the French enlightenment, and English utilitarianism.[68]

The second decisive step is the development of Spinoza's psychology,[69] with its application of the Epicurean principle to the understanding of man's mind: a man who lives according to the dictates of reason alone is a free man.[70] To be able to live according to reason man must understand his mind; he must classify his passions, understand them, and thereby subdue them. Only a slavish nature is ruled by passions. Freedom, to Spinoza, is thus insight into necessity.

It is in this scientific tradition that Freud stands. His understanding of the instinct of aggression and self-destruction,[71] and his analysis of the need for identification as the emotional tie of one person with another,[72] contain suggestions which have so far hardly been utilized in political theory. The fundamental proposition which Freud shares with Kierkegaard[73] is that our existence is shot through with anxiety. Both distinguish anxiety ("dread" in the English translation) from fear; the latter refers to "something definite," while anxiety is a state of existence produced by innocence and thus ignorance. Anxiety, the operation of the aggressive instinct, and the need for identification of the

---

[64] Lucretius, *On the Nature of Things*, Bk. 1, 6 (Munroe transl. 1919).

[65] Plato, *Republic*, c. 4 (Cornford transl. 1945).

[66] Epicurus, *The Extant Remains* 97 (Bailey ed. 1926).

[67] *Id.* at 107.

[68] On the intellectual history of Epicureanism see Guyau, *La Morale d'Epicure et ses Rapports avec les Doctrines Contemporaines* (3d ed. 1886).

[69] See Bidney, *The Psychology and Ethics of Spinoza* 372 (1940).

[70] See Spinoza, *Ethics*, Bk. 5, Prop. 20 (1677).

[71] See Freud, *Civilization and Its Discontents* (Riviere transl. 1949).

[72] See Freud, *Group Psychology and the Analysis of the Ego* (Strachey transl. 1949).

[73] See Kierkegaard, *The Concept of Dread* 37–38 (Lowrie transl. 1946); Freud, Hemmung, Sympton, Angst (1926).

isolated human being, are the psychological processes which permit the total annihilation of freedom in totalitarianism.

Yet it is possible that neither the understanding of external nature nor the knowledge of the operation of the mind will enable us to come to grips with necessity. There is no necessary correlation between freedom and an advanced state of knowledge of external and internal nature. The societal arrangements may, indeed, be such that natural science and psychology may become the handmaidens of oppression. What one calls the "moral lag" expresses this possible developmental dichotomy.

A third step is necessary: the understanding of the historical process. If we are to believe historians of history it is Giambatista Vico[74] who first attempted a scientific analysis of the structure of political freedom in the frame of an historical analysis. The subject of his theory of history is universal, not national, history. The historical process is no longer considered a theological but a social one. History is the work of man[75] within a cultural setting, the totality of material culture. History is the conflict between man, nature, and culture. Since Vico, the conception of history as universal history, and of the historical process as an intelligible development, have become primary concerns in the analysis of the notion of freedom. Similar ideas, but more mechanistic ones, have been developed by Montesquieu,[76] whose concepts of political structure are related to historical processes. Montesquieu was the first to develop the notion[77] that the actor in the historical process may by his acts produce consequences which he intended to avoid. It is he who insisted on the interdependence of all social phenomena, rejecting attempts to isolate specific features of a social structure and attribute specific consequences to them.

From Vico and Montesquieu the road goes to Hegel and Marx. Both accepted the Epicurean-Spinozist formula that freedom is insight into necessity: one who understands what happens, and why it happens, is thereby free.[78]

The cognitive formula, however, is wrong if it is conceived as obedience to an abstract and fatalistic law of history. The historical process includes man's aspiration to secure more effective control of his environment, so that historical insight is critical and programmatic. The real function of the cognitive element is to expose the possibilities for realizing the human potentialities latent in different social situations. On the one hand it prevents us from repeating empty time-honored formulae. What is progressive today and conducive to freedom may be false tomorrow and a hindrance to freedom. On the other hand it curbs utopian radicalism. Since what man can achieve is bound to the stage of social development, the realization of freedom is not at the disposal of man's free will.

The fate of two key concepts of political theory, sovereignty and property, will demonstrate the significance of the cognitive element of freedom.

Today it is fashionable to defame the concept of sovereignty. Hobbes, in particular, has never been popular in Anglo-American countries, and Bodin, the

---

[74] See Vico, *The New Science* (Bergin and Fisch transl. 1948).

[75] *Id.*, Bk. 1, No. 132–43, at 56–57.

[76] See Neumann, *supra* note 5, at xxxv–xxxix.

[77] Although, of course, St. Augustine had a similar notion.

[78] For the most recent philosophical discussion of the Marxist conception see Wetter, *Der Dialektische Materialismus* 403–08 (1952). The author is an Austrian Catholic. The book has the Imprimatur.

creator of the word "sovereignty," has been interpreted to be a mild liberal. Some hold sovereignty responsible for all the ills of our present age. Nationalism, imperialism, even totalitarianism are deemed to be direct descendants of sovereignty, with Marsilius of Padua, Bodin, Calvin, Luther, Hobbes, and, of course, Hegel, the criminals. We do not want to raise the problem of how far a theory — even the most brilliant one — can be held responsible for political developments, but will assume here that this is possible. It is clear that this view follows directly from the equation of freedom with juristic freedom, that is, absence of restraint. Sovereignty of the state means, obviously, that the monopoly of coercion rests with an institution separate from society, yet connected with it, called the state. The progressive historical function of sovereignty has never been doubted, even if there is dispute as to the limits of the state's coercive powers. In a period of feudal rule, of exploitation of peasants and cities by feudal lords, of competing jurisdictions of monarch, vassals, guilds and corporations, of secular and temporal powers, there arose one central power: the monarchy. It destroyed the autonomies, created (or attempted to create) one administration, one legal system, and transformed privileges into an equality of duties, if not of rights. How could our modern commercial and industrial society have arisen without this sovereignty which created large economic areas and integrated them legally and administratively? It was precisely middle class political theorists — Bodin, Spinoza, Pufendorf, Hobbes — who insisted on the powers of the monarch against the privileges and autonomies of estates, corporations, guilds, and churches. One may well interpret the French revolution of 1789 not as a reaction to the monarch's misuse of his absolute powers, but rather to his failure to use them. The theories of the Marquis d'Argenson, the Abbé Dubos, of the Physiocrats and particularly of Rousseau are indeed attempts to reconstitute the unity and efficiency of the central power in the state, be it monarchical or democratic, so that the freedom of the nation can be effectively realized.

The rise of the liberal theories (such as Locke's) is understandable and has meaning only if the monopoly of the state's coercive powers is no longer challenged, so that restraints upon sovereignty will no longer lead to its disintegration. I have elsewhere stated the problem of modern political theory in these terms:

> The problem of political philosophy, and its dilemma, is the reconciliation of freedom and coercion. With the emergence of a money economy we encounter the modern state as the institution which claims the monopoly of coercive power in order to provide a secure basis upon which trade and commerce may flourish and the citizens may enjoy the benefit of their labor. But by creating this institution, by acknowledging its sovereign power, the citizen created an instrument that could and frequently did deprive him of protection and of the boon of his work. Consequently, while justifying the sovereign power of the state, he sought at the same time to justify limits upon the coercive power. The history of modern political thought since Machiavelli is the history of this attempt to justify right *and* might, law *and* power. There is no political theory which does not do both things.[79]

In international relations, the concept of state sovereignty fulfilled similar functions.[80] By attributing sovereignty to the state, formal equality is attributed to

---

[79] Neumann, *supra* note 5, at xxxi–xxxii.

[80] On this see my *Behemoth: The Structure and Practice of National Socialism* 166–71 (2d ed. 1944).

all states and a rational principle is thus introduced into an anarchic state system. As a polemical notion, state sovereignty in international politics rejects the sovereign claims of races and classes over citizens of other states, thus limiting the state's power to people residing in a specific territory. The notion of state sovereignty is thus basically anti-imperialist. The equalizing and limiting functions of this doctrine appear most strikingly when contrasted with the National Socialists' racial imperialism (which rejected state sovereignty for racial supremacy) and with the doctrine of the sovereignty of the international proletariat, represented by the Third International.

Thus sovereignty in the modern period, though it formally appeared as the negation of the juristic concept of freedom, was in reality its very presupposition.[81]

Quite identical problems arise in connection with the property concept—a concept fundamental in every political theory. There is an almost universal agreement in political theory on the supreme significance of private property. But why is private property often raised to the rank of a natural right? Why should it be treated with such reverence, even in the work of the early Marx?[82]

It seems clear that it is conceived, throughout the history of social and political thought, as an instrument for the realization of the good (or at least the tenable) life. This is clearly Aristotle's position,[83] which is carried on in the whole medieval tradition.[84] It is equally the position of the more modern political thinkers—of Bodin, Spinoza, Hobbes, Kant and Hegel—whether they believe property to be a natural right or a grant by positive law. The instrumentalist character of property is probably the strongest link among these varied political theories. The connection of property and liberty is, of course, most candidly stated in Locke's theory, where liberty appears as inherent in the overall concept of property. But property is defined as labor-property, and possessory theories of property are thus rejected, the legitimation of the property resting in the transformation of external nature, particularly land, by the creative activity of man. It is precisely the labor theory of property which demonstrates its instrumentalist role and it is here a matter of indifference that Locke drew no consequences from his own theory, which he merely intended as a legitimation of capitalist property. But the recognition of the instrumentalist nature of property in regard to liberty makes it obviously necessary to redefine the social function of property in each historical stage, and thus to distinguish clearly between various types of property and of property-owners.[85] If property is to serve freedom, and if freedom pertains to man only, then corporate property, while it may or may not be necessary socially, cannot claim to be a civil

---

[81] Whether state sovereignty in domestic and international politics fulfills or can fulfill today the same function is of no concern in this study.

[82] Especially in Marx, "*Oekonomisch-Philosophische Manuskripte*" (1844) and "*Die heilige Familie*" in 3 *Marx-Engels Gesamtausgabe, Erste Abteilung* (1932).

[83] See Aristotle, *Oeconomica* *1343[a] (Foster transl. 1920); Aristotle, *Politics* *1253[b] (Barker transl. 1946) and *passim.*

[84] For a good survey see Jarrett, *Social Theories of the Middle Ages*, 1200–1500, 122–49 (1926).

[85] The very good survey, Schlatter, *Private Property: The History of an Idea* (1951), unfortunately fails in this. An interesting theory, little known and appreciated in the Anglo-American world, is that by the late Austrian President Karl Renner, first published in 1911 and translated as *The Institutes of Private Law and Their Social Functions* (Kahn-Freund transl. 1949).

right of the same rank as freedom of religion and communications. Similarly, the substrata of the property right – land, consumption goods, production goods – may require different treatment.

Most of the continental civil rights catalogues thus make a clear distinction between property and other civil rights, the protection of the latter being far more stringent that that of the former.[86] One very simple consideration will make clear the instrumentalist role of property: all constitutions permit the condemnation of private property with adequate compensation. Yet no civilized constitution could possibly permit the state to do away with a person's life or liberty for public purposes even with more than adequate compensation. The value of political freedom is absolute; that of property is merely relative to it. Thus the tasks of a political theory concerned with man's freedom are to analyze whether property fulfills its function as an efficient instrument of freedom, and to discover what institutional changes are necessary to maximize its effectiveness.[87]

[86] This was also Chief Justice Stone's position. See United States v. Carolene Products Co., 304 U.S. 144, 152 n.4 (1938); see also Schneider v. State, 308 U.S. 147, 161 (1939). Against this see particularly Justice Frankfurter in Board of Education v. Barnette, 319 U.S. 624, 646 (1943) (dissenting opinion).

[87] It is impossible to define within the system of democracy specific institutions which are potentially superior to other institutions, notwithstanding the old tradition that within the democratic system certain institutional arrangements make for the better protection of freedom: the doctrines of mixed government, of separation of powers, and of federalism.

As to mixed government, Aristotle as well as Polybius, both advocates of the doctrine, never understood by it a mere constitutional arrangement, that is, the mixing of monarchic, aristocratic and democratic elements. They correlated the constitutional distribution of power with the distribution of social power. Both had specific social goals in mind.

Montesquieu's doctrine of separate powers is equally correlated to the distribution of social power. Moreover if we look into political reality we cannot discern a coherent pattern. The English system of parliamentary democracy, which knows no doctrine of separate powers (except for the uncontested and uncontestable doctrine of judicial separateness and independence), maximizes political freedom; the continental parliamentary democracies have failed in this task; while the United States, with her presidential democracy, has maximized freedom – at least in the past. As Bentham recognized in his Montesquieu critique, the division of state functions into legislative, executive, and judicial and their allocation to three separate constitutional organs can protect freedom only if different social groups control the three agencies, the division losing its protective value if the three agencies are controlled by the same social group. See Neumann, *supra* note 5.

There exists as little correlation between political freedom and federalism. Montesquieu, probably following Plato's conception that the size of the *Polis* is determined by the reach of the Herald's voice, believed that democracies could function only in small territories. See Montesquieu, *Considerations on the Causes of the Grandeur and Decadence of the Romans* (Baker transl. 1882) and Neumann, *supra* note 5, at xliv. But since they may be threatened by external danger, confederation can give them external strength without jeopardizing the internal strength derived from their smallness. Montesquieu, *The Spirit of the Laws*, Bk. 9, ¶ 2 (1748). Jefferson followed this reasoning, adding to it his view that an agrarian society is the most stable substratum of democracy. See Jefferson, *Commonplace Book* (Chinard ed. 1926); but see Griswold, *Farming and Democracy* (1948). None of these propositions holds up to a critical analysis. There is no discernible relation between the size of a territory and political liberty, and none between federalism and democracy. England and France are centralistic democracies; the United States a federalist democracy; Imperial Germany and many Latin-American republics have or have had a federalism which served to strengthen authoritarian trends.

Such theories are expressive of what I call constitutional fetishism, the attribution of political functions to isolated constitutional arrangements which have meaning only in a total cultural, and particularly social, setting. In short, the socio-cultural bases of a system of political

To sum up: Insight into the operation of external nature permits man to master nature. Our enlarged knowledge of man's psyche permits us to understand the psychological processes activating the anxiety which deprives him of freedom and tends to make him a slave to authoritarian and totalitarian leaders. Our understanding of the historical situation permits us to adjust our institutional framework to the increased knowledge of nature and of man.

The Volitional Element in Freedom

The above formula indicates, however, that neither the juristic nor the cognitive element of freedom is really exhaustive. Law limits political power; knowledge shows us the way to freedom; but man can actually attain freedom only through his own efforts. Neither God nor history grants freedom to him. In this insight rests the theoretical formulation of democracy as that political system which permits the maximization of political freedom. The volitional or activist element is as indispensable to the constitition of political freedom as are the juristic and cognitive elements. We have said before that if political and juristic freedom are equated no case can be made for democracy as that political system where, supposedly, political freedom is best preserved, and that the constitutional monarchy might then be as good an institution − if not better.

Despite Aristotle's dislike of democracy, some kind of active participation in politics is to him the precondition for citizenship. This minimum he defines as a share in "the deliberative and judicial functions."[88] The freedom created by the *Polis*[89] can thus be attained solely through active participation in its politics − even if, for reasons of expediency, Plato and Aristotle deny full participation to the masses. In our terms, some kind of identification through action is necessary to prevent the total political alienation of the citizen.

This assumes, of course, a value judgment, namely the undesirability of political alienation. This is by no means shared in the history of political thought. The Epicurean school (Epicurus, Lucretius, Hobbes and many others) took the opposite point of view: the undesirability of political participation, thereby frankly admitting that political power, whatever its origin and form, is and will always remain a force hostile or alien to man, who should find his satisfaction not in a political system − which provides merely the outer frame of order − but rather outside it. Political Epicureanism may indeed be a necessary attitude in periods where two evil principles compete, and a third principle has no prospect of asserting itself.[90] The

---

freedom are far more important than the specific constitutional manifestations. This is today quite important because the various occupation powers in the Far East and Europe have tended to impose their specific political institutions upon the occupied countries because they attribute to bare constitutional arrangements political effects which they could not possibly exert.

The value of political democracy as a system preserving the rule of law, taking account of the increase of knowledge, and rationally changing society to keep up with knowledge, is not to be challenged; but within the system no specific institutions are, per se, more effective than others.

[88] Aristotle, *Politics* *1281[b] (Barker transl. 1946).

[89] I take it that the freedom of the *Polis* is, simultaneously, that of her citizens. See on this Foster, *The Political Philosophies of Plato and Hegel* (1935).

[90] See Max Radin's delightful study, *Epicurus My Master* (1949).

homo politicus may indeed then withdraw and cultivate his garden or his mind. As a rule, however, Epicurean attitudes will probably be expressions of either cowardice or indifference, playing directly into the hands of those bent on appropriating political power for their own ends. Whether or not one believes political power is alien to man, it determines his life to an ever increasing extent; thus the need for participation in its formation is imperative even for those who prefer the cultivation of individual contemplation.[91]

To stress merely the volitional aspect of freedom creates as dangerous a situation as does exclusive concentration on the juristic or the cognitive aspect. To define political freedom simply as individual will implies the negation of the obligations which we have toward our fellow man: one cannot assert one's will at the expense of another, nor attain one's own perfection by destroying another's. The protection of minorities and of dissenting opinions is ruled out if the activist element alone is deemed the equivalent of freedom. The juristic notion, therefore, cannot be dispensed with.

If we stress the supremacy of political action regardless of the historical situation within which the will must be realized, we arrive at a utopian putschism — the view that man can, in each historical stage, or rather regardless of the historical stage, realize his full freedom through his action. Bakunin, very strongly influenced by Fichte's philosophy,[92] espoused revolutionary action for its own sake; while Mussolini preached the virtue of a "heroic life" in contrast to the sordidness of bourgeois security.

Yet the element of political action by the individual is as indispensable as are the other two. Man can realize his political freedom only through his own action, by determining the aim and methods of political power. A monarch or a dictator may give him freedom — but he can as easily take it away. History may present magnificent opportunities for freedom, but they may be missed if one does not act or fails to act adequately.

Thus the democratic political system is the only one which institutionalizes the activist element of political freedom; it institutionalizes man's opportunity to realize his freedom and overcome the alienation of political power. All three elements of the notion of political freedom are given a chance in the democratic system. The rule of law (expressed in civil rights) prevents the destruction of minorities and the oppression of dissenting opinion; the mechanism of change (inherent in the democratic system) allows the political system to keep pace with the historical process; the need for self-reliance of the citizen gives the best insurance against his domination by anxiety. Political action obviously involves the possibility of a choice between approximately equal alternatives. Only with such alternatives can the choice — and hence the action — be free. It is this which, in turn, constitutes the connecting link between the volitional and juristic aspects of freedom. The citizen can choose between alternatives only if he can choose freely; that is, only if his personal and societal rights are protected.

The stability of the democratic system thus depends upon these three elements: the effective operation of the rule of law; the flexibility of its political machinery to cope with new problems; and the education of its citizens.

---

[91] The extent to which the volitional element is based on the corresponding philosophical trends (culminating in Fichte's philosophy) need not be discussed here.

[92] See Carr, *Michael Bakunin* (1937), particularly at 31–32.

The Present Crisis in Political Freedom

All three elements of political freedom are equally important and therefore none can be dispensed with. All three are in danger.

That none of them exists in totalitarian societies needs no comment here. In totalitarian states the individual-state relationship is reversed. There is no longer a presumption in favor of right and against coercion; rather there is a discretionary authorization of the agencies of the state to act as they see fit. Increased knowledge of man and nature is not used for the betterment of man's fate; rather, it assists in the manipulation of oppression. The active participation of the citizen in the formation of the national will is a sham. The basic elements of the structure of totalitarianism are so well known that nothing need be added here. Far more difficult, however, is the analysis of our system of democracy.

In the present period our attention is focussed on the juristic element of freedom – on the operation of the rule of law, particularly as it relates to personal freedom.

We have drawn attention to the fact that in the modern period the traditional sanctions of the criminal law are supplemented by socio-economic ones which may undermine the traditional guarantees. The problem appears in the so-called Loyalty Program and the Taft-Hartley Act.[93]

In the Loyalty Program[94] two problems naturally arise: the dismissal of civil servants suspected of disloyalty, and the refusal to appoint suspects. There can be no doubt, of course, that a government has the right, indeed the duty, to dismiss disloyal employees. The major problem is how far the rights of the employee are to be protected: how loyalty is to be defined and what procedures are to be adopted. Since no criminal charge is involved, it may be correct to say that the protective clauses in the Sixth Amendment do not apply; the dismissed employee does not, therefore, enjoy the guarantee of a fair trial, so that "without a trial by jury, without evidence, and without even being allowed to confront [his] accusers or to know their identity, a citizen of the United States" may be "found disloyal to the government of the United States."[95] This may well be law; one can argue that no "civil right" is involved and that the discretion of the executive agencies cannot be questioned. It may also be legally true that nobody has a right to a specific government position and that, therefore, executive discretion in the exercise of the government's hiring power cannot be challenged. Yet one of the political principles upon which democracy rests is that of equal access to all public offices. No doubt this principle permits the government to exclude disloyal persons from employment. But there remains the problem of protecting the rights of applicants against arbitrary action.

Similarly, it may also be legally accurate – as the Supreme Court maintains[96] – that trade unions which are private associations should have no access to the National Labor Relations Board if their officers fail to file the non-communist affidavit required by the Labor-Management Relations Act of 1947.[97]

---

[93] This brief discussion does not intend to analyze the legality of the measures but merely to hint at their political relevance.

[94] See Executive Order 9835, March 21, 1947, 12 *Fed. Reg.* 1935 (1947).

[95] Bailey v. Richardson, 182 F.2d 46, 66 (D.C. Cir. 1950) (Edgerton, J., dissenting).

[96] American Communications Ass'n v. Douds, 339 U.S. 382 (1950).

[97] See 61 STAT. 146 (1947), 29 U.S.C. S 159(h) (Supp. 1952).

Yet our analysis of the relation between the three types of civil rights — personal, societal, and political — attempted to show that even the justified denial of societal and political rights need not and should not lead to a restraint upon personal rights, which are not (or should not be) bound to changes in the economic, social or political structure. The requirement of a fair trial is the indispensable minimum of civil liberties.

That minimum is now increasingly denied by socio-economic sanctions which are probably not unconstitutional. From this it seems to follow that the juristic conception of liberty can no longer adequately perform its function. A few years ago one could indeed regard as adequate the classical interpretation of the personal rights as protecting the physical integrity of the individual from arbitrary action by the state. This is no longer possible today. Governmental sanctions against economic status are now of indefinitely greater importance. The size of government employment has grown tremendously, and if we add the private industries working for the government — where similar rules seem to apply — we must conclude that in many cases the application of economic sanctions means a sentence of economic death inflicted without a hearing.

Perhaps worse than the possibility of an economic death penalty are the psychological-social consequences of governmental action. Social ostracism may well be the result of firing — or refusing to hire — a person because of suspected disloyalty. In a period of growing political conformism the stigma attached to these governmental actions may transform the citizen and his family into outlaws, proscribed by his neighbors, shunned even by his friends.

It seems clear, therefore, that the traditional notion of juristic freedom can no longer cope with the new phenomena. Juristic freedom, indispensable though it is, guarantees merely a minimum. And this minimum, once covering a broad aspect of our freedom, although perhaps for a relatively small stratum of the people, is steadily shrinking.

Similar difficulties exist in the operation of such societal civil rights as the right of communication. The Supreme Court's decision in *Kovaks v. Cooper*,[98] the loudspeaker truck case, illustrates the problem. Justice Black, in his dissenting opinion, considered the loudspeaker van as the communication medium of the little man, permitting him to compete with highly organized ad concentrated media of communication. But even assuming that Justice Black's view had prevailed and the local ordinance had been voided, the free and equal use of societal rights would still not have been possible. The economic imbalance cannot thus be restored. The problem appears in various forms and has given rise to the formulation of a new type of civil right, the so-called "social rights" designed by various means — such as intervention of the state in behalf of the economically weak, as in various types of social security legislation, or recognition of mass organizations by the state, as in labor legislation — to restore a balance of social forces jeopardized either by the concentration of power on the one side or by awakening of political and social consciousness on the other. It is extremely doubtful whether it is wise to designate as civil rights positive demands upon the state — whether for social security, trade union recognition, or even planning. These and similar demands upon the state have their legitimation in their social utility, which must be concretely demonstrated. Personal, societal and political rights, by contrast, constitute the very essence of a

[98] 336 U.S. 77 (1949).

democratic political system and need no demonstration as to their social usefulness. But the psychological attraction of natural right doctrines, with their presentation of specific interests as natural ones, is such that the category "social rights" will probably soon find general acceptance. Whatever language we choose, however, the fact is that the exercise of civil (and political) rights requires a fair degree of equality in the control of and access to the media of communication.

These problems may not appear so depressing if one considers political power not as an alien power (as expressed in the formula citizen versus state) but as one's own – that is, if the volitional or activist element of freedom is recognized as being of equal importance with the two others. This may be expressed in the formula: no freedom without political activity. Yet it it clear – and this is the eternal contribution of individualist political thought – that no matter what the form of government, political power will always be to some degree alienated. The theories of Plato and Rousseau are thus utopias. Postulating complete identity between the citizen and the political system, they fail to take into account the fact that the conditions under which such identification can be achieved have never been realized in history. The two alternatives – the wisdom of Plato's philosopher-king, and the complete social and moral homogeneity of the Rousseauist society – are but dreams, though they be potent ones. The most exalted ruler is subject to passions; every society is charged with antagonisms. Even the most democratic system needs safeguards against the abuse of power. Yet in its tendency to minimize the alienation of political power democracy makes possible a fair balance between the interests of the individual and the *raison d'état.*

But there is equally no doubt that today the citizen's alienation from democratic political power is increasing – in Europe, at tremendous speed, more slowly, but still discernibly, in the United States. Psychologically, this fact is usually designated as apathy. The term is useful if one does not forget that three states of mind may thus be designated: the literal meaning, the "I-don't-care" attitude; the Epicurean approach, which holds that political life is not the area in which man can or should attempt to realize his potentialities; and the total rejection of the political system without a chance of effectively articulating an alternative. In varying degrees all three types of apathy play into the hands of demagogues, and all may lead to caesarism.

The last type, the most dangerous, is the result of the malfunctioning of the democratic state. Its symptoms and causes have often been analyzed: the growing complexity of government; the growth of bureaucracies in public and private life; the concentration of private social power; the hardening of political parties into machines which, because of the high cost of politics, tend to exclude newcomers from the political market.

These difficulties are enhanced by many of the remedies proposed. There is the assertion that democracy is "mass-participation in politics" and that the structure of a system of political representation makes a sham of participation. Some propose "occupational representation," a corporate system as a substitute for political democracy. But it need not be demonstrated here that corporate representation theories are mere fig leaves for dictatorships.

Others, more modest, want to transform "political" democracy into true "economic democracy" or the German trade union demand for "co-determination" in organization of the economy and the executive power. They overlook the fact that the theory of democracy is valid only for the organization of the state and its territorial subdivisions, never for any specific function. There is but one democracy, political democracy,[99] where alone the principles of equality can operate. Plans for "economic democracy" or the German trade union demand for "co-determination" in the economy may be useful, but they cannot be legitimized as democratic.

Still others, frightened by the growth of government bureaucracies, desire to democratize the administration. This is clearly desirable if to "democratize" means — as in post-1918 Germany — to eliminate undemocratic and anti-democratic elements from the bureaucracies. If it means, however, to reform the executive branch of the government by destroying the hierarchic principle or by letting "interest groups" participate in the making of administrative decisions, then such reforms not only have nothing to do with democracy but may even create new threats to it. The democratic principles of equality cannot operate in a bureaucratic structure, where the weight of a clerk must necessarily be less than that of an executive, and where responsibility has meaning only as that of an inferior to a superior. Demands for equality in bureaucracies and for responsibility downward within the bureaucratic structures tend to destroy an orderly administration.

Still more fateful is the second alternative: the participation of interested groups in the making of administrative decisions — what the Germans call functional, as against territorial, self-government. Labor administration is thus defined as democratic if the interested employer and labor groups have a voice in the decision-making process, so that the state, represented by a civil servant, appears as a kind of honest broker between opposing interest groups. This is a fairly widespread pattern of administration in Europe — but a dangerous one.[100] The danger to democracy of these and similar devices lies in the following.

The agreement of opposing interest groups on specific problems does not by the mere fact of their compromise necessarily coincide with the national interest. If such agreements are reached in fields where the government has no jurisdiction, this is, indeed, the best method of decision-making, for in such a case the government expresses by its hands-off policy the view that national interests are not necessarily involved. If the government has assumed jurisdiction, however, its reliance on agreement between interest groups and its withdrawal into the role of broker between the interests may amount to a dictate of these interests over the nation. In this recognition lies the great contribution of Rousseau: the *volonté générale* (the national interest) is not necessarily the result of a mechanical addition of particular wills. Indeed, such an addition may, if raised to a political status, pervert the general interest of the community. If, therefore, a nation has decided that a social activity needs governmental regulation, full responsibility should rest upon the government (the executive branch) as the decision-making body, and responsibility should not be shifted to interest groups by incorporating them into the administrative machinery.

The incorporation of interest groups into the administrative system may actually have the effect of weakening what some call mass-participation but what is better designated as spontaneous responsiveness to political decisions. For when the interest groups become semi-public bodies, part and parcel of the state machine, their independence lost, spontaneous responsiveness to policy decisions is

---

[99] See also MacIver, *The Web of Government* (1947).

[100] On the dangers in Germany between 1919–1933 see my *Behemoth: The Structure and Practice of National Socialism* 400–13 (1949).

weakened. The social organization turns into bureaucratic, semi-state structures, incapable of acting as critics of the state.

Thus the essence of the democratic political system does not lie in mass participation in political decisions, but in the making of politically responsible decisions. The sole criterion of the democratic character of an administration lies in the full political responsibility of the administrative chief, not to special interests, but to the electorate as a whole. The model of a democracy is not Rousseau's construct of an identity of rulers and ruled, but representation of an electorate by responsible representatives. Representation is not agency; the representative is not an agent, acting on behalf of another's rights and interests, but one who acts in his own right although in another's (the national) interest. Political action in a democracy is the free election of representatives and the preservation of spontaneous responsiveness to the decisions of the representatives. This, in turn, requires that social bodies such as political parties and trade unions remain free of the state, open, and subject to rank and file pressure; and that the electorate, if faced with serious problems, be capable of spontaneously organizing itself for their solution.

These are simple considerations — but they seem to be largely forgotten. Many of the suggested remedies against bureaucratic absolutism seem actually to strengthen anti-democratic tendencies. In short, only with a specific context is the growth of governmental bureaucratic structure a threat to democracy.

A further and deeper threat arises from the growing antagonism between the potentialities of our historical situation and their actual utilization. Technological progress (the *conditio sine qua non* of cultural progress) is used today largely for armaments. No threat to the political system of democracy can arise if the fruits of advancing technology are diverted from normal use for a relatively short period. But our historical experience tends to show that a long-range postponement of expectations is possible only in a wholly repressive system. It is difficult to be exact in determining either the time span or the intensity of the conflict between the potential and the actual. But the principle must be clearly seen; democracy is not simply a political system like any other; its essence consists in the execution of large-scale social changes maximizing the freedom of man.

Only in this way can democracy be integrated; its integrating element is a moral one, whether it be freedom or justice. This moral legitimation is perhaps most eloquently expressed in the Prometheus myth which Protagoras expounds to Socrates:[101] "After a while the desire of self-preservation gathered them into cities; but when they were gathered together, having no art of government, they evil entreated one another and were again in process of dispersion and destruction. Zeus feared that the entire race would be exterminated, and so he sent Hermes to them, bearing reverence and justice to be the ordering principles of cities and the bonds of friendship and conciliation. Hermes asked Zeus how he should impart justice and reverence among man: Should he distribute them as the arts are distributed; that is to say, to a favored few only. . . . 'To all,' said Zeus, 'I should like them all to have a share; for cities cannot exist, if only a few share the virtues. . . .' "

But there is opposed to this a second integrating principle of a political system: fear of an enemy. Fascist political thought[102] asserts that the creation of a national

[101] Plato, "Protagoras" in *Dialogues* *322 (Jowett transl. 1871).
[102] See Schmitt, *Der Begriff des Politischen* (2d ed. 1932).

community is conditioned by the existence of an enemy whom one must be willing to exterminate physically. Politics thus denotes not the construction of a good society but the annihilation of an enemy. Anything – religion, art, race, class antagonisms – may be or may become political.

If the concept "enemy" and "fear" do constitute the "energetic principles"[103] of politics, a democratic political system is impossible, whether the fear is produced from within or from without. Montesquieu correctly observed that fear is what makes and sustains dictatorships. If freedom is absence of restraints, the restraints to be removed today are many; the psychological restraint of fear ranks first.

It is the existence and manipulation of fear that transforms a people into a mob. The anti-democratic theories of de Maistre, Bonald, Donoso Cortès, Spengler and a host of others assert that democracy must, by its inner logic, degenerate into mob rule. Such necessity is a myth, very often promoted by those who wish to demonstrate the superiority of dictatorship. But the transformation from democracy into dictatorship seems to arise when the political system discards its liberal element and attempts to impose a creed upon its members, ostracizing those who do not accept it. This will be successful if, in John Dewey's words, we attain the "stage of development in which a vague and mysterious feeling of uncertain terror seizes the populace."[104]

[103] See Jefferson, *Commonplace Book* 259 (Chinard ed. 1926).
[104] 2 Dewey, *Character and Events* 819 (1929).

16. Negative and Positive Freedom

Gerald C. MacCallum, Jr.

This paper challenges the view that we may usefully distinguish between two kinds or concepts of political and social freedom – negative and positive. The argument is not that one of these is the only, the "truest," or the "most worthwhile" freedom, but rather that the distinction between them has never been made sufficiently clear, is based in part upon a serious confusion, and has drawn attention away from precisely what needs examining if the differences separating philosophers, ideologies, and social movements concerned with freedom are to be understood. The corrective advised is to regard freedom as always one and the same triadic relation, but recognize that various contending parties disagree with each other in what they understand to be the ranges of the term variables. To view the matter in this way is to release oneself from a prevalent but unrewarding concentration on "kinds" of freedom, and to turn attention toward the truly important issues in this area of social and political philosophy.

From *The Philosophical Review*, Vol. 76 (1967), pp. 312–334, by permission of the author and publisher.

I

Controversies generated by appeals to the presence or absence of freedom in societies have been roughly of four closely related kinds — namely (1) about the nature of freedom itself, (2) about the relationships holding between the attainment of freedom and the attainment of other possible social benefits, (3) about the ranking of freedom among such benefits, and (4) about the consequences of this or that policy with respect to realizing or attaining freedom. Disputes of one kind have turned readily into disputes of the other kinds.

Of those who agree that freedom is a benefit, most would also agree that it is not the *only* benefit a society may secure its members. Other benefits might include, for example, economic and military security, technological efficiency, and exemplifications of various aesthetic and spiritual values. Once this is admitted, however, disputes of types (2) and (3) are possible. Questions can be raised as to the logical and causal relationships holding between the attainment of freedom and the attainment of these other benefits, and as to whether one could on some occasions reasonably prefer to cultivate or emphasize certain of the latter at the expense of the former. Thus, one may be led to ask: *can* anyone cultivate and emphasize freedom at the cost of realizing these other goals and values (or vice versa) and, secondly, *should* anyone ever do this? In practice, these issues are often masked by or confused with disputes about the consequences of this or that action with respect to realizing the various goals or values.

Further, any of the above disputes may stem from or turn into a dispute about what freedom *is*. The borderlines have never been easy to keep clear. But a reason for this especially worth noting at the start is that disputes about the nature of freedom are certainly historically best understood as a series of attempts by parties opposing each other on very many issues to capture for their own side the favorable attitudes attaching to the notion of freedom. It has commonly been advantageous for partisans to link the presence or absence of freedom as closely as possible to the presence or absence of those other social benefits believed to be secured or denied by the forms of social organization advocated or condemned. Each social benefit is, accordingly, treated as either a result of or a contribution to freedom, and each liability is connected somehow to the absence of freedom. This history of the matter goes far to explain how freedom came to be identified with so many different kinds of social and individual benefits, and why the status of freedom as simply one among a number of social benefits has remained unclear. The resulting flexibility of the notion of freedom, and the resulting enhancement of the value of freedom, have suited the purposes of the polemicist.

It is against this background that one should first see the issues surrounding the distinction between positive and negative freedom as two fundamentally different kinds of freedom. Nevertheless, the difficulties surrounding the distinction should not be attributed solely to the interplay of Machiavellian motives. The disputes, and indeed the distinction itself, have also been influenced by a genuine confusion concerning the concept of freedom. The confusion results from failure to understand fully the conditions under which use of the concept of freedom is intelligible.

II

Whenever the freedom of some agent or agents is in question, it is always freedom from some constraint or restriction on, interference with, or barrier to doing, not doing, becoming, or not becoming something.[1] such freedom is thus always *of* something (an agent or agents), *from* something, *to* do, not do, become, or not become something; it is a triadic relation. Taking the format "x is (is not) free from y to do (not do, become, not become) z," x ranges over agents, y ranges over such "preventing conditions" as constraints, restrictions, interferences, and barriers, and z ranges over actions or conditions of character or circumstance. When reference to one of these three terms is missing in such a discussion of freedom, it should be only because the reference is thought to be understood from the context of the discussion.[2]

Admittedly, the idioms of freedom are such that this is sometimes not obvious. The claim, however, is not about what we say, but rather about the conditions under which what we say is intelligible. And, of course, it is important to notice that the claim is only about what makes talk concerning the freedom of agents intelligible. This restriction excludes from consideration, for example, some uses of "free of" and "free from" — namely, those not concerned with the freedom of agents, and where, consequently, what is meant may be only "rid of" or "without." Thus, consideration of "The sky is now free of clouds" is excluded because this expression does not deal with agents at all; but consideration of "His record is free of blemish" and "She is free from any vice" is most probably also excluded. Doubt about these latter two hinges on whether these expressions might be thought claims about the freedom of agents; if so, then they are not excluded, but neither are they intelligible *as* claims about the freedom of agents until one is in a position to fill in the elements of the format offered above; if not, then although probably parasitic upon talk about the freedom of agents and thus perhaps viewable as figurative anyway, they fall outside the scope of this investigation.

The claim that freedom, subject to the restriction noted above, is a triadic relation can hardly be substantiated here by exhaustive examination of the idioms of freedom. But the most obviously troublesome cases — namely, those in which one's understanding of the context must in a relevant way carry past the limits of what is explicit in the idiom — may be classified roughly and illustrated as follows:

a. Cases where agents are not mentioned: for example, consider any of the wide range of expressions having the form "free x" in which (*i*) the place of x is taken by an expression not clearly referring to an agent — as in "free society" or "free will" — or (*ii*) the place of x is taken by an expression clearly not referring to an agent — as in "free beer." All such cases can be understood to be concerned with the freedom of agents and, indeed, their intelligibility rests upon their being so understood; they are thus subject to the claims made above. This is fairly obvious in

[1] The need to elaborate in this unwieldy way arises from the absence in this paper of any discussion of the verification conditions for claims about freedom. The elaboration is designed to leave open the issues one would want to raise in such a discussion.

[2] Of writers on political and social freedom who have approached this view, the clearest case is Felix Oppenheim in *Dimensions in Freedom* (New York, 1961); but, while viewing social freedom as a triadic relation, he limits the ranges of the term variables so sharply as to cut one off from many issues I wish to reach. Cf. also T. D. Weldon, *The Vocabulary of Politics* (Harmondsworth, 1953), esp. pp. 157 ff.; but see also pp. 70–72.

the cases of "free will" and "free society." The intelligibility of the free-will problem is generally and correctly thought to rest at least upon the problem's being concerned with the freedom of persons, even though the criteria for identification of the persons or "selves" whose freedom is in question have not often been made sufficiently clear.[3] And it is beyond question that the expression "free society," although of course subject to various conflicting analyses with respect to the identity of the agent(s) whose freedom is involved, is thought intelligible only because it is thought to concern the freedom of agents of some sort or other. The expression "free beer," on the other hand (to take only one of a rich class of cases some of which would have to be managed differently), is ordinarily thought intelligible because thought to refer to beer that *people* are free *from* the ordinary restrictions of the market place *to* drink without paying for it.

For an expression of another grammatical form, consider "The property is free of (or from) encumbrance." Although this involves a loose use of "property," suppose that the term refers to something like a piece of land; the claim then clearly means that *owners* of that land are free *from* certain well-known restrictions (for example, certain types of charges or liabilities consequent upon their ownership of the land) *to* use, enjoy, dispose of the land as they wish.

b. Cases where it is not clear what corresponds to the second term: for example, "freedom of choice," "freedom to choose as I please." Here, the range of constraints, restrictions, and so forth, is generally clear from the context of the discussion. In political matters, legal constraints or restrictions are most often thought of; but one also sometimes finds, as in Mill's *On Liberty,* concern for constraints and interferences constituted by social pressures. It is sometimes difficult for persons to see social pressures as constraints or interferences; this will be discussed below. It is also notoriously difficult to see causal nexuses as implying constraints or restrictions on the "will" (the person?) in connection with the free-will problem. But the very fact that such difficulties are the focus of so much attention is witness to the importance of getting clear about this term of the relation before such discussions of freedom can be said to be intelligible.

One might think that references to a second term of this sort could always be eliminated by a device such as the following. Instead of saying, for example, (*i*) "Smith is free *from* legal restrictions on travel *to* leave the country," one could say (*ii*) "Smith is free *to* leave the country *because* there are no legal restrictions on his leaving." The latter would make freedom appear to be a dyadic, rather than a triadic, relation. But we would be best advised to regard the appearance illusory, and this may be seen if one thinks a bit about the suggestion or implication of the sentence that nothing hinders or prevents Smith from leaving the country. Difficulties about this might be settled by attaching a qualifier to "free" — namely, "*legally* free." Alternatively, one could consider which, of all the things that might still hinder or prevent Smith from leaving the country (for example, has he promised someone to remain? will the responsibilities of his job keep him here? has he enough money to buy passage and, if not, why not?), could count as limitations on his freedom to leave the country; one would then be in a position to determine whether the claim had been misleading or false. In either case, however, the devices adopted would reveal that our understanding of what has been said hinged upon

---

[3] Indeed, lack of clarity on just this point is probably one of the major sources of confusion in discussions of free will.

our understanding of the range of obstacles or constraints from which Smith had been claimed to be free.

c. Cases where it is not clear what corresponds to the third term: for example, "freedom from hunger" ("want," "fear," "disease," and so forth). One quick but not very satisfactory way of dealing with such expressions is to regard them as figurative, or at least not really concerned with anybody's freedom; thus, being free from hunger would be simply being rid of, or without, hunger — as a sky may be free of clouds (compare the discussion of this above). Alternatively, one might incline toward regarding hunger as a barrier of some sort, and claim that a person free *from* hunger is free *to* be well fed or to do or do well the various things he could not do or do well if hungry. Yet again, and more satisfactorily, one could turn to the context of the initial bit of Rooseveltian rhetoric and there find reason to treat the expression as follows. Suppose that hunger is a feeling and that someone *seeks* hunger; he is on a diet and the hunger feeling reassures him that he is losing weight.[4] Alternatively, suppose that hunger is a bodily condition and that someone seeks it; he is on a Gandhi-style hunger strike. In either case, Roosevelt or his fellow orators might have wanted a world in which these people were free from hunger; but this surely does not mean that they wanted a world in which people were not hungry despite a wish to be so. They wanted, rather, a world in which people were not victims of hunger they did not seek; that is, they wanted a world without barriers keeping people hungry despite efforts to avoid hunger — a world in which people would be free *from* barriers constituted by various specifiable agricultural, economic, and political conditions *to* get enough food to prevent hunger. This view of "freedom from hunger" not only makes perfectly good and historically accurate sense out of the expression, but also conforms to the view that freedom is a triadic relation.

In other politically important idioms the *range* of the third term is not always utterly clear. For example, does freedom of religion include freedom *not* to worship? Does freedom of speech include *all* speech no matter what its content, manner of delivery, or the circumstances of its delivery? Such matters, however, raise largely historical questions or questions to be settled by political decision; they do not throw doubt on the need for a third term.

That the intelligibility of talk concerned with the freedom of agents rests in the end upon an understanding of freedom as a triadic relation is what many persons distinguishing between positive and negative freedom apparently fail to see or see clearly enough. Evidence of such failure or, alternatively, invitation to it is found in the simple but conventional characterization of the difference between the two kinds of freedom as the difference between "freedom from" and "freedom to" — a characterization suggesting that freedom could be either of two dyadic relations. This characterization, however, cannot distinguish two genuinely different kinds of freedom; it can serve only to emphasize one or the other of two features of *every* case of the freedom of agents. Consequently, anyone who argues that freedom *from* is the "only" freedom, or that freedom *to* is the "truest" freedom, or that one is "more important than" the other, cannot be taken as having said anything both straightforward and sensible about two distinct kinds of freedom. He can, at most, be said to be attending to, or emphasizing the importance of only one part of what is always present in any case of freedom.

---

[4] I owe this example to Professor James Pratt.

Unfortunately, even if this basis of distinction between positive and negative freedom as two distinct kinds or concepts of freedom is shown to collapse, one has not gone very far in understanding the issues separating those philosophers or ideologies commonly said to utilize one or the other of them. One has, however, dissipated one of the main confusions blocking understanding of these issues. In recognizing that freedom is always *both* freedom from something and freedom to do or become something, one is provided with a means of making sense out of interminable and poorly defined controversies concerning, for example, when a person really is free, why freedom is important, and on what its importance depends. As these, in turn, are matters on which the distinction between positive and negative freedom has turned, one is given also a means of managing sensibly the writings appearing to accept or to be based upon that distinction.

III

The key to understanding lies in recognition of precisely how differing styles of answer to the question "When are persons free?" could survive agreement that freedom is a triadic relation. The differences would be rooted in differing views on the ranges of the term variables — that is, on the ("true") identities of the agents whose freedom is in question, on what counts as an obstacle to or interference with the freedom of such agents, or on the range of what such agents might or might not be free to do or become.[5] Although perhaps not always obvious or dramatic, such differences could lead to vastly different accounts of when persons are free. Furthermore, differences on one of these matters might or might not be accompanied by differences on either of the others. There is thus a rich stock of ways in which such accounts might diverge, and a rich stock of possible foci of argument.

It is therefore crucial, when dealing with accounts of when persons are free, to insist on getting *quite* clear on what each writer considers to be the ranges of these term variables. Such insistence will reveal where the differences between writers are, and will provide a starting point for rewarding consideration of what might justify these differences.

The distinction between positive and negative freedom has, however, stood in the way of this approach. It has encouraged us to see differences in accounts of freedom as resulting from differences in concepts of freedom. This in turn has encouraged the wrong sorts of questions. We have been tempted to ask such questions as "Well, who *is* right? Whose concept of freedom *is* the correct one?" or "Which *kind* of freedom do we really want after all?" Such questions will not help reveal the fundamental issues separating major writers on freedom from each other, no matter *how* the writers are arranged into "camps." It would be far better to insist that the same concept of freedom is operating throughout, and that the differences, rather than being about what *freedom* is, are for example about what persons are, and about what can count as an obstacle to or interference with the freedom of persons so conceived.

---

[5] They might also be rooted in differing views on the verification conditions for claims about freedom. This issue would be important to discuss in a full-scale treatment of freedom but, as already mentioned, it is not discussed in this paper. It plays, at most, an easily eliminable role in the distinction between negative and positive freedom.

The appropriateness of this insistence is easily seen when one examines prevailing characterizations of the differences between "positive" and "negative" freedom. Once the alleged difference between "freedom from" and "freedom to" has been disallowed (as it must be; see above), the most persuasive of the remaining characterizations appear to be as follows: [6]

1. Writers adhering to the concept of "negative" freedom hold that only the *presence* of something can render a person unfree; writers adhering to the concept of "positive" freedom hold that the *absence* of something may also render a person unfree.
2. The former hold that a person is free to do x just in case *nothing due to arrangements made by other persons* stops him from doing x; the latter adopt no such restriction.
3. The former hold that the agents whose freedom is in question (for example, "persons," "men") are, in effect, identifiable as Anglo-American law would identify "natural" (as opposed to "artificial") persons; the latter sometimes hold quite different views as to how these agents are to be identified (see below).

The most obvious thing to be said about these characterizations, of course, is that appeal to them provides at best an excessively crude justification of the conventional classification of writers into opposing camps.[7] When one presses on the alleged points of difference, they have a tendency to break down, or at least to become less dramatic than they at first seemed.[8] As should not be surprising, the patterns of agreement and disagreement on these several points are in fact either too diverse or too indistinct to support any clearly justifiable arrangement of major

---

[6] Yet other attempts at characterization have been offered — most recently and notably by Sir Isaiah Berlin in *Two Concepts of Liberty* (Oxford, 1958). Berlin also offers the second and (more or less) the third of the characterizations cited here.

[7] A fair picture of that classification is provided by Berlin (*op. cit.*) who cites and quotes from various writers in such a way as to suggest that they are in one camp or the other. Identified in this manner as adherents of "negative" freedom, one finds Occam, Erasmus, Hobbes, Locke, Bentham, Constant, J. S. Mill, Tocqueville, Jefferson, Burke, Paine. Among adherents of "positive" freedom one finds Plato, Epictetus, St. Ambrose, Montesquieu, Spinoza, Kant, Herder, Rousseau, Hegel, Fichte, Marx, Bukharin, Comte, Carlyle, T. H. Green, Bradley, Bosanquet.

[8] For example, consider No. 1. Perhaps there is something to it, but the following cautionary remarks should be made. (*a*) The so-called adherents of "negative" freedom might very well accept the *absence* of something as an obstacle to freedom. Consider a man who is not free because, although unguarded, he has been locked in chains. Is he unfree because of the *presence* of the locked chains, or is he unfree because he *lacks* a key? Are adherents of "negative" freedom prohibited from giving the latter answer? (*b*) Even purported adherents of "positive" freedom are not always straightforward in their acceptance of the lack of something as an obstacle to freedom. They sometimes swing toward attributing the absence of freedom to the presence of certain conditions causally connected with the lack, absence, or deprivation mentioned initially. For example, it may be said that a person who was unable to qualify for a position owing to lack of training (and thus not free to accept or "have" it) was prevented from accepting the position by a social, political, economic, or educational "system" the workings of which resulted in his being bereft of training.

Also, in so far as this swing is made, our view of the difference mentioned in No. 2 may become fuzzy; for adherents of "positive" freedom might be thought at bottom to regard those "preventing conditions" counting as infringements of freedom as most often if not always circumstances due to human arrangements. This might be true even when, as we shall see is sometimes the case, the focus is on the role of "irrational passions and appetites." The presence or undisciplined character of these may be treated as resulting from the operation of certain

writers into two camps. The trouble is not merely that some writers do not fit too well where they have been placed; it is rather that writers who are purportedly the very models of membership in one camp or the other (for example, Locke, the Marxists) do not fit very well where they have been placed[9] — thus suggesting that the whole system of dichotomous classification is futile and, even worse, conducive to distortion of important views on freedom.

But, even supposing that there were something to the classification and to the justification for it in terms of the above three points of difference, what then? The differences are of two kinds. They concern (a) the ("true") identities of the agents whose freedom is in question, and (b) what is to count as an "obstacle" or "barrier" to, "restriction" on, or "interference" with the freedom of such agents. They are thus clearly about the ranges of two of the three term variables mentioned earlier. It would be a mistake to see them in any other way. We are likely to make this mistake, however, and obscure the path of rewarding argument, if we present them as differences concerning what "freedom" means.

Consider the following. Suppose that we have been raised in the so-called "libertarian" tradition (roughly characterized as that of "negative" freedom). There would be nothing unusual to us, and perhaps even nothing troubling, in conventional accounts of what the adherent of negative freedom treats as the ranges of these variables.

1. He is purported to count persons just as we do — to point to living human bodies and say of each (and only of each), "There's a person." Precisely what we ordinarily call persons. (And if he is troubled by nonviable fetuses, and so forth, so are we.)

2. He is purported to mean much what we mean by "obstacle," and so forth, though this changes with changes in our views of what can be attributed to arrangements made by human beings, and also with variations in the importance we attach to consenting to rules, practices, and so forth.[10]

3. He is purported to have quite "ordinary" views on what a person may or may not be free to do or become. The actions are sometimes suggested in fairly specific terms — for example, free to have a home, raise a family, "rise to the top." But, on the whole, he is purported to talk of persons being free or not free "to do what

---

specifiable social, educational, or moral institutions or arrangements. (Berlin, e.g., seems to acknowledge this with respect to the Marxists. See Berlin, *op. cit.*, p. 8, n. 1, and the text at this point.) Thus one might in the end be able to say no more than this: that the adherents of "negative" freedom are on the whole more inclined to require that the *intention* of the arrangements in question have been to coerce, compel, or deprive persons of this or that. The difference here, however, is not very striking.

[9] Locke said: "liberty . . . is the power a man has to do or forbear doing any particular action according . . . as he himself wills it" (*Essay Concerning Human Understanding*, Bk. 11, ch. xxi, sec. 15). He also said, of law, "that ill deserves the name of confinement which hedges us in only from bogs and precipices," and "the end of law is, not to abolish or restrain, but to preserve and enlarge freedom" (*Second Treatise of Government*, sec. 57). He also sometimes spoke of a man's consent as though it were the same as the consent of the majority.

Why doesn't all this put him in the camp of "positive" freedom vis-à-vis at least points (2) and (3) above? Concerning the Marxists, see n. 8, *supra*.

[10] The point of "consent theories" of political obligation sometimes seems to be to hide from ourselves the fact that a rule of unanimity is an unworkable basis for a system of government and that government does involve coercion. We seem, however, not really to have made up our minds about this.

they want" or (perhaps) "to express themselves."[11] Furthermore, the criteria for determining what a person wants to do are those we customarily use, or perhaps even the most naïve and unsophisticated of them − for example, what a person wants to do is determined by what he *says* he wants to do, or by what he manifestly *tries* to do, or even *does* do.[12]

In contrast, much might trouble us in the accounts of the so-called adherents of "positive" freedom.

1. They sometimes do not count, as the agent whose freedom is being considered, what inheritors of our tradition would unhesitatingly consider to be a "person." Instead, they occasionally engage in what has been revealingly but pejoratively called "the retreat to the inner citadel";[13] the agent in whose freedom they are interested is identified as the "real" or the "rational" or the "moral" person who is somehow sometimes hidden within, or has his seed contained within, the living human body. Sometimes, however, rather than a retreat to such an "inner citadel," or sometimes in addition to such a retreat, there is an expansion of the limits of "person" such that the institutions and members, the histories and futures of the communities in which the living human body is found are considered to be inextricable parts of the "person."

These expansions or contractions of the criteria for identification of persons may seem unwarranted to us. Whether they are so, however, depends upon the strength of the arguments offered in support of the helpfulness of regarding persons in these ways while discussing freedom. For example, the retreat to the "inner citadel" may be initiated simply by worries about which, of all the things we want, will give us lasting satisfaction − a view of our interests making it possible to see the surge of impulse or passion as an obstacle to the attainment of what we "really want." And the expansion of the limits of the "self" to include our families, cultures, nations, or races may be launched by awareness that our "self" is to some extent the product of these associations; by awareness that our identification of our interests may be influenced by our beliefs concerning ways in which our destinies are tied to the destinies of our families, nations, and so forth; by the way we see tugs and stresses upon those associations as tugs and stresses upon us; and by the ways we see ourselves and *identify* ourselves as officeholders in such associations with the rights and obligations of such offices. This expansion, in turn, makes it possible for us to see the infringement of the autonomy of our associations as infringement on our freedom.

Assessing the strengths of the various positions taken on these matters requires a painstaking investigation and evaluation of the arguments offered − something that can hardly be launched within the confines of this paper. But what should be observed is that this set of seemingly radical departures by adherents of positive freedom from the ways "we" ordinarily identify persons does not provide us with

---

[11] These last ways of putting it are appreciably different. When a person who would otherwise count as a libertarian speaks of persons as free or not free to express themselves, his position as a libertarian may muddy a bit. One may feel invited to wonder which of the multitudinous wants of a given individual *are* expressive of his nature − that is, which are such that their fulfillment is conducive to the expression of his "self."

[12] The possibility of conflicts among these criteria has not been much considered by so-called libertarians.

[13] See Berlin, *op. cit.*, pp. 17 ff. (though Berlin significantly admits also that this move can be made by adherents of negative freedom; see p. 19).

any reason whatever to claim that a different concept of *freedom* is involved (one might as well say that the shift from "The apple is to the left of the orange" to "The seeds of the apple are to the left of the seeds of the orange" changes what "to the left of" means). Furthermore, that claim would draw attention away from precisely what we should focus on; it would lead us to focus on the wrong concept – namely, "freedom" instead of "person." Only by insisting at least provisionally that all the writers have the same concept of freedom can one see clearly and keep sharply focused the obvious and extremely important differences among them concerning the concept of "person."

2. Similarly, adherents of so-called "positive" freedom purportedly differ from "us" on what counts as an obstacle. Will *this* difference be revealed adequately if we focus on supposed differences in the concept of "freedom"? Not likely. Given differences on what a person is, differences in what counts as an obstacle or interference are not surprising, of course, since what could count as an obstacle to the activity of a person identified in one way might not possibly count as an obstacle to persons identifed in other ways. But the differences concerning "obstacle" and so forth are probably not due solely to differences concerning "person." If, for example, we so-called adherents of negative freedom, in order to count something as a preventing condition, ordinarily require that it can be shown a result of arrangements made by human beings, and our "opponents" do not require this, why not? On the whole, perhaps, the latter are saying this: if one is concerned with social, political, and economic policies, and with how these policies can remove or increase human misery, it is quite irrelevant whether difficulties in the way of the policies are or are not *due to* arrangements made by human beings. The only question is whether the difficulties can be removed by human arrangements, and at what cost. This view, seen as an attack upon the "artificiality" of a borderline for distinguishing human freedom from other human values, does not seem inherently unreasonable; a close look at the positions and arguments seems called for.[14] But again, the issues and arguments will be misfocused if we fail to see them as about the range of a term variable of a single triadic relation (freedom). Admittedly, we *could* see some aspects of the matter (those where the differences do not follow merely from differences in what is thought to be the agent whose

[14] The libertarian position concerning the borderline is well expressed by Berlin in the following passage on the struggle of colonial peoples: "Is the struggle for higher status, the wish to escape from an inferior position, to be called a struggle for liberty? Is it mere pedantry to confine this word to the main ('negative') senses discussed above, or are we, as I suspect, in danger of calling any adjustment of his social situation favored by a human being an increase of his liberty, and will this not render this term so vague and distended as to make it virtually useless" (*op. cit.*, p. 44)? One may surely agree with Berlin that there may be something of a threat here; but one may also agree with him when, in the passage immediately following, he inclines to give back what he has just taken away: "And yet we cannot simply dismiss this case as a mere confusion of the notion of freedom with those of status, or solidarity, or fraternity, or equality, or some combination of these. For the craving for status is, in certain respects very close to the desire to be an independent agent." What first needs explaining, of course, is why colonial peoples might believe themselves freer under the rule of local tyrants than under the rule of (possibly) benevolent colonial administrations. Berlin tends to dismiss this as a simple confusion of a desire for freedom with a hankering after status and recognition. What need more careful evaluation than he gives them are (*a*) the strength of reasons for regarding rule by one's racial and religious peers as self-rule and (*b*) the strength of claims about freedom based on the consequences of consent or authorization for one's capacity to speak of "self-rule" (cf. Hobbes's famous ch. xvi in *Leviathan*, "Of Persons and Things Personated"). Cf. n. 10, *supra*.

freedom is in question) as amounting to disagreements about what is meant by "freedom." But there is no decisive reason for doing so, and this move surely threatens to obscure the socially and politically significant issues raised by the argument suggested above.

3. Concerning treatment of the third term by purported adherents of positive freedom, perhaps enough has already been said to suggest that they tend to emphasize conditions of character rather than actions, and to suggest that, as with "us" too, the range of character conditions and actions focused on may influence or be influenced by what is thought to count as agent and by what is thought to count as preventing condition. Thus, though something more definite would have to be said about the matter eventually, at least some contact with the issues previously raised might be expected in arguments about the range of this variable.

It is important to observe here and throughout, however, that close agreement between two writers in their understanding of the range of one of the variables does not make *inevitable* like agreement on the ranges of the others. Indeed, we have gone far enough to see that the kinds of issues arising in determination of the ranges are sufficiently diverse to make such simple correlations unlikely. Precisely this renders attempts to arrange writers on freedom into two opposing camps so distorted and ultimately futile. There is too rich a stock of ways in which accounts of freedom diverge.

If we are to manage these divergences sensibly, we must focus our attention on each of these variables and on differences in views as to their ranges. Until we do this, we will not see clearly the issues which have in fact been raised, and thus will not see clearly what needs arguing. In view of this need, it is both clumsy and misleading to try to sort out writers as adherents of this or that "kind" or "concept" of freedom. We would be far better off to insist that they all have the same concept of freedom (as a triadic relation) — thus putting ourselves in a position to notice how, and inquire fruitfully into why, they identify differently what can serve as agent, preventing condition, and action or state of character vis-à-vis issues of freedom.

IV

If the importance of this approach to discussion of freedom has been generally overlooked, it is because social and political philosophers have, with dreary regularity, made the mistake of trying to answer the unadorned question, "When are men free?" or, alternatively, "When are men *really* free?" These questions *invite* confusion and misunderstanding, largely because of their tacit presumption that persons can be free or not free *simpliciter*.

One might suppose that, strictly speaking, a person could be free *simpliciter* only if there were no interference from which he was not free, and nothing that he was not free to do or become. On this view, however, and on acceptance of common views as to what counts as a person, what counts as interference, and what actions or conditions of character may meaningfully be said to be free or not free, all disputes concerning whether or not men in societies are ever free would be inane. Concerning such settings, where the use and threat of coercion are distinctively present, there would *always* by an air of fraud or hocus-pocus about claims that men are free — just like that.

Yet one might hold that men can be free (*simpliciter*) even in society because certain things which ordinarily are counted as interferences or barriers are not actually so, or because certain kinds of behavior ordinarily thought to be either free or unfree do not, for some reason, "count." Thus one might argue that at least in certain (conceivable) societies there is no activity in which men in that society are not free to engage, and no possible restriction or barrier from which they are not free.

The burden of such an argument should now be clear. Everything *from* which a person in that society might ordinarily be considered unfree must be shown not actually an interference or barrier (or not a relevant one), and everything which a person in that society might ordinarily be considered not free to *do* or *become* must be shown irrelevant to the issue of freedom. (Part of the argument in either or both cases might be that the "true" identity of the person in question is not what it has been thought to be.)

Pitfalls may remain for attempts to evaluate such arguments. For example, one may uncover tendencies to telescope questions concerning the *legitimacy* of interference into questions concerning genuineness *as* interference.[15] One may also find telescoping of questions concerning the *desirability* of certain modes of behavior or character states into questions concerning the *possibility* of being either free or not free to engage in those modes of behavior or become that kind of person.[16] Nevertheless, a demand for specification of the term variables helps pinpoint such problems, as well as forestalling the confusions obviously encouraged by failure to make the specifications.

Perhaps, however, the claim that certain men are free *simpliciter* is merely elliptical for the claim that they are free in every important respect, or in most important respects, or "on the whole." Nevertheless, the point still remains that when this ellipsis is filled in, the reasonableness of asking both "What are they free from?" and "What are they free to do or become?" becomes apparent. Only when one gets straightforward answers to these questions is he in any position to judge whether the men *are* free as claimed. Likewise, only then will he be in a position to judge the *value* or *importance* of the freedom(s) in question. It is important to know, for example, whether a man is free from legal restrictions to raise a family. But of course social or economic "arrangements" may be such that he still could not raise a family if he wanted to. Thus, merely to say that he is free to raise a family, when what is meant is only that he is free from legal restrictions to raise a family, is to invite misunderstanding. Further, the *range* of activities he may or may not be free from this or that to engage in, or the range of character states he may or may not be free to develop, should make a difference in our evaluations of his situation and of his society; but this too is not called for strongly enough when one asks simply, "Is the man free?" Only when we determine what the men in question are free from, and what they are free to do or become, will we be in a position to estimate the value for human happiness and fulfilment of being free from *that* (whatever *it* is), to do *the other thing* (whatever *it* is). Only then will we be in a position to make rational evaluations of the relative merits of societies with regard to freedom.

---

[15] Cf. nn. 10 and 14, *supra*.

[16] E.g., is it logically possible for a person to be free to do something immoral? Cf. Berlin, *op. cit.*, p. 10, n.

V

The above remarks can be tied again to the controversy concerning negative and positive freedom by considering the following argument by friends of "negative" freedom. Freedom is always and necessarily *from* restraint; thus, in so far as the adherents of positive freedom speak of persons being made free *by means of* restraint, they cannot be talking about freedom.

The issues raised by this argument (which is seldom stated more fully than here) can be revealed by investigating what might be done to make good sense out of the claim that, for example, Smith is (or can be) made free by restraining (constraining, coercing) him.[17] Use of the format of specifications recommended above reveals two major possibilities:

1. Restraining Smith by means *a* from doing *b* produces a situation in which he is now able to do *c* because restraint *d* is lifted. He is thereby, by means of restraint *a,* made free from *d* to do *c,* although he can no longer do *b.* For example, suppose that Smith, who always walks to where he needs to go, lives in a tiny town where there have been no pedestrian crosswalks and where automobiles have had right of way over pedestrians. Suppose further that a series of pedestrian crosswalks is instituted along with the regulation that pedestrians must use only these walks when crossing, but that while in these walks pedestrians have right of way over automobiles. The regulation restrains Smith (he can no longer legally cross streets where he pleases) but it also frees him (while in crosswalks he no longer has a duty to defer to automobile traffic). Using the schema above, the regulation (*a*) restrains Smith from crossing streets wherever he likes (*b*), but at the same time is such as to (make it practicable to) give him restricted right of way (*c*) over automobile traffic. The regulation (*a*) thus gives him restricted right of way (*c*) because it lifts the rule (*d*) giving automobiles general right of way over pedestrians.

This interpretation of the assertion that Smith can be made free by restraining him is straightforward enough. It raises problems only if one supposes that persons must be either free or not free *simpliciter,* and that the claim in question is that Smith is made free *simpliciter.* But there is no obvious justification for either of these suppositions.

If these suppositions *are* made, however, then the following interpretation may be appropriate:

2. Smith is being "restrained" only in the ordinary acceptance of that term; actually, he is not being restrained at all. He is being helped to do what he really wants to do, or what he *would* want to do if he were reasonable (moral, prudent, or such like); compare Locke's words: "that ill deserves the name of confinement which hedges us in only from bogs and precipices."[18] Because of the "constraint" put upon him, a *genuine* constraint that *was* upon him (for example, ignorance, passion, the intrusions of others) is lifted, and he is free from the latter to do what he really wishes (or would wish if . . .).

This interpretation is hardly straightforward, but the claim that it embodies is nevertheless arguable; Plato argues it in the *Republic* and implies such a claim in the

---

[17] This presumes that the prospect of freeing Smith by restraining *someone else* would be unproblematic even for the friends of negative freedom.

[18] *The Second Treatise of Government*, sec. 57. As is remarked below, however, the proper interpretation of this passage is not at all clear.

Gorgias. Furthermore, insistence upon the format of specifications recommended above can lead one to see clearly the kind of arguments needed to support the claim. For example, if a person is to be made free, whether by means of restraint or otherwise, there must be something *from* which he is made free. This must be singled out. Its character may not always be clear; for example, in Locke's discussion the confinement from which one is liberated by law is perhaps the constraint produced by the arbitrary uncontrolled action of one's neighbors, or perhaps it is the "constraint" arising from one's own ignorance or passion, or perhaps it is both of these. If only the former, then the specification is unexceptionable enough; that kind of constraint is well within the range of what is ordinarily thought to be constraint. If the latter, however, then some further argument is needed; one's own ignorance and passion are at least not unquestionably within the range of what can restrain him and limit his freedom. The required argument may attempt to show that ignorance and passion prevent persons from doing what they want to do, or what they "really" want to do, or what they *would* want to do if. . . . The idea would be to promote seeing the removal of ignorance and passion, or at least the control of their effects, as the removal or control of something preventing a person from doing as he wishes, really wishes, or would wish, and so forth, and thus, plausibly, an increase of that person's freedom.

Arguments concerning the "true" identity of the person in question and what *can* restrict such a person's freedom are of course important here and should be pushed further than the above discussion suggests. For the present, however, one need observe only that they are met again when one presses for specification of the full range of what, on interpretation (2), Smith is made free to *do.* Apparently, he is made free to do as he wishes, really wishes, or *would* wish if. . . . But, quite obviously, there is also something that he is *prima facie not* free to do; otherwise, there would be no point in declaring that he was being made free *by means of* restraint. One may discover how this difficulty is met by looking again to the arguments by which the claimer seeks to establish that something which at first appears to be a restraint is not actually a restraint at all. Two main lines may be found here: (*a*) that the activities being "restrained" are so unimportant or minor (relative, perhaps, to what is gained) that they are not worth counting, or (*b*) that the activities are such that no one could ever want (or really want, and so forth) to engage in them. If the activities in question are so unimportant as to be negligible, the restraints that prevent one from engaging in them may be also "not worthy of consideration"; if, on the other hand, the activities are ones that no one would conceivably freely choose to engage in, then it might indeed be thought "idle" to consider our inability to do them as a restriction upon our freedom.

Admittedly, the persons actually making the principal claim under consideration may have been confused, may not have seen all these alternatives of interpretation, and so forth. The intention here is not to say what such persons did mean when uttering the claims, but only more or less plausibly what they might have meant. The interpretations provide the main lines for the latter. They also provide a clear picture of what needs to be done in order to assess the worth of the claims in each case; for, of course, no pretense is being made here that such arguments are always or even very often ultimately convincing.

Interpretation (2) clearly provides the most difficult and interesting problems. One may analyze and discuss these problems by considering them to be raised by attempts to answer the following four questions:

a. What is to count as an interference with the freedom of persons?
b. What is to count as an action that persons might reasonably be said to be either free or not free to perform?
c. What is to count as a legitimate interference with the freedom of persons?
d. What actions are persons best left free to do?

As was mentioned above, there is a tendency to telescope (*c*) into (*a*), and to telescope (*d*) into (*b*). It was also noted that (*c*) and (*d*) are not distinct questions: they are logically related in so far as criteria of legitimacy are connected to beliefs about what is best or most desirable. (*a*) and (*b*) are also closely related in that an answer to one will affect what can reasonably be considered an answer to the other. The use of these questions as guides in the analysis and understanding of discussions of freedom should not, therefore, be expected to produce always a neat ordering of the discussions. But it *will* help further to delimit the alternatives of reasonable interpretation.

VI

In the end, then, discussions of the freedom of agents can be fully intelligible and rationally assessed only after the specification of each term of this triadic relation has been made or at least understood. The principal claim made here has been that insistence upon this single "concept" of freedom puts us in a position to see the interesting and important ranges of issues separating the philosophers who write about freedom in such different ways, and the ideologies that treat freedom so differently. These issues are obscured, if not hidden, when we suppose that the important thing is that the fascists, communists, and socialists on the one side, for example, have a different concept of freedom from that of the "libertarians" on the other. These issues are also hidden, of course, by the facile assumption that the adherents on one side or the other are never sincere.

17. Being Free to Act and Being a Free Man[1]

S. I. Benn and W. L. Weinstein

It is now something of a commonplace that to know whether a man is free we must know what he is supposed to be free from, and what free to do. The concept "freedom" includes, as it were, two variables, which must be supplied either explicitly or contextually. However, we cannot assign just *any* value to these variables, for there are certain characteristics of the concept that limit what in general one can appropriately say one is free from, and free to do. One object of this paper is to identify these restrictive conditions; another, to show that they arise in moral and political discourse, in part at least from the normative functions of "freedom." From the analysis of certain paradoxical situations, as where one wants to say that a man was not free to do something that he nevertheless did freely, we shall argue that underlying and presupposed by the concept of freedom of action there is another but related concept, that of autonomy – of the free man as chooser.

I

In a recent article, Gerald C. MacCallum questioned whether one could properly distinguish between "freedom from ..." and "freedom to ..." in relation to actions and agents, as though there were here two distinct concepts of "freedom." Whenever the freedom of agents is in question, he says, it always refers (explicitly or by contextual implication) to a triadic relation, between an agent, some preventing conditions said to be absent, and "actions, or conditions of character or circumstance" (that the agent is free to do, become, or attain).[2] MacCallum's claim is restricted to freedom of agents; there are other, dyadic uses of "free of" and "free from," as in "the sky is now free from clouds," "his record is free of blemish," but in such cases "free of/from" means simply "rid of" or "without."

Now although our present discussion will be mainly about "freedom" in political discourse, these more primitive dyadic uses suggest certain pointers. It is appropriate to say that a man is free from sin, fault, or awkwardness, but not from merit, virtue, or skill. We congratulate ourselves on being free from care, poverty, and fatigue; but cannot correspondingly complain that we are free from

From *Mind*, Vol. 80 (1971), pp. 194–211, by permission of the authors and publisher.

[1] This article is the result of discussions begun in 1966, when W. L. Weinstein was a Visiting Fellow in the Australian National University. It develops some of the ideas, here revised, from his "The Concept of Liberty in Nineteenth Century English Political Thought," *Political Studies*, vol. 13, 1965, pp. 145–162; and from S. I. Benn: "Freedom and Persuasion," *Australasian Journal of Philosophy*, vol. 45, 1967, pp. 259–275. Parts of the latter article have been incorporated into this one.

[2] See Gerald C. MacCallum, Jr.: "Negative and Positive Freedom," *Philosophical Review*, vol. 76, July 1967, pp. 312–334 [selection 16 of this book].

nourishment, riches, or rest. It seems that whenever we say of a person that he is free from X, or free of X, X is either a flaw, or it is some condition contrary to that person's supposed interest. To say that he was now free of his wealth would be to say, in a deliberately paradoxical way, that he was better off without it; indeed, it would be a way of revising accepted standards of what is in a man's interest.

What sort of things is it appropriate to say we are free to *do*? To run, to invest one's money, to to steal are all things that anyone might without eccentricity want to do, either for the satisfaction of just doing them, or because they promised some advantage. And there is nothing odd in rejoicing that one is free to do them, or in complaining that one is not. But there is something paradoxical about saying that a person is either free or not free to starve, cut off his ears, or to die; one would commonly add the ironic qualification: "if he wants to," precisely on account of the standard association between "being free" and experiences or activities normally regarded as worthwhile, either intrinsically or instrumentally. Of course, one can appropriately say that Jones is or is not free to do something, like bird-watching in the gardens of Buckingham Palace, without *his* having an actual interest in doing it. Nevertheless it is apposite to discuss whether he is free to do it only if it is a possible object of reasonable choice; cutting off one's ears is not the sort of thing anyone, in a standard range of conditions, would reasonably do, *i.e.* "no one in his senses would think of doing such a thing" (even though some people have, in fact, done it). It is not a question of logical absurdity; rather, to see the point of saying that one is (or is not) free to do X, we must be able to see that there might be some point in doing it. Our conception of freedom is bounded by our notions of what might be worthwhile doing; it is out of its element when we find its objects bizarre. Incomprehension, not hostility, is the first obstacle to toleration.

II

Since only acts that have some point are appropriate complements for "freedom to ...," the scope of the concept is governed by whatever criteria determine what such actions are. Similarly, there are criteria governing what one can appropriately complain of not being free from, *i.e.* what counts as an interference or as restricting choice. These criteria, we shall argue, also depend on standards of reasonable conduct and expectation.

> Liberty (according to Hobbes) is the absence of all the impediments to action that are not contained in the nature and intrinsical quality of the agent. As for example, the water is said to descend freely, or to have liberty to descend by the channel of the river, because there is no impediment that way, but not across, because the banks are impediments. And though the water cannot ascend, yet men never say it wants the *liberty* to ascend, but the *faculty* or *power*, because the impediment is in the nature of the water, and intrinsical.[3]

The point of Hobbes's definition was to give a meaning to "liberty" consistent with a determinist theory of human action; if the motions of material objects could be free while causally determined, so could the actions of human beings. Yet the cause

---

[3] Thomas Hobbes: *Of Liberty and Necessity*, in *English Works* (ed. Sir Wm. Molesworth) vol. iv, London, 1840, pp. 273–274.

of the water's natural motion is not, after all, contained in the nature of the water – "intrinsical," but in its gravitational relation with the earth; and if we continue to talk about free flow and free fall, it is because we are presupposing a system of normal or standard conditions, with correspondingly normal or natural motions, which may, however be deflected or inhibited by forces external to the system (like dams or parachutes). It turns out, then, that the distinction between intrinsic and extrinsic causes makes better sense in respect of agents of whom we can say that they try and decide, than it does for the motion of water or falling bodies. For whatever causal account, if any, that one may wish to give of trying and deciding, when one says "he did not go to the opera because he wanted to go to bed early instead," one implies that he could have gone had he wanted, *i.e.* he was free to go – it was his own decision, not something external to him like a car breakdown, nor something physical that just happened to him like a stroke, that made it impossible for him to go.

Now this distinction between internal and external determination takes us only a little way. For if I decide against a course of action to avoid threatened penalties am I free or unfree, determined by intrinsic or extrinsic factors? And if unfree, is the man who decides *for* that course, in spite of the penalty, freer on that account? And is the man who does the only thing the law permits him to do, but who would have done it anyway, freer than either, though one can quite properly say of him "he really had no choice"? The conception of freedom as the absence of impediments or constraints is unsatisfactory precisely because neither the man who would have acted in the same way in any event, nor the one who goes ahead despite the penalty, seems to be impeded, but only the one actually deterred; but it is odd to say that he alone is therefore unfree.

The phrase "he really had no choice" suggests that a better way of characterizing conditions of unfreedom is that they restrict choice by making alternatives unavailable or ineligible. So *all* the following cases would now qualify as instances of unfreedom:

1. Where the act done would *not* have been done had the alternative been available.
2. Where another act *would* have been done, had it not been made unavailable (the obverse of (1)).
3. Where the act enjoined and performed would still have been chosen had alternatives been available (here, however, one might say that "compliance is given freely").
4. Where the alternative is unavailable, but the agent decides to take it all the same. This is the case where the agent freely does what he is unfree to do.

(3) and (4) clearly raise new problems, which we shall explore more fully later. Before doing so, however, we have to consider what constitutes a restriction on choice. This comes close to the heart of the question "What are the criteria for freedom of action?"

III

Questions of freedom, as that concept has been used in political discourse, do not arise on *every* occasion that a man is frustrated by some impediment or external constraint. A man who is never free from arthritis suffers pain, but not unfreedom, even though he may be disabled from doing things he might otherwise do. Similarly, a man who lacks the physical means — whether muscular strength or ropes — to climb a cliff, need not be unfree but only unable to climb it, though one way of depriving a man of his freedom to climb it is to take away his ropes. Lucas has insisted on the importance of freedom

> contrasted not with verbal prohibition but with the pressure of factual circumstances. ... Avoiding action always may have to be taken, and may conflict with acting in other desired ways. Therefore it is a general condition of being able to act as one desires that one is not having to take avoiding action, that one is *free from* the necessity of taking avoiding action. ... We may define a man as being *free from* some real or apprehended evil, if the evil neither happens, nor would happen nor would be likely to happen, were he not to take any otherwise superfluous avoiding action.[4]

But the necessity to take avoiding action is surely not sufficient for unfreedom. For then anyone would be unfree who had to go roundabout to avoid a landslide, or to submit to a painful vaccination to avoid smallpox. As Lucas himself recognises, to be free does *not* mean "to be able to act without consideration of consequences"; it means rather to be able to choose among available courses bearing in mind their expected consequences, both good and ill. If, indeed, as we are now maintaining, deciding between alternative courses lies at the heart of freedom, it would be strange if the necessity to do so in the light of consequences were sufficient on its own to constitute unfreedom. "Being free from the necessity of taking avoiding action" may mean no more than not being faced with the necessity to choose — that is, not being in the kind of situation in which talk of freedom is most characteristically at home. Merely to *be* in that situation, to be confronted with opportunity costs, cannot therefore constitute a sufficient condition for unfreedom.

What counts as restricting choice in political discourse is conceptually related to the kind of functions that the concept "freedom" performs there. These are not simply descriptive, nor is this "freedom" the abstract noun, formed from the adjective "free," that we need for talking generally about being rid of or without something. It is unfortunate that there is no word "freeness" for this purpose. Lucas's "freedom contrasted with the pressure of factual circumstances" is no more than this. The moral and political concept of freedom cannot be stretched to cover every case in which it is linguistically appropriate to speak of "being free," without hopelessly attenuating it.

"Freedom" is a principle. To say that Negroes are not free, or that men are not free to express their opinions, or to buy liquor on Sunday in New South Wales, is very frequently to make a charge or express a grievance, not simply to state a fact. Even when it is not, it always invites the question: "What justification is there for that?" Consequently, if a restriction can give rise to discussions of freedom and unfreedom, it must make sense to ask "What justifies it?" Now we do not seek justification for restrictions unless we suppose that things could be otherwise than they are. One demands justification for an earthquake only if one challenges God: "Why did it have to happen?" So we say that the man stricken dumb has lost the *power* of speech; it is the one forbidden to address a public meeting who is denied freedom of speech.

---

[4] J. R. Lucas, *Principles of Politics*, London, 1966, pp. 144–145.

It is a general feature of events or conditions that can be accounted reasons for saying that a person is not free in respect of a certain kind of action, that unlike the tides they are not natural, unalterable, given, but rather that some rational being (or beings) can be held responsible for them, for bringing them about, or for allowing them to continue. On him lies an onus of justification. (But of course to say that an unfreedom needs to be justified is quite consistent with its being justifiable.)

By extending the range of restrictive conditions judged capable of alteration, the concept of freedom can itself be extended. Conditions formerly accepted as necessary may be called progressively into question; the frustrations to which they give rise come to be seen not merely as natural limitations on what is possible, but as restrictions on freedom. Consider the development of the concept of economic freedom during the last one hundred and fifty years. In the early nineteenth century it meant the absence of legal limitations on contracts of employment, pricing, and so on. The conditions of the market and the rights of property that governed the workers' bargaining power were generally taken to be more alterable than the weather, the laws of supply and demand no more restrictive of freedom than the laws of gravity. The worker was free in negotiating with his employer because, in terms of all conceivably controllable conditions, there was no restriction on his ability and opportunity to make the best *possible* bargain. Trade unionism and socialist economic theory combined to break down these presuppositions. The workers came to protest not merely against low wages or inequality, but against economic unfreedom – to do and enjoy many things they now saw as denied to them because the employing class was either unwilling or unable to change economic conditions that were none the less capable of change. This was due not simply to a greater scientific understanding of society, and therefore a greater capacity for manipulating it. At least equally important was a changing conception of legitimacy; it was a novel readiness to call into question property rights hitherto considered "natural" – not a revolution in technical but in moral possibilities – that gave a new reference to "economic freedom."

Of course, someone might admit that the economic system denies the workers certain freedoms, while justifying it on the grounds of general utility. But this move comes *after* the admission that the economic and social structure is open to question, in the sense that it is a proper subject for moral argument. Conceding that if some or all of its members so wanted they could change it, he maintains only that they would be wrong to do so. This is quite different from the view that it is impossible or unthinkable that things should be otherwise.

IV

Since freedom is a principle, whatever interferes with it demands to be justified; consequently, only those determining conditions for which rational agents (God or man) can be held responsible can qualify as interfering with it. But it does not follow that whenever one man's act influences or even frustrates another's, the characteristic demand for justification can appropriately be made. There are influences that do not restrict their subject's range of choice, and therefore do not need to be justified as interferences with freedom. There are others, like offering bribes or invasions of privacy, that do need justification, but on the grounds that they interfere with interests other than freedom.

The least problematic influence is a simple request. Suppose John asked George to lend him £50; George may have inquired why he wanted it, but it would have been out of place to ask John what *right* he had to make the request; for John did not have to have a right − everyone is at liberty to ask, just as everyone is at liberty to refuse. John's asking impaired no interest of George's (though if he agreed to it George may have impaired his own). It did not even interfere with George's most primitive freedom, to be allowed to go his own way. Nevertheless, John's request may have influenced George − George would not have given him £50 had he not asked. But that is not enough to constitute it an interference with George's range of choices; for that, it would have had to be not merely a necessary but a sufficient condition for George's decision − and we have no reason for saying it was. A request may confront one with a new alternative; but one decides oneself whether to adopt it. Suppose, however, that John manipulates George's feelings, *e.g.* of guilt about his wealth; this pressure may be a sufficient condition for George's compliance, and therefore an interference with his freedom. Of course, in some circumstances such an interference may be perfectly justified; but justified or not, it *needs* justifying, as the simple request does not.

John's influence over George's conduct may be decisive in other ways; for instance he may point out facts that he has overlooked, make clear what alternatives *are* open to him, or offer him disinterested advice. In none of these cases would John normally be called on to justify his action, though he may, of course, be required to give grounds for his opinion. Offering advice as such − even bad advice − calls for no justification; for George may disregard it if he likes; the mere offering of it puts no pressure on him. Moreover, though it may seem to George that courses that he formerly contemplated as possible alternatives have now been closed to him, those he now sees as impossible always were; and those he now sees only as undesirable are still open − his rejecting them makes them no less available to be chosen. So John has done nothing to restrict George's options and nothing, therefore, that needs justification as affecting George's freedom. However, tendering uncalled-for advice or asking for a loan may require justification because they invade not his freedom but his privacy. The liberty to act in these ways is restricted, in some cultures at least, to people standing in a particular social relation; the intruder causes embarrassment, and is thus, if in only a minor way, attacking a legitimate interest. But such an interference does not make George unfree; no option is closed that would otherwise be open. The offence, such as it is, touches him in quite a different way.

Making an offer, of trade or employment, is another way of influencing a person's action which calls for no justification since it limits no otherwise available alternatives. On the contrary, it enlarges them; one may either accept an offer or do precisely what one would have done had it not been made; one cannot be less free than before. So far, at least, there is nothing to justify.

Considering freedom as the non-restriction of options, rather than as the absence of impediments, we can readily distinguish straightforward business offers from extortion. The shopkeeper who offers eggs at 62 cents a dozen rather than giving them away might be said to impede my obtaining eggs if I have no money. But it would be odd to say that he interferes with my freedom, like the highwayman who takes my purse as the price of my passing. This is because the general framework of property relations is taken to define the normal conditions of action, and therefore the initial opportunities or alternatives available, just as the laws of mechanics determine the conditions under which we can fly. The earth's gravitation could be said to impede my flying – but it could as well be said to define the opportunities for flying available to me – *e.g.* if I have an aeroplane or a balloon, but not otherwise. Given the laws of property, I cannot complain that I am being deprived of free eggs as I can of the highwayman's denying me free passage. Having free eggs was never open to me anyway. Of course, it is a well-established move in radical argument to call in question the hitherto given initial conditions, like property institutions, by arguing that they *do* close alternatives otherwise available, because there is nothing illegitimate nor logically nor practically absurd, in envisaging a social order in which they would be absent, or at least different. Short of a revision of this kind, however, trading or market offers do not narrow options – on the contrary, they enlarge them, to the advantage of the respondent, and, *prima facie,* injuring no one else. But does not a bribe also enlarge the respondent's opportunities? Indeed, it does; but then, from the point of view of the respondent's freedom it is unobjectionable. Offering a bribe is properly an offence not because it makes anyone unfree but because it attacks the public interest, giving someone a motive for betraying a trust or neglecting a duty.

But this is clearly not the full story. For a man really desperate for money the offer of a bribe may be quite irresistible. Indeed, his defence might be that in accepting it he was not responsible for what he was doing – he was not a free agent.

Or consider the case of exploitation: Esau, faint unto death, was in no position to haggle with Jacob over the price of a bowl of soup. Though the form of an offer may suggest that the respondent can decide for himself whether to take it or leave it, it may still put pressure on him to accept it as effective as any threat. Exploitation – using some special bargaining power to demand more than a commodity would cost in some normal circumstances, or offering less for a service (*e.g.* in wages) than it is worth (by some similar standard) – is always *unfair*; but it is only when to turn the offer down would be to suffer real deprivation, so that one could say "I have no alternative but to accept" (*e.g.* Esau's situation, or that of an unemployed worker offered a poorly-paid job in a depression) that we are inclined to talk not only of injustice but also of unfreedom. Even so, it might still be objected that though Esau was not free to refuse Jacob's offer, this was because there happened to be no other alternative course that a reasonable, prudent man would consider eligible – not that Jacob had *deprived* him of alternatives to accepting. For he had not. All the same, we should certainly regard Esau as having contracted under duress, a condition sufficient to void the contract. But it is because the price is unreasonably high that one calls it duress; desperate need alone would not be sufficient if the price were reasonable. Jacob used the power fortuitously given him by Esau's abnormal situation to induce him to agree to a bargain that, by *normal standards and in normal circumstances* would be contrary to his interests, and therefore unreasonable. The concept of duress thus involves two standards, first, a standard price that it is reasonable to pay for a type of good or service; and second, a standard of what would be a reasonable alternative, in the absence of which one is vulnerable to pressure. Thus one may plead unfreedom in order to rebut contractual claims if one can argue both that the consideration one derives from the agreement is incommensurate with the sacrifice incurred, and that one would not have made such an agreement but for one's being in an abnormally weak bargaining position, that is to say, not having the kind of reasonable alternative normally available. In practice, the Courts may interpret these standards very strictly; they may be very reluctant to determine whether the consideration derived from a contract is incommensurate with the cost incurred. Our object here, however, is to point out the standards implied by a plea of duress, whether or not it is acceptable.

This analysis of duress suggests that the source of unfreedom is not merely the exploiter's price, but also the circumstances that give him his bargaining power. And this helps to explain a difference between the classical economic liberal and the socialist radical. An unemployed worker may be unable to refuse a poorly-paid job when no more favourable opportunities are open to him. But for the liberal, unless the employer has arranged things this way himself (*e.g.* by a blacklist or by monopoly), he is merely acting appropriately in economic conditions that are not of his making – he is not responsible for the other party's desperate need; neither is he committing an injustice in offering the wage he does. For the only available standard by which to judge the reasonableness of the wage is the competitive market rate. So the worker cannot complain of duress, but only of misfortune. No one makes him unfree. The radical socialist, however, claims that the worker's wage can be judged against a standard of need, or of what it might be in a different economic order. By such a standard, it is unreasonable. Moreover, he believes the system could be changed; society alone, or its ruling minority, is responsible for there being no reasonable alternative to the job offered. In the absence of such an alternative, the worker is vulnerable to pressure, and therefore under duress.

V

The most conclusive way of restricting a man's choices is to put him in chains or behind bars, or to deprive him of the necessary physical equipment for an activity, like depriving the mountaineer of his ropes. Similarly, one can prevent people from reading obscene books by arranging that there are none to read. This kind of interference, however, is limited in its range; though one can prevent a horse drinking by removing the trough, there is no corresponding way of forcing him to drink. Still, there may be other ways of compelling people to *do* things – substituting the Bible, say, for the banned works of de Sade – by manipulating not the objective but the subjective conditions of choice, as in hypnosis, or "thought reform."

However, by no means all – or even the most important – unfreedoms attacked or resisted in the liberal political tradition have been of these types. The case of exploitation already considered was clearly different. Different, too, are most interferences with freedom of speech, freedom of worship, sexual freedom, or freedom to travel; these consist most commonly of threats of penalties that make the conduct in question significantly less attractive as an option. But this is not enough to sustain a charge of unfreedom – for revenue duties or an entertainment tax may do as much; yet having to pay duty every time one goes to the cinema is not like having to pay a fine every time one goes to Church. One difference lies in what appears to be a difference in point in the two impositions; a revenue tax, unlike a protective tariff on imports, is not meant to prevent people buying the commodity; indeed, it defeats its purpose if it does so. But if the *penalty* is to do its job, it must be set so high that one could not reasonably expect the kind of people subject to the restriction to continue to see the forbidden conduct as an available option. That is not to say that penalties always do this; but if the penalty for a certain class of offence is so light that the offence does remain a generally available option, the penalty will come to be regarded as a tax. It is said that before the enactment of the Street Offences Act (1959), London prostitutes viewed the periodic 40/- penalty for soliciting in precisely this way. Typically, then, penalties and threats of reprisals have as their main point preventing people acting, or compelling them to act, in a certain way; moreover, systems like the criminal law that are sustained (in part at least) by such threats would not be thought of as restrictive of freedom if their penalties did not in general make the prohibited course so unattractive that, by ordinary standards of prudence and interest, it could be considered closed.

We are now in a position to return to two problems referred to earlier, (1) whether the man is free who would do anyway, of his own free will, what the law requires him by threats to do, *e.g.* the situation of the conscientious Church member when tithing is compulsory; and (2) whether Francis who is unfree by law to murder Gerald but does so all the same, must on that account be said to have been free to do so.[5]

The tithing case calls for a distinction between the conditions under which one can say that a man in doing something does it freely, and the conditions in which one can speak of his having freedom in that respect. If tithing is compulsory, I have no choice but to pay even though if I had such a choice, I should still pay. The range of alternatives open to me does not depend on my preference for one rather than another; consequently, to eliminate an otherwise available alternative, *i.e.* non-tithing with impunity, is just as much an interference with freedom, whether or not I should have chosen it had it been available. To abridge the possibility of choice is to abridge freedom. Nevertheless, we obviously want to be able to distinguish the man who acts as he does only *because* this is the only possibility left open, from the man who would act in the same way whatever the possibilities, to whose *action* the absence of other possibilities is irrelevant. Yet even for him, the possibility of reviewing his action, of deciding whether to go on acting in this way, or indeed of regretting having done so up till now, is closed — for it is pointless to regret the unavoidable.

We have been arguing so far as though any legal prescription to which a sanction is attached automatically puts all alternative courses out of reach. But this, of course, cannot be true, since people wittingly break the law. Nevertheless, it remains important to retain a way of distinguishing the unfreedom of the man who will be punished if (and because) he does what he wants, from the freedom of the man who will not. To have to say (as some recent behavioural political scientists have said) that "the greater an actor's desire to perform a punishable action, the penalty remaining constant, the greater his freedom to do so,"[6] is to pay too high a price for a solution to the paradox that criminals freely commit crimes they are not free to commit. Consider Hobbes's way of dealing with the problem: "All actions," wrote Hobbes, "that men do in commonwealths for fear of the law are actions

---

[5] *Cf.* C. W. Cassinelli: *Free Activities and Interpersonal Relations*, The Hague, 1966: "the frequency of premeditated murder ... raises doubts whether the law ever makes men who contemplate murder unfree to commit it" (p. 33). ". . . if Francis made an attempt on Gerald's life, the law against murder obviously had not made him unfree to do so" (p. 34).

[6] F. E. Oppenheim: *Dimensions of Freedom*, New York, 1961, p. 189. *Cf.* also C. W. Cassinelli, *op. cit.*

which the doers had liberty to omit." For to give a man an additional motive for action (*i.e.* fear of punishment) to set against whatever motives he may have, makes him no less free. He may choose to disobey if he will and take the consequences:

> as when a man throweth his goods into the sea for fear the ship should sink, he doth it nevertheless very willingly, and may refuse to do it if he will . . . So a man sometimes pays his debt only for fear of imprisonment, which because nobody hindered him from detaining, was the action of a man at liberty. (*Leviathan,* chapter XXI.)

This looks, to a liberal, wilfully perverse. Action under coercion or threat is, for the liberal, the very paradigm of unfreedom; the incompatibility of freedom and coercion is, after all, what classical Liberalism is all about. For all that, Hobbes's paradox can help to distinguish the kind of unfreedom we have been mainly concerned with so far, from that which arises from manipulation by certain techniques of persuasion and conditioning. It also illuminates the sort of action model that Hobbes, like many other liberal social philosophers, regarded as standard.

The model is that of a man wanting to do something, threatened with legal penalties if he does it, and freely deciding it would not be worth it. Still, when Hobbes remarks "that in all kinds of actions by the laws praetermitted, men have the liberty, of doing what their own reasons shall suggest, for the most profitable to themselves" (*Leviathan,* chapter XXI), he implies that in those things forbidden by the law, men are not free, at least in the same sense. It is, of course, true that there is a rule-derived sense in which a person is unfree to do anything forbidden by a rule (*i.e.* not "praetermitted"), irrespective of any sanction, as one is unfree to move a pawn backwards in chess. If A has undertaken to have dinner with B this evening, A is not free to accept another invitation. He has already limited the alternatives he is *entitled* to choose among. But he *could* break his promise, all the same — there is nothing to stop him. So he is free to decide whether to honour his obligation or not. But suppose a penalty is attached to his breaking faith; now, quite apart from wholly rule-derived unfreedom, he is not free to do what he would otherwise like to do (to do X) because he cannot now do X without also attracting the penalty (P), and X is not worth doing on those terms. Hobbes would maintain that this is consistent with freedom — A would have chosen X had it been open to him, but in fact it is not — it is X + P rather than X that is the available alternative to not-X. A sensibly prefers not-X. There *are* people who might prefer X + P and, as Cassinelli remarks,[7] it is "logically most cumbersome to say that a man is unfree to perform an activity he in fact performs." Can a conscientious objector in prison for refusing to obey orders claim that he was unfree to refuse? Yet another, less steadfast, might very well explain that, his appeal having been rejected, he was no longer free to refuse — it was quite unreasonable to expect anyone to do X if he also had to suffer P; only someone with a disordered scale of values, or one of quite superhuman steadfastness, a fanatic or a saint, would make such a choice. The unfreedom now in question is more substantial than pure rule-derived unfreedom: it is not merely that one is not *entitled* to consider X among the available alternatives; it is that X simpliciter no longer *is* available — but only X + P. The claim now is that by attaching penal sanctions to a course of action, the law has made it unavailable to any reasonably prudent man.

[7] *Op. cit.*, p. 34.

Still, even someone arguing in this way presupposes a kind of freedom – the freedom of a rational being, an economic man, making the most prudent choice he can among alternatives with different (if all rather unsatisfactory) utilities. The choice, it is true, may be rigged against him by someone with power to allot rewards or penalties (analogous to a monopolistic price-fixer), but given the conditions, he makes his own choice – he is still his own master. But if we accept this model, the man who submits to the law does so as freely, no more, no less, than the man who deliberately defies it.

How adequate a model is it?

There is a range of politically important forms of utterance in which "freedom" and "unfreedom" occur, each making its own characteristic kind of point. How far, then, do these forms all presuppose a model of rational choice? One such form has already emerged: we have shown that the man whose freedom is restricted by a law backed by a sanction may also be seen as choosing between obedience and disobedience. If he obeys or intends to obey, his account of his position as being unfree contains *an evaluation,* namely that it would be unreasonable to expect anyone in such circumstances to break the law, though admittedly some rash or unusually determined individuals might be able to break it in spite of the consequences.

This evaluation might be challenged by insisting that the law does not sufficiently foreclose other alternatives: "But you *could* still break the law." If to obey is to abandon some vital principle or some paramount interest or objective, the point of claiming "You still have a choice," in spite of the fact that choosing X incurs P, is to insist on the agent's responsibility for what he does in obeying, and perhaps to charge him with lack of will or faith. And this one does only if there is some good reason, overriding his prudential calculations, why he should disobey. So to insist that he was free to act is to alter his moral position; for example, it would expose to blame a soldier who complied with an order to torture prisoners. The point of denying that a threatened penalty is sufficient to determine the agent's action is to challenge the usual prudential defence. The agent's counter-plea that in his circumstances only a saint or a fanatic would have disobeyed, is a claim that the wrong standards are being applied to him, *i.e. he* could not be expected to disregard normal prudence.

A plea of duress in criminal law works in the same way; the accused excuses himself by claiming that he was not free to obey the law, on account of some more immediate threat that he could not reasonably have been expected to disregard. There are at least two ways of rebutting such a plea. One might deny the legitimacy of the interest defended, *e.g.* fraudulent conversion would not be excused by the need to pay off a blackmailer who threatened to expose one's own past crimes. The other way is to deny that, given the importance of the law in question, obedience would have involved an excessive sacrifice, *e.g.* in the case of the soldier mentioned above. Corresponding to the standards presupposed by the plea of duress in contract [see p. 315], there is here a kind of reasonable rate of exchange between the importance of a given law and what damage a man might reasonably be expected to risk or to suffer (for the same kind of case could be made for steadfastness under torture) rather than break that law.

The range of utterances about freedom and unfreedom which contextually assign or diminish responsibility for action all presuppose the conception of man as a chooser. Most obviously, when a man deliberately violates the law, his responsibility as an offender, which justifies imposing the consequences, rests precisely on the judgment that he acted freely. Conversely, when his compliance is criticised; as he could have chosen otherwise, he is responsible for his action. Similarly, when the act enjoined and performed is one that the agent would have chosen even though alternatives had been available; here the point of saying that he acts freely may be either to weaken the claim that the law is hostile to freedom, or to praise the agent for having a motive and an intention worthier than a mere regard for legal sanctions (or conversely, to censure him more severely than if he had acted *only* because the law required it).

VI

The possibility of choice is central, then, to the concept of freedom of action. Unfreedom is created by the restriction of choice, by physical restraints that prevent any choice because they prevent any action whatsoever, or by the loading of choices, so that some become, for ordinary practical purpose, ineligible. But choice presupposes a chooser; only a man who can be seen as a chooser is qualified as the subject of a free act. But what sort of conditions would disqualify a man in this respect? For what kind of man is the model inappropriate?

The most obvious disqualifications are the commonly accepted grounds for pleas of diminished responsibility, such as various forms of insanity. A paranoiac appears to make choices, but having a phantasy view of the world, he chooses between unreal alternatives; his choices are pseudo-choices. Again a compulsive neurotic — a kleptomaniac, say — is disqualified, because though he may appear to perceive the world as it is, the perception makes no difference to his behaviour. He has no choice, not in the sense that the alternatives have been rigged against him, but in that his behaviour is misdescribed if described in the language of choosing.

Less extreme instances, not so evidently cases of derangement, are met in dominance relationships. A submissive partner may be hopelessly disabled from choosing on a matter regarding which the dominant partner has exerted his will, not because he has freely submitted (as in certain kinds of authority relationships), but because he cannot squarely contemplate the possibility of doing otherwise than obey. It is at best a theoretical possibility — something done by others, but not his sort of thing. The dominant partner's expressed wish does not make an alternative ineligible — it makes it no longer an alternative. But suppose the conflict between his repressed aspirations and the dominant will reached some critical breaking point; would he then discover, as an existentialist might say, that he had been free all the time? The concept of man presupposed by the concept of freedom of action is that of the free (autonomous) chooser. Not to have this freedom is to be defective. Nevertheless, it may be more accurate to regard it as something to be achieved; to see it clearly as a possibility may be only the first step towards having it. There are cases, indeed, in which one clearly does not have it, cases of manipulated choice. The hypnotised subject and the brain-washed are "not their own masters," not because the objective conditions of choice have been interfered with, but because the subjective conditions have. Though the subject may believe that he is choosing, the actions of other people may still sufficiently account for what he does; he may be as externally programmed as a computer.

The brief outline we have given of conditions disqualifying a man as a chooser suggest the following three criteria (necessary but perhaps not sufficient) for freedom as autonomy:

1. A chooser must have a realistic understanding of the alternatives. Delusions are not available courses of action. Hence a certain minimum degree of rationality is necessary to freedom.
2. Motivation must not be vicarious. That A wants B to want P must not be a sufficient condition of B's wanting P. (That it is a necessary condition is fully consistent with freedom: a well-wisher who persuades me by good arguments to do P is not impairing my freedom. Neither, necessarily, is a successful commercial advertiser.)
3. B must be capable of criticising and rejecting any proposals that A offers him. This follows from 2, but it also requires that B's sources of information shall not be controlled by A, for then B's view of reality is what A chooses to make it.

These criteria may assist in the disentangling of certain problematic cases, like the legitimacy of mass advertising and propaganda, control over addictive drugs, the distinction between education and indoctrination, the relation between conscience and obligation to authority, and so on. What is perhaps difficult about some of these is not so much that the criteria of "realistic understanding," "vicarious motivation" and "capacity for criticism and rejection" are fundamentally disputable. What is at stake is the control of action in areas peculiarly crucial for the development and maintenance of the agent's capacities effectively to make choices. The objection to a man's selling himself into slavery is that by one act of choice he enables others to control the objective conditions of choice; the objection to starting on addictive drugs is that by a gradual and irreversible process the addict actually disqualifies himself as a chooser. Under certain conditions, constraint may be justified if it diminishes an individual's opportunities to do just that.[8]

---

[8] *Cf.* S. I. Benn: "Freedom and Persuasion," *Australasian Journal of Philosophy*, vol. 45, 1967, pp. 259–275, for a discussion of this principle in relation to addictive drugs and forms of therapeutic manipulation.

Part V

Equality

Introduction

The topics of the next three parts, "equality," "justice," and "rights," are closely connected, indeed interwoven, in a number of respects. As the very titles of the papers on equality remind us, it has long been thought that justice involves some form of equal treatment in an essential way. If or insofar as this is true, clarifications of "equality" will contribute to the understanding of "justice" and the converse. Some of the selections on "equality" take up "justice" explicitly, but all have a bearing on both topics. Again, it is a common point about rights, and particularly "human" or "natural" or "fundamental" rights, that in one sense or another they are and must be held equally by all human beings, indeed that justice requires that they be available to or held by all human beings. And on some views human rights are linked to respects in which it is said that all human beings are in fact equal. Here again, then, there is a good deal of explicit and implicit interplay not only within but between the next parts of the book.

The topics are also bound together by the fact that each of them is central to debates concerning utilitarianism and the moral and political theories that compete with it. Most writers, whether utilitarians or not, have agreed that justice and rights, but especially justice, pose the most difficult problems for utilitarian theory. Roughly, utilitarianism insists that the moral quality of an action depends upon the good or evil consequent upon doing or taking it; if the consequences are good (can be expected to be good) the action is a good or right one to take, if they are bad it is wrong or evil. When "good" and "evil" are interpreted as "greatest happiness," "least pain" and so on, this argument suggests that an action could be good or right despite being unjust or a violation of fundamental rights, that it could be morally right to do injustice and/or to violate fundamental rights. Many writers have believed that this is exactly what utilitarianism (not only suggests but) entails, that this implication puts utilitarianism in blatant conflict with both actual and defensible moral belief and practice, and hence that utilitarianism is untenable. As we noted in Part III, this is the view of Rawls, and, although there are important differences between them in other respects, his view is shared by Alan Gewirth, H. L. A. Hart, William Frankena, and Joel Feinberg among the contributors to these parts. Other writers, however, have tried to show that utilitarianism remains the only viable general moral theory and they have tried to formulate it so as to meet the objection mentioned above and various related criticisms. The contributions of J. S. Mill, Lawrence Haworth, the present writer, and perhaps S. I. Benn to these parts are efforts along these lines.

In narrowly descriptive terms "equality," to use a term from MacCallum's analysis of "freedom," involves at least a triadic relationship among two or more agents, objects, or entities (*A* and *B*) and a third variable (*X*) in respect to which *A* and *B* can be said to be equal one to the other. As J. L. Lucas reminds us, if the *X* in respect to which *A* and *B* are equal is not specified, at least tacitly or contextually, talk about *A* and *B* being equal is empty. To say that *A* and *B* are equal in respect to *X* is, to take a slight liberty with the Oxford English Dictionary, to say that each of them can be accurately described by one and the same formula. Thus "*A* is equal to *B* in height" means that, say, the formula "is five feet eleven inches tall" accurately describes both *A* and *B*. As S. I. Benn puts it, in the respect in which *A* and *B* are equal they are interchangeable.

What the Oxford English Dictionary actually says is that "equally" means "according to one and the same rule." This formulation links up more directly with normative issues about equality than the "descriptive" formula just mentioned. To *treat* *A* and *B* equally is to treat them according to one and the same rule. To say that *A* and *B* *should be treated* equally in a certain respect is to say that one and the same rule should be applied to each of them.

But *why* should they be treated equally? If they *are* equal in some respect we may have occasion to notice or report this fact about them. But why should they be treated equally? Why is it good or bad, just or unjust to treat them in an equal or unequal manner? When we know what it means to treat equally in some respects, what is there to convince us that we should or ought to do so? This is a general formulation of the main issue in this part.

Reasoning in support of equal treatment in respect to some *X* often links the descriptive and the prescriptive senses of equality tightly together. The fact that *A* and *B* are equal in respect to *X* is used as a warrant for the argument that *A* and *B* should receive equal treatment in respect to some *Y*. For example, the fact that *A* and *B* (or all of mankind) are accurately described by the formula "craves relief from intense physical pain" (Gregory Vlastos) might be used as a warrant for the rule "*A* and *B* ought to be furnished with a supply of morphine sufficient to give them the relief they crave." "Craves relief . . ." is the *X* in respect to which *A* and *B* are equal, "furnish with a supply of morphine" is the *Y*, the rule or policy according to which *A* and *B* ought to receive equal treatment. This equality in respect to *X* is put forward as a warrant or reason for accepting and acting on *Y*.

But why is the fact of equality in respect to *X* a reason for accepting and acting on *Y*? There is at least one respect in which a clear and indisputable answer can be given to this question, namely that, given the satisfaction of certain conditions, it would be inconsistent, a violation of a rule of logic, to treat *A* and *B* other than equally. Stating the matter in terms of what is commonly called the Generalization Principle or the principle of formal justice (hereafter GP) is a way of showing that, and why, this is the case. "If *Y* is right for *A* and if *A* and *B* are relevantly similar persons in relevantly similar situations, *Y* is right for *B*." If *Y* is right for *A* because *A* is *X*, and if *B* is also *X*, *Y* is right for *B* (unless *B* can be shown to have some further characteristics, not possessed by *A*, that make it wrong to give *Y* to *B*).[1] All the contributors to this part accept the validity of this formal principle and concede that it has value in moral and political reasoning.

The issue in dispute is the further question whether the logical or formal principle exhausts what we might call the principle of equality, the principle that, in various respects (or at least in *some* respects) it is right or just to treat men equally, wrong or unjust to treat them unequally. Granting that violations of the

---

[1] For a more detailed statement of the logic here, see section V of Gewirth's paper.

principle of equality will always be a violation of the logical principle, are they also, at least sometimes, violations of a substantive (as opposed to formal or logical) moral principle of equality? Or are they nothing more than logical mistakes that may or may not *coincide with* a violation of some moral principle in the formulation of which "equality" plays no necessary part? Although differing as to its formulation (content), Benn and Gewirth argue that there is a substantive moral principle of equality or egalitarian justice, a principle which, though it works in conjunction with the logical principle, is not reducible to, not exhausted by, the latter. As Gewirth puts it at the beginning of his paper, "Unlike doctrines of purely formal justice, which require simply that all cases falling under general rules be treated in the same way in accordance with the rules regardless of their contents, egalitarian justice puts equality into the very contents of some of the most basic rules about men's rights or treatment." In short, the fact that an action or policy treats men unequally can sometimes be an (independent and) sufficient condition of its being unjust. In this writer's essay, by contrast, it is argued that the formal GP exhausts the principle of equality; that this formal principle cannot be applied until it is decided (1) whether Y is right for X and (2) whether A and B are relevantly similar persons, and so on, that the concept of equality is of no help in making these decisions, and finally that the decisions must be made (if a moral question is involved) in terms of moral principles or reasons in and to the formulation and application of which "equality" is irrelevant. (I suggest that the relevant moral principles are utilitarian but I have hardly shown this to be the case.) Hence judgments about equal treatment are derivative of other moral judgments, and concern no more than logical relationships between or among such moral judgments. (Although he does not discuss the issue in these terms, it is my impression that Lucas would agree, if not with my mode of formulating it, with my conclusion in this respect.)

Formulations similar to Benn's are criticized in my paper. Also, Gewirth's list of standard objections to and criteria that a theory of (nonformalistic) egalitarian justice must meet apply to Benn's as well as to his own argument. Readers will want to examine the question whether Benn meets the objections and satisfies the criteria that Gewirth mentions. Finally, Lucas' strictures concerning "respect" and "humanity" bear directly on the nonformalistic egalitarian position. For these reasons I will limit the remainder of the present remarks to Gewirth's argument.

The chief difficulty with the principle of formal justice, Gewirth argues, is that it yields no nonarbitrary criterion or criteria by which to decide which similarities and differences between A and B are relevant to the question of whether Y is right for both of them. Given the many ways in which any person or action can be correctly characterized, it is always possible to escape from the requirements of GP by calling attention to differences between those who will be affected by the policy or action that is under consideration. It may be true that A and B both crave relief from physical pain, but it will always be true that they will differ from one another in some respect and that giving a supply of morphine will have different consequences for each of them. A substantive theory of egalitarian justice must supply a nonarbitrary basis on which to decide which similarities are relevant and which irrelevant to deciding whether they should be treated equally in a particular respect.

A criterion will be nonarbitrary if and only if its content is restricted "to what is necessarily and universally connected with its subject-matter." Now the subject matter of all moral claims (and some other kinds of claims as well), however much they may vary in other respects, is always and necessarily human action. Further, it is a necessary feature of human action that it involves agents who have purposes they wish to fulfill. Purposes vary from agent to agent, action to action, claim to claim, but purposiveness is a *necessary* feature of *all* action. Hence however many differences A may identify between himself and B, or C may identify between A and B, they cannot deny that, as agents advancing claims, they are equal in respect to their being purposive agents. Since it is to satisfy or fulfill a purpose that they enter into what Gewirth calls "transactions" with others and advance claims against others, the ground on which they must assert the right to do so is their desire to satisfy their purpose or purposes. Because this is necessarily the same reason that all persons enter transactions and advance claims, A cannot, on pain of contradicting himself, claim the right to do so for himself and deny that right to others. The necessary relationship between purposiveness and action makes it impossible to distinguish one person's case, including one's own, from any other person's case. Thus we have a rational, that is entirely nonarbitrary, criterion of relevant similarities and differences; this criterion gives us the basis for a substantive theory of egalitarian justice. All persons have an equal right "to participate voluntarily and purposively in transactions" and to advance claims to satisfy their purposes. Any denial of this right to any person is arbitrary and unjust.

Gewirth achieves the necessity and universality essential to avoiding what he calls arbitrariness by making use of the most general possible characterization of actions. He abstracts from all features that distinguish one action from others to features that define the category of action and hence are necessarily a part of all action. In terms of my own assessment of GP and equality he seeks to avoid having to appeal to, say, the consequences of an action to decide whether similarities and differences are relevant by characterizing actions in such a way as to eliminate all differences among them.

There is a question whether such characterizations of actions are in fact intelligible. If we abstract away all the particular, distinguishing purposes of and reasons for an action from our identification and characterizations of it, how do we recognize it as purposive? Is there such a thing as purposiveness apart from this or that purpose? (Is there such a thing as "gameness" apart from particular games and their distinguishing characteristics and features?)

But let us grant that Gewirth has established a cogent, nonderivative, and substantive principle of egalitarian justice and let us instead inquire into its moral and political import.

It is our *having* a purpose, not the specific purpose that we have, that we share with all agents. Hence this having a purpose must be the basis of our claim to participate in transaction, and it is this claim that we must concede to all others. We cannot deny others the right to participate in transactions without contradicting our own claim to a right to do so. This is clearly important. It precludes, for example, justifying the exclusion of some persons from moral and political life altogether (unless, of course, it was contended that those "persons" were not agents in Gewirth's sense, for example, that they had the qualities Aristotle seems to ascribe to "natural slaves"); it excludes treating some persons as nonpersons for moral, political, and perhaps other purposes. It may also exclude acting toward others so as to make them incapable of forming and giving expression to their purposes, of participating voluntarily and purposively in transaction, as, for example, by killing them or harming them seriously.

What it does not and cannot do is provide grounds on which to decide which of the conflicting substantive claims that persons assert (as opposed to the claim to have a right to assert the substantive claims) should in fact be satisfied. It cannot decide between substantive claims because descriptions of the substance of claims, of the particular goods which will satisfy the particular purposes people have in participating in transactions, are not allowed into the description of the action on which the application of the principles of egalitarian justice must be based. We cannot decide between or among particular claims that we are not permitted to describe in their particularity. (If everything apart from the extremely stringent criteria of "reason" that Gewirth uses is arbitrary, it seems that the moment we depart from the confines of the application of the principles of egalitarian justice we necessarily enter a realm of arbitrariness. Hence it seems that although we have perfectly rational grounds for asserting our claims, deciding which of them should be satisfied is necessarily an arbitrary business.) Thus even if we grant that the theory of egalitarian justice is cogent and compelling, it is far from a complete theory of justice and many issues that arise concerning justice, rights, and equality remain to be dealt with on other grounds.

Further Reading

Blackstone, W. T. ed. *The Concept of Equality*. Minneapolis: Burgess Publishing Co., 1969.

Charvet, J. "The Idea of Equality as a Substantive Principle of Society," *Political Studies*, Vol. 18 (1969), pp. 1–13.

Lakoff, Sanford A. *Equality in Political Philosophy*. Cambridge, Mass.: Harvard University Press, 1964.

Olafson, Frederick A., ed. *Justice and Social Policy*. Englewood Cliffs, N.J.: Prentice-Hall, Inc., 1961.

Pennock, J. Roland, and John W. Chapman, eds. *Equality*. New York: Atherton Press, Inc., 1967.

Rees, J. C. *Equality*. New York: The Macmillan Company, 1971.

Wilson, John. *Equality*. London: Hutchinson & Co., Ltd., 1966.

18. The Religion of Inequality

R. H. Tawney

... It is obvious, again, that the word "Equality" possesses more than one meaning, and that the controversies surrounding it arise partly, at least, because the same term is employed with different connotations. Thus it may either purport to state a fact, or convey the expression of an ethical judgment. On the one hand, it may affirm that men are, on the whole, very similar in their natural endowments of character and intelligence. On the other hand, it may assert that, while they differ profoundly as individuals in capacity and character, they are equally entitled as human beings to consideration and respect, and that the well-being of a society is likely to be increased if it so plans its organization that, whether their powers are great or small, all its members may be equally enabled to make the best of such powers as they possess.

If made in the first sense, the assertion of human equality is clearly untenable. It is a piece of mythology against which irresistible evidence has been accumulated by biologists and psychologists. In the light of the data presented — to mention only two recent examples — in such works as Dr. Burt's admirable studies of the distribution of educational abilities among school-children, or the Report of the Mental Deficiency Committee, the fact that, quite apart from differences of environment and opportunity, individuals differ widely in their natural endowments, and in their capacity to develop them by education, is not open to question. There is some reason for holding, for instance, that, while eighty per cent. of children at the age of ten fall within a range of about three mental years, the most backward may have a mental age of five, while the most gifted may have one of as much as fifteen.

The acceptance of that conclusion, nevertheless, makes a smaller breach in equalitarian doctrines than is sometimes supposed, for such doctrines have rarely been based on a denial of it. It is true, of course, that the psychological and political theory of the age between 1750 and 1850 — the theory, for example, of thinkers so different as Helvetius and Adam Smith at the beginning of the period, and Mill and Proudhon at the end of it — greatly underestimated the significance of inherited qualities, and greatly overestimated the plasticity of human nature. It may be doubted, however, whether it was quite that order of ideas which inspired the historical affirmations of human equality, even in the age when such ideas were still in fashion.

It is difficult for even the most sanguine of assemblies to retain for more than one meeting the belief that Providence has bestowed an equal measure of intelligence upon all its members. When the Americans declared it to be a self-evident truth that all men are created equal, they were thinking less of the

From R. H. Tawney, *Equality* (London: George Allen & Unwin Ltd.), pp. 39–48, by permission of the publisher.

admirable racial qualities of the inhabitants of the New World than of their political and economic relations with the Old, and would have remained unconvinced that those relations should continue even in the face of proofs of biological inferiority. When the French, who a century and a half ago preached the equalitarian idea with the same fervent conviction as is shown to-day by the rulers of Russia in denouncing it, set that idea side by side with liberty and fraternity as the motto of a new world, they did not mean that all men are equally intelligent or equally virtuous, any more than that they are equally tall or equally fat, but that the unity of their national life should no longer be torn to pieces by obsolete property rights and meaningless juristic distinctions. When Arnold, who was an inspector of schools as well as a poet, and who, whatever his failings, was not prone to demagogy, wrote "choose equality," he did not suggest, it may be suspected, that all children appeared to him to be equally clever, but that a nation acts unwisely in stressing heavily distinctions based on birth or money.

Few men have been more acutely sensitive than Mill to the importance of encouraging the widest possible diversities of mind and taste. In arguing that "the best state for human nature is that in which, while no one is poor, no one desires to be richer," and urging that social policy should be directed to increasing equality, he did not intend to convey that it should suppress varieties of individual genius and character, but that it was only in a society marked by a large measure of economic equality that such varieties were likely to find their full expression and due meed of appreciation. Theologians have not, as a rule, been disposed to ignore the fact that there are diversities of gifts and degree above degree. When they tell us that all men are equal in the eyes of God, what they mean, it is to be presumed, is what Jeremy Taylor meant, when he wrote, in a book to-day too little read, that "if a man be exalted by reason of any excellence in his soul, he may please to remember that all souls are equal, and their differing operations are because their instrument is in better tune, their body is more healthful or better tempered; which is no more praise to him than it is that he was born in Italy." It is the truth expressed in the parable of the prodigal son – the truth that it is absurd and degrading for men to make much of their intellectual and moral superiority to each other, and still more of their superiority in the arts which bring wealth and power, because, judged by their place in any universal scheme, they are all infinitely great or infinitely small. And, when observers from the Dominions, or from foreign countries, are struck by inequality as one of the special and outstanding characteristics of English social life, they do not mean that in other countries differences of personal quality are less important than in England. They mean, on the contrary, that they are more important, and that in England they tend to be obscured or obliterated behind differences of property and income, and the whole elaborate façade of a society that, compared with their own, seems stratified and hierarchical.

The equality which all these thinkers emphasize as desirable is not equality of capacity or attainment, but of circumstances, institutions, and manner of life. The inequality which they deplore is not inequality of personal gifts, but of the social and economic environment. They are concerned, not with a biological phenomenon, but with a spiritual relation and the conduct to be based on it. Their view, in short, is that, because men are men, social institutions – property rights, and the organization of industry, and the system of public health and education – should be planned, as far as possible, to emphasize and strengthen, not the class differences which divide, but the common humanity which unites, them.

Such a view of the life which is proper to human beings may, of course, be criticized, as it often has been. But to suppose that it can be criticized effectively by pointing to the width of the intellectual and moral differences which distinguish individuals from each other is a solecism, an *ignoratio elenchi*. It is true, of course, that such differences are important, and that the advance of psychology has enabled them to be measured with a new precision, with results which are valuable in making possible both a closer adaptation of educational methods to individual needs and a more intelligent selection of varying aptitudes for different tasks. But to recognize a specific difference is one thing; to pass a general judgment of superiority or inferiority, still more to favour the first and neglect the second, is quite another. The nightingale, it has been remarked, was placed in the fourth class at the fowl show. Which of a number of varying individuals is to be judged superior to the rest depends upon the criterion which is applied, and the criterion is a matter of ethical judgment. That judgment will, if it is prudent, be tentative and provisional, since men's estimates of the relative desirability of initiative, decision, common sense, imagination, humility and sympathy appear, unfortunately, to differ, and the failures and fools — the Socrates and St. Francis — of one age are the sages and saints of another. Society would not be the worse, perhaps, if idiots like Dostoievsky's were somewhat less uncommon, and the condemnation passed on those who offend one of these little ones was not limited to offenders against children whose mental ratio is in excess of eighty-five.

It is true, again, that human beings have, except as regards certain elementary, though still sadly neglected, matters of health and development, different requirements, and that these different requirements can be met satisfactorily only by varying forms of provision. But equality of provision is not identity of provision. It is to be achieved, not by treating different needs in the same way, but by devoting equal care to ensuring that they are met in the different ways most appropriate to them, as is done by a doctor who prescribes different regimens for different constitutions, or a teacher who develops different types of intelligence by different curricula. The more anxiously, indeed, a society endeavours to secure equality of consideration for all its members, the greater will be the differentiation of treatment which, when once their common human needs have been met, it accords to the special needs of different groups and individuals among them.

It is true, finally, that some men are inferior to others in respect of their intellectual endowments, and it is possible — though the truth of the possibility has not yet been satisfactorily established — that the same is true of certain classes. It does not, however, follow from this fact that such individuals or classes should receive less consideration than others, or should be treated as inferior in respect of such matters as legal status, or health, or economic arrangements, which are within the control of the community.

It may, of course, be deemed expedient so to treat them. It may be thought advisable, as Aristotle argued, to maintain the institution of slavery on the ground that some men are fit only to be living tools; or, as was customary in a comparatively recent past, to apply to the insane a severity not used towards the sane; or, as is sometimes urged to-day, to spend less liberally on the education of the slow than on that of the intelligent; or, in accordance with the practice of all ages, to show less respect for the poor than for the rich. But, in order to establish an inference, a major premise is necessary as well as a minor; and, if such discrimination on the part of society is desirable, its desirability must be shown by some other argument than the fact of inequality of intelligence and character. To convert a phenomenon, however interesting, into a principle, however respectable, is an error of logic. It is the confusion of a judgment of fact with a judgment of value — a confusion like that which was satirized by Montesquieu when he wrote, in his ironical defense of slavery: "The creatures in question are black from head to foot, and their noses are so flat that it is almost impossible to pity them. It is not to be supposed that God, an all-wise Being, can have lodged a soul — still less a good soul — in a body completely black."

Everyone recognizes the absurdity of such an argument when it is applied to matters within his personal knowledge and professional competence. Everyone realizes that, in order to justify inequalities of circumstance or opportunity by reference to differences of personal quality, it is necessary, as Professor Ginsberg observes, to show that the differences in quality are relevant to the inequalities. Everyone now sees, for example, that it is not a valid argument against women's suffrage to urge, as used to be urged not so long ago, that women are physically weaker than men, since physical strength is not relevant to the question of the ability to exercise the franchise, or a valid argument in favour of slavery that some men are less intelligent than others, since it is not certain that slavery is the most suitable penalty for lack of intelligence.

Not everyone, however, is so quick to detect the fallacy when it is expressed in general terms. It is still possible, for example, for one eminent statesman to ridicule the demand for a diminution of economic inequalities on the ground that every mother knows that her children are not equal, without reflecting whether it is the habit of mothers to lavish care on the strong and neglect the delicate; and for another to dismiss the suggestion that greater economic equality is desirable, for the reason, apparently, that men are naturally unequal. It is probable, however, that the first does not think that the fact that some children are born with good digestions, and others with bad, is a reason for supplying good food to the former and bad food to the latter, rather than for giving to both food which is equal in quality but different in kind, and that the second does not suppose that the natural inequality of men makes legal equality a contemptible principle. On the contrary, when ministers of the Crown responsible for the administration of justice to the nation, they both took for granted the desirability and existence, at any rate on paper, of legal equality. Yet in the eighteenth century statesmen of equal eminence in France and Germany, and in the nineteenth century influential thinkers in Russia and the United States, and, indeed, the ruling classes of Europe almost everywhere at a not very distant period, all were disposed to think that, since men are naturally unequal, the admission of a general equality of legal status would be the end of civilization.

Our modern statesmen do not agree with that view, for, thanks to the struggles of the past, they have inherited a tradition of legal equality, and, fortified by that tradition, they see that the fact that men are naturally unequal is not relevant to the question whether they should or should not be treated as equal before the law. But they have not inherited a tradition of economic equality, for that tradition has still to be created. Hence they do not see that the existence of differences of personal capacity and attainment is as irrelevant to the question whether it is desirable that the social environment and economic organization should be made more conducive to equality as it is to the question of equality before the law, which itself, as we have said, seemed just as monstrous a doctrine to conservative thinkers in the past as the suggestion of greater economic equality seems to them to-day.

And Sir Ernest Benn, who says that economic equality is a scientific impossibility, is quite unconscious, apparently, of the ambiguities of his doctrine. He ignores the obvious fact that, in some economic matters of the first importance — protection by the police against violence and theft, and the use of the roads, and the supply of water, and the provision of sewers, and access to a minimum of education and medical attendance, all of which were once dependent on the ability of individuals to pay for them — all members of civilized communities are now secured equality irrespective of their personal attainments and individual economic resources. He fails to see that the only question is whether that movement shall be carried forward, or rather, since in fact it is carried forward year by year, how quickly society will decide to establish complete environmental equality in respect of the external conditions of health, and education, and economic security. So he behaves like the countryman who, on being for the first time introduced to a giraffe at a circus, exclaimed indignantly, "There ain't no such animal." He says that equality is a scientific impossibility, and draws a sharp line between the natural and, as he thinks, the healthy state of things, under which each individual provides all his requirements for himself, and the unnatural and morbid condition, under which the community, consisting of himself and his fellows, provides some of them for him.

Such a line, however, is quite arbitrary, quite fanciful and artificial. Many services are supplied by collective effort to-day which in the recent past were supplied by individual effort or not supplied at all, and many more, it may be suspected, will be so supplied in the future. At any moment there are some needs which almost everyone is agreed should be satisfied on equalitarian principles, and others which they are agreed should be met by individuals who purchase what their incomes enable them to pay for, and others, again, about the most suitable provision for which opinions differ. Society has not been prevented from seeking to establish equality in respect of the first by the fear that in so doing it may be perpetrating a scientific impossibility. Nor ought it to be prevented from moving towards equality in respect of the second and third, if experience suggests that greater equality in these matters also would contribute to greater efficiency and to more general happiness.

"But," it will be said, "you are forgetting Pareto's law, and the logarithms, and the observational points. These are hard realities. No ingenious sophistry will enable you to make light of *them*." It is wrong, as we all know, to speak disrespectfully of the equator; and if the equator, which is a simple idea, deserves to be approached in a spirit of deference, how much more is such deference incumbent on those who venture within the awful ambit of economic law? There is, however, as St. Paul says, one glory of the sun and another glory of the moon; there are powers celestial and powers terrestrial; there are laws and laws. There are scientific laws which state the invariable relations between phenomena, and there are juristic laws which state how men should conduct themselves, and there are laws which are neither juristic nor, in the full sense, scientific, though they belong, no doubt, to the same category as the latter. Such laws neither state invariable relations nor prescribe conduct, but describe how, on the whole, under given historical and legal conditions, and when influenced by particular conventions and ideas, particular groups of men do, as a rule, tend to behave.

It is evident that, as economists have often reminded us, many economic laws are of the third class, not of the first or second. They indicate the manner in which, given certain historical conditions, and a certain form of social organization, and certain juristic institutions, production tends to be conducted and wealth to be distributed. They are not the less instructive and useful on that account, to those, at least, who know how to interpret them. But those who, though successful and rich, are not fully alive to the pitfalls which yawn for the unwary, and who are delighted when they hear of a law which jumps, as it seems to them, with their own instinctive preference for success and riches, sometimes find in economic laws a source of intellectual confusion, which it is distressing to all persons of humanity, and in particular, it may be suspected, to economists, to contemplate. They snatch at elaborate formulae in order to demonstrate that the particular social arrangements that they have been accustomed to admire are the product of uncontrollable forces, with which society can tamper only at its peril. They run to the fashionable nostrum of the moment, in order to shuffle off their responsibilities upon some economic automaton. Like a drunkard who pleads an alcoholic diathesis as an excuse for drinking, they appeal to the economic laws, the majority of which are merely a description of the manner in which, in a certain environment and in given circumstances, men tend to behave, as a proof that it is impossible for them to alter their behaviour.

How men in given circumstances tend to behave, and how, as a consequence, wealth tends in such circumstances to be distributed, are subjects about which valuable and illuminating, if necessarily tentative, generalizations have been produced by economists. But their behaviour, as economists have often told us, is relative to their circumstances; and the distribution of wealth depends, not wholly, indeed, but largely, on their institutions; and the character of their institutions is determined, not by immutable economic laws, but by the values, preferences, interests and ideals which rule at any moment in a given society.

These values and preferences are not something fixed and unalterable. On the contrary, they have changed repeatedly in the past, and are changing to-day; and the distribution of wealth has changed, and is changing, with them. It was of one kind in the France of the old régime, where a large part of the wealth produced was absorbed by the privileged orders, and quite another in France after the Revolution, where wealth previously paid in taxation and feudal dues was retained by the peasantry. It is of one kind in Denmark to-day and of another kind in England. Thanks largely to changes in fiscal policy and to the development of the social services, which Sir Ernest Benn finds so distasteful, it is different in the England of 1937 from what it was in the England of 1857, and, if experience may be trusted, it will be different again in the England of 1957. To suppose, as he supposes, that it must necessarily be wrong to aim at greater economic equality, because Pareto suggested that, under certain conditions, and leaving the effects of inheritance, fiscal policy, and social services out of account, the curve of distribution in several different countries and ages tended, as he thought, to conform to a certain shape, is a pardonable error, but an error none the less. It implies a misunderstanding of the nature of economic laws in general, and of Pareto's law in particular, at which no one, it is probable, would have been more amused than Pareto himself, and which, indeed, he expressly repudiated in a subsequent work. It is to believe in economic Fundamentalism, with the New Testament left out, and the Books of Leviticus and Deuteronomy inflated to unconscionable proportions by the addition of new and appalling chapters. It is to dance naked, and roll on the ground, and cut oneself with knives, in honour of the mysteries of Mumbo-Jumbo.

Mumbo-Jumbo is a great god, who, if he is given his head, is disposed to claim, not only economics, but the whole world, as his kingdom, and who is subtle enough to deceive even the elect; so that Sir Ernest Benn is to be pitied, rather than blamed, for yielding to his seductions, and for feeling the same kind of reverence for Mumbo-Jumboism as was inspired by Kant by the spectacle of the starry heavens and by the moral law. But the power of Mumbo-Jumbo, like that of some other spirits, depends on the presence of an initial will to believe in the minds of his votaries, and can, if only they are not terrified when he sends forth his thunders and his lightnings – the hail of his logarithms and the whirlwind of his economic laws – be overcome. If, when he tells them that a certain course will result in the heavens falling, they summon up the resolution to pursue it all the same, they will find that, in a surprising number of cases, though they may have succeeded in improving the earth, the heavens, nevertheless, remain much where they were. And, when his prophets are so much alarmed by the symptoms of increasing equality, and by the demand for its still further increase, that they declare that equality is a scientific impossibility, they ought not, indeed, to be treated unkindly, or hewn in pieces before the Lord, like the prophets of an earlier Mumbo-Jumbo; but they should be asked to undergo, for the sake both of themselves and of their neighbours, what to nimble minds, with a gift for quick and sweeping generalization, is sometimes a hardly less painful discipline. They should be asked to study the facts. The facts, they will find, show that the distribution of wealth in a community depends partly, at least, upon its organization and institutions – its system of property rights, its economic structure, its social and financial policy – and that it is possible for it to give these matters a bias either towards greater equality or towards greater inequality, because different communities, at different times, have done, in fact both the one and the other.

Perhaps, therefore, the remote Victorian thinkers, like Arnold and Mill, who dealt lightly with Mumbo-Jumbo, and who commended equality to their fellow-countrymen as one source of peace and happiness, were not speaking so unadvisedly as at first sight might appear. They did not deny that men have unequal gifts, or suggest that all of them are capable of earning, as the author of *The Confessions of a Capitalist* tells us that he earns, £10,000 a year, or of making a brilliant show when their natural endowments are rigorously sifted and appraised with exactitude. What they were concerned to emphasize is something more elementary and commonplace. It is the fact that, in spite of their varying characters and capacities, men possess in their common humanity a quality which is worth cultivating, and that a community is most likely to make the most of that quality if it takes it into account in planning its economic organization and social institutions – if it stresses lightly differences of wealth and birth and social position, and establishes on firm foundations institutions which meet common needs, and are a source of common enlightenment and common enjoyment. The individual differences of which so much is made, they would have said, will always survive, and they are to be welcomed, not regretted. But their existence is no reason for not seeking to establish the largest possible measure of equality of environment, and circumstance, and opportunity. On the contrary, it is a reason for redoubling our efforts to establish it, in order to ensure that these diversities of gifts may come to fruition.

It is true, indeed, that even such equality, though the conditions on which it depends are largely within human control, will continue to elude us. The important thing, however, is not that it should be completely attained, but that it should be sincerely sought. What matters to the health of society is the objective towards which its face is set, and to suggest that it is immaterial in which direction it moves, because, whatever the direction, the goal must always elude it, is not scientific, but irrational. It is like using the impossibility of absolute cleanliness as a pretext for rolling in a manure heap, or denying the importance of honesty because no one can be wholly honest.

It may well be the case that capricious inequalities are in some measure inevitable, in the sense that, like crime and disease, they are a malady which the most rigorous precautions cannot wholly overcome. But, when crime is known as crime, and disease as disease, the ravages of both are circumscribed by the mere fact that they are recognized for what they are, and described by their proper names, not by flattering euphemisms. And a society which is convinced that inequality is an evil need not be alarmed because the evil is one which cannot wholly be subdued. In recognizing the poison it will have armed itself with an antidote. It will have deprived inequality of its sting by stripping it of its esteem.

19. Egalitarianism and the Equal Consideration of Interests

Stanley I. Benn

Egalitarians persist in speaking of human equality, as a principle significant for action, in the face of all the evident human inequalities of stature, physique, intellect, virtue, merit, and desert. Claims pressed so tenaciously, in the face of seemingly manifest and overwhelming objections, can hardly be summarily dismissed as naive absurdities. The task for the philosopher is to look for ways of construing such claims, consistent with the evident inequalities, compatible with commonly accepted conceptions of justice, yet still with bite enough to make a difference to behavior worth contending for. I shall argue that in many contexts the claim to human equality is no more than a negative egalitarianism, a denial, a limited criticism of some specific existing arrangements. If one were to interpret such claims as implying a universal positive assertion about human rights and social organization, one would be going beyond what was necessary to make good sense of them. But because such a negative interpretation does not seem to exhaust the possibilities of egalitarianism, I shall formulate a principle that, while satisfying the aforementioned criteria, can still be applied quite generally, and can be properly expressed in the formula "all men are equal." This is the *principle of equal consideration of human interests*. I shall further maintain that this principle is

Reprinted from *Equality: Nomos IX*, editorial by J. Roland Pennock and John W. Chapman (New York: Atherton Press, 1967), pp. 61–78. Copyright © 1967 Atherton Press. Reprinted by permission of Lieber-Atherton, Incorporated.

required by current conceptions of social justice. It can be effective in public policy-making, however, only to the extent that agreement can be reached on the proper order of priority of human interests.

I

Things or persons can be equal in several different ways. In one sense equality presupposes an ordering of objects according to some common natural property or attribute that can be possessed in varying degrees. So, although objects said to be equal occupy interchangeable places in such an ordering, their equality in this respect is necessarily implied neither by their possessing this property in common nor by their common membership of a larger class of which all members possess the property. Although two cabbages happen, for instance, to be of equal weight, their equality is not a necessary feature of their both being cabbages, even though every cabbage has weight. In this sense at least, not all cabbages are equal. Things can be equal in a second sense according to some standard of value or merit. Two students' essays may be equally good, though their properties may differ, one being detailed and painstaking, the other original and imaginative. Here, differences in their properties are weighed against one another in assessing their relative merit; however, in a final ordering of all essays, in which some stand high and others low, these two occupy interchangeable places. Here, again, their equality is not a necessary feature of their both being essays. A third kind of equality is that of need, entitlement, or desert; the remuneration to which a main is entitled for his work or the dose of medicine he needs for his cough may be equal to another's, though it could conceivably have been different without prejudice to their common status as workers or sick men.

These three ways of ascribing equality — descriptive, evaluative, and distributive — are not of course independent of one another. There may be a logical connection: two knives, equally sharp, equally well-tempered, possessing indeed all relevant properties in the same degree, are equally good knives, sharpness, temper, and the like, being the criteria of a good knife.[1] However, the equal merit of the students' essays does not follow necessarily from a list of their properties but depends on a complex appraisal in the light of multiple standards. Different again is the case of two men entitled to equal pay for doing equal amounts of work. In this case, their equality depends on a particular convention; according to a different practice, if one man worked longer than the other, their deserts would be different, even though the results might be the same. In all these instances, however, though the possibility of comparison depends on the subjects being members of the same class, it is not a necessary condition of their membership that they possess the property by virtue of which they are equals in the precise degree that they do. Mere membership of the same class does not entail, therefore, that the subjects are equals in any of the three senses discussed. Consequently, although two members of a class happen to qualify for equal treatment, this is not a necessary result of their common membership.

To say, then, that two things are in some respect equal is to say that they are, in

---

[1] The phrase "possessing all relevant properties to the same degree" guarantees the tautology, of course, by exhausting all the possible criteria.

that and perhaps related respects, interchangeable — that no rational ground exists for treating them in those respects differently from each other. Egalitarians would maintain, however, that the reason for considering them equal need not always be that they satisfy some qualifying condition to the same degree; it may be because, with regard to some manner of treating them, the qualifying condition does not admit of degrees; it may be enough simply to possess the properties necessary to make them members of that class. There may then be something to which all members of a class have an equal claim, in the sense that none has a better claim than another, nor could have, given their common membership. If, for instance, all sane adults have the right to vote, and there are no other qualifying (or disqualifying) conditions, no qualified member of the class of sane adults has any better right than another, nor has any member a right to any more votes than another, by virtue of some further property than they possess in varying degrees. All qualified voters, qua voters, are equal.

II

Those who demand social equality do not necessarily take universal adult equal suffrage as a paradigm for all social institutions and practices. There may be egalitarians for whom a society without differences is both a possibility and an ideal; most, however, have more limited aims. When egalitarianism is translated into concrete political programs, it usually amounts to a proposal to abandon existing inequalities, rather than to adopt some positive principle of social justice. The egalitarian in politics usually has quite specific objectives and is critical of quite specific kinds of differentiation rather than of every kind of social discrimination. Indeed, differences are rarely called "inequalities" unless, in the first place, they affect the things which men value and for which they compete, like power, wealth, or esteem. One complains of inequality if one has to pay more tax than another man but not if, for some administrative reason, the demands arrive in differently colored envelopes. Egalitarians protest when, in the second place, they see no rational justification for differentiating a particular class for the purpose of allocating certain specific privileges or burdens. The campaign for equal pay for women is a case in point. To treat people according to their skill or productivity would not be to discriminate between the sexes, even though some women might in fact receive less than some men (or, conceivably, all women less than all men), for skill and productivity are generally recognized as relevant and legitimate criteria. Sex differentiation as such is intolerable because, it is argued, no one has yet shown good enough reasons for thinking a person's sex relevant to the income he should earn — and the burden of proof rests on the discriminator. On the other hand, discrimination according to sex for military service has been generally accepted without much question and is usually considered well-grounded; so it is rarely called an inequality.

A race, sex, religious, or class egalitarianism denies the justice, then, of some existing modes of discrimination, possibly in a relatively limited range of social practices; it does not press for the removal of all forms of differentiation. Or it may endorse existing grounds of discrimination but question whether they ought to make as much difference as they do. Of course, the conditions under attack, and the related forms of differentiation not under attack, may be contextually supplied and not explicitly stated; nevertheless, they may be perfectly well understood by all parties to the debate.[2]

III

Although most movements for equality can be interpreted in terms of protests against specific inequalities, a strong disposition nonetheless exists, among philosophers and others, to argue that whatever men's actual differences and whatever their genuine relevance for certain kinds of differentiation, there yet remain important values in respect of which all men's claims are equal. Whatever these may be — and catalogs of natural and human rights are attempts to formulate them — they are such that no difference in properties between one man and another could affect them; all men qualify simply by virtue of belonging to the class *man*, which admits of no degrees (just as, in my earlier example, all voters are equally qualified provided they are sane adults). This certainly looks like a positive and quite general claim to equality rather than a denial of specific irrelevant inequalities.

In a recent article, "Against Equality,"[3] J. R. Lucas contends that egalitarianism rests on a confusion of two principles, each sound in itself but which, if pressed, together lead to incompatible conclusions. One, the principle of formal equality, is the familiar principle underlying all forms of what I have called negative egalitarianism: if two people are to be treated differently there should be some relevant difference between them. Lucas does not regard this as really an egalitarian principle at all, because in itself it prescribes neither equality nor inequality, but, taking it for granted that there might be good reasons for treating men differently in some respects, it lays down the form that a justificatory argument must take. The other principle, that Lucas calls the principle of universal humanity, makes this assertion:

> Men, because they are men, ought not to be killed, tortured, imprisoned, exploited, frustrated, humiliated; . . . they should never be treated merely as means but always as ends in themselves. . . . We should treat human beings, because they are human beings, humanely.

But this, he says, has little to do with equality:

> To say that all men, because they are men, are equally men, or that to treat any two persons as ends in themselves is to treat them as equally ends in themselves is to import a spurious note of egalitarianism into a perfectly sound and serious argument. We may call it, if we like, the argument for Equality of Respect, but in this phrase it is the word "Respect" — respect for each man's humanity, respect for him as a human being — which is doing the logical work, while the word "Equality" adds nothing to the argument and is altogether otiose.[4]

---

[2] A favorite way of discrediting the egalitarian, however, is to make it appear that he seeks to remove forms of discrimination that neither he, nor anyone else, would for a moment question. Though the Levellers were concerned only for equal political rights, for removing monopolistic privileges in trade, and for legal reforms, they were frequently accused, despite vigorous disclaimers, of wanting to level property.

[3] *Philosophy*, Vol. XL (1965), pp. 296–307.

[4] *Ibid.*, p. 298.

I suspect that Lucas has dealt too shortly with positive egalitarianism, in representing it simply as rules about how we ought to behave in relation to objects or persons of a given class. He is perfectly right in saying, for instance, that the duty not to inflict torture has nothing to do with equality, but then, it is not a duty in respect of human beings alone but also of animals. This is not a duty we *owe* to men as men, for it is doubtful whether, properly speaking, we *owe* it to the object at all. Inflicting needless pain is simply wrong; it would not be a case of unequal treatment, but simply of cruelty. It would be a case lacking altogether the characteristic feature that makes inequality objectionable — namely, unfairness or injustice.

But some of Lucas' examples of inhumanity do seem to have more to do with equality than that. In particular, the injunction to respect all men, simply as men or as ends in themselves, unlike the injunction not to torture them, involves recognizing them as subjects of claims, and not merely as objects, albeit objects that ought to be handled in one way rather than another. To treat a man not as an end but simply as a means is to give no consideration to his interests, but to consider him only insofar as he can promote or frustrate the interests of someone else — to treat him, in short, like Aristotle's "natural slave," with no end not derived from that of a master. Now to adopt such an attitude can be said to be not merely wrong (as is cruelty), but wrong in the special way that it disregards a fundamental equality of *claim* — the claim to have one's interests considered alongside those of everyone else likely to be affected by the decision.

Now this *principle of equal consideration of interests* seems to me to involve an assertion of equality that is neither purely formal or otiose. It *resembles*, it is true, another principle, which is deducible from the principle of formal equality — therefore itself formal — and which is often called the principle of equal consideration. The principle of formal equality states that where there is no relevant difference between two cases, no rational ground exists for not treating them alike; but, conversely, where there is a relevant difference, there is a reasonable ground for treating them differently. This involves, as a corollary, that equal consideration must be given to the relevant features of each, for to have good reasons for favoring one person or course of action rather than another surely implies that there are no conclusively better reasons on the other side; and how could one know that, without having given them equal consideration?[5] This is certainly, then, a purely formal or procedural principle, for it offers no criterion for good reasons nor makes any substantive recommendation for action. The principle of equal consideration of interests, on the other hand, is specific at least to the extent that it directs consideration to the *interests* of those affected, and so lays down, as the other principle does not, a criterion of relevance. After all, if I preferred A to B because A could be of more use to me, I should still be acting consistently with the formal principle of equal consideration, provided I had first considered how useful to me B could be. But this would not be consistent with the equal consideration of interests, for I would have given thought to the interests of neither A nor B, but only to my own.

If the principle is not purely formal, neither is it otiose. For it would be

---

[5] See S. I. Benn and R. S. Peters, *Social Principles and the Democratic State*, London, 1959 (reissued as *Principles of Political Thought*, New York, 1964 and 1965), Chapter V, for a fuller discussion of the formal principle of equal consideration.

perfectly possible to consider the interests of everyone affected by a decision without giving them *equal* consideration. Elitist moralities are precisely of this kind. Although the elitist would allow that ordinary men have interests deserving some consideration, the interests of the super-man, super-class, or super-race would always be preferred. Some men, it might be said, are simply worth more than others, in the sense that any claim of theirs, whatever it might be and whatever its specific ground, would always take precedence. Such a morality would maintain that there was some criterion, some qualifying condition, of race, sex, intellect, or personality, such that a person once recognized as satisfying it would automatically have prior claim in every field over others.

The egalitarian would deny that there is any such criterion. Whatever priority special circumstances or properties confer on a man in particular fields, no one of them, neither a white skin, male sex, Aryan ancestry, noble birth, nor any other whatsoever, would entitle a man to move to the head of *every* queue. That is not to imply that any man can always claim the same treatment as any other, nor, indeed, that one man's interest could never have priority over another's, as, for instance, when we tax the rich to assist the poor. But every claim must be grounded on criteria specifically appropriate to it, and every demand for privilege must be argued afresh, since arguments valid in one field have no necessary consequential validity in others. This, I think, is the claim fundamental to the idea of social equality or equality of esteem. It is related to the claim of self-respect, which J. C. Davies has put in these words: "I am as good as anybody else; I may not be as clever or hard-working as you are, but I am as good as you are."[6] It bears also on the concept of equality of respect. No one could respect all men equally; nor does it seem likely, leaving aside the differences in respect we have for men on account of their different virtues and merits, that there is still a residual respect we owe to each merely as a man. What is there to respect in what alone is common to all men — membership of this particular biological species? It makes perfectly good sense, however, to say that, whereas we respect different men for different things, there is no property, such as a white skin, which is a necessary condition of a man's being worthy, whatever his other merits, of any respect at all. So every man is entitled to be taken on his own merits; there is no generally disqualifying condition.

That this is not mere empty formalism is clear when we contrast the case of men with that of animals. For not to possess human shape *is* a disqualifying condition. However faithful or intelligent a dog may be, it would be a monstrous sentimentality to attribute to him interests that could be weighed in an equal balance with those of human beings. The duties we have in respect to dogs would generally be discounted when they conflict with our duties to human beings — discounted, not set aside, for we might well decide to waive a minor obligation to a human being rather than cause intense suffering to an animal. But if the duties were at all commensurate, if, for instance, one had to decide between feeding a hungry baby or a hungry dog, anyone who chose the dog would generally be reckoned morally defective, unable to recognize a fundamental inequality of claims.

This is what distinguishes our attitude to animals from our attitude to imbeciles. It would be odd to say that we ought to respect equally the dignity or personality of the imbecile and of the rational man; it is questionable indeed whether one can treat with respect someone for whom one's principal feeling is pity. But there is

[6] *Human Nature in Politics*, New York, 1963, p. 45.

nothing odd about saying that we should respect their interests equally, that is, that we should give to the interests of each the same serious consideration as claims to conditions necessary for some standard of well-being that we can recognize and endorse.[7]

The imbecile has been something of an embarrassment to moral philosophers.[8] There is a traditional view, going back to the Stoics, that makes rationality the qualifying condition on which human freedom and equality depend. But if equal consideration of interests depended on rationality, imbeciles would belong to an inferior species, whose interests (if they could properly be allowed to have interests) would always have to be discounted when they competed with those of rational men. What reason could then be offered against using them like dogs or guinea pigs for, say, medical research? But, of course, we do distinguish imbeciles from animals in this regard, and although it would be quite proper to discriminate between imbeciles and rational men for very many purposes, most rationalist philosophers would concede that it would be grossly indecent to subordinate the interests of an imbecile to those of normal persons for *all* purposes, simply on the ground of his imbecility.

Nevertheless, the link between rationality and our moral concern for human interests cannot be disregarded. If the human species is more important to us than other species, with interests worthy of special consideration, each man's for his own sake, this is possibly because each of us sees in other men the image of himself. So he recognizes in them what he knows in his own experience, the potentialities for moral freedom, for making responsible choices among ways of life open to him, for striving, no matter how mistakenly and unsuccessfully, to make of himself something worthy of his own respect. It is because this is the characteristically human enterprise, requiring a capacity for self-appraisal and criticism normal to men but not to dogs, that it seems reasonable to treat men as more important than dogs.[9]

Still, we respect the interests of men and give them priority over dogs not *insofar* as they are rational, but because rationality is the human norm. We say it is *unfair* to exploit the deficiencies of the imbecile, who falls short of the norm, just as it would be unfair, and not just ordinarily dishonest, to steal from a blind man. If we do not think in this way about dogs, it is because we do not see the irrationality of a dog as a deficiency or a handicap but as normal for the species. The characteristics, therefore, that distinguish the normal man from the normal dog make it intelligible for us to talk of other men as having interests and capacities, and therefore claims, of precisely the same kind as we make on our own behalf. But although these characteristics may provide the point of the distinction between men and other species, they are not in fact the qualifying conditions for membership, or the

[7] I do not argue for this conception of interests in this paper, except by implication. I have done so explicitly, however, in " 'interests' in Politics," *Aristotelian Society Proceedings*, Vol. LX (1959–1960), pp. 123–140.

[8] For example, Bernard Williams, "I omit here, as throughout the discussion, the clinical cases of people who are mad or mentally defective, who always constitute special exceptions to what is in general true of men." "The Idea of Equality," in P. Laslett and W. G. Runciman, Eds., *Philosophy, Politics and Society*, Oxford, 1962, p. 118.

[9] If we were able to establish communication with another species – dolphins, for instance – and found that they too were engaged in this "characteristically human enterprise," I think we should find ourselves thinking of them as a fishy variety of human being, making much the same claim on our consideration.

distinguishing criteria of the class of morally considerable persons; and this is precisely because a man does not become a member of a different species, with its own standards of normality, by reason of not possessing these characteristics. On the other hand, the deficiency is more than an accidental fact, for it has a bearing on his moral status. For if someone is deficient in this way, he is falling short of what, in some sense, he *ought* to have been, given the species to which by nature he belongs; it is, indeed, to be deprived of the possibility of fully realizing his nature. So where the mental limitations of the dog can be amusing, without lapse of taste, those of an imbecile are tragic and appalling. Moreover, so far from being a reason for disregarding his interests, they may be grounds for special compensatory consideration, to meet a special need.

IV

I said earlier that an egalitarian would deny that any property could confer an automatic general priority of claim on anyone possessing it, but that this need not preclude one man's interests having priority over others' in certain respects. I want to enlarge on this point and in doing so to compare the principle of equal consideration of interests with John Rawls' account of justice as fairness.[10]

Rawls asserts that "inequalities are arbitrary unless it is reasonable to expect that they will work out for everyone's advantage, and provided the positions and offices to which they attach ... are open to all." He then seeks to show that only a practice that satisfied these conditions could be accepted by free, equal, rational, and prudent participants in it, given that they knew their own interests and that each ran the risk of filling the least favored roles. Rawls' model appears to derive justice from consent. However, what really counts is not what a man would actually accept but what, understanding his interests, he could reasonably accept. Thus objections to a practice based purely on envy of a privileged position would not be admissible, because avoiding the pangs of envy would not be an interest of a rational, prudent man. Rawls' model looks like a way of saying that a practice is just if it sacrifices no one's interest to anyone else's and makes only such distinctions as would promote the interests of everyone, given that the interests are not simply desires but conditions of well-being that rational men could endorse as such. This in turn looks rather like the egalitarian principle of equal consideration of interests. There are, however, difficulties in trying to equate the two accounts.

Rawls' model suggests an adequate schema for justifying discrimination in terms of desert or merit (the traditional problems of justice); it can be fitted, however, to modern conceptions of social justice, only at the cost of so abstracting from reality that the model loses most of its suggestiveness.[11] These conceptions are characteristically compensatory and distributive; they are implicit in the institutions and policies of welfare states, which provide for the needs of the handicapped by taxing the more fortunate. At first glance, at least, Rawls' principles of justice

[10] John Rawls, "Justice as Fairness," in P. Laslett and W. G. Runciman, *op. cit.*, pp. 132–157; and "Constitutional Liberty and the Concept of Justice," in Carl J. Friedrich and John W. Chapman, Eds., *Justice, Nomos VI*, New York, 1963, pp. 98–125.

[11] Cf. John Chapman's point that, admitting the justice of Rawls' strictures on utilitarianism, the latter has this merit, as against the contractualist theories of justice, that it can take account of need. "Justice and Fairness" in *Justice, op. cit.*, pp. 147–169.

would give wealthy but sterile people who are taxed to help educate the children of poor but fertile people legitimate grounds for complaint, as victims of a discriminatory practice that imposes sacrifices without corresponding advantages.

It could be argued, perhaps, that Rawls meets the case by presupposing in his model that all participants start equal, and that all roles are interchangeable. The restrictions that the community's practices would put on individual interests, or the sacrifices that would be accepted by some for the benefit of others, would then be such as "a person would keep in mind if he were designing a practice in which his enemy were to assign him his place." Rawls may argue that it is always prudent for the fortunate to insure against misfortune; it would be reasonable, in that case, for a man to consent to a tax for someone else's advantage, if there were a risk of his finding himself in that person's place. But which of all the features of a man's situation, character, talents, and incapacities, by which he could be at a disadvantage, are to be taken as intrinsic and irremediable, and which conjecturally subject to reallocation, as part of the "place" to which his enemy might assign him? Need the normal, healthy person really reckon with the risk of being called upon to fill the role of the congenitally handicapped? Similar questions can be asked of some socially conferred disadvantages. While the rich must, perhaps, take account of the risk of poverty, need a white man take seriously the risk of having to fill the role of a colored man in a racially prejudiced society? To meet these arguments, Rawls would need to postulate as one of the conditions of his model, not that the participants are equal but that they are completely ignorant of all their inequalities.[12]

When pressed, then, the model becomes increasingly remote from reality. Rawls' account of justice seems to rely, at first glance, on the conception of principles to which self-interested individuals would agree; it soon becomes evident, however, that these are principles to which such individuals *could reasonably* agree. Moreover, if the primary motivation of self-interest is to be preserved, we must suppose these individuals ignorant of their identities and thus unaware of any circumstances that would distinguish their own interest from anyone else's. What they are really called upon to do, then, is to safeguard a paradigmatic set of interests from a number of typical hazards. We need not now suppose a collection of egotists, so much as creatures with standards of human well-being and with both a concern for and a knowledge of the conditions necessary for achieving or maintaining it. Now the lack of some of these conditions, food and shelter for instance, would frustrate the attainment of such standards more completely than the lack of others, such as holidays or books. One must arrange human interests, then, in an order of priority, distinguishing basic from other less urgent needs. So a participant in one of Rawls' practices would be well advised to reckon with the possibility of being deprived of basic needs, as well as of being subject to a range of natural and social handicaps that would impair his capacity to supply them. Consequently, he would be rash to concur in any practice that (subject to certain proviso considered below) does not guarantee the satisfaction of basic needs and compensate for handicaps before conceding less urgent advantages to others, even if that means giving the handicapped special treatment at the expense of the normal and healthy.

Developed in this way, Rawls' model would take account of the fact that

---

[12] Or, as John Chapman has put it to me, "Rawls assumes you don't know who you are."

questions of social justice arise just because people are unequal in ways they can do very little to change and that only by attending to these inequalities can one be said to be giving their interests equal consideration. For their interests are not equal in the sense that every interest actually competing in a given situation is of equal weight, irrespective of how far each claimant's interests have already been attended to; they are equal, instead, in the sense that two men lacking similar conditions necessary to their well-being would, *prima facie*, have equally good claims to them.

This analysis throws some light on the paradoxical problems of compensatory welfare legislation on behalf of Negroes. A recent collection of essays[13] has drawn attention to the ambiguous implications of the notion of equality and, in particular, of the "equal protection" clause of the Fourteenth Amendment, for the desegregation and social integration of Negroes. Even liberal friends of the Negro have been known to argue, it seems, that the law should be color-blind, and that compensatory legislation on the Negro's behalf is discrimination in reverse. If (it is said) color is irrelevant to eligibility for jobs, housing, education, and social esteem, to make special provisions for the Negro as such would be to reinstate an irrelevant criterion, and so to treat equals unequally, or alternatively, to deny the human equality that it is so important to affirm. This argument disregards, however, a vital ambiguity. Negroes and whites are equal in the sense that their interests deserve equal consideration; they are painfully unequal in the sense that society imposes on the Negro special disabilities. So although black and white may equally need housing or education, the obstacles placed by society in the black man's way add extra weight to his claim to public assistance to meet these needs. Where society imposes handicaps, it can hardly be unjust for the state to compensate for them. Nor is it far-fetched to call this a way of providing equal protection for the interests of black and white. Where the interests of a group are subject to discriminatory social handicaps on the irrational ground of color, it is not irrational for the state to apply the same criterion in giving them protection on an appropriately more generous scale. Equal protection ought not to mean an equal allocation of the means of protection— for the protection must be commensurate with the threat or impediment.[14]

V

Finally, it is necessary to qualify the principle of equal consideration of interests in two respects, the first theoretical, the second practical.

The first corresponds to Rawls' qualification that "an inequality is allowed only if there is reason to believe that the practice with the inequality, or resulting in it, will work for the advantage of every party engaging in it."[15] The principle of equal consideration of interests provides for the satisfaction of interests in order of urgency, every individual's claim being otherwise equal. A departure from this principle could be defended by showing that it would increase the capacity to satisfy interests in general and that it would not weaken the claims of someone

[13] R. L. Carter, D. Kenyon, Peter Marcuse, Loren Miller (with a foreword by Charles Abrams), *Equality*, New York, 1965.

[14] G. Vlastos makes a similar point in connection with the right to security, "Justice and Equality," *Social Justice*, R. B. Brandt, Ed., Englewood Cliffs, N.J., 1962, p. 41.

[15] "Justice as Fairness," *op. cit.*, p. 135.

who, without the adoption of the variant practice, could reasonably claim satisfaction under the main principle. It may be expedient, but not just, that one man should starve that others might grow fat; but there is no injustice if, in allowing some to grow fat, we can reduce the number that would otherwise starve. In this way we take account of incentive arguments for distribution by desert, as well as of claims to special treatment to meet functional needs.

The second qualification applies to the practical application of the principle. I have argued that it prescribes that interests be satisfied in order of their urgency, men without food and clothes falling further short of some presupposed conception of well-being than men who have these things but lack guitars. But clearly, this principle works as a practical guide for social policy only so long as there is a very wide measure of agreement on priorities. And there is such agreement in what range of interests we most commonly call "needs," those, in fact, from which most of my examples have been drawn. But it is not easy to see how a society that had solved the problem of providing for everyone's generally agreed needs could go much further in applying equal consideration of needs as a direct distributive principle.

Throughout this paper I have been relying on a conception of interests as conditions necessary to a way of life or to forms of activity that are endorsed as worthwhile, or (what probably amounts to the same thing) as conditions necessary to the process of making of oneself something worthy of respect.[16] Now, hermits and ascetics apart, we shall probably agree on the basic conditions necessary for any good life at all. Once given those preliminary conditions, however, we shall encounter very diverse opinions on the absolute eligibility of certain ways of life, on their relative worth, on the conditions necessary for them, and on the relative urgency of such conditions, as claims to our attention. This would make it very difficult indeed to put a schedule of interests into a socially acceptable order of priority. Furthermore, it is difficult to see how an authoritative and general allocation of resources according to interests could avoid laying down an official ruling on what ways of life were most eligible. Yet, as Charles Fried has argued,[17] the freedom to judge, even mistakenly, what is in one's own interests is itself an important human interest.

This may, however, point the way out of the dilemma. My main criticism of Rawls has been that, unless amended along the lines I have indicated, his postulate of equality is either unrealistic or restrictive, removing some of the most insistent problems of social justice from the scope of his principles, by presupposing a condition that it is in the interests of justice to bring about. But in the conditions of affluence I am now considering, where basic interests are already being satisfied, and there is no further common ground on priorities, the postulate of equality would come much closer to reality. If there are equal opportunities to pursue one's interests, and freedom to determine what they are is recognized as itself an

---

[16] It is not necessary for my present purpose to discuss what could be good reasons for approving some ways of life, or forms of activity, or kinds of personality, and rejecting others. I ask the reader's assent only to the following propositions: that we do in fact make judgments of this kind, and that the notion of what is in a man's interest must ultimately be related to such a judgment, at any rate at the stage at which it is said that he is mistaking where his real interest lies. There may be sufficient consensus in a society for "interests" to function descriptively; but this is only because, at that level, the normative element is not in dispute and not therefore obtrusive.

[17] "Justice and Liberty," in *Justice, op. cit.*, pp. 126–146. See also my " 'Interests' in Politics," *loc. cit.*

important interest, even at the risk of error, Rawls' principles of justice come into their own. Rawls lays it down that a practice is just if everyone is treated alike, unless a discrimination in favor of some is of advantage to everyone. We can now translate this into the language of equal interests: If all basic interests are already being satisfied and if there is no universally acknowledged order of priority as between further interests competing for satisfaction, then, given that the individual has a fundamental interest in determining what are his own interests, a practice would be just that gave all interests actually competing in a situation equal satisfaction, save insofar as an inequality made possible a greater degree of satisfaction without weakening claims that would be satisfied without it. On this interpretation, Rawls' original account of the criteria of a just practice turns out to be a special application, in conditions where all handicaps have already been remedied, of the principle of the equal consideration of interests.

20. Equality

J. L. Lucas

Equality is a difficult notion in politics and a dangerous one. Outside politics, equality is naturally applied to *metrical* concepts. Only when we have a system of measurement does it make sense to raise the question whether two magnitudes are equal or not. We can talk of equal *lengths*, or *areas*, or *weights*, because these things can be measured. It make sense to ask whether two things are equal when, and only when, it also makes sense to ask whether one of them is twice as large as the other, etc.

It is an acceptable extension of the concept of equality to apply it to two members, say x and y, of a set, completely ordered by the transitive, asymmetrical relation R, when $\sim xRy$ & $\sim yRx$. Thus we talk of two substances being equally hard when neither will scratch the other, or of two sounds being equally loud when neither is louder than the other, even though we may have no satisfactory way of measuring hardness or loudness.

Further extensions of the concept of equality are neither helpful nor innocuous. We can apply the concept to things which could not differ in degree but might differ in kind, to mean what we normally express by the word "same" or "similar." The phrase, "Other things being equal," means "If the circumstances are the same," or "in the absence of any differentiating features." But this is not a helpful usage, for we already have perfectly good words to express the fact that two things resemble each other in respect of a certain feature, and the word "Equality" is charged with emotional overtones which obstruct clear thinking. Men are apt to be resentful if they are told that they are not equal with somebody else, when all that is being said is the perfectly acceptable truth that they are different. The word

From J. L. Lucas, *The Principles of Politics* (Oxford: The Clarendon Press, 1966), pp. 243–250, by permission of The Clarendon Press, Oxford, England.

"Equality" is a dangerous one in politics. It would be better if it were never used, but always some clearer, and less emotionally charged, synonym. But in fact it is used, and we must attempt to elucidate its various senses, and use it as clearly as we can.

The first rule for achieving clarity when the concept of Equality is involved is always to ask: "Equality in respect of what?"[1] A man may be demanding Equality in respect of monetary incomes, or, like Procustes, Equality in respect of height: he may be saying that he feels most at ease in the company of those who are (approximately) his equals in age, or among those to whom he neither gives orders nor renders obedience (his equals in rank). But always the word "equal" by itself is incomplete. It is like the word "same." We need to specify the respects in which things are said to be the same or not. Between any two things, however dissimilar, we can always find some point of resemblance: and between any two things, however similar, we can always find some point of difference. Therefore we never can say that two things are the same, or are not the same, without being ready to specify, at least to some extent, the ways in which they are, or are not, the same. And so too, in the political sense of "Equality," we can never say simply that two people are equal, or unequal, but we must have in mind the respects in which they are equal or unequal. We are all equal in some respects – we all must die. In other respects – the possession of personal peculiarities – every one of us is unequal in comparison with everybody else. Therefore all discussions of Equality will be fruitless unless there is a specification of the respects in which Equality is claimed or contested.

We can, secondly, make discussions of Equality more fruitful if we translate them into discussions of *relevance*. Although, strictly speaking, no two things are the same in all respects, we often talk of two things as being the same if they are the same in all relevant respects. What respects are relevant depends partly on the context of argument, and may partly itself be a matter for dispute. It is much easier to discuss whether a particular characteristic is a relevant one, than to discuss whether two men, or two cases, are equal. Therefore we do well to replace controversies about Equality by arguments about *criteria of relevance*.

It will, in fact, prove useful to go further, and have a two-way discussion, one about criteria of relevance the other about criteria of irrelevance. This reflects the dialectical nature of political argument, which makes it important to distinguish the cases where the onus of proof is on a man who claims a certain factor is relevant from those where it is on him who denies it. But of this more later.

Discussions about criteria of relevance and irrelevance have the further merit of emphasising that the Equalities we claim or affirm are optional alternatives, not conjoint necessities. If I choose to regard one feature as relevant and all others as irrelevant, then I shall have one sort of Equality, either as an ideal or as a fact, but at the price of forgoing other Equalities based on other criteria of relevance. We can give everybody equal access to the courts or even equally good legal aid; but we cannot, and necessarily cannot, equalise the outcome. Justice holds the scales equal; but allows one side to go down and the other up. We can provide equal rations of food for each member of the community, but at the cost of satisfying

[1] Compare Aristotle, *Politics*, Bk. III, Ch. IX, 1280a21ff.; Bk. III, Ch. XII, 1282b22; Bk. V, Ch. I, 1301a28ff.

appetites unequally, leaving boys still hungry, and old women overfed. We can give everybody an equal right to vote in parliamentary elections, but then minority communities or groups may never be represented: or we can give different communities or groups their own representatives, but then we do not give each man's vote equal weight. In the United States, the House of Representatives is constituted according to one principle of Equality, the Senate according to another. Each excludes the other. Neither is naturally right. The Founding Fathers had to *choose* which factors to take as relevant and which to disregard.

Equality is often thought to be connected with Justice, often with Legality, sometimes with Humanity. In a manner of speaking it is connected with each of these, but it is a different sort of Equality in each case. Justice (in particular cases) or Equity could, as we now see, be described, rather misleadingly, as Formal Equality: two cases that are formally equal should be treated equally; that is to say, two cases that are the same in all relevant respects should be treated, in all relevant ways, the same. This is none other than the weak principle of universalisability, the principle of rationality, which we have called Equity. It is a principle of crucial importance, but it carries no egalitarian implications, and to describe it as a form of Equality is but a bad Latin pun. The strong principle of universalisability, which we have called Legality, can also be called Equality *before* the law, which lays down that we should treat each case in accordance with an antecedently promulgated rule, which we should apply to all cases that fall under it, and which thus specifies what features are to count as relevant. Equality of Respect, or Humanity, restricts even further the factors to be taken as relevant. Only the fact that men are human is relevant when considerations of Humanity are urged, and in this respect all men indeed are equal, for assuredly they are all human beings. All these, and some other, Equalities are important. But they are different Equalities in each case, and nothing but confusion can result from regarding all these Equalities as being one and the same. The usual egalitarian argument is just such a confusion. It confuses Formal Equality with Equality of Respect. Both principles correlate human situations with possible treatments of them. Formal Equality lays down for one type of correlation that it should be one-valued; that is, that every distinction which can be drawn between treatments corresponds to some distinction which can be drawn between human situations: but this is always possible since no two human beings are qualitatively identical. Equality of Respect lays down for another type of correlation the fact that it correlates characteristics common to all human beings with characteristics common to all humane treatments. Formal Equality specifies the treatment as fully as any one, egalitarian or non-egalitarian, could want, but in doing this for the treatments, is committed to drawing too many distinctions among the human beings for the egalitarian to stomach. Equality of Respect manages not to distinguish between men, so as to gladden the heart of the egalitarian: but in saying so little about men as not to differentiate between them, it says too little about treatments to characterise them in more than a very minimal way — too little to ensure that they all will be equal in the way that the egalitarian wants. The egalitarian wants a map of the logical possibilities which is very detailed — in order to have everybody treated alike *in all respects* — and at the same time a crude outline sketch — in order to include all men together in only one constituency: but the logical manoeuvres which will give him the one will preclude him from having the other, and *vice versa*. We have no warrant for combining the minimal specification of human beings, which is the only one in respect of which we are all alike, with the maximal specification of the treatments we are to receive, which is necessary if they are all to be thought to be the same.

The central argument for Equality is a muddle. There are two sound principles of political reasoning, the weak principle of universalisability and the principle of Universal Humanity, and each has been described as a sort of Equality, Formal Equality in the one case and Equality of Respect in the other. But they are not the same Equality, nor are they compatible, and they cannot be run in harness to lead to a full-blooded egalitarianism.

Egalitarian arguments depend on not making explicit the criteria of relevance and irrelevance being propounded, so that they can shift in the course of the argument. The logical structure of the word "Equality" makes this easy. It becomes even easier if to the equivocal word "Equality" we add the vague one "Opportunity." We have no way of measuring opportunities. Often we do not know we have them, unless we take them. Success is the only certain proof of their existence. And we cannot always have success. In the face of failure, we have no sure way of telling whether our failure is due to our not having taken the opportunities open to us, or to our not having had them. Pride inclines us to the latter view. We blame external circumstances rather than our own inadequacies, and find in the failures of life fuel for fires of resentment rather than lessons in the grace of humility. Equality of Opportunity has bred envy rather than endeavour.

Like all bad doctrines, it is a corruption of a good one. It has a part, subordinate but perfectly respectable, in the structure of competitions. Competitions occur when there is some good thing, natural or artificial, in short supply, so that not everyone can have all he wants, and each attempts to obtain some to the exclusion of some others. They are a special sort of dispute. In order that they may not degenerate into conflicts, they are formalised to a greater or lesser extent, and take place according to a set procedure. We may assess the procedure of a competition, and criticise it on the score of its being unreasonable, unfair, inefficient or inexpedient; in particular, a rule or factor which confers an advantage or imposes a disadvantage not connected with the main purpose of the competition is open to the criticism of precluding Equality of Opportunity. In games, where enjoyment is the prime object of the exercise, the fun is lost if the outcome is a foregone conclusion. Therefore we arrange players or teams in "leagues" where they will be more or less evenly matched, or handicap the stronger side, so that the result shall still be open. In the serious business of life, we apply criteria of relevance, and object to irrelevant factors being given an influence on the result. We object if government contracts are awarded on the "old-boy net," because not having been to the same school as a civil servant is not relevant to a contractor's capacity to give good value for money. In order to prevent these and other irrelevant factors from operating, we require that contracts be advertised and tenders invited, thereby giving each contractor an equal opportunity in the relevant sense for this sort of competition, of securing the prize. Similarly in a beauty competition we may require the contenders to wear only bathing dresses, in order that the judges may reach their conclusion in the light of facial charms only, and not any adventitious elegancies of dress. In awarding scholarships and other educational advantages we have doubts about the propriety of taking into consideration a boy's competence at cricket or facility on the flute. But here, just because the purposes of education are many and diverse, it becomes much more a matter of dispute what factors should, and what should not, be considered relevant.

The difficulty becomes intractable when we generalize from education to life. We are not agreed on what the good life is, nor on what constitutes success in life, and therefore we cannot lay down what factors should be relevant, and what ought not to be allowed to count. We are equally uncertain when the race begins and where the finishing post is. Divorced from its proper context, Equality of Opportunity becomes viciously vague. Every contest ends in some contender winning and others not. But if every contest is succeeded by another contest, the strict egalitarian may object to the result of the first contest being allowed to have any influence on the outcome of the second. Those who pass the eleven-plus have an advantage over those who fail, when they come to compete for places at the university. So egalitarians, who were loudest in their support of the eleven-plus in the 1940s, on the ground that it gave children Equality of Opportunity, clamour for its abolition, on the ground that it denies children Equality of Opportunity.[2] Nor is it merely a matter of their taking a different time as their starting-point. Every competition must result in some being successful and others not: and therefore, if the competition proceeded on a rational basis, it not only creates a new inequality, but reveals an antecedent one. A competition in which there is Equality of Opportunity is one in which the best man wins, and therefore one in which the winner is deemed to have been the best man, and in that, crucial, respect unequal. The egalitarian takes exception to this form of discrimination, and, shifting his ground, demands that it too be eliminated. The objective, he says, should be Equality, not Equality of Opportunity.[3] This change of front reflects neither dishonesty nor outstanding stupidity on the part of egalitarians, but the internal inconsistency of their ideal, absolute Equality. We can secure Equality in certain respects between members of certain classes for certain purposes and under certain conditions; but never, and necessarily never, Equality in all respects between all men for all purposes and under all conditions. The egalitarian is doomed to a life not only of grumbling and everlasting envy, but of endless and inevitable disappointment.

Equality, and more especially Equality of Opportunity, are treacherous concepts. This is not to say that no egalitarian conclusions ever hold good, nor that we must canonise inegalitarian meritocracy. It is, rather, that we should reformulate all controversies about Equality in other less emotive and less absolute terms. We need not slogans, but detailed arguments about criteria of relevance and irrelevance. Being arguments they are naturally two-sided, and one side may be right without the other being unreasonable, and an opponent may be wrong without being necessarily wrong-headed. In the detailed assessment of argument we shall see the important truth which the idiom of egalitarianism conceals, that on most political questions we are presented with a balance of argument rather than a simple black-and-white issue. Our arguments, therefore, will yield conclusions that are more solidly based, yet more tolerant in tone. Some, but not all, the conclusions the egalitarian yearns for can be maintained on non-egalitarian grounds, better established, but less censoriously affirmed.

[2] "The central and irresistible argument against the 11-plus lies in the denial of social justice and equal opportunity which this implies." Mr. Crosland at Harrogate, 7 January 1966.

[3] So Mr. Brian Simon, Reader in Education in Leicester University, addressing the Confederation for the Advancement of State Education, as reported in *The Times*, 27 September 1965.

21. The Justification of Egalitarian Justice

Alan Gewirth

Doctrines of egalitarian justice hold that all men have certain basic equal rights. Unlike doctrines of purely formal justice, which require simply that all cases falling under general rules be treated in the same way in accordance with the rules regardless of their contents, egalitarian justice puts equality into the very contents of some of the most basic rules about men's rights or treatment. At a minimum, these rules provide that all men, irrespective of their different capacities or merits, should have equal freedom to pursue their goals without violence to other men, equal possession of the necessities of life, equal opportunity to develop and utilize their talents to the fullest possible extent, equality of political and civil rights, and so forth. To this minimum list many doctrines of egalitarian justice add further items, including greater equalization of wealth and of actual political power.

I. The Problem of Justification

Can egalitarian justice, in either its minimal or its expanded form, be justified? We can begin to get at the complex structure of this problem if we run through some steps of the dialectic which has grown up around it.

a. It is a principle of reason that all men ought to be treated alike unless there is some good reason for treating them differently. This principle rests on the still more general principle that cases which are of the same kind ought to be treated in the same way, and being human is held to be such a kind. But the principle leaves unspecified what constitutes a "good reason" for treating men differently, that is, which sub-kinds are relevant to differential treatment; and, of course, very many differences, including intelligence, sex, and color, have been held to be thus relevant, so that the principle can eventuate in drastic inegalitarianism.

b. Differences of merit, on which are based some of the most plausible objections to egalitarianism, are themselves the result of initial inequalities of opportunity which cannot be justified on moral or rational grounds. Hence, if these differences are to be justified, one must uphold at least equality of opportunity for all men. To this, however, it is objected not only that complete equality of opportunity is impossible because of the differences in men's heredity and environment, but also that insofar as equality of opportunity is possible it may eventuate in great inequalities of outcome which will be differentially rewarded. But egalitarian justice requires that, regardless of the outcome of men's competitive endeavors, at least certain equalities must be kept inviolate. Hence, the justification of equality of opportunity does not provide a sufficient basis for egalitarian justice.

c. All men ought at least *prima facie* to be treated as equals because they equally have certain needs, desires, or capacities, such as the need for food and shelter or

From *American Philosophical Quarterly*, Vol. 8, No. 4 (October 1971), pp. 331–341, by permission of the author and publisher.

the desire for relief from pain or the capacity to enjoy distinctively human satisfactions. The objection which arises here is that, quite apart from the gap between "is" and "ought," it must still be shown why these factual characteristics in respect of which men are equal or similar are decisively relevant to how men are to be treated, as against those factual characteristics in respect of which men are unequal or dissimilar, such as the capacity to reason or to attain command over others or the desire for self-aggrandizement. Hence, the degree to which some factual characteristic is distributed among men cannot of itself be the justifying ground for the allocation of rights.

d. Regardless of men's factual inequalities or dissimilarities, men are equal in intrinsic worth or dignity because they are all equally ends in themselves or children of God or possessed of uniquely human personalities. Such characterizations, however, which are directly or ultimately normative, reduplicate the doctrine to be justified, that all men have basic equal rights. If one is doubtful about the latter, one will be at least equally doubtful about the characterizations which were invoked to justify it.

Can egalitarian justice, then, be rationally justified at all? The above brief survey suggests some of the requirements that must be fulfilled by such a justification. First, insofar as the justification appeals to characteristics of men, the ascertainment of these characteristics must not involve a normative assumption which is either identical with or dependent on the egalitarian principle one seeks to justify; hence, the characteristics in question must be empirically ascertainable. Second, reasons must be given for regarding men's possession of these characteristics as the decisively relevant criterion for their having equal rights. Third, a satisfactory answer must be given to the logical question of how a normative conclusion about rights can be derived from factual premises about empirically ascertainable characteristics. I shall refer to these three requirements, respectively, as those of empirical reference, of the criterion of relevance, and of logical derivability.

I shall now try to show how egalitarian justice can be justified on the basis of rational requirements concerning the actions of agents toward their recipients.

II. Reason

In general, "reason" signifies some sort of justificatory ground: in the sphere of argument, for inferring some conclusion; in the sphere of practice, for performing some action. Persons may have many different criteria for such grounds, but the criteria I shall use in my own justificatory arguments will for the most part be quite stringent ones. They are determined by the fact that a central concern of reason and rationality is to avoid arbitrariness. In this respect, to say that some statement is sanctioned by reason is to say, negatively, that the statement does not merely reflect its user's particular preferences or desires, and, positively, that it in some sense imposes itself on the user and hence is necessary. The criteria of this necessity may be either formal or material, in that the statement's necessity derives either from its logical relation to some other statement or statements which the user has already admitted or from its reflecting necessary and universal features of its subject matter. Such necessity, in turn, may be either causal or conceptual. The statements which I shall present as materially necessary will have emerged from conceptual analysis. I shall not here inquire whether the results of such analysis, since they involve logical relations among statements we make, are also necessary by the formal criterion. It is sufficient for my present purposes to emphasize that in what I call my materially necessary statements the independent variable is intended to be the features which necessarily and universally characterize some subject-matter as we conceive it in our thinking and talking about it.

III. Action

All moral rules and judgments deal, directly or indirectly, with human actions. While morality is sometimes held to be concerned more with character than with action, men's characters consist in settled dispositions to act in certain ways, and it is by their actions that men acquire their characters. Now the realm of what is called "human action" is notoriously diffuse. We speak not only of voluntary and purposive actions but also of actions which are involuntary, inadvertent, habitual, accidental, done in ignorance, and so forth. The sphere of action insofar as it is relevant to the present discussion, however, is initially to be demarcated in terms of the possible objects of moral rules and judgments. Moral rules, regardless of their highly variable contents in different moral systems, are intended for the most part to direct or guide the performance of actions by persons who know what they are doing and who can initiate and control their movements or behavior in the light either of the rules in question or of other purposes which the agents have in view. Moral judgments are intended, at least in part, to evaluate the agent's performance of actions insofar as he is accountable for them. Hence, actions as delimited by moral rules and judgments, in the general sense of "moral," must have two main features. First, they are voluntary, in that the agent who performs them must know what he is doing and must initiate or choose and control his behavior, without his choice being forced. (The choice and control, even if lacking at the time of the immediate act, must have been present at an earlier stage, as in cases of culpable negligence.)[1] Secondly, they are purposive, in that the agent must intend to do what he does, envisaging some purpose or goal which may consist either in the performance of the action itself (whether or not it conforms to some moral rule) or in some outcome of that performance; in either case insofar as it is the purpose of his action the agent regards it as some sort of good. (The kind of goodness here in question need not, of course, be moral.)

I shall henceforth call voluntariness and purposiveness the "categorial features" of action since they characterize the whole category of morally relevant action, as against the features of more particular kinds of action within this category. Since agents are persons who perform actions in the sense just specified, it is necessarily true of every agent that he acts voluntarily and purposively. In virtue of these categorial features, the actions of any agent are characterized by freedom and welfare, where "freedom" refers to the fact that actions derive from the agent's own unforced choice and control, and where "welfare," like the "good" which the agent envisages, is relative to the purposes and criteria which he accepts, although these may fall into some sort of hierarchy such that some can be evaluated in terms of others.

[1] See the discussion of the legal "technique of moving back to a stage at which the defendant had a choice" by P. J. Fitzgerald, "Voluntary and Involuntary Acts," in A. G. Guest, ed., *Oxford Essays in Jurisprudence* (Oxford, 1961), pp. 16–21.

It will also be convenient to put this point in another way. By a "transaction" I shall mean an action in which an agent acts on at least one other person, whom I shall call the "recipient." I shall use the general word "participate" to signify the way in which both agent and recipient are involved in transactions. The agent, of course, chooses or initiates the transaction and controls his participation in it with a view to some purpose of his. It is necessarily true of every agent, then, that *qua* agent he participates voluntarily and purposively in transactions in which he is involved.

While I have here derived the categorial features of action from the necessary requirements of the objects of moral rules and judgments, such actions are pertinent not only to morality but to all practical rules insofar as they prescribe how men are to act, where the actions in question are under the control of their agents for purposes or goods they want to achieve. Such practical rules characterize the more general realm which I shall call "practice"; it comprises, besides morality, such fields as prudence, art, and technique. Hence, it is ultimately to the category of practice that what I have called the categorial features of action pertain.

IV. Right-Claims

Since, in acting, the agent initiates and controls his movements with a view to realizing some purpose of his, this purpose constitutes for him his reason for the action, and it gives his action a certain normative quality. The purpose does not provide a causal explanation of the action in the way in which a sudden pain causally explains a groan. The groaner may subsequently adduce his pain as excusing his groan. But the purpose of an action does not operate to cause the action in any such reflex or involuntary way; it is rather what for the agent gives point and appropriateness to an action which is under his control and which he unforcedly chooses for the sake of something which is good according to whatever criteria he accepts in the given context. In view of this good which is to be accomplished directly or indirectly by his action, he regards his purpose as justifying his action and hence implicitly claims that he has, at least *prima facie*, a right to perform the action.

While a full elucidation of the connections here indicated among purpose, good, justification, and right-claim would go beyond the limits of this paper, several points bearing on such elucidation should be mentioned.[2] First, I am not, of course, saying that the agent must always or even usually make his right-claim explicitly, or must explicitly declare that his action is justified by his purpose. But, for that matter, he need not always explicitly think of his action as emerging from his choice, nor need he explicitly think of whatever criteria he has for choosing one action rather than another. What I have been presenting is not a psychological description of the agent's actual or conscious thought-processes but rather a logical analysis of the features which are necessarily involved in action insofar as it is to be of the kind which can be the object of moral and other practical rules and judgments. In acting for a purpose the agent has a reason for acting which, for him,

---

[2] Some of the other necessary qualifications can be gathered from my discussion of the transition from the acceptance of factual beliefs to the acceptance of "ought"-beliefs in "Must One Play the Moral Language Game?," *American Philosophical Quarterly*, vol. 7 (1970), pp. 107–118; see especially pp. 109–111.

grounds or justifies his action. While he need not be explicitly aware of this justifying relation, the relation can nonetheless be said to be dispositionally present in that, were it called to his attention, he would acknowledge it. Otherwise, it is difficult to see how the action could be said to be subject to his unforced choice and control, as against reflex movements which involve no choice or purpose on his part.

Secondly, both "justification" and "right-claim" may be used in connection with various criteria, including not only moral and legal but also prudential, technical, and others. For example, when a heavy smoker comes to realize that he ought to cut down on his smoking for reasons of health, he may come to believe that the statistical evidence warrants the conclusion that he still has a right to smoke two cigarettes per day. Here the right is not legal or moral but prudential, for the grounds on which it is based are, on the one hand, his enjoyment of smoking and, on the other, his desire for longevity — both prudential purposes.

Thirdly, this analysis is not essentially altered by the fact that men may engage in purposive actions which they acknowledge to be unjustified because they regard their purposes as bad or wrong and hence as disjustifying rather than justifying their actions. Such cases involve conflicts among the criteria or justifying reasons referred to above. An agent may act for one purpose which, since it comprises something which he takes to be good, he regards as justifying his action, but he may also believe that the criterion which makes that purpose good is outweighed in respect to justification by some other criterion or criteria, so that, all things considered, his purpose is bad and his action wrong. For example, moral scruples may be overcome by reasons of self-interest or of law, reasons of long-range self-interest may be overcome by reasons of immediate or short-run self-interest, and so forth. Even in such cases, however, the agent still acts for a purpose which, at least in part, he takes to be good; if this were not so, he would not regard his action as having any point or appropriateness at all, so that the idea of unforced choice and control in the light of intention or purpose would be completely absent. Hence, he views himself as having at least *prima facie* a right to perform the action, although this right is here outweighed by justificatory criteria which he regards as more authoritative. But since he views his action as unjustified overall, he thereby removes it from contention in respect to what he has a right to urge others to accept, at least by way of non-interference. In the sphere of justification, as against the sphere of mere fact, his action ceases to exert any claim. Now since I am here concerned with the justification of a principle of justice, and since in establishing this justification I am proceeding dialectically in terms of what agents view as their justified claims, I shall henceforth disregard this kind of case in my arguments leading up to the principle. This is not to say, however, that agents who view their actions as unjustified overall are exempt from the requirements of the principle. The very fact that such agents consider questions of justification, and must consider them insofar as they are rational, shows that they cannot rationally claim exemption from such requirements.[3]

[3] The complex series of considerations involved in the kinds of cases considered in the text are illustrated in the following passage from an article on the drug traffic in New York City (*The New York Times*, September 23, 1969, p. 34):

A former Harlem heroin dealer who estimates he made $4,000 to $5,000 a week on sales of about four pounds was asked how he justified what he did. The dealer, whose name cannot be used, replied: "I never gave it a thought whether it was right or wrong. It was just a way of

As is suggested by this last consideration, I am here using "right-claim" in a sense in which it entails a correlative claim on the part of the agent that other persons ought at least not to interfere with the action for which the right-claim is made. For insofar as one regards one's purpose as good and hence as justifying one's action according to whatever criteria one accepts in the given context, one holds that, according to those criteria, one's action should not be prevented from occurring by any other person. As with the right-claim itself, this "ought" need not be a moral one. It applies even in prudential cases like that of the smoker mentioned above. His claim that he has a prudential right to smoke two cigarettes per day entails his claim that other persons ought (in terms of his prudential purpose) to refrain from interfering with his smoking the two cigarettes.

Since, as we saw earlier, it is necessarily true of every agent that he participates voluntarily and purposively in transactions in which he is involved, we can also put the point just made in similar terms: every agent (with the exception just noted) necessarily claims that he has a right to participate voluntarily and purposively in transactions in which he is involved. It may be objected that "having a right," like "ought," implies both "can" and "may not"; but if the agent cannot participate other than voluntarily and purposively in transactions, then it makes no sense to say that he claims to have the right so to participate. My reply is that the agent claims to have the right to participate voluntarily and purposively in the specific transactions in which he is involved, and there is no necessity that he, *qua* agent, become involved in any specific transaction. The necessity attaches only to the general mode of his participation, *qua* agent, once he does become involved; but the object of his right-claim, that to which he necessarily claims the right, is his voluntary and purposive participation in the specific transaction.

V. The Criterion of Relevance

Every right-claim is made on behalf of some person under a certain description or for a certain reason. The description or reason may be as general as that the person in question is human (as in many egalitarian doctrines) or it may be more restrictive, including even (at least according to some philosophers) that the person in question has a certain proper name or some other completely individualized property. But whatever be the description under which or the reason for which it is asserted that the person has the right in question, the assertor must admit, on pain of inconsistency, that this right also belongs to any other person to whom that description or reason pertains. This necessity is an exemplification of the formal principle of universalizability in its moral application, which says that whatever is

---

making money. I was never in any trouble. You can get into trouble by selling some bad dope. I knew I was getting good dope from the people I was dealing with."

He insisted, however, that "I never sold to kids." The dealer was disconcerted recently to learn that his teen-age son used heroin.

In this passage, the dealer's disavowal of any concern with moral justification ("whether it was right or wrong") is immediately followed by a justification in terms of prudential purpose ("It was just a way of making money"). Further elements of both moral and prudential justifications are indicated in his references to his selling "good" as against "bad dope," his not selling to "kids," and his not getting "into trouble."

right for one person must also be right for any similar person in similar circumstances. But this formal moral principle, in turn, derives from a more general logical principle of universalizability: if some predicate P belongs to some individual subject S because S has some property Q (where the "because" is that of sufficient reason or condition), then P must also belong to all other subjects $S_1, S_2, \ldots S_n$ which have Q. (This implication is, in syllogistic terms, a first-figure enthymeme with suppressed major). If one denies this implication in the case of some individual, such as S_1, which has Q, then one contradicts oneself, for in saying that P belongs to S because S has Q one implies that all Q is P, but in denying this in the case of S_1, which has Q, one says that some Q is not P.

The formal principle of universalizability in its moral application is often said to be a principle of "formal justice," and it often receives such other formulations as that similar cases ought to be similarly treated and that whatever rule one applies in one's own case one ought to apply in all similar cases. All these formulations, however, admit of a completely variable content, depending on the criterion one adopts as to which similarities are to count as relevant ones. Now the criterion of relevant similarities which gives content to formal justice is the same as the reason for which, or the description under which, a person is held to have a certain right. Hence, the question of under what description or for what reason the agent must make his necessary right-claim may also be put as the question of which criterion of relevant similarity the agent must accept from among the indefinitely variable criteria left open to him by the formal principle of universalizability. This latter question, however, assumes that there is just one criterion of relevant similarity which every agent must accept. And this assumption may well be questioned.

Many philosophers have held the following general position on the criterion of relevant similarities: since all men are similar in some respects and dissimilar in others, and since men and acts can hence be classified in many different ways, what anyone takes to be relevant qualities or similarities must be entirely relative to his own evaluations or moral principles. One familiar version of this position is found among expositors of utilitarianism, who suggest that from a utilitarian standpoint qualities of persons or acts are relevant to justice insofar as they causally affect the production of good or bad consequences. Entirely apart from the well-known difficulties which beset utilitarian attempts to provide grounds for justice, it is clear that this general position, if sound, would make impossible the project of the present essay. For since the purpose of all the steps of my argument, including the current one aiming at the rational justification of a criterion of relevant similarities, is to set forth a rational justification of a principle of justice as a basic moral principle, I cannot, without vicious circularity, appeal to my own moral principle to justify the criterion of relevant similarities.

Attempts have been made to justify criteria of relevant similarity in ways which avoid the evaluative relativity of the above general position. According to some philosophers, which qualities of persons or acts are relevant to justice are to be determined by the specific purposes of the positions, rules, or institutions for which the qualities are to be selected. Since, however, these purposes may be such as we ordinarily regard as unjust or otherwise immoral, to distinguish between qualities of persons or acts on the basis of these purposes would promote injustice rather than justice. Other philosophers have suggested that which qualities are relevant to justice is to be determined by means of reciprocal acceptability, that is, by considering whether differentiations of treatment in terms of those qualities are acceptable to persons regardless of whether or not they themselves have the qualities and regardless of whether they are on the active or on the passive side of transactions according to rules which determine treatment of persons by possession of those qualities. This criterion, however, unless specified in further ways, would prohibit acts and rules which we ordinarily regard as just or otherwise morally right, such as punishment and differential academic grading. And it would permit acts and rules which we ordinarily regard as unjust or otherwise morally wrong, for a "fanatic" may uphold various discriminatory ideals regardless of their harmful impact on his own interests if he were to have the qualities in question.

The difficulties of all the above views on the justification of criteria of relevant similarities may be summed up by noting that they all admit of one or more sorts of substantive or moral variability. I now wish to argue that it is possible to give a rational justification of a criterion of relevant similarities which avoids these variabilities and which hence shows that any agent, in claiming that he has a right to perform some action, rationally must make this claim for himself under a certain description or for a certain sufficient reason. To see how this is so, we must advert to the requirements of rational justification. It will be recalled that reason, in the stringent sense in which I am using the term, excludes what is arbitrary. But any agent's procedure in making his right-claim is arbitrary so long as he is permitted to pick and choose according to his own predilections from among the varying descriptions, contents, or criteria of relevant similarities which may enter into his right-claim. The only way to halt this arbitrariness, and hence to establish his claim on a rationally justified basis, is to restrict its contents to what is necessarily and universally connected with its subject-matter, as against what is optional or left to the agent's discretion. Now no matter in how many ways the agent in making his right-claim might choose to describe himself or to give sufficient reasons for his action, the description and sufficient reason which he cannot reject is that he is a prospective agent who has some purpose which he wants to fulfill. For it is this description which is necessarily and universally, hence invariably, connected with the category of action, which, as we have seen, is the general subject-matter of morality and practice. Hence, insofar as the agent's necessary right-claim is restricted to what he is rationally justified in claiming, his claim that he has a right to participate in the transaction in which he is involved must refer to himself *qua* prospective agent who wants to realize some purpose of his.

I shall now consider four kinds of objection to this argument.

a. It may be objected that since the purposes of agents may vary in all sorts of ways, variabilities and arbitrariness are permitted rather than removed by the criterion of relevant similarities just presented. It is crucially important in this regard, however, to note the level of generality at which the criterion operates in respect to the description of the agent which must enter into his right-claim. What the criterion declares to be alone rationally justified is the description of the agent as a prospective agent who wants to fulfill some purpose of his, as against the various possible descriptions of him as having some particular qualities or purposes. The former, categorial description is invariable and hence impervious to the relativities and arbitrarinesses whereby the agent might choose from among the latter sorts of description. And as we shall see in the next section, the criterion in terms of the categorial description of the agent also provides for moral invariability, as against the possibly immoral outcomes of more particular descriptions.

b. An objection may also be brought against my procedure in arguing that the agent's rationally justified description of himself in his right-claim is determined by what is necessarily connected with the category of action. Admittedly, if we take as one of our relata something so general as the category of action as such, then the other relatum, the description of which is necessarily connected with it, must be equally general, viz., the categorial quality of being a prospective agent who wants to realize his purposes. But, the objection goes, there is no rational necessity that the subject-matter relatum be taken in so general a way. The agent may say, with equal justification, that the subject-matter of his behavior is not action as such but rather highly intelligent action, or white man's action, or the action of someone named "X" (where "X" is the agent's name), so that the relata or descriptions which are necessarily connected with these subject-matters are, respectively, being a highly intelligent agent, or a white agent, or an agent named "X."

My answer to this objection has already been suggested. Action, in the sense specified above, is the necessary and universal subject-matter of moral and other practical rules and judgments since these all refer directly or indirectly to ways in which persons act. Hence, there can be no question that the categorial features which distinctively characterize all action are relevant to morality and practice and to the contents and criteria of moral and other practical judgments and claims. The case is otherwise, however, with more specific descriptive features which are restrictive selections from within the category of action. For there can be a question whether those features are relevant to practice, since at least some practical judgments can dispense with them. It is obviously not necessary, from the standpoint of practical rules and judgments, that the agent's action be described as highly intelligent action or white man's action or the action of someone named "X."

c. It may still be objected, however, that my stringent conception of rationality commits me to an excessive generality. The categorial description of the agent as having purposes which he wants to fulfill in action is only a necessary part of the relevant description of any particular agent, but it is not sufficient. For any particular agent obviously has many additional features which truly and distinctively characterize him; but these are all omitted by the suggested categorial criterion. Right-claims are not made by agents as such; rather, specific kinds of persons make various differential claims which they ground on specific kinds of criteria or sufficient reasons. These reasons often invoke the claimant's differential position in some institution, such as being a teacher, a husband, a parent, a policeman, and so forth. But all such specific or differential features are omitted from my criterion of relevant qualities.

In answer to this objection, it must, of course, be admitted that many specific descriptions are true of an agent's action. The trouble is that there is an infinite number of such true descriptions, and the question is how those which are held to be the relevant ones are to be selected. If the agent's own justificatory reason for his action is taken as decisively answering the question of relevance, then this admits all the relativitities and variabilities mentioned earlier. The whole point of a rational principle, however, is to subject men's choices to rational evaluation; hence, those choices cannot be themselves made the independent variables for determining such evaluation. Insofar, then, as the basis of evaluation is to be confined in a non-question-begging way to what is rationally justifiable, the only alternative is to select as the criterion of evaluation those features of the agent and his action which, because they are necessarily and universally connected with the category of action, are impervious to whatever particular purposes or principles he may himself want to advance.

This point is also pertinent to the institutional rules or features invoked in the above objection. For not only are institutions subject to great variation among different cultures, but they are not self-justifying; they require justification in terms of a moral principle which can itself be shown to be rationally justifiable. Only after institutions have been justified in this way can the differential roles which persons play in them be justifiably invoked as a sufficient reason for a right-claim.[4]

d. It may also be objected that even if we take the whole category of action as generally relevant to agents and their right-claims, we may still recognize, within this category, an important non-arbitrary distinction which marks out a certain differential and yet undeniably relevant description. This description provides a rationally justifiable criterion for claiming superior or perhaps even exclusive action-rights for certain agents, so that it gives an inegalitarian content to formal justice. While it is indeed arbitrary to invoke such properties as an agent's skin color or his proper name as a reason for his having superior action-rights, since there is no rational connection between being a superior agent and having a certain color or name, the case is otherwise with such a feature as superior practical intelligence. For persons who have this feature are superior agents, since they an act more effectively to achieve their purposes than can persons of inferior intelligence. Hence, it can be maintained on purely rational grounds and without arbitrariness that persons of superior intelligence have superior (and perhaps even exclusive) action-rights, that is, greater rights to freedom and welfare: greater power to choose and control their own and other persons' participation in transactions, and a greater degree of fulfillment of their own purposes as compared with those of other persons.

The crucial question raised by this contention is what rational justification there is for regarding possession of superior intelligence as a sufficient reason for having any action-rights at all, let alone for having either superior or exclusive action-rights. If a person of superior intelligence had no purposes, he would make no claim to have any right to act. It is hence by virtue of being a prospective agent who wants to fulfill his purposes that the person of superior intelligence makes this right-claim. To this extent, however, such a person is in no different position from that of other prospective agents, and he can claim no rational justification, simply *qua* person of superior intelligence, for any right-claim of action.

So far as concerns his having a superior or an exclusive right to action, I shall here deal only with the former, since if this is refuted, then so too is the latter, exclusivist claim. The basic argument is that if an agent has a right to act, then a superior agent (which, *ex hypothesi*, the person of superior intelligence is) has a superior right to act. Now this argument commits a *non sequitur*. The antecedent of the argument, properly expanded, says that the reason why a person has a right to act is that he is a prospective agent who wants to fulfill his own purposes. The consequent says that if one prospective agent X has greater ability to achieve X's purposes than another prospective agent Y has to achieve Y's purposes, then X has a superior right to act. This consequent does not, however, follow from the antecedent, since the reason which the consequent gives for having a superior right to act is quite distinct from the reason which the antecedent gives for having a right

---

[4] I have discussed this in some detail in "Obligation: Political, Legal, Moral," *Nomos*, vol. 12 (1970), pp. 55–88.

to act. Wanting to fulfill one's own purposes through action is not the same as having the ability to fulfill one's own purposes through action. While it is true that to act requires certain abilities, what is crucial in any agent's *reason* for acting is not his abilities but his purposes.

To justify the claim of superior right, the argument from superior intelligence would have to encompass one or both of two further assertions: (i) that those who have superior intelligence will necessarily use it for the fulfillment not only of their own purposes but also of the purposes of all or many other prospective agents; (ii) that those who have superior intelligence also have more valuable purposes. Neither of these assertions, however, is plausible. Assertion (i), moreover, would involve an implicit admission that the action-rights of the more intelligent agents, so far as they claim to fulfill the purposes of persons of inferior intelligence, must be evaluated by reference to those purposes. But since without some sorts of basic controls on the part of the inferior agents it is quite unlikely that their purposes would be sufficiently provided for by the superior agents, the claims of the latter to superior rights are further weakened.

I conclude, then, that the description under which or the sufficient reason for which any agent rationally must claim that he has the right to participate voluntarily and purposively in transactions in which he is involved is that he is a prospective agent who wants to fulfill his purposes.

VI. Justice as Categorial Consistency

It follows from this that every agent logically must accept the generalization that all prospective agents who want to fulfill their purposes have the right to participate voluntarily and purposively in transactions in which they are involved. If the agent denies this, then he contradicts himself. For he then denies what he has implicitly affirmed insofar as he is rational: that he has a right to participate because he is a prospective agent who wants to fulfill his purposes. For in this affirmation he has held that possession of the categorial feature of being a prospective agent who wants to fulfill his purposes is a sufficient justifying condition for having the right in question.

Now the recipients of the agent's action are themselves prospective agents. To be a prospective agent, it is necessary and sufficient that one be able to operate voluntarily and purposively, choosing or initiating and controlling one's conduct in the light of one's purposes, and deciding on or making for oneself the various specific rules on which one acts in the many circumstances of life. Hence, animals, children, and feeble-minded persons are in varying degrees and on different grounds excluded from the class of prospective agents. But any more restrictive qualifications would go beyond the general criteria marked out by the categorial features of agency.

Insofar as some person is a recipient in a transaction, he does not then actually choose or initiate and control his conduct with a view to fulfilling some purpose of his. Nevertheless, he still has purposes which he wants to fulfill, at least in the dispositional sense that he has wants or interests which are of concern to him. Hence, the agent must acknowledge that the generalization to which we saw that he is logically committed applies to his recipients: they too have the right to participate voluntarily and purposively in the transaction in which they are involved with him. Their right to participate voluntarily means that, just as the agent controls whether or not he will initiate the transaction, so his recipients have the right to control whether or not they will undergo the agent's initiative. Their participation in the transaction must hence be subject to their own consent, to their own free choice, so that the agent ought to refrain from coercing them. Their right to participate purposively means that, just as the agent acts with a view to attaining some purpose which seems to him to be a good of his, so too his recipients' participation in the transaction must be with a view to attaining some purpose which seems to them to be a good of theirs. This means, at a minimum, that the agent ought to refrain from harming his recipients, for if they are harmed they are made to lose something which seems to them to be some good of theirs; they are forced to participate in the transaction in a way that contravenes their own purposes.

It follows from these considerations that every agent logically must acknowledge two basic obligations. Put negatively, they are that he ought to refrain from coercing and from harming his recipients; put affirmatively, they are that he ought to respect his recipients' freedom and welfare as well as his own. The recipients have two basic correlative rights, to non-coercion by other persons, or freedom, and to non-maleficence from other persons, or welfare. The general principle of these obligations and rights may be expressed as the following precept addressed to every agent: *Apply to your recipient the same categorial features of action that you apply to yourself.*[5] I shall call this the *Principle of Categorial Consistency* (*PCC*), since it combines the formal consideration of consistency with the material consideration of the categorial features of action. The *PCC* is a necessarily valid principle in two respects. It is formally or logically necessary in that to violate it is to contradict oneself. It is also materially necessary in that, unlike other principles, the obligations of the *PCC* cannot be escaped by any agent by shifting his inclinations, interests, or ideals. Since the categorial features of action are involved in the necessary structure of agency, the agent cannot refrain from applying these features to himself and from claiming the right to apply them in his specific transaction *qua* prospective agent; hence he rationally cannot evade the obligation of applying these features to his recipient because of the latter's also being a prospective agent. In this respect, the *PCC* is unlike those moral principles whose contents are contingent in that they reflect the variable desires or opinions of agents.

It may be objected that I have not shown the *PCC* to be a necessarily valid principle. For my argument has been dialectical in that, beginning from agents' right-claims to which the universalizability principle was applied, I have shown that agents must admit that their recipients also have these rights. Since, however, agents' right-claims may be unjustified, the recipients' rights of voluntary and purposive participation also remain unproved, since from unjustified premisses, as such, a justified conclusion does not necessarily follow.

[5] In an earlier statement of this principle (in "Categorial Consistency in Ethics," *Philosophical Quarterly*, vol. 17 [1967], pp. 289–299, at p. 292) I put it in terms of "categorial rules" rather than "categorial features." While I think the former statement is in certain respects preferable, it raises complex issues about the nature of rules which may be avoided for the purposes of the present paper. In "Some Comments on Categorial Consistency," *Philosophical Quarterly* (forthcoming), I discuss some criticisms bearing on these issues. In the last section of the present paper, I repeat a few sentences from "Categorial Consistency in Ethics."

In answer to this objection, I wish to point out that the method I have followed in establishing the *PCC* falls between two extremes. The apodeictic method would deduce the *PCC* either from elf-evident premises or from assertoric premises about human nature. Such deduction obviously involves severe logical difficulties. The dialectically contingent method begins from singular claims which reflect some protagonist's particular interests or ideals, and then argues through the principle of universalizability that the claim's normative predicate must be admitted by the protagonist to apply to all other persons who fit the description or reason set forth in the subject of his claim. Since, however, interests and ideals may vary from one person to another, this method would justify claims which are quite unacceptable and even harmful to their recipients. The method I have followed in establishing the *PCC*, which I shall call the dialectically necessary method, resembles the dialectically contingent method in beginning from claims made by protagonists and then applying the principle of universalizability. In my argument, however, the contents of these claims are necessary rather than contingent, in that they reflect not some protagonist's variable interests or ideals but rather the necessary structure of action. Since the categorial features of this structure are the proximate conditions both of action and of whatever goods are attainable by action, the *PCC*'s requirement that the agent, regardless of his particular desires, extend these conditions to his recipients constitutes an indefeasible guarantee of fairness to the recipients. Such a justification of the *PCC* is all that is rationally required in order to establish it as a necessarily valid principle.

The *PCC* is a principle of egalitarian justice, for it requires of every agent that he be impartial as between himself and his recipients when the latter's freedom and welfare are at stake, so that the agent must respect his recipients' freedom and welfare as well as his own. To violate the *PCC* is to establish an inequality or disparity between oneself and one's recipients with respect to the categorial features of action and hence with respect to whatever purposes or goods are attainable by action.

Let us now consider how the *PCC* stands in relation to the three requirements which emerged above in the course of my discussion of the problem of justification. I have appealed to the characteristic of being a prospective agent who has purposes that he wants to fulfill. Whether someone has this characteristic can be ascertained empirically without making normative assumptions which are identical with or dependent on the egalitarian principle whose justification is in question; hence, the requirement of empirical reference is satisfied. So too is the requirement of the criterion of relevance, for with regard to the agent's claim that he has a right to participate voluntarily and purposively in his specific transactions, I have argued that the only characteristic which he is rationally justified in holding to be relevant to this claim is that of being a prospective agent who has purposes that he wants to fulfill. It is because my argument has satisfied the requirement of the criterion of relevance in this way that my conclusion can be an egalitarian one despite my recognition that men may be factually unequal in respect to their effectiveness as agents. As for the requirement of logical derivability, this was met earlier in my argument that purposive action entails right-claims on the part of the agent.

VII. Social Justice

I have thus far dealt with the *PCC* primarily as governing just transactions among individual persons; but it has direct implications for the justice of social institutions. The *PCC* puts a premium on equal freedom and on mutual accommodation of wants and purposes; these have an obvious application in the sociopolitical sphere as the principles of consent and of common good or public interest. The general conception of individuals and of society which emerges from the *PCC* is that of an association of free and non-maleficent persons.

While the detailed working out of the many complexities of social justice as founded on the *PCC* must be left for another occasion,[6] I shall briefly deal with one aspect of these complexities by referring to a problem of differentiation. According to the *PCC*, all men have an equal right to freedom and welfare. On the other hand, the fulfillment of men's purposes requires that there be various social institutions and rules to regulate conflicts and to govern at least those of men's transactions which affect more persons than the immediate participants; and these institutions and rules may treat men unequally by assigning superior and inferior roles, penalties and rewards, and so forth. We often regard these social institutions and rules with their concomitant inequalities as just. But can their justice be accounted for by the *PCC*?

My answer to this question is that if such inequalities are to be just ones, then the social institutions and rules from which they derive must themselves be justifiable by the *PCC*. This justification is of two main kinds. One kind is procedural: the rules must themselves have been made by the method of consent, in that they must have emerged from a process whereby all the persons affected by them have at some point been able to have an equal voice in determining the rules. The other kind of justification is instrumental: the contents of the rules must further the purposes of the persons subject to them and, more generally, the rules must be means toward fostering the kinds of characteristics in persons and in institutions that the *PCC* directly involves, namely, freedom and non-maleficence.

It will be noted that these two kinds of justification themselves derive, respectively, from the voluntariness and the purposiveness which the *PCC* requires that all agents accord to their recipients. In these justifications the makers or defenders of social rules and institutions are envisaged as agents who must accord to all their recipients, the persons subject to the rules, the same voluntariness and purposiveness which characterize the actions of the agents themselves. This approach serves to emphasize that institutions are in various ways generated and upheld by the actions of individual persons and groups composed of individuals, so that the requirements for just transactions among individuals can be applied, with appropriate modifications, to the operations of social institutions. Insofar as social rules and institutions are justified by these procedural and instrumental reasons, the different roles that the rules assign to different persons are themselves justified and constitute the criteria of relevant similarities and differences between persons.

The social rules which are procedurally and instrumentally in accordance with the *PCC* may hence prescribe that in particular cases persons be treated in ways that go counter to the voluntariness and purposiveness directly prescribed by the *PCC*. The *PCC* is thus a *prima facie* rather than an absolute requirement for particular acts, in

---

[6] I have discussed some of the sociopolitical applications of the *PCC* in "Obligation: Political, Legal, Moral," *op. cit.*

that any particular act must be in accord with the *PCC* unless the act is in accord with a social rule which is itself in accord with the *PCC*. But this requirement that social rules, to be justified, must be in accord with the *PCC* sets an important limit to the content of such rules. Whatever sacrifices of individual interests these rules may require must themselves serve to foster the freedom and welfare of each individual so far as this is compatible with the freedom and welfare of each other individual.

22. Equality and Generalization: A Formal Analysis

Richard E. Flathman

To treat people equally is to treat them in the same way. To treat people in the same way is to treat them according to a rule. "Equally" is defined in the *Oxford English Dictionary* to mean "According to one and the same rule." Philosophers, aware of this relationship, have attempted to explicate and refine the notion of equality through the notion of general rule or generalization. Historically, the salient names in this connection are Rousseau and Kant. Many contemporary philosophers have concerned themselves with generalization, but few have applied their conclusions to "equality." The purpose of the present paper is to analyze the concept of equality in the light of recent discussions of generalization. I will argue that the concept of equality can be explicated in terms of generalization, and that to do so shows that as normative concepts both equality and generalization are of derivative significance. These conclusions will lead to suggestions concerning the importance of utilitarian considerations in morals.

I

Recent work in ethics or meta-ethics has been concerned to identify and provide formalized statements of the principles and rules that operate, if only in a concealed manner, in moral discourse. The concept of generalization has been the object of substantial attention in these respects, and we now have several analyses of what has been called the Generalization or Universalizability Principle (hereafter GP). Professor Marcus Singer, who has made the most detailed study of the topic, states GP in the form we will adopt for the purposes of this paper: "What is right (or wrong) for one person must be right (or wrong) for every relevantly similar person

Reprinted from *Equality: Nomos IX*, edited by J. Roland Pennock and John W. Chapman (New York: Atherton Press, 1967), pp. 38–60. Copyright © 1967 Atherton Press. Reprinted by permission of Lieber-Atherton, Incorporated.

in relevantly similar circumstances."[1] According to this formulation, if X is right for A, it must be right for B, C, D, . . . N unless A or his circumstances is different from B, C, D, . . . N or their circumstances in a manner justifying making an exception of A. There is, it would appear, a presumption in favor of equal treatment of all persons and any departure from that rule must be justified.

One feature of GP, its "formal" or "neutral" character, requires immediate attention. Before the universal principle that GP expresses can be applied to a problem, two particular premises must be established. The first is of the form: "This X is right for this A"; the second: "This B is, vis-à-vis this A, a relevantly similar person in relevantly similar circumstances." GP states a relationship between these premises; it does not tell us how to establish them in any instance. Until they have been established, GP, although valid as an abstract principle, has no application. GP does one thing: When it has been established that X is right for A and that A and B are relevantly similar, the principle requires that it be wrong for A to act or be treated differently from B. Hence GP is formal or neutral in the sense that, taken alone, it does not prescribe the proper content of any decision. Clearly, then, the crucial problems are those involved in establishing the particular premises in specific cases. Those problems, and the question of GP's utility once those problems have been resolved, will be our primary concern. We will also give attention to an argument that a substantive doctrine of equality is concealed by the ostensibly formal or neutral character of GP.

II

It will facilitate the analysis to use a real controversy concerning equality as a source of examples and illustrations. The recent United States Supreme Court decisions concerning apportionment in state legislatures, the "one-man, one-vote" decisions, are well suited to this purpose.[2] In the Court's view, the question before it in the Reynolds Case was whether the Equal Protection clause[3] permits a state to employ a system of apportionment in which the representatives of some districts represent substantially fewer citizens than the representattives of other districts.

---

[1] Marcus Singer, *Generalization in Ethics*, New York: Alfred A. Knopf, 1961, pp. 19–20; alternative formulations are presented on pp. 5 and 31. There is a very extensive critical literature concerning Singer's book, and I have profited substantially from it. It would be impracticable to cite that literature here, but mention should be made of Alan Gewirth's "The Generalization Principle," *Philosophical Review*, Vol. 73 (April, 1964), p. 229, in which the reader will find arguments similar in important respects to some of those presented here.

[2] The leading case is *Reynolds* v. *Sims*, 377 U.S. 533 (1964). A series of companion cases follows immediately in the same volume. I would like to emphasize that it is not the purpose of this paper to present an evaluation of the Court's decisions in these cases. The arguments of the paper would be relevant to such an evaluation, and in it critical statements will be made concerning Chief Justice Warren's argument in the Reynolds case. But the purpose of these remarks will be to question the logic of the argument by which the conclusion is reached, not the conclusion itself. A competent evaluation of the latter would require a much wider investigation that I have undertaken. Also, because I am using the cases purely for illustrative purposes, I have not scrupled to ignore complexities in the Court's reasoning, which would lead beyond present purposes. It is my belief that the following interpretation of Warren's argument can be defended it terms of the text of his opinion, but I have not attempted to defend it here.

[3] Article 14, Section 1.

Although insisting that "mathematical exactitude" is neither desirable nor practicable as a standard for determining the adequacy of a plan, the majority nevertheless found that Equal Protection ". . . requires that a state make an honest and good faith effort to construct districts in both houses of its legislature as nearly of equal population as practicable."

In terms of GP, the issue can be restated as follows: "Is it constitutional for A (the citizens of legislative district A' in state Q') to have X (number of citizens per representative) if B, C, D, . . . N (the citizens of legislative districts B', C', D', . . . N' in state Q') do not have X (have Y, a larger or smaller number of citizens per representative)?" Under GP the answer could be, for example, "Yes, if X is right for A and if vis-à-vis B, C, D, . . . N, A is (the class of A consists of) relevantly different persons in relevantly different circumstances." The decision, in other words, would seem to turn on establishing the two premises we have identified. We will try to show, however, that what appears to be two tasks is in fact one — establishing the rightness of X.

Many of the arguments of Warren's opinion, by contrast, suggest that in matters of apportionment "right" and the kind of equality demanded by the equal population rule are equivalent; they collapse the first premise of GP into the second. Much of his opinion is designed to show that various differences among citizens such as class, economic status, place of residence, and other characteristics, although alleged to justify differences in treatment, are irrelevant to apportionment. The assumption seems to be that "equal" in the Constitution establishes a presumption that the equal population rule is right (constitutional), and the task is less to defend that presumption than to show that the conditions required for its application (relevant similarity of all citizens) are satisfied. If challenges to the relevant similarity of all citizens can be met, the question of "right" (constitutionality) will be answered. In common with many egalitarian arguments, in other words, Warren treats equality as a sufficient normative principle. To clarify the logic of this argument we will examine some of the key contentions that Warren offers to support his conclusion.[4]

Warren's aim is to support the conclusion that all citizens should be treated according to the rule, "Equal representatives for equal population." To do so he asserts: "With respect to the allocation of legislative representation, all voters as citizens of the State stand in the same relation. . . ."[5] Presumably this means that there are no differences among citizens or their situations that would significantly affect their opportunity to participate effectively in or the manner in which they are affected by the system of representation. But the empirical proposition crucial to Warren's argument is highly doubtful. A citizen's relation to the system of representation, his opportunity to participate in and benefit from that process, can be affected by such factors as the predominant interest pattern in his district,

---

[4] Inasmuch as Warren is interpreting a Constitution to which he must be faithful, it might be thought misleading or worse to say that *he* "treats equality" as a sufficient principle. The Constitution, it might be alleged, established the principle and Warren is required to accept it in his role as judge. If the content of "equal" in "equal protection" were entirely clear, this argument would be persuasive. We will try to adduce logical considerations to show that it is not, and hence that the language used above is appropriate.

[5] *Reynolds* v. *Sims*, 565. The sentence ends ". . . regardless of where they live." But in the course of the opinion Warren makes the same contention for all differences alleged to be relevant (there is something of an exception for existing political subdivisions) and hence it is not a distortion to broaden the passage by omitting the restriction.

whether his party affiliation is that of a majority or a minority party, difficulties of communication with political and governmental centers, informal political tradition, size (in area) of districts, and perhaps others. By adopting the equal population rule Warren *makes it* true that all citizens "stand in the same relation" to the system in the respect required by that rule. But they may stand in very different relations to the system in other respects.

It is of course possible that Warren could justify rejecting these other differences. Indeed it is certain that some of the above-mentioned factors would have to be ignored, especially in establishing constitutional requirements concerning the conditions of participation. It would be difficult and perhaps undesirable to refine those requirements to take account of all of the differences that have been alleged to be relevant.[6] But this possibility, although relevant to whether Warren's conclusion could be defended, does not support the logic of the argument by which the conclusion is reached.

More particularly, it does not support the assumption that "right" (constitutionality) and "equal" can be equivalent, that establishing the second premise of GP will establish the first premise as well. If the premise that all citizens "stand in the same relation" with regard to representation is not literally true in all respects that affect representation, then treating them according to a rule based on that premise will mean that there will be respects in which they will be treated differently (unequally). In opting for the equal population rule, Warren treats all citizens equally in the respect required by that rule. But in doing so he accepts inequalities with regard, for example, to size (in area) of electoral districts, distance from governmental centers, and perhaps others. Once again, he might be entirely justified in so doing. But his justification cannot be in terms of equality. For he has, if only tacitly, chosen between equalities. He has preferred the equality of the equal population rule to the equality of, say, size of electoral districts.[7] Inasmuch as he is choosing between competing equalities, he has, again if only tacitly, turned to some principle other than equality to make that choice, that is, to decide what is right. "Right" and "equality" are not equivalent; equality is not an independent or a sufficient normative principle.

These considerations can be generalized. They suggest that "right" and "equality" could be equivalent, that establishing the second premise of GP would also establish the first, only if the decision-maker was not faced with the kind of choice Warren had to make. This choice, however, can be avoided only if all those

---

[6] To assume difficulty or undesirability too readily, however, is to risk assuming away the issues concerning proper apportionment. It is instructive in this connection to consider the British practice, a practice that has gone to great lengths in adapting to some of the differences mentioned above. The British have evidently found this practicable, and they have rejected the conclusion that the numerical equality for which Warren opts will provide a base from which the citizen can overcome all other inequalities. For a general account of British practices see Vincent E. Starzinger, "The British Pattern of Appointment," *The Virginia Quarterly Review,* Vol. 41 (Summer 1965), pp. 321ff.

[7] Here again (cf. note 4 above) it might be argued that Warren did not "choose" between equalities but read the Constitution as *requiring* the equal population rule. Leaving aside general issues concerning the difficulty of interpreting the Constitution, the foregoing argument is intended to show that it is logically impossible for the words of the document, taken alone, to require this finding. Perhaps the usual materials of constitutional interpretation, previous court decisions, intent of the Framers, etc., support Warren's finding. Inasmuch as our concern is not constitutional law but the logic of "equality," this fact, if it is a fact, is of little relevance here and does not affect the above argument.

involved in or affected by a decision are similar persons in similar situations in *all* respects that might affect the results of the decision. Given the diversity of men and their situations, it is difficult to believe that such decisions are a regular occurrence — especially in politics where we are typically concerned with very large numbers. Hence questions arise about the significance of the principle of equality.

It might be useful to restate the foregoing argument in terms closer to those used in our preliminary discussion of GP. When GP is applied to a concrete issue, it serves to raise a comparative question — whether X is right for A *and* for B, C, D, . . . N. The foregoing argument supports our earlier contention that this comparative question cannot be answered until we have determined whether X is right for A. Warren's argument, and all arguments that treat equality as a sufficient standard of right, suggests that X can sometimes be right for A *because* A and B, C, D, . . . N are treated in a like manner. But this argument either begs the question of the first premise of GP — "Is X right for A?" — or simply restates it for B, C, D, . . . N and A. The question whether X is right for A must be independent of GP. It is not a comparative question (that is, not in the sense of GP or equality; it may be comparative in the sense of comparing the merits of alternative policies or actions) and it cannot be answered by a comparative formula or rule. If we treat A wrongly, it will not help to say that we have treated him the same as B, C, D, . . . N.

The same is true of B, C, D, . . . N. The rightness or wrongness of giving X to B, C, D, . . . N could turn on a relationship of equality or inequality between B, C, D, . . . N and A only in the circumstances specified above. (Even in those circumstances questions of ethical naturalism might arise.) Treating them equally in one respect will usually involve treating them unequally in another, possibly more important, respect. If we treat B, C, D, . . . N badly, it will not help that we have treated B, C, D, . . . N and A alike. To decide the rightness or wrongness of X for B, C, D, . . . N, we must repeat for the latter those steps taken to determine whether X was right or wrong for A.

Our reason for contending that establishing the first premise of GP is the main task should now be clear. For the procedure just described establishes the second as well as the first premise. It tells us whether B, C, D. . . . N are, vis-à-vis A, relevantly similar persons in relevantly similar circumstances. Our purpose is to discover whether X is right or wrong for both A and B, C, D, . . . N; and, by hypothesis, we have now done so. What could be more relevant than that the same policy is right or wrong for both? Indeed, what other proper answer could there be to the question of whether they are relevantly similar? The second premise of GP, in short, is properly established through the same procedures as the first, by determining the rightness or wrongness of applying X to B, C, D, . . . N. If that determination accords with the result obtained in making the same decision with regard to applying X to A, then A and B, C, D, . . . N are relevantly similar persons in relevantly similar circumstances and what is right or wrong for B, C, D, . . . N must (logically) be right or wrong for A. If the results of the two determinations differ, A and B, C, D, . . . N are not relevantly similar — and what is right for A is not right for B, C, D, . . . N.

GP demands a certain relationship between A and B, C, D, . . . N; but that relationship is a logically necessary relationship between the results obtained by the application of tests that are independent of GP. The moment we lose sight of this fact we are in danger of mistreating a person, or class of persons, on the irrelevant grounds that he, or it, is receiving the same treatment as others.

III

It might be contended that the foregoing analysis fails to consider certain dimensions and characteristics peculiar to equality questions. We have dissolved equality questions into a series of right-wrong questions connected in a *post hoc,* formal manner. At the least, it might be alleged, this analysis ignores prominent aspects of moral and political thought and practice.

The objection is justified in that one aspect of equality questions is partially masked by the foregoing discussion. The difficulty in the above account is its apparent suggestion that judgments about the rightness or wrongness of X for A are *entirely* independent of, and cannot be upset by, concern with B, C, D, ... N. There are cases in which this is obviously not true. If A and B, C, D, ... N are part of the same moral or legal system, giving X to A might have consequences for B, C, D, ... N, consequences that must be considered in deciding whether it is right to give X to A. In the cases discussed thus far, we have assumed we had accounted for the impact of X on both (all) parties or classes; but there are other types of cases to be considered. Hence the foregoing discussion is incomplete; it needs to be supplemented by an enumeration and further analysis of the combinations that logically can arise under GP. Although this will involve some repetition of earlier arguments, it should summarize the results of those arguments and show what must be added to them in order to handle the objection before us.

We will continue to assume that X is right for A taken alone (that is, without considering the impact on B, C, D, ... N, of giving X to A). Holding this constant, there are two basic types of situations (A and B) and six types of cases (A.1–3 and B.1-3) that can arise under GP.

Situation A: If X is not right for B, C, D, ... N, A and B, C, D, ... N are not relevantly similar, and what is right for A is, by hypothesis, not right for B, C, D, ... N.

Hence: A.1. To treat A and B, C, D, ... N alike would be to treat unlike cases alike and would violate GP.

This is the standard type of case in which GP is violated. The Reynolds decision illustrates the point nicely. The Court holds that the equal population rule is the "controlling criterion" under the Equal Protection Clause. All citizens must be treated equally in the respect indicated by that rule. A.1. shows that this rule can be a requirement only if it would not be wrong to treat B, C, D, ... N in this way. Critics of the decision hold that this condition is not satisfied in some states, that use of the equal population rule will lead to results of the A.1. type. To insist that all citizens be treated equally in this respect might involve treating them unequally in respects more important to the citizens in question and to the system.

To apply the equal population rule to Colorado, for example, might require that citizens of area D', an isolated mountain district with unique interests, be placed in a legislative district (D) which is uniquely large in terms of area, which poses very difficult transportation and communication problems, in which the overwhelming majority of the population have interests and political affiliations (for example, party) markedly at variance with those of the citizenry in D', and in which the citizens of D' share no mechanisms and channels of informal political activity with the other citizens of D. If these conditions do not obtain in other districts of the state, or, as posited, for other citizens in D, the citizenry of D', although treated equally in terms of the equal population rule, are treated unequally in other respects. Hence to impose the equal population rule upon them would be to treat unlike cases alike. More important, it might be to treat unlike cases alike in a manner that results in treating some groups well and other groups badly.

To treat A and B, C, D, . . . N differently in situation A, for example to give X to A but not to B, C, D, . . . N, might appear to be acceptable under GP. But this is one of the situations prompting the objection that the present analysis ignores distinctive aspects of equality questions. Before we can decide whether it is right to give X to A but not to B, C, D, . . . N, we must decide whether it would be right not to give X to B, C, D, . . . N when one of the conditions is that we are giving X to A. Although we have posited that it would be wrong to give X to B, C, D, . . . N, we do not yet know whether it would be wrong to treat B, C, D, . . . N in the proposed manner, that is, subjecting them to whatever effects would result from giving X to A.

This case (A.2.) is not covered by A.1.; it is an entirely different case and an entirely different problem. But the principle employed to decide A.1. must be used to decide A.2. (and A.3.) as well. We can decide A.2. only by asking whether it is wrong to treat B, C, D, . . . N in this manner.

Hence: A.2. If the policy of giving X to A but not to B, C, D, . . . N is not wrong for B, C, D, . . . N, a permissible classification has been made and it is right to give X to A.

A.2. is the paradigm case of the permissible classification, and a great deal of governmental action falls under it.

A.3. If giving X to A but not to B, C, D, . . . N wrongs B, C, D, . . . N, the classification is not permissible and the policy must be abandoned. Note that it is not the mere fact that A and B, C, D, . . . N are treated differently (unequally) that renders X obnoxious. Or rather, there is only one sense of "unequal" in which this is true, namely that one is treated well and the other badly. They are also treated unequally in many respects under A.2., which is unobjectionable. Again, we can decide only by looking at the effects of the policy for B, C, D, . . . N.

A.2. and A.3. are common in government. A.2. allows a degree of flexibility that is essential if government is to act widely but with discrimination. And the search for A.2.'s sometimes leads to A.3.'s instead. It would be undesirable to tax those with incomes under five thousand dollars at 90 per cent, but it would also be undesirable if we were thereby prevented from taxing multimillionaires at that rate. It would be wrong to conscript men over sixty years of age, but it might be disastrous if we were thereby prevented from drafting men under twenty-six. For another illustration, consider the problem in Reynolds. Strict adherence to the equal population rule renders it impossible for cases of type A.2. to arise in the area of apportionment. Because the rule is satisfied only if everyone in the system is treated equally in this particular respect, the rule must be right for everyone or for no one.

Situation B: If X is right for B, C, D, . . . N, A and B, C, D, . . . N are relevantly similar persons in relevantly similar circumstances, and what is right for A must be right for B, C, D, . . . N.

Hence: B.1. If X is applied to A and to B, C, D, . . . N, it does not violate GP. If Warren's argument is tenable, the equal population rule falls under this heading. Notice that this is the one and only case in which that rule is consistent with GP as it has been interpreted here.

B.2. If the policy of giving X to A but not to B, C, D, . . . N does not wrong B, C, D, . . . N, a permissible classification has been made and GP is not violated.

This is another situation that prompts an objection to the analysis. But the fact that B.2. is not fully covered by B.1. does not upset the above analysis or indicate that it cannot take account of the distinctive features of equality questions. B.2. is a different policy from B.1., and it must be evaluated independently. But nothing in the analysis prevents us from noticing and evaluating the fact that giving X to A has consequences for B, C, D, . . . N despite the fact that B, C, D, . . . N are not given X.

B.2. is perhaps the most interesting result with regard to equality. The argument is that the fact that X is right for both A and B, C, D, . . . N does not require that it be wrong to give X to A but not to B, C, D, . . . N. To prove that giving X is right is not to prove that withholding it is wrong. To show that it would be wrong to withhold X from B, C, D, . . . N while giving it to A would require a demonstration that the results of withholding X from B, C, D, . . . N, under these circumstances, would be wrong.

Consider the following hypothetical case. School districts A and B would both benefit from receiving X dollars of state aid. State resources are sufficiently great to give X to A and B without hampering other programs, but A has a large population of educationally deprived children and B does not. It would be right to give X to both A and B and to give X to A and not to B would be to treat them unequally in one important respect. But if we are right about B.2., to do the latter would not be wrong. The inequality would not lead to bad results for B and hence it would be based upon a permissible classification.

This point is at the heart of the present argument. "Equally" means "according to one and the same rule." Whenever we treat according to a rule, we will be treating equally in respect to that rule. Clearly then, the crucial question will be "according to what rule should we treat people in this case?" The principle of equality will rarely answer this question because ordinarily we must choose between equalities. If we choose to treat A and B equally in respect to educational achievement, we will treat them unequally in respect to the size of the grant awarded. This must be defended in terms of the relative importance of equal educational achievement as against equal grants of money. To dramatize the example, let us consider whether we could justify giving a larger grant to B despite the fact that B is already ahead of A in terms of educational achievement. To justify such a policy we would have to find another rule that we regard as more important than either size of grant or educational achievement. Let us say that the national defense would be served by concentrating the bulk of our resources in B. If our rule was "maximize contributions to the national defense," we could properly say that A and B had been treated equally if B received a larger grant, unequally if A and B received an identical grant. Hence one could not object to the rule on the ground that it violated the principle of equality. One could only object that the kind of equality served by the rule was less important than other kinds of equality that might have been served in the same situation. Such an objection would involve an appeal from equality to some other principle.[8]

B.3. If to refuse to give X to B, C, D, . . . N while giving it to A wrongs B, C, D, . . . N, GP is violated and the policy must be abandoned.

The problem in Reynolds is instructive concerning B.2. and B.3. If B.2. would be unobjectionable under GP, the equal population rule would not be a requirement in situations of this type. It would be acceptable to follow the rule in such cases, but it would not be wrong to depart from it. If Colorado employed the equal population rule in most of its legislative districts, there would be no *prima facie* bar to departure from that rule in dealing with cases such as our hypothetical D′. Special treatment for D′, regardless of how great the departure from the equal population rule, would be condemned only if it could be shown that it wronged non-D′s. If, say, all non-D′s, by every measure other than the equal population rule, were receiving effective representation, special treatment of D′ would no more be a problem than the special treatment we accord to some people virtually every time government acts. For the rule to be a requirement, all departures from it must fall under B.3. This is the position that defenders of a strict "one-man, one-vote" rule, or any comparable egalitarian rule, must defend.

These cases, allowing for recombination among the situations and types, exhaust the logical possibilities under GP. Although they complicate the earlier analysis, none of them upsets that analysis. If correct, the analysis shows that GP, or equality, is not a sufficient criterion of a justifiable decision. We must decide whether policies are right or wrong, good or bad; since we will rarely, if ever, be able to treat equally in one respect without treating unequally in others, to equate "right" with "equal" and "wrong" with "unequal" produces the logically absurd result that our decisions must be both right and wrong. This absurdity is avoided by using a criterion other than equality to choose between competing equalities. GP states a logical relationship between the results obtained through use of such a criterion. Hence the analysis indicates that equality is a significant normative criterion only in a *derivative* sense.

IV

The force of the foregoing analysis is primarily negative. It seeks to demonstrate that equality or equal treatment is a derivative criterion inadequate for determining rightness or wrongness. Attempts to elevate it to the status of a sufficient standard

---

[8] It has been suggested that this example strains ordinary usage; that "equally" would be used in connection with the effects of the policy on A and B, not its effects on the country at large. One response to this objection would be that the argument considers the effects of the policy on A and B in what Rousseau would call their corporate capacities. Both are members of the system; the system is affected in a particular manner; and hence both, as members, are affected in the same way. It is my view that much public policy is justified, and can only be justified, in this way. But this response concedes more than is necessary to the objection. "According to one and the same rule" is a standard meaning of "equally" and the above argument is in conformity with it. The objection that the argument strains usage could be sustained only if another interpretation of "equally" could be sustained. My suspicion is that an exchange on this point would show not that the argument strains ordinary usage of "equally" but that it departs from widespread conceptions as to which kinds of equality are most important.

involve logical errors that could readily lead to unsatisfactory decisions. The question of how rightness and wrongness are *properly* determined, of how we decide whether X is right for A, is too large for adequate discussion here; but the previous analysis has implications for that question, which we will explore briefly.

We emphasized the difficulties stemming from the fact that equality, as ordinarily understood, is concerned with comparative questions. Such questions are derivative in status and significance. But the argument that led to this conclusion included a more fundamental point, one that has application beyond equality questions. In arguing that substantive (as opposed to formal or neutral as above) egalitarian rules deal with derivative considerations, we suggested that such rules cover only one of many relationships relevant to or created by policies implementing those rules. Our immediate attack was upon the concern with a certain kind of relationship, which, it was suggested, should be replaced by concern with the consequences of treating a person or class of persons in a certain manner. But relationships with which egalitarian rules are concerned are sometimes a consequence of and are almost always affected by the adoption of a policy implementing such a rule. The argument, then, that the rightness of X for A can be determined only by examination of consequences is, in a more basic sense, an argument that egalitarian rules are concerned with an overly narrow range of the consequences of X for A. The equal population rule, for example, establishes, in advance of the application of the policy, not only the criterion of rightness that districting policy must meet but also the aspects of the policy that will be relevant to determining its rightness. A considerable range of the consequences of the policy are classed as irrelevant for purposes of evaluation.[9]

Against the narrowing effect of concern with equality, we suggest the need for a broader, indeed an – in principle – unrestricted, definition of the range of consequences potentially relevant to the evaluation. In morals and in law our primary purpose is to discover whether those affected by our actions and policies are treated well or badly by them. Because our actions and policies have a great variety of effects, any one or all of which might be morally or legally significant, it is dangerous to rule out the possibility that any one of those effects might be crucial for our evaluation.

These considerations suggest that the most general and perhaps the primary principle of moral and legal evaluation would be along the lines, "consider the consequences." Conveniently, Singer has developed a more sophisticated formulation of such a utilitarian principle. He calls it the Principle of Consequences (hereafter, PC).[10] The principle has both a negative and a positive formulation. The negative version reads, "If the consequences of A's doing X are undesirable, A ought not to do X." The positive formulation reads, "If the consequences of A's not doing X are undesirable, then A ought to do X." These two versions result in moral imperatives. There is also a non-imperative version (which Singer rejects as invalid). "If the consequences of A's doing X are desirable, then it would be good if A did X." Since the fact that an action would be morally desirable or good is not in and of itself sufficient to generate an imperative to do that action (other actions might be as good or better) the last formulation would be invalid if it concluded

---

[9] Once again, this might be a defensible *conclusion* in the Reynolds case or in related types of moral and political decisions. But it is not defensible as an assumption used in the making of such decisions.

[10] Singer, *op. cit.*, pp. 63–67.

that "A ought to do X." But if PC in general is valid, there are no difficulties with the non-imperative version, and it is of considerable importance to public policy.

The strength of PC in the present context, and the only defense that will be offered for it here,[11] is that it provides a standardized statement of some of the findings of the foregoing analysis. As with GP, it is a formal principle. It has no force in any concrete case until the particular premise of the form, "the consequences of this X for this A are desirable," has been established, and the principle itself does not aid us in establishing that premise. But the principle does direct our attention to the most fundamental considerations in any moral decision (including legal decisions with moral dimensions). Before we adopt the equal population rule, or any substantive moral or legal rule, we must test the results of the use of that rule against the requirements of PC. If they fail that test, we search for a more satisfactory rule. The equal population rule, or any other substantive moral or legal rule, will be viewed as a secondary rule useful as a guide in establishing the particular premise of PC. But if a rule fails to satisfy the requirements of PC, if it leads to undesirable consequences in a specific case, it will be abandoned or modified as a rule for that case. If a rule regularly leads to undesirable consequences, it will be abandoned entirely.[12]

With PC available, we can state earlier arguments concerning equality in a more standardized manner. GP states a logical relationship between the conclusions reached through two or more applications of PC. We determine whether X is right for A under PC, and whether it is right for B, C, D, . . . N under PC. If it is right for each, the particular premises of GP are established and what is right for A is right for B, C, D, . . . N. If not, the second premise is not established. From a moral or legal standpoint, then, GP reduces to "Don't treat people in a manner that violates PC."

If this argument is correct, the formal principle of GP is not subject to the limitations noted in connection with substantive egalitarian rules such as the equal population rule. But the argument might also suggest that GP is trivial. GP has no moral force until PC has been applied, and hence it might appear that it can teach us nothing that we cannot better learn under PC. This inference is unwarranted. If I say that X is red, I do so in virtue of certain properties of X. When I do so, I commit myself to saying that any other object that has the same properties is red. If Y has all the properties that led me to say that X is red, I must say that Y is red as well (or retract my statement concerning X). To deny that Y is red is to contradict myself. There is a logical relationship between the statements "X is red" and "Y is red."

GP states the same logical relationship between two (or more) moral judgments as obtains between "X is red" and "Y is red." The first particular premise of GP is

---

[11] Singer discusses a number of the issues that arise in connection with PC. See *ibid*., per Index. I have examined the principle in detail in my recent work, *The Public Interest*, New York: John Wiley, 1966, Chapter 8.

[12] Cf. H. L. A. Hart's notion of "defeasibility." See his "The Ascription of Responsibility and Rights," in Antony Flew (Ed.), *Logic and Language*, First Series, Oxford: Basil Blackwell, 1963. In minimizing equality and other formalist or deontological rules and considerations, the foregoing argument involves a condensed version of act-utilitarianism. There are a number of standard objections to this position, the most relevant here being that the logic of the position eliminates all moral and legal rules and requires that decisions be made exclusively on their individual merits. Hart's discussion of defeasibility rebuts important aspects of this objection, and I have discussed the objection at length in *The Public Interest, op. cit.*

of the form: "This X is right for this A." We establish this premise by applying PC. We say "X is right (or wrong) for A by virtue of the desirability (undesirability) of the consequences of X for A." The second particular premise is established in the same manner. We determine the relevant similarity of A and B by examining the consequences of X for B. Having applied PC, we say "X is right (or wrong) for B by virtue of the desirability (undesirability) of the consequences of X for B." Between the two particular premises of GP stands "must be." "Must be" has the same status as the logical rule that requires us to say "Y is red" if Y has the same properties that led us to say "X is red." GP states a logical relationship between the conclusions reached through two (or more) applications of PC. A logical relationship between two conclusions is not the same thing as the two conclusions themselves, and GP is not the same as two (or more) applications of PC.

Hence GP does not inform us concerning the moral status of any action. But it does not follow that GP lacks utility in discourse concerning morals and politics. If X has properties (P) such that we call it red, and if Y has P, we do not need a rule of logic to tell us that Y is red. When we see that Y has properties P we say that Y is red simply because it has the properties by virtue of which we apply the word "red." But in morals and politics matters are more complicated. To say that X is right for A by virtue of its having desirable consequences is not merely to describe X. It is also to evaluate or commend X. We commend in order to guide conduct, to convince people, including ourselves, to act in a manner that might be contrary to our inclinations. To say "X is right for A because P" is not simply to describe X; it is to say that A ought to do X. And hence, under the logical rule of GP, it is to say that every A ought to do X. If I say "Jones ought to give $1000 to charity because P" and if my giving $1000 to charity produces P, then I must give $1000 (or retract my statement concerning Jones). But giving $1000 to charity is apt to conflict with my inclinations in a manner that saying "Y is red" is not likely to do. I am apt to want to say that giving $1000 to charity is not right for me. But GP provides a logical principle, neutral to the moral question, that can discipline my thinking in a salutary manner. "Didn't you say Jones ought to give $1000 to charity?" "Yes." "How does his case differ from yours?" If I am unable to show a relevant difference, if I am unable to show that for A to do X produces P, whereas for me to do X produces Q, then it will be inconsistent for me to refuse to do X. Hence although I do not share Hare's lofty estimate of the significance of GP (he calls it the universalizability principle) for moral discourse, I do not see how it can be regarded as trivial.[13] Because GP is a formalized statement of the principle of equality, the same conclusion applies to that principle.

V

Our conclusion concerning equality runs counter to a pervasive and influential strand in Western thought. The primary justifications for the conclusion are those presented in the course of the analysis, but it will be useful to deal more explicitly

[13] R. M. Hare has developed these points in great detail in his two books on ethics: *Language of Morals*, Oxford: Oxford University Press, 1952; *Freedom and Reason*, Oxford: Oxford University Press, 1963. But Hare makes no explicit use of PC or any equivalent principle, and this leads to serious difficulties. See especially his discussion of "fanatics" in *Freedom and Reason*.

with some of the basic contentions with which the present conclusions conflict.[14] Conveniently, some of these have been restated in recent papers by William Frankena and Gregory Vlastos.[15] Consideration of these arguments will lead to the question mentioned earlier: whether, despite the foregoing analysis, a substantive moral principle lurks beneath the logical rule to which we have reduced GP and equality.

Both Frankena and Vlastos contend that an aspect of treating men well is to treat them equally in a non-derivative sense. In Frankena's words, "all men are to be treated as equals, not because they are equal in any respect, but simply because they are human."[16] Equal treatment in this fundamental sense is regarded as an irreducible value that depends in no way upon utilitarian considerations. Both writers concede that very dissimilar treatment is often consistent with, indeed demanded by, recognition of equal worth, and that in most cases relevant equalities are to be identified by reference to good treatment. But they insist that there are actions or policies that would be unjustified solely because they are inconsistent with "recognition of the equality or equal intrinsic value of every human personality."[17] One of Vlastos' examples is that cruel treatment, even of a cruel man, is always unjustified because it singles the man out for treatment contrary to a moral rule based not on any merits distinctive of the man but on recognition of human equality, on the man's "birthright as a human being." In such cases, if their analysis is correct, good treatment would be derivative of equal treatment rather than the reverse.[18] If I understand them correctly, it is only in respect to such cases that their position is at odds with that argued here.

As suggested by the phrase "equal intrinsic value of every human personality," Frankena and Vlastos are arguing against meritarian justifications for certain kinds of unequal treatment. Now if "intrinsic value" is to provide a meaningful ground for moral judgments, it must be identified sufficiently to allow us to know what it

[14] It should be noted that the "egalitarian tradition" is anything but well defined. For recent attempts to sort out some of the important strands in the tradition, see the papers by Richard Wollheim and Sir Isaiah Berlin in Frederick Olafson (Ed.), *Justice and Social Policy*, Englewood Cliffs, N.J.: Prentice-Hall, 1961. See also S. I. Benn and R. S. Peters, *Social Principles and the Democratic State*, Chapter 5, London: George Allen and Unwin, 1959. For a general historical survey, see Sanford A. Lakoff, *Equality in Political Philosophy*, Cambridge: Harvard University Press, 1964. Berlin and Benn and Peters make a number of arguments closely akin to those presented above.

[15] See Richard Brandt (Ed.), *Social Justice*, Englewood Cliffs, N.J.: Prentice-Hall, 1962. These papers are concerned with questions of justice and rights, and there is some suggestion in them that these questions are regarded as distinct from those of rightness and wrongness, goodness and badness, which are discussed here. (This suggestion has been made more strongly by H. L. A. Hart in another symposium related to present concerns. See the papers of Hart, Frankena, and Stuart M. Brown, Jr. in *Philosophical Review*, Vol. 64, No. 2 [April, 1955], pp. 1ff.) The present writer is not convinced that there is a radical distinction between the logics of these different concepts. It is impossible to enter into the question here, but it may be that some of the disagreements between the aforementioned papers and the present one are to be explained in this way.

[16] Brandt, *op. cit.*, p. 19.

[17] *Ibid.*, p. 14.

[18] The non-derivative, irreducible status of "all men are to be treated as equals" suggests that this imperative is unanalyzable. In this respect the argument is deontological or formalistic in character and it raises the problems associated with deontological positions generally, particularly the problem of how one could defend or justify the imperative or action taken in accord with it.

will support and when it has been disregarded or violated.[19] The task of identifying it has proved to be a difficult one, productive of considerable controversy.[20] However defined, respect for intrinsic value might require, in particular situations, that one person's intrinsic value be served, another's not served at all or disserved. If (a) the intrinsic value of one man differs in its manifestations from that of others, its manifestation as a specific need, interest, or demand might conflict with the needs, interests, and demands of others. Even if (b) the intrinsic worth of all men is the same in nature and manifestation, scarcity of resources, administrative difficulties, human shortcomings, and the like might make it impossible to serve all men equally. In the case of either (a) or (b), if a decision must be made, the decision-maker will require a principle that will allow him to justify serving the intrinsic value of one person or set of persons over the intrinsic value of others. By hypothesis, equality of intrinsic value cannot provide that principle. This is the main reason that equal rights for which equal worth provides the ground[21] are *prima facie* rights, the claim to which can be defeated in particular circumstances.[22]

The doctrine of equal intrinsic value, then, can provide a basis for moral and political decisions and policy only if the various manifestations of value are self-regarding in significance or if there is a harmony between them such that all can be served equally well. I am not prepared to deny the possibility of such cases. But moral and political questions arise primarily where other-regarding behavior and conflicts of needs, interests, and demands are present. In such cases the doctrine of equal intrinsic value cannot provide a basis for decision. To assert that particular decisions of this kind are justified because they serve equality is to assert that one kind of equality is preferable to other kinds of equality that might have been served in the same situation. If the foregoing analysis is correct, the more fundamental principle is: "Treat people well as demanded by PC."

This conclusion leads to a final problem. Assuming that the present argument is correct and that equal treatment (GP) must be interpreted through good or right treatment (PC), it nevertheless appears that GP commits us to treating everyone equally in the sense of equally well. Hence it might appear that a substantive moral principle underlies GP even as it has been interpreted here.

---

[19] Cf. Benn and Peters, *op. cit.*, especially p. 109. See also R. M. Hare, *Freedom and Reason*, especially pp. 211–213.

[20] Frankena identifies it as follows: "I accepted as part of my own view the principle that all men are to be treated as equals, not because they are equal in any respect but simply because they are human. They are human because they have emotions and desires, and are able to think, and hence are capable of enjoying a good life in a sense in which other animals are not. They are human because their lives may be 'significant' in the manner which William James made so graphic . . . : 'Wherever a process of life communicates an eagerness to him who lives it, there the life becomes genuinely significant. Sometimes the eagerness is more knit up with the motor activities, sometimes with the perceptions, sometimes with the imagination, sometimes with reflective thought. But wherever it is found . . . there *is* importance in the only real and positive sense in which importance anywhere can be.' By the good life is meant not so much the morally good life as the happy or satisfactory life. As I see it, it is the fact that all men are similarly capable of enjoying a good life in this sense that justifies the *prima facie* requirement that they be treated as equals." Brandt, *op. cit.*, p. 19. For Vlastos' statement see *ibid.*, pp. 47–52. See also the related arguments of H. L. A. Hart, *loc. cit.*

[21] See Vlastos, *op. cit.*, pp. 50–52.

[22] See especially Frankena's paper in the symposium cited above, pp. 227–232 and *passim*. See also the very important note 44 on p. 52 of Vlastos' paper.

We want to treat people equally in the sense of equally well. To determine whether we are treating people well, we examine the consequences of policies and actions and evaluate them in terms of moral standards. Satisfaction of the standard or standards selected in any case will often require treating people dissimilarly in respect to standards that have been rejected in the case in question. If we institute selective conscription, we might draft all healthy, unmarried men between the ages of eighteen and twenty-six on the grounds that such a classification best serves the standard, "Maintain national security." If we draft all those who fall into the class, and none who do not, we will be treating the citizenry equally in terms of that standard. But our policy might produce inequalities in terms of other standards. Draftee A is in the throes of a passionate love affair, the interruption of which causes him enormous psychic distress; Draftee B, on the other hand, is bored with his life and finds military service a welcome relief. Drafting them both creates inequality in terms of the standard "minimize psychic distress." We justify this inequality by arguing that the national security requires it and that in the circumstances the rule "maintain national security" is more important than the rule "minimize psychic distress." But if the national security is our standard, we cannot justify treating A differently from B in terms of that standard. If the consequences of drafting A and B were the same with regard to service of the national security, we could not exempt A on grounds of his love affair. We must treat everyone equally in the sense that we must apply our standards *impartially* to all. To defer A but draft B under the posited conditions would be to give preference to A in a manner that could not be justified in terms of the standard.

The last phrase, together with a notion of impartiality, is the key to the significance of the notion that we must treat people equally well. We attempt to decide how to treat people by looking at the consequences of different policies for them and evaluating those policies in the light of standards that we can defend. Because men are extraordinarily diverse in person and circumstance, adhering to our standards often requires that men be treated very differently. But we treat men differently because we have good reasons for doing so, namely that treating well according to the best standards that we can construct requires that we do so. Where no such reason can be offered, it would be impossible to defend or justify unequal treatment. In such cases we describe differences in treatment as based on partiality or bias. The question then becomes: "Why are we opposed to partiality and bias?"

Vlastos and Frankena contend that our opposition stems from a sense of the equal intrinsic value of all men. Granting that we have or should have such a "sense," for the reasons noted this position will rarely if ever help us to reach and defend a decision. A second position is suggested by Hare, who argues that the requirement of generalization (universalization) is a purely logical requirement and that departure from it is a logical mistake.[23] On this view we are against partiality and bias because they lead to violations of the logical rule that it is inconsistent to treat unlike cases alike and like cases unalike. We are against violations of the rules of logic. But in the moral realm violation of these rules coincides with violation of the moral rule PC. And we are against violations of PC because we are in favor of treating people well and against treating them badly. Treating them unequally in

[23] See R. M. Hare, *op. cit.*, especially pp. 10–13 and 30–35.

the sense identified by violations of GP will be to treat them badly, and hence we are against it for moral as well as logical reasons. It is because partiality and bias are productive of such results that we are right in objecting to them. Hence there is a respect in which unequal treatment is morally wrong, but it is derivative in the sense argued throughout the paper.

Part VI

Justice

Introduction

Although he is a utilitarian, it is very far from John Stuart Mill's view that justice is unimportant or that we should cease to talk about it and restrict our moral discourse and reasoning to direct applications of utilitarian principles. He identifies a distinct group of questions that typically arise under the rubric of justice, and he insists that they are the most important of all moral questions, that the reasons for doing what is just and avoiding injustice are among, if not absolutely, the strongest reasons that we have for any class or type of actions. But he does not believe that justice has absolute weight in all circumstances; he finds considerable and recurrent conflict concerning what just arrangements and policies are, and he insists that justice itself and the resolution of controversies concerning it cannot be understood apart from their relationship to the wider set of principles and reasoning that constitute utilitarianism. Justice is not reducible to utility in any simple sense, but the foundations of rational convictions concerning its importance, and the understanding and resolution of practical issues concerning it, require that we go "down to the principles which lie under justice and are the source of its authority." When such questions arise, "Social utility alone can decide the preference" or yield a reasoned position.

It is a refreshing feature of John Rawls' formidable challenge to utilitarianism that it does not begin, or for that matter end, with the charge that utilitarianism leads ineluctably to the defense of slavery, of judicial murder, of denial of all human rights, or of any of the other "parade of horribles" with which antiutilitarians have laced their arguments from the eighteenth century to the present. But Rawls does contend that utilitarianism cannot give a cogent account of justice and cannot give adequate arguments for the social arrangements that the principles of justice require or against the arrangements and practices that they condemn. Hence he sets about to construct a theory that grounds the principles of justice and the modes of applying them in considerations and arguments independent of those which define utilitarianism, in the kinds of considerations and arguments typically emphasized by thinkers in the social contract tradition. The principles of social justice are to be identified through reasoning concerning what rational men would (should) establish as the principles of judgment and decision about the social and political practices in which they and their progeny are to live their lives.

In their criticisms of Rawls' theory, Brian Barry and Lawrence Haworth[1]

[1] The primary subject of Haworth's paper, which appears in Part VII, is the theory of rights, not of justice, and he reaches Rawls' theory of justice because it yields a set of foundations for rights. It should be mentioned again that Rawls has developed his theory of justice more fully

concentrate (albeit not exclusively) on arguing that the principles Rawls puts forward would (should) *not* be accepted by rational men in what Rawls sets forth as the "general" position, that is, when establishing the principles of their social and political order. If this is the test that an account of "justice" must pass, they contend, Rawls' account cannot be correct. (Barry also argues that even if rational men in the "general" position would (should) accept Rawls' principles, they are not principles of social *justice* as that concept is used in our language, and hence that Rawls has not given an account of justice. Both he and Haworth argue that it is impossible, or probably impossible, to account for our concept of justice with, to "encapsulate" that concept in, any single formula. In this respect they might be interpreted as arguing that Mill's utilitarian account is also inadequate.) This criticism, however, leaves open the possibility that Rawls' approach to the problem of analyzing justice, that is, the approach of reasoning from the situation of men who live in a society but who do not as yet have a concept of justice, is the correct approach.[2] After one or two preliminary comments, the present remarks will attempt to raise some questions concerning the appropriateness of this approach.

First, it is worth noticing that the argument that utilitarians cannot give an adequate account of justice rests in part on the controversial assumption that reasons of justice, once we have decided what they are in any given situation, have not only a "special" but an "absolute" weight when they conflict with the "greatest satisfaction of desire" that utilitarians have emphasized. By making his principles of justice *the* criteria (or criterion) of judgment, Rawls of course guarantees that this will be true within the confines of his theory. (We return to this point immediately below.) But the belief that it is true is clearly a main impetus to the construction of a theory in which it is true. (In a later essay Rawls says, "If . . . we believe that as a matter of principle each member of society has an inviolability founded on justice which even the welfare of everyone else cannot override . . . we shall have to look for another account (other than the utilitarian account) of the principles of justice."[3]) Rawls may be correct that there could be no circumstance in which a society would be justified in doing injustice, in maintaining an injust social practice or institution in order to serve or protect the general welfare. But the belief that this view is incorrect, supported by examples plausibly interpreted as evidence that societies have thought that it was and is, has been an extremely important part of utilitarianism. When Rawls assumes that his view in this respect accords with the ordinary conception of justice he takes a short way with a fundamental aspect of his controversy with utilitarianism. (Mill makes an interesting comment on this subject, see the last paragraphs of his selection.)

The view that reasons of justice have absolute weight is an essential part of Rawls' argument that utilitarianism cannot yield a satisfactory argument against

---

in his recent book of that title (Cambridge, Mass.: Harvard University Press, 1971). In that work he responds explicitly to a number of criticisms advanced by contributors to this and the previous part.

[2] It is essential to notice that Rawls' "general" position is not a "state of nature" in the sense of a presocial situation in which it is necessary to create a full range of social and political institutions and arrangements *de novo*.

[3] John Rawls, "Distributive Justice," in Peter Laslett and W. G. Runciman, eds., *Philosophy, Politics and Society*, Third Series (Oxford: Basil Blackwell, 1967), p. 59.

slavery. His use of this assumption in making his argument brings us closer to the consequences of analysing justice by reasoning from the "general" position. The utilitarian argument against slavery is that, in fact, the advantages to the slaveholder will never outweigh the disadvantages to the slaves. This of course means that if the former did outweigh the latter the utilitarian would have to approve of slavery. On Rawls' conception of justice, by contrast, slavery is necessarily (not merely contingently) unjust because that conception "would not allow one to consider the advantages of the slaveholder in the first place."

In the "general position" that Rawls conjectures, every person is assumed to be in a position of moral and juridical equality, that is, no one as yet has any authority over or rights against anyone else. Moreover, although it is assumed that all persons are mutually self-interested and rational, it is also posited that, so far as they know in the general position, they are roughly equal in "power and ability" so that no one has reasonable grounds on which to expect that he can dominate the others. As Rawls puts the last point in the "Distributive Justice" essay cited earlier, "no one knows his position in society, nor even his place in the distribution of natural talents and abilities. The principles of justice to which all are forever bound are chosen in the absence of this sort of specific information. A veil of ignorance prevents anyone from being advantaged or disadvantaged by the contingencies of social class and fortune."[4] Thus persons in the general position have no reason to accept, it would be irrational for them to accept, principles that *could* yield a justification for slavery and hence a justification for their being slaves. Because the persons involved are rational, the principles decided upon will be such that the advantages to the slaveholder cannot be considered in deciding whether slavery is just (that is, will be the two principles of justice Rawls identifies).

It is interesting to note, first of all, that in the general position as Rawls describes it the application of utilitarian reasoning would also yield the conclusion that slavery is and must be indefensible. For in that condition, as Rawls himself puts it, his "two principles of justice define distributive shares in a way compatible with efficiency." "[P]erfectly just institutions," he goes on to say, "are also efficient."[5] Thus *under the conditions posited* utilitarianism and Rawlsian justice would be extensionally equivalent theories, would *always* yield the same practical conclusions. If this is not true when those theories are applied to the societies we know, the question as to which theory is best as regards those societies cannot be settled without considering the significance of the enormous differences between the conditions Rawls posits in the "general situation" and those under which we actually live.

The point here might be made by recurring to some of Wittgenstein's terminology discussed in the introduction to this book. The general position Rawls posits might be viewed as a language game or form of life. That language game involves, consists in part of, certain concepts such as "rationality," "self-interest," and "just," "justice," and "injustice." The way these concepts work, as with all concepts in all language games, is inseparable from the other features of the game of which they are a part. What "justice" is in that game is a function of the role that concept plays in the game. Because Rawls himself is a (perhaps the only) participant in the game (not to mention the fact that he created it!) there is reason to think that he understands how the concepts that figure in it are used.

[4] Ibid.
[5] Ibid.

What is the relationship between "reason," "justice," and so forth, in Rawls' game and in the game or games in which these terms figure in the societies we know? Rawls, of course, thinks that they are congruent, that the concepts (not just the terms) work the same way in essential respects, that his use of "justice," "reason," and so on, in his theory is an abstract, rationalized version of its use in the societies we know. The very fact, however, that the conditions under which the concepts are used are so different, and that the differences are so prominent in Rawls' discussion, is cause for skepticism on the point.

There is a further cause for skepticism, one very similar to the basis on which we raised questions concerning Gewirth's argument for a theory of egalitarian justice. Rawls says that the persons who debate and decide upon the principles of justice are rational and self-interested. And, with one exception in the case of "rational" (see his section III, third paragraph), he claims to be using these concepts in the ordinary way. But he also says that persons in the general position do not know their place in society, do not know their talents, abilities, powers, and so on. Now the question must be raised whether our concepts of "reason" and "self-interest" can be coherently used under the circumstances he describes. What would it mean to form a conception of one's interests in the "veil of ignorance" he posits? What would reasoning about those interests and the arrangements that would serve or disserve them consist of? Just as "purposiveness" seems to be inseparable from particular purposes formed and acted upon in definite circumstances, "self-interestedness" may be inseparable from the particular interests that develop in the course of interaction among persons with a place; or places, in a society, "reason" and "reasoning" may be inseparable from the agreements, understandings, facts, intentions, and so forth that form the fabric of social life. If so, it is possible not only that Rawls does not use these concepts in the ordinary way, but that he does not succeed in using them in any intelligible way. If, to carry the speculation to the point that matters most here, his notion of "justice" is conceptually dependent upon "self-interest" and "rational," it is possible that his concept of justice is (not only different from "justice" in ordinary language but) no concept at all.

Further Reading

Cunningham, R. L. "Justice: Efficiency or Fairness," *The Personalist*, Vol. 52 (1971), pp. 253–281.

Ewin, R. E. "On Justice and Injustice," *Mind*, Vol. LXXIX (1970), pp. 200–216.

Kelsen, Hans. *What Is Justice?* Berkeley: University of California Press, 1957.

Lessnoff, Michael. "John Rawls' Theory of Justice," Political Studies Vol. 19 (1971), pp. 65–80.

MacAdam, J. I. "The Precepts of Justice," *Mind*, Vol. LXXVII (1968), pp. 360–371.

Perelman, C. *The Idea of Justice and the Problem of Argument*. London: Routledge and Kegan Paul Ltd., 1963.

Rawls, John. "Constitutional Liberty and the Concept of Justice," in J. C. Chapman and Carl Friedrich, eds., *Justice: Nomos VI*. New York: Atherton Press, Inc., 1963.

———. "Distributive Justice," in Peter Laslett and W. C. Runciman eds., *Philosophy, Politics and Society*, Third Series. Oxford: Basil Blackwell, 1967.

———. "Distributive Justice: Some Addenda," *Natural Law Forum*, Vol. 13 (1968).

Rawls, John. "The Sense of Justice," *Philosophical Review*, Vol. 62 (1963) pp. 281–305.

Rescher, Nicholas. *Distributive Justice*. Indianapolis: The Bobbs-Merrill Co., Inc., 1966.

Wolff, Robert Paul. "A Refutation of Rawls' Theorem on Justice," *Journal of Philosophy*, Vol. 63 (1966), pp. 179–190.

23. On the Connection Between Justice and Utility

John Stuart Mill

In all ages of speculation one of the strongest obstacles to the reception of the doctrine that utility or happiness is the criterion of right and wrong, has been drawn from the idea of *justice*. The powerful sentiment, and apparently clear perception, which that word recalls with a rapidity and certainty resembling an instinct, have seemed to the majority of thinkers to point to an inherent quality in things; to show that the just must have an existence in nature as something absolute, generically distinct from every variety of the expedient, and, in idea, opposed to it, though (as is commonly acknowledged) never, in the long run, disjoined from it in fact.

In the case of this, as of our other moral sentiments, there is no necessary connection between the question of its origin, and that of its binding force. That a feeling is bestowed on us by nature, does not necessarily legitimate all its promptings. The feeling of justice might be a peculiar instinct, and might yet require, like our other instincts, to be controlled and enlightened by a higher reason. If we have intellectual instincts, leading us to judge in a particular way, there is no necessity that the former should be more infallible in their sphere than the latter in theirs: it may as well happen that wrong judgments are occasionally suggested by those, as wrong actions by these. But though it is one thing to believe that we have natural feelings of justice, and another to acknowledge them as an ultimate criterion of conduct, these two opinions are very closely connected in point of fact. Mankind are always predisposed to believe that any subjective feeling, not otherwise accounted for, is a revelation of some objective reality. Our present object is to determine whether the reality, to which the feeling of justice corresponds, is one which needs any such special revelation; whether the justice or injustice of an action is a thing intrinsically peculiar, and distinct from all its other qualities, or only a combination of certain of those qualities, presented under a peculiar aspect. For the purpose of this inquiry it is practically important to consider whether the feeling itself, of justice and injustice, is *sui generis* like our sensations of color and taste, or a derivative feeling, formed by a combination of others. And this it is the more essential to examine, as people are in general willing enough to allow that objectively the dictates of justice coincide with a part of the field of general expediency; but inasmuch as the subjective mental feeling of justice is different from that which commonly attaches to simple expediency, and, except in the extreme cases of the latter, is far more imperative in its demands, people find it difficult to see in justice only a particular kind or branch of general utility, and think that its superior binding force requires a totally different origin.

From *Utilitarianism*, 1861.

To throw light upon this question, it is necessary to attempt to ascertain what is the distinguishing character of justice or of injustice: what is the quality, or whether there is any quality, attributed in common to all modes of conduct designated as unjust (for justice, like many other moral attributes, is best defined by its opposite), and distinguishing them from such modes of conduct as are disapproved, but without having that particular epithet of disapprobation applied to them. If in everything which men are accustomed to characterize as just or unjust, some one common attribute or collection of attributes is always present, we may judge whether this particular attribute or combination of attributes would be capable of gathering round it a sentiment of that peculiar character and intensity by virtue of the general laws of our emotional constitution, or whether the sentiment is inexplicable, and requires to be regarded as a special provision of Nature. If we find the former to be the case, we shall, in resolving this question, have resolved also the main problem; if the latter, we shall have to seek for some other mode of investigating it.

To find the common attributes of a variety of objects, it is necessary to begin by surveying the objects themselves in the concrete. Let us therefore advert successively to the various modes of action and arrangements of human affairs which are classed, by universal or widely spread opinion, as just or as unjust. The things well known to excite the sentiments associated with those names are of a very multifarious character. I shall pass them rapidly in review, without studying any particular arrangement.

In the first place, it is mostly considered unjust to deprive anyone of his personal liberty, his property, or any other thing which belongs to him by law. Here, therefore, is one instance of the application of the terms just and unjust in a perfectly definite sense, namely, that it is just to respect, unjust to violate, the *legal rights* of anyone. But this judgment admits of several exceptions, arising from the other forms in which the notions of justice and injustice present themselves. For example, the person who suffers the deprivation may (as the phrase is) have *forfeited* the rights which he is so deprived of: a case to which we shall return presently. But also,

Secondly, the legal rights of which he is deprived, may be rights which *ought* not to have belonged to him; in other words, the law which confers on him these rights, may be a bad law. When it is so, or when (which is the same thing for our purpose) it is supposed to be so, opinions will differ as to the justice or injustice of infringing it. Some maintain that no law, however bad, ought to be disobeyed by an individual citizen; that his opposition to it, if shown at all, should only be shown in endeavoring to get it altered by competent authority. This opinion (which condemns many of the most illustrious benefactors of mankind, and would often protect pernicious institutions against the only weapons which, in the state of things existing at the time, have any chance of succeeding against them) is defended, by those who hold it, on grounds of expediency; principally on that of the importance, to the common interest of mankind, of maintaining inviolate the sentiment of submission to law. Other persons, again, hold the directly contrary opinion, that any law, judged to be bad, may blamelessly be disobeyed, even though it be not judged to be unjust, but only inexpedient; while others would confine the license of disobedience to the case of unjust laws: but again, some say that all laws which are inexpedient are unjust; since every law imposes some restriction on the natural liberty of mankind, which restriction is an injustice, unless legitimated by tending to their good. Among these diversities of opinion, it seems to be universally admitted that there may be unjust laws, and that law, consequently, is not the ultimate criterion of justice, but may give to one person a benefit, or impose on another an evil, which justice condemns. When, however, a law is thought to be unjust, it seems always to be regarded as being so in the same way in which a breach of law is unjust, namely, by infringing somebody's right; which, as it cannot in this case be a legal right, receives a different appellation, and is called a moral right. We may say, therefore, that a second case of injustice consists in taking or withholding from any person that to which he has a *moral right*.

Thirdly, it is universally considered just that each person should obtain that (whether good or evil) which he *deserves*, and unjust that he should obtain a good, or be made to undergo an evil, which he does not deserve. This is, perhaps, the clearest and most emphatic form in which the idea of justice is conceived by the general mind. As it involves the notion of desert, the question arises, what constitutes desert? Speaking in a general way, a person is understood to deserve good if he does right, evil if he does wrong; and in a more particular sense, to deserve good from those to whom he does or has done good, and evil from those to whom he does or has done evil. The precept of returning good for evil has never been regarded as a case of the fulfilment of justice, but as one in which the claims of justice are waived, in obedience to other considerations.

Fourthly, it is confessedly unjust to *break faith* with anyone: to violate an engagement, either express or implied, or disappoint expectations raised by our own conduct, at least if we have raised those expectations knowingly and voluntarily. Like the other obligations of justice already spoken of, this one is not regarded as absolute, but as capable of being overruled by a stronger obligation of justice on the other side; or by such conduct on the part of the person concerned as is deemed to absolve us from our obligation to him, and to constitute a *forfeiture* of the benefit which he has been led to expect.

Fifthly it is, by universal admission, inconsistent with justice to be *partial*; to show favor or preference to one person over another, in matters to which favor and preference do not properly apply. Impartiality, however, does not seem to be regarded as a duty in itself, but rather as instrumental to some other duty; for it is admitted that favor and preference are not always censurable, and indeed the cases in which they are condemned are rather the exception than the rule. A person would be more likely to be blamed than applauded for giving his family or friends no superiority in good offices over strangers, when he could do so without violating any other duty; and no one thinks it unjust to seek one person in preference to another as a friend, connection, or companion. Impartiality where rights are concerned is of course obligatory, but this is involved in the more general obligation of giving to everyone his right. A tribunal, for example, must be impartial, because it is bound to award, without regard to any other consideration, a disputed object to the one of two parties who has the right to it. There are other cases in which impartiality means, being solely influenced by desert; as with those who, in the capacity of judges, preceptors, or parents, administer reward and punishment as such. There are cases, again, in which it means, being solely influenced by consideration for the public interest; as in making a selection among candidates for a government employment. Impartiality, in short, as an obligation of justice, may be said to mean, being exclusively influenced by the considerations which it is supposed ought to influence the particular case in hand; and resisting solicitation of any motives which prompt to conduct different from what those considerations would dictate.

Nearly allied to the idea of impartiality is that of *equality*; which often enters as a component part both into the conception of justice and into the practice of it, and, in the eyes of many persons, constitutes its essence. But in this, still more than in any other case, the notion of justice varies in different persons, and always conforms in its variations to their notion of utility. Each person maintains that equality is the dictate of justice, except where he thinks that expediency requires inequality. The justice of giving equal protection to the rights of all, is maintained by those who support the most outrageous inequality in the rights themselves. Even in slave countries it is theoretically admitted that the rights of the slave, such as they are, ought to be as sacred as those of the master; and that a tribunal which fails to enforce them with equal strictness is wanting in justice; while, at the same time, institutions which leave to the slave scarcely any rights to enforce, are not deemed unjust, because they are not deemed inexpedient. Those who think that utility requires distinctions of rank, do not consider it unjust that riches and social privileges should be unequally dispensed; but those who think this inequality inexpedient, think it unjust also. Whoever thinks that government is necessary, sees no injustice in as much inequality as is constituted by giving to the magistrate powers not granted to other people. Even among those who hold leveling doctrines, there are as many questions of justice as there are differences of opinion about expediency. Some communists consider it unjust that the produce of the labor of the community should be shared on any other principle than that of exact equality; others think it just that those should receive most whose wants are greatest; while others hold that those who work harder, or who produce more, or whose services are more valuable to the community, may justly claim a larger quota in the division of the produce. And the sense of natural justice may be plausibly appealed to in behalf of every one of these opinions.

Among so many diverse applications of the term "justice," which yet is not regarded as ambiguous, it is a matter of some difficulty to seize the mental link which holds them together, and on which the moral sentiment adhering to the term essentially depends. Perhaps, in this embarrassment, some help may be derived from the history of the word, as indicated by its etymology.

In most, if not in all, languages, the etymology of the word which corresponds to "just," points distinctly to an origin connected with the ordinances of law. *Justum* is a form of *jussum,* that which has been ordered. *Dihaion* comes directly from *dike*, a suit at law. *Recht*, from which came *right* and *righteous*, is synonymous with law. The courts of justice, the administration of justice, are the courts and the administration of law. *La justice,* in French, is the established term for judicature. I am not committing the fallacy imputed with some show of truth to Horne Tooke, of assuming that a word must still continue to mean what it originally meant. Etymology is slight evidence of what the idea now signified is, but the very best evidence of how it sprang up. There can, I think, be no doubt that the *idée mère,* the primitive element, in the formation of the notion of justice, was conformity to law. It constituted the entire idea among the Hebrews, up to the birth of Christianity; as might be expected in the case of a people whose laws attempted to embrace all subjects on which precepts were required, and who believed those laws to be a direct emanation from the Supreme Being. But other nations, and in particular the Greeks and Romans, who knew that their laws had been made originally, and still continued to be made, by men, were not afraid to admit that those men might make bad laws: might do, by law, the same things, and from the same motives, which if done by individuals without the sanction of law, would be called unjust. And hence the sentiment of injustice came to be attached, not to all violations of law, but only to violations of such laws as *ought* to exist, including such as ought to exist, but do not; and to laws themselves, if supposed to be contrary to what ought to be law. In this manner the idea of law and of its injunctions was still predominant in the notion of justice, even when the laws actually in force ceased to be accepted as the standard of it.

It is true that mankind consider the idea of justice and its obligations as applicable to many things which neither are, nor is it desired that they should be, regulated by law. Nobody desires that laws should interfere with the whole detail of private life; yet everyone allows that in all daily conduct a person may and does show himself to be either just or unjust. But even here, the idea of the breach of what ought to be law, still lingers in a modified shape. It would always give us pleasure, and chime in with our feelings of fitness, that acts which we deem unjust should be punished, though we do not always think it expedient that this should be done by the tribunals. We forego that gratification on account of incidental inconveniences. We should be glad to see just conduct enforced and injustice repressed, even in the minutest details, if we were not, with reason, afraid of trusting the magistrate with so unlimited an amount of power over individuals. When we think that a person is bound in justice to do a thing, it is an ordinary form of language to say that he ought to be compelled to do it. We should be gratified to see the obligation enforced by anybody who had the power. If we see that its enforcement by law would be inexpedient, we lament the impossibility, we consider the impunity given to injustice as an evil, and strive to make amends for it by bringing a strong expression of our own and the public disapprobation to bear upon the offender. Thus the idea of legal constraint is still the generating idea of the notion of justice, though undergoing several transformations before that notion, as it exists in an advanced state of society, becomes complete.

The above is, I think, a true account, as far as it goes, of the origin and progressive growth of the idea of justice. But we must observe that it contains as yet nothing to distinguish that obligation from moral obligation in general. For the truth is, that the idea of penal sanction, which is the essence of law, enters not only into the conception of injustice, but into that of any kind of wrong. We do not call anything wrong unless we mean to imply that a person ought to be punished in some way or other for doing it: if not by law, by the opinion of his fellow-creatures; if not by opinion, by the reproaches of his own conscience. This seems the real turning point of the distinction between morality and simple expediency. It is a part of the notion of duty in every one of its forms, that a person may rightfully be compelled to fulfil it. Duty is a thing which may be *exacted* from a person, as one exacts a debt. Unless we think that it may be exacted from him, we do not call it his duty. Reasons of prudence, or the interest of other people, may militate against actually exacting it; but the person himself, it is clearly understood, would not be entitled to complain. There are other things, on the contrary, which we wish that people should do, which we like or admire them for doing, perhaps dislike or despise them for not doing, but yet admit that they are not bound to do it: it is not a case of moral obligation; we do not blame them, that is, we do not think that they are proper objects of punishment. How we come by these ideas of deserving and not deserving punishment, will appear, perhaps, in the sequel; but I think there is no doubt that this distinction lies at the bottom of the notions of right and wrong: that we call any conduct wrong, or employ, instead, some other term of dislike or disparagement, according as we think that the person ought, or ought not, to be punished for it; and we say, it would be right to do so and so, or merely that it would be desirable or laudable, according as we would wish to see the person whom it concerns, compelled, or only persuaded and exhorted, to act in that manner.[1]

This, therefore, being the characteristic difference which marks off, not justice, but morality in general, from the remaining provinces of expediency and worthiness; the character is still to be sought which distinguishes justice from other branches of morality. Now it is known that ethical writers divide moral duties into two classes, denoted by the ill-chosen expressions, duties of perfect and of imperfect obligation; the latter being those in which, though the act is obligatory, the particular occasions of performing it are left to our choice — as in the case of charity or beneficence, which we are indeed bound to practice, but not towards any definite person, nor at any prescribed time. In the more precise language of philosophic jurists, duties of perfect obligation are those duties in virtue of which a correlative *right* resides in some person or persons; duties of imperfect obligation are those moral obligations which do not give birth to any right. I think it will be found that this distinction exactly coincides with that which exists between justice and the other obligations of morality. In our survey of the various popular acceptations of justice, the term appeared generally to involve the idea of a personal right — a claim on the part of one or more individuals, like that which the law gives when it confers a proprietary or other legal right. Whether the injustice consists in depriving a person of a possession, or in breaking faith with him, or in treating him worse than he deserves, or worse than other people who have no greater claims, in each case the supposition implies two things — a wrong done, and some assignable person who is wronged. Injustice may also be done by treating a person better than others; but the wrong in this case is to his competitors, who are also assignable persons. It seems to me that this feature in the case — a right in some person, correlative to the moral obligation — constitutes the specific difference between justice, and generosity or beneficence. Justice implies something which is not only right to do, and wrong not to do, but which some individual person can claim from us as his moral right. No one has a moral right to our generosity or beneficence, because we are not morally bound to practice those virtues towards any given individual. And it will be found with respect to this as to every correct definition, that the instances which seem to conflict with it are those which most confirm it. For if a moralist attempts, as some have done, to make out that mankind generally, though not any given individual, have a right to all the good we can do them, he at once, by that thesis, includes generosity and beneficence within the category of justice. He is obliged to say that our utmost exertions are *due* to our fellow-creatures, thus assimilating them to a debt; or that nothing less can be a

---

[1] See this point enforced and illustrated by Professor Bain, in an admirable chapter (entitled "The Ethical Emotions, or the Moral Sense"), of the second of the two treatises composing his elaborate and profound work of the Mind.

sufficient *return* for what society does for us, thus classing the case as one of gratitude; both of which are acknowledged cases of justice. Whenever there is a right, the case is one of justice, and not of the virtue of beneficence; and whoever does not place the distinction between justice and morality in general, where we have now placed it, will be found to make no distinction between them at all, but to merge all morality in justice.

Having thus endeavored to determine the distinctive elements which enter into the composition of the idea of justice, we are ready to enter on the inquiry, whether the feeling which accompanies the idea is attached to it by a special dispensation of nature, or whether it could have grown up, by any known laws, out of the idea itself; and in particular, whether it can have originated in considerations of general expediency.

I conceive that the sentiment itself does not arise from anything which would commonly, or correctly, be termed an idea of expediency; but that though the sentiment does not, whatever is moral in it does.

We have seen that the two essential ingredients in the sentiment of justice are, the desire to punish a person who has done harm, and the knowledge or belief that there is some definite individual or individuals to whom harm has been done.

Now it appears to me, that the desire to punish a person who has done harm to some individual is a spontaneous outgrowth from two sentiments, both in the highest degree natural, and which either are or resemble instincts: the impulse of self-defense and the feeling of sympathy.

It is natural to resent, and to repel or retaliate, any harm done or attempted against ourselves, or against those with whom we sympathize. The origin of this sentiment it is not necessary here to discuss. Whether it be an instinct or a result of intelligence, it is, we know, common to all animal nature; for every animal tries to hurt those who have hurt, or who it thinks are about to hurt, itself or its young. Human beings, on this point, only differ from other animals in two particulars. First, in being capable of sympathizing, not solely with their offspring, or, like some of the more noble animals, with some superior animal who is kind to them, but with all human, and even with all sentient, beings. Secondly, in having a more developed intelligence, which gives a wider range to the whole of their sentiments, whether self-regarding or sympathetic. By virtue of his superior intelligence, even apart from his superior range of sympathy, a human being is capable of apprehending a community of interest between himself and the human society of which he forms a part, such that any conduct which threatens the security of the society generally, is threatening to his own, and calls forth his instinct (if instinct it be) of self-defense. The same superiority of intelligence, joined to the power of sympathizing with human beings generally, enables him to attach himself to the collective idea of his tribe, his country, or mankind, in such a manner that any act hurtful to them, raises his instinct of sympathy, and urges him to resistance.

The sentiment of justice, in that one of its elements which consists of the desire to punish, is thus, I conceive, the natural feeling of retaliation or vengeance, rendered by intellect and sympathy applicable to those injuries, that is, to those hurts, which wound us through, or in common with, society at large. This sentiment, in itself, has nothing moral in it; what is moral is the exclusive subordination of it to the social sympathies, so as to wait on and obey their call. For the natural feeling would make us resent indiscriminately whatever anyone does that is disagreeable to us, but when moralized by the social feeling it only acts in the directions conformable to the general good: just persons resenting a hurt to society though not otherwise a hurt to themselves, and not resenting a hurt to themselves, however painful, unless it be of the kind which society has a common interest with them in the repression of.

It is no objection against this doctrine to say that when we feel our sentiment of justice outraged, we are not thinking of society at large, or of any collective interest, but only of the individual case. It is common enough certainly, though the reverse of commendable, to feel resentment merely because we have suffered pain; but a person whose resentment is really a moral feeling, that is, who considers whether an act is blamable before he allows himself to resent it — such a person, though he may not say expressly to himself that he is standing up for the interest of society, certainly does feel that he is asserting a rule which is for the benefit of others as well as for his own. If he is not feeling this — if he is regarding the act solely as it affects him individually — he is not consciously just; he is not concerning himself about the justice of his actions. This is admitted even by anti-utilitarian moralists. When Kant (as before remarked) propounds as the fundamental principle of morals, "So act, that thy rule of conduct might be adopted as a law by all rational beings," he virtually acknowledges that the interest of mankind collectively, or at least of mankind indiscriminately, must be in the mind of the agent when conscientiously deciding on the morality of the act. Otherwise he uses words without a meaning; for that a rule even of utter selfishness could not *possibly* be adopted by all rational beings — that there is any insuperable obstacle in the nature of things to its adoption — cannot be even plausibly maintained. To give any meaning to Kant's principle, the sense put upon it must be, that we ought to shape our conduct by a rule which all rational beings might adopt *with benefit to their collective interest*.

To recapitulate: the idea of justice supposes two things — a rule of conduct and a sentiment which sanctions the rule. The first must be supposed common to all mankind and intended for their good. The other (the sentiment) is a desire that punishment may be suffered by those who infringe the rule. There is involved, in addition, the conception of some definite person who suffers by the infringement; whose rights (to use the expression appropriated to the case) are violated by it. And the sentiment of justice appears to me to be the animal desire to repel or retaliate a hurt or damage to oneself, or to those with whom one sympathizes, widened so as to include all persons, by the human capacity of enlarged sympathy and the human conception of intelligent self-interest. From the latter elements, the feeling derives its morality; from the former, its peculiar impressiveness and energy of self-assertion.

I have throughout treated the idea of a *right* residing in the injured person, and violated by the injury, not as a separate element in the composition of the idea and sentiment, but as one of the forms in which the other two elements clothe themselves. These elements are: a hurt to some assignable person or persons on the one hand, and a demand for punishment on the other. An examination of our own minds, I think, will show that these two things include all that we mean when we speak of violation of a right. When we call anything a person's right, we mean that he has a valid claim on society to protect him in the possession of it, either by the force of law, or by that of education and opinion. If he has what we consider a sufficient claim, on whatever account, to have something guaranteed to him by society, we say that he has a right to it. If we desire to prove that anything does not belong to him by right, we think this done as soon as it is admitted that society ought not to take measures for securing it to him, but should leave him to chance, or to his own exertions. Thus a person is said to have a right to what he can earn in fair professional competition, because society ought not to allow any other person to hinder him from endeavoring to earn in that manner as much as he can. But he has not a right to three hundred a year, though he may happen to be earning it; because society is not called on to provide that he shall earn that sum. On the contrary, if he owns ten thousand pounds three per cent stock, he *has* a right to three hundred a year; because society has come under an obligation to provide him with an income of that amount.

To have a right, then, is, I conceive, to have something which society ought to defend me in the possession of. If the objector goes on to ask why it ought, I can give him no other reason than general utility. If that expression does not seem to convey a sufficient feeling of the strength of the obligation, nor to account for the peculiar energy of the feeling, it is because there goes to the composition of the sentiment, not a rational only, but also an animal element, the thirst for retaliation; and this thirst derives its intensity, as well as its moral justification, from the extraordinarily important and impressive kind of utility which is concerned. The interest involved is that of security, to everyone's feelings the most vital of all interests. All other earthly benefits are needed by one person, not needed by another; and many of them can, if necessary, be cheerfully foregone, or replaced by something else; but security no human being can possibly do without; on it we depend for all our immunity from evil, and for the whole value of all and every good beyond the passing moment; since nothing but the gratification of the instant could be of any worth to us, if we could be deprived of anything the next instant by whoever was momentarily stronger than ourselves. Now this most indispensable of all necessaries after physical nutriment, cannot be had unless the machinery for providing it is kept unintermittedly in active play. Our notion, therefore, of the claim we have on our fellow-creatures to join in making safe for us the very groundwork of our existence, gathers feelings around it so much more intense than those concerned in any of the more common cases of utility, that the difference in degree (as is often the case in psychology) becomes a real difference in kind. The claim assumes that character of absoluteness, that apparent infinity, and incommensurability with all other considerations, which constitute the distinction between the feeling of right and wrong and that of ordinary expediency and inexpediency. The feelings concerned are so powerful, and we count so positively on finding a responsive feeling in others (all being alike interested), that *ought* and *should* grow into *must*, and recognized indispensability becomes a moral necessity, analogous to physical, and often not inferior to it in binding force.

If the preceding analysis, or something resembling it, be not the correct account of the notion of justice; if justice be totally independent of utility, and be a standard *per se*, which the mind can recognize by simple introspection of itself; it is hard to understand why that internal oracle is so ambiguous, and why so many things appear either just or unjust, according to the light in which they are regarded.

We are continually informed that utility is an uncertain standard, which every different person interprets differently, and that there is no safety but in the immutable, ineffaceable, and unmistakable dictates of justice, which carry their evidence in themselves, and are independent of the fluctuations of opinion. One would suppose from this that on questions of justice there could be no controversy; that if we take that for our rule, its application to any given case could leave us in as little doubt as a mathematical demonstration. So far is this from being the fact, that there is as much difference of opinion and as much discussion about what is just, as about what is useful to society. Not only have different nations and individuals different notions of justice, but in the mind of one and the same individual, justice is not some one rule, principle, or maxim, but many, which do not always coincide in their dictates, and in choosing between which he is guided either by some extraneous standard or by his own personal predilections.

For instance, there are some who say that it is unjust to punish anyone for the sake of example to others; that punishment is just only when intended for the good of the sufferer himself. Others maintain the extreme reverse, contending that to punish persons who have attained years of discretion, for their own benefit, is despotism and injustice, since if the matter at issue is solely for their own good, no one has a right to control their own judgment of it; but that they may justly be punished to prevent evil to others, this being the exercise of the legitimate right of self-defense. Mr. Owen, again, affirms that it is unjust to punish at all; for the criminal did not make his own character; his education, and the circumstances which surrounded him, have made him a criminal, and for these he is not responsible. All these opinions are extremely plausible; and so long as the question is argued as one of justice simply, without going down to the principles which lie under justice and are the source of its authority, I am unable to see how any of these reasoners can be refuted. For in truth every one of the three builds upon rules of justice confessedly true. The first appeals to the acknowledged injustice of singling out an individual, and making him a sacrifice, without his consent, for other people's benefit. The second relies on the acknowledged justice of self-defense, and the admitted injustice of forcing one person to conform to another's notions of what constitutes his good. The Owenite invokes the admitted principle that it is unjust to punish anyone for what he cannot help. Each is triumphant so long as he is not compelled to take into consideration any other maxims of justice than the one he has selected; but as soon as their several maxims are brought face to face, each disputant seems to have exactly as much to say for himself as the others. No one of them can carry out his own notion of justice without trampling upon another equally binding. These are difficulties; they have always been felt to be such; and many devices have been invented to turn rather than to overcome them. As a refuge from the last of the three, men imagined what they called the freedom of the will; fancying that they could not justify punishing a man whose will is in a thoroughly hateful state, unless it be supposed to have come into that state through no influence of anterior circumstances. To escape from the other difficulties, a favorite contrivance has been the fiction of a contract, whereby at some unknown period all the members of society engaged to obey the laws, and consented to be punished for any disobedience to them; thereby giving to their legislators the right, which it is assumed they would not otherwise have had, of punishing them, either for their own good or for that of society. This happy thought was considered to get rid of the whole difficulty, and to legitimate the infliction of punishment, in virtue of another received maximum of justice, *Volenti non fit injuria* – that is not unjust which is done with the consent of the person who is supposed to be hurt by it. I need hardly remark that even if the consent were not a mere fiction, this maxim is not superior in authority to the others which it is brought in to supersede. It is, on the contrary, an instructive specimen of the loose and irregular manner in which supposed principles of justice grow up. This particular one evidently came into use as a help to the coarse exigencies of courts of law, which are sometimes obliged to be content with very uncertain presumptions, on account of the greater evils which would often arise from any attempt on their part to cut finer. But even courts of law are not able to adhere consistently to the maxim, for they allow voluntary engagements to be set aside on the ground of fraud, and sometimes on that of mere mistake or misinformation.

Again, when the legitimacy of inflicting punishment is admitted, how many conflicting conceptions of justice come to light in discussing the proper apportionment of punishments to offenses. No rule on the subject recommends itself so strongly to the primitive and spontaneous sentiment of justice as the *lex talionis*, an eye for an eye and a tooth for a tooth. Though this principle of the Jewish and of the Mohammedan law has been generally abandoned in Europe as a practical maxim, there is, I suspect, in most minds, a secret hankering after it; and when retribution accidentally falls on an offender in that precise shape, the general feeling of satisfaction evinced bears witness how natural is the sentiment to which this repayment in kind is acceptable. With many, the test of justice in penal infliction is that the punishment should be proportioned to the offense; meaning that it should be exactly measured by the moral guilt of the culprit (whatever be their standard for measuring moral guilt) — the consideration, what amount of punishment is necessary to deter from the offense, having nothing to do with the question of justice, in their estimation; while there are others to whom that consideration is all in all — who maintain that it is not just, at least for man, to inflict on a fellow-creature, whatever may be his offenses, any amount of suffering beyond the least that will suffice to prevent him from repeating, and others from imitating, his misconduct.

To take another example from a subject already once referred to. In a co-operative industrial association, is it just or not that talent or skill should give a title to superior remuneration? On the negative side of the question it is argued that whoever does the best he can, deserves equally well, and ought not in justice to be put in a position of inferiority for no fault of his own; that superior abilities have already advantages more than enough, in the admiration they excite, the personal influence they command, and the internal sources of satisfaction attending them, without adding to these a superior share of the world's goods; and that society is bound in justice rather to make compensation to the less favored for this unmerited inequality of advantages, than to aggravate it. On the contrary side it is contended that society receives more from the more efficient laborer; that his services being more useful, society owes him a larger return for them; that a greater share of the joint result is actually his work, and not to allow his claim to it is a kind of robbery; that if he is only to receive as much as others, he can only be justly required to produce as much, and to give a smaller amount of time and exertion, proportioned to his superior efficiency. Who shall decide between these appeals to conflicting principles of justice? Justice has in this case two sides to it, which it is impossible to bring into harmony, and the two disputants have chosen opposite sides; the one looks to what it is just that the individual should receive, the other to what it is just that the community should give. Each, from his own point of view, is unanswerable; and any choice between them, on grounds of justice, must be perfectly arbitrary. Social utility alone can decide the preference.

How many, again, and how irreconcilable, are the standards of justice to which reference is made in discussing the repartition of taxation. One opinion is, that payment to the State should be in numerical proportion to pecuniary means. Others think that justice dictates what they term graduated taxation; taking a higher percentage from those who have more to spare. In point of natural justice a strong case might be made for disregarding means altogether, and taking the same absolute sum (whenever it could be got) from everyone — as the subscribers to a mess, or to a club, all pay the same sum for the same privileges, whether they can all equally afford it or not. Since the protection (it might be said) of law and government is afforded to, and is equally required by all, there is no injustice in making all buy it at the same price. It is reckoned justice, not injustice, that a dealer should charge to all customers the same price for the same article, not a price varying according to their means of payment. This doctrine, as applied to taxation, finds no advocates, because it conflicts so strongly with man's feelings of humanity and of social expediency; but the principle of justice which it invokes is as true and as binding as those which can be appealed to against it. Accordingly it exerts a tacit influence on the line of defense employed for other modes of assessing taxation. People feel obliged to argue that the State does more for the rich than for the poor, as a justification for its taking more from them: though this is in reality not true, for the rich would be far better able to protect themselves, in the absence of law or government, than the poor, and indeed would probably be successful in converting the poor into their slaves. Others, again, so far defer to the same conception of justice, as to maintain that all should pay an equal capitation tax for the protection of their persons (these being of equal value to all), and an unequal tax for the protection of their property, which is unequal. To this others reply that the all of one man is as valuable to him as the all of another. From these confusions there is no other mode of extrication than the utilitarian.

Is, then, the difference between the just and the expedient a merely imaginary distinction? Have mankind been under a delusion in thinking that justice is a more sacred thing than policy, and that the latter ought only to be listened to after the former has been satisfied? By no means. The exposition we have given of the nature and origin of the sentiment, recognizes a real distinction; and no one of those who profess the most sublime contempt for the consequences of actions as an element in their morality, attaches more importance to the distinction than I do. While I dispute the pretensions of any theory which sets up an imaginary standard of justice not grounded on utility, I account the justice which is grounded on utility to be the chief part, and incomparably the most sacred and binding part, of all morality. Justice is a name for certain classes of moral rules which concern the essentials of human well-being more nearly, and are therefore of more absolute obligation, than any other rules for the guidance of life; and the notion which we have found to be of the essence of the idea of justice, that of a right residing in an individual, implies and testifies to this more binding obligation.

The moral rules which forbid mankind to hurt one another (in which we must never forget to include wrongful interference with each other's freedom) are more vital to human well-being than any maxims, however important, which only point out the best mode of managing some department of human affairs. They have also the peculiarity, that they are the main element in determining the whole of the social feelings of mankind. It is their observance which alone preserves peace among human beings: if obedience to them were not the rule, and disobedience the exception, everyone would see in everyone else an enemy, against whom he must be perpetually guarding himself. What is hardly less important, these are the precepts which mankind have the strongest and the most direct inducements for impressing upon one another. By merely giving to each other prudential instruction or exhortation, they may gain, or think they gain, nothing; in inculcating on each other the duty of positive beneficence they have an unmistakable interest, but far less in degree: a person may possibly not need the benefits of others, but he always needs that they should not do him hurt. Thus the moralities which protect every individual from being harmed by others, either directly or by being hindered in his freedom of pursuing his own good, are at once those which he himself has most at heart, and those which he has the strongest interest in publishing and enforcing by word and deed. It is by a person's observance of these that his fitness to exist as one of the fellowship of human beings is tested and decided; for on that depends his being a nuisance or not to those with whom he is in contact. Now it is these moralities primarily which compose the obligations of justice. The most marked cases of injustice, and those which give the tone to the feeling of repugnance which characterizes the sentiment, are acts of wrongful aggression, or wrongful exercise of power over someone; the next are those which consist in wrongfully withholding from him something which is his due: in both cases, inflicting on him a positive hurt, either in the form of direct suffering, or of the privation of some good which he had reasonable ground, either of a physical or of a social kind, for counting upon.

The same powerful motives which command the observance of these primary moralities, enjoin the punishment of those who violate them, and as the impulses of self-defense, of defense of others, and of vengeance, are all called forth against such persons, retribution, or evil for evil, becomes closely connected with the sentiment of justice, and is universally included in the idea. Good for good is also one of the dictates of justice; and this, though its social utility is evident, and though it carries with it a natural human feeling, has not at first sight that obvious connection with hurt or injury, which, existing in the most elementary cases of just and unjust, is the source of the characteristic intensity of the sentiment. But the connection, though less obvious, is not less real. He who accepts benefits, and denies a return of them when needed, inflicts a real hurt, by disappointing one of the most natural and reasonable of expectations, and one which he must at least tacitly have encouraged, otherwise the benefits would seldom have been conferred. The important rank, among human evils and wrongs, of the disappointment of expectation, is shown in the fact that it constitutes the principal criminality of two such highly immoral acts as a breach of friendship and a breach of promise. Few hurts which human beings can sustain are greater, and none wound more, than when that on which they habitually and with full assurance relied, fails them in the hour of need; and few wrongs are greater than this mere withholding of good; none excite more resentment, either in the person suffering, or in a sympathizing spectator. The principle, therefore, of giving to each what they deserve, that is, good for good as well as evil for evil, is not only included within the idea of justice as we have defined it, but is a proper object of that intensity of sentiment, which places the just, in human estimation, above the simply expedient.

Most of the maxims of justice current in the world, and commonly appealed to in its transactions, are simply instrumental to carrying into effect the principles of justice which we have now spoken of. That a person is only responsible for what he has done voluntarily, or could voluntarily have avoided, that it is unjust to condemn any person unheard, that the punishment ought to be proportioned to the offense, and the like, are maxims intended to prevent the just principle of evil for evil from being perverted to the infliction of evil without that justification. The greater part of these common maxims have come into use from the practice of courts of justice, which have been naturally led to a more complete recognition and elaboration than was likely to suggest itself to others, of the rules necessary to enable them to fulfil their double function, of inflicting punishment when due, and of awarding to each person his right.

That first of judicial virtues, impartiality, is an obligation of justice, partly for the reason last mentioned, as being a necessary condition of the fulfilment of the other obligations of justice. But this is not the only source of the exalted rank, among human obligations, of those maxims of equality and impartiality which, both in popular estimation and in that of the most enlightened, are included among the precepts of justice. In one point of view, they may be considered as corollaries from the principles already laid down. If it is a duty to do to each according to his deserts, returning good for good as well as repressing evil by evil, it necessarily follows that we should treat all equally well (when no higher duty forbids) who have deserved equally well of *us*, and that society should treat all equally well who have deserved equally well of *it*, that is, who have deserved equally well absolutely. This is the highest abstract standard of social and distributive justice; towards which all institutions, and the efforts of all virtuous citizens, should be made in the utmost possible degree to converge. But this great moral duty rests upon a still deeper foundation, being a direct emanation from the first principle of morals, and not a mere logical corollary from secondary or derivative doctrines. It is involved in the very meaning of utility, or the greatest happiness principle. That principle is a mere form of words without rational signification, unless one person's happiness, supposed equal in degree (with the proper allowance made for kind), is counted for exactly as much as another's. Those conditions being supplied, Bentham's dictum, "everybody to count for one, nobody for more than one," might be written under the principle of utility as an explanatory commentary.[2] The equal claim of everybody to happiness in the estimation of the moralist and of the legislator, involves an equal claim to all the means of happiness, except in so far as the

---

[2] This implication, in the first principle of the utilitarian scheme, of perfect impartiality between persons, is regarded by Mr. Herbert Spencer (in his *Social Statics*) as a disproof of the pretensions of utility to be a sufficient guide to right; since (he says) the principle of utility presupposes the anterior principle, that everybody has an equal right to happiness. It may be more correctly described as supposing that equal amounts of happiness are equally desirable, whether felt by the same or by different persons. This, however, is not a *pre*supposition, not a premise needful to support the principle of utility, but the very principle itself; for what is the principle of utility, if it be not that "happiness" and "desirable" are synonymous terms? If there is any anterior principle implied, it can be no other than this, that the truths of arithmetic are applicable to the valuation of happiness, as of all other measurable quantities.

(Mr. Herbert Spencer, in a private communication on the subject of the preceding Note, objects to being considered an opponent of utilitarianism, and states that he regards happiness as the ultimate end of morality; but deems that end only partially attainable by empirical generalizations from the observed results of conduct, and completely attainable only by

inevitable conditions of human life, and the general interest, in which that of every individual is included, set limits to the maxim; and those limits ought to be strictly construed. As every other maxim of justice, so this is by no means applied or held applicable universally; on the contrary, as I have already remarked, it bends to every person's ideas of social expediency. But in whatever case it is deemed applicable at all, it is held to be the dictate of justice. All persons are deemed to have a *right* to equality of treatment, except when some recognized social expediency requires the reverse. And hence all social inequalities which have ceased to be considered expedient, assume the character not of simple inexpediency, but of injustice, and appear so tyrannical, that people are apt to wonder how they ever could have been tolerated; forgetful that they themselves perhaps tolerate other inequalities under an equally mistaken notion of expediency, the correction of which would make that which they approve seem quite as monstrous as what they have at last learnt to condemn. The entire history of social improvement has been a series of transitions, by which one custom or institution after another, from being a supposed primary necessity of social existence, has passed into the rank of a universally stigmatized injustice and tyranny. So it has been with the distinctions of slaves and freemen, nobles and serfs, patricians and plebeians; and so it will be, and in part already is, with the aristocracies of color, race, and sex.

It appears from what has been said that justice is a name for certain moral requirements which, regarded collectively, stand higher in the scale of social utility, and are therefore of more paramount obligation, than any others; though particular cases may occur in which some other social duty is so important, as to overrule any one of the general maxims of justice. Thus, to save a life, it may not only be allowable but a duty to steal or take by force the necessary food or medicine, or to kidnap and compel to officiate the only qualified medical practitioner. In such cases, as we do not call anything justice which is not a virtue; we usually say, not that justice must give way to some other moral principle, but that what is just in ordinary cases is, by reason of that other principle, not just in the particular case. By this useful accommodation of language, the character of indefeasibility attributed to justice is kept up, and we are saved from the necessity of maintaining that there can be laudable injustice.

The considerations which have now been adduced resolve, I conceive, the only real difficulty in the utilitarian theory of morals. It has always been evident that all cases of justice are also cases of expediency: the difference is in the peculiar sentiment which attaches to the former, as contradistinguished from the latter. If

---

deducing, from the laws of life and the conditions of existence, what kinds of action necessarily tend to produce happiness, and what kinds to produce unhappiness. With the exception of the word "necessarily," I have no dissent to express from this doctrine; and (omitting that word) I am not aware that any modern advocate of utilitarianism is of a different opinion. Bentham, certainly, to whom in the *Social Statics* Mr. Spencer particularly referred, is, least of all writers, chargeable with unwillingness to deduce the effect of actions on happiness from the laws of human nature and the universal conditions of human life. The common charge against him is of relying too exclusively upon such deductions, and declining altogether to be bound by the generalizations from specific experience with Mr. Spencer thinks that utilitarians generally confine themselves to. My own opinion [and, as I recollect, Mr. Spencer's] is, that in ethics, as in all other branches of scientific study, the consilience of the results of both these processes, each corroborating and verifying the other, is requisite to give to any general proposition the kind and degree of evidence which constitutes scientific proof.)

this characteristic sentiment has been sufficiently accounted for; if there is no necessity to assume for it any peculiarity of origin; if it is simply the natural feeling of resentment, moralized by being made coextensive with the demands of social good; and if this feeling not only does but ought to exist in all the classes of cases to which the idea of justice corresponds: that idea no longer presents itself as a stumbling-block to the utilitarian ethics. Justice remains the appropriate name for certain social utilities which are vastly more important, and therefore more absolute and imperative, than any others are as a class (though not more so than others may be in particular cases); and which, therefore, ought to be, as well as naturally are, guarded by a sentiment not only different in degree, but also in kind; distinguished from the milder feeling which attaches to the mere idea of promoting human pleasure or convenience, at once by the more definite nature of its commands, and by the sterner character of its sanctions.

24. Justice as Fairness

John Rawls [1]

I

It might seem at first sight that the concepts of justice and fairness are the same, and that there is no reason to distinguish them, or to say that one is more fundamental than the other. I think that this impression is mistaken. In this paper I wish to show that the fundamental idea in the concept of justice is fairness; and I wish to offer an analysis of the concept of justice from this point of view. To bring out the force of this claim, and the analysis based upon it, I shall then argue that it is this aspect of justice for which utilitarianism, in its classical form, is unable to account, but which is expressed, even if misleadingly, by the idea of the social contract.

To start with I shall develop a particular conception of justice by stating and commenting upon two principles which specify it, and by considering the circumstances and conditions under which they may be thought to arise. The principles defining this conception, and the conception itself, are, of course, familiar. It may be possible, however, by using the notion of fairness as a framework, to assemble and to look at them in a new way. Before stating this conception, however, the following preliminary matters should be kept in mind.

Throughout I consider justice only as a virtue of social institutions, or what I

From Peter Laslett and W. G. Runceman, eds., *Philosophy, Politics, and Society*, Second Series (Oxford: Basil Blackwell Publisher, 1967), pp. 132–157, by permission of the author and publisher.
[1] This article originally appeared in the *Philosophical Review*, 1958. Some footnotes have been omitted, others abbreviated, and the last paragraph of Section III has been revised.

shall call practices.[2] The principles of justice are regarded as formulating restrictions as to how practices may define positions and offices, and assign thereto powers and liabilities, rights and duties. Justice as a virtue of particular actions or of persons I do not take up at all. It is important to distinguish these various subjects of justice, since the meaning of the concept varies according to whether it is applied to practices, particular actions, or persons. These meanings are, indeed, connected, but they are not identical. I shall confine my discussion to the sense of justice as applied to practices, since this sense is the basic one. Once it is understood, the other senses should go quite easily.

Justice is to be understood in its customary sense as representing but *one* of the many virtues of social institutions, for these may be antiquated, inefficient, degrading, or any number; of other things, without being unjust. Justice is not to be confused with an all-inclusive vision of a good society; it is only one part of any such conception. It is important, for example, to distinguish that sense of equality which is an aspect of the concept of justice from that sense of equality which belongs to a more comprehensive social ideal. There may well be inequalities which one concedes are just, or at least not unjust, but which, nevertheless, one wishes, on other grounds, to do away with. I shall focus attention, then, on the usual sense of justice in which it is essentially the elimination of arbitrary distinctions and the establishment, within the structure of a practice, of a proper balance between competing claims.

Finally, there is no need to consider the principles discussed below as *the* principles of justice. For the moment it is sufficient that they are typical of a family of principles normally associated with the concept of justice. The way in which the principles of this family resemble one another, as shown by the background against which they may be thought to arise, will be made clear by the whole of the subsequent argument.

II

The conception of justice which I want to develop may be stated in the form of two principles as follows: first, each person participating in a practice, or affected by it, has an equal right to the most extensive liberty compatible with a like liberty for all; and second, inequalities are arbitrary unless it is reasonable to expect that they will work out for everyone's advantage, and provided the positions and offices to which they attach, or from which they may be gained, are open to all. These principles express justice as a complex of three ideas: liberty, equality, and reward for services contributing to the common good.[3]

[2] I use the word "practice" throughout as a sort of technical term meaning any form of activity specified by a system of rules which defines offices, roles, moves, penalties, defences, and so on, and which gives the activity its structure. As examples one may think of games and rituals, trials and parliaments, markets and systems of property. I have attempted a partial analysis of the notion of a practice in a paper "Two Concepts of Rules," *Philosophical Review*, LXIV (1955), 3–32.

[3] These principles are, of course, well known in one form or another and appear in many analyses of justice even where the writers differ widely on other matters. Thus if the principle of equal liberty is commonly associated with Kant (see *The Philosophy of Law*, tr. by W. Hastie, Edinburgh, 1887, pp. 56 f.), it may be claimed that it can also be found in J. S. Mill's

The term "person" is to be construed variously depending on the circumstances. On some occasions it will mean human individuals, but in others it may refer to nations, provinces, business firms, churches, teams, and so on. The principles of justice apply in all these instances, although there is a certain logical priority to the case of human individuals. As I shall use the term "person," it will be ambiguous in the manner indicated.

The first principle holds, of course, only if other things are equal: that is, while there must always be a justification for departing from the initial position of equal liberty (which is defined by the pattern of rights and duties, powers and liabilities, established by a practice), and the burden of proof is placed on him who would depart from it, nevertheless, there can be, and often there is, a justification for doing so. Now, that similar particular cases, as defined by a practice, should be treated similarly as they arise, is part of the very concept of a practice; it is involved in the notion of an activity in accordance with rules. The first principle expresses an analogous conception, but as applied to the structure of practices themselves. It holds, for example, that there is a presumption against the distinctions and classifications made by legal systems and other practices to the extent that they infringe on the original and equal liberty of the persons participating in them. The second principle defines how this presumption may be rebutted.

It might be argued at this point that justice requires only an equal liberty. If, however, a greater liberty were possible for all without loss or conflict, then it would be irrational to settle on a lesser liberty. There is no reason for circumscribing rights unless their exercise would be incompatible, or would render the practice defining them less effective. Therefore no serious distortion of the concept of justice is likely to follow from including within it the concept of the greatest equal liberty.

The second principle defines what sorts of inequalities are permissible; it specifies how the presumption laid down by the first principle may be put aside. Now by inequalities it is best to understand not *any* differences between offices and positions, but differences in the benefits and burdens attached to them either directly or indirectly, such as prestige and wealth, or liability to taxation and compulsory services. Players in a game do not protest against there being different positions, such as batter, pitcher, catcher, and the like, nor to there being various privileges and powers as specified by the rules; nor do the citizens of a country object to there being the different offices of government such as president, senator, governor, judge, and so on, each with their special rights and duties. It is not differences of this kind that are normally thought of as inequalities, but differences in the resulting distribution established by a practice, or made possible by it, of the things men strive to attain or avoid. Thus they may complain about the pattern of honours and rewards set up by a practice (e.g. the privileges and salaries of government officials) or they may object to the distribution of power and wealth which results from the various ways in which men avail themselves of the

---

On Liberty and elsewhere, and in many other liberal writers. Recently H. L. A. Hart has argued for something like it in his paper "Are There Any Natural Rights?" *Philosophical Review*, LXIV (1955), 175–91. The injustice of inequalities which are not won in return for a contribution to the common advantage is, of course, widespread in political writings of all sorts. The conception of justice here discussed is distinctive, if at all, only in selecting these two principles in this form; but for another similar analysis, see the discussion by W. D. Lamont, *The Principles of Moral Judgment* (Oxford, 1946), ch. v.

opportunities allowed by it (e.g. the concentration of wealth which may develop in a free price system allowing large entrepreneurial or speculative gains).

It should be noted that the second principle holds that an inequality is allowed only if there is reason to believe that the practice with the inequality, or resulting in it, will work for the advantage of *every* party engaging in it. Here it is important to stress that *every* party must gain from the inequality. Since the principle applies to practices, it implies that the representative man in every office or position defined by a practice, when he views it as a going concern, must find it reasonable to prefer his condition and prospects with the inequality to what they would be under the practice without it. The principle excludes, therefore, the justification of inequalities on the grounds that the disadvantages of those in one position are outweighed by the greater advantages of those in another position. This rather simple restriction is the main modification I wish to make in the utilitarian principle as usually understood. When coupled with the notion of a practice, it is a restriction of consequence, and one which some utilitarians, e.g. Hume and Mill, have used in their discussions of justice without realizing apparently its significance, or at least without calling attention to it. Why it is a significant modification of principle, changing one's conception of justice entirely, the whole of my argument will show.

Further, it is also necessary that the various offices to which special benefits or burdens attach are open to all. It may be, for example, to the common advantage, as just defined, to attach special benefits to certain offices. Perhaps by doing so the requisite talent can be attracted to them and encouraged to give its best efforts. But any offices having special benefits must be won in a fair competition in which contestants are judged on their merits. If some offices were not open, those excluded would normally be justified in feeling unjustly treated, even if they benefited from the greater efforts of those who were allowed to compete for them. Now if one can assume that offices are open, it is necessary only to consider the design of practices themselves and how they jointly, as a system, work together. It will be a mistake to focus attention on the varying relative positions of particular persons, who may be known to us by their proper names, and to require that each such change, as a once for all transaction viewed in isolation, must be in itself just. It is the system of practices which is to be judged, and judged from a general point of view: unless one is prepared to criticize it from the standpoint of a representative man holding some particular office, one has no complaint against it.

III

Given these principles one might try to derive them from *a priori* principles of reason, or claim that they were known by intuition. These are familiar enough steps and, at least in the case of the first principle, might be made with some success. Usually, however, such arguments, made at this point, are unconvincing. They are not likely to lead to an understanding of the basis of the principles of justice, not at least as principles of justice. I wish, therefore, to look at the principles in a different way.

Imagine a society of persons amongst whom a certain system of practices is *already* well established. Now suppose that by the large they are mutually self-interested; their allegiance to their established practices is normally founded on the prospect of self-advantage. One need not assume that, in all senses of the term "person," the persons in this society are mutually self-interested. If the characterization as mutually self-interested applies when the line of division is the family, it may still be true that members of families are bound by ties of sentiment and affection and willingly acknowledge duties in contradiction to self-interest. Mutual self-interestedness in the relations between families, nations, churches, and the like, is commonly associated with intense loyalty and devotion on the part of individual members. Therefore, one can form a more realistic conception of this society if one thinks of it as consisting of mutually self-interested families, or some other association. Further, it is not necessary to suppose that these persons are mutually self-interested under all circumstances, but only in the usual situations in which they participate in their common practices.

Now suppose also that these persons are rational: they know their own interests more or less accurately; they are capable of tracing out the likely consequences of adopting one practice rather than another; they are capable of adhering to a course of action once they have decided upon it; they can resist present temptations and the enticements of immediate gain; and the bare knowledge or perception of the difference between their condition and that of others is not, within certain limits and in itself, a source of great dissatisfaction. Only the last point adds anything to the usual definition of rationality. This definition should allow, I think, for the idea that a rational man would not be greatly downcast from knowing, or seeing, that others are in a better position than himself, unless he thought their being so was the result of injustice, or the consequence of letting chance work itself out for no useful common purpose, and so on. So if these persons strike us as unpleasantly egoistic, they are at least free in some degree from the fault of envy.[4]

Finally, assume that these persons have roughly similar needs and interests, or needs and interests in various ways complementary, so that fruitful co-operation amongst them is possible; and suppose that they are sufficiently equal in power and ability to guarantee that in normal circumstances none is able to dominate the others. This condition (as well as the others) may seem excessively vague; but in view of the conception of justice to which the argument leads, there seems no reason for making it more exact here.

Since these persons are conceived as engaging in their common practices, which are already established, there is no question of our supposing them to come together to deliberate as to how they will set these practices up for the first time. Yet we can imagine that from time to time they discuss with one another whether any of them has a legitimate complaint against their established institutions. Such discussions are perfectly natural in any normal society. Now suppose that they have settled on doing this in the following way. They first try to arrive at the principles by which complaints, and so practices themselves, are to be judged. Their procedure for this is to let each person propose the principles upon which he wishes his complaints to be tried with the understanding that, if acknowledged, the complaints of others will be similarly tried, and that no complaints will be heard at

---

[4] It is not possible to discuss here this addition to the usual conception of rationality. If it seems peculiar, it may be worth remarking that it is analogous to the modification of the utilitarian principle which the argument as a whole is designed to explain and justify. In the same way that the satisfaction of interests, the representative claims of which violate the principles of justice, is not a reason for having a practice (see Section VII), unfounded envy, within limits, need not be taken into account.

all until everyone is roughly of one mind as to how complaints are to be judged. They each understand further that the principles proposed and acknowledged on this occasion are binding on future occasions. Thus each will be wary of proposing a principle which would give him a peculiar advantage, in his present circumstances, supposing it to be accepted. Each person knows that he will be bound by it in future circumstances the peculiarities of which cannot be known, and which might well be such that the principle is then to his disadvantage. The idea is that everyone should be required to make *in advance* a firm commitment, which others also may reasonably be expected to make, and that no one be given the opportunity to tailor the canons of a legitimate complaint to fit his own special condition, and then to discard them when they no longer suit his purpose. Hence each person will propose principles of a general kind which will, to a large degree, gain their sense from the various applications to be made of them, the particular circumstances of which being as yet unknown. These principles will express the conditions in accordance with which each is the least unwilling to have his interests limited in the design of practices, given the competing interests of the others, on the supposition that the interests of others will be limited likewise. The restrictions which would so arise might be thought of as those a person would keep in mind if he were designing a practice in which his enemy were to assign him his place.

The two main parts of this conjectural account have a definite significance. The character and respective situations of the parties reflect the typical circumstances in which questions of justice arise. The procedure whereby principles are proposed and acknowledged represents constraints, analogous to those of having a morality, whereby rational and mutually self-interested persons are brought to act reasonably. Thus the first part reflects the fact that questions of justice arise when conflicting claims are made upon the design of a practice and where it is taken for granted that each person will insist, as far as possible, on what he considers his rights. It is typical of cases of justice to involve persons who are pressing on one another their claims, between which a fair balance or equilibrium must be found. On the other hand, as expressed by the second part, having a morality must at least imply the acknowledgement of principles as impartially applying to one's own conduct as well as to another's, and moreover principles which may constitute a constraint, or limitation, upon the pursuit of one's own interests. There are, of course, other aspects of having a morality: the acknowledgement of moral principles must show itself in accepting a reference to them as reasons for limiting one's claims, in acknowledging the burden of providing a special explanation, or excuse, when one acts contrary to them, or else in showing shame and remorse and a desire to make amends, and so on. It is sufficient to remark here that having a morality is analogous to having made a firm commitment in advance; for one must acknowledge the principles of morality even when to one's disadvantage. A man whose moral judgements always coincided with his interests could be suspected of having no morality at all.

Thus the two parts of the foregoing account are intended to mirror the kinds of circumstances in which questions of justice arise and the constraints which having a morality would impose upon persons so situated. In this way one can see how the acceptance of the principles of justice might come about, for given all these conditions as described, it would be natural if the two principles of justice were to be acknowledged. Since there is no way for anyone to win special advantages for himself, each might consider it reasonable to acknowledge equality as an initial principle. There is, however, no reason why they should regard this position as final; for if there are inequalities which satisfy the second principle, the immediate gain which equality would allow can be considered as intelligently invested in view of its future return. If, as is quite likely, these inequalities work as incentives to draw out better efforts, the members of this society may look upon them as concessions to human nature: they, like us, may think that people ideally should want to serve one another. But as they are mutually self-interested, their acceptance of these inequalities is merely the acceptance of the relations in which they actually stand, and a recognition of the motives which lead them to engage in their common practices. *They* have no title to complain of one another. And so provided that the conditions of the principle are met, there is no reason why they should not allow such inequalities. Indeed, it would be short-sighted of them to do so, and could result, in most cases, only from their being dejected by the bare knowledge, or perception, that others are better situated. Each person will, however, insist on an advantage of himself, and so on a common advantage, for none is willing to sacrifice anything for the others.

These remarks are not offered as a rigorous proof that persons conceived and situated as the conjectural account supposes, and required to adopt the procedure described, would settle on the two principles of justice. For such a proof a more elaborate and formal argument would have to be given: there remain certain details to be filled in, and various alternatives to be ruled out. The argument should, however, be taken as a proof, or a sketch of a proof; for the proposition I seek to establish is a necessary one, that is, it is intended as a theorem: namely, that when mutually self-interested and rational persons confront one another in typical circumstances of justice, and when they are required by a procedure expressing the constraints of having a morality to jointly acknowledge principles by which their claims on the design of their common practices are to be judged, they will settle on these two principles as restrictions governing the assignment of rights and duties, and thereby accept them as limiting their rights against one another. It is this theorem which accounts for these principles as principles of justice, and explains how they come to be associated with this moral concept. Moreover, this theorem is analogous to those about human conduct in other branches of social thought. That is, a simplified situation is described in which rational persons pursuing certain ends and related to one another in a definite way, are required to act subject to certain limitations; then, given this situation, it is shown that they will act in a certain manner. Failure so to act would imply that one or more of the assumptions does not obtain. The foregoing account aims to establish, or to sketch, a theorem in this sense; the aim of the argument is to show the basis for saying that the principles of justice may be regarded as those principles which arise when the constraints of having a morality are imposed upon rational persons in typical circumstances of justice.

IV

These ideas are, of course, connected with a familiar way of thinking about justice which goes back at least to the Greek Sophists, and which regards the acceptance of the principles of justice as a compromise between persons of roughly equal power who would enforce their will on each other if they could, but who, in view of the equality of forces amongst them and for the sake of their own peace and security acknowledge certain forms of conduct in so far as prudence seems to require. Justice is thought of as a pact between rational egoists the stability of which is dependent on a balance of power and a similarity of circumstances. While the previous account is connected with this tradition, and with its most recent variant, the theory of games, it differs from it in several important respects which, to forestall misinterpretations, I will set out here.

First, I wish to use the previous conjectural account of the background of justice as a way of analysing the concept. I do not want, therefore, to be interpreted as assuming a general theory of human motivation: when I suppose that the parties are mutually self-interested, and are not willing to have their (substantial) interests sacrificed to others, I am referring to their conduct and motives as they are taken for granted in cases where questions of justice ordinarily arise. Justice is the virtue of practices where there are assumed to be competing interests and conflicting claims, and where it is supposed that persons will press their rights on each other. That persons are mutually self-interested in certain situations and for certain purposes is what gives rise to the question of justice in practices covering those circumstances. Amongst an association of saints, if such a community could really exist, the disputes about justice could hardly occur; for they would all work selflessly together for one end, the glory of God as defined by their common religion, and reference to this end would settle every question of right. The justice of practices does not come up until there are several different parties (whether we think of these as individuals, associations, or nations and so on, is irrelevant) who do press their claims on one another, and who do regard themselves as representatives of interests which deserve to be considered. Thus the previous account involves no general theory of human motivation. Its intent is simply to incorporate into the conception of justice the relations of men to one another which set the stage for questions of justice. It makes no difference how wide or general these relations are, as this matter does not bear on the analysis of the concept.

Again, in contrast to the various conceptions of the social contract, the several parties do not establish any particular society or practice; they do not covenant to obey a particular sovereign body or to accept a given constitution. Nor do they, as in the theory of games (in certain respects a marvellously sophisticated development of this tradition), decide on individual strategies adjusted to their respective circumstances in the game. What the parties do is to *jointly* acknowledge certain *principles* of appraisal relating to their common *practices* either as already established or merely proposed. They accede to standards of judgement, not to a given practice; they do not make any specific agreement, or bargain, or adopt a particular strategy. The subject of their acknowledgement is, therefore, very general indeed; it is simply the acknowledgement of certain principles of judgement, fulfilling certain general conditions, to be used in criticizing the arrangement of their common affairs. The relations of mutual self-interest between the parties who are similarly circumstanced mirror the conditions under which questions of justice arise, and the procedure by which the principles of judgement are proposed and acknowledged reflects the constraints of having a morality. Each aspect, then, of the preceding hypothetical account serves the purpose of bringing out a feature of the notion of justice. One could, if one liked, view the principles of justice as the "solution" of this highest order "game" of adopting, subject to the procedure described, principles of argument for all coming particular "games" whose peculiarities one can in no way foresee. But this comparison, while no doubt helpful, must not obscure the fact that this highest order "game" is of a special sort.[5] Its significance is that its various pieces represent aspects of the concept of justice.

Finally, I do not, of course, conceive the several parties as necessarily coming together to establish their common practices for the first time. Some institutions may, indeed, be set up *de novo*; but I have framed the preceding account so that it will apply when the full complement of social institutions already exists and represents the result of a long period of development. Nor is the account in any way fictitious. In any society where people reflect on their institutions they will have an idea of what principles of justice would be acknowledged under the conditions described, and there will be occasions when questions of justice are actually discussed in this way. Therefore if their practices do not accord with these principles, this will affect the quality of their social relations. For in this case there will be some recognized situations wherein the parties are mutually aware that one of them is being forced to accept what the other would concede is unjust. The foregoing analysis may then be thought of as representing the actual quality of relations between persons as defined by practices accepted as just. In such practices the parties will acknowledge the principles on which it is constructed, and the general recognition of this fact shows itself in the absence of resentment and in the sense of being justly treated. Thus one common objection to the theory of the social contract, its apparently historical and fictitious character, is avoided.

V

That the principles of justice may be regarded as arising in the manner described illustrates an important fact about them. Not only does it bring out the idea that justice is a primitive moral notion in that it arises once the concept of morality is imposed on mutually self-interested agents similarly circumstanced, but it emphasizes that, fundamental to justice, is the concept of fairness which relates to right dealing between persons who are co-operating with or competing against one another, as when one speaks of fair games, fair competition, and fair bargains. The question of fairness arises when free persons, who have no authority over one another, are engaging in a joint activity and amongst themselves settling or acknowledging the rules which define it and which determine the respective shares in its benefits and burdens. A practice will strike the parties as fair if none feels that, by participating in it, they or any of the others are taken advantage of, or forced to give in to claims which they do not regard as legitimate. This implies that each has a conception of legitimate claims which he thinks it reasonable for others as well as himself to acknowledge. If one thinks of the principles of justice as arising

[5] The difficulty one gets into by a mechanical application of the theory of games to moral philosophy can be brought out by considering among several possible examples, R. B. Braithwaite's study, *Theory of Games as a Tool for the Moral Philosopher* (Cambridge, 1955). What is lacking is the concept of morality, and it must be brought into the conjectural account in some way or other. In the text this is done by the form of the procedure whereby principles are proposed and acknowledged (Section III). If one starts directly with the particular case as known, and if one accepts as given and definitive the preferences and relative positions of the parties, whatever they are, it is impossible to give an analysis of the moral concept of fairness.

in the manner described, then they do define this sort of conception. A practice is just or fair, then, when it satisfies the principles which those who participate in it could propose to one another for mutual acceptance under the aforementioned circumstances. Persons engaged in a just, or fair, practice can face one another openly and support their respective positions, should they appear questionable, by reference to principles which it is reasonable to expect each to accept.

It is this notion of the possibility of mutual acknowledgement of principles by free persons who have no authority over one another which makes the concept of fairness fundamental to justice. Only if such acknowledgement is possible can there by true community between persons in their common practices; otherwise their relations will appear to them as founded to some extent on force. If, in ordinary speech, fairness applies more particularly to practices in which there is a choice whether to engage or not (e.g. in games, business competition), and justice to practices in which there is no choice (e.g. in slavery), the element of necessity does not render the conception of mutual acknowledgement inapplicable, although it may make it much more urgent to change unjust than unfair institutions. For one activity in which one can always engage is that of proposing and acknowledging principles to one another supposing each to be similarly circumstanced; and to judge practices by the principles so arrived at is to apply the standard of fairness to them.

Now if the participants in a practice accept its rules as fair, and so have no complaint to lodge against it, there arises a prima facie duty (and a corresponding prima facie right) of the parties to each other to act in accordance with the practice when it falls upon them to comply. When any number of persons engage in a practice, or conduct a joint undertaking according to rules, and thus restrict their liberty, those who have submitted to these restrictions when required have the right to a similar acquiescence on the part of those who have benefited by their submission. These conditions will obtain if a practice is correctly acknowledged to be fair, for in this case all who participate in it will benefit from it. The rights and duties so arising are special rights and duties in that they depend on previous actions voluntarily undertaken, in this case on the parties having engaged in a common practice and knowingly accepted its benefits.[6] It is not, however, an obligation which presupposes a deliberate performative act in the sense of a promise, or contract, and the like. An unfortunate mistake of proponents of the idea of the social contract was to suppose that political obligation does require some such act, or at least to use language which suggests it. It is sufficient that one has knowingly participated in and accepted the benefits of a practice acknowledged to be fair. This prima facie obligation may, of course, be overriden: it may happen, when it comes one's turn to follow a rule, that other considerations will justify not doing so. But one cannot, in general, be released from this obligation by denying the justice of the practice only when it falls on one to obey. If a person rejects a practice, he should, so far as possible, declare his intention in advance, and avoid participating in it or enjoying its benefits.

This duty I have called that of fair play, but it should be admitted that to refer to it in this way is, perhaps, to extend the ordinary notion of fairness. Usually acting unfairly is not so much the breaking of any particular rule, even if the

---

[6] For the definition of this prima facie duty, and the idea that it is a special duty, I am indebted to H. L. A. Hart. See his paper "Are There Any Natural Rights?" *Philosophical Review*, LXIV (1955), 185 f.

infraction is difficult to detect (cheating), but taking advantage of loop-holes or ambiguities in rules, availing oneself of unexpected or special circumstances which make it impossible to enforce them, insisting that rules be enforced to one's advantage when they should be suspended, and more generally, acting contrary to the intention of a practice. It is for this reason that one speaks of the sense of fair play: acting fairly requires more than simply being able to follow rules; what is fair must often be felt, or perceived, one wants to say. It is not, however, an unnatural extension of the duty of fair play to have it include the obligation which participants who have knowingly accepted the benefits of their common practice owe to each other to act in accordance with it when their performance falls due; for it is usually considered unfair if someone accepts the benefits of a practice but refuses to do his part in maintaining it. Thus one might say of the tax-dodger that he violates the duty of fair play: he accepts the benefits of government but will not do his part in releasing resources to it; and members of labour unions often say that fellow workers who refuse to join are being unfair: they refer to them as "free riders," as persons who enjoy what are the supposed benefits of unionism, higher wages, shorter hours, job security, and the like, but who refuse to share in its burdens in the form of paying dues, and so on.

The duty of fair play stands beside other prima facie duties such as fidelity and gratitude as a basic moral notion; yet it is not to be confused with them. These duties are all clearly distinct, as would be obvious from their definitions. As with any moral duty, that of fair play implies a constraint on self-interest in particular cases; on occasion it enjoins conduct which a rational egoist strictly defined would not decide upon. So while justice does not require of anyone that he sacrifice his interests in that *general position* and procedure whereby the principles of justice are proposed and acknowledged, it may happen that in particular situations, arising in the context of engaging in a practice the duty of fair play will often cross his interests in the sense that he will be required to forgo particular advantages which the peculiarities of his circumstances might permit him to take. There is, of course, nothing surprising in this. It is simply the consequence of the firm commitment which the parties may be supposed to have made, or which they would make, in the general position, together with the fact that they have participated in and accepted the benefits of a practice which they regard as fair.

Now the acknowledgement of this constraint in particular cases, which is manifested in acting fairly or wishing to make amends, feeling ashamed, and the like, when one has evaded it, is one of the forms of conduct by which participants in a common practice exhibit their recognition of each other as persons with similar interests and capacities. In the same way that, failing a special explanation, the criterion for the recognition of suffering is helping one who suffers, acknowledging the duty of fair play is a necessary part of the criterion for recognizing another as a person with similar interests and feelings as oneself.[7] A person who never under any circumstances showed a wish to help others in pain would show, at the same time, that he did not recognize that they were in pain; nor could he have any feelings of affection or friendship for anyone; for having these feelings implies, failing special

[7] I am using the concept of criterion here in what I take to be Wittgenstein's sense. That the response of compassion, under appropriate circumstances, is part of the criterion for whether or not a person understands what "pain" means, is, I think, in the *Philosophical Investigations*. The view in the text is simply an extension of this idea. I cannot, however, attempt to justify it here.

circumstances, that he comes to their aid when they are suffering. Recognition that another is a person in pain shows itself in sympathetic action; this primitive natural response of compassion is one of those responses upon which the various forms of moral conduct are built.

Similarly, the acceptance of the duty of fair play by participants in a common practice is a reflection in each person of the recognition of the aspirations and interests of the others to be realized by their joint activity. Failing a special explanation, their acceptance of it is a neeessary part of the criterion for their recognizing one another as persons with similar interests and capacities, as the conception of their relations in the general position supposes them to be. Otherwise they would show no recognition of one another as persons with similar capacities and interests, and indeed, in some cases perhaps hypothetical, they would not recognize one another as persons at all, but as complicated objects involved in a complicated activity. To recognize another as a person one must respond to him and act towards him in certain ways; and these ways are intimately connected with the various prima facie duties. Acknowledging these duties in *some* degree, and so having the elements of morality, is not a matter of choice, or of intuiting moral qualities, or a matter of the expression of feelings or attitudes (the three interpretations between which philosophical opinion frequently oscillates); it is simply the possession of one of the forms of conduct in which the recognition of others as persons is manifested.

These remarks are unhappily obscure. Their main purpose here, however, is to forestall, together with the remarks in Section IV, the misinterpretation that, on the view presented, the acceptance of justice and the acknowledgement of the duty of fair play depends in every day life solely on there being a *de facto* balance of forces between the parties. It would indeed be foolish to underestimate the importance of such a balance in securing justice; but it is not the only basis thereof. The recognition of one another as persons with similar interests and capacities engaged in a common practice must, failing a special explanation, show itself in the acceptance of the principles of justice and the acknowledgement of the duty of fair play.

The conception at which we have arrived, then, is that the principles of justice may be thought of as arising once the constraints of having a morality are imposed upon rational and mutually self-interested parties who are related and situated in a special way. A practice is just if it is in accordance with the principles which all who participate in it might reasonably be expected to propose or to acknowledge before one another when they are similarly circumstanced and required to make a firm commitment in advance without knowledge of what will be their peculiar condition, and thus when it meets standards which the parties could accept as fair should occasion arise for them to debate its merits. Regarding the participants themselves, once persons knowingly engage in a practice which they acknowledge to be fair and accept the benefits of doing so, they are bound by the duty of fair play to follow the rules when it comes their turn to do so, and this implies a limitation on their pursuit of self-interest in particular cases.

Now one consequence of this conception is that, where it applies, there is no moral value in the satisfaction of a claim incompatible with it. Such a claim violates the conditions of reciprocity and community amongst persons, and he who presses it, not being willing to acknowledge it when pressed by another, has no grounds for complaint when it is denied; whereas he against whom it is pressed can complain.

As it cannot be mutually acknowledged it is a resort to coercion; granting the claim is possible only if one party can compel acceptance of what the other will not admit. But it makes no sense to concede claims the denial of which cannot be complained of in preference to claims the denial of which can be objected to. Thus in deciding on the justice of a practice it is not enough to ascertain that it answers to wants and interests in the fullest and most effective manner. For if any of these conflict with justice, they should not be counted, as their satisfaction is no reason at all for having a practice. It would be irrelevant to say, even if true, that it resulted in the greatest satisfaction of desire. In tallying up the merits of a practice one must toss out the satisfaction of interests the claims of which are incompatible with the principles of justice.

VI

The discussion so far has been excessively abstract. While this is perhaps unavoidable, I should now like to bring out some of the features of the conception of justice as fairness by comparing it with the conception of justice in classical utilitarianism as represented by Bentham and Sidgwick, and its counterpart in welfare economics. This conception assimilates justice to benevolence and the latter in turn to the most efficient design of institutions to promote the general welfare. Justice is a kind of efficiency.

Now it is said occasionally that this form of utilitarianism puts no restrictions on what might be a just assignment of rights and duties in that there might be circumstances which, on utilitarian grounds, would justify institutions highly offensive to our ordinary sense of justice. But the classical utilitarian conception is not totally unprepared for this objection. Beginning with the notion that the general happiness can be represented by a social utility function consisting of a sum of individual utility functions with identical weights (this being the meaning of the maxim that each counts for one and no more than one), it is commonly assumed that the utility functions of individuals are similar in all essential respects. Differences between individuals are ascribed to accidents of education and upbringing, and they should not be taken into account. This assumption, coupled with that of diminishing marginal utility, results in a prima facie case for equality, e.g. of equality in the distribution of income during any given period of time, laying aside indirect effects on the future. But even if utilitarianism is interpreted as having such restrictions built into the utility function, and even if it is supposed that these restrictions have in practice much the same result as the application of the principles of justice (and appear, perhaps, to be ways of expressing these principles in the language of mathematics and psychology), the fundamental idea is very different from the conception of justice as fairness. For one thing, that the principles of justice should be accepted is interpreted as the contingent result of a higher order administrative decision. The form of this decision is regarded as being similar to that of an entrepreneur deciding how much to produce of this or that commodity in view of its marginal revenue, or to that of someone distributing goods to needy persons according to the relative urgency of their wants. The choice between practices is thought of as being made on the basis of the allocation of benefits and burdens to individuals (these being measured by the present capitalized value of their utility over the full period of the practice's existence), which results from the distribution of rights and duties established by a practice. Moreover, the individuals receiving these benefits are not conceived as being related in any way: they represent so many different directions in which limited resources may be allocated. The value of assigning resources to one direction rather than another depends solely on the preferences and interests of individuals as individuals. The satisfaction of desire has its value irrespective of the moral relations between persons, say as members of a joint undertaking, and of the claims which, in the name of these interests, they are prepared to make on one another:[8] and it is this value which is to be taken into account by the (ideal) legislator who is conceived as adjusting the rules of the system from the centre so as to maximize the value of the social utility function.

It is thought that the principles of justice will not be violated by a legal system so conceived provided these executive decisions are correctly made. In this fact the principles of justice are said to have their derivation and explanation; they simply express the most important general features of social institutions in which the administrative problem is solved in the best way. These principles have, indeed, a special urgency because, given the facts of human nature, so much depends on them; and this explains the peculiar quality of the moral feelings associated with justice. This assimilation of justice to a higher order executive decision, certainly a striking conception, is central to classical utilitarianism; and it also brings out its profound individualism, in one sense of this ambiguous word. It regards persons as so many *separate* directions in which benefits and burdens may be assigned; and the value of the satisfaction or dissatisfaction of desire is not thought to depend in any way on the moral relations in which individuals stand, or on the kinds of claims which they are willing, in the pursuit of their interests, to press on each other.

VII

Many social decisions are, of course, of an administrative nature. Certainly this is so when it is a matter of social utility in what one may call its ordinary sense: that is, when it is a question of the efficient design of social institutions for the use of common means to achieve common ends. In this case either the benefits and burdens may be assumed to be impartially distributed, or the question of distribution is misplaced, as in the instance of maintaining public order and security or national defence. But as an interpretation of the basis of the principles of justice,

---

[8] An idea essential to the classical utilitarian conception of justice. Bentham is firm in his statement of it. (*The Principles of Morals and Legislation*, ch. II, sec. iv. See also ch. X, sec. x, footnote 1.) The same point is made in *The Limits of Jurisprudence Defined*, pp. 115 f. Although much recent welfare economics, as found in such important works as I. M. D. Little, *A Critique of Welfare Economics*, 2nd ed. (Oxford, 1957) and K. J. Arrow, *Social Choice and Individual Values* (New York, 1951), dispenses with the idea of cardinal utility, and use instead the theory of ordinal utility as stated by J. R. Hicks, *Value and Capital*, 2nd ed. (Oxford, 1946), Pt. I, it assumes with utilitarianism that individual preferences have value as such, and so accepts the idea being criticized here. I hasten to add, however, that this is no objection to it as a means of analysing economic policy, and for that purpose it may, indeed, be a necessary simplifying assumption. Nevertheless it is an assumption which cannot be made in so far as one is trying to analyse moral concepts, especially the concept of justice, as economists would, I think, agree. Justice is usually regarded as a separate and distinct part of any comprehensive criterion of economic policy. See, for example, Tibor Scitovsky, *Welfare and Competition* (London, 1952), pp. 59–69, and Little, op. cit., ch. VII.

classical utilitarianism is mistaken. It *permits* one to argue, for example, that slavery is unjust on the grounds that the advantages to the slaveholder as slaveholder do not counterbalance the disadvantages to the slave and to society at large burdened by a comparatively inefficient system of labour. Now the conception of justice as fairness, when applied to the practice of slavery with its offices of slaveholder and slave, would not allow one to consider the advantages of the slaveholder in the first place. As that office is not in accordance with principles which could be mutually acknowledged, the gains accruing to the slaveholder, assuming them to exist, cannot be counted as in *any* way mitigating the injustice of the practice. The question whether these gains outweigh the disadvantages to the slave and to society cannot arise, since in considering the justice of slavery these gains have no weight at all which requires that they be overriden. Where the conception of justice as fairness applies, slavery is *always* unjust.

I am not, of course, suggesting the absurdity that the classical utilitarians approved of slavery. I am only rejecting a type of argument which their view allows them to use in support of their disapproval of it. The conception of justice as derivative from efficiency implies that judging the justice of a practice is always, in principle at least, a matter of weighing up advantages and disadvantages, each having an intrinsic value or disvalue as the satisfaction of interests, irrespective of whether or not these interests necessarily involve acquiescence in principles which could not be mutually acknowledged. Utilitarianism cannot account for the fact that slavery is always unjust, nor for the fact that it would be recognized as irrelevant in defeating the accusation of injustice for one person to say to another, engaged with him in a common practice and debating its merits, that nevertheless it allowed of the greatest satisfaction of desire. The charge of injustice cannot be rebutted in this way. If justice were derivative from a higher order executive efficiency, this would not be so.

But now, even if it is taken as established that, so far as the ordinary conception of justice goes, slavery is always unjust (that is, slavery by definition violates commonly recognized principles of justice), the classical utilitarian would surely reply that these principles, as other moral principles subordinate to that of utility, are only generally correct. It is simply for the most part true that slavery is less efficient than other institutions; and while common sense may define the concept of justice so that slavery is unjust, nevertheless, where slavery would lead to the greatest satisfaction of desire, it is not wrong. Indeed, it is then right, and for the very same reason that justice, as ordinarily understood, is usually right. If, as ordinarily understood, slavery is always unjust, to this extent the utilitarian conception of justice might be admitted to differ from that of common moral opinion. Still the utilitarian would want to hold that, as a matter of moral principle, his view is correct in giving no special weight to considerations of justice beyond that allowed for by the general presumption of effectiveness. And this, he claims, is as it should be. The everyday opinion is morally in error, although, indeed, it is a useful error, since it protects rules of generally high utility.

The question, then, relates not simply to the analysis of the concept of justice as common sense defines it, but the analysis of it in the wider sense as to how much weight considerations of justice, as defined, are to have when laid against other kinds of moral considerations. Here again I wish to argue that reasons of justice have a *special* weight for which only the conception of justice as fairness can account. Moreover, it belongs to the concept of justice that they do have this special weight. While Mill recognized that this was so, he thought that it could be accounted for by the special urgency of the moral feelings which naturally support principles of such high utility. But it is a mistake to resort to the urgency of feeling; as with the appeal to intuition, it manifests a failure to pursue the question far enough. The special weight of considerations of justice can be explained from the conception of justice as fairness. It is only necessary to elaborate a bit what has already been said as follows.

If one examines the circumstances in which a certain tolerance of slavery is justified, or perhaps better, excused, it turns out that these are of a rather special sort. Perhaps slavery exists as an inheritance from the past and it proves necessary to dismantle it piece by piece; at times slavery may conceivably be an advance on previous institutions. Now while there may be some excuse for slavery in special conditions, it is never an excuse for it that it is sufficiently advantageous to the slaveholder to outweigh the disadvantages to the slave and to society. A person who argues in this way is not perhaps making a wildly irrelevant remark; but he is guilty of a moral fallacy. There is disorder in his conception of the ranking of moral principles. For the slaveholder, by his own admission, has no moral title to the advantages which he receives as a slaveholder. He is no more prepared than the slave to acknowledge the principle upon which is founded the respective positions in which they both stand. Since slavery does not accord with principles which they could mutually acknowledge, they each may be supposed to agree that it is unjust: it grants claims which it ought not to grant and in doing so denies claims which it ought not to deny. Amongst persons in a general position who are debating the form of their common practices, it cannot, therefore, be offered as a reason for a practice that, in conceding these very claims that ought to be denied, it nevertheless meets existing interests more effectively. By their very nature the satisfaction of these claims is without weight and cannot enter into any tabulation of advantages and disadvantages.

Furthermore, it follows from the concept of morality that, to the extent that the slaveholder recognizes his position *vis-à-vis* the slave to be unjust, he would not choose to press his claims. His not wanting to receive his special advantages is one of the ways in which he shows that he thinks slavery is unjust. It would be fallacious for the legislator to suppose, then, that it is a ground for having a practice that it brings advantages greater than disadvantages, if those for whom the practice is designed, and to whom the advantages flow, acknowledge that they have no moral title to them and do not wish to receive them.

For these reasons the principles of justice have a special weight; and with respect to the principle of the greatest satisfaction of desire, as cited in the general position amongst those discussing the merits of their common practices, the principles of justice have an absolute weight. In this sense they are not contingent; and this is why their force is greater than can be accounted for by the general presumption (assuming that there is one) of the effectiveness, in the utilitarian sense, of practices which in fact satisfy them.

If one wants to continue using the concepts of classical utilitarianism, one will have to say, to meet this criticism, that at least the individual or social utility functions must be so defined that no value is given to the satisfaction of interests the representative claims of which violate the principles of justice. In this way it is no doubt possible to include these principles within the form of the utilitarian conception; but to do so is, of course, to change its inspiration altogether as a moral conception. For it is to incorporate within it principles which cannot be understood on the basis of a higher order executive decision aiming at the greatest satisfaction of desire.

It is worth remarking, perhaps, that this criticism of utilitarianism does not depend on whether or not the two assumptions, that of individuals having similar utility functions and that of diminishing marginal utility, are interpreted as psychological propositions to be supported or refuted by experience, or as moral and political principles expressed in a somewhat technical language. There are, certainly, several advantages in taking them in the latter fashion. For one thing, one might say that this is what Bentham and others really meant by them, as least as shown by how they were used in arguments for social reform. More importantly, one could hold that the best way to defend the classical utilitarian view is to interpret these assumptions as moral and political principles. It is doubtful whether, taken as psychological propositions, they are true of men in general as we know them under normal conditions. On the other hand, utilitarians would not have wanted to propose them merely as practical working principles of legislation, or as expedient maxims to guide reform, given the egalitarian sentiments of modern society. When pressed they might well have invoked the idea of a more or less equal capacity of men in relevant respects if given an equal chance in a just society. But if the argument above regarding slavery is correct, then granting these assumptions as moral and political principles makes no difference. To view individuals as equally fruitful lines for the allocation of benefits, even as a matter of moral principle, still leaves the mistaken notion that the satisfaction of desire has value in itself irrespective of the relations between persons as members of a common practice, and irrespective of the claims upon one another which the satisfaction of interests represents. To see the error of this idea one must give up the conception of justice as an executive decision altogether and refer to the notion of justice as fairness: that participants in a common practice be regarded as having an original and equal liberty and that their common practices be considered unjust unless they accord with principles which persons so circumstanced and related could freely acknowledge before one another, and so could accept as fair. Once the emphasis is put upon the concept of the mutual recognition of principles by participants in a common practice the rules of which are to define their several relations and give form to their claims on one another, then it is clear that the granting of a claim the principle of which could not be acknowledged by each in the general position (that is, in the position in which the parties propose and acknowledge principles before one another) is not a reason for adopting a practice. Viewed in this way, the background of the claim is seen to exclude it from consideration; that it can represent a value in itself arises from the conception of individuals as separate lines for the assignment of benefits, as isolated persons who stand as claimants on an administrative or benevolent largesse. Occasionally persons do so to stand to one another; but this is not the general case, nor, more importantly, is it the case when it is a matter of the justice of practices themselves in which participants stand in various relations to be appraised in accordance with standards which they may be expected to acknowledge before one another. Thus however mistaken the notion of the social contract may be as history, and however far it may overreach itself as a general theory of social and political obligation, it does express, suitably interpreted, an essential part of the concept of justice.

VIII

By way of conclusion I should like to make two remarks: first, the original modification of the utilitarian principle (that it require of practices that the offices and positions defined by them be equal unless it is reasonable to suppose that the representative man in *every* office would find the inequality to his advantage), slight as it may appear at first sight, actually has a different conception of justice standing behind it. I have tried to show how this is so by developing the concept of justice as fairness and by indicating how this notion involves the mutual acceptance, from a general position, of the principles on which a practice is founded, and how this in turn requires the exclusion from consideration of claims violating the principles of justice. Thus the slight alteration of principle reveals another family of notions, another way of looking at the concept of justice.

Second, I should like to remark also that I have been dealing with the *concept* of justice. I have tried to set out the kinds of principles upon which judgements concerning the justice of practices may be said to stand. The analysis will be successful to the degree that it expresses the principles involved in these judgements when made by competent persons upon deliberation and reflection.[9] Now every people may be supposed to have the concept of justice, since in the life of every society there must be at least some relations in which the parties consider themselves to be circumstanced and related as the concept of justice as fairness requires. Societies will differ from one another not in having or in failing to have this notion but in the range of cases to which they apply it and in the emphasis which they give to it as compared with other moral concepts.

A firm grasp of the concept of justice itself is necessary if these variations, and the reasons for them, are to be understood. No study of the development of moral ideas and of the differences between them is more sound than the analysis of the fundamental moral concepts upon which it must depend. I have tried, therefore, to give an analysis of the concept of justice which should apply generally, however large a part the concept may have in a given morality, and which can be used in explaining the course of men's thoughts about justice and its relations to other moral concepts. How it is to be used for this purpose is a large topic which I cannot, of course, take up here. I mention it only to emphasize that I have been dealing with the concept of justice itself and to indicate what use I consider such an analysis to have.

---

[9] For a further discussion of the idea expressed here, see my paper, "Outline of a Decision Procedure for Ethics," in the *Philosophical Review*, LX (1951), 177–97. For an analysis, similar in many respects but using the notion of the ideal observer instead of that of the considered judgement of a competent person, see Roderick Firth, "Ethical Absolutism and the Ideal Observer," *Philosophy and Phenomenological Research*, XII (1952), 317–45. While the similarities between these two discussions are more important than the differences, an analysis based on the notion of a considered judgement of a competent person, as it is based on a kind of judgement, may prove more helpful in understanding the features of moral judgement than an analysis based on the notion of an ideal observer, although this remains to be shown. A man who rejects the conditions imposed on a considered judgement of a competent person could no longer profess to *judge* at all. This seems more fundamental than his rejecting the conditions of observation, for these do not seem to apply, in an ordinary sense, to making a moral judgement.

25. On Social Justice

Brian Barry

I

We sometimes characterize rules and laws, social arrangements and economic distributions, even whole societies, as just or injust. What are the criteria appropriate to this kind of judgement — a judgement of substantial justice or, on a large scale, social justice? Three kinds of answer have been given. In increasing order of pessimism they are, first, that some verbal formula can be devised which encapsulates this notion of justice; second, that there is a number of irreducible criteria for the satisfactory distribution of benefits and burdens, some rather vague subset of which can be subsumed under "justice"; and, third, that the whole idea of using "justice" to criticize distributive arrangements is mistaken. If the first position can be shown to be untenable and the third unnecessarily gloomy, the second is left. I shall try to support the second position, mainly by attacking recent attempts to rescue the first. . . .

The uselessness of most verbal formulae, as guides to the application of "justice" in actual situations, is so manifest that I shall not labour the point. "To each his own" — a popular classical tag — obviously gets us back to square one pretty quickly, and a popular recent formula, that justice requires "relevant differences" to be taken into account, hardly manages to get off square one at all. There is, I think, one formula which breaks out of the circle and thus carries the promise of at least providing workable prescriptions in concrete situations. Stated in the most general terms, it is that a distribution is just if those subject to it would have agreed in advance to the procedure by which it was brought about.

We can illustrate this idea most clearly from games of skill. Within certain limits, it does not matter exactly what the rules are, so long as all the players know what they are and adhere to them. Thus, if they agree to play a certain "local rule," this makes it difficult for one of the players to say afterwards that the rule resulted in an unjust outcome to the game. In his classic study, Piaget reported that his young informants soon came to realize that some of the rules of marbles — those prescribing that the marbles should be placed in a square and shot at from behind a certain line — were "due to mutual consent and capable of being altered by general opinion" (Jean Piaget, *The Moral Judgement of the Child*, 3rd ed., p. 92).

I do not think, however, that even in the very favourable case of games of skill we can contemplate *defining* a just distribution (the good distributed here being a prize or simply the intangible good of winning) as one in accordance with rules accepted by the participants at the start. For one thing, a player might accept a rule proposed by another even though he expected it to work out unjustly to his own disadvantage. Thus, suppose a man is playing golf with his boss, a powerful but erratic hitter: he might accept the suggestion that lost balls should not be penalized while realizing that his boss stands to gain from it. And even leaving aside sanctions

From *Oxford Review*, Trinity Term (1967), pp. 29–43, by permission of the author and publisher.

extraneous to the game, a man who very badly wants to play might accept disadvantageous terms in order to get a game.

Another way in which the rules might be less than just would be for the players to accept rules which gave a large role to luck (either openly or in the form of flukes) in determining the result, or in some other way made the game a poor test of skill. Piaget's informants did not think that *any* rules in marbles would be equally fair: he noted "the precedence given to justice as opposed to chance" and "of effort over easy gain." (pp. 92 – 3.) Thus, one boy said of a proposed rule "Perhaps it isn't quite fair, because it isn't very hard to take four marbles that way"; and another said "The chaps might think it [another rule] wasn't very fair because it's luck. To be a good rule it has to be skill." (pp. 65 – 6.) It should perhaps be added that one certainly can also speak of a "fair rule" where the concept of a just result has no place, as in pure gambling games: a fair rule here is simply one which gives the players equal chances of winning (or chances proportional to their stake). But this simply reinforces the point that a just distribution cannot be defined as the outcome of a fair procedure.

Finally, we should consider the possibility that even where the rules are "fair" in the sense of maximizing the influence of skill on the outcome, one player might still be so grossly unlucky on a particular occasion that one would be inclined to say that his losing was not a just outcome because it did not reflect the relative skill of the players. Even if one does not place much weight on this final point, the conclusion seems unavoidable that "justice" in the context of games of skill refers to a result in accordance with the relative skill of the players, and that all we can say about agreement on the rules is that under certain circumstances agreed-on rules will tend to produce just results. This is especially so where the players are *trying* to set up a game in which skill determines the outcome.

The criterion of agreement in advance on the rules does not provide a criterion of a just outcome, even in games. But it is still a potentially fruitful idea. Can the difficulties with games of skill be ironed out, and can the basic idea be extended beyond games of skill? Let us take up the first question. We have said that, because a certain rule could sometimes be predicted to favour one player rather than another in its working out, unfair rules might be agreed to where bargaining-power was unequal. We could try to meet this by simply adding to the specifications that bargaining-power should be equal, but this is not a very clear notion to apply in actual situations. So we could try instead to minimize the disruptive effect of differences in bargaining-power. The key to this is to *increase the area of ignorance*. Much of the trouble about local rules adopted for a particular occasion lies in the fact that it is too easy to calculate the effect of a given rule on the chances of the players. Thus, to return to our golfers, if there is a water hazard on the left of the fairway, any increase in the penalty for landing in it will be bad for players whose shots have a particular tendency to go to the left, and *vice versa*. But if players had to decide for *all* courses whether the penalty should be changed, the location of the water on any given course would be less important. There is still the difficulty that a player may confidently expect to play most of his games on one particular course and cast his vote on that basis. But the size of the problem would have been reduced. It could be eliminated altogether if we added a further stipulation to the conditions under which the agreement was to be reached, namely that the golfer either did not know what course he usually played on or had temporarily forgotten the characteristics of his own game. This stipulation would carry us over into the realms of fantasy, but it must be borne in mind that the criterion of justice for which we are looking is to be stated in terms of the agreements people *would* reach under certain yet-to-be-determined conditions. The only legitimate ground for complaint, therefore, could be that the further we get away from real human beings taking real decisions the less convincing may be our assertion that they *would* agree on so-and-so under the postulated conditions.

But there is no point in pushing this line of analysis any further until we have seen whether anything can be done about the other difficulty. Replacing questions about the justice of distributions by questions about the fairness of procedures seems to have some promise, but can it be extended beyond games of skill? I think it can, but not in such a way as to solve all our problems. Thus, instead of trying to reach agreement on the name of one man to fill a certain position, the members of a group might instead work on setting up an agreed electoral procedure for filling the position. Again, instead of trying to reach an agreement on the substance of their dispute, the parties to it might by agreement set up some mechanism for the arbitration either of this particular dispute or of all future disputes.

These would both be good examples of agreement on a procedure replacing dispute about a particular outcome. But, even if we waive all questions about agreement on the rules guaranteeing their fairness, there is still a snag which no technical ingenuity will enable us to circumvent: even less than in the case of games of skill are we prepared to say that a fair procedure *by definition* produces a just result. An election might be fairly conducted but we might still wish to say that the result was unjust because a majority of the voters had behaved unjustly in voting the way they did. Or, again, two parties might agree to refer a dispute to arbitration, and they might agree to accept the decision as binding. But they (logically) could not commit themselves in advance to believing the decision to be just. Moreover, one of the arguments used by voters on one another and by the parties on the arbitrator would very likely be that it would be just to vote or to decide in a certain way — an argument that would be impossible if the justice of the result was logically constituted by the fairness of the procedure.

II

We seem to be stuck. Procedures can be multiplied but they do not enable us to dispense with our substantial, first-order, notions of justice, inchoate though these may be. On the contrary, we apparently cannot avoid using these notions of justice as our touchstone for deciding whether or not the procedure is delivering just outcomes. But perhaps we have been too hasty. We have been looking for aggreement on some procedure that would guarantee just distributions. Why not look instead for agreement on some *principles* that would guarantee just distribution?

Go back, for example, to our two parties locked in dispute on some particular questions, who have nevertheless agreed on a procedure for arbitration. By a "procedure" we mean rules for the appointment of the arbitrator(s), the methods by which evidence should be given, whether cross-examination is to be permitted, etc. But suppose that the parties were not content with this and also wanted to limit the discretion of their arbitrator in other ways: they would then have to try to reach agreement on a set of principles to guide the arbitrator, telling him that arguments based on such-and-such considerations were to be ruled out, that great weight should be attached to such-and-such a factor, and so on. Might we not regard principles agreed on by both parties as principles of justice?

One possible answer is that we might do so, but that we would not expect the principles in question to amount to much. For if the parties are trying to do as well for themselves as they can (an assumption we have made throughout, and shall continue to make) why should they be any more ready to agree on principles than on the subject of the dispute itself? Each will put forward principles favouring itself and reject the principles put forward by the other side. No doubt there is a lot of force in this objection, but, to meet it, all that we have to do is bring back the stipulations we canvassed to deal with the parallel difficulty in reaching fair agreements about rules in games. As a first step we say that the parties have to put forward principles not merely for application to this dispute but principles which they would be willing to see applied to any future dispute in which they were involved. If this is not strong enough, we can add that while deciding what principles to put forward they are somehow made unaware of their personal qualities, position in the social structure, etc.

What we have now reached is the position maintained by Professor John Rawls. The fundamentals of this position are set out in his well-known article "Justice as Fairness." (*Philosophical Review*, LXVII (1958), reprinted in F. A. Olafson (ed.) *Justice and Social Policy* and in P. Laslett and W. G. Runciman (eds.) *Philosophy, Politics and Society*, Second Series. I shall give page references to the reprint in Laslett and Runciman, this being probably the most easily accessible.) Rawls suggests that the principles of just distribution are those principles which would be agreed on by rational, self-interested men, "sufficiently equal in power and ability to guarantee that in normal circumstances none is able to dominate the others" (p. 138), as providing a basis upon which they would be willing to have their common affairs regulated in perpetuity.

Rawls does not, I think, ever devote much space to proving that the principles agreed on in such circumstances would be properly described as principles of *justice*; still less that justice should be defined in those terms. In "Justice as Fairness" he says that "The character and respective situations of the parties [e.g. their egoism and their equal strength] reflect . . . the fact that questions of justice arise when conflicting claims are made upon the design of a practice and where it is taken for granted that each person will insist, as far as possible, on what he considers his rights." At the same time, "The procedure whereby principles are proposed and acknowledged represents constraints, analogous to those of having a morality"; for "having a morality must at least imply the acknowledgement of principles as impartially applying to one's own conduct as well as to another's, and moreover principles which may constitute a constraint, or limitation, upon the pursuit of one's own interests. (p. 139.)

The required conclusion is not, however, established by these points. What Rawls needs to show is that, if the procedure he describes were employed in the kind of situation he describes, the principles agreed on would necessarily be principles of justice. This does not follow from the passage I have quoted, which maintains only that the problem of justice arises in situations such as those he describes and that the procedure he describes automatically produces the impartiality and limitation of interest-seeking which is a minimum condition of morality. A situation in which interests conflict is no doubt relevant to justice, but it is equally relevant to all the other principles by which social relationships may be ordered; and to say that a procedure guarantees a minimum condition of morality is not the same as saying that it produces the particular set of moral principles embodied in the concept of justice.

Rawls could avoid this criticism (though at the cost of opening another line of attack) by saying that he was simply proposing to appropriate the word "justice" to refer to whatever principles would be agreed on in the situation that he depicts. But he does not take this course, for he writes that "justice is to be understood in its customary sense as representing but *one* of the many virtues of social institutions," and claims that the principles which would be chosen in the prescribed set-up are "typical of a family of principles normally associated with the concept of justice." (p. 133.) Rawls' case is, then, that certain principles would be chosen by rational self-interested men who were forced to agree, on equal terms, to the principle that should govern their relations in future; and that these principles would in fact be recognizable as falling under our ordinary concept of justice. This does not of course entail that they should fit our ordinary concept at every point; but that we would be prepared to regard them as constituting a "rational reconstruction" of our ordinary concept, a more coherent, streamlined form of it, which we should be willing to adopt in its place. Thus, the next step is to see what principles Rawls believes *would* be adopted; and to ask (a) whether there is a good case for thinking they would be adopted, (b) whether, in any case, they coincide at all closely with our ordinary concept of justice, and (c) whether, even if they do not, they are still valuable principles.

III

As far as I know, nobody has actually tried the experiment of setting up the Rawlsian initial conditions and finding out what principles emerged. Rawls does not rely on empirical evidence; but if someone challenged him with some he might reply that he is speaking of *rational* men, and if the experimental results do not agree with his own conclusions this merely shows that the subjects employed were not fully rational. Rawls' method, then, is deductive. If Martians play chess then we at once know, without any information about Martians, that a good move in Martian chess is also a good move in Earth chess. Similarly, provided that Martians have conflicting interests which they desire to pursue, they will (if Rawls is right) agree on the same principles for regulating their affairs as human beings will, insofar as they are rational in pursuing those interests.

According to Rawls, two principles would be agreed upon: "first each person participating in a practice, or affected by it, has an equal right to the most extensive liberty compatible with a like liberty for all; and second, inequalities are arbitrary unless it is reasonable to expect that they will work out to everyone's advantage, and provided the positions and offices to which they attach, or from which they may be gained, are open to all." (p.134.) The basic idea is fairly simple, though its working out can become very complicated. In order to decide what would be a just distribution, the participants in any practice start from a baseline of equality: this means a situation where there is equality in the "benefits and burdens attached to [different offices and positions] either directly or indirectly, such as prestige and wealth, or liability to taxation and compulsory services." (p. 135.)

They then ask, taking this equal position as a point of comparison, whether there is any possible system of inequalities which would make everybody better off — and that means *everybody*. "The representative man in every office or position defined by a practice, when he views it as a going concern, must find it reasonable to prefer his condition and prospects with the inequality to what they would be under the practice without it. The principle excludes, therefore, the justification of inequalities on the grounds that the disadvantages of those in one position are outweighed by the greater advantages of those in another position." (p.135.)

Let us now take up the first question: would these principles be adopted by rational, self-interested men? Two kinds of objection might, I think, be pressed. I shall call them the practical and the theoretical objection. The practical difficulty is that the ordinary uncertainty of the future is not so great that men putting forward principles for the regulation of things in the future might not be able to make a shrewd guess about their chances of being near the top or near the bottom in a system of inequalities. Thus, Rawls assumes too easily that because of uncertainty men would have to leave out of account their own positions in putting forward principles. I call this a practical difficulty because it can be eliminated by making the initial conditions stronger. As before, we can simply add the postulate that the men (or, if you like, beings) who are choosing the principles are suffering from a temporary amnesia about their personal qualities, etc.; and that all they know is that they have conflicting interests but the possibility of gains from co-operation. Rawls does not take this line of retreat in "Justice as Fairness" but he has done so since. (See "Constitutional Liberty and the Concept of Justice," *Nomos VI.*) Obviously, adding this condition emphasizes the abstract, deductive nature of the whole operation, but given Rawl's purposes it seems to me a legitimate way of clearing an irrelevant practical difficulty out of the way.

The other objection I call the theoretical one because it challenges the deduction at its core. The objection is that, no matter how perfectly the initial conditions are set up, rational self-interested men would *not* necessarily choose the Rawlsian principles, because there is no good reason why they should do so. This criticism centres round Rawls' second principle: that inequalities are to be accepted if and only if they can be expected to make the worst-off person under them better-off than he would have been under a regime of absolute equality. It is important to see exactly how Rawls arrives at the conclusion that this principle would meet with universal approval among anonymous, self-interested beings — that is to say, beings who know they have interests they wish to pursue, even though they do not know what these interests are. Rawls writes that the principles each man puts forward "will express the conditions in accordance with which each is the least unwilling to have his interests limited in the design of practices, given the competing interests of the others, on the supposition that interests of others will be limited likewise. *The restrictions which would so arise might be thought of as those a person would keep in mind if he were designing a practice in which his enemy were to assign him his place.*" (pp. 138–9; my italics.)

Now, if the sentence I have italicized is right, it must be allowed that Rawls' deduction works. A man whose place is to be assigned him by his enemy will obviously concentrate on designing the system of distributions so that the worst-off position will be as pleasant as possible. He knows that he can, and must, concentrate on this and ignore everything else, because he knows for certain that, whatever the worst-off position is, he will be occupying it. But our hypothetical principle-choosers are *not* going to be assigned their positions by their enemy. They know in fact that the allocation of places will depend (in proportions that they do not know) on personal characteristics and on luck. And since they do not at the moment remember what personal characteristics they have, they can simply regard positions as allocated by a random process.

Now the question is, if you know that outcomes are determined by a random process (or, more generally, by a process which is not directed at giving you personally one outcome rather than another) is it rational to behave as if the outcome were going to be determined by the wishes of your enemy? This is the vexed problem of decision-making under conditions of uncertainty. Rawls' solution has been put forward often as the maximum criterion: "maximin" simply refers to the fact that it prescribes the choice which *maximizes* the *minimum* pay-off. In other words, the decision-maker looks at the possible consequences of each alternative to discover the worst possible outcome that each could produce. For each alternative he asks: if everything went wrong, how catastrophic would it be? And he then picks the alternative which gives him the smallest losses if everything goes wrong. Clearly this is a play-safe strategy, a conservative strategy. Does it make sense as a universal response to uncertainty?

Let us consider a simple example. Either it will rain today or the sun will shine; and I can either take my raincoat or leave it at home. If the sun shines and I have left my raincoat, I shall be very pleased; on the other hand, if I leave my raincoat and it rains, I shall be very annoyed. If I take my raincoat and it rains, I shall be fairly pleased in that I am at least suitably clad, though less pleased than the combination of sun and no raincoat would make me; if the sun shines when I take my raincoat, I shall be somewhat annoyed, though less annoyed than I would be at having to walk through the rain without a raincoat.

The maximin criterion dictates that I take my raincoat: the worst that can happen is that the sun will shine; and this is less annoying than the worst thing that can happen if I leave my raincoat behind, namely get wet. This would obviously be the right plan if I were convinced that there was a Weather Man who took a malicious pleasure in thwarting me. But if I thought that "someone up there likes me" and was striving to make me as happy as possible, I would be more sensible to adopt a maximax policy: instead of choosing the best of the worst outcomes I would go for the best of the best outcomes. In the present case, this would entail that I leave my raincoat behind and trust in providence to make the sun shine, for my most pleasant outcome consists of the combination of no raincoat and the sun shining.

Suppose, however, that I don't believe that my decision about taking a raincoat or not will have any effect on whether it rains or whether the sun shines. How should I decide then which to do? The natural answer would seem to be that I should try to guess how likely it is to rain and should act accordingly. If there is a fair chance of its raining, I take my coat; if I think the chance of rain is very remote, I leave it behind. Exactly how likely rain has to be before it is worth taking my coat depends on the relative pleasantness and unpleasantness of the four possible outcomes and my taste for risk-taking. Fortunately, there is no need for the present purpose to go into details. The essential point is that almost anyone would think it sensible to go out without a raincoat if the probability of rainfall is below *some* level; but on the maximin criterion one would always take a raincoat if there was any chance of rain at all, however remote. The conclusion to be drawn is, I suggest, that it is not rational to follow the maximin policy except where someone *is* responding to your choices in such a way as to damage you. In other cases some sort of system for playing the percentages is more rational.

The implications for Rawls' construction are plain. It is not legitimate to say that rational self-interest requires the adoption of a maximin policy. It follows that there would not be agreement on the second of Rawls' principles. Rational choosers would look not just at the minimum but at the average and the spread around it. They would then pick a set of principles which would lead to a high average level of well-being; whether they would prefer one with more equal or less equal distribution would depend on their taste for gambling. (See William Vickrey, "Utility, Strategy and Social Decision Rules," *The Quarterly Journal of Economics,* LXXIV.)

IV

Although the two Rawlsian principles cannot be deduced from Rawls' initial conditions, they are still worth examining in their own right, first, as principles of *justice,* and, second, as principles of *distribution* in general. For, if they either embody or replace the ordinary criteria of social justice, the optimistic view that a single formula can be produced will have been vindicated — provided, of course, that we are willing to accept a single formula in two parts; and I think we ought to be, so long as the two parts are completely consistent with one another.

Rawls' two principles do not, I suggest, correspond with the main elements in the ordinary notion of justice. The first principle, that some reason has to be given for treating people unequally, is no doubt a constituent part of the concept of justice; but this is because it is a necessary condition of bringing different people's claims into a moral relationship with one another. It is not connected with justice in particular. The second principle falls into two parts: the maximin criterion and the prescription that "positions and offices" carrying privileges should be "open to all." (p. 133.) The latter part, if interpreted to mean that such positions should be open to those most fully qualified, is fairly clearly relevant to justice, though it seems oddly limited in scope to occur in a general formula for justice. The original and controversial first part seems not to be a principle of justice at all. If it were followed, the results might quite often coincide with those required by justice, but where they did not, I do not think we would be inclined to adopt the maximin criterion and drop other conceptions.

The only ground on which one can defend an inequality as just, in Rawls' conception, is that introducing it will lead to the worst off member of the society being better off than he would otherwise have been. I should like to suggest, however, that, although this would often be a good reason for saying the inequality was *justified*, it would never be a good reason for calling it *just*. For justice is not a forward-looking virtue. Justice consists in some appropriate relationship between what a person has done or what he is now and the benefits that he receives or the costs that he bears. The size of incentive payments is not determined by the criteria of just distribution. It may be considered essential to pay someone a certain amount in order to get him to do something and it may also be considered vital that he should do it. But the payment does not automatically become just when these two conditions obtain. It would be perfectly comprehensible to assert that it was unjust for anyone to be paid so much "rent" for the exercise of the talent in question, but it was right in this instance for justice to give way to public interest.

If we assume (as we have in the last example) that Rawls' maximin criterion is to be applied in a society where people are allocated to jobs and have to be got to work in them by inducements, differentials may tend to be too large for justice. But there is nothing in Rawls, formula specifying that it should be applied in a "liberal" society. People might be allocated to jobs and kept at work in them by coercion: that is to say, instead of being made better off than the norm by doing what is wanted they are made worse off than the norm if they don't do what is wanted. Under such conditions, exact equality could be maintained. Unpleasantness of work would have to be compensated for to *maintain* equality but, even so, it might be thought that justice had been infringed in the other direction from that in which a liberal society deviated. Of course, a "liberal" could argue that a directive-coercive system is so much less efficient than a liberal system that, not only would the best off under a liberal system be better off than anyone under a directive coercive system, but even the *worst* off person in a "liberal" system would be better off than anybody in a directive-coercive system. This may be true; then again it may not. And in any case it seems to me dubious to suppose that the justice of all differentials turns on the results of such an experiment.

V

The reader may have become impatient with the latest phase of the discussion. I imagine him saying: "All right, the maximin criterion doesn't correspond to the ordinary notion of justice, and we don't particularly want to give up the ordinary notion of justice. But (as you admitted in the incentive-payment example) we are willing to allow justice in this ordinary sense to be overridden. Doesn't the maximin criterion provide an acceptable overriding principle?" This is a very attractive idea, and maybe there will be some people who are prepared to stick to the maximin principle through thick and thin. I should like, however, to suggest that there is a certain arbitrary quality about it, compared with a frank recognition of multiple "ultimate" principles with no simple rule for settling clashes between them.

Rawls tells us that "in deciding on the justice of a practice it is not enough to ascertain that it answers to wants and interests in the fullest and most effective manner. For if any of these conflict with justice, they should not be counted, as their satisfaction is *no reason at all*. It would be irrelevant to say, even if true, that it resulted in the greatest satisfaction of desire. In tallying up the *merits* of a practice one must toss out the satisfaction of interests the claims of which are incompatible with the principle of justice." (p. 149, my italics.) The expressions I have italicized show how weak is the form of moral pluralism that Rawls is willing to accept, compared with what he appeared to be offering us when he said that justice is only one possible virtue of institutions. The claim that an institution satisfies wants more fully than any alternative is "no reason at all" in favour of it — irrelevant to its "merits" — if it conflicts with the requirements of justice. "With respect to the principle of the greatest satisfaction of desire . . . the principles of justice have an absolute weight." (p. 154.) Against this view, I should like to suggest that utilitarian considerations cannot simply be "tossed out" when they conflict with the criteria of justice. I shall argue this in connection with Rawls' criteria of justice, but I think the same argument could be made against the absolute priority of any distributive criteria.

I have argued above that someone rationally pursuing his own self-interest would not accept the inflexibility of the maximin criterion; and that he would insist on taking account of the whole range of positions, not just the lowest. Similarly here I wish to argue that a responsible moral agent should not commit himself to giving an absolute priority to the principles of justice, but that he should allow for the possibility that a large increase in utility might counterbalance a small decrease in justice. In terms of the maximin criterion this means that it is possible to conceive a situation in which it would be morally justifiable for someone to say: "I know I'm better off than you; but I think you ought to do so-and-so because it would be of great benefit to me and only a minor inconvenience to you." For example, suppose that one of us drives a Bentley and the other a Mini; and that we have to decide which of us is to get the big garage and which of us the small one. On Rawls' principles it might be concluded that the man with the Mini should be compensated with the big garage and the Bentley left to stand outside (since it won't go in the small garage). But this seems absurd. At the very least it does not seem unreasonable to prefer, say a large gain for the better off and a smaller gain for the worse off to an infinitesimally larger gain for the worst off and a loss for the better off — provided that these are the only alternatives.

I have followed Rawls in taking up the problem of conflicts between the maximin criterion and the principle of maximizing the satisfaction of wants, and I have suggested that it would not be desirable for the latter always to override the former. But there are other principles that can conflict with the maximin criterion, and here too one might well be uneasy in assenting to the universal priority of the maximin criterion. One of these is the notion of "desert." In arguing earlier that the maximin criterion did not coincide with the ordinary notion of justice it was the strong connection between desert and justice that I had in mind. Here, of course, we are not concerned with whether the maximin criterion is properly regarded as a principle of justice but with whether it is appropriate to treat it as an overriding principle when making moral judgements about social institutions. I do not think that desert can be written off. A survey whose findings were published recently illustrates the strong hold that desert seems to have over people, in this country at least. [1] Respondents were asked, among other things, which of three criteria for earned incomes they thought "most important." Almost half (49%) said "that people with special skills are fully rewarded," as against 41% saying "that lowest paid workers get a reasonable wage" and 10% " that incomes become more equal." And the replies to another question show vividly that the support for "fully rewarding" those with "special skills" was derived from a belief in desert — an intrinsically proper relationship between the work done and its reward — rather than a forward-looking attempt to attract labour to jobs where it was needed. For when asked "which two of these [five possible reasons] do you think are the best reasons for a pay rise?" very few respondents (16%) gave the "incentive" answer: "It's difficult to find people for the job." The most popular two reasons (especially among Conservatives and Liberals but getting a clear majority of votes among

[1] *New Society*, April 6th, 1967, page 492. Acknowledgement is made to the Opinion Research Centre and to the Editor of *New Society* for permission to quote the findings cited below.

Labour supporters too) were the two most clearly tied to hierarchical notions of
desert: "it's a responsible job" (61%) and "it's a job which needs long training"
(56%). Two less hierarchical bases of ascribing desert — "long hours" and
"difficult job" — came a long way behind in third and fourth places (27% and 21%)
leaving the need to attract labour sharing last place with the principle of
comparability ("other people doing similar work get more pay"). Ours is a society
in which the elite are rewarded not only with deference but with hard cash — and
most people seem to think that is the way it should be.

I shall not pursue this line of argument any further, since either one of the
criteria for judgement mentioned — the utilitarian one and that of desert — is
sufficient to break the primacy of the maximin criterion if one accepts that in case
of conflict one of these might be followed in preference to the maximin criterion.
Before leaving this criterion, however, I should like to say a few words in its
defence. One may concede (as I wish to do) that it is not a principle of justice and
that it is not an overriding principle of morality. One may concede further (as again
I would wish to do) that it is not an ultimate principle at all. This does not prevent
one from recognizing its attraction as one possible compromise point between two
ultimate principles, namely the utilitarian principle and the principle of equality.
The strength of the maximin criterion lies in its promise of providing a determinate
point of compromise. The only other way of reaching a compromise is to ask how
much of one value is worth how much of the other, and these weightings are in the
nature of the case almost impossible to formulate in general terms.

We can present the point most conveniently in a simple illustrative diagram.

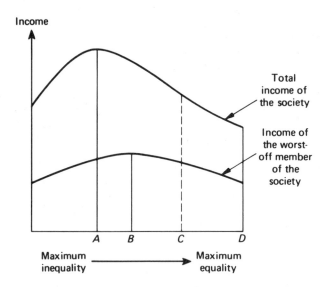

As the equality of distribution increases, from the minimum on the left to the
maximum on the right, we suppose that the total income of all those concerned
(added together) first rises and then falls, and that the income of the worst-off
follows the same pattern but reaches a maximum at a more egalitarian point. These
seem reasonable assumptions. Now, the two simple maximizing prescriptions, taken

separately, yield definite results. If we want to maximize total income we adopt A, and if we want to maximize equality we adopt D. But suppose we don't want to go overboard on either; then what point should we adopt? Rawls' maximin criterion provides a prescription which is both in effect a compromise between equality and total income and yet at the same time gives a definite result. According to this we maximize the income of the worst-off and thus adopt B. Of course, this is not the only possible compromise position; of the many possible alternatives, one somewhat more egalitarian solution is represented by C. But whereas B can be read off the diagram as the point at which the curve turns down, C depends on looking at all feasible combinations of the two amounts — equality and total income — and the judgement that the most desirable combination attainable is to be found at that point. This can be expressed technically by noting that whereas the determination of the points A, B and D does not depend on the scale — the height of the curves could be doubled or halved without altering the results — the position of C does depend crucially on the scale, since it is two amounts that are being weighed against one another and not merely one amount being maximized.

Thus, where the main considerations which are taken to be relevant to some question happen to be those of equal distribution and total income (or, less specifically, "general utility"), the maximin principle provides a determinate compromise position — it can be put forward with a certain plausibility as the point beyond which it is not "reasonable" to push equality. A good example of this may be drawn from the equalization of wages and salaries. In a recent article ("The Case for a National Minimum Wage," *The Times*, 23.3.67, p. 9) Professor H. A. Clegg has suggested that a movement towards "the redistribution of earned incomes" might be achieved by the use of a national minimum wage. The question then arises, on what basis should the level of this minimum wage be fixed? And the answer that appears to be given is: the level that maximizes the pay of the lowest paid. For Clegg writes: "The consequence of a £15 minimum would be a surge in wage-costs and prices which would benefit no one, *not even the lowest-paid*; but a minimum of £10 10s. or £11 should not be unmanageable." (My italics.)

Part VII

Rights

Introduction

Of the concepts studied in this book, few are more prominent in current discourse than is the concept of "rights." In political speeches, in the law, in the media, and indeed in the workplace and marketplace the concept is positively ubiquitous. The rights to work and to strike, the rights of consumers, of women, of children, of the accused and the convicted, of homosexuals, professors, and students (indeed of animals and trees), the right to walk safely on the streets, to know what the government is doing and why, to privacy, to medical care, to vacations with pay, to a good education, to free child-care centers, to abortions on demand, to serve on juries and to refuse to do so, to travel, to citizenship, to refuse to do military service — all of these and many, many more have been asserted and denied, exercised and waived, interpreted, respected and violated, and above all extensively and heatedly debated by and before large numbers of the members of many contemporary societies. A substantial part of the social, political, and moral action and interaction, conflict and controversy, in contemporary societies takes place in terms of the concept of "rights." It is of obvious importance that we be clear about this concept and the reasons for its prominence in the "weave of our lives."

We can make some headway in this regard by noticing distinctions that jurists, who have been intimately concerned with "rights" for a long time, have found useful in sorting out the many uses to which the concept (or at least the word) has been put in the law. The leading discussion in this respect remains that of Wesley Hohfeld, who distinguished among (1) rights in what he called the "strict sense," (2) liberties, (3) powers, and (4) immunities.[1] Hohfeld drew these distinctions in terms of the concepts that are the usual "correlatives" and "opposites" of the several uses of "rights" he found common in the law. By "correlatives," which are the most relevant here, he meant the concept that identifies the jural situation of the B or B's against whom A has a right. Thus if A has a right in the strict sense, some B has an obligation to A in respect of that right. If A has a liberty, some B has a "no-right" in respect to that liberty, that is, roughly, has no ground on which to interfere or even object to A's doing or having X. In the case of A having a power, B has a correlative liability; for example, if A has a power to disinherit his son, his son is "liable" to the exercise of A's power. Finally, if A has an immunity, for example, the immunity against self-incrimination established by the Fifth Amendment to the U.S. Constitution, then some B, say a judge, has a disability, that, is lacks any

---

[1] See W. H. Hohfeld, *Fundamental Legal Conceptions* (New Haven: Yale University Press, 1919). Hohfeld most often uses the term "privilege" for the second type or use of "right," but "liberty" has been more commonly employed by writers using his distinctions.

ground on which to require *A* to testify against himself (whereas ordinarily *B* can require *A* to testify).

Although many questions arise concerning these distinctions, they are useful and they are employed, sometimes implicitly, in the selections that follow. But they are only a first step because they do no more than identify the several senses of "rights" that require analysis and they give little clue to the centrality of the concept in our discourse.

H. L. A. Hart's attempt to take the discussion further stresses the tight, apparently logical or conceptual, connection he thinks obtains between "rights" on the one hand and freedom and justifying interferences with freedom on the other. The concept of rights as we ordinarily use it presupposes a commitment to the notion that all human beings, or at least all human beings capable of choice, have at least one natural right, the right to equal freedom. This is because, very briefly, asserting a right always involves interference with the freedom of others. When I claim a right, I am claiming that some other person or persons have an obligation (or a no-right, a liability or a disability) to act or refrain from acting in a certain manner. If the interference with their freedom that my having or doing *X* did not require justification, the notion of my having a right to do or have it, which provides such a justification, would lose its point. Because the particular rights presuppose and logically cannot themselves provide a justification for the need to justify interferences with freedom, we can say freedom itself is a natural right.

It would be very hard to deny that there is a close connection between "rights" and "freedom." Leaving aside ambiguities in Hart's discussion of this connection, the problems raised by his argument concern his further contention that the various uses of "rights" *do not* connect with concepts having to do with benefits and harms. Benefit and harm are indeed moral considerations, Hart argues, but they come from a different part or segment of morality than "rights" and are irrelevant to rights.

William Frankena agrees with Hart that the fact that *A* stands to benefit from the discharge of a duty by *B* does not itself show that *A* has a right against *B*. (Thus rights correlate with duties but duties do not always correlate with rights. On this point, see also Joel Feinberg's discussion of "Nowheresville.") He thinks, however, that there are connections between rights and benefits, namely (at a minimum), that a person can be a possible holder of rights only if he or she is "capable of" benefiting from them, that is, of deriving satisfaction or pleasure from exercising them, from having them respected, and so on. Rights are not proportionate to or justified solely in terms of benefits to those who possess them, but they are connected with benefits in the manner just indicated.

But more than this must be said against Hart's view. Unless we treat freedom itself as a benefit (and hence at once undermine Hart's thesis and risk that inflation of "freedom" we discussed in the introduction to Part IV), Hart's sharp separation between rights and benefits suggests that the question whether *A* benefits from having his or her right is irrelevant to deciding that it is a right that *A* has. It is true that *A* need not think that benefits derive from every exercise of the right or from every case in which *B* respects it. But what if *A* thinks that benefits *never* derive from the right? What, indeed, if *A* thinks that having the right is a great burden? Or what if all those in the society who are *A*'s in respect to a certain right or type of right uniformly think that the right is a burden they would rather be without?

Hart's thesis implies that we could go on saying, with a straight face as it were, that these people still have a right. And this is absurd.[2]

As Frankena suggests, a very similar point can be put in Hart's own terms. What Hart calls special rights result from promises, agreements, and other voluntary arrangements and transactions entered into by persons "capable of choice." And "general rights" are a direct, presumably intentional assertion of the equal right to freedom. In suggesting that benefits and harms are irrelevant to rights, Hart suggests that we can understand a very large class of voluntary actions, including those actions by which the members of a society create and sustain the procedures by which particular rights so often come into being, that we can understand this whole class of actions without considering the benefits and harms that the agents involved think they have derived from such actions and arrangements in the past and expect to derive from them in the future. (Or, again, he inflates the concept of freedom and restraints upon it to encompass all those benefits and harms.) This is a very strange conception of human action, and it is an understanding of "rights" that will never explain its extraordinary prominence in our affairs.

Hart is surely correct, however, that the concept does a distinctive job and that it loses its value if it is used, as it has been in recent years, in an excessively extended or indiscriminate manner. Talk about the rights of animals, of endangered species of trees, of lakes that are being polluted, indeed talk of the rights of the fetus, may be no more than a metaphorical way to talk about the rights of people to use unpolluted lakes or the duties of people toward the fetus and toward animals (and it may be no more than overheated rhetoric). Although they can hardly halt such talk, analysts must at least note the changes it works in the concept and enter a protest against its inflationary tendencies.

It might justly be responded, however, that the foregoing criticisms of Hart's theory of rights deprive analysts of any possibility of making such an analysis or entering such a protest. If such general concepts as benefit and harm are brought into the analysis of "rights," how can one object to talk about the rights of the fetus, of animals, and even of lakes and trees? For there is no doubt that the fetus can benefit from various actions and conditions (e.g., the dietary practices of the mother), that animals, lakes, and trees can be harmed (or at least damaged) by the actions of men.

In this perspective Joel Feinberg's analysis is attractive and promising. He argues that rights are a kind of claim. In expressing this claim A manifests his or her dignity as a human being. In mutually recognizing such claims, human beings manifest their acceptance of the fundamental human dignity that they express. As Feinberg's discussion of various human needs indicates, this dignity, although it most emphatically includes freedom, is not exhausted by the latter notion. We will not understand the range of legitimate right claims that have been advanced in recent years if we follow Hart in thinking that it does.

Nor does Feinberg's analysis leave us without defense against talk of the rights of animals and trees or against reducing "rights" to "welfare" and "illfare." Animals can benefit from and be harmed by many actions, conditions, and so forth.

---

[2] It is true that rights established and defined by a set of rules, especially legal rules that can only be changed by certain definite procedures, can sometimes be said to continue to hold despite widespread dislike and even repudiation of them. But we would speak of such rights only, as it were, in quotation marks and we would hardly expect to find them playing a prominent role in the society.

Although we may translate the imploring look or the sorrowful whimper into our concept of a plea or request, no animal can do so. The fetus, animals, and so forth do not engage in "performative claiming." Feinberg's "Nowheresville" would be a utopia for the creatures and entities to which the concept of rights has been (mis)applied in recent years. With further attention to the reasons why people claim the range of rights (substantively speaking) that they do, and with appropriate emphasis on the notion that the value of rights stems not *merely* from the benefits that one receives from their exercise but also from the distinctive manner in which, the distinctive conditions under which, one obtains those benefits, Feinberg's analysis can also take us a good distance toward an understanding of the special logic and advantages of the concept in discourse about human beings in a society.

Further Reading

Braybrooke, David. *Three Tests for Democracy*. New York: Random House, Inc., 1968.

Cranston, Maurice. *What Are Human Rights?* New York: Basic Books, Inc., 1962.

Feinberg, Joel. "Duties, Rights and Claims," *American Philosophical Quarterly*, Vol. 3 (1966), pp. 137–144.

Lyons, David. "Rights, Claimants and Beneficiaries," *American Philosophical Quarterly*, Vol. 6 (1969), pp. 173–185.

———. "The Correlativity of Rights and Duties," *Nous*, Vol. IV (1970), pp. 45–55.

McCloskey, H. J. "Rights," *Philosophical Quarterly*, Vol. 15 (1965), pp. 115–127.

MacDonald, Margaret. "Natural Rights," in Peter Laslett, *Philosophy, Politics and Society*, First Series. Oxford: Basil Blackwell, 1956.

Melden, A. I. *Human Rights*. Belmont, Calif.: Wadsworth Publishing Co., Inc., 1970.

———. *Rights and Right Conduct*. Oxford: Basil Blackwell, 1959.

The Monist, Vol. 52 (1968). Issue devoted to rights, including papers by W. T. Blackstone, M. P. Golding, Arnold S. Kaufman, Henry David Aiken, Kai Nielsen, and Herbert Morris.

Owens, Meirlys. "The Notion of Human Rights: A Reconsideration," *American Philosophical Quarterly*, Vol. 6 (1969), pp. 240–246.

Raphael, D. D. ed. *Political Theory and the Rights of Man*. Bloomington, Ind.: University of Indiana Press, 1967.

Srezednicki, J. "Rights and Rules," *The Philosophical Quarterly*, Vol. 21 (1971), pp. 315–333.

Wainright, W. I. "Natural Rights," *American Philosophical Quarterly*, Vol. 3 (1966), pp. 79–84.

Wasserstrom, Richard. "Rights, Human Rights, and Racial Discrimination," *Journal of Philosophy* (1964), pp. 628–641.

Weinstein, Michael. "Basic Political Rights," *Southern Journal of Philosophy*, Vol. 13 (1971), pp. 75–84.

26. Are There Any Natural Rights?[1]

H. L. A. Hart

I shall advance the thesis that if there are any moral rights at all, it follows that there is at least one natural right, the equal right of all men to be free. By saying that there is this right, I mean that in the absence of certain special conditions which are consistent with the right being an equal right, any adult human being capable of choice (1) has the right to forbearance on the part of all others from the use of coercion or restraint against him save to hinder coercion or restraint and (2) is at liberty to do (i.e., is under no obligation to abstain from) any action which is not one coercing or restraining or designed to injure other persons.[2]

I have two reasons for describing the equal right of all men to be free as a *natural* right; both of them were always emphasized by the classical theorists of natural rights. (1) This right is one which all men have if they are capable of choice; they have it *qua* men and not only if they are members of some society or stand in some special relation to each other. (2) This right is not created or conferred by men's voluntary action; other moral rights are.[3] Of course, it is quite obvious that my thesis is not as ambitious as the traditional theories of natural rights; for although on my view all men are *equally* entitled to be free in the sense explained, no man has an absolute or unconditional right to do or not to do any particular thing or to be treated in any particular way; coercion or restraint of any action may be justified in special conditions consistently with the general principle. So my argument will not show that men have any right (save the equal right of all to be free) which is "absolute," "indefeasible," or "imprescriptible." This may for many reduce the importance of my contention, but I think that the principle that all men have an equal right to be

From *Philosophical Review,* Vol. 64 (1955), pp. 175–191, by permission of the author and publisher.

[1] I was first stimulated to think along these lines by Mr. Stuart Hampshire, and I have reached by different routes a conclusion similar to his.

[2] Further explanation of the perplexing terminology of freedom is, I fear, necessary. *Coercion* includes, besides preventing a person from doing what he chooses, making his choice less eligible by threats; *restraint* includes any action designed to make the exercise of choice impossible and so includes killing or enslaving a person. But neither coercion nor restraint includes *competition*. In terms of the distinction between "having a right to" and "being at liberty to," used above and further discussed in Section I, B, all men may have, consistently with the obligation to forbear from coercion, the *liberty* to satisfy if they can such at least of their desires as are not designed to coerce or injure others, even though in fact, owing to scarcity, one man's satisfaction causes another's frustration. In conditions of extreme scarcity this distinction between competition and coercion will not be worth drawing; natural rights are only of importance "where peace is possible" (Locke). Further, freedom (the absence of coercion) can be *valueless* to those victims of unrestricted competition too poor to make use of it, so it will be pedantic to point out to them that though starving they are free. This is the truth exaggerated by the Marxists whose *identification* of poverty with lack of freedom confuses two different evils.

[3] Save those general rights (cf. Section II, B) which are particular exemplifications of the right of all men to be free.

free, meager as it may seem, is probably all that the political philosophers of the liberal tradition need have claimed to support any program of action even if they have claimed more. But my contention that there is this one natural right may appear unsatisfying in another respect; it is only the conditional assertion that *if* there are any moral rights then there must be this one natural right. Perhaps few would now deny, as some have, that there are moral rights; for the point of that denial was usually to object to some philosophical claim as to the "ontological status" of rights, and this objection is now expressed not as a denial that there are any moral rights but as a denial of some assumed logical similarity between sentences used to assert the existence of rights and other kinds of sentences. But it is still important to remember that there may be codes of conduct quite properly termed moral codes (though we can of course say they are "imperfect") which do not employ the notion of *a* right, and there is nothing contradictory or otherwise absurd in a code or morality consisting wholly of prescriptions or in a code which prescribed only what should be done for the realization of happiness or some ideal of personal perfection.[4] Human actions in such systems would be evaluated or criticised as compliances with prescriptions or as *good* or *bad, right* or *wrong, wise* or *foolish, fitting* or *unfitting,* but no one in such a system would have, exercise, or claim rights, or violate or infringe them. So those who lived by such systems could not of course be committed to the recognition of the equal right of all to be free; nor, I think (and this is one respect in which the notion of a right differs from other moral notions), could any parallel argument be constructed to show that, from the bare fact that actions were recognized as ones which ought or ought not to be done, as right, wrong, good or bad, it followed that some specific kind of conduct fell under these categories.

I

A. Lawyers have for their own purposes carried the dissection of the notion of a legal right some distance, and some of their results[5] are of value in the elucidation of statements of the form "X has a right to . . ." outside legal contexts. There is of course no simple identification to be made between moral and legal rights, but there is an intimate connection between the two, and this itself is one feature which distinguishes a moral right from other fundamental moral concepts. It is not merely that as a matter of fact men speak of their moral rights mainly when advocating their incorporation in a legal system, but that the concept of a right belongs to that branch of morality which is specifically concerned to determine when one person's freedom may be limited by another's[6] and so to determine what actions may

---

[4] Is the notion of a right found in either Plato or Aristotle? There seems to be no Greek word for it as distinct from "right" or "just" (δικαιον), though expressions like γα εμα δ ικαια are I believe fourth-century legal idioms. The natural expressions in Plato are γο εανγον (εχεω) or γα γωι οφειλομευα, but these seem confined to property or debts. There is no place for a moral right unless the moral value of individual freedom is recognized.

[5] As W. D. Lamont has seen: cf. his *Principles of Moral Judgment* (Oxford, 1946); for the jurists, cf. Hohfeld's *Fundamental Legal Conceptions* (New Haven, 1923).

[6] Here and subsequently I use "interfere with another's freedom," "limit another's freedom," "determine how another shall act," to mean either the use of coercion or demanding that a person shall do or not do some action. The connection between these two types of "interference" is too complex for discussion here; I think it is enough for present purposes to point out that having a justification for demanding that a person shall or shall not do some action is a necessary though not a sufficient condition for justifying coercion.

appropriately be made the subject of coercive legal rules. The words *"droit,"* *"diritto,"* and *"Recht,"* used by continental jurists, have no simple English translation and seem to English jurists to hover uncertainly between law and morals, but they do in fact mark off an area of morality (the morality of law) which has special characteristics. It is occupied by the concepts of justice, fairness, rights, and obligation (if this last is not used as it is by many moral philosophers as an obscuring general label to cover every action that morally we ought to do or forbear from doing). The most important common characteristic of this group of moral concepts is that there is no incongruity, but a special congruity in the use of force or the threat of force to secure that what is just or fair or someone's right to have done shall in fact be done; for it is in just these circumstances that coercion of another human being is legitimate. Kant, in the *Rechtslehre*, discusses the obligations which arise in this branch of morality under the title of *officia juris*, "which do not require that respect for duty shall be of itself the determining principle of the will," and contrasts them with *officia virtutis,* which have no moral worth unless done for the sake of the moral principle. His point is, I think, that we must distinguish from the rest of morality those principles regulating the proper distribution of human freedom which alone make it morally legitimate for one human being to determine by his choice how another should act; and a certain specific moral value is secured (to be distinguished from moral virtue in which the good will is manifested) if human relationships are conducted in accordance with these principles even though coercion has to be used to secure this, for only if these principles are regarded will freedom be distributed among human beings as it should be. And it is I think a very important feature of a moral right that the possessor of it is conceived as having a moral justification for limiting the freedom of another and that he has this justification not because the action he is entitled to require of another has some moral quality but simply because in the circumstances a certain distribution of human freedom will be maintained if he by his choice is allowed to determine how that other shall act.

B. I can best exhibit this feature of a moral right by reconsidering the question whether moral rights and "duties"[7] are correlative. The contention that they are means, presumably, that every statement of the form "X has a right to . . ." entails and is entailed by "Y has a duty (not) to . . .," and at this stage we must not assume that the values of the name-variables "X" and "Y" must be different persons. Now there is certainly one sense of "a right" (which I have already mentioned) such that it does not follow from X's having a right that X or someone else has any duty. Jurists have isolated rights in this sense and have referred to them as "liberties" just to distinguish them from rights in the centrally important sense of "right" which has "duty" as a correlative. The former sense of "right" is needed to describe those areas of social life where competition is at least morally unobjectionable. Two

---

[7] I write " 'duties' " here because one factor obscuring the nature of a right is the philosophical use of "duty" and "obligation" for all cases where there are moral reasons for saying an action ought to be done or not done. In fact "duty," "obligation," "right," and "good" come from different segments of morality, concern different types of conduct, and make different types of moral criticism or evaluation. Most important are the points (1) that obligations may be voluntarily incurred or created, (2) that they are *owed to* special persons (who have rights), (3) that they do not arise out of the character of the actions which are obligatory but out of the relationship of the parties. Language roughly though not consistently confines the use of "having an obligation" to such cases.

people walking along both see a ten-dollar bill in the road twenty yards away, and there is no clue as to the owner. Neither of the two are under a "duty" to allow the other to pick it up; each has in this sense a right to pick it up. Of course there may be many things which each has a "duty" not to do in the course of the race to the spot — neither may kill or wound the other — and corresponding to these "duties" there are rights to forbearances. The moral propriety of all economic competition implies this minimum sense of a "a right" in which to say that "X has a right to" means merely that X is under no "duty" not to. Hobbes saw that the expression "a right" could have this sense but he was wrong if he thought that there is no sense in which it does follow from X's having a right that Y has a duty or at any rate an obligation.

C. More important for our purpose is the question whether for all moral "duties" there are correlative moral rights, because those who have given an affirmative answer to this question have usually assumed without adequate scrutiny that to have a right is simply to be capable of benefiting by the performance of a "duty"; whereas in fact this is not a sufficient condition (and probably not a necessary condition) of having a right. Thus animals and babies who stand to benefit by our performance of our "duty" not to ill-treat them are said *therefore* to have rights to proper treatment. The full consequence of this reasoning is not usually followed out; most have shrunk from saying that we have rights against ourselves because we stand to benefit from our performance of our "duty" to keep ourselves alive or develop our talents. But the moral situation which arises from a promise (where the legal-sounding terminology of rights and obligations is most appropriate) illustrates most clearly that the notion of having a right and that of benefiting by the performance of a "duty" are not identical. X promises Y in return for some favor that he will look after Y's aged mother in his absence. Rights arise out of this transaction, but it is surely Y to whom the promise has been made and not his mother who *has* or *possesses* these rights. Certainly Y's mother is a person concerning whom X has an obligation and a person who will benefit by its performance, but the person *to whom* he has an obligation to look after her is Y. There is something *due to* or *owed to* Y, so it is Y, not his mother, whose right X will disregard and to whom X will have done *wrong* if he fails to keep his promise, though the mother may be physically injured. And it is Y who has a moral *claim* upon X, is *entitled* to have his mother looked after, and who can *waive* the claim and *release* Y from the obligation. Y is, in other words, morally in a position to determine by his choice how X shall act and in this way to limit X's freedom of choice; and it is this fact, not the fact that he stands to benefit, that makes it appropriate to say that he has *a right*. Of course often the person to whom a promise has been made will be the only person who stands to benefit by its performance, but this does not justify the identification of "having a right" with "benefiting by the performance of a duty." It is important for the whole logic of rights that, while the person who stands to benefit by the performance of a duty is discovered by considering what will happen if the duty is not performed, the person who has a right (to whom performance is *owed* or *due*) is discovered by examining the transaction or antecedent situation or relations of the parties out of which the "duty" arises. These considerations should incline us not to extend to animals and babies whom it is wrong to ill-treat the notion of a right to proper treatment, for the moral situation can be simply and adequately described here by saying that it is wrong or that we ought not to ill-treat them or, in the philosopher's generalized sense of "duty," that we have a duty not to ill-treat them.[8] If common usage sanctions talk of the rights of animals or babies it makes an idle use of the expression "a right," which will confuse the situation with other different moral situations where the expression "a right" has a specific force and cannot be replaced by the other moral expressions which I have mentioned. Perhaps some clarity on this matter is to be gained by considering the force of the preposition "to" in the expression "having a duty to Y" or "being under an obligation to Y" (where "Y" is the name of a person); for it is significantly different from the meaning of "to" in "doing something to Y" or "doing harm to Y," where it indicates the person affected by some action. In the first pair of expressions, "to" obviously does not have this force, but indicates the person to whom the person morally bound is bound. This is an intelligible development of the figure of a bond (*vinculum juris: obligare*); the precise figure is not that of two persons bound by a chain, but of *one* person bound, the other end of the chain lying in the hands of another to use if he chooses.[9] So it appears absurd to speak of having duties or owing obligations to ourselves — of course we may have "duties" not to do harm to ourselves, but what could be meant (once the distinction between these different meanings of "to" has been grasped) by insisting that we have duties or obligations *to* ourselves not to do harm to ourselves?

D. The essential connection between the notion of a right and the justified limitation of one person's freedom by another may be thrown into relief if we consider codes of behavior which do not purport to confer rights but only to prescribe what shall be done. Most natural law thinkers down to Hooker conceived of natural law in this way: there were natural duties compliance with which would certainly benefit man — things to be done to achieve man's natural end — but not natural rights. And there are of course many types of codes of behavior which only prescribe what is to be done, e.g., those regulating certain ceremonies. It would be absurd to regard these codes as conferring rights, but illuminating to contrast them with rules of games, which often create rights, though not, of course, moral rights. But even a code which is plainly a moral code need not establish rights; the Decalogue is perhaps the most important example. Of course, quite apart from heavenly rewards human beings stand to benefit by general obedience to the Ten Commandments: disobedience is wrong and will certainly harm individuals. But it would be a surprising interpretation of them that treated them as conferring rights. In such an interpretation obedience to the Ten Commandments would have to be conceived as due to or owed to individuals, not merely to God, and disobedience not merely as wrong but as *a wrong to* (as well as harm to) individuals. The Commandments would cease to read like penal statutes designed only to rule out certain types of behavior and would have to be thought of as rules placed at the disposal of individuals and regulating the extent to which *they* may demand certain behavior from others. Rights are typically conceived of as *possessed* or *belonging to* individuals, and these expressions reflect the conception of moral rules as not only prescribing conduct but as forming a kind of moral property of individuals to which they are as individuals entitled; only when rules are conceived in this way can we speak of *rights* and *wrongs* as well as right and wrong actions.[10]

---

[8] The use here of the generalized "duty" is apt to prejudice the question whether animals and babies have rights.

[9] Cf. A. H. Campbell, *The Structure of Stair's Institutes* (Glasgow, 1954), p. 31.

II

So far I have sought to establish that to have a right entails having a moral justification for limiting the freedom of another person and for determining how he should act; it is now important to see that the moral justification must be of a special kind if it is to constitute a right, and this will emerge most clearly from an examination of the circumstances in which rights are asserted with the typical expression "I have a right to. . . ." It is I think the case that this form of words is used in two main types of situations: (A) when the claimant has some special justification for interference with another's freedom which other persons do not have ("*I* have a right to be paid what you promised for my services"); (B) when the claimant is concerned to resist or object to some interference by another person as having no justification ("*I* have a right to say what I think").

A. *Special Rights.* When rights arise out of special transactions between individuals or out of special relationship in which they stand to each other, both the persons who have the right and those who have the corresponding obligation are limited to the parties to the special transaction or relationship. I call such rights special rights to distinguish them from those moral rights which are thought of as rights against (i.e., as imposing obligations upon)[11] everyone, such as those that are asserted when some unjustified interference is made or threatened as in (B) above.

i. The most obvious cases of special rights are those that arise from promises. By promising to do or not to do something, we voluntarily incur obligations and create or confer rights on those to whom we promise; we alter the existing moral independence of the parties' freedom of choice in relation to some action and create a new moral relationship between them, so that it becomes morally legitimate for the person to whom the promise is given to determine how the promisor shall act. The promisee has a temporary authority or sovereignty in relation to some specific matter over the other's will which we express by saying that the promisor is under an obligation *to* the promisee to do what he has promised. To some philosophers the notion that moral phenomena – rights and duties or obligations – can be brought into existence by the voluntary action of individuals has appeared utterly mysterious; but this I think has been so because they have not clearly seen how special the moral notions of a right and an obligation are, nor how peculiarly they are connected with the distribution of freedom of choice; it would indeed be mysterious if we could make actions morally good or bad by voluntary choice. The simplest case of promising illustrates two points characteristic of all special rights: (1) the right and obligation arise not because the promised action has itself any particular moral quality, but just because of the voluntary transaction between the parties; (2) the identity of the parties concerned is vital – only *this* person (the promisee) has the moral justification for determining how the promisor shall act. It is *his* right; only in relation to him is the promisor's freedom of choice diminished, so that if he chooses to release the promisor no one else can complain.

[10] Continental jurists distinguish between "*subjektives*" and "*objektives Recht*," which corresponds very well to the distinction between *a* right, which an individual has, and what it is right to do.

[11] Cf. Section B below.

ii. But a promise is not the only kind of transaction whereby rights are conferred. They may be *accorded* by a person consenting or authorizing another to interfere in matters which but for this consent or authorization he would be free to determine for himself. If I consent to your taking precautions for my health or happiness or authorize you to look after my interests, then you have a right which others have not, and I cannot complain of your interference if it is within the sphere of your authority. This is what is meant by a person surrendering his rights to another; and again the typical characteristics of a right are present in this situation: the person authorized has the right to interfere not because of its intrinsic character but because *these* persons have stood in *this* relationship. No one else (not similarly authorized) has any *right*[12] to interfere in theory even if the person authorized does not exercise his right.

iii. Special rights are not only those created by the deliberate choice of the party on whom the obligation falls, as they are when they are accorded or spring from promises, and not all obligations to other persons are deliberately incurred, though I think it is true of all special rights that they arise from previous voluntary actions. A third very important source of special rights and obligations which we recognize in many spheres of life is what may be termed mutuality of restrictions, and I think political obligation is intelligible only if we see what precisely this is and how it differs from the other right-creating transactions (consent, promising) to which philosophers have assimilated it. In its bare schematic outline it is this: when a number of persons conduct any joint enterprise according to rules and thus restrict their liberty, those who have submitted to these restrictions when required have a right to a similar submission from those who have benefited by their submission. The rules may provide that officials should have authority to enforce obedience and make further rules, and this will create a structure of legal rights and duties, but the moral obligation to obey the rules in such circumstances is *due to* the co-operating members of the society, and they have the correlative moral right to obedience. In social situations of this sort (of which political society is the most complex example) the obligation to obey the rules is something distinct from whatever other moral reasons there may be for obedience in terms of good consequences (e.g., the prevention of suffering); the obligation is due to the co-operating members of the society as such and not because they are human beings on whom it would be wrong to inflict suffering. The utilitarian explanation of political obligation fails to take account of this feature of the situation both in its simple version that the obligation exists because and only if the direct consequences of a particular act of disobedience are worse than obedience, and also in its more sophisticated version that the obligation exists even when this is not so, if disobedience increases the probability that the law in question or other laws will be disobeyed on other occasions when the direct consequences of obedience are better than those of disobedience.

Of course to say that there is such a moral obligation upon those who have benefited by the submission of other members of society to restrictive rules to obey these rules in their turn does not entail either that this is the only kind of moral reason for obedience or that there can be no cases where disobedience will be morally justified. There is no contradiction or other impropriety in saying "I have

---

[12] Though it may be *better* (the lesser of two evils) that he should: cf. p. 447.

an obligation to do X, someone has a right to ask me to, but I now see I ought not to do it." It will in painful situations sometimes be the lesser of two moral evils to disregard what really are people's rights and not perform our obligations to them. This seems to me particularly obvious from the case of promises: I may promise to do something and thereby incur an obligation just because that is one way in which obligations (to be distinguished from other forms of moral reasons for acting) are created; reflection may show that it would in the circumstances be wrong to keep this promise because of the suffering it might cause, and we can express this by saying "*I ought not* to do it though *I have an obligation to him* to do it" just because the italicized expressions are not synonyms but come from different dimensions of morality. The attempt to explain this situation by saying that our real obligation here is to avoid the suffering and that there is only a prima facie obligation to keep the promise seems to me to confuse two quite different kinds of moral reason, and in practice such a terminology obscures the precise character of what is at stake when "for some greater good" we infringe people's rights or do not perform our obligations to them.

The social-contract theorists rightly fastened on the fact that the obligation to obey the law is not merely a special case of benevolence (direct or indirect), but something which arises between members of a particular political society out of their mutual relationship. Their mistake was to identify *this* right-creating situation of mutual restrictions with the paradigm case of promising; there are of course important similarities, and these are just the points which all special rights have in common, viz., that they arise out of special relationships between human beings and not out of the character of the action to be done or its effects.

iv. There remains a type of situation which may be thought of as creating rights and obligations: where the parties have a special natural relationship, as in the case of parent and child. The parent's moral right to obedience from his child would I suppose now be thought to terminate when the child reaches the age "of discretion," but the case is worth mentioning because some political philosophies have had recourse to analogies with this case as an explanation of political obligation, and also because even this case has some of the features we have distinguished in special rights, viz., the right arises out of the special relationship of the parties (though it is in this case a natural relationship) and not out of the character of the actions to the performance of which there is a right.

v. To be distinguished from special rights, of course, are special liberties, where, exceptionally, one person is *exempted* from obligations to which most are subject but does not thereby acquire a *right* to which there is a correlative obligation. If you catch me reading your brother's diary, you say, "You have no right to read it." I say, "I have a right to read it — your brother said I might unless he told me not to, and he has not told me not to." Here I have been specially *licensed* by your brother who has a right to require me not to read his diary, so I am exempted from the moral obligation not to read it, but your brother is under no obligation to let me go on reading it. Cases where *rights,* not liberties, are accorded to manage or interfere with another person's affairs are those where the license is not revocable at will by the person according the right.

B. *General Rights.* In contrast with special rights, which constitute a justification peculiar to the holder of the right for interfering with another's freedom, are general rights, which are asserted defensively, when some unjustified interference is anticipated or threatened, in order to point out that the interference is unjustified. "I have the right to say what I think."[13] "I have the right to worship as I please." Such rights share two important characteristics with special rights. (1) To have them is to have a moral justification for determining how another shall act, viz., that he shall not interfere.[14] (2) The moral justification does not arise from the character of the particular action to the performance of which the claimant has a right; what justifies the claim is simply — there being no special relation between him and those who are threatening to interfere to justify that interference — that this is a particular exemplification of the equal right to be free. But there are of course striking differences between such defensive general rights and special rights. (1) General rights do not arise out of any special relationship or transaction between men. (2) They are not rights which are peculiar to those who have them but are rights which all men capable of choice have in the absence of those special conditions which give rise to special rights. (3) General rights have as correlatives obligations not to interfere to which everyone else is subject and not merely the parties to some special relationship or transaction, though of course they will often be asserted when some particular persons threaten to interfere as a moral objection to that interference. To assert a general right is to claim in relation to some particular action the equal right of all men to be free in the absence of any of those special conditions which constitute a special right to limit another's freedom; to assert a special right is to assert in relation to some particular action a right constituted by such special conditions to limit another's freedom. The assertion of general rights directly invokes the principle that all men equally have the right to be free; the assertion of a special right (as I attempt to show in Section III) invokes it indirectly.

III

It is, I hope, clear that unless it is recognized that interference with another's freedom requires a moral justification the notion of a right could have no place in morals; for to assert a right is to assert that there is such a justification. The characteristic function in moral discourse of those sentences in which the meaning of the expression "a right" is to be found — "I have a right to. . ."You have no right to. . . .," "What right have you to. . . ?" — is to bring to bear on interferences with another's freedom, or on claims to interfere, a type of moral evaluation or criticism specially appropriate to interference with freedom and characteristically different from the moral criticism of actions made with the use of expressions like "right," "wrong," "good," and "bad." And this is only one of many

[13] In speech the difference between general and special rights is often marked by stressing the pronoun where a special right is claimed or where the special right is denied. "You have no right to stop him reading that book" refers to the reader's right. "*You* have no right to stop him reading that book" denies that the person addressed has a special right to interfere though others may have.

[14] Strictly, in the assertion of a general right both the *right* to forbearance from coercion and the *liberty* to do the specified action are asserted, the first in the face of actual or threatened coercion, the second as an objection to an actual or anticipated demand that the action should not be done. The first has as its correlative an obligation upon everyone to forbear from coercion; the second the absence in any one of a justification for such a demand. Here, in Hohfeld's words. the correlative is not an obligation but a "no-right."

different types of moral ground for saying "You ought..." or "You ought not...." The use of the expression "What right have you to...?" shows this more clearly, perhaps, than the others; for we use it, just at the point where interference is actual or threatened, to call for the moral *title* of the person addressed to interfere; and we do this often without any suggestion at all that what he proposes to do is otherwise wrong and sometimes with the implication that the same interference on the part of another person would be unobjectionable.

But though our use in moral discourse of "a right" does presuppose the recognition that interference with another's freedom requires a moral justification, this would not itself suffice to establish, except in a sense easily trivialized, that in the recognition of moral rights there is implied the recognition that all men have a right to equal freedom; for unless there is some restriction inherent in the meaning of "a right" on the type of moral justification for interference which can constitute a right, the principle could be made wholly vacuous. It would, for example, be possible to adopt the principle and then assert that some characteristic or behavior of some human beings (that they are improvident, or atheists, or Jews, or Negroes) constitutes a moral justification for interfering with their freedom; *any* differences between men could, so far as my argument has yet gone, be treated as a moral justification for interference and so constitute a right, so that the equal right of all men to be free would be compatible with gross inequality. It may well be that the expression "moral" itself imports some restriction on what can constitute a moral justification for interference which would avoid this consequence, but I cannot myself yet show that this is so. It is, on the other hand, clear to me that the moral justification for interference which is to constitute a *right* to interfere (as distinct from merely making it morally good or desirable to interfere) is restricted to certain special conditions and that this is inherent in the meaning of "a right" (unless this is used so loosely that it could be replaced by the other moral expressions mentioned). Claims to interfere with another's freedom based on the general character of the activities interfered with (e.g., the folly or cruelty of "native" practices) or the general character of the parties ("We are Germans; they are Jews") even when well founded are not matters of moral right or obligation. Submission in such cases even where proper is not *due to* or *owed to* the individuals who interfere; it would be equally proper whoever of the same class of persons interfered. Hence other elements in our moral vocabulary suffice to describe this case, and it is confusing here to talk of rights. We saw in Section II that the types of justification for interference involved in special rights was independent of the character of the action to the performance of which there was a right but depended upon certain previous transactions and relations between individuals (such as promises, consent, authorization, submission to mutual restrictions). Two questions here suggest themselves: (1) On what intelligible principle could these bare forms of promising, consenting, submission to mutual restrictions, be either necessary or sufficient, irrespective of their content, to justify interference with another's freedom? (2) What characteristics have these types of transaction or relationship in common? The answer to both these questions is I think this: If we justify interference on such grounds as we give when we claim a moral right, we are in fact indirectly invoking as our justification the principle that all men have an equal right to be free. For we are in fact saying in the case of promises and consents or authorizations that this claim to interfere with another's freedom is justified because he has, in exercise of his equal right to be free, freely chosen to create this claim; and in the case of mutual restrictions we are in fact saying that this claim to interfere with another's freedom is justified because it is fair; and it is fair because only so will there be an equal distribution of restrictions and so of freedom among this group of men. So in the case of special rights as well as of general rights recognition of them implies the recognition of the equal right of all men to be free.

27. Natural and Inalienable Rights

William Frankena

I

Hart's paper consists mainly of an attempt to establish the thesis "that if there are any moral rights at all it follows that there is at least one natural right, the equal right of all men to be free." I shall deal with his argument step by step, together with some of the discussions incidental to it. The first main step is the contention that to have or assert a moral right is to have or assert a moral justification for limiting or interfering with the freedom of another by insisting that he act or refrain from acting in a certain way. For example, if A promises B a ride, then B has a right to that ride and thus a moral justification for insisting that A give it to him. With this step, which involves a point not often noticed, I shall not quarrel. In connection with it, however, Hart discusses the stock question of the correlativity of rights and duties in a novel way. He says that, except for rights of the kind he calls "liberties," my having a right entails someone's having an obligation. I am not sure whether he denies that obligations entail rights or not. He does, however, distinguish between *obligations* and *duties*, and he is concerned to maintain that duties at least do not imply corresponding rights seeming at the same time to hold that my having an obligation does not involve my having a duty or vice versa, and that my having a right does not imply your having a duty). He contends that those who hold that all moral duties imply correlative moral rights "have usually assumed . . . that to have a right is simply to be capable of benefiting by the performance of a 'duty.' " This seems to me questionable; deontological moralists have traditionally regarded rights and duties as correlative, but can hardly have been assuming that having a right entails standing to benefit by the action in question. Hart goes on to argue that being capable of benefiting or standing to benefit by the performance of a "duty" is not a sufficient (and probably not a necessary) condition of having a moral right. Suppose, he says, that A promises B that he will care for B's mother. Then B has a right to expect A to care for his mother, but it is

From *Philosophical Review*, Vol. 64 (1955), pp. 213–221, by permission of the author and publisher.

B's mother, not B, who stands to benefit; and A has an obligation to B even though it is not B, but B's mother, who stands to benefit.

Even if we admit that this case shows that standing to benefit from an action is neither a necessary nor a sufficient condition of having a right to its performance, it may still be that in order for B to have a right someone must stand to benefit. If we are so antiteleological as to deny this also, we should still have to distinguish, as Hart does not, between "standing to benefit" and "being capable of benefiting" by an action. It does seem to me that in order to have rights one must be the sort of being that is capable of benefiting by actions, at least in the sense of being capable of satisfaction, suffering, and the like. Hart seems to imply sometimes that only the capacity for choice is a prerequisite for having rights, but it is hard to believe this, if the capacity for choice is not accompanied by a capacity for the enjoyment of good or evil in any degree. To say that having rights presupposes a general susceptibility to pleasure, satisfaction, or benefit of some kind is not to say that rights are proportional to actual or expected benefits, or that the moral justification of a claim or act must always consist simply in a consideration of such benefits. Woven into Hart's discussion here and elsewhere is his view that we must distinguish the sphere of morality to which rights and *obligations* belong from that to which *ought* and *duties* belong. The right to have a promise kept and the obligation to keep it pertain to one of these spheres, and the duty to relieve suffering pertains to the other. In the latter there are, properly speaking, no rights, in the former no duties. Rights and duties do not entail one another, nor do obligations and duties. One may have an obligation to do something (because he promised to) and yet have a duty not to do it (because it will cause suffering), and the latter may take precedence over the former.

This is an intriguing doctrine, but Hart leaves his exposition of it somewhat cryptic and fragmentary, and I remain unconvinced that morality involves quite this kind of dualism. Two considerations seem to lead Hart to think that it does: (1) the fact that part of morality "may be appropriately made the subject of coercive legal rules," while the rest may not, and (2) his claim that "two quite different kinds of moral reason" are involved in the two spheres, by which he seems to mean that in the former moral justification consists in an appeal to the equal right to freedom, and in the latter in an appeal to actual or possible benefits, suffering, etc. The first, however, has usually been recognized by moralists who identify obligation and duty and assert the full correlativity of rights and duties, and the second is analogous to the old distinction between justice and benevolence, which also has often been recognized by such moralists. Neither seems to require us to take Hart's position.

In any case, morality does not appear to fall apart in just the way Hart suggests. He himself talks as if making a promise always conveys a right, but some promises belong to the area which is appropriately covered by law, and others do not. Here then we may properly speak of rights, even when legal coercion is not present or desirable. Again, to take a different kind of case, it seems quite proper for a person who is being made to suffer by another to say, "You have no right to make me suffer so." In some such cases it would be appropriate that there be legal coercion, while in others it would not. Possibly one should speak of a right only in the former cases, but the only reason for this would seem to be that then one would not be using the same term in two different kinds of situation, and even then there would still be rights whose recognition involves an appeal, not to the right to freedom, but to consequences in terms of suffering.

It is tempting, therefore, to deal with this whole matter, as some earlier Oxford moralists did, by speaking of prima facie as well as actual rights, duties, and obligations, and by regarding "duties" and "obligations" as synonymous and rights and duties as correlative.[1] One can then admit both of the considerations by which Hart seems to be influenced, and at the same time take care of the cases I have just cited against him. One can also, of course, provide for the fact that the duty to relieve suffering may outweigh the obligation to keep a promise (or distribute freedom), by saying that two prima facie duties (or obligations) are involved, and that in the case in question the prima facie duty to relieve suffering takes precedence over that of keeping a promise, so that the agent's actual duty (or obligation) is to relieve the suffering. Hart sees this, but rejects such a treatment of the situation on the ground that it confuses "two quite different kinds of moral reason" and "obscures the precise character of what is at stake when 'for some greater good' we infringe people's rights or do not perform our obligations to them," However, as I have already mentioned, deontological moralists have generally recognized at least two different kinds of moral reason; and, in any case. it will hardly do to assume that morality falls into two spheres in a more drastic way than they realize, for that is just the question at issue. As for the judgment that their way of speaking obscures what is at stake when the consideration of consequences in terms of good is given precedence over a right or obligation – this is much too cryptic to be decisive as it stands. So far as I can see, Hart can only say that when this happens one sort of "moral justification" is given more weight than another, and I do not see that this differs essentially from saying that one prima facie duty is regarded as more stringent than the other.

No doubt there would be some gain in having different terms where distinct kinds of moral justification are involved, especially if legal coercion is appropriate in one case and not in the other. But the gain would not consist in a greater accordance either with ordinary usage or with that of moral philosophers, as Hart seems to admit, and it is counterbalanced by the fact that morality would be made to appear more dualistic than it is. Hart himself talks about "moral justification" in dealing with both spheres of morality, and it must have a common meaning in the two areas, for, if the duty to relieve suffering may outweigh the obligation to keep a promise, duty and obligation must be somehow commensurable. Then the two spheres cannot be so disparate as he claims they are, and do not require distinct vocabularies.

II

Hart's second main step is to contend that "the moral justification must be of a special kind if it is to constitute a right" – it must consist in a direct or indirect appeal to the equal right to be free. His argumentation on this point is not entirely clear, and I shall restate it in my own way as I deal with it. Partly he seems to be maintaining that to assert or recognize a moral right is to assert or recognize a moral justification for limiting the freedom of another, and that this directly or

---

[1] For a brief statement of this view, and some references, see my paper in the American Philosophical Association volume, *Science, Language and Human Rights* (1952), pp. 196–197, 207.

indirectly involves asserting or recognizing the equal right of all to be free. But how does it involve recognizing this more basic right? Hart's answer seems to be that claiming a moral justification for limiting another's freedom involves recognizing that limiting another's freedom requires a moral justification, and that this in turn presupposes a recognition of the equal right to freedom. The first part of this answer is not obvious, but let us grant that there is a sense in which it is true. Then it shows that the recognition of any moral right in some sense entails a recognition of the right to equal freedom.

However, Hart does not stop here, as one might expect, and his reason for not doing so may be put as follows. The notion of a moral right involves a recognition that interfering with another's freedom requires a moral justification. This means that it implies (1) a recognition that all men have an equal right to freedom and (2) a claim that there often is or may be a moral justification for interfering with another's freedom. But then the notion of a right implies that the equal right of all to be free is compatible with there being a moral justification (and so a right) to interfere with the freedom of some. And then the conclusion that moral rights entail the natural right to equal freedom can be trivialized by adding that A is morally justified in interfering with B's freedom if B is colored, Jewish, etc. Therefore some restriction must be found in the very notion of a right on the kind of consideration which justifies limiting another's freedom. Else the whole point of the doctrine of natural rights is lost.

Now, I should be inclined to say that being colored, etc., simply are not considerations of a kind which morally justify restricting a person's freedom. Hart, however, is not satisfied with this. He studies various kinds of rights to see what it is that justifies limiting another's freedom in each case, arguing that, directly or indirectly, it is the equal right to freedom that does so. Take, for instance, a general right like the right to say what we think. My having this right entails my having a moral justification for limiting the freedom of another who threatens to interfere with my freedom to say what I think. Here it seems clear that what justifies my limiting his freedom is my having the equal right to be free, and so Hart has no trouble in showing that if there are general rights then there is a right to be free; in fact, as he points out, these general rights are merely "particular exemplifications of the right of all men to be free."

Now take a special right like B's right to the ride A has promised him. What is it that justifies B's insisting on A's giving him the ride? Not any moral quality in the action insisted on as such, but the fact that A promised to do it. Why does A's promising B a ride justify B in insisting on having it? I should have said it was because of the rule that promises ought to be kept. But Hart claims that A's promising confers a right on B because A "in the exercise of his equal right to be free, freely [chose] to create this claim." That is, he offers the equal right to be free as that which underlies the obligation to keep a promise and the right to have it kept. This is interesting, but again I remain unconvinced. Saying that A in the exercise of his equal right to be free freely chose to promise B a ride seems to be just a way of saying that he freely promised B a ride, and, of course, B has a right to the ride only if A freely promised it to him. A's *being* free, then, is presupposed, but it is not clear that his having the *right* to be free is. In promising, A freely confers on B the right to limit his freedom, but in what way does his doing this imply that he has a right to be free? It is possible that A can make a binding promise only if he is free to make it, not merely in the sense of not being under any constraint to do so or not to do so, but in the sense of having a right to make it, and that his having a right to make it presupposes his having a right to be free. But this is not obvious, and I am not sure Hart means to maintain it. In another place, he suggests that what justifies one man's limiting the freedom of another is always the fact that "a certain distribution of human freedom will be maintained if he by his choice is allowed to determine how that other shall act." But he does not explain how this applies in the case of rights based on promises, and it is not easy to see how it does.

Either, then, the exposition of his argument is incomplete, or it does not establish his thesis that the justification of every claim to a moral right depends on the equal right of all to be free. This thesis is plausible in the case of general rights and of special rights based on mutual restrictions, but it is not clearly true in the case of other special rights. Hart does not even really try to show that it holds in the case of rights depending on a special natural relationship, as in the case of parent and child. And if there are other rights, such as a right to be told the truth, a right to gratitude for benefits done, a right to assistance, or a right not to be made to suffer, then it is certainly not clear that all moral rights presuppose the equal right to be free, for Hart does not treat these at all. This does not mean that there is no natural right to equal freedom, but it does mean that Hart has not shown that there is, even hypothetically. It also means that he has not shown that morality falls into two parts in the way in which he claims it does.

III

However this may be, I do not wish to deny that all men have an equal right to be free, or that this is a natural right. Only I should like to assert it categorically. Hart's objection to this, which he also uses against the correlativity of duties and rights, is that "there may be codes of conduct quite properly termed moral codes . . . which do not employ the notion of *a* right," and which are therefore not "committed to the recognition of the equal right of all to be free." This is puzzling, and I am inclined to answer by taking a cue from Brown, arguing that if a people in a certain culture do not recognize moral rights they may and do still have them. In any case, however, the question whether people have moral rights or not is surely a normative question, even if it is relative to the moral code of the questioner and his culture. But if this is so, then an affirmative answer to it need not be affected by the fact that some cultures do not recognize such rights. Moreover, the objection proves too much, if it proves anything, since, so far as I can see, there may also be cultures which recognize moral rights without recognizing any natural right to equal freedom. Unless Hart is willing to regard his own thesis as blocked by such a possibility, and I should agree that it is not, it would seem that this sort of consideration is not fatal to the categorical assertion that men have natural rights, or that duties entail rights.

Yet, while I am in a sense more ready than Hart is to affirm a natural right of all to be free, I do have certain questions about it. (a) Is it our natural right? Hart does not say so, but that it is seems implied by his insistence that rights obtain only in the part of morality where the equal right to be free is the basis of moral reasoning. If this contention is questioned, however, and we have seen that it may be, then there is no reason for denying that there are also natural rights to life and happiness. Perhaps one can argue that these rights are really included in the equal right to be free. This is suggested by Roosevelt's proclamation of the four freedoms, which lists freedom from want and fear along with freedom of expression and worship. But then the right to freedom is complex in a way in which Hart seems to deny it to be complex.[2] (b) Hart says that freedom is not an inalienable right, but implies in one place that the equal right to be free is indefeasible. But just what does "the equal right of all to be free" mean? Does it mean that all men alike have the right to be free? This seems implied when Hart says that interference with another's freedom requires a moral justification. But the right to be free is not inalienable, unless it is taken to be a prima facie right, and Hart rejects such a view. Shall we say that each man has a right to be as free as any other? But this is not indefeasible either, unless it is regarded as a prima facie right. It must then be equality rather than freedom which is an inalienable right. I am not necessarily entitled to the same amount of freedom as any other man, but I am just as entitled to be free as he is, in a sense which is valid even when there is a moral justification for giving me less freedom than he enjoys. But to say this is to say that, if there is no consideration which morally justifies varying limitations on our freedom, then we are entitled to be equally free. But then why not say also that, if there are no considerations justifying limiting one's freedom, then he has a right to be completely free?

It looks, therefore, as if it would be best to say that "the equal right to be free" breaks up into two prima facie rights — a right to equality and a right to freedom, both of which are indefeasible qua prima facie rights (that is, it is always true that there must be a moral justification for not respecting them) and neither of which is always an actual right (that is, there sometimes is a moral justification for denying them).

---

[2] Even Hart regards it as complex in a way, for he holds that it exemplifies itself in a number of "general rights" Incidentally, would he regard it as wrong to speak of each of these general rights as a natural right?

28. The Nature and Value of Rights

Joel Feinberg

I

I would like to begin by conducting a thought experiment. Try to imagine Nowheresville — a world very much like our own except that no one, or hardly any one (the qualification is not important), has *rights*. If this flaw makes Nowheresville too ugly to hold very long in contemplation, we can make it as pretty as we wish in other moral respects. We can, for example, make the human beings in it as attractive and virtuous as possible without taxing our conceptions of the limits of human nature. In particular, let the virtues of moral sensibility flourish. Fill this imagined world with as much benevolence, compassion, sympathy, and pity as it will conveniently hold without strain. Now we can imagine men helping one another from compassionate motives merely, quite as much or even more than they do in our actual world from a variety of more complicated motives.

This picture, pleasant as it is in some respects, would hardly have satisfied Immanuel Kant. Benevolently motivated actions do good, Kant admitted, and therefore are better, *ceteris paribus,* than malevolently motivated actions; but no action can have supreme kind of worth—what Kant called "moral worth"—unless its whole motivating power derives from the thought that it is *required by duty.* Accordingly, let us try to make Nowheresville more appealing to Kant by introducing the idea of duty into it, and letting the sense of duty be a sufficient motive for many beneficent and honorable actions. But doesn't this bring our original thought experiment to an abortive conclusion? If duties are permitted entry into Nowheresville, are not rights necessarily smuggled in along with them?

The question is well-asked, and requires here a brief digression so that we might consider the so-called "doctrine of the logical correlativity of rights and duties." This is the doctrine that (i) all duties entail other people's rights and (ii) all rights entail other people's duties. Only the first part of the doctrine, the alleged entailment from duties to rights, need concern us here. Is this part of the doctrine correct? It should not be surprising that my answer is: "In a sense yes and in a sense no." Etymologically, the word "duty" is associated with actions that are *due* someone else, the payments of debts *to* creditors, the keeping of agreements with promises, the payment of club dues, or legal fees, or tariff levies to appropriate authorities or their representatives. In this original sense of "duty," all duties are correlated with the rights of those *to* whom the duty is owed. On the other hand, there seem to be numerous classes of duties, both of a legal and non-legal kind, that are *not* logically correlated with the rights of other persons. This seems to be a consequence of the fact that the word "duty" has come to be used for *any* action understood to be *required,* whether by the rights of others, or by law, or by higher

From *The Journal of Value Inquiry,* Vol. 4 (1970), 243–257, by permission of the author and publisher.

authority, or by conscience, or whatever. When the notion of requirement is in clear focus it is likely to seem the only element in the idea of duty that is essential, and the other component notion – that a duty is something *due* someone else – drops off. Thus, in this widespread but derivative usage, "duty" tends to be used for any action we feel we *must* (for whatever reason) do. It comes, in short, to be a term of moral modality merely; and it is no wonder that the first thesis of the logical correlativity doctrine often fails.

Let us then introduce duties into Nowheresville, but only in the sense of actions that are, or believed to be, morally mandatory, but not in the older sense of actions that are due others and can be claimed by others as their right. Nowheresville now can have duties of the sort imposed by positive law. A legal duty is not something we are implored or advised to do merely; it is something the law, or an authority under the law, *requires* us to do whether we want to or not, under pain of penalty. When traffic lights turn red, however, there is no determinate person who can plausibly be said to claim our stopping as his due, so that the motorist owes it to *him* to stop, in the way a debtor owes it to his creditor to pay. In our own actual world, of course, we sometimes owe it to our *fellow motorists* to stop; but that kind of right-correlated duty does not exist in Nowheresville. There, motorists "owe" obedience to the Law, but they owe nothing to one another. When they collide, no matter who is at fault, no one is accountable to anyone else, and no one has any sound grievance or "right to complain."

When we leave legal contexts to consider moral obligations and other extra-legal duties, a greater variety of duties-without-correlative-rights present themselves. Duties of charity, for example, require us to contribute to one or another of a large number of eligible recipients, no one of whom can claim our contribution from us as his due. Charitable contributions are more like gratuitous services, favours, and gifts than like repayments of debts or reparations; and yet we do have duties to be charitable. Many persons, moreover, in our actual world believe that they are required by their own consciences to do more than that "duty" that *can* be demanded of them by their prospective beneficiaries. I have quoted elsewhere the citation from H. B. Acton of a character in a Malraux novel who "gave all his supply of poison to his fellow prisoners to enable them by suicide to escape the burning alive which was to be their fate and his." This man, Acton adds, "probably did not think that [the others] had more of a right to the poison than he had, though he thought it his duty to give it to them."[1] I am sure that there are many actual examples, less dramatically heroic than this fictitious one, of persons who believe, rightly or wrongly, that they *must do* something (hence the word "duty") for another person in excess of what that person can appropriately demand of him (hence the absence of "right").

Now the digression is over and we can return to Nowheresville and summarize what we have put in it thus far. We now find spontaneous benevolence in somewhat larger degree than in our actual world, and also the acknowledged existence of duties of obedience, duties of charity, and duties imposed by exacting private consciences, and also, let us suppose, a degree of conscientiousness in respect to those duties somewhat in excess of what is to be found in our actual world. I doubt that Kant would be fully satisfied with Nowheresville even now that duty and

---

[1] H. B. Acton, "Symposium of 'Rights'," *Proceedings of the Aristotelian Society*, Supplementary Volume 24 (1950), pp. 107–8.

respect for law and authority have been added to it; but I feel certain that he would regard their addition at least as an improvement. I will now introduce two further moral practices into Nowheresville that will make that world very little more appealing to Kant, but will make it appear more familiar to us. These are the practices connected with the notions of *personal desert* and what I call a *sovereign monopoly of rights.*

When a person is said to deserve something good from us what is meant in parts is that there would be a certain propriety in our giving that good thing to him in virtue of the kind of person he is, perhaps, or more likely, in virtue of some specific thing he has done. The propriety involved here is a much weaker kind than that which derives from our having promised him the good thing or from his having qualified for it by satisfying the well-advertised conditions of some public rule. In the latter case he could be said not merely to deserve the good thing but also to have a *right* to it, that is to be in a position to demand it as his due; and of course we will not have that sort of thing in Nowheresville. That weaker kind of propriety which is mere desert is simply a kind of *fittingness* between one party's character or action and another party's favorable response, much like that between humor and laughter, or good performance and applause.

The following seems to be the origin of the idea of deserving good or bad treatment from others: A master or lord was under no obligation to reward his servant for especially good service; still a master might naturally feel that there would be a special fittingness in giving a gratuitous reward as a grateful response to the good service (or conversely imposing a penalty for bad service). Such an act while surely fitting and proper was entirely supererogatory). The fitting response in turn from the rewarded servant should be gratitude. If the deserved reward had not been given him he should have had no complaint, since he only *deserved* the reward, as opposed to having a *right* to it, or a ground for claiming it as his due.

The idea of desert has evolved a good bit away from its beginnings by now, but nevertheless, it seems clearly to be one of those words J. L. Austin said "never entirely forget their pasts."[2] Today servants qualify for their wages by doing their agreed upon chores, no more and no less. If their wages are not forthcoming, their contractual rights have been violated and they can make legal claim to the money that is their due. If they do less than they agreed to do, however, their employers may "dock" them, by paying them proportionately less than the agreed upon fee. This is all a matter of right. But if the servant does a splendid job, above and beyond his minimal contractual duties, the employer is under no further obligation to reward him, for this was not agreed upon, even tacitly, in advance. The additional service was all the servant's idea and done entirely on his own. Nevertheless, the morally sensitive employer may feel that it would be exceptionally appropriate for him to respond, freely on *his* own, to the servant's meritorious service, with a reward. The employee cannot demand it as his due, but he will happily accept it, with gratitude, as a fitting response to his desert.

In our age of organized labor, even this picture is now archaic; for almost every kind of exchange of service is governed by hard bargained contracts so that even bonuses can sometimes be demanded as a matter of right, and nothing is given for nothing on either side of the bargaining table. And perhaps that is a good thing; for consider an anachronistic instance of the earlier kind of practice that survives, at

---

[2] J. L. Austin, "A Plea for Excuses," *Proceedings of the Aristotelian Society,* Vol. 57 (1956–57).

least as a matter of form, in the quaint old practice of "tipping." The tip was originally conceived as a reward that has to be earned by "zealous service." It is not something to be taken for granted as a standard response to *any* service. That is to say that its payment is a *"gratuity,"* not a discharge of obligation, but something given apart from, or in addition to, anything the recipient can expect as a matter of right. That is what tipping originally meant at any rate, and tips are still referred to as "gratuities" in the tax forms. But try to explain all that to a New York cab driver! If he has *earned* his gratuity, by God, he has it coming, and there had better be sufficient acknowledgement of his desert or he'll give you a piece of his mind! I'm not generally prone to defend New York cab drivers, but they do have a point here. There is the making of a paradox in the queerly unstable concept of an "earned gratuity." One can understand how "desert" in the weak sense of "propriety" or "mere fittingness" tends to generate a stronger sense in which desert is itself the ground for a claim of right.

In Nowheresville, nevertheless, we will have only the original weak kind of desert. Indeed, it will be impossible to keep this idea out if we allow such practices as teachers grading students, judges awarding prizes, and servants serving benevolent but class-conscious masters. Nowheresville is a reasonably good world in many ways, and its teachers, judges, and masters will generally try to give students, contestants, and servants the grades, prizes, and rewards they deserve. For this the recipients will be grateful; but they will never think to complain, or even feel aggrieved, when expected responses to desert fail. The masters, judges, and teachers don't *have* to do good things, after all, for *anyone*. One should be happy that they *ever* treat us well, and not grumble over their occasional lapses. Their hoped for responses, after all, are *gratuities*, and there is no wrong in the omission of what is merely gratuitous. Such is the response of persons who have no concept of *rights*, even persons who are proud of their own deserts.[3]

Surely, one might ask, rights have to come in somewhere, if we are to have even moderately complex forms of social organization. Without rules that confer rights and impose obligations, how can we have ownership of property, bargains and deals, promises and contracts, appointments and loans, marriages and partnerships? Very well, let us introduce all of these social and economic practices into Nowheresville, but *with one big twist*. With them I should like to introduce the curious notion of a "sovereign right-monopoly." You will recall that the subjects in Hobbes's *Leviathan* had no rights whatever against their sovereign. He could do as he liked with them, even gratuitously harm them, but this gave them no valid grievance against him. The sovereign, to be sure, had a certain duty to treat his subjects well, but this duty was owed not to the subjects directly, but to God, just as we might have a duty to a person to treat his property well, but of course no duty to the property itself but only to its owner. Thus, while the sovereign was quite capable of *harming* his subjects, he could commit no wrong against them that they could complain about, since they had no prior claims against his conduct. The only party *wronged* by the sovereign's mistreatment of his subjects was God, the supreme lawmaker. Thus, in repenting cruelty to his subjects, the sovereign might say to God, as David did after killing Uriah, "to Thee only have I sinned." [4]

---

[3] For a fuller discussion of the concept of personal desert see my "Justice and Personal Desert," *Nomos VI, Justice*, ed, by C. J. Chapman (New York: Atherton Press, 1963), pp. 69–97.

[4] II Sam. 11. Cited with approval by Thomas Hobbes in *The Leviathan*, Part II, Chap. 21.

Even in the *Leviathan*, however, ordinary people had ordinary rights *against one another*. They played roles, occupied offices, made agreements, and signed contracts. In a genuine "sovereign right-monopoly," as I shall be using that phrase, they will do all those things too, and thus incur genuine obligations toward one another; but the obligations (here is the twist) will not be owed directly *to* promises, creditors, parents, and the like, but rather to God alone, or to the members of some elite, or to a single sovereign under God. Hence, the rights correlative to the obligations that derive from these transactions are all owned by some "outside" authority.

As far as I know, no philosopher has ever suggested that even our role and contract obligations (in this, our actual world) are all owed directly to a divine intermediary; but some theologians have approached such extreme moral occasionalism. I have in mind the familiar phrase in certain widely distributed religious tracts that "it takes three to marry," which suggests that marital vows are not made between bride and groom directly but between each spouse and God, so that if one breaks his vow, the other cannot rightly complain of being wronged, since only God could have claimed performance of the marital duties as his *own* due; and hence God alone had a claim-right violated by nonperformance. If John breaks his vow to God, he might then properly repent in the words of David: "To Thee only have I sinned."

In our actual world, very few spouses conceive of their mutual obligations in this way; but their small children, at a certain stage in their moral upbringing, are likely to feel precisely this way toward *their* mutual obligations. If Billy kicks Bobby and is punished by Daddy, he may come to feel contrition for his naughtiness induced by his painful estrangement from the loved parent. He may then be happy to make amends and sincere apology to *Daddy;* but when Daddy insists that he apologize to his wronged brother, that is another story. A direct apology to Billy would be a tacit recognition of Billy's status as a right-holder against him, someone he can wrong as well as harm, and someone to whom he is directly accountable for his wrongs. This is a status Bobby will happily accord Daddy; but it would imply a respect for Billy that he does not presently feel, so he bitterly resents according it to him. On the "three-to-marry" model, the relations between each spouse and God would be like those between Bobby and Daddy; respect for the other spouse as an independent claimant would not even be necessary; and where present, of course, never sufficient.

The advocates of the "three to marry" model who conceive it either as a description of our actual institution of marriage or a recommendation of what marriage ought to be, may wish to escape this embarrassment by granting rights to spouses in capacities other than as promisees. They may wish to say, for example, that when John promises God that he will be faithful to Mary, a right is thus conferred not only on God as promisee but also on Mary herself as third-party beneficiary, just as when John contracts with an insurance company and names Mary as his intended beneficiary, she has a right to the accumulated funds after John's death, even though the insurance company made no promise to her. But this seems to be an unnecessarily cumbersome complication contributing nothing to our understanding of the marriage bond. The life insurance transaction is necessarily a three party relation, involving occupants of three distinct offices, no two of whom alone could do the whole job. The transaction, after all, is defined as the purchase by the customer (first office) from the vendor (second office) of protection for a beneficiary (third office) against the customer's untimely death. Marriage, on the other hand, in this our actual world, appears to be a binary relation between a husband and wife, and even though third parties such as children, neighbors, psychiatrists, and priests may sometimes be helpful and even causally necessary for the survival of the relation, they are not logically necessary to our *conception* of the relation, and indeed many married couples do quite well without them. Still I am not now purporting to describe our actual world, but rather trying to contrast it with a counterpart world of the imagination. In *that* world, it takes three to make almost *any* moral relation and all rights are owned by God or some sovereign under God.

There will, of course, be delegated authorities in the imaginary world, empowered to give commands to their underlings and to punish them for their disobedience. But the commands are all given in the name of the right-monopoly who in turn are the only persons to whom obligations are owed. Hence, even intermediate superiors do not have claim-rights against their subordinates but only legal *powers* to create obligations in the subordinates *to* the monopolistic right-holders, and also the legal *privilege* to impose penalties in the name of that monopoly.

2

So much for the imaginary "world without rights." If some of the moral concepts and practices I have allowed into that world do not sit well with one another, no matter. Imagine Nowheresville with all of these practices if you can, or with any harmonious subset of them, if you prefer. The important thing is not what I've let into it, but what I have kept out. The remainder of this paper will be devoted to an analysis of what precisely a world is missing when it does not contain rights and why that absence is morally important.

The most conspicuous difference, I think, between the Nowheresvillians and ourselves has something to do with the activity of *claiming*. Nowheresvillians, even when they are discriminated against invidiously, or left without the things they need, or otherwise badly treated, do not think to leap to their feet and make righteous demands against one another though they may not hesitate to resort to force and trickery to get what they want. They have no notion of rights, so they do not have a notion of what is their due; hence they do not claim before they take. The conceptual linkage between personal rights and claiming has long been noticed by legal writers and is reflected in the standard usage in which "claim-rights" are distinguished from other mere liberties, immunities, and powers, also sometimes called "rights," with which they are easily confused. When a person has a legal claim-right to X, it must be the case (i) that he is at liberty in respect to X, i.e. that he has no duty to refrain from or relinquish X, and also (ii) that his liberty is the ground of other people's *duties* to grant him X or not to interfere with him in respect to X. Thus, in the sense of claim-rights, it is true by definition that rights logically entail other people's duties. The paradigmatic examples of such rights are the creditor's right to be paid a debt by his debtor, and the landowner's right not to be interfered with by anyone in the exclusive occupancy of his land. The creditor's right against his debtor, for example, and the debtor's duty to his creditor, are precisely the same relation seen from two different vantage points, as inextricably linked as the two sides of the same coin.

And yet, this is not quite an accurate account of the matter, for it fails to do justice to the way claim-rights are somehow prior to, or more basic than, the duties with which they are necessarily correlated. If Nip has a claim-right against Tuck, it is because of this fact that Tuck has a duty to Nip. It is only because something from Tuck is *due* Nip (directional element) that there is something Tuck *must do* (modal element). This is a relation, moreover, in which Tuck is bound and Nip is free. Nip not only *has* a right, but he can choose whether or not to exercise it, whether to claim it, whether to register complaints upon its infringement, even whether to release Tuck from his duty, and forget the whole thing. If the personal claim-right is also backed up by criminal sanctions, however, Tuck may yet have a duty of obedience to the law from which no one, not even Nip, may release him. He would even have such duties if he lived in Nowheresville; but duties subject to acts of claiming, duties derivative from the contingent upon the personal rights of others, are unknown and undreamed of in Nowheresville.

Many philosphical writers have simply identified rights with claims. The dictionaries tend to define "claims," in turn as "assertions of right," a dizzying piece of circularity that led one philosopher to complain — "We go in search of rights and are directed to claims, and then back again to rights in bureaucratic futility." [5] What then is the relation between a claim and a right?

As we shall see, a right *is* a kind of claim, and a claim is "an assertion of right," so that a formal definition of either notion in terms of the other will not get us very far. Thus if a "formal definition" of the usual philosophical sort is what we are after, the game is over before it has begun, and we can say that the concept of a right is a "simple, undefinable, unanalysable primitive." Here as elsewhere in philosophy this will have the effect of making the commonplace seem unnecessarily mysterious. We would be better advised, I think, not to attempt definition of either "right" or "claim," but rather to use the idea of a claim in informal elucidation of the idea of a right. This is made possible by the fact that *claiming* is an elaborate sort of rule-governed *activity*. A claim is that which is claimed, the object of the act of claiming. . . . If we concentrate on the whole activity of claiming, which is public, familiar, and open to our observation, rather than on its upshot alone, we may learn more about the generic nature of rights than we could ever hope to learn from a formal definition, even if one were possible. Moreover, certain facts about rights more easily, if not solely, expressible in the language of claims and claiming are essential to a full understanding not only of what rights are, but also why they are so vitally important.

Let us begin then by distinguishing between: (i) making claim to . . . , (ii) claiming that . . . , and (iii) having a claim. One sort of thing we may be doing when we claim is to *make claim to something*. This is "to petition or seek by virtue of supposed right; to demand as due." Sometimes this is done by an acknowledged right-holder when he serves notice that he now wants turned over to him that which has already been acknowledged to be his, something borrowed, say, or improperly taken from him. This is often done by turning in a chit, a receipt, an I.O.U., a check, an insurance policy, or a deed, that is, a *title* to something currently in the possession of someone else. On other occasions, making claim is making application for titles or rights themselves, as when a mining prospector stakes a claim to mineral rights, or a householder to a tract of land in the public domain, or

[5] H. B. Acton, *op. cit.*

an inventor to his patent rights. In the one kind of case, to make claim is to exercise rights one already has by presenting title; in the other kind of case it is to apply for the title itself, by showing that one has satisfied the conditions specified by a rule for the ownership of title and therefore that one can demand it as one's due.

Generally speaking, only the person who has a title or who has qualified for it, or someone speaking in his name, can make claim to something as a matter of right. It is an important fact about rights (or claims), then, that they can be claimed only by those who have them. Anyone can claim, of course, *that* this umbrella is yours, but only you or your representative can actually claim the umbrella. If Smith owes Jones five dollars, only Jones can claim the five dollars as his own, though any bystander can *claim that* it belongs to Jones. One important difference then between *making legal claim to* and *claiming that* is that the former is a legal performance with direct legal consequences whereas the latter is often a mere piece of descriptive commentary with no legal force. Legally speaking, *making claim to* can itself make things happen. This sense of "claiming," then, might well be called "the performative sense." The legal power to claim (performatively) one's right or the things to which one has a right seems to be essential to the very notion of a right. A right to which one could not make claim (i.e. not even for recognition) would be a very "imperfect" right indeed!

Claiming that one has a right (what we can call "propositional claiming" as opposed to "performative claiming") is another sort of thing one can do with language, but it is not the sort of doing that characteristically has legal consequences. To claim that one has rights is to make an assertion that one has them, and to make it in such a manner as to demand or insist that they be recognized. In this sense of "claim" many things in addition to rights can be claimed, that is, many other kinds of proposition can be asserted in the claiming way. I can claim, for example, that you, he, or she has certain rights, or that Julius Caesar once had certain rights; or I can claim that certain statements are true, or that I have certain skills, or accomplishments, or virtually anything at all. I can claim that the earth is flat. What is essential to *claiming that* is the manner of assertion. One can assert without even caring very much whether anyone is listening, but part of the point of propositional claiming is to *make sure* people listen. When I claim to others that I know something, for example, I am not merely asserting it, but rather "obtruding my putative knowledge upon their attention, demanding that it be recognized, that appropriate notice be taken of it by those concerned. . . ."[6] Not every truth is properly assertable, much less claimable, in every context. To claim that something is the case in circumstances that justify no more than calm assertion is to behave like a boor. (This kind of boorishness, I might add, is probably less common in Nowheresville.) But not to claim in the appropriate circumstances that one has a right is to be spiritless or foolish. A list of "appropriate circumstances" would include occasions when one is challenged, when one's possession is denied, or seems insufficiently acknowledged or appreciated; and of course even in these circumstances, the claiming should be done only with an appropriate degree of vehemence.

Even if there are conceivable circumstances in which one would admit rights diffidently, there is no doubt that their characteristic use and that for which they

[6] G. J. Warnock, "Claims to Knowledge," *Proceedings of the Aristotelian Society.* Supplementary Volume 36 (1962), p. 21.

are distinctively well suited, is to be claimed, demanded, affirmed, insisted upon. They are especially sturdy objects to "stand upon," a most useful sort of moral furniture. Having rights, of course, makes claiming possible; but it is claiming that gives rights their special moral significance. This feature of rights is connected in a way with the customary rhetoric about what it is to be a human being. Having rights enables us to "stand up like men," to look others in the eye, and to feel in some fundamental way the equal of anyone. To think of oneself as the holder of rights is not to be unduly but properly proud, to have that minimal self-respect that is necessary to be worthy of the love and esteem of others. Indeed, respect for persons (this is an intriguing idea) may simply be respect for their rights, so that there cannot be the one without the other; and what is called "human dignity" may simply be the recognizable capacity to assert claims. To respect a person then, or to think of him as possessed of human dignity, simply *is* to think of him as a potential maker of claims. Not all of this can be packed into a definition of "rights"; but these are *facts* about the possession of rights that argue well their supreme moral importance. More than anything else I am going to say, these facts explain what is wrong with Nowheresville.

We come now to the third interesting employment of the claiming vocabulary, that involving not the verb "to claim" but the substantive "a claim." What is to *have a claim* and how is this related to rights? I would like to suggest that *having a claim consists in being in a position to claim, that is, to make claim to or claim that.* If this suggestion is correct it shows the primacy of the verbal over the nominative forms. It links claims to a kind of activity and obviates the temptation to think of claims as *things,* on the model of coins, pencils, and other material possessions which we can carry in our hip pockets. To be sure, we often make or establish our claims by presenting titles, and these typically have the form of receipts, tickets, certificates, and other pieces of paper or parchment. The title, however, is not the same thing as the claim; rather it is the evidence that establishes the claim as valid. On this analysis, one might have a claim without ever claiming that to which one is entitled, or without even knowing that one has the claim; for one might simply be ignorant of the fact that one is in a position to claim; or one might be unwilling to exploit that position for one reason or another, including fear that the legal machinery is broken down or corrupt and will not enforce one's claim despite its validity.

Nearly all writers maintain that there is some intimate connection between having a claim and having a right. Some identify right and claim without qualification; some define "right" as justified or justifiable claim, others as recognized claim, still others as valid claim. My own preference is for the latter definition. Some writers, however, reject the identification of rights with valid claims on the ground that all claims as such are valid, so that the expression "valid claim" is redundant. These writers, therefore, would identify rights with claims *simpliciter.* But this is a very simple confusion. All claims, to be sure, are *put forward* as justified, whether they are justified in fact or not. A claim conceded even by its maker to have no validity is not a claim at all, but a mere demand. The highwayman, for example, *demands* his victim's money; but he hardly makes claim to it as rightfully his own.

But it does not follow from this sound point that it is redundant to qualify claims as justified (or as I prefer, valid) in the definition of a right; for it remains true that not all claims put forward as valid really are valid; and only the valid ones can be acknowledged as rights.

If having a valid claim is not redundant, i.e. if it is not redundant to pronounce *another's* claim valid, there must be such a thing as having a claim that is not valid. What would this be like? One might accumulate just enough evidence to argue with relevance and cogency that one has a right (or ought to be granted a right), although one's case might not be overwhelmingly conclusive. In such a case, one might have strong enough argument to be entitled to a hearing and given fair consideration. When one is in this position, it might be said that one "has a claim" that deserves to be weighed carefully. Nevertheless, the balance of reasons may turn out to militate against recognition of the claim, so that the claim, which one admittedly had, and perhaps still does, is not a valid claim or right. "Having a claim" in this sense is an expression very much like the legal phrase "having a *prima facie* case." A plaintiff establishes a *prima facie* case for the defendant's liability when he establishes grounds that will be sufficient for liability unless outweighed by reasons of a different sort that may be offered by the defendant. Similarly, in the criminal law, a grand jury returns an indictment when it thinks that the prosecution has sufficient evidence to be taken seriously and given a fair hearing, whatever countervailing reasons may eventually be offered on the other side. That initial evidence, serious but not conclusive, is also sometimes called a *prima facie* case. In a parallel *"prima facie* sense" of "claim," having a claim to X is not (yet) the same as having a right to X, but is rather having a case of at least minimal plausibility that one has a right to X, a case that does establish a right, not to X, but to a fair hearing and consideration. Claims, so conceived, differ in degree: some are stronger than others. Rights, on the other hand, do not differ in degree; no one right is more of a right than another. [7]

Another reason for not identifying rights with claims *simply* is that there is a well-established usage in international law that makes a theoretically interesting distinction between claims and rights. Statesmen are sometimes led to speak of "claims" when they are concerned with the natural needs of deprived human beings in conditions of scarcity. Young orphans *need* good upbringings, balanced diets, education, and technical training everywhere in the world; but unfortunately there are many places where these goods are in such short supply that it is impossible to provision all who need them. If we persist, nevertheless, in speaking of these needs as constituting rights and not merely claims, we are committed to the conception of a right which is an entitlement *to* some good, but not a valid claim *against* any particular individual; for in conditions of scarcity there may be no determinate individuals who can plausibly be said to have a duty to provide the missing goods to those in need. J. E. S. Fawcett therefore prefers to keep the distinction between claims and rights firmly in mind. "Claims," he writes, "are needs and demands in movement, and there is a continuous transformation, as a

---

[7] This is the important difference between rights and mere claims. It is analogous to the difference between *evidence* of guilt (subject to degrees of cogency) and conviction of guilt (which is all or nothing). One can "have evidence" that is not conclusive just as one can "have a claim" that is not valid. "Prima-facieness" is built into the sense of "claim," but the notion of a "prima-facie right" makes little sense. On the latter point see A. I. Melden, *Rights and Right Conduct* (Oxford: Basil Blackwell, 1959), pp. 18–20, and Herbert Morris, "Persons and Punishment," *The Monist*, Vol. 52 (1968), pp. 498–9.

society advances [towards greater abundance] of economic and social claims into civil and political rights . . . and not all countries or all claims are by any means at the same stage in the process."[8] The manifesto writers on the other side who seem to identify needs, or at least basic needs, with what they call "human rights," are more properly described, I think, as urging upon the world community the moral principle that *all* basic human needs ought to be recognized as *claims* (in the customary *prima facie* sense) worthy of sympathy and serious consideration right now, even though, in many cases, they cannot yet plausibly be treated as *valid* claims, that is, as grounds of any other people's duties. This way of talking avoids the anomaly of ascribing to all human beings now, even those in pre-industrial societies, such "economic and social rights" as "periodic holidays with pay."[9]

Still for all of that, I have a certain sympathy with the manifesto writers, and I am even willing to speak of a special "manifesto sense" of "right," in which a right need not be correlated with another's duty. Natural needs are real claims if only upon hypothetical future beings not yet in existence. I accept the moral principle that to have an unfulfilled need is to have a kind of claim against the world, even if against no one in particular. A natural need for some good as such, like a natural desert, is always a reason in support of a claim to that good. A person in need, then, is always "in a position" to make a claim, even when there is no one in the corresponding position to do anything about it. Such claims, based on need alone, are "permanent possibilities of rights," the natural seed from which rights grow. When manifesto writers speak of them as if already actual rights, they are easily forgiven, for this is but a powerful way of expressing the conviction that they ought to be recognized by states here and now as potential rights and consequently as determinants of *present* aspirations and guides to *present* policies. That usage, I think, is a valid exercise of rhetorical licence.

I prefer to characterize rights as valid claims rather than justified ones, because I suspect that justification is rather too broad a qualification. "Validity," as I understand it, is justification of a peculiar and narrow kind, namely justification within a system of rules. A man has a legal right when the official recognition of his claim (as valid) is called for by the governing rules. This definition, of course, hardly applies to moral rights, but that is not because the genus of which moral rights are a species is something other than *claims*. A man has a moral right when he has a claim the recognition of which is called for − not (necessarily) by legal rules − but by moral principles, or the principles of an enlightened conscience.

There is one final kind of attack on the generic identification of rights with claims, and it has been launched with great spirit in a recent article by H. J. McCloskey, who holds that rights are not essentially claims at all, but rather entitlements. The springboard of his argument is his insistence that rights in their essential character are always *rights to,* not *rights against:*

> My right to life is not a right against anyone. It is my right and by virtue of
> it, it is normally permissible for me to sustain my life in the face of obstacles.
> It does give rise to rights against others *in the sense* that others have or may
> come to have duties to refrain from killing me, but it is essentially a right of

    [8] J. E. S. Fawcett, "The International Protection of Human Rights," in *Political Theory and the Rights of Man,* ed. by D. D. Raphael (Bloomington: Indiana University Press, 1967), pp. 125 and 128.
    [9] As declared in Article 24 of *The Universal Declaration of Human Rights* adopted on December 10, 1948, by the General Assembly of the United Nations.

mine, not an infinite list of claims, hypothetical and actual, against an infinite number of actual, potential, and as yet nonexistent human beings ... Similarly, the right of the tennis club member to play on the club courts is a right to play, not a right against some vague group of potential or possible obstructors. [10]

The argument seems to be that since rights are essentially rights *to*, whereas claims are essentially claims *against*, rights cannot be claims, though they can be grounds for claims. The argument is doubly defective though. First of all, contrary to McCloskey, rights (at least legal claim-rights) *are* held *against* others. McCloskey admits this in the case of *in personam* rights (what he calls "special rights") but denies it in the case of *in rem* rights (which he calls "general rights"):

> Special rights are sometimes against specific individuals or institutions − e.g. rights created by promises, contracts, etc. . . . but these differ from . . . characteristic . . . general rights where the right is simply a right to . . . [11]

As far as I can tell, the only reason McCloskey gives for denying that *in rem* rights are against others is that those against whom they would have to hold make up an enormously multitudinous and "vague" group, including hypothetical people not yet even in existence. Many others have found this a paradoxical consequence of the notion of *in rem* rights, but I see nothing troublesome in it. If a general rule gives me a right of noninterference in a certain respect against everybody, then there are literally hundreds of millions of people who have a duty toward me in that respect; and if the same general rule gives the same right to everyone else, then it imposes on me literally hundreds of millions of duties − or duties towards hundreds of millions of people. I see nothing paradoxical about this, however. The duties, after all, are negative; and I can discharge all of them at a stroke simply by minding my own business. And if all human beings make up one moral community and there are hundreds of millions of human beings, we should expect there to be hundreds of millions of moral relations holding between them.

McCloskey's other premise is even more obviously defective. There is no good reason to think that all *claims* are "essentially" *against*, rather than *to*. Indeed most of the discussion of claims above has been of claims *to*, and we have seen, the law finds it useful to recognize claims *to* (or "mere claims") that are not yet qualified to be claims *against*, or rights (except in a "manifesto sense" of "rights").

Whether we are speaking of claims or rights, however, we must notice that they seem to have two dimensions, as indicated by the prepositions "to" and "against," and it is quite natural to wonder whether either of these dimensions is somehow more fundamental or essential than the other. All rights seem to merge *entitlements to* do, have, omit, or be something with *claims against* others to act or refrain from acting in certain ways. In some statements of rights the entitlement is perfectly determinate (e.g. *to* play tennis) and the claim vague (e.g. *against* "some vague group of potential or possible obstructors"); but in other cases the object of the claim is clear and determinate (e.g. *against* one's parents), and the entitlement general and indeterminate (e.g. to be given a proper upbringing.) If we mean by "entitlement" that *to* which one has a right and by "claim" something directed at those against whom the

[10] H. J. McCloskey, "Rights," *Philosophical Quarterly*, Vol. 15 (1965), p. 118.
[11] *Loc. cit.*

right holds (as McCloskey apparently does), then we can say that all claim-rights necessarily involve both, though in individual cases the one element or the other may be in sharper focus.

In brief conclusion: To have a right is to have a claim against someone whose recognition as valid is called for by some set of governing rules or moral principles. To have a *claim* in turn, is to have a case meriting consideration, that is, to have reasons or grounds that put one in a position to engage in performative and propositional claiming. The activity of claiming, finally, as much as any other thing, makes for self-respect and respect for others, gives a sense to the notion of personal dignity, and distinguishes this otherwise morally flawed world from the even worse world or Nowheresville.

29. Utility and Rights

Lawrence Haworth

The question I wish to explore is: What shows that people have rights? Along the way, it will appear that people do indeed have them — not merely legal or customary, but also moral rights (or, to put it another way, a ground for the common and commonly unquestioned conviction that there are such rights will be found); that there are even, in a plausible sense, natural rights; and that among the criteria proposed as grounds for the practice of ascribing rights, three at least — utility, equal freedom, and equal shares — are defensible. The core of the argument, once the spadework has been done, will be that a peculiar significance attaches to the idea of deciding an issue "on its merits": the commitment to proceed in such a way includes a commitment to be disinterested while assessing the alternatives; and, as I shall argue, this latter commitment cannot be met unless one regards the fact that an alternative satisfies the principle of utility, equal freedom, or equal shares as tending to show that it should be adopted.[1]

I. What Is a Right?

When one has a right, what does one have? If we follow the generally accepted analysis of legal rights, we shall say that for every right there is a correlative obligation, borne by another or others, not to interfere with some act one is at liberty to perform. The act which one is at liberty to perform, and with the performance of which another or others are obligated not to interfere, is then said

From Nicholas Rescher, ed., *Studies in Moral Philosophy* (Oxford: Basil Blackwell Publisher, 1968), pp. 64–85, by permission of the author and publisher.

[1] In developing the argument of the essay I have been helped, in ways that may not be clear to them, by discussions with my colleagues J. S. Minas and Jan Narveson.

to be one's "right." Being at liberty to perform the act means it is not wrong to perform it, and being obligated not to interfere means one ought not to interfere. As a result, one's right to do something consists in the facts that (1) it is not wrong to do it, and (2) there is someone who ought not to interfere with its being done, in the sense that by interfering he would wrong the person who has the right.

But when it is asked, "Does anyone really have a right?" ("Are rights anything more than mere conventions?") it is clear what the question means – even when it is clear what one has when one has a right. It is not at all like asking whether anyone has a pain, and the difference is connected with the fact that, unlike pains, rights are not kinds of things that can be *there*; they aren't events or objects. This leads some to hold that rights are conventions – a view that is generally made to depend on the assumption that unless a belief is descriptive, in the way "my clavicle is painful," is descriptive, or formal, in the way pure mathematics is formal, then it cannot be "true" or "known." If analysis shows that what appeared to be a descriptive statement is really a proposal, then the conclusion will be drawn that no better reason can be given for "asserting" (making) it than for denying it. And the ordinary person's assumption, that it is possible to have as good reason for making a proposal as for believing a descriptive statement to be true, is precluded by the presupposition that in any significant (non-conventional) sense there can be "good reasons" only for descriptive and formal statements.

I think it is true that the "statement" that one has a right is not a statement, but a proposal. When it is said, that a person has a right to do something, this is to be understood as the proposal that he be protected in his efforts to do it, and that others be discouraged in some way from interfering with its being done (or as an endorsement of the fact that people are so protected and discouraged). And the "truth" of the "statement" that he has the right consists in the reasonableness of the proposal. The proposal is reasonable to the extent it can be supported by good reasons. Hence it is important to know what sorts of considerations, if any, could count as good reasons for proposals of this kind.

In their most general form, the required reasons would be criteria of importance for actions, in the sense that they would identify traits of or associated with an act that make it reasonable to regard the act as sufficiently important that one ought to protect the actor in his efforts to carry it out, and to dissuade others who would interfere with its being carried out. In principle, these may be traits of (a) the actors, (b) the world created by the actions, (c) the actions themselves or their maxims, or (d) the world in which the actions arise. The most prominent form of the first is the desert theory of rights, and its most prominent exponent is Aristotle. The second is most obviously (if not exclusively) exemplified by the principle of utility. The third has many forms, but I regard the principle of equal freedom as the most promising one. The fourth could have many forms, but I regard the principle of consent as the most promising one. The desert theory, however, reduces to or is a form of the utilitarian theory (since, with Aristotle at least, the source of merit is contribution to the ends of the city, and to the question, "Why measure merit in this way?" he would seem to have no alternative to answering that it is a practice that contributes to the ends of the city). Consequently, I shall restrict my attention to the other three. Some loss of comprehensiveness results from this decision, since even if the desert theory is a form of utilitarianism it has unique and important characteristics.

II. Principles of Rights: Utility

Consider now the explicit theory that the criterion of importance for actions, which indicates the circumstances in which persons should be supported and protected in their endeavors to act, is utility. We shall say that according to the principle of utility the preferability of a proposed course of action is shown by its promise of having good consequences, where "good consequences" includes at least pleasure (in Bentham's sense of "interesting perception," so that, for example, considered in itself the "pleasure in pain" experienced by a masochist forms a good consequence); satisfaction of actual needs, interests, and wishes: and the fulfillment of goals or purposes. The intent of the classification of kinds of good consequences is that it will permit one to regard as a good consequence any but only those conditions that the individuals on whom they impinge will regard as good consequences. In a secondary sense, of course, one will want to say that conditions productive of good consequences are also good.

Two questions arise in the theory of rights to which one might suppose the principle of utility provides a plausible answer. What kind of reasons, if any, are there for distinguishing among actions and regarding some as matters of right, while withholding even the liberty to perform others? And on what basis, that is, in terms of what principle or principles, should the distinction be drawn? The distinction should be drawn, the utilitarian says, because some actions promise to have decidedly good consequences on the whole, while others promise to be extremely harmful in their effects, and it is not unreasonable to expect both that the occurrence of the former sort would be increased if a right to perform them were accorded, and that the occurrence of the latter sort would be diminished if even the liberty to perform them were withheld. And it is obvious that this contains an answer to the second question as well: those actions should become matters of right that promise to have markedly good consequences.

The utilitarian theory of rights (or, what comes to the same thing, of justice) has been objected to in more ways that can be conveniently canvassed here. I shall mention only two such objections. (1) It is said that the principle is arbitrary. Although most people accept some form or other of the principle that the utility of a course of action tends to show that it should be adopted — that utility provides a good reason for adopting it — there is no real basis for this attitude. Thus, Hume: " 'Tis not contrary to reason to prefer the destruction of the whole world to the pricking of my finger." (2) It is also objected that, for example, the enjoyment a rapist experiences tends not at all to minimize the immoral character of what he has done, so that this "good consequence has no bearing on the answer to the question, "Are there circumstances in which the act would be a matter of right?" In the same way, it is said that utility does not even tend to give one a right to "punish" an innocent person.

One wants to generalize about such cases that the promise of good consequences doesn't count insofar as the act that has them violates the rights of another. But then it does not seem possible to ground the latter rights on consequences, since their distinctive character appears to be that of holding good despite consequences. At least two courses are open.

1. Modify the principle of utility so that it becomes consistent with such rights as that of an innocent person not to be "punished" despite the prospect that good consequences would ensue. This can be done (or attempted) by making the

principle apply to rules rather than to individual acts, or by redefining (or more accurately defining) the notion of good consequences, so that, for example, some modes of distribution of goods qualify as good consequences, while others qualify as bad consequences.

2. The second course is that of defining some other (non-utilitarian) principle that is capable of accounting for those rights which we imagine people possess regardless (within limits) of their consequences — one's rights to have debts repaid and promises kept, the right of one who is not interfering with anyone not to be interfered with, the right not be to "punished" for crimes one did not commit. The two principles most often discussed in this connection are the principle of equal freedom and the principle of consent. The first has the effect deriving of rights from characteristics of the act itself, or of the maxim of the act; the second has the effect of deriving rights from characteristics of the world in which the act occurs.

III. Principles of Rights: Equal Freedom

Forms of the principle of equal freedom are found in Hobbes, Rousseau, Kant, Mill, Marx and Engels, Spencer, Popper, and Hart — to mention only those surveyed in Gewirth's useful discussion of the subject.[2] Of these, Hart is most explicit in seeking to derive rights from the principle, and in rejection a utilitarian derivation.

Hart's avowed purpose is to show that if there are any moral rights, then there must be at least one natural right — the right to equal freedom — where a natural right is defined as a right that (a) all men capable of choice possess, regardless of the character of the society in which they live, and (b) does not arise in consequence of any voluntary transaction into which men enter. This is to argue that one's possessing a natural right to equal freedom is a necessary condition of one's possessing any moral rights, a thesis that will yield the conclusion that there is at least one natural right if it is accepted that people do have moral rights. Hart assumes that this will or should be granted. The significance of the argument in the present context is that it purports to establish a non-utilitarian principle that overcomes widely-felt difficulties in the utilitarian theory of rights.

It appears, however, that Hart makes the rather elementary mistake of establishing, at best, that the right to equal freedom is a sufficient condition (or, in another class of cases, the most prominent in a group of conditions that together are sufficient) of one's having moral rights, but not a necessary one. As will be seen, this is a fatal defect, since one is left with the knowledge that if there are good reasons for ascribing to all men capable of choice a right to equal freedom, then all men have, or are eligible for, moral rights, even rights not derivable from the principle of utility as it is ordinarily understood. But this leads nowhere until, in some other way, the good reasons for ascribing a natural right to equal freedom are produced.

By an equal right to be free, Hart understands that "any adult human being capable of choice (1) has the right to forbearance on the part of all others from the use of coercion of restraint against him save to hinder coercion or restraint, and (2) is at liberty to do (i.e., is under no obligation to abstain from) any action which is not one coercing or restraining or designed to injure other persons."[3]

[2] "Political Justice" in *Social Justice*, ed. by Richard Brandt *et al.* (Englewood Cliffs, 1962).

[3] ["Are There Any Natural Rights?" *The Philosophical Review*, vol. 64 (1955), p. 175, Selection 26 of this book.]

Hart founds other rights on this right in the following manner. He first distinguishes between special and general rights. A special right is one that individuals have owing to voluntary transactions into which they enter. Thus, promises, contracts, and authorizations create special rights. A general right, by contrast, does not arise out of a voluntary transaction but merely exemplifies in a particular way the right to equal freedom. Examples are the rights to speak and to worship insofar as these acts do not involve coercing, restraining, or injuring other persons, and provided that the person for whom the right is claimed has not entered into a voluntary transaction with another that has the effect of obligating him not to perform the act.

The relation between a general right to do any particular thing that does not involve coercing, etc., others, and the natural right to equal freedom is that of part to whole. It is possible without distortion to define the natural right by saying that adult human beings capable of choice have a right to perform any action that does not coerce, etc., others — from which it follows that each general right is included in the natural right, just as from the fact there is a can containing beans of every color, it follows that the can contains a blue bean. Hart argues that "if there are any moral rights at all, it follows that there is at least one natural right, the right of all men to be free."[4] To establish this, and to show that the natural right is a necessary condition of there being moral rights, he observes that "The assertion of general rights directly invokes the principle that all men equally have the right to be free...."[5] But this is not true. One may base a general right — the general right, say, to worship — on the natural right of all men to be equally free, just as one may defend the view that there is a blue bean in a can by claiming that the can contains beans of every color. But to assert the general right to worship is not to *invoke* the natural right,[6] just as to claim there is a blue bean in the can is not to claim that the can contains beans of every color.

More precisely, Hart bases his contention, that the natural right is a necessary condition of any general right, on the relation that holds between the natural right and general rights. But this relation — that each general right is included in the natural right, or, as he puts it, is a "particular exemplification" of it — implies only that the natural right is a sufficient, but not that it is a necessary condition of there being general rights.

The same case can be made for the relation between the natural right to equal freedom and special rights. Two points must be recalled: first, the transaction that creates a special right is voluntary; second, to have a right is to have authority to limit another's freedom. Hart argues that if we justify limiting the freedom of another on the ground that the other has promised, or consented to, or authorized something, "we are in fact indirectly invoking as our justification the principle that all men have an equal right to be free. For we are in fact saying in the case of promises and consents or authorizations that this claim to interfere with another's freedom is justified because he has, in exercise of his equal right to be free, freely chosen to create this claim...."[7]

---

[4] *Ibid.,* p. 175.

[5] *Ibid.,* p. 188.

[6] To claim this is to claim something to which Hart has committed himself — that the natural right is a necessary condition of the general right to worship, so that there is no principle other than the natural right to equal freedom from which the general right to worship may also be derived.

[7] Hart, *op. cit.,* p. 190.

But, again, this is not true. One may attempt to justify interference by appealing to the principle of equal freedom, and I shall not dispute that the right that arises out of a promise, say, can be successfully defended in this way, but there is nothing to show that there are not other principles that may be used as well, even in circumstances where the promise is binding despite the fact that the principle of equal freedom is violated. That is, Hart's argument shows that if we assume one has an equal right to be free, then we may infer that when in normal circumstances one makes a promise he creates an obligation for himself and a right in another. For if in normal circumstances (that is, circumstances in which promises are possible) he makes a promise but is not regarded as having created an obligation for himself, and a right in another, then his equal right to be free is denied him. But this is not to show that if one creates an obligation by making a promise he possesses the natural right to equal freedom. For it is open to one to suppose that, say, utility is the ground of the practice of promising, and that each promise is binding (*is* a promise) because it exemplifies sound practice, in which case to claim the right that the promise creates, and the obligation, is to "invoke" the principle of utility, not that of equal freedom.

As a result, the assumption that people possess a natural right to equal freedom makes it possible to argue that they also possess numerous moral rights. But although the principle of equal freedom seems inherently plausible, so that one is strongly inclined to assume it and then, with Hart, deduce moral rights from it, so far no actual account of its plausibility, no explanation of why it is to be assumed, is at hand.

IV. Principles of Rights: Consent (Equal Shares)

The attempt to ground rights to act in characteristics of the world in which the acts occur often finds expression in the endorsement of the principle of consent as embodied in social contract theory. In the recent literature the same approach is exemplified by the theory of justice developed by John Rawls. According to Rawls, the fundamental principles of justice are that". . . each person participating in a practice, or affected by it, has an equal right to the most extensive liberty compatible with a like liberty for all; and second, inequalities are arbitrary unless it is reasonable to expect that they will work out for everyone's advantage, and provided the positions and offices to which they attach, or from which they may be gained, are open to all."[8]

Rawls associates the ideas of justice and rights in such a way that the foregoing principles are criteria for rights and duties, in the sense that a practice that allocates rights and duties is defensible if, but not unless, it satisfies the principles. The principles diverge from the principle of utility mainly in the requirement that inequalities should work out for everyone's (distributively), rather than a net, advantage. Their similarity with the principle of equal freedom is acknowledged by Rawls, but as will be seen, the real interest lies not in the principles themselves but in one of the attempted lines of derivation of them. In fact, there are at least two such lines of attempted derivation that Rawls interweaves, but one might imagine each of them to be capable of independently establishing the principles. (1) Rawls claims that "These principles [of justice] are those which account for the

---

[8] "Justice as Fairness," *The Philosophical Review*, vol. 67 (1958), p. 165.

considered judgments of competent persons concerning the justice of political and social institutions."⁹ The reference is to an earlier article,¹⁰ which develops the position that ethical theories and principles are justified insofar as they account for the practical judgments in which a specially constituted panel of "competent judges" concur. (2) Rawls also argues that "the family of principles associated with the concept of justice can be characterized as those principles which rational persons would acknowledge when the constraints of morality are imposed upon them in circumstances which give rise to questions of justice."¹¹ It is this second line of derivation that gives his theory the appearance of being based on the idea of consent. Development of the theme involves supposing that the members of a society are to attempt to agree on the principles they will use for evaluating and setting up practices, with the understanding that no principles will be adopted that are not unanimously assented to. Then various constraints are imagined to be placed on their deliberations, the principal one being that the participants are self-interested. In the circumstances, this, coupled with the requirement of unanimity, has the effect of assuring that the principles finally agreed upon will endorse a system of practices just in case the system as a whole establishes an equal sharing of risks and or prospects of gain. On one hand, an individual, being self-interested, would not accept a principle that promised to impose on him fewer prospects of gain, or more risks, than the rest. On the other hand, he could not gain acceptance by others of a principle that promised him greater prospects of gain, or fewer risks.

We are confronted then with two ideas, and it is not clear at once which is the more basic. The principles of justice are those principles that could be mutually acknowledged by rational persons subject to the constraints of morality; and the principles of justice are also those principles that promise to establish an equal sharing of risks and of prospects of gain. (1) Rawls regards the first as the more basic, but I would be inclined to say that the second — which I shall refer to as the principle of "equal shares" — is more basic. (2) Moreover, as will be seen, the two principles he calls principles of justice aren't such, by his own criterion — they would not be mutually acknowledged in the circumstances described. (3) Finally, the principle of equal shares is in fact the principle that Rawls is seeking, since this is the principle that would be mutually acknowledged in those circumstances. I shall discuss each of these points in detail;

1. That the idea of equal shares is more basic than that of mutual acknowledgment or consent may be seen in the following way. The question is raised, "What principles for evaluating practices would be unanimously assented to by individuals who satisfy the conditions of an 'analytical construction' (as Rawls calls it), marked by such stipulations as that the individuals are mutually self-interested, rational, and not envious, and that the principles assented to are to be employed impartially for the settlement of contemporary issues and also for the settlement of future issues the exact nature of which cannot be anticipated?" Then it is intended that one should be able to *deduce* the principles of justice from the analytical construction. But if one asks why each of the stipulations is included in the construction, the answer must be that if it were not included then principles

---

⁹ "The Sense of Justice," *The Philosophical Review*, vol. 72 (1963), p. 282.
¹⁰ "Outline of a Decision Procedure for Ethics," *The Philosophical Review*, vol. 6 (1951), pp. 177–197.
¹¹ "The Sense of Justice," *op. cit.,* p. 282.

might be deducible that do not involve an equal sharing of risks and of prospects of gain. The ideas of consent and mutual acknowledgment of principles have no role to play. The issue is not, "What would be consented to?" but "What *could* be assented to, in the specified circumstances?" And what could be assented to is merely what satisfies the conditions implied by those circumstances – the circumstances, that is, delineated by the "analytical construction." But the conditions are such that, taken altogether, no principles could satisfy them except ones that would establish equal shares. Consequently, to say that the two "principles of justice" are those that could be mutually acknowledged is a way of saying that they are the principles that would establish an equal sharing of risks and of prospects of gain.

One might object that this ignores the force of the stipulation that the principles of justice are to be those that could be mutually acknowledged by rational persons "subject to the constraints of morality." That is, the details of the analytical construction result not so much from the consideration, "What set of circumstances will permit the deduction of principles that establish an equal sharing of risks and of prospects of gain?" as they do from the consideration, "What circumstances must be imagined to obtain in order that the persons involved might be made 'subject to the constraints of morality'?" This is true. But then it becomes clear, as the latter question is answered by the description of the analytical construction, that the overriding idea in the conception of accepting the constraints of morality is that of not asking others to take more risks, and not allowing oneself greater prospects of gain; and when it is further assumed that one is rationally self-interested, the additional feature, that one will not willingly accept greater risks and fewer prospects of gain, is introduced. The result is the principle of equal shares.

It might seem, then, that rather than showing the priority of the principle of equal shares to the principle of mutual acknowledgment by rational persons subject to the constraints of morality, this shows instead their identity. I would not object if the following points were granted. First, the idea of actual or even possible consent or acknowledgment has nothing important to do with the latter principle, since when it is said that the two principles are identical what is meant is that the principle of equal shares explicates what a rationally self-interested person submits to when he submits to the constraints of morality. Second, the analytical construction is not to be regarded as a manner of deducing the identity, since the description of the construction itself proceeds with an eye to the fact of the identity, and is regulated by a prior understanding that the constraints of morality involve an equal sharing of risks and of prospects of gain. The analytical construction is then but a way of communicating the fact of the identity.

2. I wish to argue that Rawls is mistaken in supposing that rational persons subject to the constraints of morality (persons placed in the circumstances described by the analytical construction) must endorse the two principles of justice that he defines. The second of the two principles is the only substantial one, and it has two parts. The major difficulty attaches to the first part of the second principle. It reads: ". . . inequalities are arbitrary unless it is reasonable to expect that they will work out for everyone's advantage . . . " There is a minor problem here that I shall merely mention in passing: The persons concerned would not insist that inequalities work out to their advantage (especially in view of the stipulation that they are not envious), but at most would insist that inequalities do not work out to their disadvantage.

The major difficulty involves the respect in which this part of the second principle is related with the standard interpretation of the principle of utility. The latter principle, it is said, requires only a net advantage, and is objected to on the ground that a net advantage might be attained in a manner that involves an objectionable disadvantage being borne by a minority. Rawls's principle, by contrast, excludes the consideration of a net advantage altogether, in the sense that in terms of his principle a net advantage of any amount would be insufficient to warrant an inequality that does not promise to work out for each and everyone's advantage, or that promises to work out for the disadvantage of at least one. But surely this is too extreme. Although rational persons subject to the constraints of morality would not accept an unqualified principle of utility as the sole rule for evaluating their practices (would not accept net advantage, regardless of its distribution, as the sole criterion), neither would they accept a principle that entirely overrides the consideration of net advantage. In some circumstances the over-all gain promised by an inequality would not seem sufficient to encourage everyone to accept the inequality; on other occasions the over-all gain would seem sufficient. It would depend on the amount of gain or net advantage, on one hand, and on the extent of the disadvantage suffered by the most disadvantaged person (or, in Rawls's analytical construction, the most disadvantaged representative office-holder). If one knew in advance that he would be the one disadvantaged by an inequality, he would not be swayed by the consideration that a net advantage would be gained at his expense. But the second part of the second principle stipulates that "the positions and offices to which [the inequalities] are attached, or from which they may be gained, are open to all." And the result of this is that in advance of the relevant information concerning who will benefit from and who will suffer under any inequality, each must regard a proposed inequality that would result in a net advantage but in disadvantage to a minority (that is, less advantage than is promised by an alternative) as a *gamble*, and must decide whether accepting the inequality would be a good gamble for him by taking into account the chances of his losing (being disadvantaged by the inequality), the extent of his loss if he loses, and his share of the net advantage if he wins (if he is not one of the minority disadvantaged by the inequality). Persons placed in the circumstances of Rawl's analytical construction cannot know in advance what the values for these variables will be in all future issues, and therefore cannot be certain that an option that, while promising to disadvantage some, nevertheless forms a good gamble for everyone, will ever present itself. But neither can they be certain that it will not. And we may add that as a matter of fact good gambles of this sort do frequently present themselves. But then rational persons subject to the constraints of morality would not agree on a principle for evaluating their practices that they knew would forever deny to them the opportunity to accept such gambles.

One example should suffice. Suppose that conscription into the army during a war is entirely by lot, and that being a member of the army involves an inequality *vis-à-vis* civilians. Then I would think that the offices of soldier and civilian satisfy the requirement of openness specified in the second part of the second principle. But some of the soldiers (second lieutenants in the infantry, at least) are ultimately disadvantaged, in the sense that their share of the net gain to their country that is produced by having an army at all is more than offset by the disadvantage they suffer in the consequence of their position (they are very likely to be killed), and that this loss is greater than theirs would be under some alternative, for example, the alternative of surrendering without a fight. Thus, all things considered some people are likely to be ultimately disadvantaged by the complex practice of subscription by lot – or by most other ways of forming an army. Consequently, Rawls's second principle condemns the practice. Nevertheless, the persons who become second lieutenants in the infantry, along with everyone else in the society, might reasonably have chosen the practice of subscription by lot – in advance of the actual drawing of the numbers that assigned them their positions of advantage and disadvantage. It is possible to lose a good gamble.

Another way to make the same point is to say that it is possible to have an equal sharing of risks and of prospects of gain in a society that tolerates inequalities that, while producing a net social advantage, work out to the ultimate disadvantage of a minority within the society. This is possible, provided that the positions of advantage and disadvantage are assigned in a fair or reasonable rather than an arbitrary or partial manner, and that the probability of suffering the disadvantage is sufficiently small, or the extent of the possible disadvantage sufficiently restricted, that in view of the share each can expect of the net advantage produced by the inequality – should he be fortunate enough to avoid the disadvantage – he can reasonably assume that choice of the society with the inequality represents a better gamble than does choice of the society without the inequality.

3. It seems obvious then that the principles of justice defined by Rawls must be revised if they are to be principles to which rational persons subject to the constraints of morality would unanimously consent. The revision should have the effect of making it possible for the principles to endorse practices that promise a net advantage, at the price of disadvantage to some. But the revised principles cannot specify the point at which a promised net advantage would be sufficient to warrant paying the price, since this depends on the values for variables that cannot be known in advance. All that is possible is a principle that delineates the requirement that the system of practices that form a society should represent a good gamble for everyone. But, assuming that two qualifications are introduced, such a principle would be but a form of the principle of equal shares. The qualifications have analogues in Rawls's principles of justice. First, not only is equality desired, but equality at the highest attainable level. This is expressed by stipulating that the risks should be at the lowest point compatible with their being equal, and the prospects of gain at the highest point. Second, a system of practices that embodies an inequality is nonetheless tolerable if (a) it incorporates on balance less risk and greater prospect of gain (for the society at large) than the alternatives, and (b) none who suffers under the inequality (by bearing an unequal share of the risks or of prospects of gain) suffers more than he would under the alternatives. It will be noticed that the effect of these qualifications is to make the principle of equal shares correspond in an important way with Rawl's two principles of justice. It diverges from those principles mainly in that, unlike Rawl's principles, it does not form a criterion for individual practices, but forms instead a criterion for the system of practices that constitute a society.

Both Rawls and Hart fail, then, in two major respects. Neither succeeds in his project of defending a principle that has, as Rawls puts it, "absolute weight" over the principle of utility. In Hart's case, this results from the fact that, contrary to the requirements of his position, he has managed to establish that the principle of equal freedom is a sufficient, but not that it is a necessary, condition of one's having a moral right. If it were necessary, then no amount of utility would justify one in violating another's right to equal freedom — that right would have "absolute weight." But if it is merely sufficient, then it remains open that one may in the name of utility justify violating another's right to equal freedom; that is, that one may violate that "right" without thereby wronging him, which is another way of saying that in the circumstances it is no right of his, or it is defeated by considerations of utility, or it lacks "absolute weight." In Rawls's case, it is shown by the fact that there may be practices that form a good gamble for everyone, despite their not working out for the advantage of everyone. The second respect in which Rawls and Hart fail is that neither succeeds in accounting for or in grounding the "principle of rights" he proposes.

V. The Ground of the Principles

Nevertheless, the three principles — equal shares, equal freedom, and utility — are all inherently plausible. If in seeking to defend the claim that some action is one's right one were to introduce a consideration the force of which depended on assuming any one of these principles, it seems likely that the consideration would be accepted as relevant to the matter at hand. But how is this plausibility to be accounted for? Two ideas introduced by Rawls are capable of adaptation in a way that is promising in this connection: first, his use of the conception of what follows from one's submitting to the constraints of morality; second, his effort to identify the considered judgments of competent persons as the primitive data of ethics. These two ideas are similar in the respect that in both instances one is encouraged to consider the kind of judgments that would be made by persons placed in a situation that precludes their merely consulting their own interests. But the persons in the first case are nevertheless imagined to have a stake in the eventual decision, so that the requirements of morality have the character of restraints; while in the second case their status is that of disinterested judges whose own futures are not part of the issue. On the other hand, the working out of the first idea — that of submitting to the constraints of morality — involves identifying certain high level judgments or principles as implied by those constraints, so that one who submits to the constraints necessarily accepts the principles; while the working out of the second idea — that of taking the considered judgments of competent persons as the data of ethics — does not involve supposing that the judgments concurred in by the panel are necessitated by the setting in which they operate (in the sense that their not passing just those judgments is proof that they are not operating in the manner contemplated by the definition of the setting; that is, are not functioning as disinterested, competent judges).

Add now, to the conception of such a panel, the idea that in carrying on their deliberations they are submitting to the constraints of morality, in a sense to be explained shortly. Then I think it can be shown, not that any particular judgments concerning particular moral issues are necessitated by that submission, but that certain high level judgments or principles — in particular, at least those of equal shares, equal freedom, and utility — are necessitated, so that unless a person accepts these principles he is not actually submitting to those constraints. Then the actual judgments concerning particular moral issues made by the panel are understandable as results of a conscientious effort on their part to be guided by the principles that their position commits them to accept. It is of course not necessary that they should have a clear notion in the abstract of what those principles are.

In adapting these two ideas of Rawls's it will be useful to drop the stipulation that there be a panel of competent judges, and to replace the conception of submission to the constraints of morality by that of agreeing to discuss an issue "on its merits." The kind of issue that concerns us is that in which someone's rights are called into question; and we are to imagine that a decision-making body (either Rawls's panel or a single individual) commits itself to decide the issue on its merits. For simplicity suppose that a specific proposal is made, and that the problem confronting the decision-making body is that of deciding whether to accept or reject it. In resolving to decide the issue on its merits, the individual members of this body commit themselves (1) to inquire whether there are good reasons for accepting the proposal, and (2) to let the disposition of the proposal be regulated by the outcome of that discussion. Nothing more elaborate than this need be imagined to be involved in the decision to decide the issue on its merits. In particular, no exact notion of what a "good reason" would be like need be assumed, nor need it be assumed that there are good reasons.

In the first instance, the effect of these two very general commitments is wholly negative. Without knowing what one must do, if one is to decide the issue on its merits, one at least knows some of the things one must not do – what not deciding the issue on its merits involves. For there are some rather obvious ways in which one might violate the two commitments. Consequently, one may identify additional commitments of a negative sort that are involved in the initial commitments, and of which it may be said that unless they are kept an issue is not decided on its merits.

I shall mention only two. First, each commits himself not to force a view of his on the others. Thus, there are ruled out physical violence and exceptionally forceful emotional appeals as devices for gaining acceptance of a proposal. Secondly, each commits himself to place his own unique concerns to one side, so that they affect neither the view he evolves during the discussion nor his contribution to it. Each thus commits himself to functioning disinterestedly (that is, he need not be or feel disinterested, but he must act disinterestedly). This is not to say that the distinctive interests of each would not be taken into account, but only that none would allow the fact that certain interests are *his* to bias his contribution and response to the proceedings. Instead, the interests would be regarded as "ones" – to be sure, a "one" who has other characteristics in addition to these interests – so that if they are relevant at all it is for a reason, and the reason would show the relevance of that kind of interests regardless of whose they are, provided only that he possesses the additional characteristics that make the interests relevant.

When individuals discuss a proposal on its merits, so that each contributes disinterestedly, what, in the absence of "subjectivity" and arbitrarily introduced criteria, determines them to reach any conclusion at all? How *can* they be led to some particular view of the merits of a proposal except on the basis of their own interests, needs, drives, etc., or by appealing to criteria that, closely considered, have nothing to recommend them but are arbitrary? When the issue concerns belief of matter of fact, there remain, after personal biases and inclinations are set to one side, sensory experiences that at least *may* permit a settlement of the issue. But it may seem that no analogous material is available when the issue is prescriptive rather than descriptive, so that despite the best of intentions on the part of disinterested decision-makers, their project of deciding an issue on its merits cannot issue in a decision.

Such a position would be fanciful. It is simply a fact that people who discuss proposals do on occasion more or less achieve a stance of disinterestedness and do come to conclusions concerning the merits of the proposals. Observations are passed back and forth, and disinterested people are either swayed or not swayed by them. Nor is there any mystery in this. When a disinterested person is swayed by an observation – finds it to form a good reason in support of some practical conclusion – this can be accounted for by referring to some principle or other that is involved in his stance of disinterestedness, in the sense that his adoption of the stance finds expression in his being swayed by considerations that can be so accounted for. Three such principles are equal freedom, equal shares, and utility. To see that this is so, one need only ask the following question: If a person, purporting to be discussing a proposal on its mertis, did not accept as relevant the observations that it would have bad consequences, that it would establish an unequal distribution of freedom (or restrictions), and that it would involve spreading unevenly the risks and prospects of gain, could he be fairly described as functioning in the manner that he purported? Could he be fairly described as functioning disinterestedly? In this connection, the question is not how he feels but how he acts, what the tendency of his actions is. And it is important to notice that one can fail to be disinterested not only by giving undue weight to one's own interests, but also by showing partiality toward others.

I think it is obvious that not to be swayed by observations whose relevance is accounted for by the principle of equal freedom or by the principle of equal shares is to introduce a bias; that is, is effectively to depart from a stance of disinterestedness. For to deny their relevance is to display a readiness to accept a decision that would promote an inequality (either of freedom or of risks and prospects of gain) which one is not prepared to defend by appealing to collateral benefits realized at the cost of the inequality, or to other features of the situation that offset the inequality or minimize its seriousness; and acceptance of the inequality shows partiality for those who are to benefit from it.

The relation of the principle of utility with disinterestedness is rather more complex. A person purporting to be disinterested may effectively violate the principle in three very different ways. One of these is a straightforward example of partiality – he may accept the relevance of some "good consequences," those to himself, say, while denying the relevance of others, those to everyone else. But the other two are, on the surface at least, consistent with the idea of disinterestedness. He may depend on a principle contrary to that of utility, a principle of disutility, or what Bentham called "asceticism," in terms of which one is enjoined to maximize bad consequences; or he may deny that the consequences of a course of action – good, bad, or neutral – are in any way relevant to its preferability.

An elementary consideration indicates, however, that the second of these approaches is a way of showing partiality in just those situations where a utilitarian would find it objectionable. When the consequences of an alternative are good in their bearing on some persons, and bad in their bearing on others, but the good consequences outweigh the bad, so that on the basis of consequences at least the alternative seems reasonable to one who accepts the relevance of utilitarian considerations, then to deny effectively that consequences are relevant at all by not accepting the alternative is to show partiality for those on whom the alternative promises bad consequences. For, not to accept the alternative is, in effect, to assign greater weight to the interests of those on whom the alternative promises bad consequences than to the interests of those on whom it promises good consequences. There are of course circumstances in which, consequences aside, it is reasonable to assign greater weight to the interests of a minority than to those of a majority. But then these are also circumstances in which some principle in addition to the unqualified principle of utility applies, and in which that other principle dominates, so that the situation is not one of denying the relevance of consequences but of acknowledging the force of a more compelling consideration.

But it does not appear that one can condemn the principle of disutility on the same basis. One might hold that to maximize bad consequences is to discriminate against everyone, but it must be admitted that if this is discrimination nevertheless it may be effectively disinterested. However, the relevance of rejecting principles that are incompatible with disinterestedness is that failure to be disinterested implies failure to consider an alternative on its merits. But I think one should say that to choose a course of action because it promises to have bad consequences is to be guided not by its merits but by its demerits. Nor is this merely a bad pun, for although one may *say* whatever one thinks necessary to make a philosophical point, and thus may say that it is a mark of merit in a proposal that it promises bad consequences, if anyone purported really to believe this we would be warranted in concluding that he did not understand the meaning of the term "merit."

The force of this disposition of the principle of disutility will be lost unless it is recalled that nothing is to count as a good consequence that is not regarded as such by the individual on whom it impinges, and that, in the primary sense, everything so regarded because of what it is, rather than what it produces, is a good consequence. As a result, the principle of disutility does not claim that the only consequences that have merit and that show merit in the acts that produce them are those that as a rule people regard as bad. It claims instead that the only consequences that have merit and that show merit in the acts that produce them are those that the people on whom they impinge – including also the person who maintains the principle – regard as bad. The principle, that is, is literally perverse, a circumstance that is also identified by noticing that a sane person who sets about deciding an issue by appealing to the principle and who believes that he is deciding the issue "on its merits" is in fact confusing "merits" with "demerits." It is true, but not relevant, that no one would be so confused.

Even if the foregoing is granted – that the principles of equal freedom, equal shares, and utility are all implicates of disinterestedness – it may still be doubted that there is any significance in the fact. Thus, Alan Gewirth has objected that, "To try to justify an egalitarian, non-discriminatory criterion of justice by an appeal to what would be upheld by an impartial spectator is, obviously, begging the question. For to be impartial is, by definition, to be against discrimination and for equality of treatment."[12] But then if one accepts current views concerning the non-empirical character of philosophy, one could object in the same way to every philosophical conclusion as being question-begging, since whenever the argument is not empirical the conclusion is, or is represented as being, a necessary consequence of some concepts, terms, propositions, etc., in the same way that equality of treatment is a necessary consequence of impartiality.

---

[12] Gewirth, *op. cit.,* p. 126.

The important question is whether there is any significance in the fact that commitment to decide an issue on its merits involves commitment to acknowledge the force of the principles of utility, equal freedom, and equal shares. We know that one who does not acknowledge the principles in deciding an issue does not, so far, decide it on its merits. But what of that? What can be said of such a person?

It can be said, subject to one qualification, and in the required sense, that he ought to decide the issue on its merits, and that therefore he ought to acknowledge the principles, since doing so is a necessary condition of considering the issue in this manner. The qualification is that there are occasions when, owing to lack of information or for other reasons, it seems reasonable to decide by, say, tossing a coin. One may always make a second-level, procedural issue of whether an issue-at-hand is to be decided on its merits, and decide *that* on its merits too. It is with such procedural issues that we are concerned, and with those which when decided on their merits yield the decision to decide the issue-at-hand on *its* merits (rather than by, say, tossing a coin). Whenever this is or would be the outcome of a second-level, procedural issue, the associated issue-at-hand (the settlement of which the procedure contemplates) *ought to be* decided on its merits. It ought to be decided on its merits not because of anything to be accomplished by doing so, but merely because in part the force of saying, in the only sense relevant here, that a course of action ought to be adopted is that it is the course that would be adopted by anyone who decided the issue (of adopting it) on its merits.[13] And since this is so, to say that whenever settlement of a procedural issue on its merits would include the decision to decide the issue-at-hand on *its* merits then one ought to decide the issue-at-hand on its merits, is to say that one ought to do what one ought to do. And one ought.

Part of the force of saying that some course of action ought to be adopted is that it is the course that would be adopted by anyone who decided the issue on its merits. This may be seen in the following way. One who does not decide an issue on its merits acts on the basis of whim or interest. Suppose that such a person tells us we ought to do something, and then supports the directive by saying that he fancies our doing it, or that it would please him or some friend of his, and makes clear that he is unwilling to consider any other "reason." We should conclude that he had misrepresented his position by saying we ought to do that thing. It was not that he really thought we ought to do it, but only that for some reason or other he wanted us to do it. He will not show that he really thinks we ought to do it until, for example, he responds to the question, "Why ought we?" in a manner that he regards as constituting a consideration of the issue on its merits. In general, to say "you ought to . . . ," as opposed to "I want you to . . . ," or "you'd better . . . " is to recommend an act as being the one that would be selected following a disinterested investigation of its merits. This point concerning what is involved in recommending an act as the one that ought to be adopted could also be expressed by saying that to represent an act as the one that ought to be adopted is to impute to the recommendation that it be adopted a character of objectivity, or that it is to assert that there are good reasons for adopting it that any conscientious person would accept as decisive. When one decides an issue on its merits, one may or may not preface a description of the course decided on with the words, "This is what

---

[13] I say, "part of the force," because "ought to" here is also a directive, while in the case of deciding an issue on its merits the "ought" is replaced by the action that expresses the decision, so that the directive is acted on.

ought to be done." But given the sense those words have in that context, no other kind of decision procedure produces decisions whose descriptions may properly be prefaced by them. (The procedure of, say, tossing a coin, when this is a reasonable procedure, is an exception — it may be that one ought to do what the result of the toss implies.)

One may object that the argument is purely verbal, that at most it shows that people use "ought to" in the indicated way. The objection seems roughly correct, but does not seem to form an objection. For, it is just this sense of "ought" that one has in mind when he wonders whether he ought to decide issues on their merits, rather than on some other basis. That is, one is not wondering whether he really wants to, or whether it would be better for him to. He can discover, by considering more fully the meaning of "ought," that he ought. There is nothing more to discover. To continue by asking, "But, usage aside, ought one *really* to decide issues on their merits?" deserves the answer: "If by 'ought' is meant what would ordinarily be meant, then one ought — really; while if something else is meant the question can't be answered until it is decided what that something else is."

VI. Natural Rights

To summarize: Acknowledging the force of the principles of utility, equal freedom, and equal shares (at least these) is a necessary condition of considering an issue on its merits. Subject to the mentioned qualifications, issues ought to be decided on their merits, and consequently, the indicated principles ought to be acknowledged. It follows that people do indeed have rights. For, an act is one's right just in case its performance is sufficiently important that others should be restrained from interfering with one's efforts to perform it, and there are acts such that not to regard them as sufficiently important in this sense is to violate and therefore to ignore the force of one or another of the "principles of rights" that have been established. Thus, other things being equal, that one ought to acknowledge the force of the principle of equal freedom involves that one ought to accept the practice of restraining those who interfere with people who are not coercing, restraining, or acting in a way designed to injure others. And this means that the latter ought to be treated in the way people to whom rights are ascribed are to be treated. And so on.

But, also, associated with each of the principles is a right that has most, at least, of the characteristics traditionally associated with natural rights. Thus, associated with the principle of equal shares is a right that everyone enjoys, that does not rest on any political circumstance or voluntary transaction, and that cannot be transferred or abrogated. This is the right to an equal share of risks and of prospects of gain. There is similarly associated with the principle of equal freedom a natural right to equal freedom. And with the principle of utility there is associated a natural right to have one's own interests and concerns assigned the same weight as is assigned to the relevantly similar interests and concerns of others, so that, for example, if some course of action is in one's interest and it is the one that would be selected by the principle, then, other things being equal, that course of action forms one's natural right (there being nothing the individual or anyone else can do to make it not the case that it is his right). The "naturalness" of these rights follows from the fact that the associated principles of rights are absolute, in the sense that not only do they have moral force always and everywhere, but it is not possible for them not to have moral force. This is not to say that each is always applicable, nor that when it is applicable it inevitably dominates other considerations. The terms in which an issue is best put may be such that one or another of the principles has no relevance to its settlement (and so is not applicable). And we have not yet considered the important question of how the principles and others like them are to be adjusted to one another in cases of conflict among them.

Part VIII

The Public Interest

Introduction

Frank J. Sorauf's discussion in the first selection in this part is representative of a way of approaching conceptual problems that has been widely accepted in political and other social sciences in recent years. These are empirical sciences, and the concepts they employ must have empirical referents. To specify what these referents are and how they warrant the use of a concept is to "operationalize" that concept and hence to render it useful for political or social scientific purposes. If a concept cannot be operationalized in this empirical sense, it has no proper place among the concepts used by the social scientist to analyze political and social life. Attempts to operationalize the concept of the "public interest" have failed. Political scientists must recognize that the concept is employed in political life, but they should eschew its use in their scientific work.

The specific difficulties this view creates for the theory of the public interest are discussed in selection 30. But we may pause briefly to note the bearing on it of the more general questions discussed in the introduction to this book and in the readings in Part I. There is no logical or conceptual impossibility and no necessary incoherence involved in the approach Sorauf employs. Indeed given the understanding of the purposes of political science that underlies Sorauf's discussion of the "public interest," his conclusions concerning that concept may be the correct ones to draw. But the fact that "public interest" or any other concept does not satisfy the criteria generated by a particular conception of political science says nothing whatever about the place of that concept in any other language game — for example, the language games of political and social life that some political scientists want to understand. If we are interested in understanding the latter, Sorauf's position will have little to recommend it.

Bertrand de Jouvenel's approach to the common good, which has a pedigree going back at least to Plato, raises different sorts of problems. Recognizing the difficulties that have prompted Sorauf and others to abandon use of the concept, de Jouvenel's very different conception of political science requires him to put it at the center of his concerns. The analysis he gives of the concept, however, creates definite problems. Without claiming to have given an exhaustive account of the concept, de Jouvenel pursues and thinks he has captured its "essential constituent." When we speak of the common good or the public interest, when we say a policy, arrangement or institution serves the common good, we mean that it strengthens or develops the "social tie" in the society in question. For reasons examined earlier, the very notion that concepts have an "essential component," and particularly that concepts used as widely as are "common good" and "public interest" have such a component, is certain to raise hackles. The issue, however, cannot be settled on such general grounds. Specific reasoning must be brought forward against de Jouvenel's analysis.

If de Jouvenel is correct, if "common good" *means* "contributes to the social tie," it would follow that all policies, arrangements, and institutions that have this characteristic *must* be said to serve the common good, and that none that lack this characteristic *can* be said to do so. If we find "common good" used when this condition is not satisfied, or if we find cases in which it is conceded that a policy contributes to the social tie but is nevertheless contrary to the common good, there will be three possibilities: (1) de Jouvenel's analysis of the concept is mistaken; (2) the uses in question are incorrect and should be given up; (3) the policy in question really does or really does not contribute to the social tie.

It is no problem at all to find uses of "common good" and "public interest" involving no explicit connection with the notion of the "social tie." (If there is a problem in this respect it is to find cases in which such a connection *is* made.) But de Jouvenel's notion of the social tie is sufficiently capacious and open-textured that the third of the preceding alternatives will usually be available. The question will then be whether we would learn anything about either the common good or the social tie by insisting that they are always linked. If my own analysis (selections 33 and 34) of the use of "public interest" and "common good" is correct, they have application (positive or negative) to a very wide range of authoritative actions of government and perhaps to other actions in the public arena. It is implausible to think that all of these uses involve, or should involve, assertions or denials concerning the social tie as such. Societies have other concerns to attend to as well. The emphasis de Jouvenel places upon the social tie and how it can be maintained and extended is one of the most interesting features of his original and provocative political philosophy. But it is not very promising as an analysis of the "essential constituent" of the "public interest" or the language games of which it is part.

The basic difficulty with de Jouvenel's analysis, however, traces not to the notion of the social tie itself but to the idea that any single substantive formula could serve to explicate all the uses to which the "public interest" and the "common good" are put. Brian Barry seems to agree with this criticism in that he does not attempt to reduce "public interest" to any single substantive criterion or consideration. But he does assign it a limited range of application, and he contends that the criteria of its proper use are specific to and limited by the characteristics of the contexts or circumstances in which it is used. More specifically, he says that "public interest" is primarily an administrator's concept employed in contexts where the means to satisfy clearly defined and agreed-upon interests are being debated. Thus "in the public interest" is said to be equivalent to "those interests which people have in common qua members of the public." The "administrator's" task, then, is to show people (who may not realize it because they are not thinking of themselves as members of the public and are not distinguishing between the *policy* in question and particular *applications* of that policy to them) that they really do share interests and that the policy in question is the most eligible means of serving them. "Common good," on the other hand, which we have been treating as roughly interchangeable with "public interest," is said to be used to appeal to individuals to sacrifice their personal interests (net interests) to the service of those interests they share with others. Hence the task of those who use it is to show that there are shared interests and to convince people that those shared interests are sufficiently important, elevated, or whatever to render appealing the at first unpleasant idea of sacrificing their other interests to them.

Barry's discussion defines the range and the criteria of the use of both "public interest" and "common good" too narrowly. The generic use of both "public interest" and "common good" is to claim that there are good reasons for adopting and enforcing, through the authority of government, policies that are controversial in the society in question. "Policy X is (would be) in the public interest" is usually said when authoritative means are used (or proposed) to establish and enforce a policy that some number of persons, usually persons able and willing to express their views, oppose because they believe it to be contrary to their interests or to some other value they hold. Barry is right that there are common or shared interests. But the administrator (legislator, candidate for office, or whoever) who persuades all concerned that X is in their interests (as members of the public or in any other way) is obviating the necessity of talk about the public interest, not showing that the policy is (or is not) in the public interest. If we all agree about a policy, the kind of justification for adopting it that "it is in the public interest" is intended to provide loses its usual point in political discussion and debate.

There is another difficulty with Barry's analysis. Conflict or disagreement among those affected by a policy or proposed policy are conditions under which "public interest" is used, not criteria of X being in the public interest. But neither is "X is in the interests which people have in common qua members of the public" always a sufficient criterion of its correct use. As with de Jouvenel, if Barry's analysis is correct it would be a contradiction to affirm that "X is in the interests . . ., etc." and to deny that it is in the public interest. But Barry has no more shown that this is the case as regards "interest," than de Jouvenel has shown it as regards "social tie." Leaving aside the problems about ethical naturalism that would be raised by the attempt to do so, it seems clear that considerations other than the service of particular kinds of interests, for example, considerations of security and order, equality, moral rightness and goodness, are relevant to deciding whether a policy is in the public interest. We can inflate the concept of "interest" or of "interests which people have in common qua members of the public" to encompass all these considerations, but then we would simply have to draw the same distinctions anew under or within the rubric of the concept "interest."

The analysis of "public interest" in the final two readings in this part is intended to accommodate the fact that a wide range of policies are justified by the claim "in the public interest," hence that a wide range of considerations are relevant to supporting or refuting that justification, and yet to show that "public interest" has a definite logic, is governed by broad but identifiable rules that place significant restraints on what will count as good reasons for thinking that a particular policy is or is not in the public interest. The most obvious difficulty with the argument presented, it now seems, is that it does not trace in sufficient detail the connections between more particular characterizations of policies (more particular than "in the public interest"), and the limits these characterizations (that is, the rules governing the uses of the concepts to characterize the policy) place upon inferences made from them to or about the public interest. The lack of detailed analysis of these relationships (except perhaps in the case of the relationship between "interest" and "public interest") leaves the appearance of even greater open texture, even greater scope for personal decision and well-grounded controversy concerning the public interest, than is in fact characteristic of uses of the concept. In terms of earlier discussions in this book, more attention needs to be paid to the kinds of rules that Searle identifies in the case of promising and the implications such rules have for thought and action within the language games of which they are part.

Further Reading

Banfield, Edward, and Martin Meyerson. *Politics, Planning and the Public Interest*. New York: The Free Press, 1955.

Benn, S. I. " 'Interests' in Politics," *Proceedings of the Aristotelian Society*, Vol. 60 (1960), pp. 123–140.

Cassinelli, C. W. "Some Reflections on the Concept of the Public Interest," *Ethics*, Vol. 69 (1958), pp. 48–61.

Downs, Anthony. "The Public Interest: Its Meaning in a Democracy," *Social Research*, Vol. 29 (1962), pp. 1–36.

Fried, Charles. Two Concepts of Interests," *Harvard Law Review*, Vol. 76 (1963), pp. 755–778.

Friedrich, Carl J., ed. *The Public Interest*. New York: Atherton Press, Inc., 1962.

Held, Virginia. *The Public Interest and Individual Interests*. New York: Basic Books, Inc., 1970.

Leys, Wayne, and C. M. Perry. *Philosophy and the Public Interest*. Chicago: Committee to Advance Original Work in Philosophy, 1959.

Schubert, Glendon. *The Public Interest*. New York: The Free Press, 1960.

Smith, Howard R. *Democracy and the Public Interest*. Athens: University of Georgia Press, 1960.

Zarecor, William. "The Public Interest and Political Theory," *Ethics*, Vol. 69 (1959), pp. 227–280.

30. The Conceptual Muddle

Frank J. Sorauf

The vocabulary of politics very likely has more than its share of words and phrases whose definition lies obscured in a half-light of confusion and disagreement. Tag words such as "liberal" and "conservative" have achieved a notoriety of imprecision. Not only have they acquired a cumbersome baggage of special historical usages, but today their meaning often runs no deeper than political invective. But we are widely reassured that politics (and its study) is an art rather than a science, and that a certain genteel fuzziness — often masquerading as literary elegance — would not be out of place. As a consequence of their impressionistic study of politics and their desire to avoid recondite jargons, academic political scientists have adopted for their use much of this vocabulary of political debate and public affairs. Concepts such as that of the "public interest," therefore, reverberate both in legislative chambers and academic halls.

The propensity of political scientists to draw upon the vocabulary and concepts of everyday politics has, of course, spared their discipline an abstruse and grating jargon. Aside from the work of the "behaviorists," most of their writings are remarkably free of the polysyllabic conglomerates and esoteric usages that clog the literature of the rest of the social sciences, except history. But readability and accessibility of language have often been bought at the price of failure to develop precise and operational concepts for scholarly analysis. Generalizations, theories, and even accurate description can be no stronger and no more valid than the concepts and definitions in which they are expressed. As David Easton has written:

> A science, it is often said, is as strong as its concepts; and if this is true, the vague, ill-defined concepts unfortunately so typical of research in political science reduce the discipline to a low position on a scale of maturity in the social sciences. It is the rule rather than the exception to find difficulty in referring political concepts back to the things to which presumably they refer.[1]

In its distaste for a specialized terminology, academic political science has probably underestimated its acceptability as well as its importance. Poets and literati, after all, write without embarrassment of spondees, trochees, dactyls, and iambs.

Easton's strictures apply to few concepts in political science as aptly as they do to the "public interest." Even in scholarly usage it has assumed an astounding

Reprinted from *The Public Interest: Nomos V*, edited by Carl J. Friedrich (New York: Atherton Press, 1962), pp. 183–190. Copyright © 1962 by Atherton Press. Reprinted by permission of Lieber-Atherton, Incorporated, and Frank J. Sorauf, University of Minnesota.
[1] *The Political System* (1953), p. 44.

variety of definitional hues and shades.[2] Generally it has come to mean some criterion or desideratum by which public policy may be measured, some goal which policy ought ideally to pursue and attain. But just *whose* standard it is to be remains the problem. It may variously be an ethical imperative (such as the natural law), some superior standard of rational and "right" political wisdom, or the goals or consensus of a large portion of the electorate. Or it may be some amalgam, some almost mystical balance of narrower interests in which the final product appears to be considerably greater than the sum of its "selfish" parts.

Moreover, the meaning of public interest has extended beyond the idea of a guiding goal for policy making. A number of writers have identified it with the democratic political process of compromise and accommodation. Their public interest resides in the complex procedures of political adjustment and compromise which the democratic polity employs to represent and accommodate the demands made upon its policy-making instruments. Here the public interest as means and procedure replaces the public interest as end and goal, and one is left with an understanding of the public interest which has little to do with the wisdom or morality of public policy itself. Presumably, any policy evolved without violence or offense to the system is in the public interest; at the least, considerations of the public interest are irrelevant to it. Similarly, others have defined the public interest as a system of functional prerequisites for the operation of these accommodative processes; it here becomes a series of "the necessary conditions for the pursuit and enjoyment of interests, of the different institutional arrangements that are actually conditions for the pursuit of interests. . . ."[3]

In yet other hands the public interest assumes an elusive and ineffable content. In this regard Horace M. Gray has remarked:

> The concept of the "public interest," like the equally vague and undefinable common law "rule of reason," has validity and usefulness as a fictional device for the ordering of human affairs though we never quite succeed in defining it with scientific precision.[4]

This, then, is the public interest as a potent political myth, and as with any myth, its value rests in *not* defining it, in not drawing it out from the shrouds of mystery. By semantic shorthand the public interest also often reflects a congeries of unspecified ethical and rational interests which might be lost or disregarded in the policy-making process.

Clearly, no scholarly consensus exists on the public interest, nor does agreement appear to be in the offing. Not only do scholars disagree on the defining of the public interest, they disagree as well about what they are trying to define: a goal, a process, or a myth. Effective communication and cumulative scholarly work suffers inevitably. Add to this confusion the even greater imprecisions of the political arena — where public interest too often means, with or without elegant rationalizations, merely *my* interest — and the result is semantic chaos. Although semantic

---

[2] For a closer examination of the various meanings clinging to the public interest see Frank J. Sorauf, "The Public Interest Reconsidered," *Journal of Politics, XIX* (November 1957) 616–639, and Wayne A. R. Leys and Charner M. Perry, *Philosophy and the Public Interest* (1959), a discussion document prepared for The Committee to Advance Original Work in Philosophy. For a more general analysis of concepts of the public interest, see Glendon Schubert, *The Public Interest* (1960).

[3] *Philosophy and the Public Interest*, p. 24.

[4] Quoted in *Philosophy and the Public Interest*, p. 27.

confusion may serve someone's short-run needs in political debate, scholarly discussion and analysis need better tools than this.

Undoubtedly one of the public interest's more fundamental infirmities — its confusion of the normative and the real — contributes to this definitional tangle. In much of contemporary usage public interest means an interest possessed by (and, presumably, at least dimly perceived by) "the public" or some segment of it; in this sense it is a real, empirically identifiable interest. And at the same time it refers to a goal in the interest (i.e., "best interests" or "enlightened self-interest") of the public, whether or not that public is or is not sufficiently enlightened to grasp it. So, the "is" and the "ought" are inextricably knotted together in this single phrase, the public interest.[5] The questions of the distribution, organization, strength, and tactics of interests consequently merge with questions which arise out of the rational and ethical evaluations of public policy objectives.

Granted that we will never achieve a completely "value-free" study of politics, there is a powerful argument to be made for determined attempts to achieve a maximum degree of separation of the two. Theories and generalizations about the political process must be built with terms and concepts as nearly free as possible of normative overtones and implications. By the same token, it seems to me, the normative issues of political choice will never be illuminated by little rubrics which establish without evidence certain postulates about the existential world. Concepts such as those of the public interest, which embrace both problems, do not bridge the gulf between the two. They merely confuse the valid distinction between them.

Involved, too, in this combination of the "is" and the "ought" is the matter of the democratic ethic. If one assumes in a democratic political system that what is desirable and ethical is also a "real" organized political interest, he judges unfavorably any activities on behalf of competing interests. So to judge the competing interests in democratic politics denies the axioms that each man is his own best judge of what he wants and that the workings of the free political system will determine the final priority of interests which will be enacted into policy. As soon as one presumes to assess the ethical value of competing political interests, he reduces democratic political choice to the choice between public "right" and self-centered "wrong."

Beyond the confusion resulting from this alliance of "is" and "ought," the public interest fosters more analytic confusion by attempting to reconcile in an elusive catchword a series of very troublesome conceptual issues. At its level of generality it embraces and smothers a number of questions touching political interests, representation, and policy formation. It makes assumptions — all at once — about the nature and organization of political interests, about the responsibility of elected representatives, and about the making and administration of public policy. These are all, needless to say, problems which have troubled the practitioners and theoreticians of politics since the first recorded stirrings of representative democracy. Just the single question of whether the elected representative is to cater to the wishes and mandates of his constituents, yield to the leadership of a party, or assert his own vision of the goals of the good society remains a troublesome one. It has been and ought to be continually thought about and reflected on — but on its own terms and merits rather than on the posited concept of representation underlying someone's definition of the public interest.

[5] For an excellent discussion of this problem, see C. W. Cassinelli, "Some Reflections on the Concept of the Public Interest," *Ethics*, LXIX (October 1958), 48–61.

These, then, are among the chief weaknesses the "public interest" has as a tool of scholarly inquiry. It has, however, been argued that even though the term has restricted value to the cloistered academician, it still maintains considerable usefulness in the hurly-burly of the political arena. The world of politics is widely thought to have its own standards of clarity and its own rules of debate. Yet I am not at all sure why it should feel any lesser need than the scholarly world for unambiguous concepts and precisely framed questions. Public interest confuses general political debate to the same extent — and often for the same reasons — that it confuses academic inquiry.

At its most primitive level in political debate public interest serves as little more than rationalization for some particular group's interest. The process of rationalization may be the very human and unconscious one of erecting one's personal goals and preferences into universals. Or it may involve the calculated design of propagandizing one's interests in the most pleasing possible light and in the most prestigious semantics. There is, indeed, a proper place for universals and ethical norms in political debate, but one may doubt that such a discourse is served by trading catchwords and assertions of virtue. To argue that one's interest ought to prevail because it is "in the public interest" only steers the argument into an unprofitably circular course.

No single criterion or standard, such as the public interest, can subsume or encompass all that is good and desirable for society — regardless of the system of values one prefers or propounds. The matter of the goals of a contemporary industrial society consists in reality of a series of specific, policy-centered questions which involve the entire range of our concern, from a realistic approach to the emerging nationalism of Africa, through care for the ill among the aged, to the resolution of domestic racial conflict and tension. The answers to these policy questions will be hammered out painfully and pragmatically, and they will certainly by expressed in alternatives and wisdom considerably more specific and vastly less grandiose than the all-encompassing guise of a "public interest." If one argues that a public interest exists in all these problem areas, and if he can go the next step and identify it, all well and good. But why then resort to a concept of the public interest?

There is also a school of thought which argues that the public interest can be defined on a level of abstraction high and broad enough to touch the universal goals of man — liberty, security, food, and shelter, for instance.[6] But these abstractions have little to do with problems of public policy, little to do with the issues of American politics. The question at the moment is not "security," but whether social security coverage ought to be extended, and if so, to whom and under what conditions. "Liberty" as such is not at issue; we confront instead questions such as the jailing of individuals for refusing to answer the questions of legislative committees. If the public interest frames the political dialectic in terms of generally agreed upon symbols, the "binders" of political debate,[7] it keeps it at least one level of abstraction above the reality of actual political conflict and practical political alternatives.

The public interest promotes another oversimplification. It is no secret that Americans have long been uneasy over social and political conflict in American life. The institutions through which we wage our political conflict — parties, interest

[6] See *Philosophy and the Public Interest*, p. 23.
[7] Walter Lippmann, *Public Opinion* (1946), p. 163.

groups, "politicians" – bear a heavy burden of popular resentment for their imagined disruption and disregard of the unities of American life. As a symbol of unity and community in our politics, and as a warning to contending interests, public interest overrides the complex proliferation of interests in our political system and "solves" in one glib phrase the dilemmas of a political pluralism. Although no society gains from the exaggeration of conflict and disagreement, neither does it in the long run gain from myths which ignore legitimate differences of interest and imply that these interests are divisive and faintly antisocial. Certainly it does not profit from concepts which promote and encourage political cynicism.

Substantially these paragraphs have argued that the "public interest" works toward moralization and simplification in our political debates, even though the policy issues of concern to our democratic discussion are, to take Oscar Wilde from context, rarely pure and never simple. To reduce them to simple alternatives and black-white moralities does them the greatest violence. Nor is political maturity or the democratic ethic served by myths which ignore and deny the validity of opposing political aspirations. The practitioners of politics, just as the academic political scientists, need phrases and concepts which will clarify competing interests, separate the "is" from the "ought," shield the debate from undue moralism, and frame practicable and specific policy alternatives. Above all, they need intellectual tools for discussing the morality and wisdom of political policy, not in vague moralizations and rationalizations, but in terms of identifiable results and consequences and in terms related to policy itself. The record of the public interest has been one of lifting political debate out of the realities of our political process and away from the complicated equities of its choices.

That the "public interest" has meaning for some public officials and interest groups is an incontestable fact. That it may in these terms affect the shaping and administration of public policy is equally incontestable. Observation of American politics will also afford instances of its effective use as a unifying symbol and a social myth. Even should scholars reject the public interest for their own analysis, they must observe and record its prevalence and influence in the political system. But it is only as political datum that the public interest has a definable relevance to the study of politics and public policy.[8]

The tools of the scholarly craft are words, concepts, and hypotheses, and what the craft produces can be no better than the tools with which the scholar works. Whereas imprecision, vagueness, and mythology may serve some strategic purpose in the world of affairs, they contribute nothing to the formulation of valuable generalizations and theories about politics and the evolution of public policy. And to draw distinctions between the semantic needs of scholars and practitioners – to argue that what is not good enough for the scholar should suit the politician – does little to further the effective political dialogue which our democratic politics presumes. Perhaps the academicians ought to take the lead in drawing up a list of ambiguous words and phrases "which never would be missed." For such a list I would have several candidates, but it should suffice here to nominate the "public interest."

[8] Some particularly acute reader of the literature on the public interest, or of Schubert's analysis of it, may note that my position here is somewhat stronger and more negative than the one I took four years ago in the *Journal of Politics*. What appears to be an inconsistency is none in reality; I have simply changed my mind on a few issues touching the public interest in the intervening years.

31. The Problem of the Common Good

Bertrand de Jouvenel

There are a hundred different ways of saying that men in authority should use it in the general interest and for the common good; that the interest of the people should be the rule of their decisions and the public good the end of their actions. Exhortation of this kind never comes amiss. Traditionally it has been directed at the sole and absolute ruler, but it is no less necessary when authority is diffused, when the regime is one in which responsibility for decisions is widely spread. There is, in regimes of this kind, a temptation for individuals to regard their tiny ration of public authority as a piece of private property which they can use for their personal advantage. For that reason it is desirable to remind them that, as participants in the public authority (even if only as voters), they hold a public office and are morally bound to seek the common good in their decisions.

Salutary as the reminder is, it is not the last word in political ethics: it is only the first. To the philosopher who bids him seek and promote the general interest, the magistrate may reply: "Tell me how I may know it. Give me a clear idea of it, or supply me with criteria which may help me to select from the various open courses the one which best serves the public good." So presented, the problem is full of difficulties. But political science cannot escape the problem without renouncing its own purpose and end; let political science shirk its duty, and all it has left to do is to compile procedural manuals and commentators' monographs.

Before embarking on this problem, our first question is whether it is necessary to handle it at all, as clearly it will not be if the solution is always staring us in the face; our second question is whether there is not always an infinite number of solutions.

First Question: Is the Common Good Self-Evident?

People often talk as if men in positions of authority had only to wish to use it in the general interest for the problem of the common good to be solved. This assumes implicitly that public-spirited intention necessarily brings instant understanding both of the substance of the public good and of the means by which it may be realised.

If this assumption were well founded, politics would be an extremely simple affair. All the men in a state who cared for the public interest — the good citizens, in short — would also be in perfect agreement as to the best decision to take and the right course to adopt. The same spirit in each would bring the same illumination to each, with the result that all these "good wills" would, by being good, compose a

From Bertrand de Jouvenel, *Sovereignty: An Inquiry into the Political Good* (Chicago: The University of Chicago Press, 1957), pp. 105–116. © 1957 by Bertrand de Jouvenel. Published 1957.

single will: the "general will," which is necessarily righteous. It would not, certainly, be the will of all, because all are not public-spirited in intention. But those who have no public spirit, or have so little that it does not prevail over care for their private advantage and does not reveal to them the common good – the bad citizens, in short – would find themselves powerless in the presence of the good. Each of them would be thinking only of himself, and this very selfishness of their preoccupations would disperse their wills; by reason of this dispersal, their wills would on every occasion be found weak against the single will of the good citizens, which is compact and coherent and wears the impressive livery of virtue.

It might, of course, happen that the particular interest in question was that of persons so powerful or of a class so numerous that it would be able to block the "general will," the will of the patriots. But in that event the patriots would feel entitled to destroy the peccant social authorities and to forbid the private associations which obstructed in this way the pursuit of the common good. And anyone agreeing that the flame of their virtue had merited the revelation to them of the common good would have to allow them the right to pull up by the roots these parasitic and obstructive weeds.

Thus, the postulate of the self-evidence of the common good to patriots takes us straight to the views of Robespierre – views which have found favour with many others since. The republic will necessarily be well governed by the solid phalanx of the public-spirited, who will necessarily be in agreement among themselves and will form the only legitimate party – themselves. The only obstacle to be found is the inevitable conspiracy of the wicked: this must be broken.

Those opposing cannot but be wicked. They are not men who are only mistaken; they must have evil intentions as well. Allow to any one of them the smallest spark of patriotism and the doctrine collapses. The moment that someone who does not see the public good where we see it is given credit for public-spirited intention, the admission has been made that patriotism may go astray in its judgments; and if I admit, as regards this someone, that the patriotic conscience is not infallible, then it is not a whit more infallible in us.

This infallibility of the patriotic conscience can only be safeguarded by denying that the man in question is a mistaken patriot, for, if he was a patriot, his judgment would necessarily accord with ours. Since it is different from ours, he is a rascal whose patriotism is only a cloak, and he must be reprobated the more, the more of a patriot he seems to be. Give credence to his patriotism, and his opposition to us leads to one of two conclusions: either patriotism is not infallible – which destroys our doctrine, or we are not patriots – which destroys our reputation. For that reason, Robespierre and his like are bound to represent the dissident patriot as shamming patriotism for ulterior ends.

This has not been the predominant point of view in the countries of the West. In them it is admitted that the same care for the public good may inspire very different opinions and that equally good intentions may be found in different parties, acting though they do as respectable façades for the sectional or egotistical interests which find shelter in each of them. Once admit that good intentions are not all on one side and it becomes impossible to hold that good intention brings in its train sure and immediate knowledge of the common good. A regime in which debate is free and to whose institutions debate is fundamental implies the assumption that the men who seek the public good do not find it easily and help one another in the search by making it an object of public debate. Evidently, therefore, this is a quest in which the philosophers must take a hand.

Second Question: Is the Common Good Entirely Subjective?

But this quest is perhaps a vain one; perhaps the common good (or the general interest) is only a name which each of us gives to his own ideas or imaginings. This is a formidable difficulty. The idea that I have of the common good is something definite; the idea that someone else has of it is also something definite. But are these different ideas reflections of something which has an absolute existence, the real common good, or is there no such thing and is the common good only the generic name for a bundle of individual conceptions differing among themselves? Here once more is the old dispute between "realists" and "nominalists" about "universals." If we adopt the nominalist thesis, no two people speaking of the common good are speaking of one and the same thing and neither of them can be wrong, for, when each of them says "This is what the common good is," he is merely declaring "For my part, what I call the common good is this."

In the large family of private notions to which the name of "common good" is given by individual minds, no single one is false for the man who professes it or true for other people. It follows from this that the obligation laid on rulers, "Act for the common good," loses much of its force, for now it only means, "Act for what you call good." It cannot be said that a recommendation of this kind is altogether futile, for it instigates rulers to act with reference to their judgments of value, to consult their principles and put some coherence into what they do; but it does no more than that.

Yet, if we rejected the nominalist thesis and looked for the "real" common good, a nominalist would have good cause to reproach us with only formulating our subjective preference. For that reason we can only build solidly if we make the nominalist position our starting point.

I do not deny that the idea of the common good that I can make for myself is only my subjective preference, valid for myself only. But it is a preference in relation to something. That something I call "France," and my compatriots and I, when we speak of "France," have the feeling that we are talking at least of one and the same thing. France brings to my mind a great collection of men who have, as individuals, certain satisfactions, certain aspirations, certain discontents, certain attitudes of mind; I also envisage their relations between one another, their daily intercourse. In the complex of which I am thinking, there is more than individuals and their unceasing interaction; there are also emotions felt in common (as in a time of national disaster) and actions taken either simultaneously (as when we go to vote or pay our taxes) or in combination (as when we go to war side by side). And it is the possibility of these collective movements which makes the difference between a collection of individuals and "a people." Finally, we note that foreigners pass judgments on this whole which are collective; they speak well or ill of France and the French.

If I now declare that the virtue and prosperity of Frenchmen, the excellence of their mutual relations, their capacity to feel and act in common and their reputation in the outside world are my great preoccupations, will any Frenchman be found to tell me that these preoccupations have nothing in common with what he has in mind when he thinks of the public good? On the contrary, will he not agree that so far, at any rate, we are talking of one and the same thing, or of one and the same complex of things? That agreed, I am safe in concluding that in differing notions of the common good there is in fact a common substance.

But, I shall be told, this agreement is obtained only because of the vagueness of the statement. The reputation desired for France may vary wisely from man to man; the virtue and prosperity of a great collection of individuals may be conceived in an infinite number of different ways. Though that is true, what I have said is not that there is no room for subjective preferences, but only that, in speaking of the common good, we are talking of something with a definite meaning. I would point out, moreover, that there is one phrase in the statement which is almost entirely free from subjectivity: the capacity to act simultaneously or in combination is a concrete fact, which takes us into the domain of the objective. We can now embark on our examination of the problem.

Third Question: Is the Common Good Comprised in the Good of Individuals?

"Did you ever expect a corporation to have a conscience," asked the first Lord Thurlow, "when it has no soul to be damned, and no body to be kicked?" The radical inferiority of legal persons to men could not be more forcefully expressed. God became incarnate for the salvation not of the Jewish State or the Roman Empire but of men. It can, therefore, be maintained very plausibly that the duty of rulers is exclusively to individuals and that the good of a social whole is entirely comprised in the personal good of each of the individuals who compose it. Let us adopt this opinion provisionally with a view to seeing where it leads us.

If our rulers have been notified that the common good which it is their duty to serve consists in the particular goods of the subjects, it leaps to the eye that their difficulty will be to reconcile all the particular goods. That difficulty vanishes only if the particular good is made to consist in the acquisition of virtue, and this will not readily be conceded. Conversely the difficulty will get worse the more that the particular good is made to consist in the acquisition of scarce things, such as wealth and honours. Thus we find our attention drawn to the necessity of defining personal goods, and a road-fork comes into view.

What meaning should be given to the personal good of each? Is it what the rulers conceive to be his good, or is it what each conceives his good to be?[1]

Let us first go down the second road, which seems to show most affinities with our basic thesis. When we have exalted the individual by making him the end of governmental action, would it not be contradictory to lower him by refusing to let him be judge of his own good? So we will here treat as his good what it seems to him to be, his perceived interest. But a man ordinarily sees his good in the satisfaction of his desires, which are in conflict with those of others. The result of our instructing the public authority that its duty is to serve personal interests as perceived, and of our telling the citizens in the same breath that it is their right to set authority in motion for their own ends, is that the rulers are inevitably beset by contradictory petitions. Each man asks of them a decision which hurts others. It has often been said that the duty of the public authority was to limit and deaden the natural clash of interests; but the assertion that it is the servant of those

---

[1] It is clear that, in the case of individuals, the question of a "real good," different at once both from the good they imagine for themselves and from the good as it is conceived for them by the rulers, does not arise, for the ruler cannot possibly work towards what is for him an indeterminate end, which neither his own intelligence nor the declarations of those concerned have disclosed to him.

interests is bound to stimulate the latter to assert themselves in clamorous fashion and to encumber the forum with their scuffles.

What is the public authority to do then? It has the choice either of trying all the suits or of declaring itself incompetent and dismissing the suitors.

To try the suits is no easy task, for it has received, as the criterion of the common good which it must serve, the personal good of individuals as they themselves conceive it to be. How can it choose between two personal goods? Crudely, by reference to the volume of noise each makes, or by the subtler method of weighing the two goods? One method suggested is to weigh the respective satisfactions which the two camps at issue may gain or lose by any given decision and to return the verdict which ensures that the winners gain more satisfactions than the losers lose. As the estimates on which a calculation of this kind has to be based are very debatable and the basis itself is open to challenge, a verdict so arrived at would never be received with respect; it would serve as mask for a compromise rather than as a criterion. The long and short of it is that the public authority is merely tossed about between opposing pressures.

Will it, then, dismiss the suitors? What reason will it give? That it holds itself bound to the service of the interests of individuals only so far as they are common to all? This leads to definition of the general interest as that part of the particular interests which is held in common. But in setting off along the road of our choice we conceded that the interests in question were the interests perceived. It is possible to think that, taking the citizens' individual interests as a whole, the essential and major part is made up of interests which they have in common; but that is certainly not true when the interests to be considered are those of which they are aware. The interests which unite them are felt but feebly, whereas those which divide them are felt strongly.[2] The result is that a public authority which confined itself to serving only those particular interests which the citizens were at one in thinking important for all would condemn itself to virtual inactivity.

It thus appears that the road of our choice leads us either to handing over authority to the disorderly scrimmage of particular interests or else to a drastic curtailment of the competence of government. Let us therefore make our way back to the road-fork and take the other road which was open to us: the public authority is still conceived as there to serve individual goods, but now we shall establish it as judge of what those goods are.

We are repelled at the outset. To know each man's good better than he knows it himself is something within the competence of God alone. It is the duty of a father, ruler in his tiny realm, to perceive wherein the good of each of his sons consists and to set the feet of each in his proper path while making the others help him in the task; yet with how many blunders does even a father exercise this function! Clearly it cannot be exercised over a large population, for the indispensable adjuncts of a jurisdiction of this kind are personal knowledge of each single subject and unceasing vigilance in his regard. For this reason it may cause confusion to say "Authority is paternal," when in fact it can have neither the knowledge of the personal good of each nor the care for these personal goods such as are proper to a father.

The infirmity of human intelligence makes it impossible for the ruler to consider individual goods particularly; he can only conceive of them in general terms. Therefore he will make himself a diagram of the good and contented citizen, and he

---

[2] Hume. *A Treatise of Human Nature*, Book III, part II, sec. VII.

will reduce living people to the measure of this diagram. He will, in other words, stigmatise as misconduct all conduct deviating from that which, according to him, the citizen should practise for his good, and he will consider unjust all spontaneous relations which will not establish the citizen in the condition in which he wishes to see him. An authority of this kind will be equally detestable whether it is exercised by one man or by an oligarchic group; nor will it be less so for being borne along on a current of opinion, for it must of its nature always be persecuting nonconformist elements. If the model of particular good is taken from the past, a regime of this kind will have a suffocating effect and will act as a barrier to any sort of novelty; if the model is conceived as a dream of future bliss, it will justify sanguinary upheavals.

Thus, to put the public authority at the service of particular goods has equally deplorable results whether the goods have been conceived by individuals or by the authority. It is an idea which leads to disorder in the first case and to tyranny in the second. Our conclusion is, therefore, that it is not the office of the public authority to procure the personal goods of individuals.

Fourth Question: Does the Common Good Consist in the Social Tie Itself?

The natural effort of each to procure himself his personal good is made within a society. And the notion which he forms of this good is itself conditioned by the spectacle of society; the various goods, spiritual and material, which he sees in others, inspire in him both his noblest and his grossest objects of desire. Imitation is so powerful a principle of behaviour that God himself has made use of it, by setting before us through the Incarnation the living exemplar of our Sovereign Good.[3]

Society furnishes us with opportunities for conceiving what our good is to be; it furnishes us also with opportunities for realising it. It is in society that a man meets with the various co-operators and traders by means of whom he assures himself of a material comfort such as he could never acquire in a state of isolation. It is in society again that he finds occasions for romance, enthusiasm and devotion, in other words, his spiritual good. It is by means of social relations that moral and intellectual truths are propounded to him: the gospel was first preached in gatherings of people.

Therefore life in society is the condition of each man's individual good, indeed of his being a man at all. For life in society is natural to man in the sense of being necessary to the realisation of his true nature. Is it also natural in the sense of being primary, or is it in that sense artificial, as being the product of actions which have created it?

The greatest political thinkers, such as Hobbes and Rousseau, have called it artificial and have made us the spectators of its creation. For this they have been strongly attacked on the ground of the extreme improbability of man ever having lived in any other state; the argument comes down to saying that man was found in social formations of an elementary kind from the moment that he passed the threshold of humanity. But these great geniuses had very good reasons for

---

[3] Herein lies the seriousness of the monophysite heresy. If Jesus had not entirely assumed man's nature, if he was merely God in disguise, it would follow that human nature would be powerless to imitate him; and it is imitation of him which has been set before us.

compressing into a single day, "the day of creation" of their imaginations, a process which took a thousand years; if it is untrue that society was made in a day, it is true that it is made and unmade every day. And the myth of instantaneous creation enabled them to bring out in sharpest relief the conditions on which social life is possible.

It matters little that society was not in fact founded on one bright morning by the deliberate and simultaneous assent of each of its members, if this hypothesis makes clear that a daily, muddled, assent by each is necessary to social existence. It matters little that men did not in fact emerge from a state of war, in which their appetites clashed, into a state of peace, in which their desires are, so far as they clash, bridled, and are sublimated to tasks of co-operation; it is enough if this hypothesis demonstrates that the curbing of the ego and the awareness of the whole are essential to a viable society. Nor does it matter much more that men did not on any particular day give themselves a government and did not on another day receive a body of laws, if by means of this fable the reality of interdependence is brought out by the fiction of simultaneity.

Lastly and above all, it is better to picture society as artificial than to call it natural (in the sense of spontaneous), for only so can the point be made effectively that art is necessary to its support and development. The real purpose of those who postulated the formation of society as an act of will was to put us on guard against social dissolution; the victory which, in their account of it, was won in a single day by the forces of integration over those of disaggregation is the very victory which has to be won every day of life.

It will be noted that they have told us nothing as to the end or good which the rulers of the social edifice in being were to seek; may not the reason be that those rulers' entire task consisted in the consolidation and development of the social tie which had been formed? That, in short, the common good for which those in government were responsible, up to the limit of their powers, was the foundation in perpetuity of man's social condition?

We must never forget the admirable dictum of Rivarol: "All executive power is in the hands of individuals"; it is never possible for it to be conveyed to the rulers, for there is never a moment in which, even under the most frightful tyranny, each man does not remain the master of his own actions.[4] Therefore the social state is merely one in which the executive powers of individuals are used not to hurt but to bring mutual advantage. As this state of things can never exist completely, the social state is a matter of degree; it is always in the making just as it is always in process of coming apart.

As a working hypothesis we will admit that the common good consists in the social state itself and in its successive advances. But what is meant by "social state," and why do we speak of "social good" and "social tie"?

[4] There is a prevalent illusion that the power of constraint possessed by the authorities is great; at the worst they have only a power of intimidation, itself resting on assents on the part of the men who serve as their instruments. That, incidentally, is why a despotism always breaks down in the long run; it ceases to be served and with that it ceases to intimidate – two phenomena which are complementary to each other.

Fifth Question: Is Life in Society the Institutionalisation of Trust?

Human actions are, it is clear, based on confidence in others. The condition of a man would be miserable — it might be truer to say that he would never even have become a man — if at every moment he had to be on guard against the unforeseeable actions of every other man. Our progress in and towards the human condition presupposes that we live within a circle of peace and friendship, in which not only do we not anticipate attacks but we expect to be succoured at need.

There is in man, as in the animals, a power of affection, which inspires in him friendly behaviour. But he does not so behave to every other person without exception. It is unnatural for us to behave in friendly fashion indiscriminately; still less will those who do not give us their friendship receive ours. The very greatest saints, whose love knew no bounds and expected no return, thus acted only for the love of God. The affection which reaches directly only a small number of people is, therefore, extended to a much wider circle only by means of an intermediary — because strangers too are subject to the same loved whole. The friendly feelings inspired by the unknown family of a friend may also be inspired by the unknown members of a whole, the whole in the second case having as regards the unknown the effect of the friend in the first. In this way the fictitious person, the group, enlarges the circle of friendships, of those who will at their need receive our service and give their service at ours.

Awareness of a "we" is aroused by real affections and is in the present indicative for persons known to us; it constrains our affections to the conditional future, or to the imperative, for unknown persons who are members of the "we." The "we" breeds obligations which are really feelings of linkage. Awareness in each "he" of these obligations constitutes for each "me" a powerful safeguard. It enables "me" to have confidence in "him." This confidence is the condition on which human activity can develop.

The activities of the fisherman in his boat and of the farmer in his field do not, it is true, directly involve any other person, except in so far as both of them need to have what they produce bought by others; but most activities of men in society are based very directly indeed on an anticipated intervention by other men.

The regular and foreseeable behaviour of these others and the possibility of anticipating their reactions with the smallest margin of error are the pillars on which every individual calculation rests. Hardly any plans could be made if the degree of uncertainty in the behaviour and attitude of other people was known to be very high. Therein is the miracle of society: my calculations, though calling for the intervention of a very large number of free agents, can yet be made as if there was no question of free agents at all. Mobile as they are, these agents yet furnish me with fixed points on which to hinge my action. Life in society can be denoted by the wide range of my certainties regarding others.

To say "foreigner" is as much as to say "enemy" — an agent whose conduct is not foreseeable. It cannot be foreseen because he is not a member of our league of friendship, because his folkways and probable reactions are unknown, and, lastly and most important, because I have no surety for his behaviour.

In effect the public authority of my group is surety, as regards me, for the obligations which its subjects owe me and on which I base myself. It cannot, obviously, ensure that whatever I undertake shall end prosperously, but it has a duty to provide me with sure foundations on which I can make my plans. These foundations are the obligations to me enforced on the other members of the group, obligations to which they are required to show themselves faithful.

Clearly it is in the personal interest of each individual to be able to trust others, and to trust them in two different ways. First, he needs to be able to count on the general complaisance of others, and that presupposes a social climate of friendship; next, he must know with reasonable certainty how others will conduct themselves towards him. This personal interest, which is particular for each and the same for all, constitutes a real common interest; it cannot be said of it *a priori* that it is an exhaustive description of the common good, but at least it emerges as its primary and essential constituent.

32. Public and Common Interests

Brian Barry

The definition of the meaning of "the public interest" which I propose makes it equivalent to "those interests which people have in common *qua* members of the public." I shall treat "public" in this section and "common interests" in the next.

A hundred and thirty years ago, Sir George Cornewall Lewis offered a general definition of "public" which it is impossible to improve upon:

> *Public*, as opposed to *private*, is that which has no immediate relation to any specified person or persons, but may directly concern any member or members of the community, without distinction. Thus the acts of a magistrate, or a member of a legislative assembly, done by them in those capacities, are called public; the acts done by the same persons towards their family or friends, or in their dealings with strangers for their own peculiar purposes, are called private. So a theatre, or a place of amusement, is said to be public, not because it is actually visited by every member of the community, but because it is open to all indifferently; and any person may, if he desire, enter it. The same remark applies to public houses, public inns, public meetings, &c. The publication of a book is the exposing of it to sale in such a mamner that it may be procured by any person who desires to purchase it: it would be equally published, if not a single copy was sold. In the language of our law, public appear to be distinguished from private acts of parliament, on the ground that the one class directly affects the whole community, the other some definite person or persons.[1]

Bentham's discussion in "Principles of the Penal Code" has some extra points

From Brian Barry, *Political Argument* (London: Routledge & Kegan Paul Ltd., 1965; New York: Humanities Press, Inc., 1965), pp. 190–206, by permission of the author and publishers.

[1] *Remarks on the Use and Abuse of Some Political Terms* (London, 1832), pp. 233–234. Here is an additional example, from the many which might be given. "Pious and charitable" bequests tend to be distingushed by their "public purpose" and we find, not surprisingly, the same criterion. "A charity, in the legal sense, may be . . . defined as a gift – for the benefit of an indefinite number of persons. . . ." (Supreme Court of Massachusetts, in Jackson *v.* Phillips, 14 All 539 Supreme Court of Massachusetts, 1867.)

highly relevant for my purposes, while resting on the same general distinction as Lewis.[2]

  1st. *Private Offences.* Those which are injurious to such or such assignable individuals. An *assignable* individual is such or such an individual in particular, to the exclusion of every other; as Peter, Paul, or William other than the delinquent himself.

  2nd. *Reflective Offences, or Offences Against One's Self.*

  3rd. *Semi-public Offences.* Those which affect a portion of the community, a district, a particular corporation, a religious sect, a commercial company, or any association of individuals united by some common interest, but forming a circle inferior in extent to that of the community.

  It is never a present evil nor a past evil that constitutes a semi-public offence. If the evil were present or past, the individuals who suffer, or who have suffered, would be assignable. It would then be an offence of the first class, a private offence. In semi-public offences the point is a future evil, – a danger which threatens, but which as yet attacks no particular individual.

  4th. *Public Offences.* Those which produce some common danger to all the members of the state, or to an indefinite number of non-assignable individuals, although it does not appear that any one in particular is more likely to suffer than any other.

So much for "public" as an adjective; but how about "the public"? Here again the emphasis is on "an indefinite number of non-assignable individuals." The main (though not the only) kind of situation which gives rise to "publics" is that where people are affected as consumers, using the term broadly. A rail strike would inconvenience "the public" (i.e. it will inconvenience travellers and those sending goods by rail). "The public" (i.e. those using the park as opposed to, say, the municipal gardeners) are requested to keep off the grass in the park. For doctors "the public" is patients; for theatre managers it is theatregoers or potential theatregoers, for civil servants it is citizens (i.e. roughly, consumers of government services) and so on. Clearly, the qualifications for being "a member of the public" vary from one situation to another, and we cannot therefore speak of what "the public interest" requires until we know the particular context in which the question is being raised.[3]

Common Interests: Introduction. To say that two or more people have common (or divergent) interests is to make an incomplete statement. Nor is it complete to say that they have a common interest in a certain policy's being put into effect or a certain action's being taken. This is due to a feature which "interest" shares with "good," "welfare" and "favourably affected," namely that they are necessarily comparative. You can ask "would this policy be fair?" without introducing a comparison with some other policy. In other words, "This policy is fair" does not for the sake of completeness require expansion into "This policy is fairer than that policy." But if you ask whether a certain policy would be in someone's interest (etc.) this *does* require expansion into "Is this policy more in his interests than that

----

  [2] *The Theory of Legislation* (London, 1931), p. 240.

  [3] "The membership of the public is not fixed. It changes with the issue: the actors in one affair are the spectators of another, and men are continually passing back and forth between the field where they are executives and the field where they are members of a public." Walter Lippmann, *The Phantom Public* (New York, 1927), p. 110.

policy?" "Being in someone's interests" is at least a triadic relation between a person and at least two policies.

This phenomenon of a concept not on its face comparative being in fact comparative is quite common. Hume remarked on it in the following terms:

> That there is a natural difference between merit and demerit, virtue and vice, wisdom and folly, no reasonable man will deny: yet it is evident that, in affixing the term, which denotes either our approbation or blame, we are commonly more influenced by comparison than by any fixed unalterable standard in the nature of things. In a like manner, quantity, and extention, and bulk, are by everyone acknowledged to be real things: but when we call any animal *great* or *little*, we always form a secret comparison between that animal and others of the same species; and it is that comparison which regulates our judgement concerning its greatness. A dog and a horse may be of the very same size, while the one is admired for the greatness of its bulk, and the other for its smallness. When I am present, therefore, at any dispute, I always consider with myself whether it be a question of comparison or not that is the subject of controversy; and if it be, whether the disputants compare the same objects together, or talk of things that are widely different.[4]

It is of considerable importance to make a distinction between *standards* and *criteria* so as to avoid drawing from this wider conclusions than are warranted.[5] The criterion remains the same from one context to another; the comparison affects only the standard. The criterion for "being larger than" is the same whether one is talking about dogs or horses; it is only the standard defining the minimum size which an animal has to be before it can be called "large" which varies from one kind of animal to another. A good golfer by local standards may be a mediocre one by national standards, and a good one by national standards mediocre by world standards; but the criterion of a "good golfer" is always the ability to turn in scores lower than the average of the relevant class. Similarly, if the standards of university entrance go up, all this means is that students have to be better to gain a place; but the criteria of "being a better student" need not alter. (They may of course alter but this would be an independent change.)

The application of this distinction to "interest" (etc.) may now be traced. A certain policy can be "in so-and-so's interest" when it is compared with another alternative. The standard which the policy has to meet alters between one comparison and the other. But at the same time the criteria for "one policy's being more in somebody's interest than another" do not alter; and I would of course claim that they are as set out in the last chapter.

Neglect of the way in which all statements about "interest" carry a "secret comparison" between one policy and another is responsible for a good deal of shadow boxing in arguments as to whether or not a policy (e.g. a certain specific reduction in particular tariffs) is in my, your or everybody's interests. Two people may agree on what kinds of results any policy must have for it to count as being more in a person's interests than an alternative. They may also agree on what the

---

[4] "Of the Dignity or Meanness of Human Nature," *David Hume's Political Essays*, ed. Charles Hendel (New York, 1953).

[5] Hume, in the passage quoted, is plainly resisting the temptation to suppose that the point about comparisons proves more than it in fact does when he says that "quantity, and extension, and bulk, are by everyone acknowledged to be real things" although the comparison "regulates our judgement."

actual results of policy x will be if it is adopted. Yet they may still disagree on whether it would be in their (or everyone's) interest for it to be adopted because each is forming a different "secret comparison" between x and possible rival policies. One disputant may be asserting that x isn't in his interests because he can think of a policy that would be even better for him. Another may say that it *is* in his interests because it would make him better off than the *status quo*. And another may take an intervening position, comparing x not with all logically possible alternatives, however absurd and unlikely (e.g. prohibitive duties on toothpaste, everything else admitted free – probably the policy most in the interests of a toothpaste manufacturer) but with the half dozen or so which stand some chance of being enacted; and compared to these he may assert that x is (let us say) in the interests of most people but not all.

The same neglect is responsible for statements that there are no interests common to all the members of a society. The grounds advanced for the view are that any proposal which becomes practical politics is opposed by some group.[6] This is superficial because it ignores the question: why are some logically possible proposals never advocated by anyone at all? Why, for example, is nobody in the USA in favour of having the Strategic Air Command take off and drop all its bombs on the USA? Obviously, because nobody at all believes this would be in his interests. To point out as if it were a great discovery that all proposals *which are actually put forward* meet opposition is as naïve as expressing surprise at the fact that in all cases which reach the Supreme Court there is something to be said on each side. (If there isn't, someone has been wasting an awful lot of money.)

Once we remember that "being in A's interest" is at least a triadic relationship (between A and at least two policies) we can easily see how empty it is to talk in general about common and divergent interests. For any given proposal there is nearly always at least one that compared to it is in someone's interests and at least one that compared to it is contrary to someone's interests. To say that two or more people have a common interest is to say that there are two policies x and y such that each of them prefers x to y from the point of view of his own interest. On this definition it is safe to say that *any* two people have a common interest as between *some* two policies and *any* two people have a divergent interest as between *some* two policies; and the same is (by the same reasoning) true of groups.

Common interests are ubiquitous even among enemies[7] and so are divergent interests among allies.[8] Instead of speaking in blanket terms about people or groups

[6] For example: Arthur F. Bentley, *The Process of Government* (Indiana, 1949), p. 122: "We shall never find a group interest of the society as a whole." David B. Truman, *The Governmental Process: Political Interest and Public Opinion* (New York, 1951), p. 51: "We do not need to account for a totally inclusive interest, because one does not exist."

[7] See Thomas C. Schelling, *The Strategy of Conflict* (Cambridge, Mass., 1960), pp. 4–5, 11; and also Schelling, "Reciprocal Measures for Arms Stabilization," *Arms Control, Disarmament and National Security*, ed. Donald G. Brennan (New York, 1961), p. 169: "It is not true that in the modern world a gain for the Russians is necessarily a loss for us, and vice versa. We can both suffer losses, and this fact provides scope for cooperation. We both have – unless the Russians have already determined to launch an attack and are preparing for it – a common interest in reducing the advantage of striking first, simply because that very advantage, even if common to both sides, increases the likelihood of war. If at the expense of some capability for launching surprise attack one can deny that capability to the other, it may be a good bargain."

[8] E. E. Schattschneider, *Politics, Pressures and the Tariff* (New York, 1935), p. 224: "The very nature of tariff legislation, since it involves a vast number of independent conflicts of interest, is such as to bring out the fissures in almost any group, however homogeneous it may

with common or opposed interests, we should speak of people or groups whose interests coincide or conflict with respect to the adoption of x rather than y. If once we do this, it becomes plain that there are considerable possibilities for "common interests" so interpreted, among all the citizens of a country as well as among wider groups.

A final point in this introductory section is that a person may be affected in a number of different ways by a certain policy as he is impinged upon by it in different roles or capacities. As a motorist, tighter enforcement of the speed limit is not in his interest, as a pedestrian it is; as an importer of some raw materials it is not in his interests to have higher tariffs all round, as a seller who has to compete with foreign rivals it is; and so on. I shall therefore distinguish between a man's interests *as a ϕ* (that is, in some particular capacity) and his *net interest* in a policy (that is, how he is affected overall, striking a balance between the pluses and minuses incurred in his various capacities). So far, I have been thinking only of net interests, but the interests which people share with one another in virtue of similar roles or capacities, even if these interests are overlaid with others which diverge, are analytically and practically important too.

Common Interests in Policies. Though common net interests in particular actions even extending to a community are not impossible in principle it must be agreed that between pairs of particular actions actually proposed it is unlikely that one of them would be better for everyone than the other. This is particularly true where the benefit redounds to assignable persons, that is, where each person can say precisely what he has gained. More promising are cases where some hazard is averted which might indifferently have struck any member of the community but would probably not have struck all. For example, suppose high seas will cause flooding costing £100 per head to half the population unless the dykes are strengthened at a cost of £10 per head to the whole population. The action of strengthening the dykes would be in everyone's interest *provided* nobody knew in advance whether or not he would be among the half who would be flooded. If some know they will be safe anyway, the levy will represent to them a £10 loss rather than a bargain-rate insurance with an expected value of $(0.5 \times £100 =)$ £50.

But it is policies rather than particular actions which provide the most scope for common interests among the members of communities and this is again because the incidence of benefits and losses arising under it cannot be accurately predicted in advance. An insurance policy is an example of what I mean here by "a policy": it says that if at any time you suffer a certain loss you will be compensated. Retrospectively, each person can work out whether he has gained or lost from having his house insured against fire; but prospectively, he is simply forced to work out whether, given the premium and the risk of fire, it is worth having insurance. He knows that at the end of the year he will either be glad or sorry that he insured his house. But that is no help to him in making up his mind because he has no way of telling now whether he will be glad or sorry.

Many government programmes — medical care, unemployment relief, etc. — are

seem in other relations. Indeed, in tariff legislation it is often the interests which lie nearest to each other in the families of industries which have contradictory needs. Add to this the fact that trade associations may be formed on many bases, most of which bear no reference to the tariff, and it may be seen that interests within single groups are often complex."

of this kind. Though the benefits and costs are always specific, nobody can know whether over the course of his life he will gain from them or not so it may be in everyone's interest to support such programmes and save worry. This is the sort of thing I refer to as a *policy*; it consists not simply of a decision to give *A* ten pounds a week but to give everyone in such-and-such conditions ten pounds a week. Most laws are "policies" in this sense; indeed, laws which specify individuals to be punished are distinguished as "acts of attainder" (and prohibited under the U.S. Constitution).

Very often where there is not common interest in a specific act *x* there will be a common interest in a policy under which acts of type *x* will be carried out. For example, there may be no single road in a country to whose building cost it would be in everyone's interest to contribute; but it may still be in everyone's interest to contribute to the costs of a policy under which roads will be built all over the country wherever some criterion of "need" is satisfied.

Rousseau's use of the distinction between what he calls "laws" and "decrees" is precisely the same as that which I have been making between "policies" and "particular acts." Since in supporting a policy you are in effect writing a blank cheque which events may in future write your name on, it behoves you to be careful. Before voting to make the penalty for murder severe, remember you may some day be in the dock. Before voting to make it lenient remember you may some day be the victim.[9] In voting on particular actions, however, the people are not making a "general" judgement, because the gainers and losers are assignable. This is a job of deciding between interests and should, Rousseau says, be left to executive or judicial agencies.

The mental block against accepting this point of view which some people appear to have may arise from confusing it with a crude "harmony of interests" theory of the kind Pareto dissected as follows;

> Some writers, such as Pufendorf, Hobbes, Spinoza, and Locke, think that there is a sanction for natural laws in the fact that the individual who violates them does harm to Society and hence to himself as a member of society. The fallacy lies (1): In disregarding the amounts of gain or loss, on the assumption that *all* individuals are to act in one way or *all* in another, and in not considering the case where some individuals are to act in one way and some in another. (2) In going to extremes along the line of the above and considering gains only, or losses only. In fact, let us adopt the premise that if *all* individuals refrained from doing *A* every individual as a member of the community would derive a certain advantage. But now if all individuals *less one* continue refraining from doing *A*, the community loss is very slight, whereas the one individual doing *A* makes a personal gain far greater than the loss he incurs as a member of the community.[10]

Pareto's strictures do not, however, apply to Rousseau (or, I suspect, to the authors mentioned by him). Rousseau does not deny that it may be in your interest to *break* a law which benefits you *qua* member of the community; all he says is that it is certainly in your interests to *vote* for it, and that if you have voted in favour of a certain punishment for a certain crime you have no business to complain if your

---

[9] Cf. John Rawls, "Justice as Fairness," *The Philosophical Review*, LXVII, No. 2 (April 1958), pp. 164–194, reprinted in Olafson (ed.), *Justice and Social Policy*.

[10] Vilfredo Pareto, *The Mind and Society (Tratto di sociologia generale)* ed. Arthur Livingston (New York, 1935), pp. 945–946.

wish for a certain general policy is applied to you in a particular case. Exactly the same point may be made about contracts: it is in your interests to enter into some contracts even though it would be even better for you if you could avoid performing your part of the agreement.

The complexity of modern society makes it hard to see this principle at work, so I offer this example:

The Eskimos living in the Coronation Gulf live mainly on seals. Small seals are taken home by the hunter and cooked; the wife

> either invites the neighbors to join in a meal at her house or sends portions of cooked food to families that are known to be without fresh meat.
>
> When a hunter secures a bearded [large] seal he does not take it home but stands on a small ice hummock with hands outstretched long enough to turn around three times slowly. All hunters who see him doing this gather, and the most influential of them cuts the seal into as many pieces as there are hunters present.[11]

The hunter gets the last piece, the divider next to last — an interesting solution to the "problem of fair division."

The policy described probably could not be changed so as to make everyone better off so long as everyone played the game. If some slacked or stopped sharing, this would be in the short run good for them but the rest would soon call a meeting to decide what was to be done, and no doubt everyone would find that the only policy which could command unanimous agreement would be one of *enforcing* the old rules. It would be in everyone's interest to agree to this rather than be excluded, since an individual hunter is quite likely to starve sooner or later between catching one seal and another; but it would of course be even better to agree and then break the rules. Everyone is better off in the first position than the second except undetected rule-breakers; so far the "harmony" theorists are right. Everyone is better in the second position than the broken-down form of the first position; this is what Hobbes and Rousseau point out. But if you can escape detection in the second position you may be even better than keeping the rules in the first position; and if you can break the rules in the first position without this having a perceptible effect on others (either in the direction of joining the racket or beating it) this is best of all: thus Pareto.

But if the popular error is to underestimate the areas of common interest in policies, this is no reason for going to the other extreme and supposing that the uncertainty of the future is the password to the rehabilitation of common interests in all areas of social life. This is an error which can be generated by confining one's attention too exclusively to the simpler parts of the criminal law (e.g. the law prohibiting murder) and "much of our Road Traffic law."[12] There are many other matters where a person's qualities affect his prospects under different policies.

Consider qualities such as being highly educated or not, skilled or unskilled, intelligent or unintelligent, white or coloured. These are unlikely to alter very much over one's life-span, at least without considerable effort, and they will inevitably place their owners differently under different general arrangements. A white man could hardly be counted on to oppose Negro slavery on the grounds that he might

---

[11] Vilhjalmur Stefansson, "Was Liberty Invented?" *Freedom — Its Meaning*, ed. Ruth Nanda Anshen (New York, 1940), p. 400.

[12] John D. Mabbott, *The State and the Citizen*, p. 67.

later turn into a Negro, for example. Thus, many of the basic issues on which there is a *prima facie* conflict of interest are not alleviated much by the fact that the future is unpredictable. People voting on political and economic arrangements are not simply choosing a set of roles on the understanding that they will have an equal chance of getting assigned any role; they have a fairly distinct idea of the general position they will occupy. And in practice I believe that it is impossible to explain actual voting behaviour unless we do assume that people are willing to count on getting one role rather than another. For example, suppose that the Southern representatives at Philadelphia had been asked to choose between, on the one hand, a ¼ chance of owning three slaves and a ¾ chance of being one (or generally a $1/n$ chance of owning $n - 1$ slaves and an $n - 1/n$ of being one); and on the other hand the certainty of neither being nor owning a slave. I suspect that most would have chosen the latter alternative; yet the Southern representatives certainly did not take the opportunity to press for slavery to be ruled out by the new constitution – on the contrary.[13]

Common Interests in Rules for Choosing Actions and Policies. Must the idea of "common interest" stop at policies? Not necessarily. Under favourable conditions it may be that everyone can reasonably expect to gain if a higher-order policy is adopted which specifies some criteria and says that *any* action or policy which satisfies these criteria is to be put into effect. An example would be a general rule to the effect that aggregatively justified changes should always be made. The classical economists, from Bentham to Edgeworth, often adopted this line of justification for utilitarian recommendations,[14] and in spite of Lord Keynes's dictum that "in the long run we're all dead," J. R. Hicks revived the idea in the 1940s.

> If the economic activities of a community were organized on the principle of making no alterations in the organization of production which were not improvements in this sense [that is, changes where the gainer *could* compensate the losers and still be better off] and making all alterations which were improvements that it could possibly find, then, although we could not say that all the inhabitants of that community would be necessarily better off than they would have been if the community had been organized on some different principle, nevertheless there would be a strong probability that almost all of them would be better off after the lapse of a sufficient length of time.[15]

[13] See William Vickrey, "Utility, Strategy, and Social Decision Rules," *The Quarterly Journal of Economics*, LXXIV (1960), pp. 507–536). Another point made by Vickrey is that even if the impossibility of predicting future roles were complete, people might still vote for different role-sets unless they had identical feelings about risk and identical ideas about the marginal utility of money at different incomes. (I think these are intuitively distinct concepts even if there is no way of distinguishing them operationally.) Otherwise, one man might prefer a role-set which gave him a big chance of a low income and a small chance of a high income, while another might prefer the reverse and a third a certainty of some intermediate income. A corollary of this is that even if *laissez faire* produced the highest real income measured in, say, expected-value terms, a rational agent might still prefer a lower expected value if he preferred a certain income to a gamble with a higher expected value but carrying the possibility of destitution.

[14] See Gunnar Myrdal, *The Political Element in the Development of Economic Theory*, tr. by Paul Streeten (London, 1953), pp. 211–212.

[15] "The Rehabilitation of Consumers' Surplus," *Review of Economic Studies*, VIII, No. 2 (February 1941), p. 111.

The limitations on this approach are fairly easy to see: some decisions would have such large effects on distribution that it would be idle to expect them to be more than cancelled out by small changes. Nevertheless, where decisions have fairly small effects on distribution and do appear to be justified on general utilitarian grounds public authorities often carry them out with general approval, and it is plausible to think that underlying this is a general assumption that in the long run everyone will gain if public authorities always act on this basis.

Instead of rules such as that just canvassed, which would still have to be applied, a group might find a common interest (compared at least with the prospect of not settling them at all) in settling things according to some automatic procedure, such as chance or voting. With chance each person might hope to be favoured by the winning policy as much on the average as anyone else, while with voting he might hope to be in the majority more often than not. . . .

It should be observed that where such a higher-level policy is in operation, it is that which is "in the public interest" and not the particular policies and actions which are carried out because they satisfy it; i.e. that it is the "majority-principle" or the "principle of utility" which is "in the public interest," rather than this or that application. In just the same way, where some particular policy is in everyone's interest in its own right . . . , it is incorrect to say that the specific actions carried out under it are in everyone's interest. For example, even if it is in everyone's interest to hang murderers, it is obviously not in any given murderer's interest to be hanged.

Public Good and Common Good

. . . I wish to turn aside briefly to extend the analysis of "public interest" and "common interest" already given to "public good" and "common good."

"Public good" presents few problems; it appears to work in exactly the same way as "public interest" inasfar as the meaning of "good" diverges from that of "interest." That is to say that whereas "the public interest" tends to be restricted to contexts where the means of general want-satisfaction are at stake, "the public good" can be used more widely as in the Obscene Publications Act already quoted, which allows "science, literature, art or learning" as elements of the "public good." Between the most typical uses of "common good" and "common interest," however, there seems to be a wider difference than can be accounted for by the different shades of meaning represented by "good" and "interest." This can be seen in two differences between typical uses of "common good" and "common interest" which, though related to the difference between "good" and "interest" themselves, are not wholly reducible to those differences.

The first difference is that the common interest of the members of a group is often held to lie in something which would benefit them at the expense of someone else.[16] The common interest of employers is formulated with reference to

---

[16] The tendency is even stronger with "the national interest," which extremely often refers to the interests of the inhabitants of a certain country in that country's relations with others. Even where this is not superficially so, as when wage claims or speculation in foreign exchanges are said to be "contrary to the national interest" it is still usually the external relations of the state which are being thought of, e.g. its balance of payments or its exchange rate.

"The national interest" may either mean the interests of the members of the state which

employees, and *vice versa.* "Common good," on the other hand, seems to be used almost exclusively for talking about the relations *within* some group rather than the relations between the members of a group and those outside the group.

The second difference is that "the common good" is invoked in order to justify a particular allocation of scarce resources but not to justify an arrangement whereby incentives and deterrents are fixed with the object of modifying behaviour. A system of rewards to encourage work or of punishments to discourage law-breaking might well be supported by saying that it was "in the public interest" but hardly that it was "for the common good." There is another way of putting what is, I think, the same point. "The public interest" is used where an institution or a political action is to be defended; *par excellence* it is an administrator's concept. "The common good" is typically used in a very different way, namely in the context of an *appeal* to individual people to do something or other which is contrary to their net interests. Thus, where a greater use of incentives might be supported as being "in the public interest," the alternative of an appeal to those concerned to work harder without extra pay would be couched in terms of "the common good." Of course, for there to be a net sacrifice involved in doing something "for the common good" the result to be brought about plainly cannot be in the net interests of everyone concerned; it must rather be in their interest (or "for their good") in the "as a ϕ sense. In other words someone who is asked to make a net sacrifice for the common good is being asked to place those elements in his own good which he shares with others above those elements the pursuit of which benefits only him.

I have taken the case where the pursuit of the common good entails a net sacrifice as being more typical. But it is possible to conceive situations where a "natural identity of interests" obtained, especially in a small group, such that a man's net interest lay in pursuing those interests which he shared with the rest of the group. For example, if there are six people in a lifeboat and all of them must either row or pump if any is to survive then the common good and each individual's good coincide in requiring the same actions. But such cases are surely unusual. Where the group is larger and the conditions are less extreme (so that results are "more or less" rather than "all or nothing") it is more likely that the amount of damage a person does himself *qua* group member by pursuing his private interests exclusively will not on balance make it worthwhile (from a purely self-interested point of view) for him to further the interests he shares with the group at the expense of those he does not. A man who makes a fortune selling substandard goods to the army in a war, for example, makes defeat more likely, let us say; but the increased probability of defeat is so fractional that it is not likely to be more significant *to him* than the certain fortune he can make. T. H. Green appears to have laboured under the belief that before someone could be expected to pursue the common good he must somehow be convinced that he was thereby pursuing his own greatest (net) good.[17] It is surely more consistent with common sense to say

---

they have in common *qua* members of the state, or it may sometimes mean the interests of the members of the state considered as a group for aggregative purposes. ... I notice a way in which "public interest" degenerates into an undifferentiated aggregative concept; but it is far easier to treat "the nation" as a (fictitious) entity having a single "interest" than it is to treat "the public" in the same way.

[17] It was in order to make this work that he declared a man's greatest good to lie in a desire to pursue the common good; unfortunately, "the common good" can then only mean a community where everyone has such desires.

that people may put the common good before their own individual good for purely altruistic reasons or from a belief that it is only fair to make a contribution to those sources of one's own good which are provided by the efforts of others. For example, if others shovel snow off the pavement in front of their houses "for the common good" so that one benefits from cleared pavements, it is surely fair to shovel the snow outside one's own house too. Similarly, if others burn smokeless fuel "for the common good," thus giving one the benefits of a less smoky atmosphere, it is fair to do the same oneself.[18]

Notice that these are (or, at least, may well be) true cases of a divergence between the common good and an individual's own good in that the amount of benefit *he* would get from clearing *his own* pavement will quite likely be not worth the effort. Of course, the benefit from *everyone's* clearing his own pavement may still be greater for each person than the cost in effort to each person of clearing his own pavement; indeed, if this were not so for at least most people it would be better (on aggregative grounds) for nobody to bother about clearing the snow at all. But unless he thinks his own decision will affect others by example this calculation has no relevance for a purely self-interested individual deciding whether or not to clear his own pavement.

If appeals to "the common good" were ineffective it would be possible to introduce a rule with sanctions requiring everyone to clear the pavement outside his house (cf. Smokeless Zones). This would be supported on the grounds that it was "in the public interest" and it might well be in the *net* interest of everyone to vote for it. If it were once passed, there would no longer be any need to appeal to "the common good" in order to get people to clear their pavements; provided the sanctions were great enough and were enforced against a high enough proportion of offenders it would be possible to rely on self-interest (i.e. the fear of a penalty).[19]

[18] These examples can be brought under the principle put forward by John Rawls in "Justice as Fairness" to the effect that if one enjoys the benefits of a practice there is a *prima facie* obligation to undertake the burdens prescribed by the practice also; but in order to do this one would I think have to widen Rawls' notion of a practice. The benefits of smoke control and snow clearing do not depend upon there being a rule saying everyone (or everyone in a certain category) should do it. Even if only one man burns smokeless fuel or clears the snow outside his house this helps; and the essential point is that additional people following suit help strictly in proportion to their numbers. (This is always on the assumption that uncleared pavements are merely inconvenient. If there were only a path and if one uncleared stretch made it impassable there would be no point in anyone clearing his section unless everyone did. Under *these* circumstances one would have the makings of a Rawlsian "practice.")

[19] It is the existence of this phenomenon which explains how there can be both a "natural identity of interests" in some matter and an "artificial identity of interests" in the same matter. There can be a natural (i.e. independent of any law) identity of interest in *having* a law with penalties to make everyone do so-and-so or refrain from doing so-and-so (i.e. a law that will produce an artificial identity of interests). Lindsay, for example, decries the Benthamites' espousal simultaneously of natural and artificial identity of interests: *Modern Democratic State*, p. 142. His own confusion is sharply brought out in his virtual equation of anarchy and *laissez faire*: *laissez faire* is the theory that everyone will gain relatively to any other economic policy if everyone pursues his own interests within a certain framework of laws (e.g. enforcing contracts). It is thus a good example of natural *and* artificial identity. The same failure to appreciate that there may be an identity of interest in maintaining a coercive structure incidentally vitiates Lindsay's strictures on Hobbes in the same volume.

33. Public Interest and Political Discourse

Richard E. Flathman

I

Congressman Jones, in a speech to the American Medical Association, says "The Medicare Bill is in the public interest." What is the force of his statement? His audience might respond that the statement demonstrates Jones's lack of the necessary qualifications for public office. The President of the United Americans for the Defense of Senior Citizens might regard it as evidence of Jones's deep understanding of social problems, his compassion for his fellow man, and the high priority to be assigned to his request for campaign assistance. The sophisticated political analyst is likely to interpret the statement as evidence that Jones is beholden to the President, who ranks the bill first on his legislative program, or that Jones has a large populace of senior citizens in his constituency. But there are two points on which all of these respondents agree: the force of Jones's statement is to express, however sincerely, approval, approbation, or commendation of the measure in question; and his approval carries the special force of commending the measure as one that could properly be made the law of the land. They would agree that "public interest" is employed to express approval of public policy or proposed public policy.

It could be contended that these respondents are mistaken, that "public interest" is not, or is not always, employed to commend. Perhaps Jones is using it as a purely descriptive category. It is perfectly good English for Jones to say "The public interest in this matter is A, but my interest is B, and I am doing everything I can to bring B about." As a matter of fact, we do not always approve of everything that is in the public interest, and our language allows us to state that this is the case. But if behavior contrary to the public interest is common enough, statements announcing such behavior are rare indeed – and positively unheard of from congressmen. The reason is precisely that "public interest" is a term ordinarily used to commend or approve; the primary function of the concept in our language is to convey approval or commendation of public policy. Hence, if an English-speaker applies it to a measure or policy, thereby conveying to other English-speakers that he believes the measure is deserving of approval, but then expresses personal disapproval of it, his behavior is odd if not contradictory. What is more, his behavior will carry a strong suggestion of immorality.[1]

From *The Public Interest: An Essay Concerning the Normative Discourse of Politics* by Richard E. Flathman, pp. 5–13. Copyright © 1966 by John Wiley & Sons, Inc. Reprinted by permission.

[1] These remarks do not mean that "public interest" can be employed only to express approval. Consider the following. "It is widely believed that X is in the public interest." "Is X in the public interest?" "At first I was persuaded that X is in the public interest, but now I'm not so sure." None of these locutions would make sense to a person who did not understand that "public interest" is most commonly used to express approval or commendation. It should

At a minimum, then, we can say that "public interest" is used to express approval or commendation of policies adopted or proposed by government. Starting from this rudimentary position, we can investigate what philosophers call the "logic" of the discourse of commendation in the area of politics. A beginning can be made by asking why it is that we utilize a specialized vocabulary in political discourse. We speak not of the satisfaction or service of "interest," but of service of the "public interest"; not of "good," but of the "common good"; not of welfare, but of the "general welfare."[2] A partial explanation for the presence of the adjectives lies in a fact concerning the political order. In political life, one agent, government, acts in the name and on the behalf of all of the members of the system, and its actions apply to all. The actions of government are in principle universal (within the system) in application.[3] The concepts we use to express our evaluations of these actions are adapted from more general commendatory language in recognition of this fact.

We can explore this question further by examining the relationship between "public interest" and other major concepts of political discourse. A good starting point is the concept of "rights." This concept and the concept of "duties" are correlative. No one can have a right unless other persons have corollary duties.[4] If I claim that I have a right to strike against my employer, I *mean that* the other members of the political system in question have a duty not to interfere with my efforts to strike. Furthermore, rights and duties together imply a system of sanctions which supports rights and enforces duties. If I claim the right to strike as a legal right, I mean that the exercise of my right is guaranteed by law and others will be preventing from or punished for violating their duty to respect that right. If I claim this right as a moral right, I mean that other individuals have a moral duty not to interfere and that it will be proper to apply moral sanctions, for example the expression of moral disapproval, against those who do not perform that duty.

The relevant aspects of this argument can be summarized by saying that rights are relational in character and create new interdependencies and extend existing

---

also be noted that "public interest" performs a number of more specialized functions. The Federal Communications Commission, for example, is charged by Congress to regulate broadcasting as the "public convenience, interest, or necessity requires," And the Commission itself has said, "The public interest to be served under the Communications Act is the interest of the listening public in the larger and more effective use of radio." (The examples are taken from Arthur S. Miller, "The Public Interest Undefined," *Journal of Public Law,* Vol. X, p. 184, 1961. See the Symposium of which this article is a part for a variety of examples of uses of the concept.) In these examples, the concept performs a somewhat special function defined by the legislation or context in question, but the specialized function depends upon the general commendatory use of the concept and would be incomprehensible without it.

[2] "Public interest" is now the most common of these locutions, although all three remain in use. (We use the term "national interest" in discussing foreign affairs.) . . . [W]e will treat the first three expressions as synonymous.

[3] In practice we regularly use classifications that restrict the force of laws to classes of people with specific characteristics. But we insist that the laws apply to any and all members of the system who have or come to have the characteristics which define the classification. What is more, we are particular about the principles of classification used. This is the problem of "permissible classification" within the framework of the rule of law.

[4] This relationship has received considerable attention. See, for example, T. H. Green, *Principles of Political Obligation* (London: Longmans, Green, revised edition, 1941); Wesley N. Hohfeld, *Fundamental Legal Conceptions* (New Haven: Yale University Press, 1923); H. L. A. Hart, "Are There Any Natural Rights," *The Philosophical Review,* Vol. 64, No. 2 (April, 1955).

ones. By definition, granting a right to an individual or class of individuals has consequences for others. The worker's right to strike means that his employer has a duty not to prevent him from striking; the employer has a duty not to prevent the worker from bringing the conduct of his business to a halt.

The key concepts used in this brief discussion of "rights" and duties are normative. If I say "I have the [legal] right to strike," I am not merely stating a fact concerning the legal order under which I live. Even if this were the case, or more obviously if I were claiming that such a legal right were my due, I would also be saying that I ought to be allowed to strike and others ought not to be allowed to prevent me from striking. Consider the challenges my claim might have to meet. If my employer says, "I am aware that present legislation establishes your right to strike, but the legislation ought to be repealed or altered for the following reasons . . . ," I must be prepared to offer warrants in defense of the legislation which exists (or which I contend should exist). If I am not prepared to do so, I place myself in the position of seeking benefits under a law which I tacitly concede to be indefensible. Since this law has a marked impact upon others, the warrants I offer must take that impact into account; they must be normative warrants.

This is the point at which the concept of public interest becomes important. If my assertion of a right is successful, it will affect, in principle, all members of the system in which I live. A law will be enforced against any and all members of the system who interfere with my efforts to strike. It might be agreed that the benefits to the individuals with the accorded right are a consideration in deciding whether the law in question *ought* to be enforced, but this consideration is an insufficient warrant for the law. It does nothing to take into account the restrictions placed upon individuals prevented from interfering with strikes and the very real harm strikes might do them. The criteria used to evaluate actions of government must take account of the full range of the effects of those actions. The adjectives "public," "common" and "general" reflect recognition of these effects. This means that we can properly apply "public interest" to a measure only when we have considered the full impact of the measure and have marshaled normative considerations relevant to justifying that impact.[5]

These remarks can be broadened by examining the relationship between "public interest" and a second characteristic feature of modern political systems, representation. The members of the representative's constituency will make conflicting demands which he will be unable to reconcile completely. Yet he will often be required to reach a single decision which must apply to all of his constituents, hence he will be forced to choose among the demands of his constituents and use the power of government to support some of them and frustrate others. If he does so simply because he has a personal preference for one part of his constituency, he will be rightly accused of partiality. This might make it difficult to justify demanding compliance from those who opposed the policy. But avoiding partiality is only one precondition of properly demanding compliance. The representative must justify his decisions in light of his position as an agent whose decisions will be enforced against all of the members of the system. He certifies that

---

[5] The discussion of rights supports an additional conclusion, the importance of which will emerge below. As far as legal rights are concerned, the logic of our use of the concept "rights" requires the presence of a more general commendatory concept such as "public interest." It is only when we are prepared to say "establishing this right and these duties is in the public interest" that we can justifiably assign the right.

he is able to do so when he states that the measure is in the public interest. [6] Since this is the function of the concept, the representative is required to offer considerations of the type discussed in connection with rights. If he applies "public interest" to a measure without marshaling such considerations, he has violated the logic of the concept.

The represented also need the concept, and they too must respect its logic. They must decide how to cast their ballots and what to ask of their representatives. It may be that most individuals formulate their decisions and demands on the basis of purely self-serving considerations. A number of problems would be created if all political activity took this form. Recall the position of Thomas Hobbes. In his system individual citizens pursue their interests as vigorously as possible, and it is the responsibility of the sovereign to care for the institutions and conditions which are shared by the members of society. The individual, in other words, has no need of "public interest" and is obligated to discipline his political activity in the name of public interest only as he is commanded to do so by the sovereign. This position might be expected to lead to ineffective government because of the constant conflict between government and the citizenry. The position also suggests that the individual, group, or corporation ought simply to consume the benefits of life in a political order and make no conscious effort to contribute to them. No degree of clarity concerning "public interest" will prevent men from behaving in this manner. Clarity about the concept, however, will help us appreciate the consequences of such behavior.

This discussion suggests the following generalizations concerning the function of "public interest" in political discourse. The concept relates closely to the problem of the one and the many. [7] The "many" are the great diversity of individuals and groups found in any political system. Their interests, demands, and needs regularly conflict, but geography and biology, if not more, force them to live together and create extensive interdependencies. Interdependence makes necessary an authoritative agent to control conflicts and tend to interrelationships. This agent is the "one," or government. It is a public agent; it exists not merely for the sake of single individuals or groups, but for the many. Its actions are directed to all the members of society, and they are enforceable against all. This means that government will not be justified in acting partially. Yet the very fact of diversity in society means that government cannot assign rights and duties or make any authoritative decision without serving some interests, demands, and needs, and restricting others. The individual citizen may be obligated to obey governmental actions that conflict with his interests, but government is expected to justify its decisions and actions in terms of a standard appropriate to the position which requires those decisions, its position as a public agent. The function of the concept "public interest" is to provide such a standard, and its logic corresponds to that function.

[6] Hence it is difficult to imagine how the representative could function if he had no such concept at his disposal.

[7] See J. Roland Pennock, "The One and the Many: a Note on the Concept," in Carl Friedrich, editor, *The Public Interest* (Nomos V) (New York: Atherton Press, 1962).

II

... "Public interest" is used to express evaluations of public policies, and the logic of the concept requires assessment of the consequences of policies for the members of the public. This means that the general difficulties of evaluation, as well as problems peculiar to politics, arise in connection with use of "public interest." Hence it comes as no surprise that a number of writers have reached very pessimistic conclusions concerning the concept. These writers concede that the concept is widely used in political discourse. It is a political "datum" of which the political scientist must take cognizance. But because of its functions the concept can never be given "operational meaning," either by political actors or by political scientists. Once we have begun to answer the question "What is the status, significance, and function of 'public interest,'" we will see that there can be no rationally defensible answer to the question "What (policy, decision, action) is in the public interest?" Since the concept is used to commend, it can only be used to express personal (or group) preferences.

The argument, it should be stressed, is not simply that the concept is sometimes, often, or even always used to express preferences or for purely propagandist purposes. The misuse of the concept (and its ancestors) is as old as politics and requires little documentation.[8] The argument takes a more radical form: the concept *can only be* used to express subjective preference or as an honorific label. The nature or character or essence of the concept excludes the possibility of its having any trans-subjective content. These commentators urge political scientists not to attempt to determine "what is in the public interest"; indeed, they argue that political scientists should banish the concept from their analytic vocabularies.[9] Assessment of the validity of these conclusions will be a secondary concern throughout the remainder of this discussion.

III

Since "public interest" is used to express commendations and justifications, the analysis that has been done of other commendatory terms, whether political or not, is likely to be useful to understanding it. In his analysis of the word "good" R. M. Hare has drawn a distinction between the "primary" or "commendatory" force of the term and its "secondary" or "descriptive" force. Whenever we say that something is "good" our primary purpose is to convey commendation. This is true whether we are speaking of a fountain pen as good because it writes smoothly or of a man as good because he is virtuous, kind, and altruistic. What is more, we are able to understand the commendatory force of "good" even when we know nothing of its descriptive meaning in a specific case.

---

[8] Thucydides, for example, noted that, "Leaders of parties in cities had programs which appeared admirable ... but in professing to serve the public interest they were seeking to win prizes for themselves," *The Peloponnesian War* (Rex Warner, translator, Penguin Classics, Baltimore, Md.: Penguin Books, Inc.,) III, 5, p. 210.
[9] See especially David Truman, *The Governmental Process* (New York: Alfred A. Knopf, Inc., 1951), pp. 50–51, Glendon Schubert, *The Public Interest* (New York: The Free Press of Glencoe, 1960), *passim;* Glendon Schubert, "Is There a Public Interest Theory," and Frank Sorauf, "The Conceptual Muddle," in Friedrich, *op. cit.,* pp. 162, 183.

To teach what makes a member of any class a good member of the class is a . . . new lesson for each class of objects; but nevertheless the word "good" has a constant meaning which, once learnt, can be understood no matter what class of objects is being discussed. We have . . . to make a distinction between the meaning of the word "good" and the criteria for its application.[10]

Hare's distinction is clarified by the reasons he offers for terming the commendatory meaning primary. First, the commendatory meaning is constant despite great variation in the descriptive meaning. We commend fountain pens for very different reasons than we commend men, automobiles for reasons other than television sets; yet we can use the word "good" in all cases, and our listeners or readers will be able to understand that we are using it in part to commend. The second is that

> . . . we can use the evaluative force of the word ["good"] in order to *change* the descriptive meaning for any class of objects. This is what the moral reformer often does in morals; but the same process occurs outside morals. It may happen that motor-cars will in the near future change considerably in design. . . . It may be that then we shall cease giving the name "a good motor-car" to a car that now would rightly and with the concurrence of all be allowed that name. How, linguistically speaking, would this have happened? At present, we are roughly agreed . . . on the necessary and sufficient criteria for calling a motor-car a good one. If what I have described takes place, we may begin to say "No cars of the nineteen-fifties were really good; there weren't any good ones till 1960." Now here we cannot be using "good" with the same descriptive meaning as it is now generally used with; for some of the cars of 1950 do indubitably have those characteristics which entitle them to the name "good motor-car" in the 1950 descriptive sense of the word. What is happening is that the evaluative meaning of the word is being used in order to shift the descriptive meaning; we are doing what would be called, if "good" were a purely descriptive word, redefining it. But we cannot call it that, for the evaluative meaning remains constant; we are rather altering the standard.[11]

This analysis might appear to support the view that commendatory expressions are employed in a highly subjective, nonrational manner. It would appear that we can commend anything without failing to communicate. Regardless of what we call good, our audience will always understand the force of our expression – even if it has no idea why we are commending. Partly for this reason, some commentators have classified Hare's ethical theory as "emotivist," as a theory holding that moral statements have no cognitive content and are best understood as expressions of emotive states or attitudes.[12] This interpretation misconstrues the (admittedly difficult) relationship between the primary and secondary meanings of "good."

The logic of the word "good," that is the logic of the manner in which "good" is actually used in ordinary language, is such that we misuse the word if we commend

[10] R. M. Hare, *The Language of Morals*, p. 102. (London: Oxford University Press, 1952). See Part 2 of this work for a full discussion of the distinction in question. For an alternative analysis of "good" see Paul Ziff, *Semantic Analysis* (Ithaca, N.Y.: Cornell University Press, 1960), Part VI. The two analyses conflict in important respects, but I do not find that Ziff has upset Hare's conclusions. (Ziff does not mention Hare's work.)

[11] Hare, *op. cit.,* p. 119.

[12] See for example, Richard Brandt, *Ethical Theory* (Englewood Cliffs, N.J.: Prentice-Hall, Inc., 1959), pp. 221–5.

when we are unable to supply a descriptive meaning in support of the commendation. To see this we have only to construct an appropriate response to a commendation. "It always makes sense, after someone has said 'That is a good motorcar,' to ask, 'What is good about it?' or 'Why do you call it good?' "[13] If the commender responds, "Well, I just like it, that's all," he demonstrates that his first statement was simply an expression of preference. It would then be appropriate to say that the commender had misused the word good. He should have *begun* by using, "I like that motorcar" or "That motorcar suits my fancy" or some other typically preferential locution. But if he responds, "It handles well at high speeds, gets 30 miles to the gallon of gas, and requires a minimum of maintenance," he has supplied a descriptive meaning which supports the commendation. To answer the question "Why do you call it good?" is "to give the properties in virtue of which we call it good."[14]

This account raises some extremely thorny questions. Most important, the "in virtue of which" in the last sentence quoted from Hare involves us in the problem of "naturalism," the problem of the relationship between statements of fact and statements of value. It might be unproblematical to call a motorcar good "in virtue of" the *fact* that it can deliver 30 miles to a gallon of gasoline. But if we make comparable statements such as, "X is a good father in virtue of the fact that he sends his children to Sunday school" or "measure X is in the public interest in virtue of the fact that it will serve to increase GNP," it becomes apparent that we are in the throes of the hoary problem of moving logically from the "is" to the "ought."

But Hare's account does solve some problems. He shows that use of commendatory expressions does not necessarily bring reasoned discourse to an immediate halt or reduce us to an exchange on the "I like it — Well I don't" model. The fact that the logic of "good" requires a descriptive meaning opens the way for, indeed renders mandatory, some discussion of why "good" was applied. The content of this exchange will vary according to the subject matter in question — the descriptive meaning varies while the primary meaning holds constant. But the fact that providing a descriptive meaning is a requirement of the proper use of "good" distinguishes moral discourse from discussions of the merits of peppermints versus chocolate creams.

Hare's distinction applies directly to "public interest." The primary function of the concept is to commend, and it is primary for the reasons indicated by Hare in connection with "good." The requirement that a descriptive meaning be supplied corresponds to the demands of the logic of "public interest." The descriptive meaning will vary in content from case to case, but the characteristics of political life discussed above establish general criteria which any descriptive meaning must satisfy. Hare's terminology provides an economical means of discussing these features of "public interest," and we will utilize it.

Hare's analysis is also enlightening concerning the question, "What is in the public interest?" It shows that this question *cannot* be properly answered by an unsupported statement of preference. It also teaches us not to expect any single, all-inclusive, once-for-all-time answer. The content of the descriptive meaning, to repeat, will vary. Finally, when combined with the earlier analysis, it suggests the

---

[13] Hare, *op. cit.*, p. 130.
[14] *Ibid.*, p. 130.

possibility of defining general criteria which any answer to the question, "What is in the public interest?" must satisfy.

IV

We have emphasized the commendatory function of "public interest," but the significance of the concept is not exhausted when this aspect of its use has been analyzed. Some men take justification seriously, and their behavior cannot be understood unless this is recognized. Similarly, the political landscape is crowded with institutional arrangements which reflect concern with justification and which cannot be comprehended if their relationship to the problems of justification is not observed. Hence even those willing to forgo evaluation and justification in politics must recognize that others do not do so. Perhaps this is what Frank Sorauf intends when he concedes that "public interest" must be recognized as a political datum.[15] But it is difficult to grasp what it can mean to "recognize" the concept if not that political scientists must understand the manner in which it functions and concern themselves with the problems that surround it.

The analysis thus far indicates why the concept presents such puzzling difficulties. Public interest is a normative standard, and it raises the whole panoply of problems associated with standards in general. The history of moral philosophy testifies that problems of standards are not easily solved. There is no reason to think that they will be easily solved in the case of public interest. But difficulty of analysis is not ordinarily considered a valid reason for abandoning a problem. The problems associated with "public interest" are among the crucial problems of politics. Determining justifiable governmental policy in the face of conflict and diversity is central to the political order; it is a problem which is never solved in any final sense but which we are constantly trying to solve. The much discussed difficulties with the concept are difficulties with morals and politics. We are free to abandon the *concept*, but if we do so we will simply have to wrestle with the *problems* under some other heading.

[15] Friedrich, *op. cit.,* p. 190.

34. The Public Interest: Descriptive Meaning

Richard E. Flathman

I

The issue of public policy to be considered here is whether to build an expressway to serve intraurban traffic in a middle-sized city in the United States. It would be a joint project involving federal, state, and municipal funds.

Such an issue is likely to involve numerous interests. There will be road-building buffs who find the construction of expressways "interesting"; commuters and property owners who have a personal material stake in the expressway and who are very much aware of it; taxpayers in distant parts of the country who may be unaware of the proposal but who are nevertheless compelled to help pay for it; members of groups such as the Council to Promote Road Safety who might have an other-regarding or disinterested concern. Some of these individuals and groups will be for the proposal, some against; some for one route and some another; some for an elevated-type construction, some for a subway or a depressed roadway. All will insist that their position represents the public interest.

The issue, of course, will allow a certain degree of horse-trading: an elevated construction in one area, a subway in others, passage through area X but with no accesses in that area, a route inconvenient for one group but with a commitment to improve the existing arteries that group utilizes. But there is a decision whether to build an expressway, and this decision and all its consequences will be imposed upon all of the interests by the force of government. How do the stewards of the public interest decide what ought to be done?

The interests and objectives of the individuals and groups affected will prompt the emergence of the issue and provide a starting point for public consideration of it. Since the issue is whether the expressway is in the public interest, the expression of these interests and objectives must be generalized. The person whose concern has been aroused by the slow and dangerous character of his drive to work must transform this into a concern with problems of all commuters, and he must state this concern in terms of the high economic and human price of an inefficient transportation network. The property owner threatened by the construction of the expressway must attempt to see his problem as a part of the general desirability of maintaining stable residential neighborhoods or avoiding unnecessary interference with property acquisition and maintenance.

The process of generalization will take place in part because of the tactical importance of finding allies in the controversy. Positions that cannot be subsumed under a rule applicable to large numbers are likely to be disadvantaged. This consideration is a partial explanation for the fact that we rarely hear: "I'm against this expressway because I don't want my house condemned." Rather, such issues prompt the formation of associations such as the Azure Hills Friends of the Family Neighborhood or the Citizens League for Progress. But whatever the explanation for these facts, the reason generalization ought to take place is that a politics of public interest requires it. If the citizenry does not transform its interests into claims in this manner, the burden will fall entirely on those in authority. If those in authority are not equal to it, it will be impossible to offer justifications for public policy.

Interests are generalized under a rule or maxim, and the rules under which they are subsumed will ordinarily be community values. This is close to a truism. The individual will want to identify his interest with those things valued by large numbers of the members of the community, and those things so valued are, by hypothesis, community values. Hence the process of expression and generalization of interest will identify many of the community values relevant to the decision. (It may not identify all of the relevant values if only because some interests may not be expressed or generalized. Again, this is one of the reasons that authority is necessary.) Without this step, further proceedings would be impossible. Contextual factors must be investigated in order to discover the consequences of the policy or policies under consideration. But in the absence of a specification of relevant values, it would be impossible to know which factors to examine. An investigation presupposes criteria of relevance and principles of judgment.

But it is equally the case that the values, taken alone, will not provide a basis for a decision concerning the merits of the proposal. For the question is not whether fast and safe traffic flow or preservation of family neighborhoods is in the public interest. The question is whether building *this* expressway is in the public interest. The latter question would never arise if the former questions were not of concern to members of the society. But abstract answers to the former questions only raise, they do not properly answer, the latter. Before a decision can be made as to whether building *this* expressway would be in the public interest, we must know whether (or to what extent) this expressway would in fact contribute to a safe and speedy flow of traffic, disrupt neighborhood life, raise or lower taxes. Detailed studies would have to be made of existing traffic flow and accident rate, factors likely to increase or decrease them in the future, types of construction feasible in the area, and availability of property for relocation of facilities the expressway would destroy.

On occasion these steps, the expression and generalization of interest, assertion of relevant values, and the examination of the contextual considerations, will be conclusive in regard to the descriptive meaning of "public interest." Let us say that the interests have been fully expressed and appropriately generalized; that investigation shows, first, that there is a serious traffic problem which is costly in time, money, and human lives and that construction of an expressway will greatly relieve this problem; and, second, that a route is available which will minimize neighborhood disruption and other disadvantages sometimes associated with expressways. Conversely, suppose studies demonstrate that an expressway will make no appreciable dent in a traffic problem which can be solved only by a public transit system and that it will require scarce land resources, divide and demean stable residential districts, and deplete tax rolls. In such cases the public interest will have been determined.

This might appear to be an unwarranted conclusion. Dispute and disagreement will continue and adoption of the indicated policy will create dissatisfaction on the part of some. In the case of the decision to build the expressway, it is apt to be impossible to implement the policy without resort to sanctions or the threat of sanctions. Recall, however, that it is in part because disagreement is rarely if ever eliminated that we have the concept "public interest." When we say, "X is in the public interest," one of the things we are saying, to put it harshly, is that "X can justifiably be imposed on all of the members of society — whether they like it or not."[1] And "justifiably imposed" means "X can be imposed because it meets the best available standards for judging public policy." This in turn is why the descriptive meaning of "public interest" has been determined in the hypothetical cases in question. Strongly felt objections might remain, but if those objections do not alter the fact that the policies in question meet the best available tests or criteria of a justifiable public policy, they do not upset the judgment concerning the public interest.[2]

Cases of this type are perhaps unusual. It is rare to find all of the contextual facts on one side of a public policy issue. Or more precisely, it is rare for such a matter to become an *issue*. Yet the unusual case enlightens the ordinary or commonplace. The point of the foregoing discussion is that the descriptive meaning of "public interest" can sometimes be determined without making a ranking, either permanent or temporary, of the values involved in or affected by the policy or policies in question. The decision to build the expressway in the first of the above instances need not reflect a preference for fast and safe traffic flow over neighborhood stability. It might simply reflect the fact that the expressway in question would serve the former and not damage the latter appreciably. If it is rare for the evidence to be as overwhelming as is posited in the example, this evidence is often sufficiently conclusive to allow a decision to be reached without ranking values. It is in part because this is the case that contextual factors are a necessary consideration in determining the descriptive meaning of "public interest."[3]

These conclusions bear upon two larger topics. They are important in connection with the nature of the value structure of society. Community values are general in character, and there are sometimes conflicts between them. We have heard a great deal, for example, about the conflicts between liberty and equality and the difficulties created by that conflict. To the extent that this is a genuine issue, the discussion of the expressway offers a partial answer. It suggests the possibility of valuing both liberty and equality in the abstract and of deciding some policy questions on the basis of the evidence of which value will be most effectively served in the situation at hand. If this were not possible, it is unlikely that a society could maintain a genuinely pluralistic value system for long. If each particular decision demanded a ranking of conflicting values, the value structure would become hierarchical.

Second, our findings concerning the expressway are important to the question of the degree to which public policy decisions are amenable to reasoned analysis and

---

[1] This does not mean that X can be imposed in any manner whatever. "Expressway X is in the public interest" justifies the state in taking A's property if it is a necessary part of building the expressway. But it does not relieve the state of the obligation to use justifiable procedures — for example, paying a fair compensation arrived at through a due process — when it takes that property.

[2] There is one suppressed premise in this argument which will be discussed below.

[3] These aguments do not support the view that the descriptive meaning of the public interest can be determined on the basis of the facts alone. It is because a policy serves a value or set of values that it is justifiable or not.

adjudication. Some decisions concerning the public interest can be made on the basis of "instrumental" rationality. Even if it were true that ends or goals or values are unamenable to reasoned analysis and adjudication, reason would still have a place in determining the instrumental relationship between values and particular policies designed to serve them. Therefore, it cannot be said that reason has no place in making public policy decisions. This may be a trivial point, but it has real implications for the view that "public interest" can never be made operational and hence ought to be "abandoned."

II

There are cases in which a full investigation of the contextual facts proves to be inconclusive, in which it is possible to serve competing values equally well, or in which the comparative importance of the values in question is properly in dispute. In such cases the decision hinges in part upon an estimate of the relative importance of the competing values as served or disserved in the case at hand. Decisions of this kind raise the question whether, to what extent, or how it is possible to find trans-subjective grounds on which to adjudicate value conflicts.

Three observations will be offered as preliminaries. We have rejected the notion that "public interest" has any single, all-inclusive descriptive meaning. We must also reject the notion that "public interest" has one and only one descriptive meaning in every decision-making situation. To say that a policy is in the public interest is to say that it meets standards and satisfies principles. There is no reason to think that there is one and only one policy which will meet those standards in each of the myriad policy-making situations which arise in a modern polity. Perhaps several routes or types of construction, for example, meet the tests we have discussed. This does not mean that the selection of one of the policies will be simply arbitrary; it will be possible to justify the imposition of the policy selected with reasoned argument. But it might be true that the arguments for the policy selected would not be conclusive arguments against the other policies which had survived earlier tests. To this degree an element of arbitrariness – in a very loose sense of that word – would enter. This is a secondary, or perhaps tertiary, reason for authority. When some decision is necessary and a number of policies satisfy the best available tests of a justifiable policy, the dilemma is resolved by the principle of authority.

It is important to see the question that remains in proper perspective. If all of the policies seriously considered serve values and interests which have been generalized in the manner indicated, it is difficult to imagine them leading to serious consequences for the system. This is not to deny the importance of decisions which require a ranking of values. They are likely to involve matters of great concern to the members of society, and they are likely to influence value commitments which in turn influence many later decisions.

A full discussion of the means of adjudicating between values requires a detailed analysis of many of the basic questions of value theory. . . . What follows . . . will be some of the basic propositions of an argument which will be more fully developed and defended . . .

So far we have appealed, albeit without much attention to labeling, to two formal moral principles and a substantive moral rule. The principles are the

universalizability principle and a general utilitarian principle (discover the consequences!) which we will call the Principle of Consequences (PC).[4] The rule is:
"Serve community values except when doing so violates the universalizability
principle [hereafter 'U' or 'GP' for generalization principle], PC, or other formal
principles." These criteria are anything but irrelevant to deciding issues requiring
adjudication between values. But there are limits built into the very structure of
arguments grounded upon such criteria. These limits stem from the fact that we can
avoid an untenable identification of "is" and "ought" only if community values are
tested by GP and PC. However, the fact that GP and PC are formal means that
neither has any force until its particular premises have been established. There are
two such premises in GP. They are of the form: "This X is right for this A," and
"This A and this B are similar persons similarly situated." PC contains one
particular premise: "The consequences of this A doing this X are undesirable."
Neither principle can itself aid us in establishing these premises in any particular
instance.

This appears to produce an insoluble dilemma. Substantive rules must be tested
by formal principles, but there are issues which cannot be decided by reference to
formal principles without antecedent decisions concerning substantive rules. One
solution is to posit basic substantive principles which require no testing either by
formal principles or by lesser substantive rules. Such principles would provide the
criteria by which all lesser rules and decisions could properly be judged. Platonic
forms perform this function. But one does not have to be a Platonist to adopt a
view of this type. Hedonistic utilitarianism, in most respects worlds apart from
Platonism, depends on an argument very similar to Platonism. Bentham accepts
something like PC, but he argues that the particular premise of PC is always
properly given content by calculating which action produces the greatest quantity
of pleasure and the least quantity of pain. "Maximize pleasure and minimize pain"
is a substantive moral rule which is not subject to question. The felicific calculus is
a means of solving the practical problems of implementing the rule in particular
cases.

Bentham's position allows us to restate the problem before us. We accept the
formal basis of the utilitarian position, PC, but reject as incomplete the classical
utilitarian solution to the problem of establishing the particular premise of that
principle, namely hedonism. No substantive rule or value (or set of rules or values)
whether pleasure, freedom, justice, the social tie, or whatever, is itself beyond
question in particular cases, and therefore no such value can constitute an adequate
final criterion for all other decisions. But this leaves a serious gap in our theory.
Arguments already presented[5] show that this gap cannot be filled with a
substantive rule. We require a principle or criterion that is not substantive but is less
restricted than GP and PC. To meet this need we turn to the principle on which all

---

[4] Stated formally, this principle reads, "If the consequences of A's doing X are undesirable,
A ought not to do X." Or, in positive terms, "if the consequences of A's not doing X would be
undesirable, A ought to do X." I take the language from Marcus George Singer, *Generalization
in Ethics* (New York: Alfred A. Knopf, Inc., 1960), pp. 63 ff,

[5] The reference is to the argument that equating public interest with a single substantive
principle (or set of principles) violates its function as a general commendatory concept. This
argument rests upon the logic of language and it is a complete answer to the Platonic or
Benthamite position only if the purpose at hand is to account for the logic of
language. . . .

principles, and hence all nonarbitrary decisions, rest, the principle "give reasons." If the tests suggested above prove to be inconclusive, if it is necessary to decide which of two or more competing values is to be served, the choice is to be made and defended by *giving reasons.*

To ask what is gained by requiring that we "give reasons" is in part to ask how the English words "give reasons" (and cognate expressions) are used. (To suggest that the requirement is meaningless or vacuous is to suggest that these words have no accepted use, that English speakers do not communicate anything when they use these words.) We can begin with the dictionary, which indicates that a "reason" is "a fact or circumstance forming, or alleged as forming, a ground or motive[6] leading, or sufficient to lead, a person to adopt or reject some course of action or procedure, belief," etc. To give reasons is to adduce facts or circumstances as grounds for doing or believing something. To require that we decide by giving reasons is to require that we not decide without a ground, "for no reason at all." But giving reasons involves more. To give reasons is to engage in the act of reasoning, it is "to reason," "to employ reasoning or argument with a person in order to influence his conduct or opinion." It is "to think in a connected, sensible, or logical manner," and it is to be "reasonable," which is to be "sensible, sane . . . : not irrational, absurd, or ridiculous." To require that decisions be made by giving reasons is to require that the decision-making process be governed by the canons of logic and evidence.[7] It is to rule out "I want" as a basis for a decision and insist upon "I want because . . . "; to forswear "you must" and require "you must because. . . . " It is to insist that criteria be met in filling in the ellipses in any particular case.

Although general, these requirements are not vacuous. To require that the grounds of a decision meet the canons of reason is to require something which we all understand and without which we could not live together. The generic character of these requirements is a virtue, not a vice. It means that the requirements will be relevant to judging all aspects of all types of decisions. GP and PC are specific principles, whose formulation and application must meet the general requirement of reasonableness. But they provide a more detailed test which can be applied to particular aspects of a decision. Once these principles have been validated, we can use them instead of the generic requirement in the area of their applicability. But where we have no specific principle, we fall back on the general requirement.[8]

The foregoing remarks are an unfortunately abstract statement of a position that is quite straightforward and not likely to be questioned in most contexts. Notice that the requirement, "give reasons," is assumed in the earlier discussion of

[6] The use of "motive" in this entry is misleading. We do use "reason" in the sense of motive, but this refers to a psychological process, not a proposition which is verifiable or supportable. The present use of "reason" will be exclusively in the latter sense. See Stanley Caveil and A. Senonske, "Moral Theory, Ethical Judgments and Empiricism," *Mind,* Vol. 61, p. 551, New Series, 1952. See part 2 of this article for an argument similar to that presented here.

[7] As will emerge more fully below, we are using "logic" in the general sense of orderly thinking, not in the technical sense in which professional logicians use it to refer to their subject matter.

[8] For an excellent discussion of "reason" and its place in practical discourse, see John Ladd, "The Desire to Do One's Duty," in H. Castenada and G. Nakhnikian, editors, *Morality and the Language of Conduct* (Detroit: Wayne State University Press, 1963), especially pp. 325–42. Ladd treats reason as a motive, but the substance of his discussion indicates that this involves no more than a terminological difference with the present argument.

"instrumental rationality." (It is the suppressed premise referred to at the end of that discussion.) Contextual considerations sometimes lead us to conclude that one value will be served and another not disserved by a policy. But this is possible only because there are standards or criteria which can be used to determine what the contextual considerations show and what they do not. If asked to describe these criteria, we might well respond that they are the "canons of reason," that arguments of this type require that we support our interpretation of the evidence by giving reasons to show that a particular conclusion is justified. Evidence does not speak for itself. We might go on to explicate, "give reasons," in terms of canons of logic and avoidance of irrational or absurd consclusions. We would be likely to respond in this manner for the *good reason* that this is the vocabulary we all use as a matter of course in referring to the standards employed to judge the validity of arguments and conclusions.

But there appears to be an important difference between the "instrumental" reasoning of our earlier example and reasoning in defense of value rankings. In the former, the content or substance of the "grounds" to be tested by the canons of reason is not in doubt. The "grounds" consist of the facts and predictions concerning the policy in question. The canons of reason are necessary to judge whether those facts have been marshaled and interpreted in a defensible manner. But in the latter case, by hypothesis, the facts are inconclusive, and the values are in conflict. To return to the example, the expressway will greatly facilitate traffic flow and safety, but it will seriously divide and disrupt stable residential neighborhoods with a predominance of single family dwellings (SRNPSFD), reduce property values substantially, and force large numbers of people to move to less desirable areas. Policy *A* (building the expressway), in other words, will serve one value or set of values and disserve another. The effects of *B* (not building the expressway) will be the converse of *A*. How can a justifiable decision be reached?[9]

If those in authority attempt to follow the dictates of a politics of public interest, the first step would be to make the most fully reasoned case for each of the values in question. How does one make a reasoned case for a value commitment, that is for "valuing" or "considering of worth or importance" (*OED*) a particular condition or phenomenon? What could be said in defense of valuing SRNPSFD's?

B might offer the following argument:

> Such neighborhoods are conducive to friendship and community interaction, which foster the development of the individual. Crime and delinquency rates are lower. Schools and other community activities are better because people have roots in the community and are willing to work and sacrifice to

---

[9] One decision strategy might be to adopt some variant of the view that "Value decisions are matters of personal preference and are unamenable to reasoned analysis." This would have the virtue of simplifying the process of decision making. If asked why decision *X* had been reached, those in authority would reply, "because it accords with our personal preferences." They would then hope that their preferences coincided with the preferences of a substantial part of the citizenry. They would also hope that those whose preferences led them to disagree with *X* would be led by other preferences to decide not to resist implementation of *X*. Finally, they would hope that a substantial number of the citizenry would have preferences such that they would be prepared to support the decision makers in the application of sanctions against those whose preferences led them to reject *X* and to resist its implementation. There are two related things which this strategy would not require: the first would be to give reasons in justification of *X*, and the second would be to say that *X* was in the public interest.

improve them. Property values tend to be steadier, making it possible for families to invest in a home with confidence, which in turn contributes to stability.

B's strategy is to list the major consequences of maintaining such neighborhoods and to attach value to those consequences by demonstrating a positive relationship between them and conditions he values and believes to be valued by others. He attempts to show as fully as possible what is involved in maintaining stable neighborhoods; in so doing, he tries to show that to refuse to value stable neighborhoods is to refuse to value friendship, community, and low crime rates. He tries to win appreciaton for the fact that a substantial price must be paid for disagreement with his position. Would we say that B's argument was a reasoned one? If we found that his facts were correct and that there were no logical flaws in the conclusions he drew from them, surely we would.

How can such an argument be tested or attacked? How does A respond when faced with this argument for preserving SRNPSFD's? His most likely strategy, aside from making an argument in favor of his value, is to attempt to show that B is mistaken in his assessment of the consequences that follow when SRNPSFD's are maintained.

People just stick to thier own yards. There is less community interaction than in apartment-house districts where everyone must make use of common facilities. In point of fact the crime rates are not any lower. And the schools are worse because such neighborhoods soon come to have a majority of people whose children have finished school. These people refuse to support tax increases and bond issues. Rather, they have their own little nests and will not contribute to or participate in community projects of any kind. Show me a city full of SRNPSFD's and chances are you've shown me a city with a starved public sector.

A contends that B's reasons are not good reasons because the facts on which they rest are faulty. To do this he must go beyond the contextual considerations special to the policy issue in question and examine available evidence concerning the general consequences of serving B's value. If that evidence disproves B's contentions, B's reasons for considering SRNPSFD's of worth or importance will be undercut, and the canons of reason will require that B produce new reasons or cease to value SRNPSFD's.

A might also take the more radical course and agree with B's estimate of the consequences of maintaining SRNPSFD's, but argue that those consequences ought not to be valued.

All of this emphasis on community interaction is a mistake. It leads to the mass conformism which is stifling our society. Where is the personal and family privacy in the neighborhood you want to preserve? The neighborhood replaces the family as the basic unit of life; the children are educated and learn their morals in the streets rather than from their parents; and everything is reduced to the lowest common denominator. It is no surprise to hear you extolling the merits of stable property values. This is just a facet of the cult of the material which flourishes in the type of neighborhood you admire. The fact that this expressway will divide some of these neighborhoods and force people into other types of areas is not much of an argument against it.

A indicates his willingness to pay the price *B* had tried to attach to the rejection of his value. Again, *A* has reasons for doing so. His reasons consist of considerations designed to demonstrate that *B* had not fully considered the implications of community, friendship, and stability. Although often thought valuable, *A* in effect says, SRNPSFD's undermine more important aspects of life such as individualism, family solidarity, rigorous moral training, and appreciation of the nonmaterial dimensions of life.

At this point, *B* would be obliged to show either that *A* is wrong in holding that friendship and community require a sacrifice of individualism and family solidarity or that the former are more valuable than the latter, and to give his reasons for thinking so. A new exchange would begin, with both *A* and *B* attempting to offer evidence for thinking that community did or did not undermine individualism, that individualism did or did not lead to certain other consequences. In short, *A* and *B* would be forced to look ever more deeply into human relationships, attempting to specify the ground on which they were committed to certain views and to support those views with the evidence which, perhaps in a not very systematic manner, led them to adopt those views to begin with. At every stage of the discussion the range of relevant experience would enlarge, and the difficulties of gathering and marshaling it would increase. *A* and *B* would be driven from the particular problem of the expressway to the problems of political philosophy.

Attention must be given to a number of problems (for example, "infinite regress" and "circularity") thought to be raised by these arguments. For our immediate purposes, two points will suffice to conclude the discussion.

1. The major purpose of the example is to show that reasons can be offered in support of and in opposition to value positions. Although we might disagree with the remarks of *A* and *B*, they would not fall into the category of "ridiculous" or "absurd" statements. To offer such arguments in support of a proposed policy would be to meet the requirement of "giving reasons." Moreover, the arguments presented can be tested by the canons of reason. Factual assertions which can be checked into are presented, and conclusions are drawn from the facts in a manner which can be tested by logical criteria. By moving outside the considerations peculiar to the particular policy decision, the problem of producing "grounds" which can be put to intersubjective tests can be overcome.

2. Reasoning of this kind will only rarely produce unanimity among those concerned. But this does not mean that the reasoning has been inconclusive vis-à-vis the public interest. Since reasoning is relevant to supporting and attacking value choices and positions, there is no reason to believe that it will always be inconclusive. If *B* opposed the expressway because SRNPSFD's gave people ample space to wash their cars on Sunday afternoons, we would have no doubt that *A*'s arguments were superior. If he rested his view on the fact that children in such neighborhoods generally had better suntans in the summer, we would still have few if any doubts. If he could show a slightly lower incidence of serious illness, we would at least give him a serious hearing. At some point it might become very difficult or impossible to be sure. But must we construct our entire theory around that "some point"? Must we throw out the host of cases in which we can decide value questions in a rational manner because of the possibility (a question yet to be examined) that there are some cases in which we cannot? We know that decisions which involve value choices are made. We know that the values of individuals, groups, and societies are implemented, modified, and sometimes transformed. Once

we know that reasons are logically relevant to value choices, is there anything but blind prejudice to make us think that a rational or irrational considerations alone influence this process?

But let us assume cases in which reasoning is genuinely inconclusive. *A* and *B* debate at great length and "ultimately" reach a point at which they are reduced to an irreducible or unanalyzable statement of preference. Such an outcome does not demonstrate that the process of reasoning which preceded it was meaningless or insignificant. *A, B,* and their audience are in a better position to make a judgment after the exchange than before it. If a governmental body chooses policy *A*, *A*'s reasons put it in a preferable position vis-à-vis *B* than it would be without them. Remembering that "arbitrary" means "based on mere opinion . . . ; capricious," it would be inappropriate to say that the decision was entirely arbitrary.

Value decisions are properly made by giving reasons. All who know the language know in a rough way what reasons are, and no one could act effectively without them. Furthermore, we all believe — and our lives sometimes depend on our being right — that we can distinguish valid from invalid reasons. But our judgments often differ substantially. This is true of reasons in support of descriptive generalizations as well as those justifying decisions with a value dimension. It is not to be expected that disagreement concerning the descriptive meaning of "public interest," including disagreement based upon careful use of the decision procedure discussed here, will be entirely eliminated. But if such reasoning is not as conclusive as the deductions of a geometer, it is surely preferable to "I want" or "I like." It does provide trans-subjective considerations which minimize if they do not eliminate the element of whim and caprice to which we are otherwise reduced. It is because exclusive reliance upon whim and caprice is incompatible with the manner in which "public interest" is employed in our discourse that the procedures discussed here are required by the logic of "public interest." More important, it is because whim and caprice have such destructive consequences in the public realm that we have the concept "public interest" and that we employ it in the way we do.

III

We conclude that "public interest" is a general commendatory concept used in selecting and justifying public policy. It has no general, unchanging, descriptive meaning applicable to all policy decisions, but a nonarbitrary descriptive meaning can be determined for it in particular cases. This descriptive meaning is properly found through reasoned discourse which attempts to relate the anticipated effects of a policy to community values and to test that relation by formal principles. We also conclude that the concept is neither a vacuous phrase nor a verbal device useful only for propaganda purposes. It performs a function in political discourse, and it has a logic which, if taken seriously, will influence the kinds of policies adopted and rejected and the character of the political process utilized to adopt and reject those policies. A politics which takes the logic of the concept seriously, a politics of public interest, will differ in a significant and predictable manner from a politics which misunderstands or "abandons" the concept.

. . . [L]et me add a word concerning the argument that *political scientists* should abandon the concept (except to observe it as a political datum). It may not be entirely clear that the foregoing conclusions meet that argument squarely. "Public interest" does not provide a divining rod or philosopher's stone for determining proper public policy. There will be cases in which the most conscientious efforts will not eliminate legitimate disagreement. This is apparently what is meant by the charge that the concept cannot be rendered "operational."

The question is whether the appropriate conclusions are drawn from the facts in question. Absolute certainty and unanimity concerning the descriptive meaning of "public interest" may sometimes be unattainable. But does it follow that we should *therefore* abandon the attempt to achieve justifiable policy? Certainly no logic would support such an inference. (How many questions would remain if we applied this test, that is, the possibility of achieving absolute certainty, to the subject matter of political science?) But if we do not abandon the attempt to justify policy, what is to be achieved by abandoning the concept which we use to communicate about the problems of justification? (We might substitute some other verbal formula, but the problems are with morals and politics, not with the concept, and verbal substitutions would solve nothing.)

There is a temptation to explain the argument for abandonment in terms of substantive attitudes toward politics. The uncertainty, inconclusiveness, and occasional inefficacy of rational deliberation and discourse are upsetting, and observers throw up their hands in despair at a crucial part of the process. It might be contended that lurking behind the abandonment argument is an urge for irrefragable answers. Having been disabused of hope in this respect, these observers over-react and argue for giving up the entire enterprise of evaluation and justification.

But this explanation misses the mark. The "abandon public interest" school of thought is not concerned with politics or justification at all, but with a more tender growth known as political science. Desiring to turn political science into a hard science on *their* model of the natural sciences, these writers wish to cut away all concepts, questions, and concerns which, in their view, hold political science back from this goal. *Political science* ought to eschew value judgments and cut away all concepts stricken with the cancer of ambiguity and imprecision generated by value judgments. If politicians, journalists, or citizens wish to concern themselves with the public interest, political science will not object. But the discipline itself must remain pure and exclude from its conceptual apparatus such prescientific curiosities.

This approach rests upon a fundamental confusion concerning the concept itself. "Public interest" is not a tool developed by political science for analytic purposes; it is a part of political discourse. The decision to abandon or retain the concept is to be made not according to standards which the academic discipline sets for its analytic vocabulary, but according to the facts concerning and the problems involved in understanding the political order. If political scientists conclude that the concept has no meaning and serves no function in politics, they will justifiably decide not to pay attention to it. But if the concept performs a function in politics, political scientists will be obliged to become as clear as possible concerning it – simply because it is the task of political science to achieve clarity and understanding concerning the political order. The fact that dispute over the descriptive meaning of "public interest" cannot be completely eliminated is irrelevant to whether political science should deal with the concept.